OVERLAND
TO VIETNAM

An 11,500 mile adventure on a
74-year-old classic motorcycle

To Paul Wood

GORDON G. MAY

All the best,

[signature] May

2019

Editor

JANE GREGORY

Rixon Groove

Rixon Groove
464 Stockport Road West
Bredbury
SK6 2EE
United Kingdom

© Text, Gordon G. May, 2016
© Photographs, Gordon G. May, 2016

Paperback ISBN: 978-0-9561168-8-8
Hardback ISBN: 978-0-9561168-9-5

www.overlandtovietnam.com

In memory of Kay Thi Han
1947 - 1999
A courageous woman and wonderful friend

7 YEARS DEVELOPMENT

AND A MAJOR ADVANCE IN MOTOR CYCLE DESIGN

MODEL G/3L
350 - O.H.V.
with
TELEDRAULIC FORKS

FROM its first introduction in 1935 the Matchless Model G/3 has undergone a process of steady and continuous development. There have been no "fashion" changes in design, made merely for the sake of change, but each year has seen the introduction of worth-while improvements that have given better performance and still greater reliability.

Now as the latest result of this seven years' development is the MATCHLESS Model G/3L—combining all the reliability of the tried and tested G/3 with a major advance in design—the already famous Teledraulic Front Fork.

Designed to be equally suitable for road or cross-country work and possessing superb steering and road-holding properties, the Matchless G/3L is already proving its outstanding reliability in the hands of thousands of riders.

MATCHLESS

RIDE TELEDRAULIC – AND ALL ROADS ARE SMOOTH

ASSOCIATED MOTOR CYCLES LTD. • PLUMSTEAD ROAD • LONDON, S.E.18

Above: 1942 advertisement for the new Matchless G3L.
Pages 7 - 8: WWII Matchless promotional images extolling the virtues of the G3L.

Acknowledgements

The team at Andrew Engineering, based in Atherton, UK, played a huge role in the restoration of the Matchless. All their replacement parts were manufactured to the highest standard and admirably stood up to the rigours of the journey. Probably more important, however, was the support of owners Malcolm and Joan Lee and their daughter Vikki. Their expertise, experience and positive response to every situation was invaluable and nothing was ever too much trouble for them. I returned from each of my regular visits to their factory laden with new parts for the bike, my spirits buoyed, my knowledge expanded and my bloodstream coursing with coffee!

I met friend Derek Thom and his lovely wife Liz at the 2007 *Netley Marsh Eurojumble*. Derek became a key contributor to both the *Overland To India* and *Egypt* projects, earning himself the nickname Mr. Bracket along the way for his prowess at fabricating fixings for those bikes. His participation in the ventures was always way more than just making brackets, however, and that was also the case with restoring and preparing the Matchless. Derek's contribution of time, knowledge and capability ensured the bike was ready for the off. His calm, rational and creative response to challenges was highly valued and his uncanny ability to dig genuine Matchless parts from the depths of his garage or spare bedroom at exactly the right moment appreciated beyond measure.

Another friend, Andy Berry of Preston, was vitally important to the project. I first met Andy when he became the pivotal contributor to *The Bullet-In*, a magazine I founded in 2001, and he's worked on my bikes ever since. Andy did a brilliant job building the Matchless's engine and its success in reaching Vietnam is testament to his skill, patience and methodical approach to the task. Moreover, Andy's input went far beyond the engine as he oversaw the reassembly of the motorcycle, ensuring its every function was up to the task ahead. His engineering savvy, problem solving wherewithal and desire to see the old bike succeed were priceless. When I experienced mechanical challenges during the shakedown period and at various stages of the ride, Andy was steadfast in his commitment to the enterprise and unfailingly came up with exactly the right advice. Without Andy, taking classic motorcycles on overland journeys would be out of the question.

This book would not exist were it not for Jane Gregory who, as with my other two travel books, applied herself to editing it, an endeavour she undertook with dedication and adroitness. She grasped hold of each daily offering and crafted it into something richer. Furthermore, as Jacques's mother, Jane bore the brunt of my three month absence and it is to her eternal credit that she then invested so much of her time and consideration into producing this book. I don't know how I will be able to repay her.

Caroline Gregory generously volunteered to proofread the finished manuscript. She transformed desert into dessert, cahoots into cohorts and, not least in importance, gave height to the 5" lady! I'm extremely grateful for her patience, proficiency and prudence with this essential and not inconsiderable task.

Many individuals and companies that I've come to know through my involvement in the motorcycle industry responded brilliantly to my requests for assistance and advice. Their belief in both me and the journey to Vietnam helped my confidence enormously. They generously contributed their time and, in some cases products, to the endeavour and in acknowledgement I have listed their details in a separate section in the back of the book entitled *Suppliers Pages*. I am a great believer in using quality parts and gear in all aspects of motorcycling and travel. These people, businesses and their products certainly proved that the principle works.

I was overwhelmed by the encouragement I received from motorcyclists who heard of my plans. One thoughtful chap I met at the *Rufforth Autojumble* brought me a handful of US$1bills in case I urgently needed small change at border crossings and another, encountered at the *Popham Megameet*, gave me a £5 note, saying he would like to pay for the first petrol I used on the ride! A big thank you also to members of the *BSA Owners Club* North Staffs section and the *Norton Owners Club* Howden branch. Both of these groups held surprise whip-rounds to help with the journey expenses. I carefully kept their money aside and it gave me great pleasure to use it when paying for petrol… their generosity got me all the way from the UK to Odessa in the Ukraine!

Friends Alan Graham and Brendan Layton did so much to help with preparations in the frenetic months before departure, going far beyond the call of duty. I'm extremely grateful for their time, thoughtfulness and especially their humour during the busiest periods. Brendan also kindly updated blog posts when I had no internet access at various points along the way. Thanks also to my wonderful parents, Iain and Martha May, for diligently posting books during my absence and David Wood of Horsham for conscientiously running other aspects of my business.

Many of my most long lasting and treasured memories come from the benevolence, hospitality and ready friendship of strangers I met along the way. Although none of them are ever likely to know it, I hope that in writing down my experiences and recalling the kindness and humanity of these otherwise unsung heroes, I can, in some small way, repay them.

Gordon G. May
October 2016

From a Signals D.R. on the Italian Front :—
'I would like to place on record my sincere thanks to you, both designers and machinists, for providing what I consider the best W.D. Motor-cycle yet issued . . . Thanks again for a very fine bike, well suited to the job.'

From a Workshop Staff Sergeant in the C.M.F :—
' The concensus of opinion by our band of enthusiasts is that the Matchless is easily the best machine for all-round work we have out here to-day.'

From a Flying Officer :—
' Upon landing in North Africa, I was fortunate enough to have the use of a MATCHLESS G/3L. It proved its weight in gold. The engine is a fine piece of engineering and one of the sweetest 350's I have ridden. This motor-cycle gave faultless service during the three months I had possession of it, covering considerable mileage. . . In conclusion I should like to thank you for an excellent product which is highly praised by D.R.'s.'

SAND

The arch enemy of all machinery is undoubtedly Sand ; yet under the conditions which prevailed in the North African Campaign — probably the worst possible — the MATCHLESS predominated in reliability and performance. That was to be expected, as the MATCHLESS is designed for all conditions.
Picture shows a G/3L on Active Service in the Libyan Desert.

★

MUD

In the Battle of France, torrential rain turned the tracks into a veritable morass, through which MATCHLESS-mounted Despatch Riders had to keep on the move to maintain vital communications.

Picture shows a Despatch Rider mounted on a MATCHLESS G/3L ploughing his way through the mud, near Caen shortly after 'D' Day.

★

From an R.A.S.C. Captain in France :—

' I must say that your ' wheels ' are performing magnificently. Everywhere one sees them—many most misused and badly ridden under the most appalling conditions—and they just go like ' bats from Hades' and with clockwork regularity. The Boys in my Company adore them.'

From a Corporal in the M.E.F :—

' I need not dilate on the Teledraulic Forks—abler pens than mine have already lauded them. Suffice to say I am delighted and charmed—they are a source of never failing joy to me, and just how good they are I didn't realise until I had a short ride yesterday on my old . . . which was newish and not bad, but I was amazed at the difference in navigation and comfort . . . I am given to understand the engine develops 15 b.h.p., they are a very energetic 15 horses anyway.'

From a Lance Corporal in Paiforce :—

' The difference in road-holding on these loose bumping roads between a Teledraulic Matchless and any other Army machine is outstanding. It has to be seen to be believed. Congrat's on a super-bike.'

Introduction

I fall to sleep every night with my mind ruminating over potential motorcycle journeys. My head is filled with maps, possible routes, border crossings, sea passages, desert pistes, mountain passes and, of course, the wonderful machines I'll make the expeditions on, almost exclusively old British thumpers. My brain's permanently wired with the language of motorcycle travel, a lexicon of two-wheel and expedition terminology that often finds me awake in the wee hours, fizzing with ideas for future ventures.

It all started in 1988 when I rode a 350cc Royal Enfield Bullet around India and Nepal for four months, living a charmed existence miles from the rat race. Twenty years later I took my own British Royal Enfield, a 1953 500 Bullet, from the UK to India culminating in a visit to the current Royal Enfield factory in Chennai. This adventure resulted in the book, *Overland To India* which, much to my great delight, people seemed to enjoy reading. Two years later I was off again, this time riding a diminutive BSA Bantam to Egypt and back, facing altogether different kinds of challenges, mostly mechanical, but nonetheless loving every moment of it.

"Where next Gordon?" I was asked countless times at the motorcycle shows and autojumbles where I primarily earn my living. The answer was clear in my mind... to South Africa, down the west coast.

It was an ambition dogged by delays right from the start. Preparation of the bike, the same Royal Enfield I'd ridden to India, took forever as we tried to make it more suitable for riding on the dirt trails of rural West Africa. Then Nigerian bureaucracy threw up an obstacle. I soon discovered it wasn't possible to get a visa without a letter of invitation and I couldn't find anybody willing to provide one. Due to instability and insurgency in Niger, Chad and the Central African Republic, Nigeria is the kingpin for southbound travellers as there's no easy way to ride around it. Eventually, after months of work and literally hundreds of emails, I received a reply from the president of a Lagos motorcycle club who said he'd write me the letter, but by then, another issue had arisen.

My absences have always distressed my son, Jacques. Although I don't live with him and his mum, Jane, we are a family and except when I'm away working, I spend every evening with them. It's easier for him to rationalise things as he gets older, but he's still troubled when I'm not present. A couple of months before I was set to leave on the African ride, Jane asked me if there was any chance I could postpone it. Surya, Jacques's sister, was due to take a gap year before going to University and Jane thought it would be better for him if I made the trip when she was at home. It was a difficult decision, and much planning went out of the window, but it was the right thing to do. A year passed and, in October 2013, I began sending off for visas all over again.

Throughout that year an outbreak of Ebola in West Africa had become increasingly serious. Whilst my passport was at the Sierra Leone embassy in London, the situation in Guinea, Sierra Leone, and Liberia became critical when the virus took hold in the cities rather than being contained in remote villages as it had in previous outbreaks. A couple of cases were reported in Nigeria and Cameroon almost immediately closed its borders with its northern neighbour. The risk of contracting Ebola seemed relatively low for a traveller but the cessation of movement across this key frontier put an end to my plans. When my passport came back, complete with its visa, I put it away. My ride down the west coast of Africa would have to wait until another time.

Of all my would-be journeys, two stood out as being next in line, one riding the length of North and South America and the other tracking across Central Asia, ending in Vietnam. Although preparations for the former would be simpler, with fewer visas and no carnet required for the bike, the latter captured my imagination as it would give me the chance to see how Vietnam had changed since my previous visits in the mid-1990s and 2004, and also allow me to ride through Myanmar.

Formerly known as Burma, Myanmar had only recently opened its borders to foreigners travelling with their own vehicles, albeit with restrictions. For 12 months I'd been following online reports as the first cross border visits were successfully completed. By 2014, the cat was out of the bag and several parties of motorcyclists and overland 4x4 drivers crossed from India to Thailand and in the opposite direction. This was made possible by using the rather expensive services of a couple of travel agencies who were able to work around the country's bureaucracy and negotiate the necessary permissions from the Ministry of Tourism. I had no idea how long it might last, whether the country's strides towards democracy and freedom of movement would continue or be quashed by the military junta, and I concluded there was no better time to do it. Decision made, I headed to the back of my shed, pulled off a cover and sat on the saddle of the bike I would use, telling my 1941 G3L Matchless she was going on an adventure!

The wartime G3L was widely regarded as the favourite motorcycle of despatch riders. It was lightweight, had a nippy engine and was, thanks to its telescopic front forks, relatively comfortable. Compared with heftier machines used in large numbers by the services, such as BSA's M20 and Norton's Model 16H side-valves, it was a thoroughly modern motorcycle. 80,000 were produced between 1941 and 1945 and deployed to many countries around the world. As Matchless's publicity stated, 'Absolute reliability is the first essential of the military motorcycle and this reliability must be maintained in the sands of the desert, the mountains of Italy, the mud of the Western Front and the jungle of Burma. In all these theatres of war, the Matchless G3L has given outstanding service, often under terrible conditions and with the minimum of skilled attention.' This final point was a vital one for me as reliability would be crucial to the expedition. The consensus of opinion amongst those in the know was that the G3L had been built strongly enough to be abused by squaddies and simple enough to be repaired by them, so it should stand up to anything that I could throw at it.

I'd owned a 1948 AJS Model 18, a direct descendant of the WWII

Matchless, for 5 years when I lived New Zealand. It still sported the wartime Matchless's patented Teledraulic forks and rigid rear end, although the engine was larger at 500cc. The AJS was produced by Associated Motorcycles (AMC) in its factory in Plumstead, south east London, which claimed to be the world's largest factory devoted solely to the manufacture of motorcycles. An example of what was known at that time as 'badge-engineering', it only bore a few minor variations in design and finish from its Matchless counterpart. The Ajay was a smashing bike to ride. Happy to motor at 85kmph, it handled impeccably and was very handsome to look at. I reluctantly sold it when moving to the UK in 1999, vowing that one day I'd have another, or if not, one of its Matchless stablemates.

It never occurred to me that the next bike might be a military version, having always preferred lustrous black enamel and chrome over drab olive green or sand camouflage colours. However, when I spotted a wartime G3L for sale by a chap called Barry from Slough, its unusual history piqued my interest. Accompanying the advert was a copy of the letter that had tempted him to buy it a year earlier. Written by John Hacker, a motorcycle enthusiast from Forest Row, it read,

'Two years ago I went on a holiday with my family to Burma. I came back with more than I bargained for... a shipping container with 20 old British bikes. Most of the bikes have now been sold and all I have left is this 1941 Matchless G3L, a 1968 BSA A50 and a 1961 BSA B40. The Matchless's engine turns over and its gears appear to select. It has very low compression and a broken fin on the engine. The bike comes with import duty paid and the appropriate documentation. It's amazing to think that this bike was being used in Burma just a few years ago.'

There were photographs showing the bike as it'd been found by John then later being loaded into a shipping container en route to the UK. There were also up-to-the-minute photos of the transformation Barry had brought about in twelve months of ownership and it now looked very much a military machine, although incomplete. According to Barry, it just needed a magneto, a carburettor and a battery plus a few minor finishing touches and it would be ready to run. I loved its history and snapped it up. It had languished in my shed ever since, a project I'd get round to one day. Now that I'd plumped for the ride to Vietnam, its day had come.

I also had personal reasons for wanting to travel through Myanmar. In 1989 I founded a clothing company called Rixon Groove. Based in Wellington, New Zealand, we quickly grew from making limited edition neckties with a reputation for zany designs to producing shirts, many made-to-measure, along with a wide range of men's accessories. Within four years we had our own shops in Wellington, Christchurch and Auckland, all fully stocked by our own small factory in Wellington. More by chance than design, as the business grew the factory workforce expanded predominately with women from South East Asia. Typically, there were two Burmese, three Vietnamese, a Cambodian, a Malay, two Indians, a Filipino and an Indonesian as well as couple of Polynesians and Pakeha Kiwis, New Zealanders of European descent.

Lunch breaks were always a great time, especially on a Friday when the staff had a ritual of each bringing food from their own country or region, which they shared as a communal meal. It gave me a great deal of pleasure to have brought a group of such splendid people together. The fact that everyone got on so well was a blessing and many times we would assemble for parties or celebrations at their homes where, along with the usual gastronomic pleasures, we would also partake in that great Asian phenomenon, karaoke.

One lady from Burma, Kay Thi Han, stood out. On her first day, using hand gestures and mouthing words slowly, I tried to explain how I wanted a pair of boxer shorts sewn. She looked up at me and, in a chirpy voice, said,
    "So you mean you would like it perpendicular?"
We soon became friends, connecting on many levels. Kay Thi was exceptionally bright, hard working and keen to help the business grow and in 1996 I made her the factory manager. She was the daughter of a doctor from Lashio, the largest town in the northern Shan State, was well educated and, as I'd discovered, like many Burmese spoke faultless English. In Myanmar she'd been frustrated by the lack of opportunities for women which resulted in her working in a silver mine with no chance of career advancement, and also by the constraints placed on the people by the military government.

When Kay Thi was diagnosed with cancer in 1990, her younger sister, Theingi, a theatre nurse who'd recently moved to New Zealand, was able to invite Kay Thi to join her on compassionate grounds. She received lifesaving treatment and, unable and unwilling to return to her homeland and its restrictions, settled in Wellington. A prominent member of the New Zealand Burmese community, Kay Thi was called Ma Kay by many, a sign of respect meaning 'big sister Kay.' At first I misheard this as 'Maggie' and it wasn't until some time later that I was informed of the correct salutation and its meaning, although Maggie stuck as a nickname shared between us.

The following year, when my long-term relationship ended, Kay Thi gave me her shoulder to cry on. Her endless support and encouragement were invaluable and a better friend I couldn't have wished for. Being a buddhist who prayed and meditated every day, Kay Thi was philosophical and wise, writing me notes with quotes or inspirational messages to help me get through those hard times. Between us there grew a deep platonic love, her kind heart, it seemed to me, saw me almost like a younger brother.

One of the bonuses I created in my clothing business was travelling to South East Asia two or three times a year to buy textiles. Many of the markets I visited again and again but Vietnam was more difficult, as was Myanmar. In 1995 I visited the former and loved it, and in 1997 made it to Myanmar where I was able to meet Kay Thi's charming family.

In 1999 I moved to the UK to pursue a new relationship... enough said! I sold the retail side of Rixon Groove to the Wellington shop manager and his partner but retained the manufacturing side, somewhat reduced in size and operating mostly with outworkers, which Kay Thi continued to manage. Just four months later, I received the news that Kay Thi's cancer had returned. I promptly flew back to New Zealand and spent most of her last weeks with her in a hospice. Kay Thi died on November 11th 1999.

In 2003 I returned to Burma and revisited Kay Thi's family. By now her father had passed away but her mother was still alive and I was able to pay my respects to her as well as her sisters, brother, nephews and niece, who lived in a small Yangon apartment. Although four years had passed, their sadness at losing Ma Kay was still very raw. When I left, I promised I would visit again, although my own family and work commitments meant the gap grew far longer than I'd envisaged. Riding to Vietnam via Myanmar would give me the opportunity to honour my pledge and Kay Thi's memory.

A birthday party with a group of Rixon Groove factory workers.
Rear row, from the left: Caroline (Burma), Grace (Malaysia), Cobich, Kim and Nhung (Vietnam).
Front row, from the left: Rena (Philippines), the author, and Kay Thi (Burma).

THEY'RE ON A GOOD THING FOR 'CIVVY' LIFE !

G3/L 350 c.c. O.H.V.
G80. 500 c.c. O.H.V.

MATCHLESS

CLUBMAN G3/L
NOW IN PRODUCTION

THE overwhelming praise for the Army G3 L by thousands of service riders undoubtedly proves that it is the forces' choice.

The enthusiasm for the G3 L by service riders during the past six years of war was something to write home about—and they did. That is why we know that over 80,000 Army Matchless Motorcycles have produced 80,000 devotees, many of whom will soon be back in ' civvy ' life, wishing they still had their trustworthy G3 L. Well, we can meet their wishes, for the civilian edition of the famous Army G3 L (which will be known as THE CLUBMAN G3 L) is in production and is now on view in the dealers' showrooms. Go and see it in its gleaming black and chromium—a feast for the eyes indeed.

In the meantime write for the Catalogue Folder M2 M (enclosing 1d. stamp) which describes THE CLUBMAN G3 L—350 and the G.80—500.

ASSOCIATED MOTOR CYCLES LTD. ● PLUMSTEAD ROAD ● LONDON S.E.18

1945 advertisement for the civilian Matchless G3L.

Preparations

Straight off, I take the bike to show to Derek Thom, a good friend who'd helped get the Royal Enfield ready for the India ride and was pivotal in preparing the Bantam ahead of the Egypt journey, including buying the bike as an act of generous sponsorship. Derek has owned AJS and Matchless motorcycles for donkeys years and I know his involvement in this project will be critical.

He looks the bike over, pointing out several rare, original War Department parts, such as brass handlebar levers, and some modern replacements, not that they'll be much of an issue as I've already decided to civilianize the bike... travelling along sensitive international boundaries in Central Asia on a military motorcycle might create too many difficulties.

"You won't believe your luck, Gordon," he says as he walks around the olive green machine, checking out the cylinder head. "Only a couple of weeks ago I met a man who had the best part of a wartime Matchless for sale. It was in bits and going cheap so I bought it, thinking I'd use what I could for my own bike's restoration then sell the rest on. Let's make a list of what you need then see what I have..."

What an unexpected and excellent start!

"That looks alright, Gordon," Andy Berry says as I lift the cover of the Matchless and he sees her for the first time. Andy, born and bred in Preston, Lancashire, is a cheerful guy who lives and breathes old motorcycles, especially Royal Enfields. He has a large collection of interesting machines and has restored over a hundred engines for other owners, all to the highest standard. I'd run the change of plans from Africa on a Bullet to Vietnam on a Matchless past him on the phone only a couple of days earlier and he'd been as keen as mustard to get started on the restoration, clearing a day from his diary for work to commence.

We unstrap the bike from my trailer and wheel her into his workshop, raising her high on a hydraulic workbench. Examining things more closely, Andy notices the missing magneto.

"I've already asked Tony Cooper to supply a refurbished one," I tell him.

Five minutes later, spanners in hand, we set to work on the big strip down, not getting far before problems with the bike's recent overhaul become apparent.

"What on earth are these?" Andy exclaims, wielding an adjustable spanner to remove the square Meccano-type nuts from the rear engine plates. "Look at this... whoever built it has used anything they had to hand... Metric, Whitworth, BSF, plumber's fittings!"

Things continue to go downhill when the footpegs come off.

"Look at these spacers... they've been made from copper gas piping. They're not even cut square!"

The engine soon lifts out and together we carry it to a worktop. The piston's loose in the bore and the con rod has chunks knocked out of it. Worse still is the timing-side crankcase half of which sports a ragged hole large enough for a little finger to pass through. It's directly underneath the timing side bush and leaves a sizeable chunk of it unsupported.

"There's not a hope that engine would have run... well, not beyond the end of the street anyway as it'd certainly not have had any oil," Andy bemoans.
I'm aghast... but he's seen it all before.

"Some people assemble engines with no care, as long as it looks OK, they're happy. They obviously never intend to ride the bike, or at least not go more than a couple of miles at a time."
In this case, however, the previous owner had done it up to sell and the damage is inexcusable. The crankshaft itself proves to be in no better shape, the rounded drive side crankpin nut tightened on with a hammer and chisel and the flywheels badly bruised by more hammer work.

"You're going to have to start afresh with everything in the engine," Andy announces.
I agree, there's no point doing it if it's not done right.

With the bike in pieces and a list of replacement parts stretching to five A4 pages, I set about finding a supplier. My research shows several companies selling AMC spares but I want to work with one that will be sympathetic to the quest. I consult Derek who tells me they're all good but the owners of the firm most local to us, *Andrew Engineering* of Atherton in Lancashire, are especially knowledgeable, efficient and friendly. I pen a letter to them, explaining the venture, my previous rides and the need for a vast quantity of parts. Finally, I ask if they would be able to offer a trade discount if I buy everything from them.

First thing next morning the phone rings.

"Hello Gordon. It's Malcolm Lee from Andrew Engineering. I've received your letter but you didn't need to include a copy of Overland To India as I've already read it."
In his lilting Lancashire accent, he continues,

"When can you come in and have a chat about it?"
11 o'clock the following morning is agreed.

The company is located just a few miles off the M60, Manchester's orbital motorway. Delayed by the ever-present congestion on the bridge that crosses the Manchester Ship Canal, I arrive just in the nick of time at a solid, red brick two-storey building. Visible through large ground floor windows is an impressive engineering workshop full of lathes, milling machines and CNC equipment. Accessed via an outside iron staircase are the first floor offices and storerooms. I climb them, to be greeted by Malcolm's wife, Joan, an incredibly warm and friendly person who chats while we wait for Malcolm to finish machining some parts. He soon breezes into the room in navy overalls and firmly shakes my hand. We talk about my rides, the Matchless, and then about their business.

"It's a hobby gone wrong," begins Malcolm, Joan philosophically nodding in agreement. "I started out making parts for my own Matchless G12. At my local bike club people would say, 'can you make me this or can you make me that?' And it just grew from there."

At first Malcolm made parts by night, using the machinery of the engineering works where he was a manager, then, deciding he could make a go of it as a business, set up in his garage. As the business grew, they moved into an old mill and then the current premises, which were built in 1922 to be a Co-op bakery and dairy, complete with an area for loading dray horses.

"That was thirty odd years ago and we've broadened our range considerably since then, we also supply the trade as well as mail order direct to customers. We incorporated Britan Lathes some time ago and we've made lots of things that have nothing to do with motorcycles as well, such as screens for theatres and exhibition centres, and also huge welding jigs for Sellafield nuclear power station and Caterpillar earthmovers. Over the last few months we've even been making test equipment for the oil industry."

Crunch time comes. A trade discount would be great but to have the ongoing support of these people, who are so knowledgeable about the bikes and steeped in quality engineering knowhow, would be invaluable.

"What we've decided, Gordon, is to support you as much as we can," Malcolm begins, "We won't see any benefit as a company because by the time you've done the ride and your book is out we'll have retired, but we have all these parts sitting here and would really like to be involved. Anything you need that we've made, you can have for free. If we've bought it in, we'll ask you to pay for it. It'll be a kind of swansong for Joan and me."

I'm hardly able to believe my ears and struggle to find the appropriate words to respond, "thank you" seeming seriously insufficient.

"So when are you off?" asks Joan.

"Next August," I reply.

"In nine months?" she questions, obviously surprised.

I nod back.

"You'd better get your parts lists to us as soon as possible then!" she laughs.

Malcolm asks about the bike's forks and I tell him the stanchions are badly corroded. He disappears into the storeroom, returning with a shiny new pair of main tubes wrapped in stretchy nylon protective sleeves.

"Take these," he says, handing them to me. "We're getting low on stock and I don't know when we'll be making more."

I thank them again, shaking both their hands.

"And call me when you know what you're going to do about your crankshaft. We have the axles here but no flywheels or con rods," Malcolm shouts as I head to the stairs.

I feel as if I'm floating on air.

That night, I fortuitously find a secondhand set of G3L flywheels listed on eBay and immediately order them. They arrive a couple of days later and to my eye look good but I take them straight to Andy, an hour's drive away, so he can check them over.

"Listen," he says, tapping one with a spanner.

It produces a tuneful ring.

"Now listen to this one," he says, picking the other up.

In comparison, it sounds dead flat.

"It's not conclusive, you could have them properly tested, but my guess is this one has a hairline fracture."

We bounce options backwards and forwards, Andy suggesting we get the whole crankshaft custom made.

"With a billet crank and matching crankpin, roller big end and all new bearings and shafts, the bottom end of the engine will be indestructible."

I agree and call Max Nightingale at *Alpha Bearings*, a 70-year-old West Midlands engineering company renowned for its superior crankshafts. Enthused by the project, he readily agrees to machine a new crank for the Matchless using donor axles provided by Andrew Engineering. He even goes so far as to put us to the top of his waiting list, a real bonus. Whilst this is in hand, there's little else that can be done to the engine so Andy busies himself with the worn out gearbox. Fortunately, Derek has a couple of spare Burman CP boxes, one of which has seen little use, so Andy sets to swapping over some of the gears. At the same time, Derek begins fabricating parts, such as a rear lifting handle, luggage rack and sump guard, and Joan and Vikki begin working their way down my lists, prioritising the parts I'll need first.

Meanwhile, I set to tackling some of the more major logistical challenges. The biggest problem appears to be getting the bike into Vietnam itself, which is a bit of a blow considering riding there is the primary object of the journey. There are, it transpires, severe restrictions on taking a foreign registered machine into the country. Some online reports border on scaremongering, with 'Nothing larger than 250cc is allowed on Vietnamese roads,' and 'Even if you do succeed in getting it across the border, which may involve bribing officials, you'll be stopped by police and have your oversize bike confiscated,' just two of the many warnings I read. They might be the voices of doom, but if they're giving fair warning, it doesn't bode well.

Then I read a write up by a couple of Americans who'd ridden their Harleys in Vietnam a couple of years earlier. According to their blog, they'd used a travel agency to sort all the paperwork in advance, and although they had to be accompanied by a company representative at all times, they had a great trip free from fear of their bikes being impounded. I contact the company they'd used only to find its prices prohibitive.

'Sorting the paperwork is very difficult and we haven't done it for some time,' their representative writes back. 'Providing we can still get approval, a 10 day tour of Vietnam, following the route you outlined, will cost US $6400 and we'll need to have one of our staff accompany you.'

I'm keen to get there, but not that keen!

Further research produces one more agency that offers the service. Based in Hanoi, *Mototours Asia* is primarily a company catering for groups that fly into Vietnam and take a week-long organised guided motorcycle tour. Best of all from my perspective, they're the only company in Vietnam that uses Royal Enfields so we're off onto a good footing straight away. Their reply to my enquiry soon lands in my inbox and fearing more exorbitant prices, I open it apprehensively. Joy of joys, the price to organise my visit is roughly a quarter of their competitor's, the main difference being that they will only send a guide to the borders to ease the bike's import and export. When it comes to the majority of my trip, riding between Hanoi and Ho Chi Minh City, I will be left to my own devices. Perfect!

Crossing China is the next procedural nightmare. Although you can fly into China, buy a local bike and ride it around unaccompanied, it's not possible to enter the country with your own vehicle without the services of an accompanying guide/escort. This, I learn, is more expensive for motorcyclists as the guide has to have his own car, and in many cases, a driver as well. Typical crossings from Kyrgyzstan to Pakistan are run over five days, with two of those days spent in the city of Kashgar while the company organises a driving license and temporary vehicle registration. To try to reduce costs I head to the overland traveller's favourite website, *Horizons Unlimited*. It's a great place to find information and tips about riding anywhere in the world and its *HUBB* forums are brilliant for researching every topic imaginable, from tyre choice for riding in the Arctic to locating a mechanic half way up the Amazon. It's also very useful if you want to connect with fellow 2-wheel travellers, so I click onto its Northern Asia regional forum and begin searching for other trans-China bikers that I can share costs with. A group, I soon discover, is being put together to transit China in early September so I make a note of their posts, wondering if I should ask to join them.

The third tricky country to cross is, of course, Myanmar. In a short time, the border-to-border escort business has blossomed with a whole raft of companies now offering the service, although some don't appear to have much of a track record. I write to three, giving estimated dates for my arrival at the border with India and exit point to Thailand, asking each to provide a proposed itinerary and quote. All reply, one being outrageously expensive, the other two fairly similar in price. The representative of *Burma Senses*, Min Min, takes the time to explain many facets of the transit process and when I respond saying I'll need to speed the crossing up to reduce the cost, quickly replies with suggestions for less sightseeing and more miles per day. He even puts me in touch with another party of motorcyclists that will be crossing with them around the same time. I contact the group's organiser to discuss their plans but in the end, taking my old bike into account, decide it's sensible to travel on my own. I confirm dates with Burma Senses, delighted to have this key stage of the journey agreed so early in the project. It's a considerable weight off my mind.

Assembling the bike is a case of two steps forward and one and a half steps backwards. So many of the bigger parts are at the end of their life and need replacing, which is especially difficult with tinware. The primary chain case cover turns into a sieve when bead blasted and removing the paint from both mudguards reveals masses of plastic filler and badly welded joints. The brake pedal snaps in half when being straightened in a vice, one of the alloy fork bottoms has a hairline fracture, the steering crown is so worn that the bearing cups slop around and even the frame proves to be bent. On the rear sub frame, where the wheel spindle sits, is a forging that's partially machined to accept the screws that move the wheel backwards, thus adjusting the chain tension. When he inspects it, Andy discovers one side has worn badly and has been bunged with an oversize bolt. There's not much supporting metal left around it and as it's unlikely we'll find a replacement frame at such short notice, he machines a proper insert which he then taps to accept the correct size adjusting screw.

"I'm not totally happy about it, Gordon, but it's a forging and can't be welded or even filled with braze. The only thing that reassures me it'll survive is the quality of the metal originally used in the frame. It's really good stuff, so it should be able to flex and absorb the impacts," he explains whilst tightening up a bracket to mount the voltage regulator.

It's exceedingly fortuitous that most of the components which need replacing are found in Derek's house. Like pulling rabbits out of a hat, he produces a replacement alloy timing cover, rear mudguard carriers, alloy top yoke off a later competition model, second toolbox and a chainguard. When it comes to restoring the petrol tank I discover the original has been filled with lead and both of its rear mounts have been butchered

"Fear not," says Derek. "I have a spare in better condition and we can swap them over."

Rear numberplate carriers are hard to source so Derek fabricates one, skillfully peening its edges until it becomes indistinguishable from an original item. The peppered primary chaincase outer cover is proving harder to replace but Derek comes up trumps, spotting one for sale at the *Stafford International Classic Motorcycle Show*. Not only is it in terrific shape, it's a later version with removable bulged section which allows easy adjustment of the clutch. I lose count of the hours he puts into the project and the number of times I thank him.

"What are you doing about rear wheel bearings?" asks Malcolm during one of my many visits to Atherton.

I explain I'm currently searching for new-old-stock items, a hard to find taper roller arrangement.

"We make a conversion kit for later AJS and Matchless front wheels that upgrade them to a modern sealed bearing setup. Considering all the luggage you'll be carrying on the back of a rigid bike, how about I make a one-off sealed bearing kit for your rear? I'll use EN24 steel for the spindle, which'll be extra strong, and I'll make you a spare one as well, just in case."

I know how busy he is but it's impossible to say no to such a generous offer and within days he sets to work on the task.

There's a larger AMC front wheel hub for sale at the *Bristol Classic Motorcycle Show*. It has a 7" drum on a half-width hub, a short lived configuration used at the end of the 1940s and early 1950s before the design was changed to a full width hub. It may only be 1" larger in diameter than my rather oval looking 6" wartime brake but because of the extra load on the bike, any additional stopping power will be welcome so I buy it. Real progress is made in March, six months before departure, when I drop both hubs at *Central Wheel Components* to be built with new rims and spokes and everything else at *Redditch Shotblasting* to be powder-coated gloss black. The vapour cleaned crankcases come back from *CC's Carburettor Cleaners* looking like new and with the precision made crank collected from Alpha's, Andy sets to work on the engine.

Complications soon arise. The replacement cylinder, a new-old-stock item covered in seventy-year-old War Department grease, hasn't been machined with cutaways at the bottom of its liner to allow the con rod to move freely. Furthermore, the replacement piston needs its skirts shortening to clear the new, larger diameter Alpha flywheels. When he's resolved these, Andy discovers a problem with the position of the camshafts. I go to look.

"Both cams are worn out because they've been over-meshing. The camshaft spindle centrelines and the crankshaft centreline are too close together," he tells me, vernier gauge in hand

This isn't a recent thing, they were machined like that back in 1941. After much head scratching he takes it to local automotive engineering legend, Bill Bannister, who machines offset bushes to compensate. Andy, who's never content to put his name to something unless it's done properly, is very pleased with the solution.

"Proper job, that. They're not going to wear out now," he says, showing me how smoothly everything turns over.

The front forks take considerable work to make good. We fit springs slightly longer than standard to give a little extra travel and Andy makes a special tool to attach to the damper rods. Sweating and cursing, we put our backs into pulling the rods up then frantically screw the top nuts down, miraculously only trapping our fingertips once, a pig of a job. When we come to attach the petrol tank, we find its mounting points aren't level and it rocks on the frame. We have a set of rubbers from Andrew Engineering that would work perfectly if the tank was square, but to level things up, order some Royal Enfield Model G tank rubbers, which Andy mixes and matches with the Andrew Engineering items until everything sits flush.

"A bit of Royal Enfield on the bike!" Andy, an ardent Enfield lover, chirps.

It's actually the second item as the replacement foot brake pedal, selected as it will sit flush with the frame, came off an Indian made Bullet. When the tank's bolted on, I go round all four corners and dab spots of different coloured paint on each of the rubber configurations, ensuring I'll be able to take it off and easily put it back together in the future.

Transported back to my flat, the bike, meaning its frame and engine plus a few attached cycle parts, is heaved up a flight of stairs and deposited in my lounge. As I'm not blessed with a heated indoor garage, it's the best place available to work on her... I can constantly evaluate progress and if I have a spare few minutes, she's at hand. Best of all, it's a warm environment in which to work on the coldest days. Derek visits to help with some of the more challenging aspects of putting her together, including assembling the overly complex front wheel taper bearing and spacer arrangement when the gleaming black rims arrive back from Central Wheels.

A couple of weeks later, when I've done all I can, I face the challenge of getting her downstairs again so call upon the help of Brendan Layton, a friend I've made whilst working at motorcycle shows. Tall and strong, Brendan cheerfully arrives one evening with his 15-year-old son, Jacob, a smashing lad who's keen to be involved. After a pizza, we wheel the Matchless through my front door, struggling to manoeuvre her down the communal hallway and stairs without being caught in the act by any of my neighbours. Jacob guides the front wheel, I hold onto the handlebars and Brendan brings up the rear, taking the bulk of the strain on a leather belt threaded through the subframe. Just when we think we're on the home straight, the belt snaps but I'm on the front brake in a flash and happily, disaster is averted. Having pushed the bike to my shed, we return to laugh about the escapade before the pair head over the hills back home to Chesterfield.

At my next visit to Andrew Engineering, Malcolm has a present for me. They don't stock petrol and oil tank caps for the wartime machines and I only have one, which is currently on the petrol tank. Handing me a strange lump that looks more like a meteorite than a motorcycle part, Malcolm explains it's been sitting on his desk for more than 30 years and its odd shape is down to layers of hardened grease.

"It's a brass cap and it'll fit your tank once it's cleaned up and polished. I'd like you to have it and use it on the ride."
I'm thrilled, another personal touch going onto the Matchless.

"And you should know," reveals Malcolm, "that thanks to you I've started riding again."
Apparently, a painful leg had kept Malcolm off his bikes for more than two years and he had wondered if he'd ever ride again.

"Talking to you made me realise how much I've missed it, so I went for a short run last weekend... it was brilliant. How would you feel if I ride with you for a few miles at the start of your journey?"
It's a great idea!

Before I leave, Vikki hands me some chopped up rubber tubing which I can use to repair any broken oil pipes and Joan digs out spare clutch plates to carry in my bags, just in case climbing mountains proves too much for the first set. Each visit I make to their premises becomes longer, not because I need more parts but because they're such good company and we sit around chatting for long stretches of time until, remembering the size of my workload, I'm forced to leave.

We're ready to start the bike for the first time in May, a keenly anticipated moment. With Andy standing next to me, I swing my boot on the kickstarter, acutely aware of the rapid tat tat tat noise made by every tooth on its ratchet. There's a marked pause before she catches then a lovely, rich booming sound emanates from her exhaust, echoing melodiously off the adjoining wall. I'm over the moon. Squatting, Andy adjusts the carburettor air screw then begins undoing the rocker feed pipe to check oil is pumping to the top end. Nothing comes out for what seems like an age, then eventually, the tiniest of dribbles oozes forth.

"I'm not happy with that!" Andy exclaims. "I know most British bikes suffer from low oil pressure but this is ridiculous."

That night I undertake some research, discovering an article in *RealClassic* magazine in which Frank Westworth wittily described his experiences with AMC oil pumps:

'If you really want to raise your blood pressure over the lack of oil pressure, detach the rocker oil feed pipe and observe how much of Mr Shell's finest

heads north to the rockers... there was no danger of drowning in the sea of oil.'
His words give me a degree of reassurance that all's as it should be but I have a hell of a long way to ride with the engine, so seek further information. I send an email to Simon Warner, an enthusiast from Kent who rides a WD Matchless and recently started a website dedicated to assisting owners in finding the correct spare part numbers for them. He kindly offers to video the oil flow to the cylinder head of one of his own G3Ls so I'll have something to compare with mine. A couple of days later, the video arrives. The oil flow on Simon's engine could hardly be described as gushing but it's much better than ours. I talk the problem through with Malcolm, who, as a back up, gives me a replacement oil pump and front end cap. The original pump seems to be working fine but the tiny holes on the end cap are better aligned on Malcolm's replacement, so we swap them over and are instantly rewarded with standard AMC oil flow, for what it's worth.

"Don't worry Gordon," Simon says on the phone. "They've always run on that amount of oil. I can assure you, even when these bikes were completely worn out, they still kept going, and so will yours!"
His encouragement is very much appreciated.

A lot still needs doing to make the bike rideable. Derek spends hours attaching the mudguards, both of which he's had to heavily modify, fabricating horn and indicator brackets and making fixings to mount a front crashbar. Each visit to his home in Runcorn moves the bike another stage forward but there's just so much work involved. When I'm not trailering the bike to Derek's, I'm at Andy's, checking and improving its every function, making sure all is properly aligned and up to the task.

I've closely followed the progress of the party crossing China in September. It's now grown from five to twelve members, each individual's financial contribution reducing every time a new name is added to the list. On several occasions I've been tempted to get in touch but I just can't imagine that, on their modern, high performance bikes, they'll want me slowing them down. The thought of having a mechanical problem and holding the whole party up is untenable. On *Horizons Unlimited* I notice a post by a German biker called Christian Vogel who's planning a round the world journey. He's also hoping to minimise the cost of transiting China so I get in touch, mentioning early on that I'll be riding a classic British bike. Despite him being on the absolute antithesis, a BMW R1200GS, we agree to travel together for five days and split the fee. The tour company I've selected, *Newland Travel*, is based in Kashgar and are more than happy to accommodate the two of us. A date's fixed to meet at the Chinese border in September.

Organising visas is one of the most challenging aspects of the preparations. The biggest problem is that most visas are only valid for 90 days from the date of issue, meaning that many will have expired by the time I reach countries in the latter stages of the ride. Arranging them all at the last moment isn't feasible as I need ten in total and some embassies can take two to three weeks to process applications. The solution is to use two passports simultaneously. I have both New Zealand and British passports but swapping nationalities midway through a journey could be tempting fate... eagle-eyed immigration officials might spot the swap and dual citizenship is sometimes treated with suspicion. In the end, I apply for a second British passport which the UK Passport Office is willing to grant to travellers if they can prove it's a necessity. The second passport allows me to split the journey in two, with all early visas in one and all the later visas in the other. I choose Kyrgyzstan as my changeover point as British citizens don't need a visa there and I hope my passport won't be too closely checked on arrival.

Several visas need extra work. Azerbaijan demands a letter of invitation, which costs 50 euros from a Baku travel agency. Tajikistan requires I apply for a GBAO permit for travel through the Gorno-Badakhshan Autonomous Region, which is the mountainous area that the Pamir Highway passes through. Turkmenistan has me worried... overland travellers are only granted a five day transit visa and it's date specific. Late arrival at the border with only three days of the visa left would almost certainly result in me being be turned away. Of even more concern, I read several reports online saying that travellers have been refused visas without explanation when applying at Turkmenistan embassies in Iran, Kazakstan, Turkey and Uzbekistan. One blog report says the applicants had initially been refused but a polite follow up letter to the Turkmenistan ambassador had got them a positive result. In light of their experience, I write an ultra polite email to their London embassy explaining the journey and asking for advice and assistance with my application. I embellish it with a list of places of beauty or cultural interest I want to visit during my five day sojourn and am rewarded straightaway by a positive response from the consul. Because of the date specific nature of the crossing, I decide to leave getting this visa to the very end.

Some visas are easy, Myanmar only takes four days and China five. Some are expensive, India topping the charts at £140 for a multiple entry visa, but others are cheap, with Nepal's £15 single entry fee the best. The London Nepalese embassy's appeal for tourists to return to the country after its shattering earthquakes of the previous year is saddening. On its homepage is an explanation that only three regions were badly affected and it is now safe to visit the country. Moreover, it's crucial that tourism returns to past levels if their economy is to recover from the devastation. This contrasts sharply with the warnings on the FCO (British Foreign and Commonwealth Office) website where travel advisories warn against all but essential travel to Nepal, which, it states, is still unsafe to visit. The FCO always err on the extreme side of caution so, undaunted, I send the embassy my passport in accordance with the visa timeline pinned to my lounge wall.

Pakistan is the other major concern. The visa application process has changed since I rode there in 2008 and a letter of invitation is now needed. A guest house / travel agency based in the north of the country offers the service online for US$50. I email my details to them, transfer the payment via Paypal and a few days later receive a letter of invitation accompanied by a completely fictitious tour schedule. Before making my application, I face a dilemma... tell the truth about crossing from China, which will reveal a planned route through areas with known problems, or tell a lie, stating that I'll enter and exit from

India. I weigh the pros and cons of both and even though I know that once obtained, I can legitimately use a visa at any border as they're not entry point specific, decide that honesty is the best policy. I make an appointment to visit the company that now process visas for Pakistan, situated directly opposite Old Trafford cricket ground in Manchester. My application is accepted without question and a week later I'm told my passport's available for collection, complete with a tourist visa.

Fitting an air filter to the Matchless proves a real headache. *Ram Air* supply three of their superb foam pod filters but there's just no way to squeeze one in. As Andy points out, bikes from this era didn't bother with air filtration and once the carburettor's attached to the cylinder head, there's no room for anything else. It's an obstacle we revisit several times, trying all kinds of tubing to mount the filter remotely, all without success.

One night, way after bedtime, I get a call from Andy who's still diligently working on the problem in his workshop.

"I think I've solved it Gordon," he says enthusiastically. "I've mounted two Royal Enfield Electra X right angle air hoses onto a connecting pipe then with some flexible hose, taken the feed round to the battery carrier. The filter fits perfectly inside it but we'll need Derek to make a mount to hold it in place... oh, and relocate the battery as well."

It's typical of Andy to be up late searching for a solution and although moving the battery is a pain, it's worth it to have a proper air filter.

The next day I head to Derek's so he can take measurements for a battery carrier that'll reside underneath the saddle, leaving him with my new *Shorai* Lithium Ion battery which saves a noticeable amount of weight and space compared with an old fashioned lead acid unit.

"Not a problem," he says in his usual unruffled way. "Leave it with me, I'll have a stainless steel one sorted in a couple of days."

As for mounting the air filter pod, that's quickly resolved by cutting up a piece of plastic drain piping which happens to be the perfect diameter. He shapes a steel mounting plate and spot welds a bolt through it. Bob's your uncle, another problem's solved!

Before I leave, Derek unveils a new rear brake plate that he's just collected from the metal spinners.

"Yours had an edge like a razor blade, Gordon," he says. "It was a health and safety fail if ever I saw one! This'll do the job."

Superb!

By mid June I know I'll be struggling to leave on time. The bike, only just running, needs so much doing to her and with my work commitments mounting, an on-time departure becomes unrealistic. Revised spreadsheets soon created, I study weather patterns to estimate how late I can possibly leave before encountering heavy snows that will close the high passes in Tajikistan, Kyrgyzstan and Pakistan. The latest I dare risk, I calculate, will be the second week in September. I set myself a new and final date for the 8th September and promptly contact Christian, who's now on the American leg of his RTW ride. Apologising for letting him down, I receive a reply the same day in which, to his enormous credit, he attempts to shift his dates back to match mine, claiming he's doing his best for Anglo-German relations. He only concedes defeat when he realises his Chinese visa will have expired if he delays by too much. Thankfully, Newland Travel are quickly able to pair him up with an American travelling in a jeep close to our original crossing date. Now, irrespective of the cost, I'll have to cross China on my own.

One of the biggest expenses for overland travellers with their own vehicle is a Carnet de Passages en Douane. In effect, it's a temporary import license for your motorcycle which needs completing each time you enter and exit a country that's a member of the carnet scheme. A substantial financial guarantee ensures you'll leave that country with your bike rather than selling it illegally, avoiding import taxes and local duties. Costs vary from country to country, India being the most expensive on this trip with an import factor of 400%, which effectively means I have to indemnify the bike for four times its agreed value. Try as I might, I'm unable to convince the RAC, the UK's issuing body, that the Matchless is worth less than £3000, which makes me realise just how expensive a business this can be... imagine the cost if I owned a brand new adventure motorcycle or a Land Rover! However, before I can take out the necessary insurance policy which underwrites the carnet, I need to go through the process of making the bike road legal.

Registering a historic vehicle in the UK is no longer as simple as going to your local DVLA office and filling in a form. The DVLA now work hand in hand with owners' clubs and it's necessary to get a certificate from one of these organisations to validate your motorcycle's authenticity before making an application. Roy Bellett of the *AJS & Matchless Owners Club* responds smartly to my request for assistance, posting a certificate as soon as I send him photographs and pencil rubbings of the bike's frame and engine numbers. The certificate dates the Matchless as leaving the factory on the 26th November 1941, meaning we'll celebrate her 74th birthday somewhere on the ride, possibly in Myanmar, which would be most serendipitous. The bike's date of manufacture is based on her frame number, her engine not being made until 1943. That doesn't come as a surprise as it's the norm for WWII machines not to have matching numbers. Each time a motorcycle needed a repair or overhaul during the war, it was sent to the *Royal Electrical and Mechanical Engineers* (REME) workshops. There, engines went one way and frame and cycle parts another, with no attempt being made to marry up original components when the bikes were later reassembled.

Despite the certificate, the DVLA still want the Matchless inspecting and, depending on where you live, it can take weeks to get an appointment. Lady luck is with me as the local travelling inspector is a keen motorcyclist who readily agrees to slot me in on his way home from another inspection. We meet up one sunny evening in July.

"Lovely old bike," he says immediately.
Within five minutes, the frame and engine numbers are confirmed and we're one step closer. The V5 registration document is delivered by post a few days later, revealing the Matchless's new number as YXG 183. It's an age related

number that wasn't allocated in the era when 3 numeral, 3 letter plates were the order of the day. Relieved, I get on the phone to Tippers Vintage Plates so they can begin making a beautiful set of front and rear black and silver number plates.

Running the engine in and checking everything else has bedded properly, a process known as a shakedown, isn't straightforward. I live in an urban area plagued with traffic lights and roundabouts and the roads are usually clogged with slow moving local traffic. Sitting stationary for long periods, becoming increasingly hot, is a far from a perfect beginning for a rebuilt cast iron engine. I do the first 20 miles one Sunday morning, looping in a 3 mile circuit around my flat. The Matchless feels quite different from my old Ajay, especially her gearbox. There's a definite clunk when shifting from neutral to first, then moving up to second and third requires slow, deliberate actions. It's almost as if I can feel the selector moving into neutral from where my foot has to guide it on and into the next gear. Third to top is seamless but moving back down the gears, especially from third to second, comes with a solid jolt. After a couple of rides in the middle of the afternoon where I'm stuck in queues of school traffic, I employ a new tactic, taking the bike out at night when the air is cooler and traffic virtually non existent. After spending my usual couple of hours at Jane and Jacques's cottage, I head home around 10pm, climb into riding gear and hop on the Matchless, usually riding for an hour around the same 3 mile circuit, each cycle adding 18 miles to the tally.

After a couple of weeks of this, and with 134 miles on the clock, I figure I need to build up the mileage more rapidly. In the middle of a fine day I set off on a longer run, heading towards the Peak District. I ride for 16 miles then stop in a layby on the far side of Whaley Bridge to let the engine cool, proactively spending the time fitting an alarm and mirrors, both of which I'm carrying in my backpack. Once everything's done I ride towards Buxton on the A6, motoring along a 3 mile straight section of dual carriageway that heads up a deceptively steep hill. Circling a roundabout, I head back downhill, the engine running sweetly. My logic says I should call it a day and head for home but on the spur of the moment, thinking it a shame to miss the opportunity of getting more miles under my belt, I spin around another roundabout and recommence the 3 mile climb. Half way up I feel a tug from the rear wheel and the engine cuts out... the piston has nipped up! I'm gutted, coasting to a halt then calling Andy from my stricken position at the roadside. As the piston's already freed itself he suggests I let everything cool then ride home as carefully as possible.

I'm on tenterhooks the whole way back, riding as smoothly as I can, but the Matchless feels no different, running flawlessly. The next day I load her onto the trailer and take her to Andy's where he immediately whips out the spark plug. It's completely bright blue, a sure sign of sudden and intense heat

"I think I know the cause," Andy announces.

He removes the recently chromed filler cap from the petrol tank and inspects the breather hole on its top.

"I reckon you've had a heat seizure caused by this..."

Blowing then sucking, he demonstrates no discernible air movement through the tiny pinprick of a hole.

"As a vacuum builds in the fuel tank and less petrol reaches the carb, it'll run leaner and leaner. That plug must have been glowing hot to get so blue!"

After enlarging the hole, we turn our attention back to the engine, using Andy's flexible camera, a mechanic's endoscope, to peer inside the cylinder. Anxiously watching the image on a laptop screen, score marks soon become visible... everything needs taking apart! With the head, cylinder and piston removed, Andy leaves to visit Bill Bannister whilst I set to scraping silicone from every surface then wiping them all spotlessly clean with a rag soaked in brake cleaner.

"Bill reckons you'd have got away with this," Andy reports on his return. "The score marks are light and would probably have polished out within a thousand miles. Still, it's not worth the risk so he's given the cylinder a light hone and dressed the piston. It's got a fraction more clearance now and I don't think it likely you'll be able to seize it again, no matter how hard you try."

We set to reassembling everything and a couple of hours later, to my huge relief, the Matchless fires up beautifully. Against the odds, only 24 hours after the incident, we're back in business.

With only three weeks to go, I receive an email from Vladim, my contact at *UKRferry*, the shipping company that operates on Black Sea routes. Apparently a revised schedule has just been announced for September with only one weekly sailing to Georgia instead of two. I'd planned to sail on a Sunday crossing but that's been cancelled and instead, I must sail three days later or four days earlier. I study my timetable but can see no way to leave any sooner so decide I'll delay my departure by two days, effectively giving me one more additional day crossing Europe. Once again I contact the three travel agencies with revised dates. Both the Vietnamese and Burmese companies are relaxed about the changes, I've paid deposits to both but as my arrival is still so far away, they haven't submitted any paperwork yet. Newland Travel, however, is concerned by this third change in dates and ask me to confirm this is the final one as they're about to tender documents to the relevant government departments. I give them my assurance it's the last change and cross my fingers.

Two weekends before the off, I trailer the bike to Derek's and he sets to work fixing on a couple of extra brackets, one at the rear for a *Tutora* chain oiler and one at the front for the cylinder head temperature gauge I'll be using to monitor overheating in the hottest places. That done, we prepare to go for a ride, something I've been really looking forward to. Derek wheels out 'old faithful', a 1957 Matchless G80 that he's owned for many years. To the accompaniment of a raucous duet of popping Plumstead exhausts, we head out, the sun warming our backs as we go. Derek's a former police motorcyclist who rides with precision and care so I follow behind, enjoying the feeling of biking with no purpose other than the pleasure of doing it. After a brief rest beside the Bridgewater Canal, where long-boaters sunbathe on deckchairs or take shelter under awnings from the late summer heat, we wend along country roads back to his home. Before I departed for Egypt on the Bantam, Derek said,

"I expect that bike to come back with battle scars all over it... in fact, I don't want to ever see it looking like this again. It should be covered in muck and oil and look as though it's really been through it."

This time, however, he's more circumspect, the journey ahead obviously a much more challenging one.

"Just make sure you have a great time and get back in one piece," he says as we shake hands.

I get up early the following morning, check the Matchless over then set off on her longest preparatory run to date, riding on gently undulating and twisting roads to Macclesfield, Leek, then the hamlet of Ramshorn and the home of Johnny and Wendy Brittain. Johnny, a former Royal Enfield works trials rider, is the oldest living winner of the *Scottish Six Days Trial* and the only surviving member of the last British team to win the *ISDT*, the Olympics of Motorcycling, in Czechoslovakia in 1953. Now in his eighties, he's still passionate about classic motorcycling and he and Wendy have been the loveliest of hosts to Jane, Jacques and myself on the several occasions we've visited them. The Matchless runs without fault the whole way, a real confidence booster, and is much admired by Johnny. He's got more knowledge about riding off road in his little finger than I've gained in my whole lifetime's experience and vividly recalls competing in trials against opponents on the postwar variants of my G3L, greats such as Hugh Viney and Gordon Jackson.

"I had an advantage over them in the early part of my career as my Royal Enfield had a spring frame, They were still riding on rigids like your Matchless and my rear suspension made such a difference," he tells me, hand resting on the Matchless's tank. "I'm sure you'll feel every stone and bump when you're riding off-road but I'm equally sure your engine will last... AMC engines were always very strong."

They're encouraging words, although I wish I had even a smidgin of his riding skill to help me on my way. After a cup of tea and a sandwich I say my farewells, and under clear blue skies, ride home non-stop, thrilled with the bike's performance. There are now almost 500 miles on the clock, she's starting first kick and not getting especially hot when held up at traffic lights. I feel I can dismiss any concerns about her not being ready... the ride is most definitely on!

Just a couple of jobs are left outstanding. I take the bike to Andrew Engineering so Malcolm can customise a sidestand to fit her. The standard item allows the bike to lean too far over so with the help of a blowtorch, he heats one up and in small increments bends it to a more suitable angle, testing each subtle adjustment until happy with the result. The next day I meet up with Andy and we put the bike on a dynamometer. This is the second time she's been tested, the first test carried out a couple of months ago by the friendly team at *Hitchcocks Motorcycles*. They'd done a great job for the initial set up but now things have bedded in we want to ensure the carburettor's optimised.

"Don't rev it above 4000," Andy implores the machine's operator as he climbs onto the Matchless's saddle and prepares for the first run. Most people put their bikes onto a dyno to tune them for maximum power and performance, we just want to make sure the air-fuel mixture is perfect at my most frequent riding speeds, 30, 40 and 45mph. It doesn't take long for Andy to make a couple of tweaks before giving his verdict.

"Bob on! We won't get better than that, Gordon," he declares.
Andy gives the rest of the bike a final check over and pronounces her fit for active service. His parting words as I climb into my car and say goodbye are,

"And remember, if it ain't broke, don't fix it... just keep an eye on the plug and points every so often and change the oil."
With a cheery wave, he leaves.

I work the last weekend before departure at the *Netley Marsh Eurojumble* and the giant *Beaulieu International Autojumble.* I really could do with staying at home, packing and finalising arrangements for my absence, but earning money for the trip is a higher priority. I share a hotel room with Alan Graham, maker of *Spitfire Fuel Catalysts.* Before dinner on the Saturday evening, we spend a couple of hours packaging my sales stock and labelling the envelopes so orders can be fulfilled whilst I'm away. Twice I say,

"Enough Alan, let's go and eat," but both times he tells me we'll crack on until they're all done, a fabulous help. It's not the first occasion he's put himself out on my behalf, only three weeks earlier he'd driven over 100 miles to pick some work up for me. He's a real gent.

On the Monday I take Jacques to Alton Towers for the day. Roller coasters scare me silly but he loves them and, like many times before, he goes on the rides whilst I wait at their exits for him to return, hair askew and cheeks glowing red. Whilst he's whooshing around, inverted or falling vertically from the skies, I spend time on the phone, chasing down my passport which still languishes in the Turkmenistan embassy, organising various aspects of business and calling friends to say cheerio. Jacques enjoys the day immensely but his pleasure is only surface deep. He's very upset about me going, emotion which has emerged as a mixture of tears and anger over the last few weeks. I've tried various strategies to mollify him, beginning with rationalisation and ending, inevitably, with bribery and the lure of a future trip to the *Harry Potter* studios as compensation. Most important, though, is a promise to be home for Christmas. When I rode to Egypt in 2010, I missed Jacques's eighth birthday which he still hasn't forgiven me for. Anniversaries and us all being together at Christmas mean a lot to him, so I know that missing it is not an option. There are times when he's so upset that I wish I could cancel, it hurts too much to see him distressed, but this far down the track it just isn't possible.

I'm run ragged for the last two days, working my way through lists that never seem to get any shorter, and finally packing my bags. Everything fits... just! The amount of oil, dehydrated expedition food and muesli I'm carrying will shrink as the journey progresses but the volume of medical supplies, including military type trauma bandages, coagulant patches, burn gels, splints, dental kit and three lots of antibiotics, take up a large amount of space that I'm seriously hoping won't be reduced. Pretty much the same is true of the spare parts I'm taking, everything from a piston and small end to replacement spokes for the wheels, spare inner tubes to a *Thorspark* electronic ignition unit that will provide the sparks should my magneto fail. I try to squeeze as many of them into the bike's two toolboxes as I can but the saddlebags, when I test them, still weight a good 15kg apiece.

As usual, I spend my evenings with Jacques and Jane, compartmentalising everything else that's going on and trying to act normally. When I get home there are still things to be done and I'm often up until the small hours in order to complete the day's tasks. The final evening is strained, it's impossible to act as though everything's hunky dory and that I won't be off in the morning. Leaving is far from easy. Jacques and Jane give me a hug, Jane quietly reminding me that my son needs his dad and to make sure I return safely. I have every intention of doing exactly that.

I finish everything on today's list just after midnight, a new one sitting on my desk for the morning. Heading to bed, I lie down in the hope that sleep comes soon.

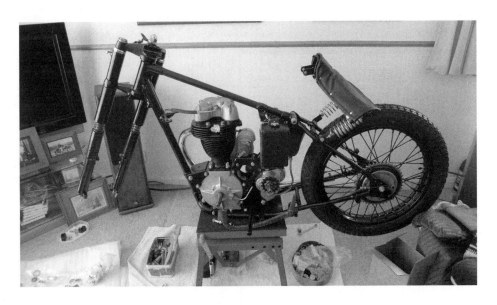

The Matchless being assembled in my lounge... where else?

Start	Manchester, uk
1	Hull, UK
2	Gescher, Germany
3	Nordhousen, Germany
4	Colditz, Germany
5	Bautzen, Germany
6	Niemodlin, Poland
7	Kraków, Poland
8	Lancut, Poland
9	South of Lviv, Ukraine
10	North of Tolstoye, Ukraine
11	Chisinau, Moldova
12-13	Odessa, Ukraine
14	Ilichevsk port, Ukraine
15-16	Crossing Black Sea
17	Mtskheta, Georgia
18	Shamkir, Azerbaijan
19-21	Baku, Azerbaijan
22	Crossing Caspian Sea
23	Turkmenbashi, Turkmenistan

Top left: Malcolm pressing new bearings into the Matchless's rear wheel.
Top right: Andy and his 1936 500cc Royal Enfield JF with 4-valve bronze head.
Bottom: Derek and his 1957 Matchless G80 beside the Bridgewater canal.

Day 1. Stockport to Hull. 124 miles.

Sitting bolt upright to the beeping alarm, a cascade of thoughts frenetically railroad through my head... it's 6.30am and there's still a huge amount to do. By 9.30am, buzzing on a third mug of coffee, I'm eventually able to apply myself to loading the Matchless. In the process of attaching the saddlebags, I hear the unmistakable sound of an air-cooled twin approaching. A grinning Malcolm, astride his Matchless G9, pulls around the corner closely followed by Joan and their friend Stephen, who've come by car.

"Not loaded yet?" asks Joan, looking surprised.

In my dreams!

Strapping the remainder of the luggage and spare tyre on is a long winded task so I make good use of Malcolm's skills. First he reattaches the side stand, which I'd removed yesterday in order to give it a coat of paint, then greases the magneto chain. Last boarding for tonight's ferry isn't until 7.00pm, which means time isn't too pressing, but checking and double checking everything seems to take an eternity and pressure begins to build. At 11.45am, with a lurching stomach, I lock up the flat and don my crash helmet and gloves. We're ready!

Joan gives me a hug and Malcolm heads up the driveway, the bark of his exhaust quickly diminishing. I check the odometer, which reads 535 miles, then prepare to start the Matchless. She does her usual thing on the first kick... taking a moment to consider whether she'd like to run or not, then deciding she might as well. I break into a grin, further anthropomorphising my motorcycle by thinking that if she knew what lay ahead of her, she'd be cowering in the darkest recesses of her shed! With the engine immediately settling into a steady rhythm, I turn a tight circle and roar up the driveway but not to the top... I'm filming the start of the journey so have to park up, run back and collect the tripod and camera, stow them away and set off again.

I'm feeling neither anticipation nor liberation and Vietnam's the last thing on my mind. Initially riding uphill, my attention's totally focused on the bike. Decidedly light on the steering, things nevertheless settle down once I'm on level ground and the weight of the luggage, approximately 55kg, doesn't seem to have tempered her acceleration one bit. One immediate concern is that the right hand saddlebag, sitting a scant three inches above the exhaust, doesn't slip lower and touch it. Pausing at the first set of lights, I ask Malcolm to check and after a thumbs up, we press on.

Driving towards Marple, I use the empty road to test the handling and brakes, both of which will take some acclimatising to now the bike's fully fuelled and loaded. With Malcolm squarely positioned in my mirrors, we ride onwards, the road paralleling the gentle bends of the River Goyt as we head for the High Peak town of New Mills. Pulling into its railway station car park, Malcolm stops alongside me and hops off.

"I can't believe how fast you're going with all that weight," he exclaims.

Neither can I, she's pulling magnificently!

"It's been great to get out on my bike again after so long, Gordon. I've really enjoyed it." he says, looking around. "But I think I'll head back now and let you get on with your trip."

Before he departs, he checks the sidestand retaining clip he'd recently fabricated. It needs tightening and I haven't a clue where to find the correct allen key amongst all my bags. Malcolm tells me to wait and disappears, soon returning with a full set he's purchased from a nearby ironmongers. Deftly making the adjustment, he tells me to keep the key as a spare, just in case. We shake hands and with a wave, he's gone.

A couple of short hops through traffic lights sees me join the A6 then 15 minutes later, I swing onto the Matchless's former nemesis, the dual carriageway where she'd nipped up just a few weeks ago. Careful not to overdo it, I build momentum gradually, settling for 40mph as we begin to climb. There's no noticeable change in the engine note, just the healthy brrm of the exhaust as we unwaveringly ascend, and to my delight, it's only necessary to drop into 3rd gear as we slow for the roundabout that marks the turnoff to Buxton. Aiming towards the first exit, I pat the bike's tank in appreciation then join the A623, the road across Tideswell Moor which scythes through the middle of the Peak District National Park.

Straddling the southern reaches of the Pennines, the Peak District was created in 1951 and holds the distinction of being Britain's first National Park. In this region, the heathland that borders the road is a mass of late flowering heather, verdant mosses and long wild grasses that sway in the afternoon breeze. The road dips and rises, turns sharply then tracks Roman-like for miles before falling steeply into Chesterfield. The Matchless devours the tarmac effortlessly, completing the first 38 miles of the journey without a hitch. I turn off before reaching the town's famed crooked spire and follow the satnav to Brendan's business unit.

"What kept you, Mr. G?" asks Brendan before admitting he'd actually thought I'd be running even more behind schedule.

He heads off to get me a cheese sandwich while I walk around his bike, a 2012 Honda Transalp that I've only previously seen partially obscured by a cover. It's equipped with robust alloy panniers complete with strapped on fuel and water bottles, an alloy topbox and a dry bag that's bungeed onto the rear seat. At the front are a pair of LED spotlights and squarely mounted onto one of the panniers is a GoPro camera. I look towards the G3L and smile, thinking that if you polled 100 random bikers about which of the two motorcycles was about to commence a 12,000 mile overland journey, it's doubtful any of them would plump for mine when Brendan's machine has the unquestionable appearance of an archetypal adventure bike.

Underway by 2.30pm, we follow a 5 mile stretch of dual carriageway then take a sharply climbing B road that serves as preliminary practice for crossing the Pamirs. We're soon on a succession of fast A roads, unfalteringly tracking in a north easterly direction through the sweeping farmlands of Nottinghamshire and Lincolnshire. Brendan takes the lead, using his mirrors to synchronise with my pace of 40 to 45mph, a task he accomplishes superbly in view of the mismatched power of our two machines. It's like having my own personal convoy outrider, a role that the Matchless was herself built for 74 years ago!

After a while, Brendan pulls into a layby to film me riding past. My Garmin, which has recalculated our route several times while following him, immediately directs me to turn off. In my mirrors, I see my confused friend raising his hand palm upwards, questioning the route change. Twenty minutes later, he passes me and his sat nav, a TomTom, instantly takes over, leading us onto another A road. Again, my Garmin begins plotting a revised course. It's interesting that two leading GPS units, both programmed to take the shortest, non-motorway route, should repeatedly attempt to take us along completely different roads, but whichever, the end result will be the same and the miles quickly pass as we get closer and closer to the North Sea.

Most of the time we're buffeted by a gusting headwind but the cloudless skies and warming sun more than compensate for the discomfort. Turning onto the majestic Humber Bridge, we're suddenly assaulted by a gale-strength crosswind that threatens to whip the wheels out from underneath us or worse, blow us sideways onto the vertical steel barriers that guard the edge. At 2,200 meters wide, it's one of the longest single span suspension bridges in the world, making our crossing a protracted dice with danger that neither of us enjoys.

"That cross wind wasn't much fun, was it?" says Brendan as we pause at the toll booths.

"You're not kidding... it's lined with bacon slicers," I reply breathlessly. "They'd be picking up thin slivers of us if the wind had gusted any more!"

Rush hour traffic's at its peak as we turn towards the city of Hull, filtering for miles between two rows of crawling vehicles that are further hampered by roadworks, then follow signs for the port.

"You do realise I've ridden one percent of the journey already," I remark as, standing next to our respective bikes, we pose for photos in front of the ferry.

"Piece of cake," he replies, tongue in cheek.

We both know today's ride was probably one of the easiest I'll have but I still feel mightily relieved to have completed it without any problems.

With a hug we say goodbye and Brendan departs post haste. Prodding the kickstarter, I set off too, riding the last couple of hundred metres to the boarding area where I fall in line behind an orange VW Karmann Ghia, its characteristic chirping engine harmonising almost melodiously with the deeper bupp-bupp-bupp of the Matchless. Boarding card and room key soon issued, I slide them into my tank bag's map pocket and continue towards the towering P&O ferry, The Pride of Rotterdam.

Gingerly advancing onto the ship's ramp, I turn a tight corner on damp checkered steel decking and head towards a line of motorcycles corralled two-by-two in a central bike park. Stopping the engine, I lower the Matchless onto her side stand and begin removing bags. There are probably 15 other bikes parked ahead of us, the riders of the ones immediately in front still strapping them down with greasy ratchet straps. The air's full of their excited chatter as they relive their ride here and two distinct groups swap details of their immediate plans.

"Where you off to, mate?" the guy nearest me asks.

To my great surprise, I suddenly feel uncomfortable... it seems embarrassing, ludicrous even, to state my destination. I mumble somewhat vaguely that I'm hoping to reach Germany tomorrow then change the subject by complementing his red Ducati. Soon left to myself, I haul the Matchless onto her rear stand and in an exhibition of overkill, use four tie downs to secure her.

Once in my cabin, having lugged three loads of gear to and then from the lift, I grab a shower and get dressed in my crinkly new travel clothes. Heading out to the bar, the crispness of them brings a wave of nostalgia as I remember being a boy at the beginning of our family summer holidays, wearing for the first time, the new clothes my mum and dad had just bought me. They were happy days.

A week ago, it seemed impossible that all my preparations would be completed in time and almost inconceivable that I'd be sitting here sipping a chilled beer, the sweet-running Matchless safely ensconced in the hold. As I gaze down the Humber Estuary, tinges of red spreading across the sky behind the fading outline of the suspension bridge, I can't help wondering which crucial things I have possibly forgotten.

Ready for the off, with Malcolm and Joan.

Day 2. Rotterdam, Holland, to Gescher, Germany. 170 miles.

For first time in months, my head's not full of to-do lists, problems to overcome and the dreadful feeling that time's rapidly running out. My world has shrunk to the joyful simplicity of two wheels, a frame, petrol tank and engine plus a pile of bags. A colossal weight has lifted off me and as I tuck into a breakfast of pain au chocolat and coffee, I realise I'm at last feeling free and unencumbered. Sailing slowly past a seemingly endless line of docks and hundreds of acres of heavy industry and petro-chemical works, we dock around 8.30am. I again struggle to find the optimal loading sequence, this time trying the tyre on top rather than under the mound of dry bags. All but one of the bikers leave, as do the hundreds of cars and vans parked on our deck. Finally done, I escape the stifling hold just a few seconds ahead of the last remaining traveller, a laid-back motorcyclist on a Honda who doesn't seem to be in a rush to go anywhere.

Once on dry land, I repeat,

"Ride on the right! Ride on the right!" as I filter past the immigration checkpoint then round a succession of lesser port exit roads.

Heading east from Europoort, the city of Rotterdam irrevocably draws me into its clutches. The downtown area's surprisingly modern with an open and airy feel. but a formidable sequence of traffic lights and pedestrian crossings on its main thoroughfare slows progress into a stop start rhythm that soon becomes tedious. On the far side I spot a Shell service station and decide to fill up. Having paid, I return to the bike and wheel her across the forecourt to a small rest area where I check the level of the oil and eat a snack. When it's time to leave, I flick the sidestand up and, carefully balancing the bike with my left hand, hoist my right leg into the air and karate kick it forwards aiming for the short gap between the petrol tank and my luggage. I don't quite get it right, the heel of my boot just catching on the top of the saddle. More of a glance than an impact, it's nevertheless enough to nudge the bike's centre of gravity and she begins to tip over. As if in slow motion, I lose my grip on the handlebar rubber and she crashes hard onto the concrete. Damn!

It gets worse... the cap flies off the oil tank and precious 20/50 begins glugging onto the ground. With no chance of lifting the bike on my own, I watch powerlessly as she bleeds herself dry, an unsightly process that takes no more than 15 seconds. Spotting my plight, a man runs over from his car and helps me right the bike then rather sheepishly, I return to the forecourt shop to ask for some cleaning equipment. The tolerant teller abandons his post, following me to the Matchless with a bucket of sawdust which he efficiently spreads on top of the gradually widening oil slick.

"Don't worry, it's not a problem," he says, returning inside to serve the queue that's formed during his short absence. In reality, it's not much of a problem for me either as I have more oil and can quickly refill the tank but I could kick myself for my clumsiness as well as the waste and the mess. Lesson learned the hard way, I resolve from now on to use the sidestand whenever I'm getting on or off the bike and to regularly check the tightness of the oil cap.

Holland is the most densely populated major country in Europe and travel along its busy highways and byways is plagued by endless sequences of traffic lights all devilishly choreographed to halt traffic flow every few hundred metres. It's far from the best scenario when it comes to keeping a cast iron, air-cooled engine the right side of melting point. However, in the early afternoon I reach my first planned stop, the city of Arnhem. It's a place I've always wanted to visit, primarily because of the major battle that was fought here during the Second World War. Known as *Operation Market Garden*, the object of the Allied attack was to secure several key bridges over rivers and canals, thus enabling ground forces to advance into Germany as the northern arm of a massed pincer movement. At Arnhem, troops of the British 1st Airborne Division and elements of the 1st Polish Independent Parachute Brigade were dropped behind German lines on 17th September 1944. Their mission was to capture and hold the Arnhem road bridge which crossed the Nederrijn, the Dutch part of the River Rhine. The paratroops encountered fiercer resistance than expected and although a small force of 740 men were able to reach the northern end of the bridge, they were overrun three days later. Failed attempts to resupply by air and the inability of ground reinforcements to break through the superior German opposition ultimately led to withdrawal for the remainder of the surviving soldiers, approximately 2,400 in total, who daringly crossed the Rhine by night in relays of small boats.

I've watched *A Bridge Too Far*, the excellent Richard Attenborough film depicting the battle, several times but my interest in it is also, unsurprisingly, motorcycle related. The Royal Enfield 126cc Model RE 'Airborne' was a diminutive, spindly framed two-stroke motorcycle that, when encased in its own purpose-built cage, could be parachuted into enemy territory. All a paratrooper had to do on landing was open the cage, turn the handlebars 90°, start the engine and ride off. It was soon labelled the 'Flying Flea' and as well as being used in several other theatres of war, was deployed most notably at Arnhem. I have a Dutch friend in the *Royal Enfield Owners Club* who has both a wartime Flea and its rare parachute cage, which he actually dug up at Arnhem and restored. Some years ago, I bought one of the immediate post-war versions of the bike, a 1948 model that was ostensibly the same simple motorcycle with a three-speed hand change gearbox but civilianized with regular road lighting and gloss black paint. Tremendously interesting as it was, I struggled to get on with it as viable means of transport. Trying to brake, change gear and give a right turn hand signal all at the same time with impatient city traffic bombing past was neither easy nor enjoyable. I sold it a couple of years later as I needed the money to invest in a more rideable machine but I've often looked back with regret, wishing I'd been able to keep it, if only for the novelty factor.

Reaching the city limits, I head straight for the river and its famous bridge, which is actually a replica. The original Arnhem road bridge was destroyed by American aerial bombing in October 1944, a month after *Operation Market Garden*, but its replacement, completed in 1948, was built in exactly the same style. In 1977, it was renamed the John Frost Bridge in memory of the British commander, Major General John Dutton Frost, who was in charge of the British paratroops during its short-lived capture. The bridge's gently curving centre is immediately recognisable and riding towards it, I'm soon swept along in the flow of traffic, unable to stop until I reach the river's northern bank. Turning around, a not-so-straightforward manoeuvre that entails puttering through a high-rise housing estate, I head back across the bridge, scanning the approaches for a way down to the riverbank and its Airborne Memorial. Unable to find one, I go full circle around a roundabout and give it another go. After four crossings, I feel I've got to know the bridge quite well, but as there's no evident vehicular access to the area immediately below it, I cross for one last time and keep going.

The day has been largely spent accelerating through 3rd gear, momentarily shifting into top before having to brake hard at the next intersection, a sequence that's been repeated ad infinitum. Not far beyond Arnhem, my route changes to a lesser road and for the first time, I ride uninterrupted, enjoying the sensation of gliding through a cool forest before emerging at speed into the sunshine. Parking up on a grass verge that runs alongside a cycle lane, I decide I'm long overdue a rest and amble to the rear of the bike. One of the indicators is hanging loose... its aluminium stalk has fractured into two, doubtless the result of vibration. Disappointed, I unpack my tools and just as I begin to undo it, see a BMW K100 shoot past. It returns within seconds and stops next to me.

"Just checking you're OK?" the rider says, climbing off and giving me the biker handshake. I thank him for his concern and show him round the Matchless.

"No problem man, us bikers have to look out for each other," he replies.
At that moment, a sports bike flies past, its brake light goes on and after a swift about-turn, a second rider joins us.

"Hey," says a woman, lifting up her visor.

"Hey," we both reply (when in Rome!)

"What's happening?" she asks, climbing off her bike.
I explain about the indicator.

"If any more bikes stop, we'll have a biker's party," she says, going on to introduce herself as Melissa.

It's heartening they both turned around and also to know that camaraderie remains a watchword of the motorcycling community. As they make ready to depart, Melissa points to a patch on her leather jacket which says BACA, explaining it stands for *Bikers Against Child Abuse*, an international organisation she campaigns for. She quickly digs out flyers, stickers and business cards and hands them to us. Then, with smiles, laughter and another round of handshakes, they both zoom off, leaving me in a sudden vacuum of silence.

The border between Holland and Germany comes as something of a surprise, occurring in the middle of a small village. I slow, make a U-turn, and head back into the Netherlands then do the same again, returning to Germany. There are houses situated just a couple of metres either side of the invisible dividing line. How odd, I think, for one's immediate next door neighbour to be in another country.

"What's the weather like in Germany today, Gunther?" I muse, imagining a conversation over a garden fence.

"Not bad, and how's it over there in Holland, Pieter?"

"Oh, can't complain..." !

Dusk's creeping in and I struggle to know which to search for first, petrol or a place to stay. Fuel wins, so spotting a road sign which says 'Gescher 3km', I turn off the main road, hoping the town will have a petrol station. It does and after filling up, I ask the friendly shop worker if there's a hotel nearby.

"I'm sorry, I don't live here so I don't know. Let me check for you," she says, extracting a smartphone from her handbag.

"Yes, look, there is one here, near the church."

She holds it out to me and points at the map. Thanking her, I return to the Matchless and motor just a couple of hundred metres to the front door of the Domhotel. I'm greeted by an exceedingly chatty man whose name sounds like Hoover, but with the H barely discernible. He seems to be an all-in-one waiter, receptionist, barman and porter and fortunately, he's appreciative of my bike, opening a garage at the rear so I can lock her away for the night.

It quickly turns dark and by the time I'm washed and changed, the streets are deserted. (H)oover tells me that the town's claim to fame is its tradition of bell making, there's even a Bell Museum but that's already closed. Optimistically, I go for a walk, twice circuiting the towering St Pankratius's walls. Gescher proves to be a cosy off-the-beaten-track kind of place and with nothing to see or do beyond another lap of the church, I return to the hotel for a meal and an early night.

Airborne Enfields

The 125 c.c. Royal Enfield Model R.E. has been used in the various Airborne operations since D-Day, being transported by Glider and dropped by Parachute in a tubular Crate ; Motor Cycle and Crate being made throughout in the Enfield Works. In addition to Airborne operations the Model R.E. has been used by other branches of the Service with very great success, frequently negotiating "impossible" sections of country which larger machines could not possibly cope with.

The Model R.E. will be available to the public in the near future.

Royal Enfield

"MADE LIKE A GUN"

THE ENFIELD CYCLE Cº Lᵗᴰ Head Office & Works. REDDITCH.

Royal Enfield advertisement for the 125cc Airborne 'Flying Flea'.

Day 3. Gescher to Nordhousen. 215 miles.

This morning's maintenance chores are time-consuming. The biggest challenge I'm facing involves the rear brake. The steel rod that connects it to the brake pedal stands proud off the chassis and the left-hand saddlebag sometimes presses against it. I checked the wheel hub and brake plate a few of times yesterday and both were disconcertingly hot, a sure sign that the brake's inadvertently being applied for extended periods. Thankfully I'm not short of Rok Straps and after a couple of failed experiments, I succeed in attaching two of them in a way that tensions the rear of the saddlebag so that it sits slightly further away from the frame. Despite getting up early, it's 10.40am before I've completed all the tasks and am ready to leave.

Blessed again with gloriously sunny skies, I'm soon gliding through a quiet rural area, enjoying the peace of an empty road. Unexpectedly, I come upon a huge garage complex that's set back within its own park-like grounds. One word jumps out from the sign adjoining its entrance, 'Oldtimer', which is used in Holland and Germany to describe classic vehicles, both cars and motorcycles. Here, in the middle of nowhere, it's an unlikely find but I decide to have a look, hoping I can replace the oil I'd lost yesterday. Turning around, I set off down its long driveway and come to a halt at a showroom with 'Rezeption' painted above the door. Inside there's an intoxicating assortment of classic sportscars for sale plus an open plan shop selling a cornucopia of expensive four wheeled memorabilia.

Empty oil can in hand, I approach the counter and ask the receptionist if they sell oil. A phone call results in a young mechanic joining us. He's dressed in immaculately pressed snow white overalls that look as though they've never been within a mile of an engine. He indicates that I should follow him, leading me into an expansive workshop where an open top Bentley and a couple of other ancient cars that I'm unable to identify are being worked on by equally pristine technicians. The place is extraordinary, clean as an operating theatre and equipped with all manner of hydraulic ramps, powertools and electronic equipment. The mechanic leaves me wandering around in awe while he enters a side room, soon returning with the bottle now full of thick, yellow lubricant. Perfect. Back in the shop, I'm charged three times more than I've ever paid for oil, but it's worth it for the peace of mind of not running out at a later date.

Our route takes us towards Münster. It's not a place I'd planned to visit and under normal circumstances, I'd save myself the grief of contending with heavy traffic and bypass it. However, the city's familiar because of the rugby team of the same name, which from memory has had considerable success in the Heineken Cup and European Championships, so I opt to ride through it. As I stop outside a downtown coffee shop, it suddenly dawns on me that Germany is hardly the heartland of international Rugby Union. My brain's synapses got their wires crossed... the Munster rugby club is, of course, Irish! Feeling a bit of a twerp, I sit at an outside table and sip an espresso as I regard the colourful bill posters pasted onto an adjacent wall. There's obviously some sort of local election in the offing as there are similar placards plastered around the town.

The middle-aged candidates all look cast from the same mould: expensive suits; Grecian 2000 hair and Photoshop-white overstretched smiles. Wouldn't trust one of them!

Entering the Harz region, the topography rapidly changes from flat squares of pasture to gently rolling hills, lush woodland, snaking rivers and picturesque lakes. A mountainous area dotted with spa towns, Harz is popular with visitors who enjoy outdoor activities such as walking and rock climbing in summer and skiing in winter. Rail enthusiasts also flock here as it boasts a network of narrow-gauge railways with a 120 year heritage that still uses steam locomotives. Today's a saturday and a different type of tourist stands out. There must be thousands of motorcyclists on the roads, easily outnumbering cars by five to one. I receive repeated waves from riders heading towards me, often in long drawn out groups where I simply keep my left hand hanging in the breeze in continuous acknowledgement. I'm overtaken by just about as many, practically every one wagging their right boot in salute as they pass. It's little wonder they congregate here as the roads afford a magnificent opportunity to swoop up and down, track flowing contours and dart round knee scraping bends... motorcycling heaven. Although she's by far the slowest on the road, the Matchless is nevertheless a joy to be on. Undoubtably, her engine's freeing up and as we make one long ascent after another in top gear, I can actually sense her legs lengthening.

After more than 80 uninterrupted kilometres of sheer pleasure, we stop for petrol and a drink in a sleepy village then hit the road again. Half way up a steep climb, my attention's grabbed by the odometer. It's reading 998.7 miles. Only half observing the road, which is virtually straight, I watch with great anticipation as each digit changes and 999.9 makes a fleeting appearance. Tantalisingly slowly, from right to left each 9 smoothly transforms into a 0 and as if by magic, a 1 appears on the left.

"Good on yer, Peggy," I enthusiastically tell her as I squeeze the petrol tank with my knees. Then I realise what I've done, I've reverted to my pet name for the BSA Bantam I rode to Egypt. Laughing, I caress the side of the tank and hope she'll forgive me!

In the early evening, millions of minuscule insects take to the wing and for the most part of an hour, it's like riding through fine arthropodal drizzle. They crawl down my neck, inside my helmet, into my ears, around my eyelids and up my nose... delightful! I keep an eye open for a campsite but don't see any signs at the roadside. One sign that appears with increasing frequency, however, counts down the distance to the city of Nordhausen, the terminus for the Trans-Harz Railway. I make it my destination. Just 4km from its centre and still surrounded by countryside, I spot a huge hotel complex with a coach and a couple of trucks parked outside its restaurant door. I slow, half tempted to stop, then decide to carry on, hoping to find something more characterful in the old quarter of the city.

The centre, when I reach it, is fairly compact and overrun with one way streets, several of which are cobbled. Following my nose, I end up in a large market square but there's not a hint of accommodation anywhere. Heading down a smaller lane, I come to a dead end with nothing but a polished stone pathway leading through to the next road. As I'm turning around, an Audi pulls out of a sidestreet. The driver opens his window and asks if I'm OK. I explain I'm looking for a hotel and he offers to lead me to one. Following hard on his tail, we begin a circuitous route that once again encompasses the full scope of the central one-way system. Ten minutes later, we join a main road and turn north-west, soon reaching Nordhausen's thinning outskirts. It suddenly registers that this is the road I arrived on almost an hour ago and it doesn't take a genius to guess where he's taking me... the large roadside hotel I'd rejected earlier! Pulling up alongside the Audi at a set of red lights, I thank him for his trouble and explain I want to stay within the city itself. He shakes my hand and when the lights change, continues on. I turn around and retrace my steps.

Back in Nordhausen, I eventually I find a hotel near the railway station. It's fairly big but has nowhere to park the Matchless except on the pavement. Disappointed, I make a third circuit around increasingly familiar streets and briefly catch sight of a hotel on a parallel one-way road that's heading in the opposite direction. Eureka! It takes a while to track round to it but finally, I park up at its entrance.

"Nien, nien parken," the receptionist says apologetically.

Opening my arms and turning both palms upwards, I look around, gesturing as best I can for "Where?"

"Ah, eine minute bitte," she replies then, after checking her phone book, makes a quick call.

"Eine garage ist sechs euro," she triumphantly says after hanging up, then proceeds to write the name 'Zur Hoffnung hotel' and 'garage 6 €' on a piece of paper.

"Ein, zwei, drei, vier ampeln," she says, opening and closing her hands in a flashing movement to represent traffic lights, then adds, "rechts abbiegen," while furiously pointing right. Finally she indicates with a shooing motion that I should keep going straight on, "direkt... direkt!"

It's immensely helpful and I think she can tell by the intensity of my response that I'm extremely grateful.

"Bitte schön," she says, bowing slightly then waving goodbye.

Hopping onto the bike, I count four sets of traffic lights, turn to the right and accelerate down a long stretch of straight road, grateful that I'll finally have accommodation for both me and the Matchless, just in the nick of time too, as it's almost dark. A school set back from the roadside and an advertising hoarding for VW cars triggers a memory and I instantaneously realise where I'm heading... straight back to the same confounded roadside lodge! With resignation, I stop swimming against the tide and pull up at its front door a couple of minutes later. A good two hours have passed since I first dismissed it but I suppose I've had a good tiki tour round Nordhausen in the meantime.

The hotel proves to be much more homely and authentically German than expected and the promised garage is just the job. Enjoying dinner and a German beer, I reflect on the day, delighted by how well the Matchless coped with the extended Harz hill climbs and the protracted slow haul riding round the city this evening. It bodes well for the coming weeks.

Day 4. Nordhausen to Colditz. 124 miles.

The day begins with another attempt to find the optimal position on the bike for each piece of luggage. This time I think I've arrived at the best solution with the spare tyre now strapped almost vertically at the back, resting on the rear number plate carrier. Even though the result appears overly tall, the bulk of the weight is now lower and further forward which will give improved stability. A couple of locals stop to chat while I'm getting ready to leave and one inevitably asks where I'm heading. I face the same dilemma as the other day: do I simply answer with today's destination, Colditz, or do I risk ridicule by divulging that my goal is Vietnam? One is evasive and the other simply doesn't sound credible. I decide to reveal my plans, listing the sequence of countries I'll need to ride through. They both slap me heartily on the back and wish me well. It's an encouraging start to the day.

The Matchless fires first kick, always a good sign, and after handing in the garage padlock key, I turn once more towards Nordhausen. The satnav wants to take us a northerly route to Colditz but that means riding through the centre of Leipzig, the largest city in the state of Saxony with a population of over one million... no thanks. I opt instead for a more south-easterly course, inserting a waypoint for the town of Freyburg into the routing. The roads are even quieter than yesterday and the traffic lights at all minor intersections have been switched off, entrusting the crossing of these junctions to the motorists' own judgement... a marvellous idea!

Freyburg, chosen purely because of its location on the map, turns out to be a gem. From on high, Schloss Neuenburg, a rambling 11th Century castle, overlooks a historic town centre crammed full of tall, Germanic houses topped with steeply sloping red tile roofs. The stunning nucleus is the Romanesque parish church of St. Mary that's crowned with eye-catching verdigris spires. In just about every direction, terraced vineyards are staggered up the surrounding hillsides, testament to the town's status as a leading wine producer. I ride slowly along its narrow streets then, as I come to the sign that marks the end of town, cross paths with a trio of outstanding old motorcycles: a shaft-drive, flat twin Zundapp, an Ardie complete with Steib sidecar and a gorgeous late 1930's BMW R51. All three riders look authentic in period pudding basin helmets, fish eye goggles, arm-engulfing gauntlets and flapping leather greatcoats, creating a fabulous spectacle, as well as a satisfying sound, when they chug past.

With over a 150km under our belt and only 30-odd left to ride, I take the wrong exit off a roundabout and find myself on a slip road that leads straight onto an autobahn. Worse still, we join at the beginning of a long incline with traffic flying along at blistering speed. Sweating both literally and metaphorically, I press myself flat onto the tank bag and push the Matchless hard, edging up towards 80kmph. In this area of national parks and forests, the next turnoff could easily be 20km away and I rue my mistake as another fast approaching car misjudges our speed, pulling out from behind us with just milliseconds to spare. Thankfully, respite comes in the form of a junction that's less than 3km further on and we're able to break free. At the first suitable resting place, I stop and give the bike a chance to recover.

Serenely perched on a shady tree stump surrounded by berry bushes, wildflowers and butterflies, a feeling of wellbeing washes over me. My thoughts have been completely in the present throughout the ride thus far, monitoring the bike, observing road conditions and taking in all that's around, whether that be the heady smell of cut grass, the jet-stream of an airliner as it slices across the azure sky, the warmth of the sun on my shoulders or the friendly waves from a family of bicyclists as they pedal past. Vietnam, and any of the deadlines I'll need to meet in order to get there, have not entered my head since the conversation at the hotel, they're all far too distant, too peripheral to today's experiences to contemplate. Taking the journey minute by minute is proving rewarding and relaxing... if only I could live like this all the time!

Located on the banks of the Zwickau Mulde river, Colditz is a nondescript town except for one outstanding feature. It's claim to fame is the notorious Schloss Colditz, a Renaissance castle which dominates everything in sight from a prominent position atop a rocky spur. With the Matchless's exhaust pulsating off the walls of the buildings that line the town square, I ride around, searching for the illusive road that leads to its entrance. On my second circuit, I identify the narrow approach, coming to a halt at the castle's lower gates beside a pair of customised Harley Davidsons. I make a beeline for the outer courtyard and the Youth Hostel it now contains, fervently hoping there's still a bed available. I needn't have worried... I'm allocated a 4-bed room all to myself and there appears to be space for hundreds more guests!

The original castle was first constructed in the 12th Century but twice destroyed by fire. The current building, reconstructed in the 16th Century, has through the years seen service as an administrative centre, hunting lodge, workhouse, sanitarium for the wealthy and hospital for the mentally ill. Most notably, during WWII, Schloss Colditz was a Prisoner of War camp designated Oflag IV-C. It was, however, not an ordinary POW camp, but rather the supposedly escape-proof gaol where 'bad boys' were sent, trouble-making officers who'd been recaptured after escaping from other oflags. It has a special place in my heart because as a boy I was endlessly fascinated by it, watching the film and TV series several times, playing the board game whenever I could find a willing opponent and from the age of 9, repeatedly reading The Colditz Story, a highly entertaining book by Captain Pat Reid. One of the first contingent of British soldiers to be interned at the camp in November 1940, Reid orchestrated many escape attempts before audaciously succeeding in spiriting himself beyond its walls in October 1942. Four nights later, mostly travelling by train while disguised as a Flemish collaborator, he crossed into Switzerland.

Reid's book is full of tales of daring, skill, determination and resilience as the interns tried every ploy imaginable to outwit their captors. Would-be escapees shimmied down rope ladders, hid in straw mattresses, crawled through sewers, dug tunnels, scaled the roofs, dressed as female visitors, impersonated German soldiers, leapfrogged fences, foiled sniffer dogs and constructed numerous escape hatches and false walls. Some went to extremes, such as feigning insanity, starting a tunnel from within the Commandant's own office and even constructing a glider which would have been launched from the castle's roof had the sound of the allied advance not persuaded its builders to wait for liberation. This came by way of American forces arriving at the castle gates on 16 April 1945 but just days later, the Americans withdrew, the Russians arrived and Colditz fell behind the Iron Curtain, first used as a regular prison then as a nursing home.

Without delay, I head to the ticket office, pay my entrance fee and walk into the tiny inner courtyard which is where appells (roll-calls) were held three times a day. Sitting on a bench, I look around at the rows of windows sunk into the imposing walls, behind which are the rooms where captives slept, socialised and whiled away the hours planning their breakouts. After a while, I go to investigate the castle's WWII museum. Displayed here is all manner of escape paraphernalia, from forged documents and replica Reichsmark to copies of German uniforms. Each prisoner in Colditz seems to have specialised in one skill that he contributed to the overall escape operation. Some became expert tailors, creating replica civilian clothing from Allied military uniforms, others concentrated on photography, calligraphy, reproducing maps or the manufacture of various tools. Then there were the risk takers, the tunnellers, lookouts (known as stooges) and those who tested doors, windows, drain covers, indeed every nook and cranny, for a weakness and possible escape route.

Pat Reid's forte was fabricating trapdoors which he was able to camouflage so effectively that they became invisible amongst fake cracks in walls or ceilings. He named each of these contraptions 'Shovewood'. Centrality positioned in the museum is 'Shovewood IV', the trapdoor that Reid constructed for the escape of fellow British officer, Airey Neave, the first Briton to complete a 'home run' from the castle. In August 1941, Neave hid underneath the camp's theatre stage in the middle of a noisy performance. He dropped through the disguised trapdoor which was set into the ceiling of a unused room in a section of the castle occupied by the guards. Accompanied by a Dutch lieutenant, both dressed as German officers, he bravely walked down several flights of stairs and eventually right out of the castle, accepting salutes from the sentries as he passed through the final gate. Later to become a Conservative MP, Neave was killed outside The House of Commons in 1979 when his car was blown up by the IRA, Looking at 'Shovewood IV', I find it remarkable that such a random item has survived all these years, then I read a sign on the wall which explains all. The camp commandant, aware that he held the cream of allied escape artists under his roof, preserved, photographed and documented every escape attempt, sharing the information around other POW camps so that their guards would know what to look out for!

The museum closes at 5pm and as the last remaining visitor, I reluctantly leave. Back at the Youth Hostel, which is situated in the building known during the war as the Kommandantur, the German commandant's headquarters, I tell the receptionist I'm heading into town and ask if there's a nighttime curfew.

"No," he says, "you can come back anytime you wish."

Then, reaching under the counter, he extracts a large key and hands it over.

"Here, you'll need this," he continues. "It's the key to the outer gate so you can easily get in and out when everything's locked up."

Barely able to conceal my delight, I head back outside, key to the castle in hand, thinking what those courageous escapees would have given for one of these!

Failing to find a restaurant in town that fits the bill, I return to the hostel and dine in its canteen, a subterranean chamber criss-crossed with long communal benches where the only other diners are some American backpackers and an English guy who's recently arrived on his BMW GS1200. The food's simple, inexpensive and manifestly healthy. Later, sitting on a settee in a ground floor common area, I strike up a conversation with three Cumbernauld ramblers spending a week in the hostel as part of a twin town cultural exchange. We're soon joined by the two Harley owners, one Scottish and the other a Geordie, who are spending a week touring Germany together. The chance to interact with people from all walks of life is one of the many plus points of Youth Hosteling, a much more sociable way of travelling than being isolated in one's own hotel room.

When I finally hit the sack, I select the lower berth on a set of pine bunk beds. Comfortably recumbent on a foam mattress, I consider the sleeping arrangement of the WWII prisoners and feel incredibly grateful that I'm not lying on a straw palliasse with half the bed boards missing above and below me, sacrificed to shore up the walls of an escape tunnel!

Day 5. Colditz to Bautzen. 101 miles.

The dining hall is half full when I enter but none of my fellow motorcyclists are there. As I'm crunching my way through a second round of toast the two Harley riders arrive and join me.

"Thought you'd be outside with your spanners," says the Scot.

"Let him eat in peace, he'll need all the strength he can get," jokes the Geordie. "Be out there for hours once he gets started."

These days, I'm seasoned in this sort of banter about the reliability of classic British motorcycles, and in some respects it might be right. However, my Royal Enfield made it all the way to India in 2008 without any serious problems and the Matchless has been so reliable thus far that I feel the last laugh might just be on me.

"I'll be loaded and long gone before you've finished your breakfast!" I tell them with confidence.

Tool roll in hand, I uncover the bike and set to work. Actually, what I have to do is fairly routine. I add a little grease to the gearbox, check the oil level in the primary chaincase and adjust the rear chain tension. Within 10 minutes I'm checking the tappets, the final task. It only takes a moment to work out that they need adjusting. Where they should spin freely at Top Dead Centre, mine are rock solid. I search my tools and discover a problem… I need two identical 5/16" Whitworth spanners but I've only packed one. As a make-do, I try using my small adjustable spanner instead but it's too thick. The Harley riders arrive, load up and set off with unstifled laughter.

Sometime later, the BMW rider comes over to say good morning and tells me he's about to do a tour of the castle. Wishing him well and a safe journey home, certain I'll be gone by the time he returns, I put my head down and, with great concentration, try to make the necessary adjustments. To my dismay I'm still at it when he comes back to his bike and straps his luggage onto the rear seat. Wiping the figurative egg from my face, I shake hands with him and he also rides off.

After much sweat, bruised knuckles and two-spannered jiggering I manage the correct settings. Another Whitworth spanner is a high priority. It begins to rain so I push the Matchless under the castle's entrance archway and go to retrieve my luggage from the hostel, returning to find the place full of schoolchildren. The noise is deafening and the teachers, who are attempting to roll call, find themselves completely unable to quieten the excitable crowd. I leave my bags beside the bike and return to my room for a second load. When I get back the noise has increased by umpteen decibels. After a final trip to collect my riding gear, I'm aghast to see another group of forty or so schoolchildren, all with their luggage, squeezed under the archway. They're now so tightly packed around the bike it's hard for me to reach it. The volume is unbelievable… a shrieking, screaming, shouting and laughing wall of noise, amplified considerably by the arch above. How the teachers bear it is beyond me, it'd drive me crazy. I can hardly think straight let alone load the bike. To my relief, the children are led away in groups of four and although only a few remain by the time I kick the bike over, I take great satisfaction exacting my revenge as the booming exhaust reverberates around the walls.

In dense, misty rain I wind downwards from the castle along glistening streets, pausing at the junction with the town's main thoroughfare. Directly opposite is an Aldi supermarket. It has a long canopy which partially covers a cafe. My stomach is rumbling, so despite having ridden only a few hundred metres, I head for shelter and sustenance. Halfway through my sandwich with a big slice of cake still to go, I look up and to my horror see a familiar party of schoolchildren crossing the road and boisterously heading my way. Most of them follow a teacher into the supermarket but half a dozen grab a table next to me, giggling and chasing each other around. I devour what's left of the food and make a hasty escape.

Riding in heavy rain is something I thoroughly enjoy. The added jeopardy it brings sharply focuses my mind and in extreme downpours like today's, it's impossible to think of anything other than the job at hand as I engage in a moment to moment battle with the elements.

After a 20 minute climb the road plateaus at around 400 meters, the trees that had protected us from the vicious crosswind peter out as the sides of the road open up to large ploughed fields. The wind blasts harshly from the right and I have to lean into it to maintain a straight line. The rain's now horizontal, lashing the timing side of the Matchless. In my mirrors I make out the headlights of two trucks gradually closing in on me before they pull out and overtake, leaving a dense spray in their wake that's impossible to see through.

The engine coughs. I can't pretend it hasn't happened but fervently try to will it away. It misfires again and all too soon settles into an unwelcome rhythm. Pulling over onto a farm track, I hunker down next to the bike but find it impossible to see or do anything due to the force of the rain. Deflated, I climb back on and turn for Colditz, praying the bike will at least keep running as it gasps and chokes the entire 6km back to the town centre. Eventually, we come to a soggy halt once again under the canopy of Aldi's cafe.

Buoyed with black coffee and rhubarb cake I set about tracing the problem which doesn't take long. Removing the HT lead from the magneto pickup, it's obvious that everything inside is thoroughly soaked. A couple of napkins soon have it mopped up and once reassembled, I coat it with a thick protective ring of silicone.

By the time I'm ready to set off again the wind and rain has miraculously abated and as we slowly begin the climb out of Colditz, the sun peeks through the heavy clouds. In what seems like no time at all we roar past the farm track entrance and continue eastwards amongst gently rolling countryside.

I'm still hoping to make it to the Polish border today but despite my best efforts and several halts to study the map in more detail, I just can't seem to avoid Saxony's capital, Dresden. Twice I try to turn off and track around its southern limits but on both occasions I find myself heading once more towards its centre. It seems to have an inexplicable gravitational hold on the Matchless.

Resigning myself to the inevitable, I follow a multilane highway right to the heart of the city.

Just three months before the end of World War II, Dresden suffered four major bombing raids, the worst of which caused a firestorm. Estimates are that between 22,000 and 25,000 people died. Nearly all of the historic buildings in the city centre were destroyed along with approximately 12,000 homes. Given that after the war Dresden was part of East Germany, I anticipate a centre full of grim Soviet-era buildings. A set of traffic lights marks the end of the highway and almost immediately we travel along broad cobbled streets then across a market square, bouncing over shiny tramlines, my eyes peeled for the clanking trams that scoot along them. In every direction the buildings have considerably more charm and character than I'd expected.

Crossing the Elbe and exiting the city proves difficult. The road east is narrow and now crowded with rush-hour traffic. The rain that drenched Colditz must have passed through quite recently as the road surface is still wet and the tramlines treacherous. It's early evening before we're clear and back in open countryside. Noticing the sun is getting low in the sky, I'm anxious to make progress before nightfall, but where to? I pull over to study the map. Due east, in a straight line along the road I'm currently on, is Bautzen. A huge grin of recognition spreads across my face because I camped one night in this very town only a year ago. Rather unusual circumstances took me there to collect a motorcycle and I certainly never thought I'd be passing through it again. An increasing number of cars have turned on their headlights so I prod the Matchless's kick starter and head for my new destination.

As I ride into Bautzen, the sunset's final glow rests warmly on the terracotta rooftops of the churches and medieval towers that make up the old town centre. Crossing over a river I spot the illuminated city walls then continue to the far side of town where, by contrast, thousands of grey concrete flats have been built along the left side of the road in a kilometre long line. Just beyond their end is the turnoff into narrow lane which leads to the campsite gate. It's after eight and my fears that the office will be closed are thankfully unfounded. A light is on and I can see the outline of a woman's head moving about. Last time I stayed here I noticed some small Scandinavian-style cabins that were rented out to campers. My luck is in as one remains unoccupied and only costs three Euros more than pitching my tent. The cheerful manageress even gives me a kettle so I can quickly prepare camp food... and sells me a couple of locally brewed bottles of beer to boot.

Day 6. Bautzen, Germany, to Niemodlin, Poland. 181 miles.

The early morning sun pours through the window, lighting up the cabin's pine walls and ceiling. I jump out of my bunk bed with renewed energy to prepare for the day ahead. My next destination is the Polish city of Kraków and as it's over 300 miles away, I need to load up and get underway as soon as possible.

Since crossing into what was East Germany I've seen just one Trabant. My journey to the Polish border is only 30 miles yet in that time I spot three of these battered old cars, each of which leaves a substantial plume of smoke in its wake. The factory where they were manufactured for over 30 years lies just a couple of hours drive away in the town of Zwickau. More than 3 million were made before the reunification of Germany in 1990 brought production to a gradual halt. Although widely ridiculed for their cheap construction, poor reliability and underpowered 600cc twin cylinder, two-stroke engine, there's something about these idiosyncratic vehicles that I really like. This morning, I also like the fact that the Matchless is powerful enough to easily overtake them.

I'm soon at the Polish border. After the Second World War, the German town of Görlitz was split in half along what was known as the *Oder-Neisse line*. The eastern section, now in Poland, was renamed Zgorzelec. My Garmin leads me through Görlitz's centre, across a bridge that spans a small river then without pause or any break in the architecture, through Polish Zgorzelec. I notice a change of script on signposts and the predominance of Polish registered cars, but apart from these markers, could easily fail to realise that I'd ridden into another town, let alone country.

Changes do, however, become more apparent as I ride further east into a rural area. The Matchless's exhaust sounds especially loud as we pass through small rundown villages where very little seems to be happening. The road condition also deteriorates. Within an hour it transitions from smooth tar to a surface through which it's impossible to see the original road due to the immense number of patches that have been applied over many years. The bike's rear repeatedly bounces hard on the uneven surface and I get the first indication that its rigid frame is going to prove uncomfortable for parts of the journey. Indeed, I have to drop my cruising speed from 70kmph to 40kmph in order to ride in sympathy with both my machine and my body.

After 60 kilometres of discomfort, I enter a town and pull into a BP petrol station to fill up and grab something to eat. There's a small seated area at one side of the counter where food and drinks are served. Over a cup of coffee and a cheese toastie, I occupy myself by watching some of the other diners. It's apparent that several are not simply taking lunch on the run whilst buying their fuel... they've arranged to meet here, using the petrol station as a cafe. I can't help smiling as I ponder their arrangements:

"Let's meet for lunch."

"Great idea, where shall we go?"

"I know, how about the BP."

"Yeah, Brilliant!"

On leaving, it soon becomes evident that the road is too dangerous to continue on as Warsaw-bound trucks overtake within inches of the bike. I pull over and reset the satnav to take the shortest, rather than fastest, route to Kraków. Immediately turning off, we're straight back onto patched, bumpy lanes. I slow when the Garmin tells me to take another right turn onto a road that becomes even narrower as I enter a hamlet. At the sound of our approach three large dogs wake from their slumbers, leap to their feet and lunge for me. Their noisy pursuit lasts for over a hundred metres before they run out of puff. Atop a small hill ahead is a large windmill with a winding track leading to its front door. Judging by the number of windows, each trimmed with pretty curtains, I guess it's been converted into a residence. Unquestionably it's a perfect lookalike for the home of Caractacus Pott and his children in the famous musical, *Chitty-Chitty-Bang-Bang*!

Just a few hundred metres further I arrive at a small cottage. An elderly man leans over his garden fence and watches my arrival with bemusement. Beyond the cottage the road dissolves into a completely overgrown, metre-wide bridal track. My sat nav says I have to travel 6km before I turn left! Halting, I point ahead and laugh. He shrugs and gives me a knowing toothy smile. It seems unnecessary for us to communicate in any other way. I turn the bike around, give him a wave and ride back past the windmill, doing my best rendition of Lionel Jeffries singing "Port Out Starboard Home, POSH with a P," at the top of my voice before racing past the dogs once more.

Some time later I come to a halt at an intersection with a dual carriageway. I need to turn left at the staggered junction which means crossing two lanes of fast traffic. After checking both ways, I let out the clutch and set off. My intuition screams stop! I haul the brakes on hard and snap my head round to look left once more. Bearing down on me at great speed is an Audi overtaking a Volvo and I'm smack bang in the middle of the Volvo's lane... a case of the proverbial rabbit caught in car headlights. The Volvo's bonnet dives down as its driver applies the full force of his brakes and swerves into the outside lane behind the Audi, centimetres to spare. In a nano second they're flying past me, horns blazing. Stunned and sickened, I get across the road and pull over to steady myself. Still trembling, I go over and over what happened, trying to work out if it was my fault. Perhaps I'd looked right-left-right, which would be habitual for someone who normally rides on the left of the road, instead of left-right-left. Or maybe the cars were going so fast that anyone in my situation would have been caught out. Either way, if I'd not stopped, the Audi would have inevitably hit me. Images of a smashed hip and pelvis, torn arteries, and my body flying over the top of the car imprint themselves on my mind. The course of my life would have been irrevocably changed in an instant. I'm deeply shaken.

I remount the Matchless and after a short distance leave the dual carriageway. Accelerating uphill, I engage third gear and immediately notice that the gearchange lever hasn't returned to its central position. Flicking it with my foot, I can engage either second or fourth but in both cases the gear lever stays projecting upwards or downwards. No matter how many times I try, it won't centralise. Coasting onto a petrol station forecourt, I get my phone out and call Andy.

"Sounds like the selector mechanism springs have either broken or come out of their cages," he says. "If you've got some bungees you can try to rig them one above and one below the lever so they act like an external spring and centralise it every time you change gear."

I don't have any bungee cords on the bike. I use Rok straps to secure my luggage as they're strong, adjustable and their simple fixing system means there's no risk of injury from a metal hook should they fly off. I go into the filling station shop to see what they can offer. Hey presto, they sell bungees! After parting with a few zlotys, I return to the bike and tightly attach them to the gear lever. Climbing on, I try changing gear but the problem persists so I remove the bungees to see if relocating them will help. It's immediately apparent that they have too little spring in them... just a couple of stretches leaves them permanently flaccid. The elastic bands frequently dropped by the postman on my doorstep have more ping than these. Unable to understand why anybody would waste their time manufacturing something so useless, I walk over to a bin and throw them away, figuring I can quite easily manage with the gearchange as it is. Seeking comfort in a bar of chocolate, I head off again.

Approaching the edge of a small town I'm struck by the unusual shape of a large church. Its clock tower jags skywards at odd angles and parts of the building seem disconnected in an strange block-like fashion, a bit like Picasso's cubist art. Directly opposite is a pedestrian crossing. I slow to allow a lady to cross then select first gear and move on. When I push downwards for second gear, nothing happens. The bike is jammed in first. Traffic is starting to queue behind me but all I can do is crawl forward at a paltry 15kmph. With no parking on the main road, I have to painfully travel the whole length of the town centre before I can turn off.

Testing the gearbox, I'm able to select neutral but can't get it into second either by foot or hand. As it's late afternoon I decide to find somewhere to stay then investigate it further, so retrace the full stretch of the main street still in first gear. There don't appear to be any hotels.

My first two attempts at asking passers-by for help are unsuccessful... people smile and shrug but simply don't understand me. The third person I ask, a teenager on a bicycle, only grasps what I'm searching for when I lean my head to one side, rest it on hands with palms pressed together, close my eyes and make stupid snoring noises. Eureka! He laughs, points ahead, curves his hand to suggest I cross a bridge then indicates I should turn right. I wait for a break in the traffic then embarrassingly head off, once more at a snail's pace.

The hotel is set well back from the road with a small gravel car park in which I can chain the Matchless to a bench. As soon as I'm in a room, I dig out my phone and give Andy another call.

"Where are you?" he asks.

I have to be honest, I don't know. My response brings a laugh from him. I explain the problem.

"You're going to have to take the gearbox apart and have a look Gordon. It's probably something simple like the selector mechanism's jammed, maybe with one of the springs that caused problems earlier, but we won't know for sure until you open it up."

Gearboxes and their workings are a black art as far as I'm concerned. I've never taken one apart and the complexity of all those cogs, dogs, ratchets, selector forks, pawls and the like, scares me.

"I'm worried that it'll never go back together again," I tell him seriously. His faith in me is touching.

"You can do it Gordon, I know you can, and I'll talk you through putting it back together if necessary. But for starters take the cover off and let's see what you find."

It will be dark soon so I defer the trauma until tomorrow morning. I thank Andy and say good night.

The hotel receptionist, a lively young man with spiky jet black hair, called Mariusz, tells me we're in Niemodlin.

"I spotted a pizza restaurant in town. Is it any good?" I ask him.

"Sometimes."

"Er... does that mean sometimes it isn't good?"

"Sometimes."

I continue my inquisition,

"So which is the best restaurant in town please?"

"The pizza restaurant."

It had to be... I smile and resign myself to eating at Niemodlin's best!

All the shops except for a small convenience store are now closed. Apart from a couple of people making their way home with bags of shopping and a group of four youths walking ahead of me, I have the place to myself. The pizzeria is open and, joining two families who are already tucking into their evening meal, I pass the time by reading my workshop manual. Andy had already warned me on the phone not to get my hopes up, saying,

"The gearbox section is so useless it might as well be a recipe for baking fairy cakes."

He's right. Its vagueness only serves to worry me further. There's nothing of Niemodlin to see in the dark so I wander back to the hotel.

"How was the pizza?" asks Mariusz.

"OK. Not great but not awful."

"This is what I try to tell you," he answers with a grin.

Once in my room I go online to do further gearbox research. There's some discussion on the *AJS & Matchless Owners Club* forum about Burman gearboxes and in particular the selector mechanism but without any photographs or illustrations it doesn't really move me any further forward. I fall restlessly to sleep, a vision of cluelessly sitting beside my bike with a handful of unidentifiable gearbox parts in my hands going round and round in my head.

Day 7. Niemodlin to Kraków. 133 miles.

The morning heralds a stronger frame of mind and I'm determined to get the job done, whatever I'm confronted with.

After breakfast I walk to a supermarket and buy more cloths and cleaning products than I'd use in a whole year of domesticity. Back at the hotel I wheel the Matchless to a shady corner, spread a raft of newspaper over the gravel, lay out the tools and prepare my camera to photograph the sequence in which the parts come out.

With all the securing nuts undone, I prize the cover off as gently as possible. My heart's in my mouth as I pull it away, desperately trying to hold everything together as gloopy grease oozes everywhere. Needing to reuse it, I conscript my breakfast spoon to scoop as much of it as possible into my breakfast bowl. Fortunately the kickstarter coil spring stays wound in place but the same cannot be said for the selector mechanism which immediately falls apart.

Over the next hour I familiarise myself with its operation. The four springs that centralise the lever actually seem OK but it's obvious that what my parts book calls the 'indexing rocking pawl' is worn, allowing it to jump out of its locating hole and jam the gearlever. Once certain I've reassembled everything correctly, I make a dry run of putting it back onto the gearbox. Holding everything together is tricky and I could really do with not only a third hand but x-ray eyes. The biggest challenge is aligning the central ratchet tooth of the selector mechanism quadrant with the correct tooth on the camshaft pinion, which is marked with a dot that has to be set at the 9 o'clock position. I can't see it once the outer cover begins to slide into place which is further complicated as, simultaneously, I need to align a groove in the invisible clutch operating arm and hold the sprung kickstart ratchet in the correct place. Blimey Charlie!

After much wiggling, everything slides into place. I can't believe it... I can select all four gears and the lever is returning to its central position! Better still, I haven't had to take the inner cover off and disembowel the main part of the gearbox, a major relief.

Removing it once more, I begin the laborious task of scraping silicone sealant off all surfaces then wiping them down with cleaner to ensure a good seal. On goes fresh silicone, and again, I blindly slot everything into place. Once I judge the silicone has cured, I tentatively try selecting second gear. It works! Overjoyed, I dance a jig around the bike, glancing surreptitiously around as my euphoria recedes to make sure no one's seen me. Gathering several bags of slimy cloths, I pack my tools away and cheerfully go to share the good news with Mariusz.

Obviously pleased, he helps me lug everything down from my room, brings me a cup of coffee and stays to chat while I begin loading the Matchless. He tells me he spent five years at university getting a degree in tourism but unfortunately hasn't been able to find a job that makes full use of his skills. Indeed, I'm the first English-speaking guest he's met at this hotel and he's worked here for more than six months. Twice he's had seasonal apple picking work in Holland which he informs me pays four times as much as his current job without the gruelling 24-hours shifts he's presently forced to do. He has many friends who work in the UK and Holland, which is not surprising when he explains how hard it is to make a decent living in Poland.

A man walking past the gate sees the bike and comes into the courtyard to have a closer look. He's got straggly long hair and wears an AC/DC T-shirt. Mariusz introduces him as Teddy and translates his questions and my answers during which time Teddy repeatedly shakes my hand. Full of energy, he bounces off down the road to return within 10 minutes carrying a huge red and white Polish flag that has AC/DC painted in black and gold across the centre. He takes great pride in pointing out Angus Young's signature in one corner and 'Monsters of Rock, Castle Donnington 1991' in another. Throwing the flag over his shoulders, he holds it high in the air and begins singing his favourite AC/DC songs whilst jumping exuberantly up and down. What a whacky guy! I laugh along with him as he ties the flag tightly around his neck and begins playing air guitar, chanting "Na nana nana na na, Angus!" It takes me a long time to get ready when I'm being so enthusiastically entertained.

It's mid afternoon before I say my farewells and ride south in the direction of Opole. The traffic is crazy. Not only are cars and trucks passing me, they're in constant battle with each other, aggressively diving in and out of their lane. On a couple occasions there are almost head-on collisions as opposing motorists create four lanes out of two and play chicken with each other. Teddy's presence still being fresh in my mind, I repeatedly bawl AC/DC's 'Highway to Hell' until I'm able to turn off onto a quieter road and head into the aromatic shade of a pine forest.

Less than an hour later the gear lever stops self centering again. Once more I tell myself it'll be fine... as long as it doesn't jam in first gear. Next comes the city of Katowice. I slow at the third set of traffic lights in as many minutes, easing the gear lever into neutral as gently as possible. The city looks enormous and with the current rush hour stop-start traffic, I envisage taking a couple of hours to cross it. At each gearchange I'm on tenterhooks waiting for the gearbox to lock solid again. The satnav indicates I should turn left and to my surprise I swing onto a six lane highway. Traffic is absolutely bombing along and I open the Matchless up to a hearty 75kmph. It handles the speed beautifully and, with warm air blasting my face, I enjoy a long break from nervously changing gear. 25km later, with the highway reduced to a dual carriageway, I pull off beside a roadside restaurant to give the engine chance to cool and me my first meal of the day.

By the time I'm ready to ride again I know there's no chance of reaching Kraków, still more than 80km away, before nightfall. I really don't want to ride at night but prepare, just in case. This means putting on a hi-viz vest, switching to clear goggles and sticking a flashing red LED light onto the rear of my luggage. I decide I'll go as far as possible before nightfall and then make a decision.

The dual carriageway continues roughly half the distance I need to travel and the Matchless cruises faultlessly the whole way. I count down the miles on my odometer until it shows I've travelled exactly 1000 miles since setting off and my mouth spreads into a wide grin.

As darkness settles on the road, it narrows further to a single lane. Traffic remains light and the bike is running so well, I decide to press on. First seen as an orange glow in the distance, Kraków is much larger than I expect and the outer suburbs host several large hotels offering affordable rooms. However, as I want to explore the historic centre in the morning, and as the roads are now so well lit, I keep riding. Just before 9pm I begin to cross tramlines and see the shape of buildings change from modern to old. It's stinking hot, the handlebar thermometer showing just over 30°, as I park up and try a hotel. It's full, as are the next two.

By now I'm weary and soaked in sweat but just don't want to drive back out of the city centre. The fourth hotel I visit has a room but it's too expensive. They suggest I try the Ibis which is just next door. They also have rooms available with the bonus of secure underground parking, but like their neighbour they're much more than my budget allows.

"Do you have anything cheaper, or can you recommend somewhere nearby that's maybe €20 less?" I ask the receptionist.

"Let me see," she replies then taps away on her computer. "We have a discounted special rate we can offer you that is €25 less. Would you like it?" Utterly grateful, I get myself a car park pass and begin to unload. The best is yet to come... a porter arrives in the car park with a luggage trolley onto which we load everything before taking the lift all the way to my room. It's an unexpected joy that for once I don't have to manhandle several loads alone.

Over a late-night chilled beer, I call Andy to update him on the gearbox. He's delighted that I was able to fix it this morning but surprised the selector mechanism was the culprit, as he explains that it was the best part of the original gearbox.

"The layshaft, mainshaft and all the gears were knackered and if you remember I replaced all of those using Derek's donor box. The selector mechanism seemed completely serviceable but if it's now worn you'll have to look at getting a replacement sent out." he explains.

I follow up with a call to Derek who once again comes to the rescue.

"I'm sure I've enough spare parts to make up a selector mechanism," he says in his usual unflustered way. "Give me another call tomorrow and I'll let you know what I've found then we can work out where to send it."

There's no doubt that without true friends supporting me, there'd be little chance of completing a long journey like this on such an old bike as the Matchless.

Day 8. Kraków to Lancut. 117 miles.

Soon after 7am I'm out and walking the streets, keen to make the most of my stay. Heading towards the old town, I spy a bakery where local workers are choosing breakfast from a counter displaying a fabulous selection of pastries. Without hesitation I join them and, perched on a stool beside a window, am soon feasting on almond and strawberry croissant accompanied by an obligatory espresso. Regular customers walk in, cheerfully greet the staff and breakfast in hand, head back into the sunshine. The ambience is so friendly, I remain long after I've finished my meal.

During the Renaissance, Kraków was one of the largest cities in Europe and capital of Poland until, at the end of the 18th Century, that status was bestowed on Warsaw. Numerous wars and occupations led to its decline and near ruination but today its historic centre is a UNESCO World Heritage Site and a major tourist attraction. Rynek Główny, the city's magnificent 13th century main square, is dominated by a huge 15th Century trading house, the Cloth Hall. Next to it is an equally imposing structure, a clock tower that's the only surviving remnant of the city's old town hall. Parked on each side of the square are delivery vans restocking the many cafes and shops that service visiting tourists. Half visible behind them, cafe tables are being wiped down and laid with menus, napkins and condiments as the delivery drivers weave between them, pushing loaded trolleys and carrying boxes on their shoulders.

I sit at the base of the statue of Polish romantic poet, Adam Mickiewicz, and with the sun gently soaking into my bones gaze at the uneven Gothic towers of St Mary's basilica. With the air still fresh and the promise of a hot day not yet realised, I amble out of the square, eventually coming to a small fruit and vegetable market constructed from cast iron pillars and glass. Sitting on the pavement opposite are a cluster of poor looking older women selling flowers. Most have only two or three bunches for sale and it's hard to imagine how they make anything more than a few zlotys a day.

I wander back towards the main square arriving at a large intersection, where I lean on railings for at least 15 minutes watching the wonderful old trams, now almost bursting with commuters, as they cross tracks and lurch off in different directions. Around the fringes of the main square large coaches have started to arrive, disgorging flocks of tourists and their guides onto the streets. Shuttle buses, advertising trips to Auschwitz and Oskar Schindler's factory, sit in wait. How quickly the morning's changed… an hour ago I could rest quietly at the foot of the clock tower, now I can't get near it for the hordes of people milling around. It's time to head back to the Matchless.

Leaving the hotel, we immediately take a bridge across the Vistula river which offers a great view of Wawel Castle, a grand 16th century Renaissance palace. In no time, we're out of the city and heading east towards the Ukraine border. The afternoon is piping hot so after about 70 kilometres I stop to fill up with fuel and find some shade for the bike to cool down. Within twenty minutes, we're accelerating along the slip road and back onto the busy E40. Just as I change into top gear, a set of traffic lights 50 metres ahead turns to red and I have to brake hard to stop in time. When I set off, second gear is nowhere to be found... the selector mechanism has gone again!

To the right is a McDonalds restaurant and a large sports complex so I find a patch of pavement that's out of the sun, organise myself, and repeat yesterday's process. This time I manage it in just over two hours but although all gears seem to select freely, the lever simply will not centralise. It's beginning to look as if I have an ongoing problem.

With the afternoon almost gone, I ride back to the main road and begin climbing a steep hill. As I round the top and continue to accelerate, I click into 4th gear. Ten seconds later the engine revs madly in 3rd... it's jumped down a gear. I put it back into 4th but within a hundred metres the same happens. Next attempt, I keep my foot gently pressed on the gearlever and it stays in 4th, however, as soon as I release the pressure, it jumps back into 3rd again. I can only guess that with my vision inevitably obscured as before, I've failed to align the selector quadrant properly. The lack of any sensation through my foot or any tell-tale sounds suggests that using my boot to stay in 4th isn't causing damage, so with darkness approaching, I decide to risk it and keep riding.

My map shows that the E40 will merge with the A4 motorway just before the Ukraine frontier. I imagine that it'll be an exceedingly busy crossing so have decided to turn off onto minor roads and cross at a quieter border post 20km to the south. The last vestiges of daylight have shrunk from the horizon as I approach my turnoff and the road I should take on the right is dauntingly black. Pausing at the junction, I look to my left and there before me sits a large hotel complex. Perfect. Riding to the front entrance, I'm pleasantly surprised that such an upmarket place offers modestly priced rooms. Fifteen minutes later, with the Matchless securely parked in front of the receptionist's window, I head for an extremely welcome shower.

With dinner over I call Derek, who's amazingly managed to assemble a replacement selector mechanism. I then rack my brains for a safe, reliable place he can send it to and, late into the night, search the Internet for a suitable hotel in Odessa together with courier options for getting it there.

Day 9, Lancut, Poland, to E40 Ring Road, South of Lviv, Ukraine. 112 miles.

A flash of realisation wakes me with a jolt. The couriers I researched last night all require the sender to print shipping labels and Derek doesn't have a computer. Eating breakfast, I mull over the options and as soon as it's a suitable time, try phoning Andrew Engineering. Thankfully they start work early.

Malcolm immediately agrees to ship Derek's selector mechanism and furthermore says he'll hunt through his own collection of used parts to see if there's anything he can contribute. I call Derek, another early riser, who readily agrees to drive the 45 miles to Atherton at lunchtime enabling the parts to be shipped today.

Booking the hotel in Odessa has made me conscious that the gearbox problems are putting me behind schedule. In my plans I've kept a couple of days up my sleeve but the Black Sea ferry, a once-a-week sailing, leaves in five days and there are still between 600 and 700 miles to ride depending on my route. With this in mind, I reconsider the idea of taking minor roads to the border and decide that urgency requires I get on the motorway as soon as possible in order to both clock up some miles and reduce the need for gear changes. The A4 lies just 4 miles north of my present position and I determine to head straight for it.

The Matchless starts first kick every morning which gives me a great feeling of pride. Today is no exception and we're soon puttering through Lancut's charming centre. Within 10 minutes, high on an embankment, I spot the motorway. There's a small roundabout with a slip road leading to it but to my dismay, it's closed. Looking upwards, the only signs of movement are a group of workmen in hard hats and two bright yellow bulldozers. On the assumption that this intersection is being repaired, I consult my map and decide to ride in a dog leg to the next junction, which is just 5km away. It takes a quarter of an hour to get there via a series of back roads but the closer I get to it, the more baffled I become. The road I'm on should go underneath a motorway overpass. Instead there's open sky. The motorway bridge is only partially built and it dawns on me that the A4 is still under construction. This is very strange as it shows a complete, solid line on my paper map and Google maps, and the Garmin certainly wants me to travel on it. The cartographers are obviously ahead of themselves!

Reverting to my original plan and with 40 minutes wasted, I retrace my steps to the hotel and set off down the minor road I'd balked at last night, reaching the frontier at Medyka an hour and a half of bumps and vibrations later. Stationary trucks and cars wait on the approach road in a straggling double line, easily half a kilometre long. A policeman waves me around the last car, so I ride right to the front of the column and through the two broad gates that form the entrance to the immigration compound. I edge forward and join the back of one of four queues which lead to the border control booths, turn off my engine then dig out my passport and motorcycle registration papers.

I'm only sixth in line but with no shade and the sun fiercely beating down it still takes more than an hour before it's my turn. A staunch female inspector checks my passport then examines the bike, scrutinising the engine and frame numbers. The latter, which is thickly coated with paint, causes her concern. I shine my torch on it to see if that helps. To my eyes, the number is very clear but she's not satisfied and walks away to consult with colleagues who all stop their work. Everything is happening so slowly it feels like either Poland or the EU don't want us to leave. I pity the people in the tailback outside the compound as they're obviously in for a very long wait.

A customs officer approaches the group in the midst of which my immigration officer is talking. He's an imposing figure, clad in a blue and grey camouflage jacket with matching trousers tucked into black combat boots. On his head is a camo Kepi hat and he carries a black rubberised torch. Taking one look at me, he nods and launches into an animated discussion with the immigration officer. He authoritatively points at me then makes gestures towards the Ukrainian halls. Although I understand no Polish, I interpret the gist of what he's saying to be along the lines of:

"Look at him. Look at his riding clothes and all his luggage. He's just some guy on a tour with an old motorcycle, not a smuggler. Stop wasting time. Let him be on his way and let's start dealing with this backlog."

Within seconds the group disperse, the immigration officer hands all my paperwork back and tells me to go.

Having taken almost 2 hours to exit Poland, I'm heartened by the efficiency of the Ukrainian immigration and customs staff. Both sets process me quickly whilst being cheerful and friendly, a really positive introduction to a new country. The only downside is the lack of a bank for changing money so I set off, hoping I can get by on credit cards for the rest of the day.

Exiting the compound, I'm struck by the radical change in scenery. Where Poland's roads were full to bursting with motorists and its countryside a patchwork of farmed fields pockmarked with towns and villages, my first impression of the Ukraine is one of a deserted road passing through uncultivated, wild country. There are no people, junctions, roundabouts or traffic lights. Apart from the road itself, which is wide and as smooth as a billiard table, the only vestiges of human existence are the frequent signposts written in Cyrillic script, their lower halves painted the bright blue and yellow colours of the national flag.

A small petrol station eventually appears on the opposite side of the road. Halting next to a pump, I try to fill up. An elderly man comes to the office door, his arms waving. It seems that I have to pay for my fuel before the pump will work, which means guessing how much I need. As the tank's fairly empty I plump for 10 litres, paying by Visa. However, after 8 1/2 litres it's full to the brim and as my spare fuel bottles are currently filled with oil, I resign myself to wasting the balance. The man, and a lady I presume to be his wife, look puzzled. They run a small shop with three cafe tables all within the same building. I ask for a cup of coffee but they have none. I ask for food, putting my fingers to my mouth several times to indicate I want to eat. They look embarrassed as they point to a shelf upon which a few packets of crisps and chocolate biscuits are scattered. Too hungry to refuse, I stock up on these meagre rations. As I'm about to leave, the man comes running out with an empty water bottle in his hand which he proceeds to fill for me with the unused portion of my fuel. What a gent.

Despite having to keep my foot pressed down on the gearlever when in 4th, my spirits are high as the bike's cheerful exhaust roars down the empty road and I'm thrilled to have covered 60km in just over an hour. The first signs of habitation are a couple of villages in which small, simple houses lie spread unevenly along dusty streets. Absolutely captivating are the glorious Russian Orthodox churches which are gaily painted or adorned in polished metals and topped with enchanting onion-shaped domes.

The closer I get to the city of Lviv, pronounced el-vive, the more traffic begins to build. We slow at our first set of Ukrainian traffic lights before turning onto a ring road which ultimately heads in the direction of Kiev, the Ukraine's capital, now heaving with rush-hour traffic. After a little while I take the chance for a break when I spot a garage specialising in tyres and puncture repairs. Swinging off the highway, I come to a halt in a large wooden building. Two mechanics dressed in oily, navy blue overalls approach the bike and give it a once over. I point to their compressor and indicate that I would like my tyre pressures checked. Within a minute it's done with just a squirt of air required in the rear. Then it dawns on me that I don't have any Ukrainian Hryvnia to pay them. Feeling very awkward, I rub my fingers together then open my hands wide in a gesture for 'how much?', hoping they will accept euros or zlotys. Gesticulating avidly, they indicate that for my old motorcycle their service is free. I shake their hands, and for good measure shake those of the three onlookers that have joined us. With fascination, they watch my starting procedure. I wave, let out the clutch and head back out to the road.

Modern European cars are interspersed with battered old Ladas, huge artics and rumbling old Russian jalopies. Steadily, we move forward together in one continuous flow. A battered old Soviet truck, its exhaust emitting clouds of black smoke, trundles painfully up a sharp incline. As everything slows further, I try to drop down to second gear but nothing happens. This is a new one... I'm now jammed in third. Disengaging the clutch, I let gravity pull us to a rapid halt then at the last moment, steer onto the dusty grass verge. There's no option but to strip the gearbox here.

Setting a new record, I do the job in just 70 minutes with an uninterrupted flow of drivers gawking at me through their windows. A flippant thought alleviates the stress. Whilst driving in the UK, I often listen to *Radio 2* for regular traffic reports so idly imagine, floating across the Ukrainian airwaves, an update akin to:

"There are long delays on the anticlockwise carriageway of the E40 south of Lviv. A vintage motorcycle has broken down at the side of the road and is creating a considerable tailback as traffic slows to watch the rider attempting to repair it!"

The sun is low on the horizon as I pack everything away and kick the Matchless into life. A rare gap appears in the trail of passing vehicles, so I lunge out onto the road and resume my climb. Cresting the summit, the road gains a middle lane and I overtake several trucks in third then go for top gear. It's not there. I can't conceive of covering any significant distance with only three gears and realise that I'll need take the whole thing apart again. As I glance to the right, there before my eyes, another huge hotel stands welcomingly in the fading light. Without hesitation, I ride into its car park and check-in.

In my room, I call Malcolm for an update on Derek's selector mechanism.

"What a time we've had Gordon," he tells me. "Derek phoned to arrange his visit but by then I'd already found an almost new gearbox that I robbed the selector mechanism from. Saved Derek driving all the way here."

Malcolm goes on to explain that DHL, who almost certainly operate the largest international courier network in Eastern Europe, wanted him to have the parts professionally steam cleaned and certificated before they would ship them!

"We phoned several other couriers but none of them deliver to the Ukraine. Then I had the idea to call our own courier, just a local guy who taps into a bigger network. He instantly agreed to take it. The upshot is it left at 4pm and it should be at your hotel by Tuesday."

I don't know how to thank him enough.

"You need to keep that Matchless going and get yourself onto that ferry, Gordon," he says. "Oh, and before I forget, there's a present in the parcel for you… a 5/16" Whitworth spanner for your tappets!"

Brilliant.

E40 south of Lviv. Gearbox fixed and ready to leave, desperately hoping it'll work.

Day 10. E40 Ring Road, South of Lviv, to a field next to the E85, north of Tolstoye. 138 miles.

Next to some rubbish bins in the furthest corner of the car park, I embark on fixing the gearbox. This time I do a dry run without the cover but fit the gearchange lever and hold a spanner onto its nut. Using a black marker pen, I outline the position of the spanner on the engine's timing cover when the ratchet and cam are properly aligned. Assembling the gearbox once more, I use these pen guides and my spanner to ensure correct alignment and joy of joys, the result is four fully operational gears.

There's a choice of routes to the Moldovan border. The first option follows major roads in a looping arc via the city of Ternopil but a more direct south-easterly cross-country route is, according to my satnav, at least 80 miles shorter. Once underway, opting for the latter feels like the right decision as for the first 40km we follow a road that's recently been resurfaced and the Matchless glides gracefully along. The change to a poorer surface is gradual, the most obvious difference being large ripples that appear at the edges of the road where heavy trucks have made waves out of hot tar. I need to keep my eyes peeled; the outcome of hitting one of those could equal me flying off the bike.

Next come 3km of major reconstruction, the surface composed of nothing but thick gravel making it a struggle to keep the bike upright. It's difficult to see ahead as each of the cars coming towards me kick up a cloud of choking dust. My hopes for a return to some sort of normality are dashed at the end of the roadworks where the old road is completely shattered. There's barely any recognisable top surface left and it's so potholed and stony that I find myself riding on the wrong side in search of the best line. Looking ahead, I see a car making its way up a hill towards me. He's doing the same thing, bouncing up and down on what is theoretically my side of the road. At some point, as we move towards each other, we both swap over to our respective proper sides. The whole thing makes for a hot and difficult endeavour.

After riding through the centre of a small town the surface, almost unbelievably, becomes worse. The Matchless is being battered by the sharp edges of potholes and the many exposed large rocks that make up the road's foundations. It's impossible to keep both mirrors upright and I give up on trying to right them as all my concentration is needed to steer the bike around obstacle after obstacle. Lifting my eyes for a second, I notice that the speedometer has stopped working which I hope is caused by nothing more serious than its cable shaking loose. An hour into the ordeal, I stop under some trees to rest and check the bike over. The speedo cable is still attached which means the speedometer is broken. Furthermore, the ammeter is smashed, I've lost a bar-end weight and the second indicator has broken off the back of the bike.

Progress has been so slow that within 10 minutes I feel it's imperative I get back on board, instantly engrossed again in picking the optimal route along the fractured highway. Over an hour later, having only covered 20 kilometres, I come to a petrol station, fill up and buy peanut snacks for a late lunch. Returning to the Matchless, I notice there's a gap where my sleeping bag was and it's obvious it must have been shaken off. There's no way I'm going back down that dreadful road to search for it but it's a blow.

As I head in a new direction and pass through a drawn out village, things get worse. There's no vestige of tarmac left on the surface and for 20 minutes I inch my way forward, following a once white Lada with its rear suspension jacked high. Like me, it zigzags repeatedly to negotiate the ridges and holes. For the next two hours I'm permanently in first and second gears, the bike's taking a hammering and I'm increasingly exhausted. These are the worst roads I've ridden on anywhere in the world.

Passing through another town, with more decrepit, rusty old bangers than your average scrapyard, the Garmin instructs me to turn right and head up a long winding hill. 2km later, the lane peters out and turns to white, chalky gravel. The satnav's set to avoid unpaved roads so I'm not at all sure what the mapmakers think this is. Slithering and sliding this way and that, it's difficult to prevent the bike from toppling over and there are still 15km to go until the next turn. I try to relax and keep my hands soft but fear of falling and the combined effects of heavy luggage, the clammy heat and my aching muscles cause me to flounder. For the third time I almost lose the front-end when the wheel lurches sideways as it hits a thick pile of gravel. Heart pounding, I slow to a halt for a much-needed rest. Leaving the Matchless on its sidestand, I walk up and down, shaking my arms and hands and rotating my neck and shoulders as I mumble to myself that I'm going to have to start choosing my route more carefully rather than let the satnav decide where I go. After a few minutes, I become conscious that I've parked the bike smack in the middle of the road but it's not a problem as apart from a train in the distance and a few birds overhead, I've seen no movement for the last half an hour.

By the time the gravel track meets a sealed road it's early evening. At the edge of a tiny village I pull up and ask two passers-by if there's a hotel hereabouts. There isn't, so I keep riding. A short rise in the road brings me to a T junction with what's obviously a more major highway. Turning onto it, I roar through the gears and with real delight, hit top for the first time in six hours, fresh air wafting up the sleeves of my jacket, cooling my sweat soaked body.

5km further on, the satnav wants to take me onto another unpaved road. No way! I pause at the junction to check my map and suddenly, with an unusual squeaky sound, the engine cuts out. I try to kick it over but the kickstarter won't budge. The engine's so hot from hours of slow riding that I can't even get my hand close to it and it hits me that the piston has seized.

On my side of the road is a turnoff to a small farm track. Looking behind the shelter-belt of tall trees that line the road I see a hidden flat area where grass cuttings have been dumped. Wearily I push the stricken Matchless a few metres down the track and onto the compacted grass, get out my phone and call Andy.

"If it's got that hot and nipped up Gordon," he says, "I think you're going to

have to strip it down and use your spare piston."
Not the best news.

"But let's just check if it frees itself up first," he adds.
I try but it still won't turn over.

"Take the plug out and pour some oil down the bore to see if that helps," Andy suggests.
I call him back a few minutes later to tell him the piston's now free.

"Excellent, but I still think you'll need to swap it. It sounds like a pretty serious seizure and I reckon the piston'll be quite damaged."
We agree that as it's almost dark, I should reassess things in the morning.

In the distance, a farmer ploughs his field and I notice he's put his tractor headlights on. Doublechecking that I can't be seen from the road, I return to the bike, quickly unload and pitch my tent. All of a sudden, I hear voices close by. Alarmed, I creep to the end of the trees and peer around the corner. On the opposite side of the road, at the start of the lane the satnav wanted me to take, I can just make out the outline of three men trying to hitch a lift. Having seen many people hitchhiking at the outskirts of towns and villages today, I tiptoe back to my tent feeling no threat from them but am still ill at ease. Ideally, when wild camping, I carefully select a safe place where nobody's likely to find me but tonight it's more a case of by default, as the Matchless has given me little option but to stop here.

Covering the bike, I quietly prepare something to eat then in the inky darkness climb into the tent and get myself horizontal. I try not to think too much about the seizure as there's nothing I can do until tomorrow. Instead, I send text messages home, one of which inspires a jokey reply from Brendan telling me that he and Alan have already started planning a rescue mission! As it's still over 30°, the loss of my sleeping bag is no impediment and, exhausted, I'm fast asleep within minutes.

Forced encampment next to the E85, Ukraine.

68

Day 11. A field next to the E85, north of Tolstoye, Ukraine, to Chișinău, Moldova. 238 miles.

Dawn reveals a shroud of mist that has settled on the surrounding fields. I breakfast hastily, pack the tent and assemble my gear. The carpet of grass cuttings that formed our soft sanctuary for the night may have provided comfortable bedding but would make a terrible surface to strip a motorcycle engine on. If the Matchless will fire up and run, I resolve to ride it and see how far we get, rationalising that when it does seize again, I can look for a more suitable place to repair it.

Following Andy's suggestion, I add a few drops of oil to the petrol for extra top end lubrication then give the kickstarter a strong boot. Amazingly, she bursts instantly to life. I tentatively rev the engine for a minute and as the cylinder doesn't appear to be getting especially hot, think she might just be rideable. Twenty minutes later, with all my stuff secured, I head out onto the road. Nearly every muscle in my body is clenched tight in anticipation of the horrible grinding noise that accompanies an engine seizure. However, it doesn't come and the Matchless miraculously motors on. I don't exactly relax, and the road condition is far from perfect, but as the kilometres pass, my optimism begins to grow.

Despite the satnav repeatedly trying to divert me onto lesser roads, I stick to the E85 like glue, pausing twice to give the engine precautionary cooling stops. At the second such halt, I sit on a fence underneath a tree and watch the world slowly making its way by. A cyclist, half a dozen bottles of water in a handlebar basket, stops. Wearing a frayed, white sailor's cap, he's thin as a beanpole and has the wizened face of a nonagenarian. Dismounting, he tries communicating with me. Unable to understand most of what he says, I discern that he's Moldovan and cycling towards the frontier at Criva, which, according to his finger count, is 22km away. We shake hands and he wobbles off down the road.

Next, a young man on a motorbike pulls up. The bike is brilliant, a Chinese-made 125cc cruiser that he's customised with blue LED lights, spinning pink and chrome handlebar grips, tassels, prism-like stickers and my favourite, hidden horns that at the touch of a button give vent to all manner of strange electronic whoop whoop sounds. He's intrigued by the Matchless and hands me his phone to take a photo of him standing beside her. An elderly man chugging along on an ancient moped joins us and my new friend immediately introduces him as his dad, George. Once father and son have posed for more photos, they ride off.

My focus has now shifted from the fear of another seizure to my stomach. I still have no Ukrainian money and my tummy's rumbling loudly as it's been impossible to buy any food using credit cards today. With my riding gear on, I'm about to kick the bike over and head for the frontier when I hear the repeated tooting of a weak sounding horn. Looking over my shoulder, I see George reappear on his moped. He draws up alongside me, hops off and begins to unstrap a large cardboard box from his rear seat. Lifting the lid off, he reveals, rather magician-like, a huge chocolate and cream gateau, about 15 inches in diameter and 6 inches in height. Signalling with his hand, I work out that he needs a knife. The blade on my Leatherman would be totally inadequate but my spark plug spanner has a long flat handle which should serve the purpose. He looks rather dubious when I hand it to him but proceeds, nonetheless, to cut a whopping triangular chunk from the cake. Oh so grateful, I accept his gift and sink my teeth into it. Obviously on a mission to get it home before it melts, he straps it back onto his bike, wishes me well then putters off down the road. Meanwhile, I luxuriate in the unexpected decadence that's been so generously bestowed upon me then wipe, very carefully, around my mouth!

110km from my makeshift campsite I reach the border, over the moon that the bike's made it. Processed efficiently once again on the Ukrainian side, I go a short distance and come to the sleepy Moldovan checkpost. Three other vehicles are in the process of crossing together with half a dozen pedestrians. Immigration comes first followed by a police check. While I'm waiting my turn at customs, a young Moldovan man gets out of the car behind me and strikes up a conversation. He too finds the poor state of Ukrainian roads hard to believe, assuring me I'll fare better in Moldova. He asks where I'm going so I remove the map from my tank bag and show him my proposed route.

"You know not to travel through Transnistria, don't you?" he asks. Transnistria is a partially recognised region sandwiched between the River Dniester and Moldova's eastern border with the Ukraine.

"The police and customs will give you a very hard time if you go through it. It's quite dangerous, please do not go there."

I was aware of the peculiar status of this breakaway state but hadn't realised there were any risks associated with travelling through it. From experience, I suspect that if I were travelling from there to here, the people and officials of Transnistria would most likely be friendly and welcoming, doubtless warning me of the brigands and corrupt administrators I'd face in Moldova! However, as catching my ferry is the priority, I decide to take his advice and avoid any potential delays in Transnistria. Incredibly helpful, he locates a pen and paper in his car glovebox and, returning with his father in tow, sketches a route south from the capital, Chișinău. Writing in a script with curly accents above and below words, he details the towns and junctions I'll need to look out for. The crossing point back into the Ukraine is close to the shores of the Black Sea at a place called Palanca... which isn't even printed on my map.

I take to Moldova instantly. The roads, although not A-grade, don't have potholes, traffic's light and the man who serves me at the first petrol station I come to is incredibly friendly. I still haven't been able to change any money but can at least pay by card for some snacks. Already mid-afternoon, I've no idea how far I can ride before sunset and hardly dare hope that I'm out of the woods with the engine.

Purring on fresh *98 Super*, the best fuel since Germany, we follow near empty roads that rise and fall over huge hills. The countryside, at first unfarmed, eventually becomes quilted with large orchards and without effort, the Matchless makes it to the outskirts of the city of Balti. With still over an hour of daylight left, and incredulous that the engine has managed to run so beautifully, I continue on and aim for Chișinău. The burning orange ball of the sun casts an immaculate shadow to my left and I glance at the silhouette of myself and my bike fluidly rolling southwards.

We don't quite make it by nightfall but get close enough for light pollution and streetlights to help illuminate the way. On the final approaches, the single lane road I've followed all afternoon becomes firstly a dual carriageway and then a packed six lane monstrosity with traffic lights every couple of hundred metres. It takes two or three changes at each set of lights for me to reach the front of the queue and I'm on pins in case the piston gives out.

A large customised motorcycle edges past, its rider giving me a wave. Pulling alongside him at the next set of signals, I ask if he knows of a hotel nearby.

"Follow me," he responds brightly and indicates to the right.

He leads me down a slip road, picks up speed as he leans into a roundabout then exits onto a much quieter dual carriageway. Pausing at the next set of lights, he tells me to turn left and that I'll find a hotel at the first roundabout. Before I can thank him, he does a smart U-turn and heads back up the road, the rumble of his exhaust gradually fading into the night.

The hotel has no parking but the manager helps me clear space on a patio and together we push the Matchless up a wheelchair ramp, securing her to a couple of tables. After the terrors of yesterday, it's hard to rationalise that we've not only negotiated a border crossing but managed to clock up the largest number of daily miles thus far on the journey. Overwhelmed by her valiant performance, I plant a kiss on the old girl's petrol tank.

Day 12. Chișinău, Moldova to Odessa, Ukraine. 124 miles.

The bike ran so unbelievably well yesterday, with even the beleaguered selector mechanism behaving itself, that apart from a quick check for any loose nuts and bolts, I don't do any maintenance and am ready to depart Chișinău post haste. In the process of putting on my back protector and jacket, I turn around as a fellow hotel guest greets me and we fall into conversation. It transpires that Serge has lived in the UK for over 10 years with his Moldovan girlfriend. They've just married, with the formal ceremony in Britain followed by week-long family celebrations here in Moldova. I tell him how pleasant I've found everybody, from truck drivers and filling station workers to hotel and restaurant staff.

"We Moldovans take great pride in being friendly and hospitable. It's part of our national identity," he says with pride.

I wish him and his new bride the best of luck and he helps me roll the Matchless off her stand, holding her steady while I climb on.

According to my map, the hotel is ideally situated for a quick escape from the city centre. Taking the first exit off the adjoining roundabout, I follow a wide boulevard for a kilometre then turn left onto a road which will eventually become the main highway south. Within moments I see a long multicoloured line of tents and makeshift shelters that's spread along the pavement in front a large government building. Hundreds of people have camped here for months as part of anti-corruption protests over the disappearance of more than a billion US Dollars from Moldovan banks. According to the hotel manager, who gave me the lowdown over breakfast, the protesters are demanding early elections. I halt at a pedestrian crossing swarming with work-bound people, outwardly oblivious to the small band of picketers, placards in hand, gathered nearby. Things seem very quiet and peaceful. I look to my left and a van driver, his window down, gives me a thumbs up. As the last of the pedestrians scuttle off the crossing, the lights change and I continue on my way out of the city.

A bit further on, at the outskirts of a small town, I spot a petrol station and decide to fill up. The man who serves me turns out to be a bit of a joker, making quips to his two coworkers who've joined us next to the Matchless. He speaks excellent English and for some inexplicable reason, steers the conversation onto Barack Obama, whom he blatantly dislikes.

"But I like the British Prime Minister, he is good. You like him too?" he asks.

"No. Not really. But in the UK some like him and some don't. That's always the way with politicians, eh?" I reply.

Having seen the protests in the city, I ask him what the Moldovan Prime Minister is like. Almost as if pausing for comic effect, I notice the edges of his mouth begin to twitch then he replies,

"He has no hair."

He translates for his colleagues and like me, they fall about laughing.

The road soon narrows and begins to twist and turn through verdant countryside dotted with farmhouses and small villages. The final 20km run to the border is on flawless tarmac… almost as if the Moldovans are putting on a good show for visitors from the Ukraine. Low-key formalities on the Moldovan side of the crossing take under five minutes because I'm the only person there. With a fresh exit stamp in my passport, I ride to the Ukrainian controls where again I'm the sole traveller. It takes 10 minutes to clear immigration but then there's no one behind the desk in the customs booth. Seeing me mooching around, the immigration officer hollers for someone to come and attend to me at which point a uniformed man emerges from the main building. He gives my bags a cursory pat, then asks,

"Gun?" while pulling his own pistol out of its holster. "You have gun in here?" I laugh whilst shaking my head vigorously in denial. It's a new question for me and definitely more macho than the usual one about alcohol and cigarettes. Satisfied, he waves me on my way.

Straight out of the border compound, the road is so bad it's almost hilarious. Forget potholes… it has craters. What a contrast to Moldova! After a few kilometres I see glimmering blue water in the distance, the shoreline of a large lagoon that swells inland off the Black Sea. Turning left at a roundabout, I set off in a north-easterly direction but am soon stopped at a military checkpoint. Rolls of barbed wire and mounds of sandbags block the road with only a narrow gap left for traffic which is guarded by soldiers in flak jackets, their matt black assault rifles at the ready. My registration number is written in a ledger and onto a slip of paper which I'm duly handed. Beckoned through, I enter some kind of militarised transit zone.

Unsure why this particular area, so far away from conflict in the east, is heavily guarded, I ride the next 15km without stopping, only coming to a halt when I reach another fortified check post. This time, the soldier at the barrier holds his hand out so I give him the piece of paper with my registration number on it. Unsmiling, he signals me on. At that very moment, a fierce Alsatian dog appears from its roadside kennel and with bared teeth, snarls viciously. As I shift my balance and move my right foot to select first gear, it lunges for me, barking furiously. I turn sharply to the soldier for his support but he completely ignores me. I yell at the dog, it backs off momentarily then charges forward again. The soldier continues to look away so I rev hard and attempt to ride off but the animal changes its position and now moves almost in front of the bike, repeatedly thrusting forwards. I'm frightened. Giving it a continuous blast of my horn and shouting at the top of my voice, I take my chance as it momentarily retreats and blast forward, accelerating at unprecedented speed on the Matchless, its frustrated barks soon drowned by the retaliating bark of my exhaust.

Nearing the city, I'm flagged down by one of four policemen standing in a small traffic island at the edge of a roundabout. They encircle the bike, all asking questions at once. It's quite intimidating as none of them seem particularly friendly. I just smile, say "Britanskaya," which is Russian for British, several times then point forward mouthing "Odessa." They ask for papers, so I reluctantly give them my passport. Another flurry of incomprehensible questions follows. I just keep smiling, my hand held out all the time in the direction of my passport. Eventually my lack of comprehension and persistent smiles win through and they give up, relinquishing it. Careful not to show any undue haste, I steadily ride away.

Figuring that such a long hold up with my engine still running won't have done the piston any good, I pull over at the first opportunity to let it cool before tackling city traffic. I stop at a petrol station where a lone attendant paces backwards and forwards. With gestures, I ask if it's OK to sit and rest for a while, to which he nods with a warm smile. Sipping water from my Camelbak as I perch on the edge of some stone steps, I watch three cars pull in at once, the attendant instantly rushing from one to another in an attempt to serve them simultaneously. The cars are typical of what I've seen in the Ukraine to date. Two are 1990s Mercedes and the other a shambolic wreck of an old Russian car that barely holds together. Both Mercedes have missing front bumpers and are covered in scratches and dents. One has a cracked windscreen and the other a replacement door panel painted a completely different colour from the rest of the car. All tanks filled, the pump attendant strains at the rear of the Russian car and eventually manages to roll it forward... it needs a bump start to get it going again!

Jolted by cobbled streets and ever watchful of the long trams that swing unexpectedly around tight curves in the road, I head towards the Aleksandrovskiy Hotel, exceedingly grateful that the satnav seems to be guiding me unerringly to its doorstep. A cut above my usual accommodation, I'm greeted by a smartly uniformed doorman who helps me get the Matchless onto the pavement and parked at the foot of the steps to the hotel. She's technically still on the street but he assures me she'll be safe as he'll be on duty all night. Removing the luggage, I padlock my spare tyre to the rear wheel then observe how the bike gains invisibility as I throw the cover on. Before, passers-by were slowing or stopping to look at her but now they walk past without a second glance. It's an indispensable piece of kit for a travelling motorcyclist.

Early evening, I go for a walk in search of the seafront but all I can find is a vast dockyard which stretches into the distance. As I stroll into a cliff top park which overlooks the port, I notice an open-air photographic exhibition and thinking its artwork, saunter across. I'm shocked to see graphic images of the civil war that's being fought in the Donbass region of the Ukraine. There, armed pro-Russian insurgents, apparently assisted by Russian special forces, are engaged in battle with the Ukrainian army. At the back of the display is a sobering list of hundreds of names, obviously troops that have been killed in action.

Back at the hotel, I research the war online. With the Crimean peninsular, which does have a majority of ethnic Russians, already annexed by Russia, it's hard to know what will happen in Donbass where ethnic Ukrainians make up the larger percentage of the population. Demographics aside, in human terms the fighting is abominable, a sad manifestation of nationalism taken to the extreme. The situation is locked in stalemate and seems set to enter another freezing winter of conflict.

Day 13. Odessa. 0 Miles.

I decide to have a lie-in and sleep until 8am. First job of the day is to check for the arrival of my gearbox parts. Reception hasn't been contacted by a courier so I head back to my room and try to track the parcel online. The tracking details aren't recognised on the company's website so I phone the Manchester number that Malcolm has emailed me. The lady who answers confirms that the tracking number is correct and refers me to the London clearing office they use for international shipments. I call them immediately and am put through to someone called John. Before I get further than introducing myself, he says,

"Oh, hello. I've got your parcel here. It was supposed to fly out yesterday. I don't know why it was delayed but it'll be on its way to you today."
Biting my tongue, I explain that I'll be on a ferry tomorrow and sending it today will be a waste of time. I go on to tell him about my ride and the necessity for the spares.
"No problem," he answers, unfazed. "Tell me where you're heading to next and I'll forward it there."

With thanks, I assure him I'll be back in touch soon and immediately begin to research hotels in Azerbaijan. It seems to take forever… the tablet computer is so small and my fingertips too big and clumsy to use it effectively. I reproach myself yet again for the misjudgment of choosing it over a laptop in an effort to save space. How people cope using mobile phones online is beyond me... must be an age thing!

I choose a hotel in Baku, hoping it will have a helpful reception desk should the parcel arrive early and forward the details to John. It's lunchtime before I first cross the hotel doorstep and set off in search of a replacement sleeping bag. Camping stores aren't commonplace, indeed an online search by the receptionist only produces one possibility. I reach the shop but find that all their bags are synthetic, which makes them both heavy and bulky. The owner's very helpful and draws a map showing me how to get to his competitor's store. It's a half-hour walk and by the time I get there, I'm pretty crook... my stomach's feeling decidedly dodgy. This second camping shop is even more disappointing. It too, is devoid of down sleeping bags and the best is only usable at -5°. In the heat of the day, I traipse all the way back to the first shop and make my purchase.

Returning to the hotel, I'm grounded for the next three hours, glued to the toilet seat. I've got a strong constitution and it takes a lot to knock my stomach so, delicious as last night's pizza was, I'll be passing on it tonight.

Around 5pm, feeling somewhat revived and keen to take in as much of Odessa as possible, I go for another walk. The city certainly seems far more affluent than any other part of the Ukraine I've visited, with numerous top-of-the-range imported cars half parked on pavements and plenty of well-dressed people to match them. There are lots of things I like about the place: the many grand imperial stone apartments, offices and theatres; Potemkin Stairs, an imposing granite stairway that descends to the docks; cobbled tree-lined boulevards gaily lit by night and buzzing with open-air cafes and restaurants; groups of young sailors from the naval academy, attired in crisp white uniforms with blue stripy bibs and enormous pancake hats, that briskly stride up and down the streets; scores of well fed cats sprawled lazily in doorways and a multitude of dog walkers idly chatting in public gardens and on street corners; electric trams that move unsteadily along heat-warped tracks and trolleybuses, with standing room only, that skitter beneath sagging overhead cables. I roam long into the balmy evening, contentedly absorbing the atmosphere.

Heading back to the Alexandrovskiy, I climb into bed at 10pm. As my head sinks into the pillow, I suddenly remember that I need to pay for tomorrow's ferry in cash, so hurriedly put my clothes back on and dash out into the street in search of a currency exchange booth. Thankfully the first one I try is open 24 hours and I soon return to the hotel, my money belt bulging with ₴7,500 in crumpled 20 hryvnia bills.

Potemkin Stairs, Odessa.

Day 14. Odessa to Ilichevsk port. 12 miles.

Ilichevsk ferry terminal is situated 19km south of the city centre. It would seem that many travellers have difficulty locating the *UKRferry* booking office as, along with my reservation, I was emailed photographs of the building together with its GPS coordinates. In no time I'm in the vicinity of the port, the hubbub of Odessa a distant memory. Despite satnav assistance and the photos, I still ride past the office and into a dusty housing area where yet another dog takes a dislike to my exhaust and gives chase. Turning around and approaching from the opposite side, I now recognise the building and park up.

At least a dozen truck drivers are loitering in the entranceway and there's a short queue of them at the ticket kiosk inside. I wait in line and eventually meet my contact, Mrs Natalya, who gives me a form to fill in and asks that I tender the balance of my bill to the cashier at the adjoining window. I'm a little confused as the amount owing is less than I was quoted. The cashier laboriously types on an ancient computer then prints everything on a continuous ream of paper that issues forth from a dot matrix printer, its electronic chirping sound something I'd long forgotten. When I scrutinise the final bill, it's now higher than expected, the difference caused by the cashier charging her own fee for processing my payment! Protestations drawing a blank, I'm left with no option but to change a €10 note into hryvnia at an appalling exchange rate. Receipt in hand, I return to the first window and enquire when boarding will commence.

"It depends on how many passengers there are," Mrs Natalya replies.

"When will it sail?" I ask.

After a pause, she earnestly responds,

"I cannot tell you. Tonight... maybe?"

She hands over my ticket along with instructions for boarding the ferry:

‘FROM OFICE "BOREY" ONE LINE ROAD TO CUSTOM (5 MINETS).

FOR 10 METERS BEFORE BRIDGE THROUGH WATER TO THE RIGHT.

CONCRETE ROAD TO CUSTOM (SMALL WHITE BUILDING).’

Clear as mud!

For some reason the Matchless decides she doesn't want to start and while I build up a sweat kicking her over, the truckers congregate in an ever thickening circle around me, cheering in unison when the engine finally catches. I depart with Mrs Natalya's instructions prominent in the map pocket on top of my tank bag, soon coming to the bridge. There is no turnoff '10 meters before bridge' so I go over it, in the process overtaking a touring cyclist, accoutred in brightly coloured Lycra, who I guess is heading to the same place. Once past him, I pip my horn and give a friendly wave. Taking the turnoff immediately after the bridge, I ride past a long line of parked trucks and locate the promised 'small white building'. Through the front door I see an empty office with a sliding window and to the right, a pulldown chrome barrier that's firmly shut.

At that moment, the cyclist arrives. He leans his laden bike against the office wall, pulls off his peaked cap revealing a sweat-soaked, shaved head, and comes to say hello. Hans is from Switzerland and plans to ride to Ethiopia taking a rather unusual route through Georgia, Armenia, Iran, UAE and Oman before flying to the Sudan and continuing south. It soon becomes clear that he's spent the majority of this adult life cycling around the world, with brief interludes in Switzerland to work as a chef and save money for further expeditions. He started this current venture two months ago and hopes to be away for another six. We have an immediate rapport and chat non-stop for the next couple of hours.

Two more cyclists appear, a man and a woman, who teeter to a halt and struggle to dismount due to their huge backpacks. Serge is a ship's navigator and with his newlywed wife, Anna, is heading to Georgia for a two-week camping holiday. Fun and games begin around midday when the port officials show up. A woman sits behind the sliding window and a man in a shiny navy tracksuit perches on a stool adjacent to the barrier. Nothing happens for a while and the first two people that approach them with questions are quickly rebutted. Eventually, Serge goes to the window and politely asks what's happening. A minute later he rejoins us and, with patent exasperation, translates the lady's answer.

"She says she doesn't know what's happening. They are both waiting for someone to tell them what to do."

Hans and I look at each other and laugh as Serge continues.

"Some things haven't changed. It's the old Soviet way... people are frightened to act or think for themselves."

At 1.20pm there's movement. A motley crew of truck drivers, a dozen or so pedestrians, a Georgian car driver, the Ukrainian cyclists plus Hans and myself slowly filter through the barrier, our names ticked off a list by the man. Following a bare concrete corridor, we congregate in a gloomy chocolate brown room with bench seating around three walls, no windows and a door on the far side that's missing its handle. A while later, a man enters and asks if we've had our tickets stamped at the window next to the entrance. None of us have and the tracksuited official had failed to notice. En masse, we troop through the barrier, queue at the window and once our tickets are stamped, file back past it once more.

Seated again in the chocolate room, we're all so busy talking that for some time I fail to notice that the truck drivers are missing. When I do realise, it occurs to me that they've gone through another way, probably with their trucks and that, as the owner of a motorised vehicle, I should be with them. Heading outside, I spot three artics slowly making their way over an inspection pit. I push the Matchless towards them and attempt to follow but am promptly halted. It seems that I'm missing a vital piece of paper but no one can explain where I should get it.

Returning to the waiting room, I ask Serge if he would mind acting as an interpreter. A man on a mission, he leaps to his feet, exits to the corridor and begins questioning two people. Obviously dissatisfied with their answers, he requests that I follow him up some stairs where we find three administrative offices. We're shooed straight out of the first by a man on his phone but in the second encounter three women. One is sending a text, another's reading a magazine and the third staring out of the window. Serge points to me and enquires about my paperwork, provoking a histrionic outburst from all three. It transpires that their computers won't be working until 3pm. There's nothing they can do about it and we're sent away with fleas in our ears.

Accepting this rather strange situation, I thank Serge and return to sit beside my bike. What seems like an age later, an energetic young man dressed in jeans and a Nirvana T-shirt asks me what I'm doing. I describe my predicament and he tells me to wait, explaining that he is one of the port expediters and will see what he can do to get things moving. A few minutes later he returns, leads me to a room where my passport and motorcycle documents are photocopied, then summons me up the stairs to the office Serge and I had previously visited. This time the three women are hard at work. Glancing at my watch, I see it's 3:07pm and am delighted to find that their computers are now fully operational. Five minutes later, with the required documents duly printed out, I reclaim my bike and push her unhindered past the inspection pits.

Next up is the ecological station. I'm concerned this will entail some form of antibacterial cleanse for the Matchless but in fact, nobody even looks at her. The photocopies of my documents are stamped and I'm waved away. Where to now, I wonder, as I look across a vast empty dock? The expediter appears from nowhere and tells me to head to some buildings in the distance where I'll need to clear customs.

When I get there, the Georgian car driver is hanging about in an empty corridor. He tells me only one person at a time is allowed in the senior customs officer's room, so we stand around waiting to be called. When his turn comes, he is in there for 20 minutes, shaking his head in disgust when he's eventually released. I knock on the door then tentatively enter. A stern looking silver haired man, impeccably dressed in a bold blue uniform, signals me to sit opposite his desk and holds his hand out for my papers. Painfully, he one-finger types my details onto a computer then asks where my VIN number is. I take the papers back from him and point to my frame number. Apparently displeased, he gets up, walks to the door then hollers down the corridor. We're quickly joined by two men and a discussion ensues about the validity of my documents. One of his colleagues informs me that the computer system requires a 17 digit number in order to process clearance and my bike's five digit frame number is unacceptable.

I explain about its age and archaic numbering system but this just causes more consternation. The expediter and another man also come into the office, which begins to feel rather claustrophobic. All five of them seem to be competing for dominance in an argument. Reluctantly, the official relents and finishes typing, repeating the letter X 12 times after my frame number. With disdain he gives back my paperwork and I assume I'm free to go.

Alas no, one of the group of men, dressed in a black suit, charcoal shirt and black tie, asks for my passport then intensely questions me about what I'm carrying... drugs, armaments, large sums of money, contraband? Am I involved in people trafficking or prostitution? Not satisfied with my first answers, he goes through the list once more, his fervent eyes locked on mine. In the end I say,

"Please come and look at the bags on my bike. You're welcome to inspect everything."

At that, he hands back my passport and tells me I can go. What a palaver.

Outside, I'm surprised to see Hans standing behind the Matchless.

"Having fun?" he asks. "We've been on the boat for more than three hours and I think you're the last to load. I've had a shower and something to eat so I thought I'd give you a hand carrying your bags once you get the bike on. By the way, when I was allocated my cabin I asked if we can share. It saves either of us being landed with a drunken lorry driver for a roommate."

Putting my helmet on, I prepare to ride towards the ship. Just as I kick the bike over, a port agent runs across and orders me to stop. Apparently the bike has yet to be inspected. During the next 20 minutes a new group of men assemble, stand in a circle chain-smoking cigarettes and cast glances in my direction. One comes over to look at the frame and engine numbers. He returns to the group and a round of discussions takes place before they all wander across to study the Matchless. I see a look of amusement on Hans's face as they walk away, huddled together in some sort of cahoots. The expediter reappears and after the briefest consultation with the group, tells me the customs procedure is complete... now I need to visit immigration. Crikey, the process has been so protracted and my passport viewed by so many people, I've failed to notice that it hasn't been stamped.

Finally, I'm allowed to board. Carefully riding between railway tracks up a long wooden ramp and past a soldier who's guarding the ship, I'm halted by two stevedores next to a humongous steam roller. The rest of the deck is packed full of railway carriages, a long line of trucks and the Georgian's Mercedes. Enormous rubber chocks are placed on both sides of the wheels, my new sleeping bag put on top of the saddle and an industrial strength ratchet strap torqued down across it. Even in the roughest of seas I feel confident she'll be secure, so with Hans's help, set off for the cabin.

After a refreshing shower I find Hans on the top deck and watch the sun's incandescent glow expire as it sinks into the horizon, casting rippling orange shadows on the sea's oily surface as the ship finally sets sail.

Dinner is a communal affair and all passengers are called to the dining room simultaneously. Two rows of six tables, each seating seven passengers, have been shoehorned into the room and two waitresses hurriedly move up and down the aisle serving the hungry crowd. Hans and I join a table of five burly Ukrainian truckers who watch in amazement as Hans, at only 5' 6" yet built like a weightlifter, proceeds to out-eat them. Not content with his first serving, he asks for seconds and once they're polished off, clears the remnants from my plate. The drivers laughingly scrape all their leftovers onto another plate and offer him that as well.

"When I'm riding in Europe," he tells me between mouthfuls, "I eat about 5000 calories a day, but when I get to hot and challenging places like Africa, that can increase to 7000. I don't put weight on because I burn it off. I think it's the same for all long distance riders."

The drivers try hard to understand what he's saying and Serge is called over to translate. They stand in unison, telling Serge that they're off to the bar to work hard on their calorific intake.

Not much later, I climb onto the top bunk in our cabin and begin to read a book I picked up in Odessa, Hemingway's *To Have and Have Not*. There were only a few English titles to choose from and I selected this to read at sea as it has a nautical theme. Soon, the gentle swaying of the ship makes my eyes heavy, and after the book falls onto my chest for the second time, I give in to sleep and switch the light off.

The last vehicle onto the Black Sea ferry, Ilichevsk port.

Days 15 & 16 at sea.
Approximately 565 nautical miles on MV Kaunas Seaways.

Several theories exist regarding the origin of the Black Sea's name. One is that black is a general term for north in medieval Turkish and the Black Sea forms the northern boundary of Turkey. Another is that sailors of old named the sea after the sudden, bleak storms that have always raged there in winter. As light dawns on the first morning of the voyage, I climb to the promenade deck, take a deep, salty breath and scan the horizon. The sky is clear and bright yet the water appears dark and inky. Although far from black, its hue provides an even more obvious possibility for its name.

Ship life revolves around meal times with calls to breakfast, lunch and dinner all eagerly anticipated. In between, I lie on my bunk and read, stroll up and down the decks and even have an afternoon nap, my excuse being that it's the first day in months I've had the opportunity to really switch off. Highlight of the day, while leaning over the lower deck railings to watch the frothing waves, is spotting a pod of silken porpoise fluently breaking the surface three times before diving perilously close to the bow. I yell out in excitement and run to starboard for a last glimpse before they finally disappear into the depths.

Some of the technology I'm using comes into its own during the crossing. I unpack my *Garmin* and climb to the top deck. Straightaway it locates our position due south of the Crimea peninsular, even showing our current speed which is 24 kmph... there were many times in the Ukraine when I couldn't equal that on the Matchless! I'm also carrying a *Delorme InReach*, a brilliant device that communicates via text messages using the Iridium satellite phone network. Theoretically, no matter where I am in the world, I'll be able to let my family know I'm safe. Furthermore, the monthly subscription includes an SOS function that sends your coordinates to the *International Emergency Response Coordination Centre* (IERCC) which can then mobilise local rescue services to find you; perfect for a motorcyclist who's fallen into a ditch or experienced any other sort of mishap! It's great to send a message home from the middle of the Black Sea... and even better to get one back.

The passenger list is dominated by truckers. The five drivers who share our dining table could best be described as 'rough diamonds'. They pass bread, water and condiments around the table in a mannerly way and are always polite to the waitresses but with each other tend to be overtly masculine and gruff. Once the tables are cleared, we spend a hilarious hour as Hans attempts to bridge the language gap through play acting. Eventually everybody leaves except for the guy sitting next to me, Andre, who's a strapping 26-year-old with crinkly, smiling eyes. He removes a smartphone from his jeans pocket and spends the next 30 minutes flicking through pictures of his wife, two children and parents. Next he brings up Google Maps to show me his hometown of Mykolaiv, which lies approximately 130km north east of Odessa. He generally drives in 8 day stretches, this ferry crossing being one of his most frequent routes, though it's evident he misses his home life very much.

Later, in the ship's bar, there's a movie's starting. The plot's too trite to hold my interest so instead I watch Hans planning his route using an offline Russian GPS system. It seems incredibly detailed and unlike my maps, depicts the terrain. Even when he's plotting his journey, the guy's such a livewire it seems hard for him to sit still. When I ask if he ever slows down, he reveals that he's recently been diagnosed with rheumatoid arthritis. At 52, he's determined to continue cycling and believes that come what may, he'll still be travelling for many more years.

In the early afternoon of the second day, I sit reading my book on one of the reception area sofas. On the surrounding laminate walls are maps of the Baltic Sea marked with dotted shipping lanes that represent crossings between Danish, Swedish and Finnish ports. Passenger information and safety instruction boards are all written in what must be a Scandinavian language and I can only deduce that the Kaunas Seaways is a new acquisition for UKRferry. Stirring, I take a few steps to the reception desk and ask a member of the crew what time we'll be docking in Batumi. If we're on schedule, it should be around 9:30pm.

"Sorry sir," replies the purser, "we cannot get a berth tonight. The captain has already slowed the ship and we will dock sometime tomorrow morning. Dinner and breakfast will be served at the usual times."

Fine by me... saves having to pay for an overnight stay in Batumi.

Lying in our bunks, Hans and I discuss many topics. It suddenly occurs to me that German's his native language.

"Hans," I say, "what does Gute fahrt mean?"

"Good journey," he replies. "Have a good journey or good trip. Like Bon Voyage. Why?"

I tell him about the many signs I've seen at German petrol stations which say Gute fahrt, then ask,

"Do you know what a good fart is in English?"

"No," he answers naively, so I enlighten him.

He starts laughing.

"Good fart!" he roars. "You know what, I'm going to be rich. I will make a T-shirt with Gute Fahrt printed on the front and Good Fart on the back. Fantastic!"

By now, there are tears streaming down both our faces. Twenty minutes later, still chuckling, we turn our lights off and try to get to sleep.

Day 17. Batumi to Mtskheta, Georgia. 224 miles.

Hans is first in line at the lift, his waterproof bags neatly heaped beside its steel door. He returns to our cabin and helps me lug all my possessions along narrow corridors, forming a considerable pile next to his. The ferry docks an hour after breakfast and we wait patiently for Georgian officialdom to board. After what seems like an age, the lift light turns to red and, accompanied by a loud humming sound, its door opens to reveal five uniformed officials who walk straight past us and into the Captain's Bar. Once the ship's paperwork has been dealt with, the tannoy announces that all passengers are to proceed to the bar for their passports to be inspected by immigration.

It's a simple exercise, five of us being processed at a time by the officers who quickly enter our details onto laptops then unceremoniously plonk bright red stamps in our passports. Minutes later, I join Hans in the lift then we begin ferrying our bags in relays to the open stern door, the fresh morning air wafting in from the dockside competing with the hot fumes from the ships generators.

With motorbike and bicycle loaded, Hans asks Serge to take a photo of us beside our respective two wheelers, arms around each others' shoulders and grinning like a couple of schoolboys. The all clear to disembark is given and we formally shake hands in farewell. As Hans rolls forward onto the ramp, he turns and shouts over his shoulder,

"And Gordon... remember... always have a good fart!" before quickly disappearing from sight.

My turn soon follows, the faithful Matchless starting with a puff of smoke at the second kick. I carefully descend the ramp then park next to the Customs building. Inside, bike papers held high, I ask who I should see.

"Nobody. It's okay, you can go," a man answers.

Excellent!

Back on the bike, I cross railway lines and head towards the port gates, taking one last look behind me at the Kaunas Seaways. Through the gates, I halt and gaze to the right where Alphabetic Tower, a stunning 130m edifice constructed in a DNA double helix type pattern, is topped by a glimmering silver orb. To its left is Batumi Technical University Tower, Georgia's tallest building and the first skyscraper in the world to be built with an integrated ferris wheel which slowly rotates close to its shard-like pinnacle. My 30 second visual tour of the city complete, I turn left to follow the coast north, a row of palm trees and stony beaches bordering the roadside for the first few kilometres.

Traffic is light and I find myself singing all the songs I know that relate to Georgia... the US state, that is. When the 'Midnight train' has left for the fourth time, I decide to give up and concentrate on where I'm going. Heading inland, the road climbs through shady woodland before twisting downhill and once more hugging the shoreline in the direction of Poti. It feels fantastic to be back on the bike and I revel in riding round sharp bends, leaning over with confidence on the even tar surface. As I approach the turnoff to the east, my mirrors reflect a long line of trucks... my companions from the ferry. With horns blasting loudly and avid waves through their windows, one by one, they overtake.

Soon after, I unexpectedly turn onto a motorway. It seems to have been built quite recently and luckily, I have it all to myself. There's a strong crosswind which requires constant pressure from my arms in order to keep the bike upright and the radiated heat off the-near white tarmac results in both the Matchless and me becoming unhealthily hot. After 20 minutes, I pull off, find a tree to shelter under and test my jaw on a slab of peanut toffee which constitutes lunch. Rejuvenated and with a much cooler engine, we head out onto the highway once more.

The motorway comes to an abrupt end at a long stretch of road works. In the hazy distance is the barely discernible outline of the Likhi mountains, a spur which connects the Greater Caucasus mountains in the north with the Lesser Caucasus range in the south. From where they rise at the town of Zestafoni, I have 66km to run before descending to a valley on the other side. At first it's a pleasant experience, swooping round long bends as we gradually climb, but we soon run into a headwind that threatens to pull the front wheel out from underneath. It's worst on left-handers where, having been temporarily sheltered by the hillside, we're suddenly exposed to mighty gusts that almost blow me off the bike.

Progress is made considerably more treacherous by fellow road users. Cars are mostly 1990s Mercedes or BMWs that I guess, by the number of faded NL and DE country roundels on their tails, are second-hand European imports. The Georgian mindset seems to be overtake and be damned. Time and again, two cars try to overtake me at once, pulling in at the last possible moment from their vehicular jousting before tearing into the next corner. Twice, on the apexes of blind bends, the overtaking cars dive back into lane so close to my front wheel, I'm almost run off the road. Futile as the exercise might be, my voice becomes hoarse from shouting in outrage at their recklessness.

I've been told several times that Georgians are an incredibly friendly people, which is evident as cars pull alongside, their windows down and the occupants cheerfully waving at me. However, I'm shocked by their simultaneous lack of consideration as they consistently squeeze me into the dirt at the side of the road. At least a dozen times I look to my left and see that they've slowed down so they can watch and wave, seemingly oblivious to the hammering I'm taking on the rutted, stony verge. Then a car drives parallel no more than half a metre from my left leg, its front and rear passengers exuberantly shouting greetings at me. I wave back then encourage them to move ahead. Instead, the front passenger lifts his mobile phone and begins filming. Inches from the edge of the road and with tree trunks flashing past my right arm, I wave them on more forcibly but they ignore my perilous predicament. With a bend approaching, I shout and wave frantically. They finally race ahead only to slam their brakes on moments later to sharply take an exit to the right. With all I've got, I haul my brakes on in an emergency stop to avoid crashing into their bumper. By the time I reach the far side of the mountains and join a dual carriageway, I'm seriously frazzled.

An hour before sunset there's a turnoff signposted for Tskhinvali, the capital of South Ossetia, a disputed region that's recognised as an independent state by Russia but regarded by all but three of the other UN member countries as part of Georgia. Its closest boundary lies just a stone's throw north of the road I'm travelling on, however, I think it highly unlikely I'd be allowed to cross it as the most recent South Ossetian War in 2008 resulted in Russian troops being widely stationed there.

When it comes to conflict in the Caucasus, this de facto state is sadly not on its own as several other territories continue to be afflicted by the consequences of long-running struggles for autonomy. 70km north of Poti on the Black Sea coast is the partially recognised state of Abkhazia. Although the Georgian government considers it to be theirs, since the 1992 - 93 war it's been wholly controlled by its own separatist administration. Immediately north of Georgia, the Russian Federation's southern region contains the republics of Chechnya, Ingushetia, Dagestan, North Ossetia and Kabardino-Balkaria, all of which in recent times have suffered calamitous war or ethnic violence, sometimes both. To the south, the chaotic dissolution of the Soviet Union resulted in Azerbaijan controlling a small landlocked enclave known as the Nakhchivan Autonomous Republic, which is separated from the greater part of Azerbaijan by Armenia and the disputed region of Nagorno-Karabakh, itself locked in a frozen war. It's a huge mess and one that we in the West rarely hear about.

Pausing on the hard shoulder, I swap goggles, put on my hi-vis vest and steel myself for night riding. The dual carriageway remains fairly quiet as I countdown the distance markers to Georgia's capital, Tbilisi, from 34 to 12km. Traffic starts building and my search for a roadside hotel intensifies. When I spot one, I'm virtually upon it so have to brake hard and swing sharply, skidding to an ungraceful halt on its gravel driveway. There's no one at reception and after a couple of shouts of "hello" and in Russian, "Zdravstvujtye", which I hope will cause no offence as I don't know the Georgian equivalent, a woman descends a flight of stairs. A room is available but they don't accept credit cards and as yet I have no Georgian lari. Thwarted, I get back on the bike and head out to the road only to find another hotel 100m further along. The story's the same here and despite offering dollars and euros, I'm turned away.

3km later, I pick out the bright lights of a block-like building that looks like another hotel. Taking the next exit, I work my way back towards it, coming to a stop in a dimly lit courtyard. Before I can turn the engine off, a large Alsatian tears towards me, it's deep throated barks and large teeth extremely intimidating. Flicking out the sidestand, I slip off the Matchless, using it as a barrier between myself and the dog. A man comes running out of a door and pulls it away.

"Reception please?" I ask with relief.

He doesn't understand any English so I act out my usual sleep routine. Vigorously shaking his head, he points to the building then pretends to eat. It's a restaurant. The disappointment must be evident on my face and he begins pointing down the road I've just come off, signalling 5km with his right hand. To the sound of further barking, I turn in a circle and set off again.

The twisting road follows the contours of a dark lake. After an estimated 5km, I come to a junction where a bridge crosses one of its tributaries. Immediately to my right is a petrol station with a single pump and no canopy. The attendant, when I ask for directions, sends me over the bridge then left onto a narrow lane. 500m later, I climb a cobbled ramp to the Hotel Mtskheta Palace's entrance. The night manager speaks English and is incredibly helpful. Slightly flustered when the credit card machine fails to work for the third time, she tells me not to worry as she has a taxi driver friend who can take me into the nearby town to use an ATM. She then proceeds to help me carry my bags up two flights of stairs and shows me my room, its Art Deco furnishings very much at odds with the rest of the modern hotel.

"That'll do nicely," I tell her.

Back at the reception desk, she introduces me to her friend whose taxi sits outside close to the covered Matchless. We soon pull up in front of a convenience store which has an ATM next to its door. Happy to have a pocketful of lari, I climb back into the taxi and am deposited at a secluded courtyard restaurant with just four open-air tables. Now 9:30pm, I'm concerned it might be too late to eat. The chef unhurriedly comes out of her kitchen, takes my order and 15 minutes later, I'm eating my fill. Catching another taxi back to the hotel, I notice a subtly illuminated church set on one side of a flagstone quadrangle that's surrounded by stone walls. The night manager explains that Mtskheta was the capital of the Georgian Kingdom of Iberia until the 5th Century, the birthplace of the first king of Georgia and is still the headquarters of the Georgian Orthodox and Apostolic Church. It certainly looks worth a longer visit in the morning.

Day 18. Mtskheta, Georgia, to Shamkir, Azerbaijan. 126 miles.

Opening the curtains, I discover I have a small balcony with fabulous views across the murky Kura river, a lengthy goods train with rusty boxcars unhurriedly trundling along its southern bank. Beyond, a monastery sits atop a high ridge. Dragging myself away, I grab breakfast and prepare the Matchless.

The church I spotted last night is easy to locate and now, thanks to the night manager, I know that it's Svetitskhoveli Cathedral, a Georgian Orthodox cathedral which dates back to the 4th Century. According to legend, the clothes Jesus wore to his crucifixion were removed by four soldiers who divided them amongst themselves. One of those soldiers then sold Christ's mantle, his outer cloak, to a Jewish rabbi from Georgia named Elioz, who carried it to his home town of Mtskheta. To this day, it's said to be preserved in a crypt below the cathedral.

Damaged several times by war and earthquake, the cathedral's built from a dull yellow stone, has a cone-shaped dome in its centre and is surrounded on all four sides by a head-high castellated wall. I park the bike and sit on some steps that lead to a long paved broadway, in the middle of which is the cathedral entrance. An elderly priest with a long white beard arrives and is assisted up the steps by a young woman who holds his arm. With his claret coloured robes and cap a vivid contrast to the surrounding ochre stonework, he reaches the cathedral entrance and stands under an archway, talking to small groups of people who approach. It dawns on me that it's Sunday and his arrival heralds a morning service.

Heading out of town and back to the bridge, I fill up with fuel at the open air station where I got directions last night then follow the road back to the Tbilisi highway, noting that the lake I'd perceived in darkness is actually the slow-moving confluence of two rivers.

The dual carriageway soon expands, ultimately stretching to four lanes. Maintaining a fast cruising speed, 72kmph, I stay in the second lane... the inside lane has too many taxis and buses that intermittently come to abrupt halts. I need my wits about me as the aggressive and inconsiderate driving resumes. Entering a gorge, we pass beautifully designed polished steel and glass contemporary structures erected next to grim, moss covered concrete tower blocks that incongruently crowd in close to the roadside.

Tbilisi seems to be an incredibly long, drawn out city, but finally clear of it, I carry on in the direction of Rustavi. At the turn off to its centre, the eastbound road double backs on itself for at least a kilometre then begins to climb, plateauing out on a wild-looking plain, the surrounding grasslands burnt to a crisp. Half an hour later, I descend and begin the final run to the border, the road arrow straight for almost 20km. Whizzing along, I'm delighted with how the day's progressing, the Matchless engine purring gratifyingly beneath me. Something suddenly flies past my left knee. It takes a few seconds to realise that it's come off the bike. Screeching to a halt, I discover that the left-hand side of my front number plate has vibrated off. I jog back up the road just in time to see it run over by a truck. Gathering it up, I decide it looks serviceable enough so put it inside a saddlebag as a job for later.

It's a familiar story at the border... long lines of vehicles backed up with their engines off and passengers visibly wilting in the heat. I pull up at the back of the queue but within moments am approached by a man who says,

"What are you doing? Why wait here? Go to the front."

Stopping at the head of the line, it seems the exhaust has only just emitted its last pop when I'm tapped on the arm by an official and told to ride to one of the immigration booths. Firing the bike up again, I putter 50m forward and halt beside a window. In the office, a man swivels round on his chair and greets me, holding his hand out for my passport. Three other border guards gather round the bike and begin chatting with me about my impressions of Georgia. Two minutes later, my passport's handed back complete with an exit stamp and I'm free to go.

Prodding the kickstarter, the engine catches then immediately cuts out. Thinking I've turned the fuel off, I check both taps but they're in the on position so retard the ignition slightly and kick again. This time there's no compression, my leg flying downwards with a painful jerk. The official onlookers appear puzzled so I hop off and self consciously push the malfunctioning machine a hundred metres forward until I find some shade next to a duty-free shop. Baffled rather than worried, I check the spark plug then test if the clutch is releasing properly, but there's still no compression.

"Houston, we have a problem," I say to Andy when he picks up the phone. After I've explained the symptoms, he gives me an alarming prognosis.

"Sounds to me like you've either got a stuck valve or one's burnt out."

I'm daunted by the thought of having to strip the top end of the engine in no man's land, especially if I can't fix it.

"My money's on it being stuck, either because it's gummed up or something's jammed it slightly open. I once had a stuck inlet valve because the nipple had come off the end of my choke cable."

Our conversation ends with Andy suggesting I check the tappets first, just in case it's as simple as that.

I take a few moments to think the situation through rationally. Rather than trying to troubleshoot the problem while in geographic limbo, it seems sensible to start the process of entering Azerbaijan during which time the engine can cool down. I begin to push and five scorching minutes later, reach the gates to Azerbaijan. The soldier on duty tells me to wait a few moments while he lets some cars pass, then signals me to follow. Guiding the bike through the entrance, I see a very steep climb ahead and brace myself.

"Wait," shouts the guard. "We must take a photo first."

At the bottom of the hill are two sleek cameras mounted on steel posts, part of an automated system that won't work on the Matchless because, of course, she has no forward facing numberplate.

"Turn round please," directs the guard. I manhandle the fully laden bike in a three-point turn so that her rear number plate can be photographed. A minute later, I'm instructed to proceed up the hill so with a running start, set off.

I barely make it, the incline almost defeating my legs which tremble as I come to rest at the top. Parking under a canopy, I'm approached by a soldier who thankfully speaks excellent English. After patting my bags, he tells me to take the bike's paperwork to a nearby window. Once there, it's hard to see the customs officer inside because of the sun's reflection on the glass and I wait patiently for a couple of minutes until he finally slides a partition open. The face of a baldheaded man, sporting a moustache I can only liken to Hitler's, looks out and with a serious expression begins to speak in Azerbaijani. I smile and hand over my paperwork but no smile returns. After studying my V5, he appears unhappy and calls over the English-speaking soldier.

"He wants to know the year of your motorcycle," he translates.

"1941," I reply, pointing to the relevant line on the document.

The two Azerbaijanis speak together and although nearly all of it is unintelligible to me, I do discern the word 'transit'.

"I have a tourist visa, not a transit visa," I tell the soldier, fishing my passport out of my pocket to show him.

"Not you transit," he answers. "The moto. It can have three days to transit."

I see that the customs official is already filling in a form.

"No. Three days is not enough. I'm catching a ship to Turkmenistan, maybe in four or five days time but as there are no regular sailings I can't say exactly when."

Pausing to catch my breath, I then add,

"I read online that visitors to Azerbaijan with their own vehicles get 28 days."

After some consultation, the soldier translates again.

"You are right, you do get 28 days but only if your car is less than 10 years old. For a very old one like yours, you only get 3 days."

I begin to protest, but the customs official gives a curt answer and continues to fill in the form.

"He says you can leave it at the docks in Baku in three days and collect it when you catch your ship."

This is serious. Pleading my case in earnest, I explain that ships across the Caspian Sea can leave from any one of three ports and I have no idea at this juncture which I'll be sailing from. He still carries on writing my details on the form.

"My bike is an antique!" I say, getting desperate. "If I leave it in a port, half of it will probably be missing by the next day. I cannot leave it in a port. Please give me five days..."

Looking totally fed up, the customs man stops writing, rises and walks out of his office.

"He's going to ask others what to do with you," the soldier informs me then also walks away.

I go back to the bike, take all my luggage off and begin to check the tappets.

Quarter of an hour later, the soldier returns and tells me that the customs officer is now on the telephone to the chairman of the border post, seeking his advice.

"We have another problem," he continues. "The photograph of your

90

motorcycle number didn't work. Please go back and do it again."

Putting my tools away, I make a huge pile of my bags and riding gear, climb on the Matchless and coast back down the hill. The soldier who'd let me through earlier is waiting. I turn the bike around, spit on my finger and attempt to clean the registration number. Eventually, I'm told I can go. I brace myself for another big push.

"Why don't you ride?" asks the soldier as he sees what I'm about to do.

"Oh, it's much simpler this way." I tell him, nothing being further from the truth.

Back at the top, drenched in a fresh film of sweat, I catch my breath then set to work again on the engine. Accompanied by the soldier, the customs officer approaches.

"The photo is still not good." He points to the officious customs man and says, "He will take you himself."

Heavens... I'm not sure how long I can keep this pretence up but dread to think what might happen if he discovers the bike's broken down!

Trying to behave as casually as possible, I set off downhill with him, the Matchless between us. Not a word is said and I sense he's getting pretty brassed off. After ten minutes of positioning the rear number plate at various angles to the cameras, he signals that we're finished and can go back to the top of the hill. Once more I'm asked why I'm not riding it, the guard translating my answer to the customs man.

"This is a lot easier than riding," I pant. They shake their heads in bemusement.

I follow them back to the office window and once inside, the customs guy hands me a form I need to sign. Tensely I scan it, looking for some clue as to what it is. My eyes stop at the words '28 dat'. I look up and can't help smiling. Even Mr Grumpy Pants, transformed, smiles back, evidently pleased to have been able to help. I sign my temporary import licence on the dotted line then shake his hand. Phew!

After having my own photo taken and passport stamped, I buy $10 insurance then complete loading the bike. Just as I'm about to push off, a chit that'll get me out the compound held between my teeth, I look to the left and see my new friend, the customs official, who's come out of his office. He's waves then cheerily shouts,

"Azerbaijan good!"

I happily wave back, worry for the Matchless temporarily forgotten, then freewheel until I'm out of sight.

Parking in shade between two artics, I quickly call Andy.

"You know Gordon," he says. "I really think it's most likely a stuck valve. Why don't you take the plug out, kick her over a dozen times, then put it back in and see if it's cleared."

I give it a go and, to my delight, some compression returns. Turning on the fuel and tickling the carb, I swing solidly on the crank. She fires up straight away... hallelujah!

A soldier, rifle slung over his shoulder, has been watching me for the past 10 minutes. As I set myself to leave, he disappears into a building and returns with a handful of tissues for me to clean my oily hands, a welcome kindness. I ride out through the gates and into Azerbaijan.

In the late afternoon, as the light softens, Arcadian scenes play out around me: three men in white shirts pitchfork sheaves of wheat onto a wooden flatbed trailer; on a hilly smallholding, a gang of turkeys with bright red snoods are herded towards a shed by a woman wearing a floral headscarf; two rickety carts bumble along the road towed by tall grey donkeys. I begin to close in on an old Lada that's moving at a snail's pace and as I make ready to overtake, notice its rear seat and open boot are overflowing with bright green, stripey watermelons. The rear suspension is visibly sagging under the strain and its bumper scrapes the ground each time it goes over a pothole.

Thirty minutes later, still on the same quiet road, a policeman darts out from behind some trees and begins waving a baton that resembles a giant lollipop. Slowing to a halt, I pull off the road and wait for him to approach. Surprisingly young, he tells me in a high-pitched voice that I was speeding.

"I don't think so," I reply in a puzzled tone, careful not to confirm my actual speed at this point.

"95 kilometres," he states.

I laugh out loud... if only!

"On radar. We have you on radar at 95 kilometres."

"No. Absolutely not."

He watches intently as I extract my V5 from the tank bag and point to the age of the bike.

"95 impossible, it doesn't go that fast," I say. "Moto 1941. Slowly, slowly. 60 kilometres only."

"Radar," he persists.

"No," I state firmly. "No radar. Show me," I add, gesticulating with open arms.

"Go! Go!" he shouts while waving me away, then turns his back and returns to his hiding place behind the trees, ready to pounce on his next victim.

I'd read online that in these former Soviet states, it's vital to observe speed limits at the peripheries of towns and villages. Police tend wait there to catch speeders and their on-the-spot fines are severe. Fair enough... but there was no mention of them fabricating an offence.

Riding on, my satnav tells me there are just 25 minutes until sunset. I pass through a village where the road widens to include a second lane that opens inwards like an extended layby. Carefully keeping my speed below 50kmph, I move into it, allowing a shabby white Lada to pass. Emerging from the other side, I spot a 90kmph signpost and start to accelerate. Sirens begin to wail and in my mirrors I see a police car tearing up behind, blue lights flashing brightly on its roof. I pull to the side of the road and wait.

Two officers get out of the car and walk over. They ask for my driving licence, which I can't immediately lay my hands on. Searching my tankbag and pockets, I ask,

"Is there a problem?"

"Come," says one, pointing towards the car. I get off the bike and follow him to the front passenger door. He lifts out a clipboard and draws a diagram from which I assume I shouldn't have ridden on the inside lane through the village.

"Papers. Licence," he demands again.

I go back to the bike and take several bags off searching for them. Once retrieved, I return to the car and see the policeman's half way through filling in a charge sheet.

"One hundred and twenty five dollars," he tells me.

What? Unbelievable! I say I have no manat, which is true, and also that I have no dollars, which isn't.

"Get in car," he orders, pointing to the back seat. "We go to ATM and you get dollars. You give money, you get driving licence back."

I look at my bike and the two open bags on the grass verge... there's no way I'm just going to leave it.

"I do not understand. Show me again what I've done wrong."

Once more the clipboard comes out but this time the driver draws a diagram. I watch him outline a no-overtaking road sign, then using the previous illustration, sketch my bike overtaking a car. I'm incredulous, having overtaken nothing since the watermelon Lada half an hour ago and furthermore, it was me that was overtaken when passing through the village.

Outraged, I raise my voice and bluster,

"How dare you! I haven't overtaken anything. My motorcycle's from 1941," I add while pointing vigorously at my V5. "I go slowly everywhere. You never saw me overtake. This is a farce!"

Taken aback, the driver begins to speak but by now I'm in full flow.

"I'm a visitor to your country. You are the police, you should uphold the law not lie! It's disgraceful that you try to make me pay a fine for something I didn't do. You should be ashamed of yourselves! When I go back to my country, do you want me to tell everybody that the Azerbaijan police do this? I will not go to an ATM. Take me to a police station, I want to see your chief of police."

Thankfully, they can't understand most of what I'm saying but my tone and righteous indignation are very clear. The driver gathers my driving licence and V5 then throws them at me across his companion's lap and through the open door. Without another word, they make a u-turn and drive away.

Rather shakily, I pick them up off the road, walk back to the bike and begin to repack everything. I'd been aware for some time that we were being watched by a shepherd, his flock of scraggy sheep pressed against a wall on the far side of the road. He now climbs over the wall and offers me a cigarette. Looking up the road in the direction the police car has driven, he pats me on the back then mutters,

"Polis," and spits to the ground.

The sun has set by the time I'm riding again. After about 20 minutes I come to a large roundabout, a huge Azerbaijan flag in its middle and a petrol station on its far side. Pausing, I ask a car driver where I can find a hotel. He's joined by a couple of other men and they all point back to the roundabout, indicating I should take the third exit. I follow their directions and as the road begins to climb, it widens into two lanes. Strips of lights have been placed at ground level on both sides and along the central reservation, giving it the look of an airport runway at night. At the top, I circle around some buildings then stop to ask a family the way to the hotel. They point ahead and I see it, indeed, could hardly miss it as it's enormous.

I know straight away it'll be too expensive as it looks like a five-star tropical resort hotel, not something I'd expect to see here. Riding through the grotto-like illuminated gardens, I pull up at the marble front entrance where I'm met by a doorman wearing a red and gold tunic and top hat. Walking into the airy foyer, I'm greeted by an exceedingly polite concierge who accompanies me to the reception desk.

"Please can you tell me the room rate for one night," I say to the clerk.
The answer, in manat, is meaningless as I don't know the exchange rate.

"It's approximately 148 US dollars," she advises.

"I'm very sorry, but that's more than I can pay." I reply.
Turning slightly to include the concierge, I add,

"Please can you direct me to another hotel which will be cheaper."
The concierge asks me to wait then instructs the desk clerk to make a phone call. She speaks in Azerbaijani for a few moments then hands the phone to me. An urbane male voice says,

"Good evening sir. Welcome to the Excelsior Hotel, Shamkir. I am the general manager. My staff tell me that you'd like to stay with us."
I briefly explain my journey, that I'm trying to get off the road as it's dangerous in the dark, but that the room rate is beyond my budget.

"Sir, in certain circumstances I can offer a discount. Would $95 be acceptable?"
It's a lovely looking hotel but all I really need is a shower, a clean bed and somewhere safe for the bike. I thank him but decline, asking again if there's a cheaper option in town that his staff can direct me towards.

"Here's what I can do. I can offer you a room and we will pay the government tax on your behalf. That will make the room approximately $75. Can you stay now?"
After the day I've had, it's too good an offer to refuse and I give in to a night of luxury.

Day 19. Shamkir to Baku. 252 miles.

I resist getting out of such a sumptuous bed, determined to make the most of the enveloping luxury of the hotel. However, motivated by hunger, I rouse myself and head downstairs for breakfast. I'm greeted by Joey, an engaging Filipino waiter who tells me he's worked the night shift but stayed on late because he speaks English! The hotel, he informs, was opened two years ago by the president of Azerbaijan. One of three Filipino staff, he's been here exactly one year and is due to fly home soon to visit to his family... his first holiday. Previous hotel jobs have been in Russia and Saudi Arabia but this is his favourite as he likes the Azeri people and has already become fluent in the language. Shamkir, according to Joey, hosts an annual chess championship and has several archaeological sites nearby, but the hotel has been built to accommodate visitors to a new business park which is still under construction. I guess this explains why I'm the lone diner in a room that could seat a hundred.

The Matchless overnighted in a covered VIP parking area. I wheel her out, load, then hand my room key in at reception. Back outside, after kicking her over, I look behind and am touched to see five members of staff lined up at the entrance waving me off. Flying back down the 'runway', its strip lighting now off, I note rows of freshly built but seemingly empty office buildings as well as a new-looking roadside fairground. On reaching the roundabout I stopped at last night, I turn right and resume my journey eastwards.

The morning's first encounter with police occurs at a dual carriageway checkpost where traffic is forced to slow to a crawl. An officer in the centre of the road picks me out of line and instructs me to park on the right. Another officer comes over and tells me I was speeding... apparently, I was doing 87 in a 60 zone! I go through the same rigmarole as last night, producing my V5 to show the bike's age. The policeman notices my satnav and begins scanning through its screens, looking for a record of my speed. As luck would have it, last night I put it in my jacket pocket and when I later came to charge it, found I'd accidentally deleted all its history. I watch with bated breath as he examines it, hoping that any new maximum speed won't be taken as proof of lawbreaking. He locates the relevant screen... all the boxes such as maximum altitude, total distance covered, and most importantly, maximum speed, are blank. He gives up, reverting to verbal accusations. Like his predecessors, he repeatedly claims to have caught me on radar. I have seen speed cameras above the road this morning but am 100% certain I've always been well under the limit and firmly deny the charges. Once again, I'm grudgingly released.

I've become used to dogs chasing me but today I experience a particularly daft mutt. This one waits at the roadside, head turning from side to side as it judges the speed of passing traffic. When I approach, it makes a last minute dash for the opposite pavement, tearing across the road feet in front of me before coming to an exuberant if ungainly halt on the nearside pavement. Spinning around it sits, head cocked sideways, waiting for its next hair raising sprint. I can't help thinking that its days are numbered, but I sincerely hope not.

The surrounding countryside flattens and to my eye, looks impoverished. At the roadside, fruit stalls begin to appear with green apples and an assortment of melons stacked on vertical shelving the size of football goalposts. As I continue, other vendors sell live turkeys and where there are rivers or streams, boys stand on the hard shoulder waving freshly caught fish with bright orange fins, their iridescent silver scales glinting in the sunlight. When crossing the border yesterday. I'd expected more of the same heedless driving that I'd experienced in Georgia, but have been surprised by how respectful Azerbaijani drivers are, generally giving me lots of room when they overtake. Although many have waved in the process, they've done so without putting me at risk and my spirits are high as the kilometres pass to the steady beat of the Matchless's engine.

I stop for petrol on the Ganja ring-road. A tall man rushes to serve me and we soon get into conversation.

"Would you like a drink?" he asks after a few minutes. Before I can get any words out, he disappears into an adjoining cafe, soon returning with a glass of lemon tea which I slowly sip while he fuels a car. Sitting on a plastic chair beside the Matchless, I casually cast my eye over her. Something about the rear numberplate carrier seems out of place so I get up to have a closer look. Its top bracket has fractured just below the taillight and hidden underneath the registration plate is a secret stash of 200 euros. Considering myself very lucky to have spotted it, I dig out cable ties and secure the two halves of the broken area firmly together. The pump attendant comes back over and studies my map. He points sadly to the disputed region of Karabakh explaining that it's his erstwhile home, then asks me where I'm heading. I indicate the more northerly of two roads that lead to Baku.

"No, you mustn't go this way. The road is very bad and climbs into the mountains. You will not reach Baku today. Instead, take the southern route. It's a greater distance but the road is good and it will be much faster."

I thank him for his help and kindness and we shake hands before I depart.

Heeding his advice, I take the southern turnoff at the city of Yevlakh. By now, the dual carriageway is continuously under radar surveillance, overhead gantries loaded with cameras every kilometre. I frequently come up behind dumper trucks loaded with stones that travel just a couple of kilometres per hour slower than me. Because of the speed traps, I'm reticent to overtake but remaining in their dusty wakes for long periods would be seriously unhealthy. With my eye hardly straying from the satnav speedometer, I accelerate past each one before pulling in and resuming a constant speed. Twenty minutes later, I'm flagged down by yet another traffic cop, this one much more senior in years, who stands waving his lollipop beside a small police station.

"You are speeding," he says, unsurprisingly, pointing to a distant 50km sign. By now I'm an old hand at this game and refuse to get stressed or be intimidated as I'd seen the sign and slowed accordingly. Instead, I laugh, telling him that I'd love my slow old motorcycle to go fast, shaking my head in a knowing kind of way each time he mentions radar.

"Okay, I will let you go," he acquiescences after just a couple of minutes.

"But first, please, be our guest for a cup of tea..."

Moving on, the road gradually turns to the north and a thin blue line, the Caspian Sea, appears to my right. As we get closer, short choppy waves that fragment its aquamarine surface become visible and there's a familiar seaside smell to the air. I can't think of any songs with Caspian in them and, without forethought, start singing *The Beatles'* Yellow Submarine. Several rousing choruses later, I progress to other Beatles' songs. An overhead sign gives the distance to Baku, however, the name has changed to what I presume is a local spelling, Baki. My musical renditions then reach a new low with Baki-n the USSR!

Following the foreshore for 50km, we reach the city limits just as the sun sets, brilliantly illuminating two futuristic towers as it dips behind a hillside crammed with white painted houses. I have a route to my hotel mapped in my head but thought I'd be approaching it from the North. Coming in from the south instead, I ride along the main seafront boulevard and guess a point where I need to turn inland. However, as I slow, I see that the junction is a one-way street with the flow of traffic against me. Taking the next turn, 300m later, I begin to track backwards then head north for a couple of blocks, coming to a halt immediately past a Rolls-Royce dealership. Noting the surrounding upmarket shops and merchant banks, I presume I must have made a big miscalculation so, stopping the first person who walks past, a young man in a paisley shirt, I ask,

"Excuse me, do you speak English?"

"Of course."

"Do you know the way to the Du Port Hotel? It's next to the Red Lion Pub?"

He shakes his head but immediately whips out his smartphone and begins to search, skilfully manipulating a 3-D map with his fingers. After a minute he stops, positions it so I can see the screen and points.

"It's just around the corner on the next street, 70m from here."

Fan... blooming...tastic!

I pull up outside the Du Port, wheel the bike onto the pavement and go inside. Although I've arrived a day ahead of my reservation, the receptionist finds me a room, the last one available. There's no private parking but as this is a wealthy, central area, each street has its own 24-hour parking attendant. When I explain about the Matchless, the hotel manager leads me outside, waves the attendant over and introduces me. Shaking my hand, he refuses to take any money but promises he'll keep an eye on the bike. It's parked against the wall right next to the hotel's front door and is illuminated by two spotlights sunk into the surrounding pavement. My mind at rest, I fasten the lock around the bike's rear wheel and throw the cover on. It suddenly occurs to me that the gearbox selector mechanism, while still not centring, has miraculously been jam free since its last fix in the Ukraine. With the replacement due to arrive tomorrow, I'm delighted to have completed this leg of the journey and feel optimistic about the next.

Day 20 & 21. Baku. 0 miles.

There are no timetables for Caspian Sea ships, they simply leave when fully loaded. Generally, one sails to Turkmenbashi in Turkmenistan every second day but delays tend to be frequent due to bad weather or problems getting a berth in the busy ports. Hold-ups can have serious ramifications for people like me travelling on date-specific Turkmenistan transit visas. Warnings on the Internet report that late arrival in Turkmenbashi, with either an expired visa or not enough time remaining to transit the country, will result in deportation back to Azerbaijan and potentially onwards to Georgia.

Travel on board these ships is far from comparable to a regular ferry. Caravanistan.com, a website dedicated to assisting travellers in Central Asia, forewarns, 'A less exciting part of the journey will be your first encounter with your cabin. Some boats are not too bad (even clean) when it comes to hygiene. Others are awful. Shower and toilet are in the same place, and are usually not too clean, Bring a sleeping bag, as your mattress and pillow are not guaranteed to be clean. You might not need it, but to be safe, bring some food. Once the food runs out (if they open at all), you're on your own. Seeing how you can get stuck in the harbor for days, it would be wise to pack plenty of food. Don't forget water!!'

Tickets can only be bought the day the ship sails, but acquiring them is complicated. According to *Caravanistan.com,* there are three ticket offices but directions to them and their opening times are vague. Their advice is, 'You can find out when the ferry leaves by leaving your phone number at the ticket office, having someone call everyday (twice a day is better) or turning up yourself and asking "Is there a boat today?" Don't trust what they say, though, keep asking around, you will hear many contradictory stories. Be persistent, don't get fooled.' Hardly reassuring!

The most reliable agent appears to be Vika (Victoria), who's a legend amongst overland travellers as she's been organising crossings for almost 10 years. Straight after breakfast, I ask the hotel receptionist where I can buy a local Sim card.

"No need," he answers, "please use my phone."
He hands his cellphone over and I dial the Baku ticket office number. Vika herself answers but has no news of any sailings for today or tomorrow.

"Please call me back at 1pm," she says at the end of our conversation.

The next challenge is getting my gearbox parts. I ask the receptionist if he'll accept the package for me should it arrive whilst I nip out.

"Of course," he replies. "I cannot guarantee they will accept my signature but I will try for you."
Heading off, I briskly walk three blocks to a cafe and enjoy sitting in some shade, returning to the Du Port 20 minutes later. I'm gutted when the receptionist reveals that DHL has been. His desk is empty and I feel I've blown all the hard work people have put into getting the parts here. Then his face creases into a smile and from underneath the desk he produces a small

cardboard box. Brilliant!

On the dot of 1pm, I try Vika again. There's no change in the situation and she asks me to phone her first thing in the morning, explaining that she thinks there might be a boat tomorrow evening. I try a couple of other ticket telephone numbers but they both ring without an answer.

Next to the hotel is the entrance to a dark courtyard which services the backs of shops and provides access to several small apartments above. Wheeling the Matchless across to its brightest corner, I scavenge some cardboard from a wheelie bin, to protect the ground from stains, and prepare to do the gearbox. The selector mechanism change goes swimmingly well, the gearlever now self centering for the first time since Poland.

As I'm wiping my greasy hands, two young women attired in scanty dresses emerge from a door, sit on plastic chairs and get out their cigarettes. One of them stands up and walks over to say hello.

"Would you like a drink?" she asks. "We have black tea or coffee."
She returns with an ornate cup of coffee nestled in a matching saucer, two biscuits balanced on the side. I thank her, she smiles then rejoins her friend.

With the gearbox done, I set about changing the oil, substituting fully synthetic for mineral now that the engine is well run in, and simultaneously swap the oil filter. Another woman comes out of the same door the other two had used. She wears an even tighter fitting dress that's so revealing, I avert my eyes. She parades around in front of me in a blatantly seductive manner and I can't help wondering what kind of establishment this is.

Minutes later, a svelte young man with a sharp haircut exits the same door and approaches me. Pointing at my tin of grease, he asks if he can have some. It's a strange request, and I'll need all I have to maintain the gearbox for the rest of the journey. However, I tentatively nod in agreement, wondering what he wants it for. He dashes back through the door then returns holding a set of electric hair clippers. The mystery's solved and I admonish myself for my erroneous assumptions… they're obviously hairdressers! Lightly greasing the clippers, he thanks me then goes back to his job. Continuing with the task at hand, I replace the air filter, adjust the rear chain and check every single nut and bolt on the bike. Three hours after starting I get up and stretch my body, feeling very satisfied with the afternoon's work.

The next morning, with a mixture of apprehension and hope, I call Vika again.

"Sorry, these are difficult times. There is a new Turkmen registered ship that I can get you on but it's not due to dock until the weekend. It's still possible that another ship will arrive this evening, but I don't know yet whether it can take any passengers. Please phone me at 1pm."

After a long stroll along the seaside boulevard I saunter onto a pier, the sound of gently lapping waves drifting up from below the boardwalk. My head's spinning as I try to work out what to do next. To have come this far and be forced to abandon the journey due to missing my visa deadline is an unthinkable prospect. I decide to try the ticket office with the best online directions, so return to terra firma and begin walking along the seafront until, a kilometre later, I reach a port. No one stops me at the gates but once inside I see nothing that resembles a ticket office. A uniformed man approaches and asks if he can help.

"Sorry, the ticket office you ask about closed many months ago. I don't know where there is another."

Dejected, I walk back to the hotel and send a couple of emails to other contacts for tickets, then for want of anything better to do, repack all my bags.

Opening the first dry bag, I'm startled to see that it contains my sleeping bag, the one I thought I'd lost in the Ukraine! Feeling a bit of a numpty, I go through everything else, spreading the contents out across my bed and a large part of the floor. I realise my waterproof rainsuit and mitts are missing at which point I remember that I'd dried them out in Bautzen, the same night I last used my sleeping bag. I must have inadvertently swapped dry bags when repacking everything. With two sleeping bags, I'm never going to get cold camping but waterproofs are an essential component for staying warm in the mountains. I Skype Brendan, who stocks rainsuits amongst a myriad of other motorcycle paraphernalia, and ask for his help with replacements. Another search for a suitable delivery address follows. I plump for Dushanbe in Tajikistan and set to work trawling the Internet for a hotel.

My afternoon call to Vika produces mixed results. There's no ship today but she's certain about one for tomorrow. It's now becoming routine that I should call her in the morning, at 9am. I spend the afternoon walking the streets, surprised by the affluence of the people and the shops, which include Versace, Hackett, Burberry and even a Ferrari showroom. I'd no idea the place was so prosperous, but Baku, as I discover, is sometimes referred to as the Dubai of the Caucasus. All around are signs of redevelopment and looking up from Neftçilər Prospekti, the main seafront road formally known as Stalin Avenue, the crystal skyline is packed with glitzy glass towers and opulent international hotels. Baku hosted the 2012 *Eurovision Song Contest* and only months ago, attested by the many banners that still hang at the roadside, the 2015 *European Games*. The city's future looks bright, with *Formula One* races commencing in 2016 and *Euro 2020* football championships now a certainty. Oil and gas have played a huge part in this new wealth, and although 6% of Azerbaijanis still live in penury, which is hard to stomach with all the surrounding prosperity, it's far better than during the immediate post-Soviet era when supposedly 57% survived below the poverty line.

Back at the hotel, I struggle to get to sleep knowing that time is running out... my 5-day Turkmenistan visa becomes active in little more than 24 hours.

Day 22. Baku to Alat Port. 44 miles.

The day starts with what feels like a make or break phone call to Vika. Again she tells me there's the possibility of a sailing today, but I must call her back at 1pm. I need to take action, so after a final online revision of ticket office locations, set off walking to the closest port. This time I find somebody who knows where the ticket office is situated... 11km northeast in a larger port. Outside, I flag down a taxi and climb into the front passenger seat. The driver, probably in his forties, is huge, his shoulders as broad as an ox, his head almost touching the roof. Although his comprehension of English is rudimentary, he quickly grasps which port I need and sets off with a screech, pushing his Opal Astra to the limit. I lean surreptitiously to check the speedometer and am shocked to see that we're doing 130kmph. The driver seems incredibly laid-back, one hand on the wheel, the other lighting a cigarette.

"Police... radar... problem?" I ask, pointing to the speedo.

He laughs and without slowing, stretches across, flips open a glovebox lid and begins rooting inside. Grateful the road is three lanes wide, I'm horrified as he continues his search, thick smoke in his eyes and barely a glance through the windscreen. From underneath a large black pistol, he pulls out a thin blue wallet and hands it to me. Opening it, I see a military ID card, a black and white photo of his angular head in the corner.

"Karabakh veteran," he says. then adds "Sergeant," while pointing to his chest.

"Booooom!" Throwing both hands upwards off the wheel to demonstrate an explosion, he loudly repeats the sound, "Booooom!"

Then, as we're flying along, he grabs hold of my left hand and gets me to tap the side of his head. Under his short, greying hair is a scar and the feel of his skull is unnaturally flat. Next he gets me to hit his hip, where another steel plate's obviously been inserted. Finally, both hands off the steering wheel, he pulls up his left trouser leg to reveal a prosthetic limb.

"Azerbaijan President give me taxi. Hero Karabakh. I show police," he continues, pointing to the identity card on my lap, "speed no problem."

We both laugh, then I ask his name. He tries half a dozen times to get me to say it but the sounds are alien to my tongue and defeat me. There seems to be a 'zo' in there somewhere and the name Zorro pops into my head, which couldn't be more appropriate.

Upon reaching the port we draw a blank, the dark stone building which was the ticket office now silent and empty. Asking around, Zorro gets directions to its new location so we climb back into his taxi and, a fresh cigarette wedged in the corner of his mouth, set off at a blistering pace. A few minutes later, he pulls up outside more docks which are located less than half a kilometre from where we originally set off!

At the entrance, I note five touring bicycles heaped together, a Land Rover and a Toyota Land Cruiser parked close behind. It has to be the right place, so

I thank Zorro profusely and give him a well-deserved tip. He salutes, spins around in a sharp u-turn then hightails it away. A guard leads me through an x-ray machine and I set off in pursuit of four people that I guess are from the cars. They take a complex course around office buildings and stacks of shipping containers. Catching them up, I say hello and they tell me they're from Germany and South Africa. We come to a halt outside a portacabin where five cyclists sit, legs stretched out and their backs against its walls. The car people stop to chat, so with a wave, I knock on the portacabin door and enter. I introduce myself to a man and woman who sit at adjoining desks.

"Ah, you are Gordon," says the woman. "I am Vika. Pleased to meet you."
We shake hands then she grabs hold of a phone which is ringing loudly. A few minutes later, as I sit in a chair in the corner of the otherwise bare room, she comes over to update me on the situation. There is a ship today, but it's carrying oil and it'll be difficult to get me on board.

When I emphasise how desperate my position is, with my Turkmen visa starting tomorrow, she expands on the problem. Apparently, several of the trans Caspian Sea ships are not well suited to crossing open water as they're too top heavy. A few years ago, the Merkuriy-2, a ship carrying oil in railway tank wagons, foundered in a storm when some of the carriages broke free. Forty-two lives were lost and the shipping company has subsequently been reluctant to put paying passengers on this type of vessel when transporting oil.

"But I have asked for a favour," she continues. "The woman I'm talking to is a friend and she's going to try to help you. Please wait."

Shortly afterwards, the call goes out for the cyclists to come inside and get their tickets. Comprising Australians, Americans and a French woman, they produce their passports, pay the requisite number of dollars and are issued with paperwork. As they discuss their ride down to the port of Alat, the Land Rover driver, overhearing, offers to take their bags. Meanwhile, one of the American cyclists comes over and asks if I'll be on their ship to Kazakhstan as well. I explain I'm travelling to Turkmenistan which results in everybody suddenly gathering around as all five cyclists had applied for Turkmenistan visas and been turned down.

"I've led tours from Europe to China for 10 years," adds the Land Rover driver. "Every time we've travelled through Turkmenistan and there's never been a problem getting a visa. This year I was refused and no explanation was given. You're very lucky to be going there!"
I feel it, and give silent thanks to the Turkmen consul in London.

All nine Kazakhstan-bound passengers head for the door, plans for the redistribution of the cyclists' luggage filling the air. The phone gives a shrill ring and as Vika answers, I cross my fingers that it'll be good news for me. She says a few words in Azeri, then begins nodding towards me, her face creased with a smile. What a star! At the end of the call she says,

"OK. You need to get going. Let's get your ticket sorted fast as you must be at the port in two hours time."
Her assistant launches himself into action and within five minutes my passes are produced on a printer. Simply saying thank you doesn't seem enough as

Vika has certainly saved the day, but it's all I can do as I plant a kiss on her cheek then run for the door.

A taxi gets me back to the hotel in under 10 minutes and it takes another 25 minutes to get ready. Taking a steadying breath, I start the engine then bounce off the pavement. Once on Neftçilər Prospekti, I accelerate hard, clicking up into third and then fourth... except fourth gear isn't there. Once more the selector mechanism is misaligning and I've only got three gears. Cursing, I pull over to the side to think but as there's nothing that can be done in the time available, set off again minus a gear.

Once clear of the city, I take the southbound side of the dual carriageway I'd followed into Baku 3 days ago. Sitting in the hard shoulder at a relentless 50kmph, the engine running faster that I'd ideally want it to, I only swing out into the main carriageway to avoid broken glass, jettisoned tyres and the occasional grisly roadkill. Arriving at the port turn off, I follow signs along an empty road until reaching a large roundabout. In its centre lie three loose dogs which leap to attention on hearing my approach. I pause, searching for an exit signpost leading to the port. There are none and I'm already 20 minutes later than Vika advised. The dogs, barking raucously at the edge of the roundabout, are waiting for me. I make a decision about exits, wind up the engine and go for it. They all charge at once, getting dangerously close to my right shin as I lean into the roundabout, but once I'm clear and can shift into third, they give up the chase and begin scrapping amongst themselves.

Official proceedings are relatively straightforward as I'm the only person at the checkpost. Once the guard has ascertained that I have a visa for Turkmenistan, he stamps me out.

"Now you have left Azerbaijan, you cannot come back." he says with finality. Customs is even easier, my temporary import licence painlessly clearing the way, and I'm soon riding in the direction of two ships moored side-by-side. Arriving in front of them, I see that only one has its aft door open, so, carefully manoeuvring myself into the middle of railway lines, ride up a ramp and come to a halt where a sailor is flagging his hand.

"What are you doing?" he asks, sounding perplexed.

"This is the Agdam isn't it?" I reply, digging my ticket and motorcycle boarding pass out of the tank bag. "I'm going to Turkmenbashi."

"We have no passengers," he says, skimming through my paperwork. He radios the bridge and I wait patiently, absorbing the fact that the ship's completely empty and there was no need for a mad rush to get here after all.

"The captain says you are okay, ride over there to the side."

A rough looking character joins us. As I kick the Matchless over, he grabs hold of the throttle and begins wildly revving the engine while looking upwards to the main deck from where an unkempt bunch of sailors egg him on. Pulling in the valve lifter to stop the engine, I suppress my strong urge to yell at him, get off and begin to push.

Once I've assessed the best place to stow her, I ask a deckhand for ratchet straps. Their aren't any. Jovially, he touches a giant chain with his boot, its iron links each 10" long and obviously used for securing rail carriages to the deck. I unload all my bags then, with the bike on the rear stand, drag her a few inches sideways until she's pressed up against the steel hull. Removing most of my Rok straps, I use them to secure her against a variety of hooks and cleats. Certain everything's firmly fixed, I ferry all my gear up greasy steel staircases and after relinquishing my passport, am led to my cabin. Three sets of bunk beds crowd the small space, two with grubby sheets and pillows, the remainder unpleasantly stained bare mattresses. Hiding my luggage underneath one of the bunks, I visit the bathroom to wash my hands. Though not quite as bad as I'd feared, the loo has no seat and the shower just a piece of rubber hose pipe. I tell myself it's only for a short while... I hope!

Wandering into the compact dining room, one of the crew explains that I've missed dinner but kindly gets me a cup of tea from a samovar. Glad I've heeded the online warnings and brought my own supplies, I make do with flatbread, cheese and tomatoes. A tour of the ship doesn't take long and as night falls I lean against railings on the aft deck, peering down into the open hold where, lit by floodlights, the Matchless looks minuscule. Activity commences when three crewmen, walkie-talkies in hands, move purposefully towards the rear door. Accompanied by screeches and loud clanging, the first two trains of oil tankers are shunted on, jerkily changing direction as they run over on-board points and slip down both sides of the ship, leaving the central two tracks empty. An hour later, they're still loading and I'm amazed by how many carriages they manage to cram in... it's like a maritime tardis!

By now it's after 10pm so I call it a day. In the cabin I find a woman in the process of removing the dirty linen and preparing a fresh bed for me. Long after I'm asleep, the ship slips its moorings and heads out to sea.

Day 23. Caspian Sea to Turkmenbashi, Turkmenistan. Approximately 180 nautical miles on MV Agdam and 7 miles ridden.

The ship's engine, a bass hum that resonates through the cabin walls, wakes me early and I leap out of bed to check our position. As far as the eye can see there's nothing but deep blue water. After a little while, appearing as a vague shadow to the north east, I make out the hazy skeleton of an oil rig. Overhead, three gulls keep pace with the ship, mostly gliding off the stern but occasionally swooping low over the top decks. Carefully descending the greasy stairwell, made doubly treacherous after a night exposed to the elements, I squeeze between rows of oil tankers and inspect the bike. All's good.

The day passes slowly. At one point I'm invited onto the bridge but as neither of the officers speak English, I simply stand at the back and watch for a while. Returning to my cabin, I fish out the satnav and locate our position approximately halfway between the two shores. As I'm about to turn it off, I notice something unexpected... our altitude is 35m below sea level. I'll have to think about that one.

I spend a couple of hours reclining on the only available deck seating, a covered life raft, until around midday, a crewman arrives to tell me lunch is being served. In the canteen, half a dozen men are already eating. The offering is simple: lentil soup; bread; salad and fizzy lemonade, but much better than expected. The sailors, who'd appeared as such a rowdy bunch of sea dogs last night, seem far more friendly today, inviting me into their mess after we've finished eating. The spartan room has a cream coloured carpet (which necessitates everybody taking off their boots), a few chairs, a small TV and an old VHS video. The action movie currently playing is dubbed in Azerbaijani so as soon as I deem it polite, I make my excuses and go back outdoors. The rest of the afternoon is spent walking up and down the deck, oil rig spotting and hanging over the aft rails to watch the churning wake.

Late afternoon, I notice a higgledy-piggledy line of five ships at anchor then soon after, a sand coloured line materialises on the port horizon... Turkmenistan. I expect us to slow and wait our turn behind the other ships but we steam on, round a headland then steer at full speed towards a distant harbour. Unchecked, we slow at the harbour entrance, and with the whole ship vibrating noisily, turn around and dock.

After I wheel the Matchless off and ride towards the immigration complex, a lanky soldier instructs me to park nearby and indicates that he'll guard the laden bike. Through the doors, my passport's checked then I'm guided to an adjoining window where a staunch female officer extracts $8 from me. Receipt in hand, I return to the first officer and my passport's stamped. Next I'm sent to the far side of the hall, the customs area. An official, noting my clothes and crash helmet, takes charge and leads me into a small side office where a casually dressed man, feet on desk, watches television. He produces a thick, tear-off document pad and begins filling in the Matchless's details. He then asks which route I plan to take. From research I know there are three options and I've already decided to take the shortest due to only having four days left on my visa. It's a 700km ride, tracking north east in a straight line and crossing into Uzbekistan at Köneürgench. On the way, I'll pass through Kaplankyr National Park, an area rich in wildlife, and follow a dramatic road alongside the Yangykala canyon.

"Sorry, that border crossing closed in June and I don't know when it will reopen," he says.

It's a blow. He produces another document on which is printed a basic outline map of the country. The remaining two route choices appear as thick black lines, both of them heading through the capital, Ashgabat. I opt for the most direct one which exits at Turkmenabat, a distance of over 1200km. Getting his calculator out, he taps a few keys then tells me I have to pay a fuel surcharge of $86. I was expecting this and hand the money over. When I've signed all the forms, he formally warns,

"Understand, you cannot deviate from this route. The police will check as you travel. Also, you must give this document in when you leave the country or there will be fines."

I nod in agreement.

"Enjoy your stay in Turkmenistan," he ends warmly.

Customs follows, which involves rubber stamping several more sheets of paperwork, repeated computer form filling and additional dollars changing hands. Everyone is exceedingly courteous and affable, and, despite the bureaucratic entry requirements being by far the most complicated to date, I'm free to leave in under 90 minutes.

The Matchless's guard, still standing next to the bike, shakes my hand and points to the exit. The port gates are opened and I ride out of the compound. Slapping the Matchless on the petrol tank, I jubilantly shout,

"You've made it to Asia, old girl!"

One of the customs officials has given me the name of a hotel and directions to it. I follow the main road for a couple of kilometres then enter a quiet shopping district. Pulling up, I ask four young men about the hotel. They point ahead where, at least a dozen brightly lit stories high, it sits at the end of the road. Sweeping up its crescent driveway, I kick out the side stand and head into a foyer thronging with activity. At the main desk, I'm informed that the hotel is full due to a large wedding reception, then given directions to another big hotel just 10 minutes away.

"Is that 10 minutes walking or 10 minutes driving?" I ask the lady.

"It's the same," she replies.

Umm...?

Along the seafront, the roadsides are mainly devoid of buildings. After a kilometre, I notice a large tower block 200 metres up a hill to my right. Turning off and riding into an empty car park, I'm halted at a dead end and can't find a way to get any closer. As it has no obvious entrance or visible signage, I decide it must be a residential complex and head back onto the main seaside road. Ten minutes later, I make a U-turn, fearing I've gone wrong. While I'm pondering what to do next, a sleek white Mercedes pulls up, its front window opening to reveal a suited, young driver. He asks me a question in Turkoman then, upon realising that I don't understand, says,

"Can I help you?"

I tell him of my search for the elusive hotel and he immediately offers to lead me there. Leaning over his shoulder, he talks to somebody in the back. A darkened rear window glides open and the head of his wife, babe in arms, appears. She smiles at me and says,

"Please follow my husband."

Soon we arrive back at the tower block. The Mercedes driver's window wafts open again and he explains that the rear of the hotel faces the sea. He points to a dark lane on the right, saying that I'll need to follow it to the entrance, which is on the landward side. After warmly shaking my hand, he turns the car round and drives away leaving me with a great first impression of Turkmen hospitality.

Following the lane, I turn a corner and am relieved to see the usual glitz of a large hotel entranceway. Upon checking in, the Matchless is afforded a special concession due to her age and I'm allowed to park up next to the hotel's main revolving doors. It's too late for the restaurant so I head to the subterranean bar in search of snacks. None are available so I ask for a beer to take to my room. The barmaid produces a can of *Carlsberg* and requests payment. I ask for a glass.

"Sorry, glasses cannot leave the bar," she answers and turns away, our conversation evidently at an end.

The only other patron, who leans heavily on the bar looking slightly worse for wear, slugs back the rest of his beer then slams the empty glass down in front of me. In a slurred Russian accent, he says,

"Here. Take my glass. There are too many rules in the world," then immediately orders another beer for himself.

Back in my room, I dine on the stale remnants of my ship food, sip lukewarm beer and doze off to a cowboy film.

23	Turkmenbashi, Turkmenistan	44	Sost, Pakistan
24	Serdar, Turkmenistan	45	Gulmit, Pakistan
25	Ashgabat, Turkmenistan	46	Chilas, Pakistan
26	Mary, Turkmenistan	47	Uchar Nala checkpost, Pakis
27-28	Bukhara, Uzbekistan	48	Keyal police station, Pakista
29	Samarkand, Uzbekistan	49	Abbottabad, Pakistan
30	Qarshi, Uzbekistan	50	Rawalpindi, Pakistan
31	Termiz, Uzbekistan	51	Lahore, Pakistan
32-33	Dushanbe, Tajikistan	52-53	Amritsar, India
34-35	Khorog, Tajikistan	54	Chandigarh, India
36	Sasyk-kel Lake, Tajikistan	55	Meerut, India
37	Murghab, Tajikistan	56-57	Jhankat, India
38	Karakul, Tajikistan	58	Bhimdatta, Nepal
39-40	Sary Tash, Kyrgyzstan	59	Lalamativa, Nepal
41-42	Kashgar, China	60	Chandranigahapur, Nepal
43	Tashkurgan, China	61	Siliguri, India

62	Alipurduar, India		81	Mai Chau, Vietnam
63	Guwahati, India		82	Hanoi, Vietnam
64-65	Dimapur, India		83	Thai Hua, Vietnam
66	Imphal, India		84	Son Trach, Vietnam
67	Moreh, India		85	Hue, Vietnam
68	Gangaw, Myanmar		86	Hoi An, Vietnam
69	Bagan, Myanmar		87	Quy Nhon, Vietnam
70	Naypyidaw, Myanmar		88	Nha Trang, Vietnam
71-72	Yangon, Myanmar		89	Mui Ne, Vietnam
73	Kin Pun Sakhan, Myanmar		90	Ho Chi Minh City, Vietnam
74	Mae Sot, Thailand		91-92	Bakod village, Cambodia
75	Thung Salaeng Luang, Thailand		93	Phnom Penh, Cambodia
76-77	Vientiane, Laos		94	Siem Reap, Cambodia
78	Phou Khoun, Laos		95	Aranyaprathet, Thailand
79	Namnern, Laos		96	Bangkok, Thailand
80	Na Meo Border, Laos			

Day 24. Turkmenbashi to Serdar. 223 Miles.

Over breakfast I delve into a guidebook to gain further insights into Turkmenistan and my new route. Looking up Turkmenbashi town, I see it was formally known as Krasnovodsk. In 1993, 'president for life', Saparmurat Niyazov, renamed it after his own self-proclaimed title, 'Türkmenbaşy', which translates as 'Leader of all Turkmen'. Reading further on, I learn it wasn't the only name Niyazov altered... he changed the names of the months to the names of members of his family! Some of Türkmenbaşy's more whacky laws included expelling dogs from the capital, Ashgabat, because of their 'unappealing odour', and prohibiting opera, ballet and circuses as well as music on car radios due to the being 'un-Turkmen-like'. He decreed that men couldn't have long hair or beards, news reporters shouldn't wear make-up on television and gold teeth be frowned upon as people should chew on bones to strengthen their teeth! When he gave up smoking after major heart surgery, all his ministers had to give up too.

His costly personality cult manifested itself in statues and enormous portraits of himself being erected all over Turkmenistan, including one giant gold statue in Ashgabat which revolved to always face the sun. He funnelled the country's gas profits into extravagant projects such as a huge man-made lake in the Karakum desert and an immense cypress forest grown in an attempt to change the desert climate. The construction of central Asia's largest mosque, The Turkmenbashi Ruhy Mosque, close to his palatial home, cost of over $100 million. Under his rule, dissidents were jailed, sent into internal exile or detained in psychiatric hospitals, the media tightly controlled and internet access highly regulated. Calling the period of his rule the 'Turkmen Golden Age', Türkmenbaşy's slogan was 'Halk, Watan, Türkmenbaşy', meaning 'People, Nation, Me'... uncomfortably close to Hitler's 'Ein Volk, Ein Reich, Ein Fuhrer.' He died of a heart attack in 2006 and his body now lies in an ostentatious mausoleum.

With over 750 miles to cover in the next four days, I drag myself away from his outlandish yet compelling tale and commence fixing the gearbox for what I hope will be the last time. In Baku I'd been careful. This morning I'm meticulous, with fresh pen marks on the timing cover to aid with alignment. Before refilling with grease and putting everything away, I kick the engine over and test all four gears. Satisfied, I load up and ride into the heat of the day.

Heading out of town takes me straight past the port entrance, where I note the Agdam has already weighed anchor, then up a winding hill. On the other side is a much needed petrol station. Filling up with 95, I make a quick calculation of the costs. Fuel is conveniently one Manat per litre which converts to about 20p... suddenly last night's surcharge doesn't seem so punitive. Underway again, I head out into desert proper. Everywhere looks the same, with hardly any variation in hue or tone... there's sand, rocks and more sand. The road, which parallels a rocky massif to the north, has recently been resurfaced and although the occasional tar ripple catches me out, it's relatively flat and smooth. I sit at an unwavering 70kmph for a peaceful hour until a concrete-block roadside eatery emerges from the heat haze. There's absolutely nothing else around.

Iced drinks are available but food choices are limited. Through an open window a motherly woman shows me the options, gesticulating that she herself has baked a large chocolate cake which has a yellow centre. She's pleased when I choose it and carves me a king-sized wedge that's greater than a quarter of the cake. Moist and full of eggs, it constitutes a meal in itself. I sit on a bench and, continuously swiping at a couple of opportunistic flies, eat the lot.

Back on the road, the temperature is in the mid-30s and I'm thrilled by how the Matchless is coping with the heat. As long as air's continuously passing over her cast iron cylinder, everything seems to be rosy. I am concerned, however, about radiated heat off the road because my tyres and wheel hubs are quite hot. Slowing down as I approach the city of Balkanabat, where policeman with pancake-like hats stand, their traffic batons at the ready, I decide to check my tyre pressures. On the far side of town, I catch sight of an open-fronted tyre shop and head towards it. As I pull up, four men surround me, one by one shaking my hand. I point to my tyres and make "psst... psst" sounds. One of them drags an air line outside and we all squat down to see the pressure readings. Both tyres, despite the intense heat, are a little on the low side so I have them topped up. Reaching into my pocket, I pull out some Manat and ask,
"How much?"
They refuse adamantly. At that moment, a Toyota pickup arrives. The driver's door opens and a large man steps out and smiles. Kemran, it transpires, worked on oil rigs for a number of years, which is how he comes to be fluent in English... with a mild Australian twang. When I ask again about paying for air in my tyres, he has a quick word with the men then translates their answer,
"They do not want you to pay. You are a guest in our country and it is their honour to serve you."
After looking the Matchless over, he invites me for a cup of tea inside the adjoining building, a motor factors, where his friend is the manager. Without any doubt I know that the bike and all my possessions will be completely safe in the care of these men, so after saying thank you, I follow Kemran.

Opening the door, the crisp iciness of air conditioning hits like a shockwave. The manager offers me a seat and pours three cups of green tea from an ornate teapot. As the perspiration in my t-shirt turns chilly, I'm asked first where I'm from then where I'm going. As of yet, I'm not sure about the latter as I want to get as close to Ashgabat as possible before nightfall. I tell them I'm considering camping in the desert.
Kemran calls a friend and after a protracted conversation, reports,
"The town of Serdar is 200km from here. On the right is a brand-new hotel. If it's dark, you will see it has many coloured lights. There's nowhere else to stay before then."
Bracing myself for another dramatic switch in temperature, I thank them for their hospitality then head outside, and after a series of photographs taken on all four tyre workers' phones, toot my horn and leave.

Back in the wilds of the Karakum, I spot a few sand dunes then the first gangly, graceful camels, which graze on patches of spiny vegetation. Seeing them sets me wondering how these exotic creatures live. I imagine they're someone's property, a valuable asset no doubt. Unrestricted by fences, I notice they're not hobbled and contemplate how the owners keep track of their movements. I consider that, in small herds, they might be territorial but it's equally possible they just roam wherever they can find food and water. Hardly one of the greatest mysteries of the universe, but in unrelenting desert with so few other stimulants, such thoughts occupy the mind and most importantly, keep me awake.

With sunset only half an hour away, I see a small town way out in the wilderness, a singletrack road leading in an arrow straight line to its edge. It's the first habitation I've seen in the last 50km and I become concerned that it's Sedar. Two men stand close to the turnoff so I change down and brake. It's not until I'm within 20m that I recognise them as police officers. Worse still, one of them is holding a radar gun. There's no way I was speeding on this 100kmph highway but my immediate fear is that they'll think my rapid deceleration a sign of guilt. They look puzzled as I stop next to them.

"As-salamu alaykum."

"Wa-Alaikum-us-Salaam," they reply in unison. Without cutting the engine, I remove my right glove and hold my hand out to be shaken. Like all the men in Turkmenabat, their handshakes are featherlight.

"Serdar?" I ask, pointing down the side road.

Determinedly shaking his head, one removes a pad of charge sheets from a shoulder bag.

'Oh-oh... here we go again,' says a voice inside my head. Smoothly, he tears a page out and on the back writes 'Serdar 40km' in bold letters then points further down the main highway. I smile as I ride away... what a contrast to Azerbaijan.

At 7.20pm I reach the outskirts of Serdar, a small town straggled a couple of houses deep along the roadside. The sun set half an hour ago and the cloudless sky appears the deepest shade of blue before blackness closes in. Within a couple of minutes, I notice a building on the right boasting "many coloured lights" and gratefully turn onto the hotel's driveway, overjoyed to have covered so many miles, the gearbox performing perfectly all day. My lofty, airy room, costs just 30 Manat, a little over £6 and the cheapest of the ride so far. Weary from a day fully exposed to the sun, I choose to eat in the hotel's restaurant. The only diner, I have the full attention of the chef-come-waiter-come-dishwasher, who cheerfully prepares a spicy meal comprising bulgur wheat, tomatoes, tinned peas and broad beans that tastes infinitely better than it looks. While I'm eating, familiar advertisements appear on a television mounted high on a wall. They're the same toothpaste, car, soft drink, painkiller and flatscreen TV commercials shown everyday on British TV, except that Turkoman words come out of European mouths... rather disorientating.

Before bed, I go outside to check the Matchless is safe then caress her tank through the cover, whispering,

"Thank you."

Day 25. Serdar to Ashgabat. 151 miles.

Turkmenistan is an hour ahead of Azerbaijan and four hours in front of the UK, I'm finding it difficult to adjust to forward changes in time zones and rising at 7.00am this morning leaves me sluggish and groggy.

Today's first stop is at a lonely petrol station set back 200m off the highway. Fuel choices are 95 or 80 octane... something of a no brainer. After filling up, I ask the attendant if there's a toilet. He points to a distant blockhouse.

"Turkmen type toilet only," he says in an apologetic tone.
I wheel the Matchless under the shade of a cypress then head to the loo. It's a simple composting long drop, a popular meeting place for the local fly population, but for all that, clean. The pump attendant intercepts me as I walk back to the bike.

"Drink? Coffee?"
I accept his offer and he returns from his tiny office a few minutes later with a steaming mug in his hand, then rushes back to serve a new customer. A dilapidated Russian tanker stops close to the bike. It looks like a relic from the 1950s. Both of its front wings are badly dented and the domed cab roof has more rust than paint. At the rear is a large oval shaped tank which, judging by the clear liquid leaking onto the forecourt in alarming quantities, is full of water. The driver and his companion climb down, appreciatively inspect the Matchless then perch next to me on a whitewashed kerbstone. It's immediately apparent we've no common language. After a couple of dust drawings and guessed words, the driver opens both his arms, palms upward, and looks around in a enquiring way which I take to be a question about where I'm from.

"UK... England," I say, to which they both nod. "Near Manchester," I add.
Their faces instantly light up and they call out in unison,

"Manchester United!"
We all laugh. I don't follow football but have always found that a residential association with either of Manchester's two well-known teams makes a great icebreaker. As I finish the coffee, they shake my hand, return to the tanker, and under a cloud of oily black smoke, rumble westwards.

Aside from occasional bumps over the small bridges which cross dry stream beds, the highway is in good condition and the Matchless glides comfortably along. Around 1pm we reach a roundabout at the outskirts of Gokdepe. The road ahead is guarded by police who seem to be checking all the through traffic. A signpost, a rarity indeed, indicates I must take the third turn for Ashgabat. After a few minutes, the road begins to gently curve and I realise I'm on a ringroad. The surface gradually worsens and I'm too far into it before I register there are no cars... the diversion around town is for trucks.

The bike takes a pounding. I keep going in first and second gear, crunching and bouncing over sharp ridges and deep holes for at least half an hour. The overhead sun reflects silver off the cracked concrete making it hard to see ahead and twice the jolts are so severe that I'm almost thrown over the handlebars. My arms hurt and despite standing on the footpegs, I feel every impact through the bike's rigid frame. Drenched in sweat from my exertions, I curse out loud as an artic dramatically veers across to my side of the road in a last-minute attempt to avoid a rocky patch. Inhaling a suffocating mixture of dirt and diesel, I swing out of its path and straight into a crater.

Across bare fields on the right I see glints of sunlight flashing off cars as they speed along the main highway. Desperate to join them, I spot a dusty trail that leads in their direction and taking a chance, slowly navigate down it, skirting the edges of a sun baked farm. With considerable relief, we rejoin the Ashgabat road. My energy sapped, I halt under a tree, climb off and inspect the bike. All the luggage straps need re-tensioning and at the front, both rubber gators are torn in half... the forks must have repeatedly bottomed out as we dropped into potholes or hit their hard edges on the way up, tearing trapped gators on the rebound. More repairs for tomorrow! Energy renewed by a drink and a muesli bar, we rejoin the traffic heading east.

There are no further signposts and in quick succession the road forks twice. Taking pot luck, I ride on for a further 15km, gradually accepting that I've no idea where I am. According to the map, there's a bypass to the south of the capital and it's quite possible I'm already on it. Pulling over at a remote bus stop, I flip up my goggles and above the unfaltering pop pop pop of the Matchless, holler,

"Azkaban? Azkaban?" while pointing along the road.
The five people look puzzled. A young man steps forward and asks,
"What do you want, please?"
"Is this the way to Azkaban?"
He turns to his compatriots but support is not forthcoming.
"This road is to Ashgabat," he says with a degree of confusion.
I thank him, wave at the rest and, trying to stifle a laugh which may cause offence, set off as fast as possible. Jacques, a huge *Harry Potter* fan, will be delighted to hear that his dad's been for asking directions to the famed dark prison for errant wizards.

Ashgabat appears out of the sand as a shining white city, standing in stark contrast to the darker rocky hills that ring it to the north. After an admiring pause, I ride towards its centre where a smattering of hotels is located and first try the Hotel Dayhan, a shabby former Soviet establishment. Up three wide staircases of threadbare carpet, I'm led to a depressing room with a sagging steel frame single bed and an adjoining bathroom in which the bath has a full-length germ ridden crack. At $50 it's a definite miss. Back downstairs, I ask if there are any rooms that have been renovated. By way of an answer, the redoubtable manageress slams her sliding office window shut in my face. A man follows me outside and gives me directions to a better hotel, the Paygagt. With traffic police loitering on every street corner in the locale and no U-turns allowed, I work my way around the block then head north until I find it. Enormous, it sits at the rear of a huge empty square. I dismount and push the Matchless close to the main entrance. After checking a room, I enquire where I can leave the bike.

"On surrounding streets only," I'm told. "If you leave it outside our entrance or in the square, the police will take it away."

Dispirited, I wrest my arms back into a sweaty jacket, jam my head into a damp helmet then push the Matchless around the hotel and out onto Ashgabat's wide boulevards. A kilometre away, directly opposite the Turkmen State Circus, a stunning concrete building which looks like a cross between a big top and a flying saucer, sits the Ak Altyn Hotel, the antithesis of the two previous accommodations. It's modern, tastefully decorated and has a doorman who directs me to park under the main entrance canopy. Perfect. After a quick shower, I set out to explore on foot before the light fades.

Ashgabat is a queer kind of place. The pavements are virtually devoid of pedestrians and although there are modern and expensive cars flying around, traffic is light. I walk towards Independence Square. At its edge are gardens with enormous monoliths and fountains and in the distance, the golden dome of the Palace of Turkmenbashi, Niyazov's former place of work. I take a couple of photos of the Earthquake Memorial, a bull with the earth tossed high on its horns, then walk towards the palace. In this vast space of still quietness, there's no movement... it feels as if I'm the last man on earth. I wander onto a road. It too is lifeless, or so I think until a policeman jumps out from behind a wall and asks what I'm doing.

"Tourist," I say, pointing all around.

"No photo," he tells me sternly.

Conscious of his gaze on my back, I reach the strangely named Ministry of Fairness which sits aside the Majlis, Turkmenistan's parliament building. At the bottom of its steps, I open my backpack and reach for my guidebook. A voice shouts loudly, causing me to jump. Looking behind, I see a soldier waving his rifle through railings... although I can't understand the words, 'buzz off' is clearly his message. Head down, I walk quickly back across the vacant square and decide to look for a place to eat.

This takes some time. There are numerous official buildings, opera houses, museums and monuments, all grand and impressive, but few eateries. Eventually locating a pizza joint, I eat then head back in the direction of my hotel. A theatre opens its doors just as I pass and a small crowd, some of the great and good of the city, exits. Most noticeable are the women, nearly all of whom have a mass of dark hair tied up under colourful patterned scarfs. Long sleeves and ankle length skirts are de rigueur, making them appear especially tall and elegant.

Further along, reaching a junction with an underpass, its steps and passageways all at odd angles, I take a wrong turn. Back at ground level, things just don't feel right and after a hundred or so metres I stop and return to the junction. It's impossible to get my bearings and I ask a young man passing by if he knows the way to the circus. Nodding, he suggests he walks with me as it'll give him a great opportunity to practice his English.

A 17-year-old student, Armin's a fast walker and I struggle to keep up with him. After answering the fundamentals about my family and work, we talk about his education and dream of becoming a lawyer and moving to America. Out of the blue, he unselfconsciously begins to sing in a really sweet, falsetto voice. His favourite singer, he reveals, is Justin Timberlake... I'm completely out of my depth as I don't know any Timberlake songs. He looks equally bemused when I answer his questions about my favourite music. He shakes his head at Led Zeppelin, then at the list of other bands I go on to name. We laugh at the generational chasm between our musical tastes. Once in sight of my hotel, we shake hands and he sprints off in the direction we've just come so his mother won't worry about him being home late.

After a final look at the night vista from my seventh story window, I turn on the TV, climb into bed and become increasingly fascinated by a political channel. The incumbent president and successor to Türkmenbaşy, Mr. Gurbanguly Berdimuhamedov, is shown sitting behind a high desk, somewhat akin to a judge's bench, which is draped in garlands of flowers. He dictates non-stop to an audience of a couple of hundred delegates and politicians, all dressed in conservative suits. I watch as heads down, they write Berdimuhamedov's words, seemingly verbatim, in identical notepads. Occasionally, one of them will raise their head, thoughtfully nod in agreement, then continue diligently writing. Fifteen minutes later, they're still at it and the president, or Arkadag, his self-given title meaning 'protector', hasn't even paused to catch his breath. It's fascinating as I'm so culturally removed from it, however, I find it increasingly soporific so switch off the TV and fall asleep, my brain circulating images of fork gaiters.

Day 26. Ashgabat to Mary. 232 miles.

I hope to find a discarded car tyre inner tube for making long lasting repairs to the fork gaiters but as an interim measure, wrap gaffer tape around the torn sections. While the doorman kindly ferries all my bags to the bike, I discreetly wipe a couple of drips of primary chain oil off the marble paving and prepare to leave. The grid pattern layout of the city and close proximity of its central railway station makes navigating to the northbound highway easy and in no time we're flying down a spanking new dual carriageway.

Motorcycles are generally not allowed in the capital and during my short stay I didn't see a single one apart from mine. Out on the open road, however, I notice several Urals, boxer sidevalve twins derived from BMW's pre-war R71 and still made today at the IMZ-Ural plant in Irbit, Russia. Bobbing along in dusty trails beside the main road, they all have wooden flatbed sidecars attached, some empty, others heavily laden with fruit, boxes of goods, or recycled bottles of a yellow liquid I presume to be petrol. Although they're all in a poor state of repair, it's nonetheless great to see these venerable old machines still in use.

During the morning I clock up some serious miles, not stopping until the fuel tank needs refilling. Turkmenistan is mostly desert with the majority of its 5 million inhabitants domicile in towns that ring its borders. In its bleakly beautiful centre, oases are sparsely dotted along the main highways. After a second stint of over a hundred kilometres with hardly any deviation in the stark surroundings, I reach the oasis town of Tejen, an uninvitingly hot outpost swept by stinging airborne sand.

On the far side of town I finally find what I'm looking for, a tyre shop. This one is situated in the middle of a long strip of open fronted workshops, many of which seem to be repairing broken down lorries. Turning off, I backtrack along a sandy, cluttered sidewalk and pull up at its open entrance. A smell of burning rubber and the sound of hammering and arc welding fill the air and out of the adjoining doorway, sparks fly as a heavy grinder is set to work. Three men, their tracksuits smeared with oil and dirt, come out of the workshop and gather round the bike. Repeating my 'psst, psst,' routine, I soon have an extra squirt of air in my tyres. Next I point to the gaiters, the gaffer tape already torn partially open, then with a scissor-like gesture, walk towards a truck inner tube that's lying inside the doorway. One of the men picks it up and I can see that squares have already been cut out to be used as puncture repair patches. With a knife, he cuts two long strips for the Matchless.

Once more, money is refused when I try to pay them and I'm invited to share a cup of tea. Four tiny plastic stools are plonked on the ground and we sit in a circle, drinking green tea poured from a large flask. Our ability to communicate is extremely limited but I'm able to answer the men's most pressing questions, which all relate to the bike... its value, age and type of fuel it uses. After 10 minutes the conversation, such as it was, runs dry so with handshakes all round, I climb back on the Matchless which, sitting in the sun, is now burning hot. Three residential blocks later, we're back out in the desert.

Within five minutes, I come to a police check post, the fourth today. As I slowly approach a stop sign, I'm signalled to park in front of a small white office. Two policemen come over. One doesn't seem especially interested, repeatedly glancing back towards the passing traffic. The other has a look in his glassy eyes that all my instincts tell me to get away from. He first asks for cigarettes. I smile and shake my head apologetically. Next he asks if I have dollars. Feigning ignorance, I smile, laugh, tell him I'm a tourist, thank him, then ask,

"OK. I can leave now? OK to go?" while pointing down the road.
He hesitates... this obviously isn't how Turkmen drivers respond.

"Thank you, thank you," I repeat in an upbeat tone, offer my hand, which he's obliged to shake, and with a wave, set off.
Marvelling that I got off so lightly, I look in my mirrors and see him watching intensely as I gently accelerate away,

The engine temperature must've spiked whilst stationary at the checkpost. Within half a kilometre, changing down gear to swap sides of the road and enter a contraflow, the Matchless lets out a huge backfire and stalls. In the sweltering heat, I push her 200m to the shade of a tree and let her cool. After a quarter of an hour, I can get the spark plug out without burning my fingers, so I give it a clean then check the points. The gap should be around 12 thousandths of an inch when fully open but mine are at 8 thou. Digging out my magneto spanners, a cluster of six miniature spanners on a keyring, I discover that the one I need, size 5, is missing. A thorough search through the tool roll and its drybag fails to locate it, so with some fine wet and dry paper, I clean the points. When I finally kick her over, the engine immediately catches and 'normal service is resumed'.

Soon, the scrubby desert morphs into cotton fields and orchards and a few haphazard stalls selling watermelon and grapes appear at the roadside. The area is irrigated by the 1,375 kilometre long Karakum Canal, one of the largest irrigation projects in the world, which also delivers all of Ashgabat's drinking water. I pass Hanhowuz Reservoir, a huge lake created to store overflow from the canal and the Tejen river. Between the road and its shore is a swampy area where cows wade up to their haunches, stopping here and there to munch on grassy outcrops. With the desert as a backdrop in the far distance, it is quite a spectacle although the moment is slightly tainted by a dramatic increase in insects hovering above the road.

I don't stop again until we reach Mary, pronounced Mah-ree, an oasis city constructed by the Russians close the site of the ancient silk road city of Merv. It's a centre for cotton production and also a supply town for nearby gas fields. The streets are crowded and with only an hour of daylight left, I'm keen to get a hotel as soon as possible. Stopping outside a large linen shop, two men immediately approach and give me detailed directions to Hotel Margush. Ten minutes later, I pull off the road and swing round its flag lined driveway, statues of deer prominent in the surrounding garden.

In fading light with torch in hand, I cut two long rectangles of inner tube rubber, gaffer tape them into cylinders, and secure them under the top jubilee clips of the existing fork gaiters. Hopefully they should keep the worst of the dust out for the foreseeable future. Next, using the file on my Leatherman, I work on a smaller magneto spanner until it's opened up to the correct size to fit the points securing nut. Ten minutes later, I've reset the points gap and feel mighty contented with my evening's work.

In the hotel's restaurant I do some online research about tomorrow's border crossing. Apparently, codeine based drugs are banned in Uzbekistan and customs searches are thorough, with harsh penalties for anyone caught out. I'm carrying Co-codamol painkillers in one of my first aid kits, which get flushed down the toilet as soon as I return to my room. There's a challenging day ahead... failing to exit Turkmenistan on time will result in a $200 fine and to reach the frontier, I'll have to cross a river on a pontoon bridge which closes at 6pm. An early start is a must, so I set my alarm for 6am, climb into bed and am contentedly in the Land of Nod before 9pm.

Welcome to Mary, Turkmenistan.

Day 27. Mary, Turkmenistan, to Bukhara, Uzbekistan. 249 miles.

Loaded and ready to go by 7am, I double-check my route with the hotel receptionist and set off. Circling a couple of roundabouts, I arrive at the promised slip road for the M37 highway. It's shut. There are no diversion signs so three times I stop and ask people how to find the road. All of them point straight ahead, however, the first directions take me to another roundabout, the second a T-junction and the third a fork in the road. Eventually reaching the town of Bayramalay, I find the next entrance to the M37. There's an offramp, with a line of cars queueing to exit, but again the on-ramp is closed, this time covered in rubble.

The centre of Bayramalay is horrid, a confusing mess of congested local traffic, windblown litter and dust. Stopping once more, a helpful man tells me to cross the railway tracks then take the first left along a narrow street I'll need to follow for over 10km until it joins the main highway. Rattling over the train lines, I turn onto it thinking that he surely can't be right. It looks as though it's recently come under mortar fire, and what top surface remains seems to be formed from hardened mud. Tentatively nosing my way along it, I hear feverish barks as a huge dog comes bounding out of a house and runs straight at the bike. Without accelerating hard I'm sure it'll have me! Shifting into third gear, I manically bounce in and out of huge potholes... it's like riding a rodeo bull and little short of a miracle I don't fall off. Intuitively, I stop after a few hundred metres and look back. I'm no longer being pursued but my red dry bag has been thrown off the back during the frantic escape.

Nervously I head back, my heightened senses fully anticipating a repeated canine attack. Instead, I see a man who stands in the middle of the road waving, my dry bag held high in his other hand. I'm so grateful to him, not only for finding the bag but for staying with me while I strap it back on, an ally should the dog return. When eventually clear of the last dwellings, the street marginally improves and I soon reach the highway. It's 9:30am and, frustratingly, I've travelled less than 40km. Just as I'm about to join the northbound lane, it occurs to me to check the fuel level. I peer into the tank and see there's only a splash left in the bottom so my priority becomes finding a petrol station.

With nothing but desert ahead, I turn right, thinking it more likely I'll find petrol back in the direction of Mary. Almost immediately, I see a hitchhiker, a middle-aged man in a dark grey suit with a simple embroidered skullcap on his head. I ask if he knows where I can buy benzine.

"Three kilometres north of here, at a house on the left," he says with such conviction I've no hesitation in trusting his directions so turn around.
Right on cue, I see a large wooden home set back in a leafy courtyard, two aged petrol pumps under its shady veranda. While waiting my turn to fill up, an elderly lady in a striking cobalt blue dress approaches. Silver hair tied in a bun, she has a wizened, sunbaked face, bright eyes and a lovely smile which

reveals a line of gold teeth. Without asking, she hands me a cup of tea and a small packet of biscuits. Minutes later, as I stand beside the Matchless sipping my drink, I watch her leave, walking sprightly to the highway, a large thermos flask swinging from her left-hand. I can only guess that she's just brought morning refreshments for the staff.

Out in the Karakum, I ride without pause for the next 130km. The air feels cool and refreshing, blowing though the open weave of my pants and up the sleeves of my jacket. All around is sand implanted with manmade squares of reed that keep it from drifting onto the road. The Matchless seems to be enjoying the ride as much as me, effortlessly devouring the miles, its engine purring. I love the solitude, the shimmering heat haze, the softly rounded form of the sand dunes. Stopping in the middle of nowhere, the silence of the desert seems strangely comforting but the sun, beating down fiercely, is proving much hotter than I expected. Checking my thermometer, I see its needle is almost touching 40°.

Travelling at a constant 75, I notice a faint line on the horizon which swells into a murky brown cloud as we get closer. A sandstorm looks imminent. It continues to grow in size over the next few minutes then I spot a tall white stack in its centre out of which spouts a virulent plume of smoke... it's a foul cloud of pollution from a large factory, not a sandstorm. Soon, the road bears to the right leaving the culpable chimney behind and we enter Turkmenabat, Now an industrial city, it's been settled for over 2000 years. Known in ancient times as Amul, it was a crossroads on the silk route between Bukhara, Khiva and Merv. Today its throughroad is four lanes wide and has traffic lights every couple of hundred metres. We catch every single one at red, and after almost 20 minutes, I begin to fear the engine will cook.

In due course we reach a quieter part of town where humble shops line the side of the road. I pull over in the hope of finding lunch but all that's available is water, packets of sunflower seeds and peanuts. Sitting on the pavement, hidden from passing traffic by the bike, I make the most of it. Once under way again, finding the route to the bridge over the Amu Darya river proves to be a challenge and a half. On its far bank lies the town of Farab, so I repeatedly stop, pointing ahead and asking,

"Farab? Farab?"

The answer is always the same, straight ahead, but it's not quite that simple. Eventually, after several wrong turns, I come to a small building situated down a side street, the ticket office. Twenty minutes of bureaucracy on, during which I show all my documents, fill in three forms and make a payment of $14 (only US banknotes accepted), I'm given a ticket and directed to the start of the bridge.

I ride up a dusty bank, halting at the top to take in the scene before me. The pontoon appears about 300m long and its surface consists of rows of steel plates, each approximately 4m square, which lie at odd angles to each other. There's a gentle swaying movement as a truck makes its way across, rattling each section it passes over. Slipping the clutch, I edge anxiously onto the first plate. Shining in the sun, its dark polished surface is covered in a fine layer of slippery sand so I keep my right boot down, sliding it along for extra stability. As I reach the first joint, I'm shocked to see there's a gap of approximately 6 inches to the next plate and that one's proud, its sharp edge jutting menacingly forwards. Bathed in a tense sweat, I take it one plate at a time, ever fearful of punctures as first the front then rear wheel catch the protruding joints. Picking a careful path sometimes takes me onto the wrong side of the bridge and I stay in first gear the whole way. With a deep sigh, I roll the Matchless off the far end and pat her tank in appreciation of her stable and well mannered handling.

I'd expected the road to the frontier to be a major route. Instead, it's a dusty country backroad which 20km later leads to a dirt track. At the end is the border post, a group of large buildings in front of which are a few parked trucks and three colourfully attired women traders carrying bags of merchandise. Stopped at a security post, a soldier inspects my passport, counting the number of days since my arrival on his fingers. He looks almost disappointed that I've made it within my time allocation! In the immigration hall, the exit procedure takes 25 minutes and with no further delays, I ride towards the Uzbek compound. Checking my watch... it's 5.05pm.

My passport is stamped quickly but fun and games start at customs. First of all I have to fill in a declaration form, the likes of which I haven't seen for years. On one side, I list all my electrical goods, including model numbers, estimate the value of each then total them up. This, I suppose, will be checked against the actual items when I leave. On the back of the form I must declare all my cash, breaking it down into different currencies. Finally, there are lots of checkboxes, one of which asks if I'm carrying medicines.

The customs officer, a young woman with short black hair, is impossible to talk to as she interrupts every sentence before I can complete it.

"You have bags?" she asks.

"Yes, they're on..."

"Get them now."

"Is it OK to leave my...?"

"Go now. Bring your bags here."

Returning a few minutes later, she tells a male officer to go through my things. On an office desk, he rummages in my rack bag, pulling out the first-aid kit and two boxes of tablets. Carefully, he opens each one and looks at the contents. Apparently satisfied, he puts them down on the desk and begins rooting inside my tank bag. The female officer comes over and picks up the medicine boxes. Taking them to her own desk, she tips the contents out and begins systematically reading labels. From a drawer in her desk, she produces a book and from time to time uses it to cross-reference some of my medications. Spread everywhere are three different types of antibiotics, a raft of antimalarials, assorted analgesics, antihistamines, diarrhoea relief capsules, throat lozenges, etcetera, etcetera. Crucially, there are no codeine based drugs. Undeterred, she meticulously inspects all the plasters, dressings, burn creams, eyedrops, rehydration salts and even the contents of my dental kit.

"You have more pills?" she asks.

I laugh... I could almost stock a pharmacy with what's in front of her.

"No more," I reply.

She gets up, walks towards my bags and begins searching inside them.

"In here, more pills?"

"No."

"In here?"

There's a fine line between being thorough and overzealous. This lady seems to have an obsession as she goes back to her desk and commences rechecking every sachet and strip of pills. Finally, after what seems like an age, she says,

"Now go outside with this man to check your bike."

The officer she refers to has been reading the Matchless's documents. Following me through the door, he takes one look, smiles and says,

"Very nice motorbike. Welcome to Uzbekistan. You are free to go now."

We shake hands and he returns to his office.

I ride out of the compound at 6:20pm. The sun is low in the sky and including twilight, I estimate 50 minutes to an hour before nightfall. Bukhara, according to a signpost, is 98km away. Wasting no time, I accelerate down a freshly sealed dual carriageway. The road clear, we eat up the initial 35km. With the sun now gone, I'm slowed at the first small town where traffic is more dense. With 50km still to go, it turns pitch black. My headlight, with a modern LED replacement bulb, runs on a lowly 6 volts and although it emits a bright light that can be clearly seen, it doesn't project a powerful beam and oncoming cars, many of which have full beam headlights permanently on, blind me.

It seems such an unkind coincidence that the road turns bad as soon as it gets dark. Ballast is clearly visible through cracks that spread in every direction along its splintered surface and it's been so relentlessly patched with small globs of black tar, it's like riding on cobblestones. Juddering terribly, I drop into second gear and attempt to ride in the dirt track at the edge of the road but come up against pedestrians, bicycles without lights and animals being led along it. Feeling very unsettled, I stop to gather my wits and immediately realise that the dry bag which fell off this morning has disappeared again. I turnaround and slowly work backwards, shielding my eyes with my left hand whilst scanning both sides of the road. Traffic blasts dangerously close, and after 10 minutes, although I really don't want to, feel that for safety's sake I should give up.

"Come on Gordy, stop... it's gone." I say gently, out loud, but keep riding.

A minute later I coax myself again.

"Stop. Come on, let it go... let it go."

Reluctantly, I come to a halt, overwhelmed by it all.

Dreading the resumption of my now lengthened journey, I put the bike on its side stand, dig out my torch, which has an adjustable beam, and tape it onto the dry bag in front of the handlebars. Pointing slightly downwards, the light will hopefully be cast just a few metres ahead of the bike and increase my chances of avoiding the bigger splurges of surplus tar. As I make a final check to see that the tail light's working, my left leg catches on something. In the darkness, I stretch out my hands and find my lost dry bag hanging by a backup knot I'd tied to the loose end of its strap! It's been swinging there all the time, just inches above the exhaust.

The find boosts my flagging spirits and I set off with renewed determination, reaching the environs of Bukhara a slow, strained hour later. I can't see anywhere that resembles a city centre, so keep following the main road until I come to an enormous, oval shaped roundabout. Spotting three men standing beside a parked car, I brake hard, stopping just a few metres past them. Over my shoulder, I ask if they speak English and know of a nearby hotel. The answer to both questions is in the affirmative.

"See this road," says one, pointing to a turn off I've just passed. "A hotel is just 100 metres further. It's a very good one."

I ride full circle around the roundabout and take the exit, within a minute pulling up outside the Caravan Hotel. Two young men who work the nightshift, both students by daytime, bound outside to look at the bike. Their welcome is fabulously warm and cheerful, and within five minutes, we have the Matchless parked in the driveway of the hotel owner's house, which is next door. Stout wooden doors close behind her and all three of us carry my bags into the hotel. Nothing is too much trouble for my hosts, who change euros into Uzbekistan som and give me directions to a late night restaurant used by locals.

Exhausted, I walk to the recommended eating place with legs like jelly. Delighted to have a foreign visitor, the waiters run around trying to make me comfortable and serve food I'll enjoy. Eating bread and drinking peach juice as I wait for my main course, I'm surprised when a waiter comes back to my table and asks if I'd like a beer. The menu doesn't list any alcohol and there's none in the drinks fridge. When I say yes, he disappears outside, returning ten minutes later with a chilled can. I don't know where it's come from at this hour, but I'm not going to let that put me off... I deserve it after the day I've had.

124

Day 28. Bukhara. 0 miles.

Muzaffar and Izzatbek, the two members of staff who made me so welcome last night, are still on duty when I descend to the basement restaurant for breakfast. While dishing out eggs and toast, they tell me they're both economics students. Working at the hotel certainly seems to give them the opportunity to put their studies into practice... first I see them open their wallets to change money with a couple of Russian tourists, then minutes later, they do the same for an Australian man!

I'm gobsmacked when I step outside. Directly opposite stands the Ark of Bukhara, the fabulous remains of a fortified royal town. Unlit by street lighting, it had appeared as nothing but black space when I stopped in front of its twin towered ceremonial entrance to ask directions last night. Now, lit by the warm glow of morning sunlight, its towering earthen ramparts, curvaceous bulwarks and arch-shaped parapets are a sight to behold.

Occupied from the 5th Century, its history is remarkable - sacked by Genghis Khan, home to a great library and a succession of poets, mathematicians and astronomers, including Omar Khayyam, it played its part in 19th Century Great Game intrigue when, watched by a huge crowd, the ruler, Emir Nasrullah, made British diplomats Colonel Stoddart and Captain Connolly dig their own graves outside the main gates before beheading them. The citadel was bombed by the invading Red Army in 1920, which left most of its interior in ruins.

Bukhara is located on the ancient Silk Road and has been a centre of religion, scholarship and trade for over 2000 years. The old town, which begins just 50 metres from the hotel, is a UNESCO World Heritage site. I set off to explore and am instantly grabbed by its beauty. Within a couple of minutes I reach the Po-i-Kalan complex. Here stands the Kalyan Minaret which architecturally looks like a giant chess piece. It's 47m high and at the time it was built, in the 12th Century, may well have been the tallest structure in Central Asia. Even though I back away to a far corner of the square, it's hard to frame its entirety in my camera's viewfinder. The minaret stands close to Kalon mosque which is topped with a sublime turquoise mosaic dome and large enough to hold 10,000 worshippers. Directly opposite is Mir-i-Arab Madrassa, a centre of religious learning that sits behind a grand facade. Above it, a pair of ornate, onion-shaped domes rest on towers adorned with geometric patterns and calligraphic writing. Walking to some sheltered steps at one side, I sit in reverie for an hour, tracing the graceful lines of the surrounding buildings and absorbing the peaceful ambiance.

It's the tail end of the tourist season but there are still a few foreign visitors mulling around. Walking deeper into the old town, I come to a handful of traders who've set up sidewalk stalls. Selling skullcaps, enamelled plates and teapots, paintings and in one small, atmospheric bazaar, carpets, the vendors are laid back, content for me to browse rather than trying to push their wares. Sadly, the Matchless is so heavily loaded, I've no space for souvenirs.

There are several other imposing mosques and mausoleums, all within a few minutes walk, my favourite being Char Minar. It's the former gatehouse to a long gone madrassa and has identical towers at its four corners, each topped with small, green, bulbous domes. Although constructed later than most of the other major sites, there's something about its isolation, simplicity and slightly crumbling state of repair that I find alluring... in my mind's eye I can picture it standing in the remote corner of a desert, a caravan of camels approaching from the south.

I grab a late lunch close to Lyab-i Hauz, one of Bukhara's few remaining ponds. With a reputation for spreading disease, this and similar ponds supplied all of Bukhara's water until the Soviet era, when most were filled in. Afterwards, I continue wandering about, occasionally resting in shade and drinking coffee. As the sun goes down, I revisit some of the larger mosques, which, if anything, seem even more glorious in the last golden light of the day.

After dark, an open air circus gives a loud acrobatic performance outside the Arc, with young members of the cast collecting donations from the hundred or so spectators. Back at the hotel, I spend the remainder of the evening reading and washing clothes. Thoughts of tomorrow go round and round in my head. Contrary to erroneous information on *Google Maps*, the only open southern border crossing into Tajikistan is approximately 600km to the south east. However, due east is the fabled city of Samarkand, which I'd love to visit. After my terrible experience last night, I'm nervous about the prospect of a 260km detour on rough surfaces. I decide to resolve my equivocations in the morning.

*Kalon mosque,
Bukhara.*

Day 29. Bukhara to Samarkand. 193 miles.

As a boy of thirteen, I read *Eastern Approaches* by Fitzroy Maclean. A British diplomat in Moscow, Maclean undertook four intrepid journeys into then forbidden regions of the southern USSR. The second of these expeditions, in the autumn of 1937, was to the fabled city of Samarkand. His adventures, full of derring-do in mystical places, made a huge impression on me. I wake this morning with my decision made... how could I come all this way and allow the prospect of a few bad roads stop me visiting Samarkand!

Before going anywhere I need fuel. The boys at the hotel inform me that a high percentage of Uzbek cars run on LPG and warn that at this time of year, petrol is scarce. It happens to be cotton picking season which means, for reasons unexplained, that many fuel stations will be completely dry. Setting off under blustery grey skies, the first facility I pass is closed. The second only has 80 octane.

"Is good!" proclaims the man at the pump. I think not!

Stopping next to a taxi, I pat my petrol tank then open my arms questioningly and look around. The driver points ahead and to the right, saying, "UzGazOil! UzGazOil!"

Soon locating it, I stare in astonishment at the queue... there must be over 30 cars in a long line that stretches out and onto the road. Parking at the back, I hurry inside and enquire through an open cash office window,

"Do you have 95?"

"Nobody has 95 in Uzbekistan," one of the tellers replies. "We usually have 91 but today we only sell 80."

Using 80 RON would be like running the engine on paraffin, and despite a belt and braces combination of liquid additive and a *Spitfire Fuel Catalyst*, both of which lubricate the valves and boost octane levels, I doubt it would cope.

One of the pump attendants walks over and I explain the problem.

"Come," he says, looking around to see if we're being watched. "Bring your moto."

Retrieving the Matchless, I push her past the line of cars and next to a pump that's currently filling an old Lada with 80 grade. Once finished, he switches to another pump, telling me it's some of their reserved 91, and fills the tank to capacity. Greatly in his debt, I thank him sincerely. He holds his right hand to his chest and says,

"It is my duty."

How funny, I think as I ride away. In the UK I'd never put such low quality fuel in any of my bikes, yet relative to the alternative, I'm delighted to have it. Fortunately, there's no pre-ignition and the Matchless's performance seems unaffected.

The roads are in fair shape but riding conditions are made difficult by the gusting wind which strengthens, blowing from the south and across my path. It's a hot wind, the air full of sand and dust that partially obscures the sun behind a veil of murk. Most of the cotton fields seem to have already been picked, leaving nothing but bare, dry earth behind. I pass an old tractor that's ploughing a field. A thick pall of soil is picked up behind it, whipped around in the air then showered across the road... and all over me. Into view comes the first unharvested cotton with fluffy white dots growing high on dark, stringy plants. Uzbekistan is one of the world's largest producers of cotton but it comes at a high environmental and humanitarian cost. The thirsty crop requires constant irrigation and during the Soviet era, when the spread of 'white gold' was at its height, rivers were diverted to supply the farms. In north-western Uzbekistan and southern Kazakhstan is what remains of the Aral Sea, formerly one of the largest lakes in the world. Since the 1960s, it's been reduced to less than 10% of its original size, with much of the exposed seabed now wasteland. The environmental disaster has destroyed communities, with once thriving fishing villages left isolated many miles from the lakeshore, as well as ravaging delicate ecosystems, the result of the greatly increased salinity of the remaining water. In addition, many people's lives are negatively impacted each year by the mandatory harvesting of the cotton crop. Prices are kept artificially low by the government and most farmers cannot afford modern machinery. State sponsored forced labour, including the use of schoolchildren, is widespread. There's been massed international condemnation of the practice and several major retailers have banned the purchase of Uzbek cotton.

As the day progresses, it becomes even hotter. Anything moving west creates swirling squalls of dust and in the adjoining fields, donkeys, herds of goats and ox-drawn ploughs all contribute to the problem. The Matchless powers on, undaunted, and in the face of the challenge, I feel exhilarated, after all, I'm on the road to Samarkand! Stopping at the far side of a village, I find a cafe that's sheltered from the worst of the elements. I swing my leg off the bike and check the thermometer. It reads 40°.

My *Barbour* jacket, which until now was black, has adopted a silty brown colour, with lines of ochre in all the creases around my elbows and pockets. After a cursory attempt to dust myself down, I walk to one of four empty tables and ask for a menu. There isn't one. The young lady takes me inside the kitchen and points to a fridge. Through the glass door I see one row of chilled soft drinks and three shelves of raw horse meat on the bone. I opt for a Coke and sit outside. At an open air workbench, a man rolls pastry, creating somsa pasties from chunks of pink meat. Next to him is an old cast iron oven that's heated by a crackling wood fire. Making eating gestures with one hand, he points to a pasty. I smile and shake my head. Then he points upwards towards overhanging trees abundant with yellow plums. I nod in assent. Raising his voice, he speaks to the only other customers, three men drinking tea. Without hesitation, they get up, one of them grabs a long wooden pole and they proceed to pull a branch low enough to pick some fruit. Half a dozen juicy plums are placed in front of me... they're deliciously sweet. When I come to pay, I'm only charged for the Coke as the fruit is a gift. Refreshed, I head back out into the full force of the baking hot gale.

70km before Samarkand, with just over an hour of daylight left, I lean into a bend that's sheltered by swaying trees. All of a sudden, an agonizing pain

Still a non-runner, 'restored' in army trim.

battered and patched bike as she
found in Myanmar.

Gleaming… the restoration is almost complete.

ly Berry working on the steering head.

Derek Thom attaching horn brackets.

The team at Andrew Engineering. Left to right: Rachael Herrera, Vickki Lee, Malcolm Lee, Joan L
Eric Jones and Jim Price.

Above: Brendan, Hull.   Below: Ukraine.   Below: Hans.   Above: Colditz.   Below: Gearbox wo

pical highway scene in Azerbaijan… Ladas and fruit sellers.

titskhoveli Cathedral, Mtskheta, Georgia.

Deserted marble city. Ashgabat, Turkmenistan.

ssing the Karakum desert, Turkmenistan.

Kalyan Minaret and Kalon mosque, Bukhara.

Friendly Uzbeks, Shah-i-Zinda, Samarka

The incomparable Registan seen at night. Samarkand, Uzbekistan.

tton picking, Uzbekistan.

A welcome lift. Munavar, Tajikistan.

al, Murgharb, Tajikistan.

Corrugations on the Pamir Highway, Tajikistan.

auty and silence at 4,000m on the Pamir Highway, Tajikistan.

In the middle of reloading the bike after coming off on ice at 3500m. Kyrgyzstan.

Rough terrain. Pamir Highway, Kyrgyzstan.

Electric scooters and Chairman Mao, Kashg

100km of broken roads to Tashkurgan, China.

The Khunjerab Pass, 4730m.

rakoram Highway, Indus Kohistan, Pakistan.

Magnificent Bedford truck. GT Road, Pakistan.

eat hosts. Keyal police station, Pakistan.

e of many rockslides after the earthquake, Pakistan.

Beating the Retreat, border closing ceremony. Looking from India towards Pakistan.

A cup of tea with us? Friendly Pakistanis.

Nek Chand's Rock Garden, Chandigarh, Indi

Only recycled materials were used by Nek Chand.

Filthy and exhausted. Jhankat, Indi

sears through my left inner thigh... it feels like someone's pressing a lighted cigarette onto my bare skin. Braking hard, I kick out the side stand, jump off the bike and hop round to the near side. Frantically, I unzip my jacket and pull my trousers down. The white skin of my thigh is punctuated by an angry red circle, about the size of my fist, which has a swollen clear pimple in its centre. I've been stung and there's no sign of the culprit. Somewhere in my bags are antihistamines but the thought of taking everything off the bike to search for them in these dusty conditions is too much to contemplate. I limp back round the Matchless and press on.

The blurred outline of Samarkand emerges from the encompassing flat landscape, the streets of its poorer suburbs heady with blue woodsmoke from fires lit to cook evening meals. I aim towards the centre, following brown signs that declare 'Registan'. Missing the turn on a roundabout where speeding cars make it too dangerous to cut across, I have to backtrack around a one-way system then approach the roundabout again, this time angling for the outside much sooner. Now dark, I follow a wide boulevard for about a kilometre then steadily close in on a large colourfully illuminated area. Slowing down, I come to rest directly opposite the Registan. Lit up like a fairytale castle, it has to be one of the most magnificent and enchanting sights I've ever seen. Most nights I've been exhausted when I reach my destination, but not tonight. I sit in awe... the whole ride would be worth it just to experience this moment of magic.

Tearing myself away, I continue a couple of hundred metres further, spying a small hotel amongst a row of shops that's below street level. I leave the bike on the road to nip inside and am greeted by the friendly, bearded proprietor who offers me a room and safe parking for $20. Just as we shake on it, a young man breezes in, addressing me with an Eastern European accent.

"Your bike? I'm a biker too. KTM"

I say hello.

"Don't stay here, it's rubbish. Come with me. I'm in a cheaper place than this, it's not far away," he says, meanwhile extracting a hotel business card from his pocket which he hands over.

Steamrollering on, he continues,

"Where are you going?" and without waiting for an answer, "I'll be heading to Tajikistan in a few days, Why don't we ride together."

His manner is overwhelming and my host looks alarmed at the prospect of his newly acquired customer being wrenched away. Handing the business card back, I thank the man, explaining that I've just shaken hands on a room and feel I must honour my commitment. I also elucidate that he might find my riding speeds a bit on the slow side were we travelling companions. With a 'suit yourself' shrug, he leaves just as briskly as he arrived.

After offloading and taking a welcome cold shower, I apply cream to the angry bite rash which has now expanded to the size of my outspread hand. Finding a restaurant nearby, I eat a hearty meal of vegetable dumplings then return to the Registan. From a viewing platform, I spend what remains of the evening enjoying its majestic beauty.

Day 30. Samarkand to Qarshi. 93 miles.

The Registan looks totally different in daylight, but every bit as magnificent. Three richly decorated madrassas, each with elegant, imposing fronts, grace three sides of a large, open quadrant. Taking more than two centuries to complete, they've survived wars and earthquakes and are undoubtedly one of the most widely recognised ensembles of muslim architecture anywhere in the world. Wandering across the square, I try to imagine how it looked in times past, when most likely it was the site of a thriving bazaar, vibrantly teeming with people.

Moving on, I walk a kilometre to Bibi-Khanym Mosque, a vast congregational mosque that's visibly crumbling, nearly all of the decorative tiles on its once grand facade now missing. Legend has it that Bibi-Khanym, the Chinese wife of warlord, Timur, who founded of the Timurid Empire between 1370 and his death in 1405, had the mosque built as a surprise. Its architect apparently fell in love with her and refused to finish his work unless he could give her a kiss, which he planted on her cheek with such passion that it burned a mark. Timur, upon seeing it, had the architect executed and decreed that forthwith, women should be veiled so as to avert temptation.

Further ahead, atop a small hillside, I come to the avenue of mausoleums, Shah-i-Zinda, which translates as 'The tomb of the living king'. Through its arched entrance, the passageway's so narrow that to take a photograph of the first tomb I have to climb some steps at the side. Sitting on a rickety bench next to the tomb's door are four Uzbek men, three wearing Duppi, traditional black skullcaps with intricate silver woven patterns. They notice me lining up a photograph and, thinking they're in the way, begin to get up. I wave them to sit down and pointing upwards, call,

"It's OK. I'm not taking pictures of you, I'm photographing the mosaics at the top of the shrine. Please, no need to move."

Grinning, one of them shouts back,

"Not photographing us...why not? Is there something wrong with us?"

"No, no," I reply, laughing.

"Then please, you must take a photo of us!"

I oblige, jump down and after shaking their hands, show them the photo on my camera. They look happy.

There are more than a dozen tombs in the necropolis, each wonderfully adorned with intricate mosaics, scrolled religious scripts, complex geometric patterns and exquisite terracotta tiles. A myriad of blue has been used in the mosaics, some rich and striking, others subtle and delicate, and the overall effect, as I walk below the beautifully proportioned arches and domes, is ethereal. There's a hushed quiet as I near the end of the shrines, only broken by the whispered prayers of an elderly man in a long brown coat who sits, head bowed, outside the tomb of Kusam ibn Abbas, cousin to the Prophet Mohammed. A large tour party arrives and the enchanted spell is broken so I leave, catching an electric shuttle bus part way back to the Registan.

In a supermarket I stock up on lunch provisions; bread, cheese, bananas and a carton of pomegranate juice. At the checkout I hand over a 20,000 Som note. I'm given change to the nearest 1000 Som, the odd balance made up with a handful of sweets and chewing gum dropped into my carrier bag from a brass bowl. Eating in the hotel's covered courtyard, I can't finish all of the juice so pour the remainder into my Camelbak, reasoning it'll make a pleasant change from plain water when I'm riding. The hotel, I discover, is run by a family. The young woman in charge stands and chats while I check over the bike, revealing that she lived and studied in England for four years. She recently moved back to Samarkand to get married so I ask if she misses the UK.

"My sister is still there, in Milton Keynes, and I miss her. I liked England but not the weather... it rained too much."

I can't argue with that!

Setting off around 1pm, I struggle to find the route south, stopping to ask at several open fronted shops until certain I'm on the right road. Locating petrol is once again a problem; there seem to be so many LPG stops but hardly any petrol stations. At a third fruitless halt, where GAZ is all that's available, I'm directed to an adjoining business which looks more like a car repair yard. Pretty sure I'm wasting my time, I wheel the Matchless across a compound full of broken down cars and stop next to a pump that's hidden from the road.

"91?" I ask a man who comes out of his office.

"Yes. 3600 som a litre."

It's 20% more than I was charged yesterday but I'm in no position to argue and gratefully fill up.

Free from the city's closed-in streets, the road opens wide, passing through wild steppe where herds of goat graze on tussock. A fresh layer of bitumen has recently been laid which adds to my happiness as I power round long bends and up gentle hills. There's a mild headwind, little more than a breeze, but it helps keep me cool when around 3pm the temperature peaks at 36°. Hardly any cars appear to be travelling long distances, with just a handful of vehicles evident around occasional small towns. Nothing to detain us, my splendid Matchless motors non-stop for almost a hundred kilometres.

Accelerating out of a small settlement, there's a visible line in the road where the good seal stops and a vibration-inducing, broken old surface starts. Suddenly narrow, it's so badly repaired, a patchwork of different shades of tar, that it's impossible to gauge which part of the road is original. I come upon a highly unskilled road crew, two young men and a group of older women all dressed in their own clothes. From a steaming wheelbarrow, they plonk molehills of tar into small potholes and pat them down with their spades. Hitting these protruding repairs at speed is just as bad as bouncing through the actual potholes they fill and I'm compelled to slow to avoid damaging the bike. To find myself juddering along again at such a retarded pace is somewhat demoralising.

After 40km, the road improves as it enters Qarshi, a nondescript city of 200,000 well-known for carpet production. At every set of traffic lights, I talk to car drivers through their windows, asking if they know of a hotel. Everyone directs me towards the far side of town where, as part of a shopping complex set well back from the road, sits a modern hotel. I head straight inside and secure a room. A porter then leads me around the rear to show me where I can store the bike but it's nothing more than a building site with open access to a nearby market. Back at reception, I ask if they can make alternative arrangements but the answer is a regretful no. Accompanied by three members of staff, I go back outside and show them the bike. Several passers-by get involved in the ensuing discussions. A middle-aged man, who doesn't speak English, turns out to be an unexpected ally, championing the Matchless's cause. The staff seem reluctant but he doesn't give in, imploring them to allow her inside the hotel's porch. Acquiescing, they help manoeuvre her around a tight corner and along to the far end of the vestibule. Satisfied, my supporter shakes my hand and continues on his way. When all my gear is off and the cover on, I head into the foyer where to my surprise, a line of five staff stand to attention waiting to formally greet me. With a flattering sense of occasion, the manager introduces me to everyone and welcomes me to their hotel... something that's never happened to me at a Travelodge!

In the evening, I descend to the foyer to get Wi-Fi access. Sitting on a settee, I'm distracted when a fellow guest changes channels on a large wall-mounted TV. There appear the cheerful faces of *Wheeler Dealers* Mike Brewer and Edd China, busily renovating a BMW. It's riveting. Their vocals have been been overdubbed in Russian giving Mike a deep guttural voice and Edd a particularly high-pitched, squeaky one. Great!

In the adjoining restaurant, I'm again faced with no menu. Fortunately, I'd earlier spoken to one of the hotel's night staff, a gentle young man who recently graduated with a degree in philosophy. Walking back to reception, I ask if he minds translating for me. Five minutes later, my order for a noodle dish in hand, I ask the nervous young waiter if I can have a coffee.

"Chernyy," (black) I add, using one of my few Russian words.

He soon returns, setting a cup and saucer in front of me. I almost choke on my first sip. It's disgustingly sweet. Calling the waiter, I hand it back to him and say,

"Sucre, niet," repeating it several times in the strange notion he'll understand the mixture of French and Russian.

He takes it away then returns shortly with the same cup plus a bowl of sugar and a spoon. I try explaining again and some locals at a nearby table join in. The poor lad becomes totally confused. I get up, walk next door, and ask the helpful receptionist if he can intervene. He returns with me and issues instructions to the young man.

Five minutes later he returns to my table, confidently placing a fresh cup of coffee in front of me. Standing stiffly upright with his hands behind his back, he waits for my reaction as I take a mouthful. I gag and spit it into a napkin. It's like syrup, he's put even more sugar in it. I give up.

After eating my noodles, I'm handed the bill. Scrutinizing it, I see I've been charged for two cups of coffee, one napkin and an additional 10% for service. The amounts are relatively small and it's simply not worth complaining so I pay up and go to my room.

Day 31, Qarshi to Termiz. 197 miles.

After dragging the bike out of the porch, I begin my search for the nearest UzGazOil. Set on a corner and ringed by four lanes of queuing cars that cause a blockage on the road, it's a surprisingly easy find. I join the back of the shortest queue and begin counting the vehicles ahead... there are 37. After a while I realise I've made a mistake in choosing a line that contains four modern, posh cars whose drivers are rich enough to completely fill up. The neighbouring lanes, almost exclusively containing long-in-the-tooth Ladas, move forward so much faster as their drivers can only afford a few litres. It takes over half an hour to be served, but at least it's with good ol' 91.

For 80km we travel east on level roads and apart from a couple of brief police checks, it's plain sailing. Turning south on the M39, we begin to climb. To the right, the land falls away steeply and I can see clearly for several miles. On the horizon, across empty, arid earth, a vertical wall of sand materialises. This time it's unquestionably a sandstorm. Due to the frequency of police inspections, I've not been wearing my helmet camera in case its presence causes problems, so I pull over, fish it out of the tank bag and begin to film the distant mass of turbulent air. Although I've been through relatively mild sand and dust storms before, I've never witnessed anything quite as dramatic as this. Moving at pace across the ground like a terrestrial tidal wave, its vastness is of biblical proportions, the kind of meteorological phenomenon shown on the National Geographic channel or in a BBC documentary about the Sahara.

Ahead of its clearly defined front, everything looks normal but as it advances in a straight line across the countryside, it devours all in its path. With the alarming realisation that it's coming our way and a simultaneous awareness of its frightening speed, I kick the bike over and move hell for leather, revving hard uphill. Immediately below the roadside, perhaps three hundred metres away, a small village comes into sight, the layout of its houses and unpaved streets clearly visible from my vantage point. One second it is there, the next, it vanishes, the dense, dark cloud of airborne sand swallowing the community whole. The race is really on. I overtake two trucks then look again. It's almost upon me and in a flash the consequences of being caught tear through my mind... the engine would be completely choked and I'd be forced to stop, the steep drops on either side rendering me at the mercy of any cars or trucks attempting to drive through it.

Speeding on at over 80, which is approaching warp speed for the Matchless, I glance in my mirrors. Less than 100 metres to the rear the road has disappeared under a solid brown cloak. Ahead to the right, the storm's hostile front expands over a barren hill, threatening to outflank us. The road swings to the left, giving us a fraction more leeway, but when it straightens a minute later, our contest resumes and the road immediately behind is once more engulfed. Climbing then dipping, we angle closer to its clutches before curving away again. Riding like the devil, it takes a good quarter of an hour to outrun it. Clear, I slow to a more sensible speed and with the release of

pressure bellow,
    "Yes!"
What a mightily exhilarating ride!

Some time later, I cruise into a small, dismal town consisting of rows of soulless concrete houses, fronted in many instances by piles of rubbish and the rusty skeletons of abandoned or crashed cars. The groups of urchins that play at the roadside look malnourished and their clothes are little more than rags. The town centre, which is equally miserable, seems to almost exclusively contain wedding shops, their crusty windows displaying rows of ivory, blancmange-type wedding dresses. Hundreds of kilometres distant from Uzbekistan's major cities and surrounded by rocky, barren steppe, it's the most unexpected and uninspiring nuptial centre imaginable!

Riding on, the road begins climbing in earnest and major roadworks commence. It takes half an hour to ascend to 1100 metres and most of the way the surface is stripped bare. It's like riding on a bed of flint, my front wheel deflecting off larger clumps of rock or sliding where patches of gravel are prominent. Mile after mile I labour up the incline, standing on the footpegs, shifting backwards and forwards between first and second gears. Dripping with sweat from the effort, I'm showered by a fresh layer of chalky dust each time a car or van comes in the opposite direction. I weave through a craggy gully and in momentary disbelief, behold, stretching out before me, a straight descent on proper, smooth tarmac. Pulling in the clutch, I whizz downwards, giving the spitting hot engine a long blast of cool air.

At the bottom, the road points heavenwards and the tar seal disappears once more. Slithering and sliding, we scramble upwards, 1000, 1200 then finally 1500 metres. At the summit, a ravine blasted through a bleak escarpment, I stop to make a sandwich and stretch my legs. I'm filthy, my boots and trousers grey with dust, my face blackened by grime blended into a tacky sunblock paste. The poor bike doesn't look much better, her glossy shine now completely lost. Everything around is the colour of lime and the track, too appalling to be called a road, comprises a layer of shiny rocks embedded in hard clay. A truck slows to check I'm OK, its driver leaning out of his window and waving encouragingly for me to continue. When the Matchless dutifully starts first kick, I ride over the crest and again am greeted with new, perfect asphalt... a sight for sore eyes. Within a kilometre of freewheeling downhill, we're halted at a major military station where armed soldiers check everyone passing through and, while I flop in a comfortable office chair, all my details are recorded on a computer. No wonder the truck driver seemed confused by my desolate choice of picnic spots!

Leaving 30 minutes later, I continue to descend and soon come to a turnoff on the left. I've studied maps for the last few days but have been unable to make a decision about whether at this point, I should take a short cut due east. Alternatively, I can stay on main roads, travelling in a large V south east this afternoon then north east tomorrow, which will add an additional 140km to the journey. Information about what lies east is scant except that it's a remote area with one town of 26,000, Boysun. The road is uncategorised, never a good omen, and the much larger town of Denau, the last major habitation before the border crossing into Tajikistan, 120km away. Although parts of the M39 have been atrocious, the new sections have, in equal measures, been sublime. With preservation of the bike my primary concern, I decide to try the shorter route cross country on the proviso that I'll turn around should bad conditions prevail.

It starts well, and although narrow, the road's surface is fine for the first 5km. However, in short increments it deteriorates until it becomes so deplorable that I'm once more standing up in second gear, the poor machine shaking dreadfully. After ten minutes, I call a halt to it, turn around and begin to retrace my steps. Concentrating on the road, I perceive the slightest of peripheral movements and, abruptly swivelling my head to the right, catch sight of a large white hound just a few feet from my ankle, stretching to its fullest in the hope of taking a bite. Descended from high-country sheepdogs, the wild-looking pooches in this region are very wily, having learnt not to give themselves away by barking. A quick spurt of gas gets me clear but it's a close run thing.

Five minutes later, I rejoin the highway, rolling straight onto pristine tar. The route south proves to be a mixture of everything experienced to date: kilometre-long stretches of roadworks with not a machine or worker to be seen, the scarred surface a jagged, harsh trial for tyres and frame alike; incredible descents on immaculate black tarmac where, with the engine off, we fly along; an old road dimpled with so many makeshift repairs the bike hums with vibration. The further we travel, the more prominent small bridges become and we fall into a taxing routine of accelerating on new seal, reaching perhaps 60kmph before braking hard and dropping off an edge onto potholed, gravelly rock. Skittering over the remains of a bridge, there's 30 metres more rough stuff before we thump up a sharp tar ridge and back onto another beautifully laid section. Half a kilometre later, the same is repeated... again and again. Weary, I'm delighted to come to the outskirts of Termiz, where, at another major checkpost, all the cars are thoroughly searched. My passport's inspected but security checks are skipped... both me and my belongings are taken on trust.

Termiz is Uzbekistan's only border crossing point with Afghanistan and its streets have a wild west feel to them. Approaching the city centre in darkness, the pavements are empty except for a few small groups of men hanging around on street corners. I stop beside three guys who are sitting on steps near the central clocktower smoking cigarettes and ask if they know of any hotels nearby. Following their directions I manage to find the Surhan Atlantic, a concrete communist-era towerblock. Inside, I'm welcomed by a gracious man who offers me a basic room, no TV, or a deluxe room, with TV. I'm so shattered it makes no difference so opt for the former, handing over the equivalent of $8. There are two archaic lifts but only one's serviceable and it rattles so noisily I reckon its days are also numbered. The room's tired to say the least, but the shower works and I'm grateful that for once the towels are not brilliant white... dark green disguises the filth that continues to rub off me no matter how many times I scrub with soap!

Heading out in search of food I find a lone, cheap and cheerful fish restaurant that serves heaped plates and large pitchers of local beer. When I come to place my order, I realise I'm getting low on Som. As I still need to buy fuel tomorrow, I ask the waitress if I can pay in dollars. Looking concerned, she walks from table to table requesting help. At the third try, a dark skinned man with a thick moustache nods, asking how much I'd like to change.

"Only $10," I tell the waitress apologetically.

She relays my reply and the man leaves his seat, returning five minutes later having visited a friend who's willing to take the dollars. I'm gobsmacked when he offers an exchange rate of 4500 to 1 as the best to date through official channels has been 2600. I wish I'd changed on the black market sooner!

Before bed, I re-cream my bite, a hard pale circle the diameter of a tangerine in the middle of a raw rash now so big that it almost reaches my knee, and hope for better roads tomorrow. I'm not sure how much more the bike can take.

Bleak, barren and extremely rough going on the road to Termiz.

Day 32. Termiz, Uzbekistan, to Dushanbe, Tajikistan. 163 miles.

A close inspection of the Matchless reveals another break in the rear number plate carrier, which I soon fix with cable ties and gaffer tape, and that several loose nuts and spokes need retightening. After yesterday's exploits I'm astonished the bike got off so lightly. After saying farewell to the amiable hotel manager and his wife, I visit the local UzGazOil. One of the pump attendants spots me in line and comes over for a chat. He's a student who speaks English fluently and is adamant that all their 91 octane was used up last week. He gravely assures me that nobody has anything but 80 RON in Termiz.

"But eighty's good!" he insists.

I pull out of the queue, push the Matchless to one side of the forecourt and wait. I've learnt that often, in tricky situations, a little patience goes a long way and I'm sure a solution will reveal itself. Within a few minutes, a small crowd has gathered around and the student, wandering over, explains my dilemma to them.

"Try Mustang Gas," suggests one man, "Maybe they have 91."

The student looks dubious but gives me directions, finishing by telling me to come back for 80 should I fail in my quest.

Mustang Gas is roughly a kilometre away on the road out of town. A small station, it has two pumps, one bearing the number 80, the other 91. There's no queue so I draw up next to the 91 pump and expectantly ask the attendant to fill her up. He shakes his head, pointing to the 80. Almost immediately, a car stops on the other side of the pump and the attendant begins to fill it with 91! Nonplussed, I follow the man to the cashier's window where he fills his name in a book then pays. The cashier, when I ask if I can also buy 91, explains they have a limited supply and it's reserved for regular customers. I try again, but he firmly shakes his head in answer. Entreating him for help, I make explosive sounds to demonstrate the effect of 80 octane on the Matchless's engine then write its age on a notepad that sits on his counter. He begins to waver. The clincher comes when I explain that I only need 10 litres. He relents, instructing the attendant to serve me. Phew! If all goes to plan, this should be my last top up in Uzbekistan.

The route north, the M41, parallels the Tajikistan border and follows the snaking course of the Surkhandarya river. It's such a pleasant surprise to find the road, the size of an average British B-road, in reasonable nick and we comfortably chug along at a steady 60. Gradually we close in on another motorcycle, one of the few I've seen in Uzbekistan, the trail of blue smoke it leaves in its wake a clear sign that it's a two-stroker. As I pull alongside, the rider and I wave to each other and I take in the attributes of his run down machine: it's a characterful old MZ with a once red tank now sunbleached pink, rear shock absorbers close to collapse and an engine that sounds like a bag of nails. What I really fall for are its throw-over saddlebags, which, made from handwoven carpet, are the type used on mules and donkeys in Afghanistan. Classic!

The sun's out but the road's largely shaded by tall bushes and trees that line the edge of the surrounding fields and thanks to the natural irrigation of the adjacent river, everything is wonderfully green and fertile. There are vineyards, extensive watermelon patches, fields of ripe corn and most prevalent, long reaches of cotton plantations. After approximately 70km, I rest on a strip of dirt at the roadside and eat a snack. In the field opposite, women in brightly coloured floral dresses, all wearing small, triangular headscarves, squat between the rows of plants, wicker baskets at their sides. Cotton picking looks like backbreaking labour! Underway again, we ride through a series of small villages between which animals, mainly small herds of goats but sometimes sheep, are being led. Donkeys are also common, carrying loads or pulling small carts. It's the most relaxing, undemanding ride in weeks and when we eventually pass the turnoff to Boysun, I'm glad I didn't pursue it yesterday. Despite saving 130km, it would have meant missing this lovely part of the world.

Stopping outside the bazaar in the middle of a small town, where men stand talking in clusters whilst they wait for minibuses, I ask for directions to the Tajikistan border.

"Where are you going?" asks a middle aged man with soft eyes set in a gentle face, a traditional duppi prominent on his head.

"Dushanbe," I reply. His face registers understanding and he gives detailed instructions for the complex route to the border.

"Where from? Where from?" he chirps.

The UK doesn't seem to mean anything, so I try again,

"Angliya," I say, using the Russian name for England.

His face lights up and all the men around begin calling out,

"Angliya!... Angliya!"

I find myself shaking many hands before finally riding away.

Locating the frontier post, there are two tiny, stand-alone offices that I need to pass in order to reach immigration. The soldier at the first requires a quick check through my passport to ensure I have a visa for Tajikistan and the man at the second wants to inspect receipts from all the hotels that I've stayed at since arriving in Uzbekistan. Fortunately, I've been forewarned of this and have everything close to hand. Five minutes later, with a familiar 'kerchunk', my passport receives its exit stamp. The chaps at customs are more interested in checking the subject matter of my books than the medications my bags may hide. I pull out a guidebook for Central Asia, which holds little interest for them. When one insists on checking my bags himself, I offer up the Matchless's workshop manual and spare parts book.

"No books pictures women?" he asks, revealing the true nature of the search.

Hardly likely!

They've no interest in verifying that all my electronics and cash marry up with what's declared on the customs form and forty minutes after arriving, I'm told I can go.

The Tajik compound lies at the top of a steep hill. Parking in front of large iron gates, I climb unsteady wooden stairs and enter a tiny office that's raised on tall concrete stilts. It's very basic but the three officials who stand around the solitary piece of furniture, a battered steel desk, are incredibly welcoming. Fresh ink is rubbered into my passport and they wish me a great time in their country. Through the gates, I'm directed to customs. Inside the building is a series of connecting offices where I'm passed from person to person without actually achieving anything. Finally shown into the 'boss's' room, I sit at a large wooden table and am invited to watch a Russian film on the television. For the next 30 minutes, a stream of officials and Turkish truck drivers come and go, getting pieces of paper initialed. The head honcho, smart in a crisp shirt with golden epaulettes, sits at the head of the table, jovially conducting business on two mobile phones, sometimes on both simultaneously. My head's just starting to nod when two more officials arrive and one of them begins tapping the Matchless's particulars onto a computer. After relinquishing $10 tax for the bike, I can finally depart. I'm in Tajikistan!

Exiting the border post, I quickly pull into a bus stop and set about stowing my documentation more carefully. A passing car slows, does a sharp u-turn then parks alongside. It's an old 1990's Daewoo 3-door hatchback with lowered suspension and go-fast stripes painted along its flanks. The three teenagers that climb out say hello then try, with a combination of curiosity and shyness, to engage in conversation. This proves difficult. By means of a series of points and gestures I ask the closest, who wears a Bentley t-shirt, where his Bentley's parked. Their guileless young faces all crease with laughter. One of the others sports a Porsche t-shirt, so I repeat the same act with him, resulting in more hilarity. We part as friends and I climb back on the Matchless, turning in the direction of Dushanbe.

The 70km long capital bound highway is as smooth as silk and although hilly, we keep up enough momentum to ride the whole way in top gear. I've memorised a route through the city centre and without too much difficulty, am able to recognise landmarks and negotiate the widening roads and increasingly frantic traffic. I locate the sleepy suburb where my hotel's situated but need assistance to find the dirt lane that leads to its door. Obviously spotted on CCTV, large gates swoosh open as I arrive outside.

Two brothers run the Atlas Guest House, one of whom, Firuz, greets me as I cut the engine.

"Ah, Mr. May. Yes, I remember your name. You're not due to arrive until tomorrow."

"Is it OK to stay tonight as well," I ask, expecting the answer to be yes.

"We have a large contingent of aid workers staying with us at the moment and I'm afraid we're full."

Before I can ask if there are any alternatives, he continues,

"But please don't worry. A family friend runs a hotel just a kilometre from here. It's the same standard and price as ours. I'll happily lead you there in my car, then tomorrow, you can either stay there or come back here, whichever suits you best."

It's an excellent solution and I begin to wheel the Matchless around so she's ready for the off.

"Oh, before I forget," he adds. "I have a parcel for you... it's been here three days already. I'll put it in my car and give it to you when we get there." Great news!

Inside his friend's hotel 10 minutes later, Firuz hands over the package then tells me to call him in the morning... he'll help me with everything I need to arrange while I'm here. After he departs, I begin the check-in process, ordering a takeaway pizza at the same time. I'm so bushed I can hardly string a sentence together, let alone go searching for food. It arrives just as I step out of the shower, the night manager handing it over along with a chilled bottle of lager.

"This came from the owner's personal supply," he says by way of explanation. "He thought you might enjoy it."
I'm beginning to think I must have 'just give me a beer' emblazoned on my forehead, but it's a welcome and very generous gift.

Once sated, I open the parcel from Brendan. Inside is a yellow rain suit, so fluorescent fellow motorists will need sunglasses to cope with the glare. Wrapped within it are waterproof overmitts, replacing those also lost in the Ukraine, and two pairs of thermal gloves. Underneath he's enclosed four laminated photographs of Jacques and Jacob, taken when he and the boys recently visited Chester Zoo. In the last frenetic days of activity before departure, I'd overlooked loading recent pictures of Jacques onto my tablet so I'm over the moon to have these. I send Brendan a text, thanking him for the parcel, photos and especially for taking Jacques out.

'It's no great hardship to make a boy happy by taking him for a day out at the zoo,' he replies in his usual kind way.

Day 33. Dushanbe. 0 miles

I'd never imagined that the roads up to this point would be so awful and riding a rigid framed bike certainly hasn't helped matters. I know from prior studies that what comes next, the road between Dushanbe and Khorog, will probably be the worst of the whole trip. There are two routes, one of which is being reconstructed and is at this time virtually impassible. The other, used by heavy Chinese trucks, has a stretch with corrugations, potholes and rock that's almost 400km long. Already much has broken on the bike and for the last couple of weeks I've had serious concerns about whether she will survive this next key stage. In Bukhara, I briefly met a Dutch and German couple travelling round the world by bicycle. They were certainly no softies and had cycled the high altitude passes of the Pamirs 6 weeks ago. But, they told me, they'd skipped riding from Khorog to Dushanbe, putting their bikes in a hired Landcruiser for fear of breaking them. They were glad they had, saying it was an utterly awful journey.

I've decided to do the same. My objective is to ride the Matchless to Vietnam, not to some remote region of Tajikistan where I destroy it... the rear forged section of the frame, that Andy made the best of a bad job with, is particularly vulnerable and were it to fracture, it'd be game over. From Khorog I'll still be able to ride along the most beautiful and remote parts of the Pamir Highway, including all the passes, on roads that I'm told are fair. It feels like the right decision.

Just before 8am, the hotel receptionist arranges a taxi to take me to a bazaar where all the commercial Khorog-bound vehicles congregate. The driver, his face half hidden behind an enormous walrus moustache, leads me to his battered old Mercedes. After a quick stop at a cashpoint, where I get enough Tajikistan Somoni to make a reasonable deposit, he drives to a closed-in square jammed with chaotic lines of MPVs and 4x4's in various knocked-about states.

My first impression is that it's a den of thieves, for as soon as I step out of the car, I'm mobbed by men trying to get my attention, shouting, pulling at my arm and jostling to get nearer. The stalwart taxi driver sticks by my side, fending off the solicitations of some of the more physical touts. One man, an advocate I don't entirely trust, speaks some English and tells me he can organise the right vehicle. With a crowd in tow, he leads to an old Landcruiser but when the rear door's opened, it's obvious I'll not get a motorcycle in the back. Still giving me lots of sales patter, he points towards another group of vehicles, stopping at a Hyundai people carrier. I'm introduced to its driver, a quietly spoken young man with a steady look in his eyes. I ask, via the fixer, if he's fast. The driver shakes his head vigorously at the suggestion and my intuition about him being on the side of the angels rings true. In the back of the car, the clever design of its seats mean they twist and fold out of the way and I'm certain it'll hold the Matchless. Checking round the rest of it, I note four decent tyres and despite a significant crack in its windscreen and a door that doesn't close properly, it appears reasonably well cared for in comparison to the surrounding jalopies. We strike a deal, I pay a deposit to the intermediary and arrangements are made for an early start from my hotel tomorrow. I can hardly believe it's been so easy and I'm back in my room by 9am.

Hopping on one of the hotel's bicycles, which turns out to have a buckled front wheel and a pedal that repeatedly falls off, I cycle along dusty streets, visiting three banks to use their ATMs, as the maximum amount I can withdraw at any given time is ridiculously low. Relieved the stomach cramps that have troubled me for the last couple of days have retreated, I grab an early lunch then wobble my way back to the hotel.

I"m carrying a second rear tyre, a road legal Heidenau K67 Trials type with a nice chunky tread pattern that'll give lots more grip on the rough stuff. This afternoon I plan to fit it onto the bike and rather than spending a couple of hours sweating, cursing and doubtless grazing my knuckles, hope to find a motorcycle shop with a tyre changing machine. Firuz, who's amazing considering I'm not even staying at his guest house, has kindly offered to drive me in search of such a place. I set to work taking the rear wheel off, made easy by the quickly detachable mudguard, which, upon loosening four nuts, pulls away complete with luggage rack, light and number plate. Once the chain's removed, the wheel slides out. I leave the now naked looking Matchless in the safe keeping of the hotel's security guard and give Firuz a call to let him know I'm ready.

We drive for 10 minutes in his luxuriously air-conditioned RV to a dark workshop, one of only two known motorcycle repair outfits in Dushanbe. They don't have a tyre changing machine but offer to do it by hand. Instead, we opt to try the second place, Taj Moto Wave Bike House. Pulling up outside, a young man, with a breezy air and a jolly face that looks almost Tibetan, greets us.

"What's this?" he says peering into the boot. "Hey... that's old school!"
Calling his two assistants out of the shop, they lift the wheel onto the ground and begin laughing about its flimsy pressed tin brake plate, narrow spindle and skinny tyre.

"You're not riding on the Pamir with this!" teases the first man. "What's the rest of the bike like!"
Their jesting continues and when we enter the shop, I immediately see why they're so amused. A BMW F650GS, complete with alloy panniers, stands beside two purposeful-looking pairs of DRZ400s and XTR 250 dirt bikes, all of which are for hire. On the walls are flags, paintings and photos of visiting travellers on large BMW, KTM and Triumph adventure bikes. Like the first place, tyre changing will need to be done by hand but their fee's reasonable and they're nice guys so I agree. I thank Firuz who gives me a hug and leaves to return to his duties at the Atlas.

All joking's put aside when they start the job, which they do with concentration and care, even going so far as to wrap the tyre levers in gaffer tape to reduce the risk of damaging my black rims. It takes all three of them to get the knobbly on, one levering and the other two standing on the carcass... I don't fancy trying to replicate that if I get a puncture in the mountains! Thirty minutes later, they pump it full of air and to my relief, it stays up. Tipping them, I say farewell and catch a taxi back to the hotel.

Putting everything back together goes smoothly, the wider replacement tyre fitting with just a couple of millimetres to spare at each side. A new split link in the chain, I tighten everything up then grab my riding gear and set out to buy petrol. Following Firuz's directions, I locate a thriving central service station that sells 95, and with my tank and fuel bottles full of decent petrol, ride back through the dusk in good spirits.

Known as Stalinabad when Tajikistan was part of the USSR, I don't feel that I've seen much of what Dushanbe has to offer. I reflect, however, as I eat dinner in a busy restaurant packed with office workers, that in many ways I've probably experienced its best attribute... the people. My guardian taxi driver; fantastic Firuz; the cheerful mechanics; the petrol pump attendant who found me an empty water bottle to fill with extra fuel; the couple at an ATM who interrupted their third withdrawal to offer me a turn in case the machine ran out of money and the stranger on a bicycle who crossed the road simply to shake my hand and say "salaam," before carrying merrily on his way. Every one of them is a credit to this intriguing country.

On the road to Khorog.
The Pyandzh river separates Tajikistan (left) from Afghanistan (right).

Day 34. Dushanbe to Khorog. 372 miles (not ridden).

Munavar, my driver, arrives at 6.45am on the dot accompanied by the fixer and two strong men to help load the bike. All the rear seats fold away and the Matchless fits diagonally with a couple of inches to spare. As we're tying her down, an old Mercedes pulls up and my taxi driver from yesterday gets out. He's come to check everything goes okay... what a gentleman! With the bike secure, all my luggage is loaded into the remaining space along with some freight, three large polythene bags packed with clothing. Payment has to be made in advance and although I don't feel happy about it, this means handing everything over to the tout. The taxi driver and I stand side-by-side and watch from a distance as he forms a huddle with the men, first paying off his two helpers, then giving the lion's share to the driver. Business complete, everybody leaves except Munavar who waits 10 minutes while I grab a speedy breakfast.

Soon out of the city, we comfortably drive along a fast dual carriageway, heading first east then turning southwards. Munavar doesn't speak much English but we communicate well enough. In-car entertainment is initially provided courtesy of his two western CDs, Beyonce and Christina Aguilera. Munavar smiles and with universal hand movements, traces the outline of female curves. Enough said. It's a relief when they finish and he moves on to traditional Tajik and Afghan folk music.

We're pulled over by police who wait in a layby. Munavar seems to be anticipating this, slowing in advance. He jumps out of his seat and after the briefest of chats, hands over a small amount of money. Driving away, I ask how much was demanded. His answer equates to roughly £2 and by his phlegmatic reaction to my disgust, I take it that dealing with petty corruption is simply part of his everyday life.

With few undulations and little to see but nondescript pasture, the first 200 km pass in a couple of hours and I begin to question myself as the highway has so far been almost perfect. Pulling up in the small town of Kulob, Munavar sets off to buy some provisions so I get out to stretch my legs. On the pavement are three tiny shops constructed from sheets of anodised steel, each about 1 1/2m² in size. A diminutive young man arrives, says hello with a smile then proceeds to unlock the nearest metal box, which he enters via a raised side door. He lowers the hinged storefront to reveal a mobile phone kiosk then steps outside, removing his tie and shirt to expose a small white singlet and his bony frame. Climbing back inside, he settles onto a stool and waits for customers. I can't help feeling for him. Sitting in a tin cube subjected to the summer sun all day long must be somewhat akin to being cooked alive, and in winter...

Munavar returns with a kebab, drinks and three huge round flatbreads which he puts on top of the dash. Underway again, the road rapidly worsens. There's gravel giving way to long stretches of nothing but hardcore and although none of it is any worse than what I've ridden on already, the big difference is the length of the bad bits... they go uninterrupted for 30 to 40km at a time. For all that, the Matchless would have coped and I find myself perversely willing it to worsen in justification of my decision to transport the bike.

Noticeably changing direction, our route twists and turns towards the north east following the banks of the Pyandzh river, a natural frontier with Afghanistan. Stopping at a remote military checkpost, my passport's inspected but Munavar, who seems well known by the soldiers, is exempt. He gives two of the fresh loaves to a soldier, possibly another example of palm greasing. As we restart, we enter the Gorno-Badakhshan Autonomous Oblast (GBAO), a vast region which comprises over 45% of Tajikistan's territory but is home to only 3% of its total population. In the last three decades its people have fought fiercely for independence and there've been renewed clashes between the military and militants in recent times. The FCO 'advise against all but essential travel' to this area but I made my decision to come based on the rationale that if the Tajik government is willing to grant me a GBAO permit, it should be safe enough to visit. The permit was issued without question or warning when I applied for my visa in London and here I am.

To my surprise we hit a 55km belt of smooth tarmac, a section highly susceptible to landslides that's recently been reconstructed in a joint project with Turkish engineers. We glide over its superlative blacktop for half an hour before crunching joylessly back onto dirt.

Only the creamy blue mountain waters of the fast flowing river separate us from Afghanistan. I'm captivated by the tiny villages, pinned in by the surrounding valley walls. Shaded by weeping willows, each modest enclosure of stone dwellings is hemmed by a few market gardens and where room permits, a small flat football pitch or communal area on the riverbank. The dusty tracks that link each settlement together are mostly travelled on foot or by donkey but from time to time, I watch lightweight motorcycles carefully moving along, trails of dust thrown up by their wheels. Mid-afternoon, we stop for a toilet break in the back of beyond. I pick up a round stone and throw it as hard as I can. It soars over the river and lands in a rocky, barren bit of Afghanistan.

Through the late afternoon and evening we follow a gorge, all the while gently climbing. From time to time the snowcapped peaks of distant mountains make an appearance but soon vanish behind the towering rock sides of the valley. As the road surface crumbles further, the car leaps around so much that petrol leaks from the Matchless's tank. I try to stem the flow with polythene bags taped under the petrol cap but they're quickly turned to pulp by the caustic fuel. The fumes begin to take their toll and both our heads start to ache across the temples. Pulling up at a village of only a dozen houses, Munavar scours the street, returning with two empty plastic bottles. Meanwhile, I pour the remainder of my water into my Camelbak which adds another two vessels to the tally. Draining the tank of 6 litres of petrol makes a huge difference and in due course the smell diminishes.

Kalaikhum to Khorog is hell and for large tracts of the 240km long ordeal we travel sub 20kmph. Munavar constantly weaves from one side of the road to the other to avoid huge rocks or broken islands of old road, some chunks standing 10″ high in splendid isolation. The Chinese trucks that use this route to return home tow enormous empty trailers which create jarring corrugations. Following them in the dark becomes frustrating, the way ahead obscured by dense shrouds of hovering dirt, and our attempts at overtaking through the murk make it a white knuckle ride. As well as being a likeable chap, Munavar seems to have endless patience and energy and, fuelled by his second can of Red Bull, we continue into the night.

It's 11.50pm when we reach the Lal Hotel in Khorog. Waking the owner, we unload the bike, wheel her into a yard protected by two dogs, then with Munavar's help, ferry my belongings up a wrought iron spiral staircase and into a room. With a well deserved tip in his pocket, which from his reaction is unexpected, Munavar wishes me well and hands me his phone number, scribbled on a scrap of paper, in case I encounter any difficulties during my stay in Khurog.

Lying in bed, waiting for the stomach cramps that came on during the latter part of the drive to recede, I reflect on the day, knowing that I made the right decision. That road could easily have taken me 4 days to negotiate, and most likely broken the bike, me... or both of us.

Day 35. Khorog. 0 miles.

The sound of workmen drilling and cutting wakes me abruptly. I clamber into my clothes and walk along the first floor hallway with bleary eyes, yawning. Opening the door, I take a step and freeze. The spiral staircase I'd climbed in the dark is missing and there's now nothing but air below my outstretched right foot. To have fallen would I have been the stuff of comedy... or tragedy, but fortunately I keep my balance and place the hovering foot back onto the carpet. The staircase, lying on its side, is in the process of being cut up by two men with a grinder. Turning on my heels, I walk to the far end of the corridor to a second door through which another set of steel steps leads down to the courtyard where the Matchless is stored. One of two dogs, a savage wolf-like creature that was snarling in a cage when I arrived last night, comes tearing across the yard and up the steps. Slamming the door shut in the nick of time, I hear it baying with unbridled rage as I return to the first doorway and holler for help!

Khorog is the administrative centre of the GBAO region, a town of approximately 30,000 nestled between barren rock peaks at the confluence of the Ghund and Pyandzh rivers. I walk into the nearby central park where there's a PECTA tourist information booth. The knowledgeable lady sells me a map of the Pamirs and provides information about where I'll find petrol en route to Kyrgyzstan. Before leaving, she asks me to sign the visitor's book. October is certainly the end of the trekking season and I note there are only a dozen or so tourists listed since mid-September. I'm the first to add my name in 3 days.

The park backs onto a fast flowing grey river. Someone has bravely climbed hundreds of metres up the steep rocky scree on its far shores to write a giant message with white stones. Alas, I've no idea what it means. Following poplar lined walkways to a bridge at the far end of town, I turn around and backtrack along the main street, home to a bank, basic shops, local government offices and an internet cafe. Khorog's a peaceful place apart from the minibus station on the far side of the Lal, a hive of activity where 4x4s serving outlying villages jockey for prime position. At 2,200 metres, the heat of the sun warms my bones but there's a freshness to the air so I keep several layers of clothes on.

The latter part of the morning is spent in my room preparing for the next six days. I've researched more about what immediately lies ahead than any other part of the journey and have lugged a lot of gear specially for it. As well as all my camping equipment, I've packed a water filter, a Primus stove that runs on petrol, freeze dried expedition food, nuts and protein bars, merino wool underclothes and socks, winter gloves and a down jacket. What I don't need will be shipped back to the UK from India to reduce weight.

In the afternoon, the hotel manager secures the guard dog in its cage from where, lips curled to reveal yellow teeth, it fixes its eyes on me. After topping up with oil and refilling the petrol tank, I change the bike's carburettor main jet to a smaller one, to compensate for the thinner air, and fit a new air filter. Finally, I check the rest of the machine over and thankfully she's made it through yesterday's tribulations unscathed.

Heading out for food, I bump into two men, a Swiss and a German travelling in an old Land Rover Defender. They've spent the last 4 days driving from Kyrgyzstan along the route I'll follow. Their up-to-the-minute information about the absence of snow on passes, the state of the roads, night temperatures and where to wild camp is particularly helpful.

"But beware," one warns. "In a village about 10km away is the fastest dog we've ever seen. It chased us for ages, running alongside my door at 42kmph like a cheetah."

One of my biggest concerns about the ride is Acute Mountain Sickness (AMS). When I was younger, I trekked to 5400m in Nepal but that took 22 days, allowing plenty of time for my body to acclimatise. On a motorcycle, the rate of ascent is obviously much more dramatic and when riding for two weeks in Ladakh as part of Royal Enfield's 2009 *Himalayan Odyssey*, I suffered badly with altitude sickness. Memories of the drowsiness, headaches and wretched projectile vomiting are still with me. I've brought a prescription drug for the forthcoming climb called Diamox. Although it doesn't prevent AMS, it increases the speed at which the body adapts to higher altitudes, which for a motorcyclist is highly beneficial. My first dose is a precautionary 1/2 tablet taken with dinner.

I'm really up for the challenge the coming days will bring, starting with crossing a 4,200 metre pass tomorrow. As the sun takes an early bow behind the mountains, I gaze to the west and hope that the gathering clouds are not the harbingers of snow.

Day 36. Khorog to Sasyk-kel Lake. 126 miles.

With the bike loaded, I push her past the caged lupine and onto the street. Hot inside multiple layers of clothing, I take a glug of water from my Camelbak then immediately spit it out. It's fizzy and slightly sweet and when I drip some onto my palm, it has a visible pink tint. There, undoubtedly, is the cause of my stomach cramps. Returning to my room, I empty it into the sink, observing an increase in organic matter near the end... that'll be the last time I make the misjudgment of putting fruit juice into a hydration pack! After several rinses, I take it to the breakfast room and half fill the reservoir with boiling water, hoping it will clear out any bacterial residue, then shake, drain and refill with 3 litres of mineral water.

First stop today is Khorog's only petrol station where I fill up with 91. It requires less than a litre but even that small amount may prove vital in the mountains. Turning around and riding east, the town quickly disappears from my mirrors and pulling strongly, the Matchless begins to climb. After a brief stop at a remote army checkpost we come to a diversion, a rough track carved into the dark rock face. Damp and slithery, the trail undulates as we carefully edge round a recently formed lake... unusually high temperatures in the first weeks of July had led to significant glacial melting and a massive flood. Further downstream, the resulting mudflow had blocked the Gunt river, forming a lake which took out the road and destroyed several houses. For almost 6 weeks the Pamir Highway was closed until the completion of this detour. The new lake, which from my elevated position appears deep and silty, remains a threat to Khorog should it swell further and burst its temporary banks.

Clear of the obstruction, the road continues to parallel the river, wending its way along a gorge lined with maples and poplars, their leaves tinged with the yellow of autumn. In charming stone-built villages, children wave or sometimes, rather alarmingly, run into the road and extend a hand for me to give them a flying high-five. At approximately 3000m, with nothing around except distant mountains and the river coursing through its wide, boulder-strewn floodplain, I make my second toilet stop in an hour. Diamox, I'd been warned, increases the speed at which the kidneys function and subsequently, the need to pee rises dramatically. I also notice the beginning of another side effect, slight tingling in the tips of my fingers, but both seem a small price to pay for avoiding AMS. A car carrying half a dozen schoolchildren stops while I'm getting ready to depart. Through his open window, the driver says "As-salamu alaykum" then offers me a large green apple. I accept the gift and they depart, the animated youngsters waving excitedly through the rear window.

Cruising in third, I'm delighted by the lovely riding conditions and as we exit the last of the villages and enter a more barren region, feel a thrill at being alone in such a remote place. Approximately three hours after leaving Khorog, we arrive at a sharp, rising bend in the road and I notice that half way round the surface changes to rock and gravel. From here, the ride to the Koitezek pass is going to be much tougher so I pull over, let the engine cool and to counter the keen wind, wrap up in a further layer. At 3960m, the air's noticeably thinner and my breathing shallow. I take another Diamox pitstop, remount and head for the summit.

The climb has a steep gradient but the Matchless, plugging steadily upwards in second gear, is more than up to it. The surface, comprised mainly of loose gravel on dirt, isn't overly challenging and within ten minutes we've made it to 4272m, the top. I pause but there's little to see on the flat, windswept plateau, and as the engine's struggling at tickover, push straight on. The next couple of kilometres are fairly horrid, the bike jumping around as she hits stones and rocks and I criss cross the track trying to pick a better route. Out of nowhere, a strip of beautiful asphalt appears and we zoom ahead, my spirits soaring at the thought of the worst being over.

It's not. Two minutes and we're back on the rough. Everything is thrown at us... rugged ridges, rocks the size of rugby balls, slippery shingle, potholes, corrugations and sand. In the distance I spot a huge moving cloud, the aftermath of a column of enormous Chinese trucks that pound the loose surface like a seemingly unstoppable force. As they pass, the ground shudders and we're enveloped in thick, suffocating dust. Up on the foot pegs, I strain to keep the bike going, sweating profusely with the effort and because we're going so slowly, my goggles repeatedly steam up. Arms hurting, the recurrent impacts render my hands and fingers ineffective and my legs turn to putty. The atrocious conditions go on, and on, and on.

What feels like an eternity later, but according to the satnav is only 48km from the start of the pass, the track crests a rise and a sealed surface lies before me, looping its way down the side of a large bluff. In the far distance are two verdigris lakes, the furthest being my target for the day. I check the time and am astounded to calculate that over two and a half hours have passed since our last stop. With nightfall fast approaching, there's no time to rest so I let go of the brake lever and begin to descend.

Reaching the ecru coloured plain, a dramatic ring of snow topped mountains visible all around, I snick up to top gear and head towards the lakes, my hands becoming numb as the sweat in my gloves chills. According to the Garmin, we're at 3870 metres and the sun's due to set at 17.36, which is just twenty-five minutes away. There's no traffic for as far as the eye can see which affords a pocket of privacy for secreting myself into a camping spot... but it's quite not as easy as that. Built on foundations of large stones, the road's been raised higher than the surrounding ground and it's impossible to get the Matchless off it. As I continue, I keenly scan the verges for a way down but for 5 kilometres there's not a single opportunity. Just when I'm beginning to despair, the highway angles right but straight ahead, sectioned off by a line of rocks, is a stretch of cracked old road. Much closer to ground level, it continues due east, rejoining the curving new road in the far distance. Overshooting it, I make a quick about-turn, squeeze between two large stones, and ride until I discern a suitable campsite close to the shoreline.

Parking the Matchless, I step onto the dirt, quickly testing its firmness with my boots. There appears to be black sand underneath a thick crust but it's certainly rideable. Back on the bike, I ease off the road and head in the direction of a dip which fortuitously contains two deep hollows, one bike sized and the other almost made-to-measure for a tent. Standing, I can still make out the road but once squatted inside the dip, it disappears. Perfect. I ride into the smaller hollow and the rear wheel digs through the top layer, burying itself in sand as the engine stalls with a bang. The ensuing silence is dramatic. The Matchless stays upright even when I climb off but I wedge a couple of large flat stones under the sump guard to make her extra secure for the night. As the daylight's almost gone, I hurry round setting up the tent and throwing everything inside, then with my head torch on, unpack my stove and heat up dinner.

It doesn't take long for the air to turn bitterly cold. I climb into a double layer of sleeping bags and through the tent's open door, stare at the sky. With zero light pollution and no moon, the fulgent stars overlap in layers of unimaginable depth. The wind gradually increases in strength, rousing me from my reverie so I zip the door up and snuggle down, sleep taking hold as my brain adjusts to the gentle flapping sounds of the flysheet.

Camping beside Sasyk-kel Lake.

Day 37. Sasyk-kel Lake to Murghab. 77 miles.

When I first awaken my watch informs me it is -6°. Last night's wind has blown itself out and all's quiet. Although it's light, there's no point rousing myself before the sun's risen above the mountains and heated the tent, so I roll over, bury my head in soft down and slip back into sleep. Within an hour, a rapid transformation takes place as the first warming rays turn my little haven a warm orange. Within 10 minutes the inside temperature soars to 12° and I get up. As I eat breakfast, I admire sharp reflections on the chilly cyan waters of Sasyk-kel, then pack everything away and tackle the marooned bike. Extracting the stones from beneath the sumpguard, I wedge them under the rear wheel and rather wheezily rock her backwards and forwards until there's enough momentum to roll out of the trench. As though in slow motion, I heave her onto firmer ground and thrust another flat stone under the sidestand then step back and catch my breath.

Once everything's strapped on, I kick her over then pick a careful path to the old road, twice almost sinking back into the sand. Putting the rest of my riding gear on, I give unheard thanks to Brendan for the second pair of gloves he sent... the ones I rode with yesterday are still wringing wet with perspiration. I pull down my goggles and set off towards the new highway, the sound of the exhaust inharmoniously reverberating through the vast empty landscape.

North of the Hindu Kush, south of the Tien Shan and east of the Karakoram and Himalayan ranges, the Pamir mountains are known locally as the 'roof of the world'. The greatest part of the range is situated within Tajikistan, four of its peaks towering above the 7000m mark. The Pamir Highway, classified as route M-41, traverses the Pamirs from Khorog to Osh in northern Kyrgyzstan, and is the world's second highest international road, after the Karakoram Highway. Work started on the route in the 18th Century when the Russian Empire, as part of its Great Game strategy, constructed a track to expedite the movement of troops to their southern boundary and thus counter the threat of the ever-expanding British Empire. Between 1933 and 1934, the USSR fully tar sealed the road, no mean feat in those days, again to facilitate the faster transportation of its army. Much neglected, with many sections missing all their top surface, it's hoped that China will assist with reconstruction, especially in view of the damage caused by Chinese trucks in recent times.

Riding takes all my concentration as the road has many concealed dips. At 50kmph, I suddenly hit an unseen shallow trough, the bike jolting hard as it bottoms out, flinging me up off the saddle. Almost simultaneously, blows shoot up my arms, jolting my shoulders and neck as the front wheel hits the top of the rise and returns to a level surface. Some of the depressions are like shell holes, more easily avoided but nonetheless frightening when passed at speed. It proves to be a very physical experience and I work hard, constantly weaving the bike around the dips, the waves and the ripples. Heading west, two loaded trucks, a Pajero and a Landcruiser are the only other road users we encounter... just as well in view of my need to utilise the full width of the highway.

Under intensely blue skies, which have a brittle quality I can only attribute to the altitude, the surrounding meadows are covered with dry looking shrubs peeking a few inches out of the ground. Large rounded hills and rocky outcrops, a dusting of snow on their north facing sides, provide a sharp contrast to the muted ochre tones and gentle contours of the central flats they border. I adore the puffy white clouds that blow across the sun, causing raw umber shadows that flit over the landscape. In their shade, however, the air temperature falls dramatically and I find myself slowing and accelerating as I follow patches of sunshine along the road. Running faultlessly, the Matchless feels like a friend, my companion in this largely uninhabited land and with increasing regularity I hold one-sided conversations with her.

According to the map, there should be two more passes at approximately 4100m before I reach the town of Murghab. With the altimeter hovering around 4000m most of the time, I'm still anticipating a steep climb when, on a distant hillside, white dots burgeon into the shapes of houses. I'm quite taken aback... it's Murghab already. Minutes later, I come to a barrier across the road, a small blockhouse to one side. No one comes out so I knock on the door and enter. The first room's empty apart from a desk and chair so I walk into the back room where three soldiers playing cards sit next to an oil heater, their untidy cot beds pressed against the far wall. Without checking my passport, which is highly unusual, one of the men reluctantly gets up, leads me outside and raises the barrier.

The town doesn't have a clearly defined centre so I ride along its eastern road in search of a petrol pump. High above to the left I spot a house, a large blue sign along its eaves proclaiming, 'Erali Guest House.' Instinctively, I turn towards it and ride up a steep clay trail, the Matchless only just making it to the top in first gear. On hearing my arrival, a young man, Ahmed, comes out of the weatherbeaten front door and welcomes me. Not entirely sure why I've ridden here, as my intention's to camp again tonight, I nevertheless follow him inside and instantly fall in love with the place. There's one sunny room most of the way across the front, the guests' lounge / dining room. It's just wide enough to house a long, low table down its middle with embroidered cushions placed on each side for seating. The bedroom, bedecked with rustic rugs, old wooden cabinets and tin chests, contains a pile of rolled futons. It's so charming and cosy it is hard to say no and at under £5 per night, I plump for staying.

Settling into the guests' lounge, I begin reading a book. A lady enters, introducing herself as Apal. Dressed in velvety purple robes and a simple white flowery headscarf, she's the head of the family that runs the homestay. Giving me a warm smile, she places a large enamel teapot, a tiny handleless teacup and a plate of biscuits on the table. It's green tea, a great remedy for a weary traveller, and as she pours a cup, a cluster of leaves settles to the bottom. She then asks if I'd like a shower.

"Wait one hour please," she replies when I say yes and sets straight off to begin preparations.

Through the windows I watch Apal carrying several bucket loads of water to a small wooden outhouse, smoke chuffing from a blackened chimney at its side. Sipping cup after cup of tea, I gaze across the valley then get out my maps and consider the journey's progress. I'm filled with respect and admiration for my old bike, which has taken a huge amount of stick but is still going strong. I'm also pleased with how my body's bearing up, showing no negative symptoms due to altitude beside shortness of breath and no aches and pains from the bad roads that a couple of Ibuprofen can't fix. Tomorrow I'll cross a pass at 4600m and I still have a day up my sleeve before the scheduled crossing into China.

Some time later, Apal pokes her ahead through the door and tells me the shower's ready. Entering the smoky wooden shack is like stepping into a sauna and I can hardly get my thermals off fast enough. The shower room's simplicity itself, a floor of open timber decking and an old steel boiler standing in a corner, heated by the embers of a wood fire. From a tap, I half fill an old tin pail with boiling water then top it up with cold until it reaches optimal temperature. Taking a plastic scoop, I throw piping hot water over myself. It's basic but absolutely wonderful and I don't stop until all the water's gone.

With portentous clouds closing in once more, the sky darkens and night settles on Murghab. Somewhere nearby, a generator fires up and a few flickering lights come weakly to life. After dinner, another sachet of dried camping food, I peruse the guest book for some time then head for the bedroom where two heavy cotton duvets have been placed on top of a rolled out futon... I couldn't wish for more.

Day 38. Murghab to Karakul. 77 miles.

Breakfast is a fried egg with inch thick crusty bread that I tear into strips and smear with sticky home-made apricot jam followed by lashings of green tea. As I'm ready to leave, Apal hands me a piece of paper on which she's written the name of a homestay in Karakul, her brother-in-law's place. I stash it away just in case I decide not to camp. Saying a fond farewell, I descend to road level, a rather hair raising experience, then head to the bazaar. Skittering down narrow unpaved lanes formed between houses, I arrive at the main shopping street... about 20 rusty shipping containers strung along a gravel path. Inside each one is a shop selling everything from paraffin to hats. From the sparse choice of fresh food, I manage to stock up with enough provisions for a couple of lunches, closely watched by groups of older men who stand around chewing the fat. Riding one street level lower, I find the gas station, a rundown joint where the aged generator that powers the fuel pump is coaxed back to life each time a customer arrives. As we begin to fill the tank, alarm bells ring. The petrol smells off. There's nothing to be done as they're the town's only supplier and I ride away praying that it won't cause a problem.

Out on the open road, I'm aware of a lag in acceleration but it could just be my mind playing tricks, so I try to let go of my concerns and immerse myself in the spectacle of the Pamirs. At first the road is fair and, apart from one speeding 4x4, deserted. The ascent from Murghab, at 3600m, is gradual and encircled by unforgettable lunar landscapes. We make good progress, taking an hour and a half to climb to 4400m where the asphalt vanishes and the incline becomes severe. Swinging round a tight, shingly S bend in first gear, I'm confronted by a rise so steep it resembles an Olympic ski jump. With no momentum to speak of, I gun the engine and lunge forward but our speed's quickly quelled by the frightful gradient. Willing the bike on, the engine slows until the pop pop pop of each revolution feels like a struggling heartbeat. It's a close run thing but just in time, the grade flattens, we pull over a lip and gradually pick up speed.

Aided by a tailwind, we continue towards the summit. The road's now grievously potholed and, as the rear wheel kicks out of one gravel filled hole and the front plunges into another, I hear a loud clang behind. Stopping abruptly, I flick out the stand and run back down the hill, desperately trying to outpace the momentum of a red fuel bottle that's been thrown out of a saddlebag. Clutching my dented but still intact prize, the walk back uphill's far slower and with no other sounds, the noise of laboured breathing rasps loudly in my ears. I tie it back into its pouch then, with bated breath, attempt to restart the bike, which at these heights and with duff fuel could well be a problem. The redoubtable machine settles into a regular rhythm at my first try and five minutes later we reach the Ak-Baital Pass... 4665 metres!

There's little worth photographing, the pass narrow and hemmed in with sandy rock formations, so after the briefest of pauses to savour our moment of triumph, I ride on. The gentle downslope soon flattens, opening out to expansive flatlands with rounded knolls edging the horizon. The road, now dead straight, is corrugated, with hard ridges about 30cm apart that shake the bike ruthlessly. Washboarding, as it's known, is one of the most detestable surfaces that a motorcyclist will experience. For a rigid framed machine, it's nothing short of the work of the devil. I try every conceivable line of attack to lessen the vibrations but nothing makes any difference. We shake, rattle and judder horrendously. I've read that if you ride over corrugations fast enough, it's possible to nullify their effects by skimming over the tops of the ridges. I try but it makes matters worse, causing the rear wheel to jump and kangaroo so I slow back down. There's nothing to be done but grit it out in 1st and 2nd gears, stopping to rest every twenty minutes or so. The stunning backdrop vanishes from my perception as I focus on the Matchless's survival and staying upright. Thirty two kilometres later it ends and tarmac, beautiful, sweet, heavenly tarmac recommences. I'm almost inclined to get off and kiss it.

As we descend further, swooping joyfully round long bends, snowcapped peaks appear ahead, then, way below in a valley, Lake Karakul, an electric blue tract of water with a ramshackle collection of houses close to its eastern shore. Slowly approaching the village, I avoid clumps of fresh manure across the road and stop. Checking the time, which is 3.40pm. I consider whether I should camp or try Apal's recommended homestay. Camping's great, but once it's dark, in approximately 2 hours, I'll have little to do but sleep. Staying in accommodation will not only give me a chance to meet more local people, it'll also help them financially and with winter just around the corner, I guess any additional income will be welcome. I ride into town and begin searching for the guest house.

Karakul's like a ghost town, but when I turn round and take a second run along the central road, I spot an elderly woman, swathed in many thick layers, collecting dung in a bucket. I tell her the name of the homestay,
    "Aigerim," but she looks bewildered.
She takes the proffered piece of paper out of my hand but can't read so instead, leads me around the back of a whitewashed house to a man who's fixing his station wagon. He inspects the paper and instantly recognises the name, calling out,
    "Aigerim... Aigerim."
I'm certain that's exactly how I said it! Laughing, I say thanks and follow his directions, pulling up outside the homestead which proves to be practically the last building in the village.

The owners come out of their home, a wizened man and his younger wife, the lady tenderly nestling their one month old daughter who's swaddled in a blanket tied over her mother's shoulder like a sling. Their greetings are warmly attentive and they unlock a side gate so I can park the Matchless within a small compound before ferrying my bags indoors. Stiff and cold, it takes a while to get my boots off but finally I step inside and follow the patiently waiting lady to the back room. Lit by a solitary glowworm bulb, its walls are covered in traditional colourful hangings and the floor in layers of deep red scatter rugs on top of which sit neat piles of bedrolls and blankets. To one side there's a low square table and in the centre of the room, a radiantly hot steel stove, its glowing flue travelling crookedly up to the ceiling. As the owner leaves to get me a pot of tea, I look at the huge pile of luggage on the floor and shake my head, not for the first time thinking I'm carrying way too much.

On the far side of the table, blankets move and a woman's head groggily emerges from beneath... I realise it's not just my gear after all and as I look more closely, see that her *Ortlieb* bags probably outnumber mine! Introducing herself as Tara, a cyclist from Canada, she tells me she's taken 2 days to ride from Murghab having previously stayed 4 nights at the Erali as she'd been sick. With little dignity, I lie on my back to wriggle out of my motorcycle trousers. After then extracting myself from multiple layers of tops. I join her at the table where, along with the tea, we're brought bread and homemade blackcurrant jam.

Tara's been on the road for almost six months, having flown from her home in Canada to Ulan Bator in Mongolia with her bright yellow bike named Dozer. Her ride to date has taken her through Mongolia, China, Pakistan and northern India. Due to visa difficulties, she had to fly to Dushanbe, and having ridden the Wakan valley and Pamir Highway for almost 4 weeks, she plans to catch a flight from Kyrgyzstan to Greece where she'll work as a volunteer on an organic farm. She explains she'll be known as a WWOOFer, the acronym for people working under the banner of *World Wide Opportunities on Organic Farms*, an organisation set up to give first-hand experience in organic and ecologically sound growing methods. After wintering in Greece, her intention is to ride to Cape Town.

Around 6pm, dinner is brought to the table. It consists of a heaped plate of sliced boiled potatoes smothered in thick yellow butter, which I presume to be unpasteurised. My intuition is to give it a miss so I ask for boiling water and have another expedition meal instead. Tara wolfs hers down, confessing that she's struggled to get enough to eat in the last couple of weeks,

"There's only so many tins of fish and pots of peanut butter I can carry on my bike," she remarks when I offer her my plate of spuds too.
She eagerly dispatches it all.

A couple of hours fly by in non-stop conversation, mainly travel related. Working as a tree planter in the extreme north of Canada to save for this trip, Tara's spent numerous nights alone in her tent, sometimes spotted by locals who've taken her in and on more than one occasion, by police who've made her pack up and move to a hotel. Long distance cycling, as I've already heard from Hans, is hard yakka, and the combination of icy temperatures, thin air and tough climbs make this region especially arduous... motorcycling's a breeze by contrast. Like me, she'll leave for Kyrgyzstan in the morning, estimating two days to reach the town of Sary Tash. As I'll spend my spare day before the Chinese border in Sary Tash, we arrange to meet up at another homestay she's heard of, The Pink House.

At about 9.30pm, I make a last visit to the outside loo. With my headtorch on, I open the door of the open-roofed stone dunny and carefully position my feet on wooden boards each side of a black hole. Looking upwards, the heavens once more putting on a fabulous show, I shiver in the sub zero temperatures, suddenly appreciating my own bathroom in a whole new way. Back in the room, lying snugly under copious thick blankets with the glow of the flickering fire dancing on the walls, I say goodnight to my roommate and slip into a deep sleep.

32km of hard packed corrugations en route to Karakul.

Day 39. Karakul, Tajikistan,
to Sary Taşh, Kyrgyzstan. 69 miles.

The owner comes into the room just before 7.00am and lights the fire with a combination of dried roots and dung. Ten minutes later she returns with our breakfast - fried egg, bread and the mandatory pot of green tea. I drag myself out of the warmth of my bed to join Tara at the table. I was half aware of her torch flicking on and off during the night and she wearily discloses that the greasy potatoes have devastated her stomach. Having spent several miserable hours on the loo, (god... that loo, I think to myself), she doesn't feel strong enough to ride today.

Overcast, the air temperature is noticeably chilly when I step outside. Unlike previous mornings, the Matchless hasn't been heated by the sun and the engine oil has thickened. It takes full choke and six of my biggest kicks to spin the flywheels fast enough for her to fire up. Tara and all of the homestay family come outside to wave me off. Waving back, I let out the clutch and turn north.

Underneath the dark clouds, Lake Karakul looks dulled and a howling wind forms choppy waves around its shores. The same wind bites indiscriminately into me, numbing my nose and fingers as the Matchless plods on, steadily climbing up the narrow road. The first pass, at just over 4300 metres, is still on sealed roads but once we begin to descend, all bitumen disappears and washboard once again rears its ugly head. My joints, especially in my hands, are still aching from yesterday's trials so I rest for a minute, pop a couple of Ibuprofen, then gird my loins and bounce onto the corrugations.

This time they only last around 6km, morphing into gravel, which is much more manageable. The road twists and turns skywards and on the apex of a bend, I kill the engine and take in the panoramic spectacle of statuesque mountains capped with snow, the ribbon of a river glinting far below in the sandy floor of the valley. Downing my last packet of nuts, I check the bike over, tighten the luggage straps, then continue. As I round the corner, I see a cluster of buildings ahead. The Tajik borderpost, at the summit of Kyzyl-Art Ashuu Pass, is no more than 200m away.

At some heavy steel gates, I halt. Two scruffy men wander out of a building and ask me to accompany them inside. Undoubtedly, they're the most unkempt pair of border officials I've ever seen. Parking the bike, I follow. Without removing helmet or gloves, I pass through the outer door and am instantly taken aback by the disorder and squalor... rusty tin cans, screwed up newspapers and food packaging are scattered around the dirt floor and the charred remains of a fire smoulders in one corner. Through another door, there's a stark room with just a table and one chair. A third official, who stands up to greet me, is wearing stained tracksuits pants, a tatty coat and a wooly hat with long ear flaps. Dutifully, he hands me a form to complete in order to clear customs then politely asks for $10 ecology tax. It's quite likely a scam but in this inhospitable place there's no way I'm becoming involved in protracted negotiations, so cough up the remainder of my Somani, which is considerably less than $10. He gladly accepts it and I'm left to find my own way back to the bike. Outside, the gates open and I exit the woebegone hole.

I'm immediately halted by a young soldier who looks to be somewhere in his late teens.

"Stay on bike," he says as I pull up the valve lifter. "I take passport inside."
I hand it over then wait. Returning with it stamped just a couple of minutes later, he asks,

"Cigarettes?"
I shake my head. With little hope in his voice, he tries once more.

"Chocolate?"
If I had some, I'd certainly give it to him. Talk about getting the short straw in postings... at 4280m it's one of the world's highest and most remote border crossings. On such a bitterly cold day, I can't help wondering what kind of miserable existence he must endure through the freezing winter months. With a hangdog look, he waves goodbye.

The Kyrgyz frontier post at Bor Dobo is 25km further on. Starting with a steeply winding downhill track, the route through no man's land is a treacherous amalgam of rocks and gravel. Surviving a series of slippery switchbacks, I rotate my shoulders to release tension then, as the road flattens out, pass a solitary stone house beside which a man strenuously chops wood with a Herculean axe. I wonder if, residing between countries, he considers himself Kyrgyz or Tajik... though possibly, in wilderness such as this, raw survival is considerably higher on the agenda than a sense of nationality.

The view ahead is stupendous, a steep sided valley set amongst sharp peaks, all tainted green by lichen and dusted with snow. Thrown around on more rough stuff, I continue until the trail halts at a river. I stop to assess the fast flowing waters, about 3m wide and 30cm deep. The riverbed, formed from rounded rocks, seems rideable but the steep shingly banks are a concern. I roll down in first gear, concentrate as we swoosh along the bottom then accelerate hard up the far side. A doddle and clean tyres to boot! Stopping, I look back up the valley and am wowed by the sight of what we've just ridden through... the dominating mountains, forbiddingly dark and crusted with ice and snow, seem close enough to touch.

Twenty minutes later I spot more buildings. With just a couple of hundred metres left to ride into Kyrgyzstan, a Landcruiser races past, kicking up a trail of stones that showers the bike. It's the first vehicle I've seen heading in either direction all day and sod's law personified, the driver pips me to the border by 30 seconds! Pulling up next to it at a lone booth that's not much bigger than a telephone box, I join a queue formed by its four passengers. According to the decal on the car's door, they're aid workers from the Aga Khan Foundation. When their passports have been stamped, each says hello then hurries back to the warmth of the car. Within five minutes, it's my turn.

This border crossing could be tricky as I'm switching from one passport to another and holding two passports is something that officials sometimes find suspicious. Brimming with forced bonhomie, I meet the eye of the officer and begin prattling, trying my damnedest to distract him as he flicks through the pages of my passport. Fortunately, he appears more interested in reading the names and addresses of my nearest and dearest, which I've written in the back, than looking for a Tajik visa or exit stamp. With a nod he impresses his mark onto a blank page and hands the document back. I'm able to breath freely again!

Customs present reams of paperwork but I'm given a comfortable chair in a warm office so I can fill it in. Finally I'm told I have to pay another $10 tax for the bike and as I've very little left in US Dollars, ask if I can pay in Euros. Obligingly, the official accepts, giving me change in Kyrgyzstani Som, a welcome endorsement of the legitimacy of the charge and his honesty.

The final stages of the journey to Sary Tash are on an exposed road that slopes gently uphill, straight into a fierce headwind. Pressing myself as flat to the tank as possible, I ride it in 3rd, the engine working hard to overcome the force of the elements. My first impression of the town doesn't inspire. With no uplifting colour, everything appears grey: the road; buildings; countryside and even the sky. Nobody's out on the streets and a recently crashed truck sits abandoned in the middle of the road, its driver's side wing and window crumpled inwards. Dark clouds roll down gullies in the nearby hills as I scan each side of the road searching for a sign saying The Pink House or Homestay. At the far end of town, amidst all the dreariness, a single colourful building stands out. It's not actually called the pink house... it is one! Swinging off the road, I pull up beside a vibrant fuchsia single story dwelling.

The owner, a bandy legged man with a crinkly face, invites me inside. He can't speak any English but is soon joined by his granddaughter who can. I'm shown a room with two single beds, wall to wall shelving full of pictures and basic household possessions and a coal-burning steel box stove that's pumping out heat. It's ideal. Her grandfather then leads me back outside and indicates where I can store the Matchless in his coalshed. The entrance is at the side of the house through an area covered in slippery green patches which indicate the recent presence of some sort of livestock.

As night falls, I nip outside to the loo, a shed fabricated from open wood paneling that's located at the bottom of the garden. To reach it I have to hop down steps made from tread-bare car tyres packed with soil then cross a stream on a single plank bridge. When I emerge and begin making my way back to the house, it's started snowing. Tomorrow's a day off but snow on the roads could have repercussions for days to come. My border crossing into China is critical to the journey and from here there's no way of contacting the company who've arranged it should conditions shut everything down. I decide that crossing the bridge to the toilet will suffice for today and try my best to put it out of mind.

Day 40. Sary Taşh. 0 miles.

Just before 8am the granddaughter wakes me from my slumbers and asks me to move to another room... it transpires that I'm actually in her grandparents own bedroom as, unknown to me, a female Malaysian cyclist was in the main guest room last night. I get dressed then go outside to check the weather.

Viewed from the elevated top end of town, the godforsaken appearance of Sary Tash is softened by the velvety snow, which continues to fall gently from leaden clouds. The road, I'm relieved to see, is completely clear and I observe a truck throwing dirty spray up from its rear wheels as it trundles past. It's heading in the direction of the capital, Bishkek, which my brain insists on twisting to fishcake.

Clad in a bright yellow jacket and carrying her cycle helmet, a petite woman pushes an overladen bicycle round the corner and quietly says hello. She can't be much taller than 5' and the bike, a pole at its rear resplendent with a row of brightly coloured flags, appears enormous next to her. Securing her helmet, she says goodbye and sets off uphill towards Osh, quickly disappearing from sight behind a mantle of snowflakes. These long-distance cyclists are made of tough stuff!

My new room is an assault on the eyes. Packed to bursting, it contains a long wooden table beside a settee easily big enough to seat seven. The settee's draped in a lurid crimson flower-pattered throw and has equally garish fleecy cushions scattered along it. One end wall is dominated by a giant open-fronted cupboard packed with stacks of gaudy blankets and pillows that sport all the colours of the rainbow. Pinned along its top are sixteen green, gold and red rosettes which clash with everything else and hanging down from the ceiling are metre-long orange and silver satin twizzles. The remaining walls are completely covered in screaming loud carpets and a shelf running along one of them supports four stuffed minks and two animals that look like pigmy badgers. Squeezed onto the brightly carpeted floor are three single beds plus four rolled up mattresses. It's not to my taste yet, in a quirky sort of way, it's delightful.

The granddaughter enters to ask what I'd like for breakfast. I struggle to grasp her name in Kyrgyz but she offers an evocative translation into English.

"It means 'The sun coming up.'"

How exquisite!

'The sun coming up' returns shortly with sticky jam made from whole apricots, half a loaf of bread, a fried egg and a pot of aromatic black tea which has a rich, smoky flavour. The egg's like rubber and sits in a pool of oil. Picking it up by a corner, I let the worst drain off, thinking there's enough to lubricate all the bike's cables, a chore I must undertake soon. I dab it dry with a tissue and look for somewhere to place it but the corner tears off in my fingers and most of the egg slaps into the pool of oil! Back to the drawing board.

After sorting through all my gear and drinking a leisurely second pot of tea, I wrap up warm and head out to the shed where I do oil the Matchless's cables

170

then adjust the brakes, change the spark plug, re-waterproof the magneto pick up and check the tyre pressures. The thermometer reads 1° so with coagulated oil in mind, I wheel her outside, onto the main road then freewheel 100m downhill to the town's only petrol station. It's as drab and ramshackle as the rest of Sary Tash but the owner's helpful, changing some euros for me and filling the tank. Even though I'm only at 3170m, pushing back uphill takes all my strength and a few metres before the shed's entrance, I'm forced to stop. Kicking out the side stand, I bend double over the saddle, my chest painfully heaving for more oxygen.

Once the bike's safely locked away, I walk across the road to a forlorn looking shop. The goods available inside are extremely limited, with household utilities such as buckets and brooms, large trays of white eggs and packets of biscuits most prevalent. There are no fresh vegetables whatsoever. Three children, two boys and a girl still in their school uniforms, are in charge and with much teasing and goading from the others, the oldest does her best to talk with me. A man, wearing a traditional black and white tall felt hat known as a Kalpak, walks in and approaches the counter. Without a word, he points to a bottle of vodka that sits next to two shot glasses on a silver tray. One of the boys fills a glass, collects a few som in payment then waits for the man to knock it back and return the empty glass. My eyes nearly pop out of my head as I watch the scenario unfold but to them, it's normality. I spend the residue of my som on waxy milk chocolate and leaving the children giddily chasing each other behind the counter, head for the pink house.

A bench outside the front door has so far provided shelter for a scraggy dog. It's nowhere to be seen and the grandfather and two of his cronies are sitting on the seat. Snow settles delicately on their heads and shoulders as they smoke their strong smelling cigarettes and shoot the breeze. The grandmother, a rotund woman dressed in what looks like a floral dressing gown held together by a wide belt, opens the front door and yells at them. She's obviously not to be messed with as all three jump up simultaneously, two scuttling off down the road and her husband hurrying indoors. As I'm about to follow him, a herd of dark brown silken goats descend from the road and cut across the front of the house. With bells clanging, they pass an old Russian truck parked in the adjoining garden then gather in a small compound, filling the air with their high pitched bleats.

The rest of the afternoon passes peacefully as I sit in warmth, my feet up on the sofa. Around 5pm, there's a muffled noise as the outside door opens and a woman's voice faintly calls,

"Hello?"

I open my bedroom door and there, cloaked in snowflakes, stands Tara.

"You're a madwoman!" I say, laughing. "How on earth did you get over that pass in this?"

"I didn't.... a car picked me up and I can tell you I'm incredibly glad it did," she answers.

While I help with her luggage and secure her bike next to mine, she tells the tale of her journey.

"I rode most of the way up the first pass but the snow became so thick I had to get off and push. I didn't want to give up but it was impossible to continue. Just as I decided to turn around and head back to Karakul, a 4x4 arrived and offered me a lift. The driver strapped my bike to his roof and charged me $20 to get here. I couldn't have done it any other way, in fact, there were times we were sliding around so much that I thought we might not make it. He was a really experienced driver though and here I am!"

We head to the garage so Tara can change money then walk to the store where the children have been replaced by a ruddy faced woman. Once she's stocked up with snacks, we go back to our room and settle in for another night of vociferous travel talk.

To get to the Chinese border crossing at Irkeshtam tomorrow, I have to go over a pass at 3900m. The road is approximately 75km long and has recently been rebuilt in cooperation with the Chinese government. I'm expected to meet my guide at 11.00am, so set my alarm for 6.30. On my final visit to the loo, I gaze upwards at clear skies then across at the road which appears jet black. It all looks good for the morning.

Snow's on its way! Sary Tash.

Day 41. Sary Taşh, Kyrgyzstan to Kashgar, China. 197 miles.

Although the sky's brilliantly clear as I wheel the Matchless out of the coal shed, the sun hasn't yet reached this corner of Sary Tash and the thermometer reads -5°. Wearing copious layers of warm clothes, I struggle to get my waterproofs over my shoulders so Tara comes to the rescue, tugging them into position. Once loaded, I attempt to start the bike but the engine feels as if it's lubricated with tar. It takes many attempts before she hesitatingly fires, at which point Tara takes over throttle duties while I put on my facemask, helmet and gloves. Lowering goggles into place, I say farewell to her for the second time then manoeuvre out of the gates, taking the left fork onto the China highway.

Surrounded by a dazzling white landscape, the road's an asphalt delight that steadily climbs out of town. Within 20 minutes I've completely lost contact with fingers and toes and have to stop, first jogging up and down the road while intermittently stamping my feet, then toasting my hands on the engine. The altimeter reads 3315m when I swing my leg back over and set off again. Neither the cold nor the gradient slow the Matchless and I watch our altitude reach 3400 then 3450 meters. Silvery patches of frozen snow begin to appear on the road but they're easy enough to steer around. At 3,520m they become more of a nuisance, great long strips that broaden then taper again. I slow for a right hand bend that has a solitary dwelling with a rusty bulldozer set back on the left. Ahead, completely covered in sheet ice, the frigid road shines like glass so I brake hard and pull over near to the house. Climbing off to test the surface, I almost come a cropper... it's totally unridable.

Alerted by the sound of the Matchless, three rough looking men I guess to be road workers come out of the building and crunch their way towards us. One points to the road, vigorously shaking his head from side to side. He squats and draws a curved line in the snow which I take to be the route of the main highway. Adding a straight line, he forms it into a D shape then points down a snowy trail that branches off to the left. It's a barely discernible track that, crucially, heads slightly downhill. Following more hand gestures from the man, I grasp that this is a 12km shortcut that avoids the 3900m pass. There's no option but to take it so I shake all their hands and remount the bike, setting off with considerable trepidation.

Stones and small rocks poke through the snow in places but generally the covering layer is hard and slippery, the result of heavy vehicles passing over it yesterday then freezing overnight. In 1st gear, I guide the bike forward, repeating over and over again in my head,

"Don't touch the front brake. Don't touch the front brake."

Ahead, my eyes trace a line of telegraph poles but there are no other distinguishable features beyond the faint pearl white track which lies in front of an imposing, mountainous backdrop.

Further on, a thicker drift of snow covers most of the path so I ease over towards its right edge. One second I'm riding, the next my shoulder crashes into the ground as the Matchless tumbles over, settling hard on top of my left leg. The engine stalls and I'm immediately conscious of sharp, rapid breathing resounding inside my crash helmet. Nothing moves except my slowly spinning front wheel and when it stops, there's boundless silence. From under the tank bag I see petrol trickling down the tank and dripping onto the snow. It jolts me into action. Time to get up. My left leg's caught under a saddlebag so I kick hard with my right boot until it shifts far enough backwards to drag my trapped foot out... try doing that with aluminium panniers!

Getting to my feet, I quickly scan the route I've taken. The start of the track's at least a kilometre back, completely out of sight, and nothing's coming uphill towards me. I'm absolutely alone and there's no hope of righting the Matchless with all my luggage on, so I begin unclipping straps and hauling everything off as quickly as possible. When only the saddlebags remain, and with a jet of fuel still shooting out of the filler cap breather, I take hold of the bike and heave her up. Careful not to slip, I wheel her to the side of the track and rock the rear stand into place. Safe, I take a minute to slow my racing heart and assess the damage - none to myself and only slightly bent crashbars and timing-side footpeg on the bike. I then take a panoramic look around at the frozen wilderness. What on earth am I doing here in these conditions? Paramount to anything is the fact that it's China or bust, so piece by piece I begin loading everything back on.

Half an hour after the fall, I tensely recommence the ride. The front wheel instantly slips and we dance sideways across the trail, the rear eventually biting enough for me to regain control. A crosswind hits as we round a craggy outcrop and a flurry of whipped up snow drives into us. The Matchless slides again and I stamp down hard with my boot, just managing to stay upright. Ever so gradually, as we lose height, the snow and ice dissolve and more bare earth begins to show through, making conditions far less harrowing. We toil along in 1st and 2nd gears until ahead I see an incredibly sharp rise with a warning triangle tied to a post on its upper lip. Hoping it leads to nothing too perilous, I roar up it and like the cork popping from a champagne bottle, become momentarily airborne before landing on the main highway. As I stop to find my bearings, I behold the most awesome scene. To my right, snow and ice spill down the jagged peaks of the Pamirs, like rich white sauce down the sides of Christmas pudding, into a deep valley way below the level of the road.

"Wow... wow... oh wow!" I call out loud as we get underway, my eyes only half looking in the direction we're heading as I try to impress the sublime beauty into my memory forever.

The black tarmac, winding downhill, is completely clear and with no further hindrance, I reach the Kyrgyzstan border post. There's a chain across the road under which a couple of men carrying old card suitcases duck with agility. I approach the soldier on duty and ask if there's a problem.

"Closed. Eat," he says. "Open two."

It's only 12.20pm. Enormously frustrated, there's nothing for it but to wait. I check the bike over again then seek shelter from the biting wind behind a concrete blockhouse, making myself a sandwich from Pink House bread and cheese. At 2.00pm precisely, the soldier nods to me and drops the chain to the ground. With the Matchless already running, I engage 1st gear and ride towards the immigration department. My passport's stamped in under a minute and the casual, cheerful soldiers tell me there's no need to bother with customs! As I gleefully shoot up a hill towards the Chinese border, I reflect that I'm not too far behind schedule and hopefully my escort will still be waiting. Exiting a corner, I see a grand building on the left crowned by a Chinese flag, bold red with 5 yellow stars, that flaps loudly on its roof. A glass fronted sentry box is positioned at the roadside and a 3m wrought iron gate, resplendent with golden dragons, completely closes the way ahead. Halting, I first take in its substantial padlock then notice a soldier in the guard box who stares straight ahead with a fixed gaze. Pulling in the decompressor, I prepare for another delay, my head shaking in exasperation at the stupidity of unsynchronised lunch breaks on an international frontier.

At 2.45pm the gates open and I accelerate through, pass a line of waiting westbound trucks then ride for a further kilometre until I reach the upper Chinese immigration post, stopping under a corrugated iron canopy that's adjacent to a large office building. A spiky haired soldier in a bright green uniform comes out. Ethnically Han Chinese, his facial features are strikingly different from those of the Kyrgyz's and Tajik's I've seen over the last week or so. The way that dramatic cultural and ethnic changes play out either side of a man-made political boundary always fascinates me and is usually one of the thrills of travel. In relation to The People's Republic of China, however, I'm aware it's a contentious issue.

The soldier's mouth opens into a toothy smile so wide that it creases all of his face and he shouts inside for more of his colleagues to join us. As they gather around the bike, I hear a voice calling from a distance. A young man in jeans and a navy leather jacket bounds over, waving a sheaf of papers at the soldiers. It turns out to be Amzulla, my escort.

"Where have you been?" he asks. "I have been so worried, you are four hours late!"

I begin to explain about the crash and mismatched lunch breaks but he urgently interrupts,

"Quick. We must hurry. This is only the upper border post. We must travel 140km to the lower station where immigration and customs are. They close at 5 o'clock so come on, let's get going!"

The soldiers, however, have other ideas. They want to check through all my gear so instruct me to take it off the bike and carry it inside. Amzulla leaps into action, relaying each piece through the door as I unfasten it. When I finally follow him inside, tool bag and spare tyre in hand, I'm shocked by what I see... the modern concrete building is nothing but an empty shell. There's no furniture, no fittings, the walls are bare and only four naked light bulbs dangle from the ceiling. In the centre is a tin wastepaper basket where paper and fragments of timber are being burned. The soldiers begin rooting through my possessions and a senior officer joins us, asking to see my camera. I hand it over and he begins scrolling through the photos on it. Satisfied it contains no indecent or anti-Chinese images, he then asks if I have a computer. I produce my tablet which he switches on, going through the same routine. Next comes my video camera. Fortunately, I recently installed a new memory card and there's very little for him to waste time looking through. After 15 minutes they've run out of steam and with more big smiles, tell me I can leave.

Amzulla's stress intensifies when I reveal the Matchless's speed.

"You must go faster," he says.

"Sorry, it isn't possible. If you carry all my luggage in your car, I should be able to climb hills quicker, but that's all."

He rushes over to the car with two of my drybags but the driver refuses to accept them. As fast as I can, I begin strapping the saddlebags onto the bike. By now Amzulla's in a bit of a tiz. Anxiously hopping from foot to foot as he scrutinises my progress, he loses patience and runs back to the car, entreating the driver to take my belongings. The man grudgingly relents and at breakneck speed, we cram everything into the boot.

The lower border post is at 1800m but it's not all downhill. We descend to 2400m then begin climbing, reaching 3050m before the road plateaus. In my haste to get going, I'd omitted to put my balaclava under my crash helmet and there's a thin line of exposed flesh between the top of my goggles and the rim of the helmet. Without even the accompanying pleasure of eating ice cream, I develop brain freeze through this tiny sliver of skin, an icy raw pain that sears into my forehead. Then, thankfully, the road drops at an incredibly steep angle and freewheeling on blacktop as smooth as a billiard table, we hit 86kmph, our fastest yet. The surrounding rolling hills are bare and sandy, the fast dipping sun casting eerie dark shadows across them, Far from being stressed, I'm invigorated by the race against the clock. One brief police checkpost temporarily slows us then we're off again, the Matchless giving a virtuoso performance, powering up hills, gliding round bends and swooping through deep gorges.

At 5.25pm we arrive at the main border post, its tinted sliding doors still wide open. Amzulla comes running over, slapping me on the back.

"We've made it by five minutes! My office phoned them and they agreed to stay open until 5.30. Come on, bring your passport and let's get inside."

We enter a cavernous hall dotted with a variety of desks and booths, a line of offices and duty-free shops down both sides. It looks more like an international airport concourse than a remote Asian frontier crossing. A uniformed official beckons me to his desk and I present my passport. In no time it's stamped. Meanwhile, Amzulla has been searching for customs. He rejoins me with three officers in tow, explaining they want to examine the bike. We all traipse outside and careful checks are made that the frame and engine numbers correlate with the paperwork. Once done, I'm instructed to gather my luggage, load it onto a trolley and wheel it inside. With Amzulla's help, I feed it through an x-ray machine then out of the hall's far doors and straight back into the boot of the car, which has been driven around the building.

Riding the Matchless to the same spot, I park then wait... and wait... and wait. Eventually, a harassed-looking Amzulla emerges with his phone pressed to his ear, deep in conversation.

"There's a problem," he says when the call's over. "One customs official is very stubborn. He says we are rushing him too much and he wants to go home.

He has decided you must leave your motorbike here tonight and he will finish the paperwork in the morning."

"Where will it be kept?" I ask, looking around for a secure building.

"Right here," he says pointing at the ground.

Within the large compound are several trucks, one moving, others parked up for the night. There are builders still at work in one corner and other people loitering around. I'm far from thrilled by the prospect of leaving her exposed overnight and explain to Amzulla that if anything's broken, it's highly unlikely I'll find a replacement.

"How about we go back in," I suggest. "Perhaps together we can persuade him to sign it off."

We re-enter the hall and walk its full length. There's not a soul to be seen... everyone has gone home.

"I'll camp here next to the bike," I tell Amzulla when we return outside. "You can go home and come back in the morning to help with the paperwork. I have a tent and food and will be quite comfortable"

This causes him considerable consternation and he calls his office. Moments later, he hands the phone to me.

"Hello Mr Gordon. Adiljan here. Amzulla has explained the problem but unfortunately you cannot camp. It is not permitted in China. The police will come and make you leave. You must stay in a hotel. We will bring you back first thing in the morning so you can claim your bike."

I look around again. There are no fences at the perimeter and anyone is free to come and go as they please. All my instincts say I shouldn't leave her and I explain this to Adiljan. In deadlock, I give the phone back to Amzulla and sit beside the Matchless. After a while, he flops down beside me, head in hands, and says,

"I am so sorry this has happened. Bureaucracy in China makes me very angry. There is no real reason why this man should not allow your motorcycle through. All the paperwork is correct."

I feel sorry for the lad, who's obviously doing his best, but unless a building can be found where I can safely lock her up, I'm not willing to leave. More than an hour later, after another heated call to his office, Amzulla tells me to stay put. He's going to drive around to see if there's anyone else who can help with the paperwork.

Now we're no longer at high altitude, I occupy myself changing the carburettor main jet back to the standard size. Once it's done, I walk up and down, wondering how things are going to pan out. With a screech of brakes, Amzulla and his driver return. I can tell by the grin plastered across his face that everything's been resolved.

"I found someone else in an office over there who's much higher ranking," he says pointing into the distance. "He's cleared everything for us to leave. Let's go."

What a superstar!

Our first requirement is petrol. Following their car, a model known as a 'Great Wall', we enter the town of Ulugoat, its wide streets brightly lit with enough colourful neon and fancy LED lights to give Blackpool illuminations a run for its money. The first petrol station we stop at, called 'Smile', only sells 91 octane and Amzulla's certain we can do better. Driving round the block, we come to another, larger establishment. Amzulla hops out of the car and goes to check.

"Good news... they have 97!" he says when he returns. "But there's something I haven't told you yet. In China, you're not allowed to fill a motorbike from the petrol pump. Some years ago, I think in Shanghai, one caught fire while filling up and people were killed by an explosion. Since then it's been banned. We have to fill a kettle with fuel then transfer it to the bike. Some petrol stations will allow you to do this near to the pump, but not this one. You'll have to keep the bike on the street and I'll carry the kettle backwards and forwards. How much do you need?"

Somewhat nonplussed, I plump for 8 litres and Amzulla begins his task, shuttling 2 litres at a time in a dented tin kettle. When the tank's full, we pour the excess into one of my fuel bottles then with a thumbs up, make ready to depart for Kashgar, 95km to the east.

Leaving town, we turn straight onto a dual carriageway, the Great Wall vehicle following close on my tail with its headlights projecting a brilliant halogen path ahead. There are few other motorists and apart from slowing at a couple of police checkpoints, we motor at a steady 70 for over half an hour. Pulling alongside, Amzulla waves his hand to the right. They overtake, their indicators flashing as they swing down an exit ramp and onto a bumpy backroad.

It's painful, each jolt catching me unprepared as I simply can't see the terrain ahead. The driver puts his full beam lights on, which helps a little, but fails to dip them on the approach of other cars, who flash their headlamps, blinding me. I stop and ask,

"How far is it to Kashgar?"

"About 50 kilometres," replies Amzulla.

"Is it like this all the way?"

"Mostly,"

I grill him further.

"Adiljan told me the roads were modern and smooth right into the city. Is this a shortcut?"

He assures me it isn't and we set off once more.

Shuddering, the Matchless rattles down the road at a lowly 30kmph and without any luggage on the back, her rear kicks and jumps into the air each time she hits a pothole. I'm going so slowly that heavy trucks overtake dangerously close and despite the cold, I begin sweating. I spot lights to the right and realise they belong to cars flying along a dual carriageway. Stopping to rest my hands from the vibrations, I ask Amzulla again if this is the only route.

"Yes, this is the road we must take."

"What about that dual carriageway? I'm sure I've just seen an overhead sign on it for Kashgar!"

"It's not possible for us to go that way... not possible."

Pounded for the next hour, the road improves by degrees when we turn north, allowing me to speed up. From time to time the dual carriageway seems to be paralleling us but now it comes into full view, traffic queuing at a brightly lit toll booth. I call another halt.

"Amzulla," I say, "that is the dual carriageway to Kashgar that we came off, isn't it? Why didn't you tell me the truth instead of making me ride that awful patched road?"

His head hung low, he confesses that their office doesn't give them any money to travel on a toll road. I keep my cool as I fully understand why he didn't reveal this earlier. Saving face plays a big part in many eastern cultures. However, I ask him to promise he'll tell me in the future so I can pay for such things.

For a city of only 350,000, Kashgar seems enormous, the sides of its main roads dressed with cheerful red lanterns and still thronging with traffic at this late hour. There are dedicated lanes for motorcycles, all of which are electric powered, indeed, apart from people with special permission, petrol engined motorbikes are banned from the city. Much to the annoyance of several car drivers who try to force me out of their way, I stay out of the bike lanes, sticking to the rear of the Great Wall like glue. At 10.50pm we finally reach Kashgar's giant central square, coming to rest outside a marble tower block, the Dongfang Hotel. The concierge directs me to park the Matchless inside its rear courtyard then, when she's covered up, I wheel all my gear into reception on a wobbly-wheeled trolley. Thanking Amzulla for his considerable efforts, we arrange to meet in the morning and shake hands. I take the lift, shuffling like a somnambulist into the comfort of my room... it's been quite a day!

Day 42. Kashgar. 0 miles.

The early morning view from the 13th story window is of a cityscape which gently emerges as the sun's warmth dissolves the mist shrouding the lower buildings. Walking like a zombie, I catch the lift to the 5th floor breakfast dining room, meal ticket at the ready. The doors open and I'm faced with a line of stainless steel electronic booths similar to those at an underground station. Scanning the ticket, barriers flip open and I enter an area packed with rows of bench seating arranged around enormous displays of food. Empty plate in hand, I wander up and down the offerings feeling somewhat at sea... apart from fried eggs, I don't have a clue what any of it is. After a couple of passes, I opt for dumplings, three different types, of which the best has a yellow gooey centre, and a green leaf pyramid parcel tied with string which it transpires is packed with sticky rice. It's a sure winner and I go back for seconds and thirds.

As I'm a bit early for my meeting with Amzulla, I poke my head outside and decide to go for a walk across People's Square, which commences just a few steps away. In its centre is a rather European-looking Castle surrounded by greenery and a moat that's spanned by a traditional asian arch bridge. Around the whole area are giant circular lanterns, about 3m in diameter, and vivid red banners proclaiming the 60th anniversary of Xinjiang Uyghur Autonomous Region, of which Kashgar, also known as Kashi, is the capital. Across the main road perimeter is a giant statue of Mao Zedong flanked by a row of regal-looking Chinese flags. Standing 24 metres high, a waving Chairman Mao is depicted wearing a greatcoat and his trademark cap. I pause and consider its message to the people of China's largest autonomous state in which Han Chinese are still in the minority, if only just. The majority, mostly Uyghurs, have shown much resistance to centralised control over the last 60 years. As if on cue, police begin to arrive in the square, first two-up on motorcycles then followed by cars and a couple of armoured vehicles. Walking to the roadside, I turn around and watch as they assemble into an assault-rifle-toting squad, three wide and twelve deep, and as the sergeant calls the beat, they march backwards and forwards, chanting loudly to each step.

Ambling back towards the hotel, I take my eyes off the parading navy blue uniforms and focus on the road. Four lanes of cars are sandwiched between two cordoned strips for motorcycles. A constant stream of battery-driven two wheelers flows in dense clumps within these confines and the silence with which they travel is, to my ears, remarkable. Outside the hotel, I watch a car sweep across the motorcycle lane and screech to a halt. The lady passenger swings her door open without heed for the passing bikes and although she causes three scooter riders to swerve violently, she doesn't even flinch. As I witnessed last night, the rights of two-wheelers seem to be of no consequence to some of the more affluent car owners. So far, my experience of modern China feels alien, a bit like being on a different planet, yet I'm invigorated by its unfamiliarity and bustling energy.

Amzulla arrives and we climb into his car, pulling up 10 minutes later outside the offices of Newland Travel, the company that's arranged my escorted crossing of China. Adiljan, the manager, is waiting for me. He issues instructions to Amzulla who duly departs for a day spent in government offices arranging my vehicle insurance, temporary Chinese driving licence and number plate. Finally, he needs to make a payment for health screening, an odd necessity considering there's no requirement for my presence during the process! After a quick tour of the office, we drive back to my hotel then find a cafe where I quiz Adiljan about how his company helps foreign motorcyclists. Apparently, there's stiff competition between the few businesses that have a permit to escort riders and Newland Travel brings approximately half a dozen groups a year across the same route I'm taking to Pakistan. They also take one or two others on much longer journeys, either exiting to Nepal via Tibet or further east, into Laos, both of which incur eye-watering costs. Although one or two overlanders have been successful in arranging everything themselves in the past year, the complications of paperwork and translation makes it a challenging and protracted process that doesn't work out much cheaper than employing an agency. Adiljan doesn't see things changing any time soon.

We say goodbye and I head off for lunch at a place he's recommended. Sitting in a dark wooden booth in a first-floor restaurant I'd never have found by myself, I stare at a menu written totally in hanzi. Flummoxed, I smile at the waitress, pen and paper poised, and ask for assistance in English. She deftly whips out her iPhone, taps it several times, then hands it to me.

"Can I help you?" is written across the screen.

I type a reply which it instantly translates and within a couple of minutes we've worked out my order. Another wonder of modern technology!

In the afternoon I make a beeline for Kashgar's old town, a warren of narrow streets that wind backwards and forwards in the district behind Mao's statue. The first street contains small artisan workshops, single room units where wood is turned, copper beaten, steel welded and glass cut. It's not a walk that can be rushed as every skilled worker is worth watching. Following my nose, I head deeper into narrow lanes where ornate wooden houses stand squeezed between mosques and open fronted restaurants. In a small square I sit on a bench beside a merchant who's squatting on top of a wooden trailer attached to the back of his motorcycle. From two large hessian sacks he scoops coal into small bags which he sells for a few yuan. Opposite him is another motorbike trader, this one selling watermelons. There seems to be a regular motorcycle minibus service that passes every couple of minutes and I'm captivated by the sight of low-powered bikes that somehow haul up to a dozen people in trailers complete with ornate canopies. Some children playing football in the square entreat me to join in. I spend a contented quarter of an hour kicking a ball backwards and forwards with them.

My only regret is that today's a Wednesday and I would have loved to have been here on a Sunday when Kashgar's famous Sunday market takes place. A regular fixture for over 2000 years, it was visited by Marco Polo in 1275. In *Book of the Marvels of the World*, he remarked, 'The inhabitants live by trade and industry... the starting point from which many merchants set out to market their wares all over the world.' It's still frequented by traders and farmers from far beyond Xinjiang's borders, reputedly swelling the city's population by as many as 100,000 for just one day a week.

Returning to the hotel, I wash my laundry in the shower, scrubbing practically every stitch of clothing I possess. Next, I lavish the Matchless with all the maintenance treats I'd promised her during yesterday's taxing ride, continuously calling her,

"Old girl," in appreciation.

Satisfied she's ready for the challenges ahead, I set off for the 7th floor restaurant to grab an early dinner.

In its foyer, a glass wall holds about 50 backlit A4 photographs of meal choices. Opposite is a long neon counter behind which stand three young women in peach coloured silk waistcoats. Bowing at my arrival, one addresses me in Mandarin. My reply in English is as incomprehensible to her as her communication to me. She points to the wall but it's difficult to recognise what each dish contains. One of my favourite foods is tofu and as yet I've not had any on this trip. My first attempt at asking for it results in three blank expressions so I set to trying as many pronunciations as I can think of:

"Tuffoo... Too-foo... Towfew..."

The harder I try, the more they giggle. Then I remember the quick-witted waitress at lunch and ask if any of them has a phone. In a flash, three smartphones appear and as I point at each photo, translations materialise on their screens. After consideration, I type 'tofu' onto one of them.

"Ahh... tofu," they cry in unison at the Chinese translation.

I've been through this before!

A giant plate of tofu and ginger, a heaped dish of greens in soy sauce and a third carrying a mound of plain rice are brought with chopsticks to my table... enough to feed three people. Sipping on a litre of incredibly cheap beer, I eat all I can manage as I watch surprisingly good videos of Chinese love songs on a jumbo TV screen.

The hotel's wifi is painfully slow and only works in the lobby. Searching for an internet cafe turns out to be a fruitless task... there aren't any due to the endemic use of smartphones. My only option proves to be a dark gaming den lit solely by the flashing colours which emanate from rows of widescreen monitors. Over 100 exclusively male patrons, reclining in purple velvet armchairs and isolated from each other by bulbous headphones, are engrossed in fast-paced computer games. It takes 15 minutes for the manager to enter all my details, including passport information, onto his system before I can park myself amongst the gun brandishing, cop killing, spaceship flying, football playing gamers and incongruously attend to my long list of messages.

Day 43. Kashgar to Tashkurgan. 199 miles.

The hotel, like all the government offices, railway stations, airports and banks, runs on Beijing time, which is two hours ahead of Kashgar. Breakfast accordingly commences at 8.30am... 6.30am local time. Needless to say I panic when I first see the restaurant clock, thinking I'm two hours late, but breathe a sigh of relief as I remember the bureaucratic idiosyncrasy. Amzulla's waiting punctually in the lobby. Today he's both driver and guide, loading my belongings into his own Great Wall, a battered MK3 version that appears remarkably similar to an old Suzuki Rav4. It's not the first Chinese car I've seen with design influences drawn heavily from European or Japanese models. In the hotel's car park sit dead ringers for a Jaguar XF and a Audi A4 and yesterday I saw a couple of new Mini lookalikes. Less salubrious, whilst walking through the old town I'd clocked a brace of Del Boy Reliant Robin knock offs... lovely jubbly!

Fuel tank full to capacity after another encounter with a kettle, we make our way out of the city with its sprawling industrial suburbs and onto the start of National Highway G314, the Karakoram Highway. Widely referred to as the KKH, its construction through the heart of the mighty Karakoram mountain range took place between 1960 and 1982 and cost the lives of more than 1000 workers. Tracing the path of one of the ancient silk routes to India, it links Kashgar with the city of Abbottabad in the Khyber Pakhtunkhwa Province of Pakistan, south of which the tentacles of the Pakistan road network spread in all directions. Blasted through rock for hundreds of miles, it presented such a formidable engineering challenge that it's regarded as a contender for eighth wonder of the world.

Beginning as a dual carriageway, the road soon narrows to single lane, heading in a straight line through abundant agricultural land and orderly villages. With Amzulla following close behind, we maintain a good speed until we're slowed by increasing numbers of small motorcycles, each one with a long-handled spade strapped to its seat or carried by a pillion. Entering a region with woodland on one side of the road and a ditch on the other, we come upon hundreds of parked motorbikes, their riders and passengers all diligently digging amongst the trees, on the verges or in the depths of the ditch. Fervent activity continues for at least 8 kilometres involving thousands upon thousands of people. As we stop in a village to buy bread and fruit, I quiz Amzulla about them.

"These people are paid by the government to tidy up the roadsides and surrounding land. They work two days a week and get paid 500 yuan a month," he explains.

"I thought it was the Kashgar gold rush," I reply, then doing a bit of mental arithmetic add, "That's about £53 a month. How can they possibly survive on that?"

In answer, he simply shrugs his shoulders.

88km into the journey, we reach the mountains, the way ahead blocked by a fortified checkpost. Amzulla presents my paperwork and once we're through, we stop beside a Chinese army copy of a US Humvee for a briefing about what's next.

"The following hundred kilometres is really bad. It's all being reconstructed and you'll see many stretches of new road but we're not allowed to travel on any of them until the whole highway has been completed."
I brace myself.

At first it's not too bad, parts of the surface are chewed up but other narrow stretches prove easily manageable at 50kmph. However, it soon deteriorates so dramatically that it's back to standing on the foot pegs as we labour forward. I thread the Matchless through rocks and rubble on an unfinished surface diabolically rutted by the transit of bulldozers and heavy work vehicles. From time to time our route runs side by side with kilometre long stretches of new tar, all cordoned off, but it's mainly just grey stones, dusty gravel and swathes of churned up, hardened mud. After 40 minutes I tire and sit back down for a while. Suddenly there's a twang and my seat sags. Pulling up to inspect the damage, I see that all the bouncing up and down has broken one of my saddle's mattress springs and another is half hanging off. I tighten the dislodged spring back into place, let some air out of the tyres to cushion the ride, then rejoin the road.

After a shattering 15km, we stop at a quiet checkpoint so I can rest. Warmed by the sun and sitting on the ground with my back against a boulder, I ask Amzulla, who's 22, about his work and aspirations.

"I've enjoyed doing this for two years but feel like a change. I think I might join the army."
Surprised, I look at a couple of soldiers who are painting the outside of the building and think back to the ones I'd met at the lonely Kyrgyzstan border.

"I imagine many army jobs are not very glamorous," I say, nodding towards the painters. "Having had so much freedom working with foreigners, do you think you'd enjoy doing this?"

"If I become an officer, my life is made. I'll have a good income and excellent prospects when I leave the army. And it will be me telling men to paint and go on guard duty. Anyway, that's not the only reason. Most of all I want to hold a piece."

"A piece of what?" I ask.

"A piece... you know... a gun. I just want to hold one... and shoot it sometimes," he adds excitedly.

"Can't you just visit a rifle range?"

"It's not the same as the possibility of shooting at people."
The conversation falters as I'm at a loss for how to respond... maybe he's been playing too many computer games!

I strain my right thigh climbing back onto the bike and almost as soon as we set off, a brutal headwind gets up. It's so fierce that there's no way I dare risk standing up... my arms wouldn't be strong enough to prevent me being plucked off the bike, like a child. Another mattress spring snaps and more time's wasted while I reposition the remaining ones so the gaps are evenly spaced. Slogging forward, the Matchless receives a savage beating and so do I.

We reach a particularly rugged area with towering mountains closing in on both sides of the bulldozed trail. Two lines of huge concrete columns up to 40 metres tall have been erected. They wind up the valley floor before disappearing from sight behind a huge craggy prominence. Our track turns alongside it, revealing lengthy sections of a raised concrete road that sit on top of the pillars. The elevated highway snakes from side to side between the rock faces, following the contours of the steely grey ravine for over two kilometres. Evocative of some Roger Dean fantasy artwork on a prog rock album cover, only more monochromatic, I find it extraordinary that so far from civilization in these cold, inhospitable altitudes, such a dramatic sky-road would be constructed. Whatever the rationale, the cost must be astronomical. I'd love to ride it once it's finished.

The journey continues to be gruelling, the howling wind lifting chalky dust off the endless roadworks and driving it downhill, straight into me. More than three and a half hours after entering the mountains, the roadworks end and we reach Lake Kara Kule at 3300m. As the gale rages, the windchill factor becomes a serious concern. Sheltering behind the Great Wall, I re-jet the carburettor, change the clogged up air filter and get moving as fast as possible. The road descends for a while and on the nearby hillsides, herds of Bactrian camels wander peacefully around, their shaggy chestnut coats rippling in the wind. Soon we begin climbing in earnest, the gradient reducing me to 2nd gear even when I slipstream behind Amzulla. To the right I notice a large complex where several heavyweight artics are parked. It's Kalasu Port, the China border control 14km east of the Kulma Pass crossing into Tajikistan. Open solely to Chinese freight, it's just 80 km due east of Murghab. I give a wave to Apal and we continue our ascent.

My hands and feet get so cold I can no longer feel them and I start shivering. Parking behind some roadside boulders, I run up and down the highway, forcing myself to do physical jerks to get everything moving. Panting and still wearing my helmet and gloves, I climb into the Great Wall where Amzulla puts his heater on full blast. Ten minutes later we resume, passing a glacier which forges a path so steeply down the side of a mountain, it looks like a frozen waterfall. The altimeter edges past 4000m and keeps going, peaking at 4060m. In front of us lies a tremendous panorama, the road twisting and turning downhill, surrounded on all sides by bleak, ice capped mountains. Without hesitation I slip into neutral and begin to descend.

Thawing out for a second time in the car, I ask Amzulla if he met a German motorcyclist called Christian Vogel who was due to cross China a month ago.

"Yes! Christian... I escorted him to the Pakistan border too. He was riding a real motorcycle, a BMW. Wow, that was beautiful. So fast too!"

Feeling suitably put in my place, I explain how Christian and I had initially planned to travel this leg together.

"Christian had bad luck. We teamed him with an American tourist in a 4x4 and they reached Kashgar at the start of a long public holiday. Government buildings were closed and they were stranded for five days. I think it took them eight days to get from Kyrgyzstan to Pakistan."

Looking away, he adds,

"But he had a great time and gave me a big tip."

This is at least the dozenth time that "big tips" have been casually dropped into the conversation and I smile weakly in acknowledgment.

Orbiting the shores of another lake, the road turns sharply to the right and enters a dark canyon. Minutes later we emerge onto a plain, the wind finally abating. Dusk produces a sky with a copper red hue and I stop beside a road sign, the first I've seen for Tashkurgan, to change my goggles. There's still 60km to run but at least it's on smooth asphalt and within an hour, I see a colourful glow on the horizon, the decorative lights of the town. Just before 8pm we reach our hotel where I ensconce myself in a hot shower. Thoroughly defrosted, I locate Amzulla then together we hop into his car and drive to a restaurant.

For dinner we share three dishes highly recommended by him: a plate of spicy tofu; another of crispy fried green beans in a garlic sauce and the last, his favourite, shredded potatoes with chillies in soy sauce. Hungrily working our way through it, I ask where he learnt to speak English so well.

"A little at school," he replies, "but mostly from television. NCIS... do you watch it? I've seen every episode over and over again. All my best English words come from detective work and post-mortems!"

We laugh about the unsuitability of this vocabulary for his current job.

"Maybe you should join the police and not the army," I suggest "That way you can carry a gun and use all your favourite English words!"

Totally wiped, I make poor late night company, incapable of even finishing a solitary bottle of Tuborg. Back at the hotel, I dose myself with more Ibuprofen and Diamox and climb into bed, wondering when I'm going to have an easy day's ride.

The Matchless's Chinese registration plate.

186

Day 44. Tashkurgan, China, to Sost, Pakistan. 131 miles.

I knock on Amzulla's door. He looks grim having spent much of the night incapacitated by diarrhoea and stomach cramps and can't face breakfast, so I head to the dining room alone. After another coffee fiasco, this time involving milk as opposed to sugar, Amzulla surfaces and we load the Great Wall for the final time. After first visiting a fuel station, we drive to the town's border control post, an enormous concrete complex. Arriving in its almost empty car park, I pull the Matchless onto her rear stand then follow Amzulla to the smoked glass doors of the immigration hall. A group of around 40 people, nearly all Pakistani men with stacks of sacks and boxes of goods purchased in Kashgar, mill around the entrance waiting for proceedings to commence. Twenty minutes on, the doors swing open and we file into another building that's styled on an airport terminal. While Amzulla feeds my bags through an x-ray machine, I join a queue pressed between rope cordons that leads to the passport inspection desk.

A soldier keeps guard beside the line, from time to time admonishing some of my fellow travellers for talking too loudly, not standing smartly enough in line or touching the rope! There's a blatant contrast between the two cultures, the Chinese orderly, disciplined and controlled, the Pakistanis chaotic, impassioned and dissenting. This incongruity catches me on the funny bone and I struggle to hold in my laughter. With my passport stamped but temporally held, I'm instructed to ride the bike around the building to load it on the other side.

When I arrive there, I park next to three minibuses of varying sizes and a couple of 4x4s.

"They will form a convoy and you will have to ride all the way to the border with them and an army escort," explains Amzulla.

At my speed, that's going to be fun for everybody!

Carefully attaching everything to the bike, I wait for my passport to be returned. Eventually an officer arrives with it, telling me that I'm free to go and can travel to the border on my own. Amzulla's jaw drops - it's the first time in two years he's seen this happen. I'm delighted. I tell him how much I appreciate all his hard work and as we say goodbye, hand him the gratuity he's been hinting at since we first met. It's hard to tell from his low-key reaction if it's as 'big' as those from my predecessors, but I shake his hand and thank him again. He leaves to recover his car and begin the return journey to Kashgar.

From 3100m, we have to climb to over 4700m. I decide not to consider the altitude but focus instead on distance. The frontier lies just over 120km south and because of the intense cold, I mentally break the journey down into segments of 50, 30 and two lots of 20 kilometres. Departing under clear skies, the road's perfectly straight. At first there's little around but frosty grassland but as we gradually climb, the distant white peaks get closer, creating a jaggedly magnificent spectacle. On the outskirts of a neatly laid out settlement, I discern what appears to be a flock of goats milling around in the middle of the road. Braking, I drop to 2nd gear and am just about upon them when I realise there're actually a pack of eight or nine large shaggy dogs. Revving hard, my thumb firmly on the horn, I ride straight into them. Resembling skittles hit by a bowling ball, they scamper off in all directions just in time. Immediately past the 50km mark, having been desperately holding out for ten freezing minutes, I reach a couple of remote dwellings and stop. Using them as shelter from the strengthening wind, I do some heat generating exercises, eat bread and dry cake for energy then wriggle into my fluorescent rainsuit which I tie around my waist, hoping it'll at least keep my legs warm.

To my surprise, I achieve almost 40km on the next stint before succumbing to the bitter wind. Jiggling my arms and legs by the side of the road to get my blood circulating, I receive toots from a couple of passing trucks, the only vehicles on the road except those from the immigration hall, all of which had passed me within five minutes of leaving Tashkurgan. I'm now above the snow line at 3640 metres, with 1100 metres still to climb in just over 30 kilometres. The strain on the inside of my right leg is very painful from groin to knee and climbing on requires a great deal of lip-sucking as I use my hand to delicately lift it over the saddle. Thankfully, the pain vanishes as soon as I'm on the bike.

Counting down the kilometres to the border, I manage to keep going without taking any further stops. The incline increases dramatically and I steer the bike backwards and forwards around precipitous zigzags, the rock face we're ascending affording us welcome relief from the icy wind. Struggling in 2nd gear but revving too fast in 1st, I shift up and down between the two. Finally appearing in the distance is a small collection of buildings, the frontier. From here to there, however, ice and snow increasingly covers the road until there are stretches of up to a hundred metres long with no clear path. On each expanse, I pick a line and doggedly stick to it. With my right boot sliding along the surface for extra stability, I strike a constant speed in 1st gear. The rear tyre loses traction and slips sideways but the tracks left by the chunky tread of 4x4 tyres gives us purchase and within a couple of seconds I'm back in control.

Beside an austere two-storey building, a steel barrier has been lowered across the road. A youthful soldier marches out of his sentry box, shouting loudly as he approaches me. Astounded, I'm at a loss for how to respond. Aggressively swinging his rifle butt towards my chest, he makes shooing noises then begins yelling again. Turning the rifle round so the business end's pointing at me, he uses it to gesture that I should leave... now! Fumbling because of my gloves, I finally manage to extract my passport from my breast pocket and open it to the China visa page. He snatches it out of my hand, steps back a pace and without taking his eye off me for a second, makes a call on his walkie-talkie. My bafflement at his extreme reaction lessens as I consider my appearance: oil stained yellow pants knotted round my waist; filthy jacket; greasy sunblock smeared across my face and the pièce de résistance, snot dripping from a numb nose into my bushy beard. My motorcycle's hardly in showroom condition either, caked in accumulated layers of road grime, oil, dust and icicles. I don't know who or what he thinks I am, but I'm obviously not the well-dressed international traveller he's accustomed to seeing.

Given the all clear, he hands my passport back and without a by your leave, returns to the barrier and raises it. I exit China fascinated by my whole experience, and despite this final encounter, am charmed by its people. I certainly intend to come back.

The road turns and climbs along the Khunjerab Pass. I pause under a grand pagoda that straddles the summit, a welcoming or farewelling gesture from The People's Republic. I'm overjoyed by our achievement... 4730m, the world's highest international border crossing and the Matchless is still faithfully purring along. It's an unforgettable moment. Descending 100m over a elongated patch of slush, I come to a red and white drop-down pole that extends across the highway from the side of a single room dwelling. A Pakistani soldier emerges, welcoming me with,

"As-salamu alaykum."

Under his belted brown leather jacket he wears traditional shalwar kameez, on his head's a black beret and slung over his shoulder is an AK47. With dashing looks somewhere between Omar Sharif and Imran Khan, he smiles calmly, gives my offered passport a cursory glance then wishes me a safe journey to the village of Sost, 86km south, where I'll need to complete formalities. It's all so unbelievably easy.

"Please remember to drive on the left," he says, waving me goodbye. Following a month and a half riding on the right side of the road, it's a necessary reminder.

It feels good to travel at speed after the ponderous chug uphill. Within a minute, the road turns sharply left and we bomb down a long switchback, the bike cornering gracefully before picking up her coattails and storming towards the next u-bend. Over the edge, tantalisingly layered below each other, I catch glimpses of a succession of hairpins yet to come... whey hey!

Our descent continues along a deep gorge, the road clinging to the side of an almost sheer rockface and overlooking a racing river, its milky green glacial waters the only variation amidst the all encompassing shades of grey and white. More breathtaking hairpins follow then the KKH settles into a less vertiginous downslope, the road surface pure perfection bar occasional indentations caused by large loose rocks that have tumbled down from high above. Appearing like a wavering pencil line on the opposing canyon walls, a crumbling narrow path mirrors our own route. It's the ancient silk road. Wide enough for only for a camel or mule, its perilous trail disappears from time to time where landslides have wiped it out.

An hour later, with the air temperature still hovering around freezing, we arrive at another police check post with a chain across the road. Two policemen invite me into their tin roofed shack and ask me to make myself comfortable in a chair. They need to take my photo and scan my passport but all their computer equipment is switched off. With a generator noisily providing power from behind the office, they turn everything on but the scanner refuses to work properly and they spend the best part of 20 minutes re-plugging and wiggling various cables. Repeatedly apologising for the hold up, one of them offers me a cup of chai from a smoke blackened kettle. I drink the milky tea and wait. Eventually, mugshot taken, my passport's handed back and I'm free to go.

Hidden 200m round a bend lies another barrier, this one marking the entrance to the Karakoram National Park. Wearily kicking out the side stand, I enter a large hut with illustrations of the park's flora and fauna pinned to its walls. A friendly young man politely requests that I pay a park entrance fee of $8.

"I beg your pardon," he says in his best Queen's English,"for asking you to render this sum, as you will only be a visitor to the park for one kilometre."
Not much hope of spotting Marco Polo sheep, lynx, ibex, grey wolf, or even an illusive snow leopard, then!

The final 35km to Sost fly past and I spot what I assume to be the border control buildings set next to a gravel car park. Sliding to a halt beside two men, I ask which office houses immigration. A tall, noble looking gentleman wearing a woollen pakol hat decorated with a peacock feather and a cocoa brown cashmere blanket that's wrapped round his shoulders, replies,

"Customs is still open but immigration is closed. They have all gone home."
Passport in hand, I look around, wondering what to do.

"The chief Immigration officer is my friend. I will phone him for you."
After a quick discussion via his cell phone, he reports back,

"He's coming. Please wait here," then resumes a conversation with his companion.

Ten minutes later, showing no sign of irritation at being dragged out of the comforts of his home, the official arrives, warmly shaking my hand. Leading me inside, he unlocks a small glass walled room and switches a computer on. Joined by another fellow, they try logging onto the passport control system but have trouble with their password. Making a call to head office in Islamabad, they're given a complex set of instructions to follow. Joined by a third man who one finger taps everything onto the keyboard, they still can't get it working.

"Please will you go to customs and clear your paperwork while we get this sorted," the head honcho requests.
I walk to the adjoining building where I meet its sole occupant.

"Immigration always comes first, but in the circumstances, I will break with formality," I'm told by the well spoken official. Within 5 minutes, my carnet's stamped and Bob's your uncle, I'm cleared through customs with no need for inspections of the bike or my belongings.

Back in the first office, the men have progressed no further.

"Where are you staying in Sost?" asks one.
I give him the name of a hotel I've been recommended.

"Ok. Leave your passport with us, go there now and unpack, have a shower, relax. When our blasted computer is working, we will phone the hotel and ask you to come back."
What service!

One of them sets off on foot, saying he'll meet me at reception and explain why I have no passport. He's there before me and with the help of the manager, we cart everything into a basic room. Just as I'm about to strip off some layers, the reception phone rings, the caller requesting I return to immigration. It doesn't take long to get there as Sost is nothing more than a 100m strip of small concrete shops with a couple of larger buildings at the perimeter. When I arrive, I'm greeted like an old friend and, after another photo session, my visa's franked.

"Enjoy your stay in Pakistan," I'm wished by all three men.

There's no hot water and my room's frigid, so after an oily meal which I fear will have serious repercussions for my gut tomorrow, I climb into bed. Despite wearing socks, long johns, a couple of layers on my torso and a balaclava, I struggle to get warm. My body, having used up its daily quotient of energy shivering, has few reserves left. I pull the covers over my head and wait for sleep to come.

The Khunjerab Pass, looking back towards China and the pagoda which marks its frontier.

Day 45. Sost to Gulmit. 49 miles.

Knock, knock, knock.

"Hello, sir. Good morning. Hot water ready, sir."

Knock, knock, knock.

"Hello, shower ready sir."

I'm already up, dressed and about to go downstairs for breakfast. I open the door and explain, trying to edge past the manager. He blocks my way, hopping from side to side as I try to dodge round him.

"Hot water ready for you, sir."

"I'll get it later thanks, after breakfast."

"No after breakfast, sir. Take shower now, sir!"

"I'd like to eat now... I'm already dressed."

"No now... now sir! Hot water ready for you sir."

He manhandles me back into the room, firmly clicking the door shut behind him... crumbs, it feels as if I'm in a Fawlty Towers sketch but I do as I'm told!

When I do make it downstairs, the farce continues. The manager hands me the breakfast menu and after a quick look, I say,

"I'll have porridge please."

"Sorry sir, no porridge today."

Looking at it again,

"Ok, I'll try the American breakfast."

"Very sorry sir, no American breakfast today."

"Ah, well, just toast and jam with black coffee please," I concede after another scan through the list.

"Very sorry sir, no toast and jam today."

"Maybe it's easier if you tell me what is on the menu."

"Yes sir. We have paratha sir."

"Anything else?"

"Yes sir. Today is paratha."

Guess it'll be paratha then.

"Coffee sir. Black coffee. No milk sir."

The cup's ceremoniously placed in front of me followed moments later by two paratha, unleavened flat bread doused in ghee then cooked on a skillet. Before I've taken my third bite, the manager returns with the bill, bows, puts it on the table then taps it twice with his index finger. I nod in acknowledgement and keep eating. He retires to a chair resting against the nearby restaurant wall and watches me intently. It's rather disconcerting as this is exactly what he did over dinner last night. Two minutes later, he's back up on his feet, joining me at my table.

"Paratha good sir? Coffee good sir?" again tapping the bill expectantly.

It's odd behaviour and I'm glad when I've finished and can leave.

Climbing the staircase, my prediction from last night seems to be coming true: my stomach's turning summersaults and my bowels feel decidedly dodgy. I've been delaying visiting the loo since I got up as I know it's not going to be a good experience but there's no way I can stave off the inevitable any longer.

"It is your destiny, Master Luke," I say in my deepest Darth Vader voice and turn a corner at exactly the same moment as four men coming the other way. In their mid 20s and dressed in light coloured cotton salwar kameez, I can tell by their initial expressions that they must have heard my weird words but to their credit, each one formally shakes my hand and wishes me a pleasant stay in Pakistan. I hurry along the corridor, more pressing things on my mind than their perceptions of crazy Westerners.

The clouds are low, the atmosphere's heavy and it looks as if snow's imminent. Pushing the bike to the hotel's front steps, I begin loading. Three locals spot me from the road and enter the courtyard, curiously examining the Matchless. One of them is deaf and dumb, and after shaking my hand, he begins to help, following my lead as he duplicates each of my movements with straps on the other side of the bike. Dextrously, he positions every one correctly at the first attempt. Usually when people try to help it ends up taking twice as long as I have to discreetly redo most of their work. It's a real pleasure to have this chap's assistance and my spirits rise accordingly.

The incomparable KKH continues south and the valley opens out as we cross a bridge onto the west bank of the Hunza river. Flashing silver in occasional shafts of sunlight, the twisting waters remain narrow but the silty, rocky floodplain broadens considerably. Iron grey Karakorams rising menacingly above, the sloping valley sides gradually transform to green, with poplars and apricot or mulberry orchards appearing as we lose more altitude. From high above the river, I look down onto small terraced fields of potatoes and buckwheat and a few miles on, as I lift my eyes skywards, behold the sight of one of the world's most stunning mountain spectacles. It's known by several names, Tupopdan Peak, or Passu Cones, Cathedral Peak and Passu Cathedral, and consists of a series of cone shaped pinnacles which, layer upon layer in glorious natural symmetry, point to the heavens. They resemble, with little imagination, the stacked pipes of a cathedral organ and there isn't a superlative grand enough to do them justice. I first saw them when I visited Pakistan in 1988 and they look just the same 27 years on... I wish the same could be said of me!

Underway again, constantly glancing across the river in awe, I come to Passu village itself, a widespread assembly of simple dwellings set amidst small holdings, each delineated by low level stone walls. With trees tinged the vibrant colours of autumn and the fields still abundant with crops, it appears picture postcard perfect, a veritable land of milk and honey. Indeed, since first visited by the British army in the 1870s, the Hunza valley has enjoyed almost mythical status as a utopian paradise, a place where people living frugal lives in isolation from the modern world and eating healthy locally produced foods were reputed to have regularly lived to ages between 120 and 150 years. I remember long ago listening to a cassette program called *Dead Doctors Don't Lie* by Joel Wallach. Addressing man's quest for disease free health and longevity, one of its main tenets was the importance of vitamins and minerals. The Hunzas of this region were put forth as a prime example of Wallach's theories in action, with crops watered by the valley's mineral rich glacial waters the key. It certainly convinced me to buy numerous expensive tubs of colloidal minerals! Although the value of vitamins and minerals remains undisputed, much of the Hunza legend has sadly been debunked in recent times.

As I continue southwards, I'm surprised by the lack of traffic on the highway. In Sost I saw a couple of parked Chinese trucks but I haven't seen any heavy haulage, either Pakistani or Chinese, since. A couple of long distance land cruisers went past this morning but apart from the odd minibus or local motorbike around the villages of Jamalabad, Kyber, and Jahanabad, I have the road to myself, not that I'm grumbling.

Continuing beyond the outwash plain of Passu's retreating glacier, we climb for a while before gently descending towards river level at the village of Gulmit. I pass a sign for the Gulmit Tourist Inn and slowly ride through the tiny bazaar. Soon leaving it behind, I press on, my target for today the provincial capital, Gilgit, which lies 150km southeast. A long aqua body of water comes into view. It's Attabad lake and I'm most probably going to have to cross it on a vessel not much bigger than a rowing boat. The lake was formed by an immense landslide adjacent to Attabad village on January 4th 2010 which dammed the Hunza river, completely blocking its flow for over 5 months. Twenty people died but significantly, more than 6,000 were displaced from upstream villages, their fields washed away and livelihoods decimated. Twenty-five kilometres of the KKH were also wiped out. At its peak, before it began to flow over the top of the landslide dam, the lake was more than 100m deep and since then, a flotilla of small boats have carried vehicles between the undamaged sections of the highway.

Over the last three years, a 7km long series of tunnels has been constructed by China as part of a detour around the lake. Called the Pakistan-China Friendship Tunnels, I know they're due to open soon but don't have any up-to-date information. I stop the bike just before a curving bridge that leads to the rocky entrance of the first tunnel then look down at the lake where a small boat is puttering towards a wooden jetty. There are no barriers across the road to suggest the tunnel isn't open and yet boats are evidently still in operation. Uncertain what to do, I cautiously ride towards the tunnel. The lights aren't working and it's pitch dark inside but in under a minute, I emerge into daylight on the other side. A couple of tents and some earthmoving equipment are situated at the side of the road then I notice a pole that's lowered across it. An armed policeman steps out and begins flagging me down... maybe we're in for a boating adventure after all!

"Where are you going?" he asks.

"Gilgit," I reply.

"I'm sorry, not today. The road is closed."

"Do I take a boat?"

"No, no. The tunnels are all open, the Prime Minister presided over an opening ceremony on September 15th. The Karakoram Highway is closed today due to public order issues. You cannot go forward, even if you take a boat. Please come back tomorrow."

It's certainly not the answer I'd expected. By now, we've been joined by another policeman and a civilian. They're all friendly but unwavering in their assertion that I can't progress.

"You can find somewhere to stay in Gulmit or Passu, then return here tomorrow morning," I'm told. "It's not safe for you on the road today."
Thwarted, I thank them, make a tight U-turn and retrace my steps.

Riding back through Gulmit, a light drizzle begins to fall. As I'd spotted the Gulmit Tourist Inn just over half an hour ago, I make it my first port of call. A young man greets me. He's rather surprised by my arrival as the tourist season's finished and they've had no guests for over two weeks. I'm shown a room upstairs with spectacular views across the river and up towards Passu Cathedral, its highest peaks now hidden by low cloud. I couldn't wish for anything better and readily agree to the modest room rate. After the bike's covered up and I'm showered, the man returns with a pot of green tea and some bad news... there won't be any power until late afternoon and they only have one book in English for me to borrow. That's not a problem as it's a Dan Brown novel that'll easily keep me entertained. Wrapped in layers of warm clothing and with my torch shining onto the book's pages, I recline in an armchair next to the window and spend several hours cocooned, sipping cups of jasmine tea, my attention flitting backwards and forwards between the pages and the sublime view.

I try to send a text but can't get a signal on my phone. Wandering downstairs, I meet the hotel's owner, Mohammed, who's also the village's retired schoolmaster. He succinctly explains why I've been turned back from the tunnels. This weekend marks the end of the Muslim festival of Ashura which is celebrated by Sunni and Shia Muslims alike but for completely different reasons. For Shi'ites, it commemorates the killing of Hussain ibn Ali, the grandson of the prophet Muhammad. The streets of Pakistan's cities and towns will see many public assemblies and processions where some will self-flagellate in mourning rituals. The village of Ganish and several others south of the lake are expected to be obstructed most of the day by such gatherings.

Phone in hand, I ask if I'll be able to get a signal if I walk into Gulmit bazaar.

"Sadly no. Two days ago, a Shi'ite mosque was bombed in the Baluchistan province and many were killed. To foil remote-controlled bombings amongst crowds of people celebrating Ashura, the cellphone networks have all been suspended by the government. You should get a signal later this evening... Inshallah."

Sectarian violence is a serious problem in Pakistan but I'm soon put at ease.

"Please do not worry. We are Ismailis, as are the majority in the upper Hunza valley, and we are known for being tolerant and peaceful. We're a tight knit community and you are entirely safe with us. Tomorrow, everything will be back to normal and you will be able to continue your journey."

The Ismailis, I know, are a minority branch of Shia Islam. Prince Karim Aga Khan, the same man whose benevolent foundation provided the aid workers I met at the Kyrgyzstan border, is the 49th hereditary Imam of the Ismaili

Muslims and his lineage can be traced directly back to the Prophet Muhammad. I thank the manager and return to my room.

Throughout the afternoon, the clouds drift unerringly lower and the rain beats down with increasing intensity. Around 5pm, my light suddenly comes on and within minutes, I'm brought an electric heater which transforms the room, although its safety is something of a concern. In lieu of a plug, two bare wires are wiggled into position in the wall socket. Mmm. After dinner in the otherwise empty dinning room, I return to my quarters and make it past the novel's half way point before calling it a night. Just 24 hours ago I'd longed for an easy day's ride... as the saying goes, I tell myself, I need to be careful what I wish for!

Attabad lake, south of Gulmit, blocked the KKH for over 5 years.

Day 46. Gulmit to Chilas. 159 miles.

A heavy drumming noise draws me from my sleep. I lie in bed trying to convince myself it's the sound of the nearby river but it's obviously not. When I open the curtains, rain's lashing down, forming large puddles over the footpaths and flooding the hotel's gardens. The mountains are hidden by a low cloud base and most worryingly, from about a hundred metres upwards, the precipitous scree on the east bank of the river is white with snow.

In vain hope that the weather improves, I delay my departure and take a leisurely breakfast, talking with a young man from Lahore who's just stepped off a bus to take up a post as an NGO worker in Upper Hunza. His input on my route south couldn't be more timely.

I have two options. The first is to travel 230km along the KKH through the district of Indus Kohistan. Before 1988, Kohistan was a tribal area where Pakistani law held little force but since then, it's been incorporated into the North West Frontier Province. Largely populated by Pashtuns, it's a wild area that follows the Indus river through a deep gorge. Sectarian tensions simmer in Kohistan and three years ago, a bus was stopped by Sunni militants. Twelve men identified as shia were dragged off and shot. Foreigners travelling along the notoriously rundown highway are advised not to leave the road and usually receive a police escort. I remember Tara telling me that in July, she wasn't allowed to bicycle through it and along with her bike, was put on a bus which travelled in a convoy for the whole 650km journey between Gilgit and Islamabad. The second option is a 100km shorter route which forks into the mountains just before the town of Chilas, at the beginning of Kohistan. It climbs to 4170 metres, crosses the Babusar Pass then descends through the Kaghan valley, rejoining the KKH beyond Kohistan's southern boundary at Mansehra. The mountain road is generally considered safer for foreigners and I won't need a police escort, but like the Khunjerab Pass, it's completely closed from early December to mid May. As the first snows of the year are presently falling, I'm unsure of its viability over the next few days, but without question, if it's open, I'll take it.

"The bus I was on was supposed to cross Babusar Pass," the yawning man tells me over a cup of tea. "Halfway up, the police turned us back as it had snowed heavily and many vehicles were already trapped. We had to return most of the way to Islamabad, get onto the Karakoram Highway and join a convoy through Kohistan. I spent three uncomfortable nights on that bus." he concludes, before heading to bed.
Indus Kohistan it is!

Back in my room, I hum and ha about setting off. The downpour continues and there's no shelter under which to load the Matchless. I can tolerate getting wet when I'm riding but it seems daft to be soaked through before I even set off. Nipping outside to get a first hand feel of the rain's strength, I hide under the bike's cover and apply a new layer of gaffer tape protection around the mag pickup before returning to my room to watch and wait. Around 11am the rain finally thins... then sleet begins to fall. Time for action, I carry my belongings downstairs and get ready to leave.

Riding warily through the water pouring from the cliff faces that edge the road, I'm soon back at the first tunnel. Briefly sheltered from the elements, I re-emerge into daylight and halt beside the same two policemen I met yesterday.

"Welcome back," one says affably, shaking my hand and grinning broadly.

"Now you can go, but beware of landslides on the road."

Saying goodbye, I ride into the next tunnel which proves to be the longest at over 3km. Not yet fully operational, the lack of lighting and ventilation make it an unpleasant experience. Minutes later, accelerating towards the expanding circle of light at the end of the final tunnel, I become aware of a man standing in the middle of the road windmilling his arms. It's a policeman and he warns me of large rockfalls ahead. Almost immediately, I see two enormous boulders, both bigger than the Matchless, embedded in the highway. Loosened by the heavy rain, their impact on the new tar seal is staggering... the craters they've formed are about a foot deep. I navigate past them and continue southwards with extra caution.

The rain has lightened by the time I reach Ganish, a small village where a few men take shelter in the central bazaar. They look cold, wet and miserable. Hanging limply from flagpoles attached to the fronts of several houses, I notice solid black flags. Prevalent on the Internet and news channels, solid black flags with an emblem or patch of white arabic script have in recent years become synonymous with jihadist extremists. The black flags here are, fortunately, quite different. Each identifies a Shi'ite household and they are, in many ways, a brave statement considering the sometimes victimised minority status of Shia muslims in Pakistan.

A few kilometres on, the rain stops completely and I see the first signs of Karimabad, a large village popular with tourists, perched half way up the valley side. I've good reason to remember Karimabad from my visit in 1988. During the evening of my second night there, I listened to the BBC World Service news on my transistor radio. An announcement was made that the president of Pakistan, General Zia-ul-Haq, had perished in a plane crash and foul play was suspected. Martial law was immediately imposed and by the time I reached Gilgit, there were strict curfews. At that point, security very much in mind, I decided it was time to exit Pakistan post-haste and head for India.

With these rekindled memories floating round my head, I continue south. As the highway dries, I push the Matchless faster and faster, revelling in riding the smooth, twisting mountain roads on a bike that's cornering as though on rails... the plus side of a rigid frame. Crossing the umpteenth bridge, I climb a couple of hundred metres then stop, awestruck by the sight of spartan stone houses amidst strips of terraced cultivation. The entire village seems to defy gravity, precariously clinging to the mountainside on the opposite bank of the river.

I reach the turn off to Gilgit just before 3.30pm. An overhead sign indicates that Chilas lies just 122km to the south. I estimate there's more than two and a half hours until nightfall which, on these roads, should be a breeze. With a fleeting glance towards the nearby provincial capital, I keep going. 15km further on, a petrol station comes into view. I've been so engrossed in riding that I've completely overlooked the need for fuel so pull off the highway and peer into the tank. There's some swilling around in the bottom but certainly not sufficient to reach Chilas, so I ride onto the station forecourt and park beside a pump.

While I search my pockets for my rapidly dwindling supply of rupees, the pump attendant approaches. I find 120 in one pocket but can't locate two further 100 rupee notes I'd stashed in a hurry yesterday. I begin to get flustered and eventually ask the man for a paltry 120 rupees worth. One and a half litres of petrol take just moments to pour and, when he extracts the nozzle, I look in the tank and assess how much I've now got. I still don't think there's enough and for once, wish I had a fuel gauge. After another fruitless search for my remaining rupees, I ask,

"I need more petrol, can I pay by credit card?"
This gets a firm shake of the head.

"Dollars? Can I pay in US dollar?" I ask, brandishing a $5 note extracted from my wallet.

"Sorry, not possible," says the man, turning around and walking slowly to a small wooden office building.

Sitting on the bike, I consider my options and come to the conclusion that the only sensible course of action is to turn around and ride 25km north to Gilgit. There I'll be able to find a currency exchange office and spend the night. As I put my helmet back on, another man leaves the office and heads my way.

"You need 200 rupees of petrol?' he asks when he reaches me.

"Yes. I can give you $5 but not rupees."

"No, no money," he says.
He lifts the hose from the pump and points it towards the Matchless's tank.

"It is my gift to you."
In disbelief, I remove the fuel cap and watch the gauge as it clicks round to 200 Rp.
When he returns it to the pump, I try to press the $5 note into his hand, saying,

"Please take this."
He shakes his head and, backing out of reach, replies,

"It is my duty to help you,"
I know that one of the five pillars of islam, called zakat, obligates muslims to make charitable contributions of two and a half percent of their income and wealth. However, I'm far from a charitable cause, the cost of this journey alone is probably greater than the combined average annual income of 10 Pakistanis. I begin to explain this to the man.

"No, not zakat. You are a visitor to my country. I am honoured to help you," he says earnestly.
I'm temporarily lost for words. We shake hands and I ask his name.

"I am Muhammad Sharif and it is my pleasure to meet you. Enjoy your visit to Pakistan."

"Thank you for your kindness," I manage to say. He smiles, touches his right hand to his heart, then heads back to his office with a wave.

The flawless KKH gently curves to the east following the frothing waters of the Gilgit river. After 18km, we come to its confluence with the fast-flowing

Indus, the river which gave its name to India. Staying on the west bank, we glide ahead for another 10km until stopped at a police checkpost. As I fill my details into a leather bound ledger, one of the policemen asks where I'm going.

"To Chilas."

"Ah, it's 65 kilometres away."

That's excellent news as I still have almost two hours of daylight left.

"How long will it take to get there?" I ask.

"Maybe one hour... inshallah."

I resume the journey with confidence.

Soon I swing over Raikot bridge and wave to a couple of policemen sitting in a pickup truck. Behind them, a gravel track turns off the highway and immediately begins to climb. Called Fairy Meadows Road, its poetic sounding name belies the fact that it's one of the worlds most dangerous roads. Quickly turning into an unmaintained narrow track, it provides climbers with access to Nanga Parbat, at 8,126 metres the second highest mountain in Pakistan behind K2. Nanga Parbat has a formidable reputation... numerous mountaineering deaths in the last century resulted in its epithet, 'killer mountain', and in 2013, a Taliban group dressed in scouts uniforms killed ten foreign climbers at its base camp. Although the views of its peak from Fairy Meadows Road are said to be unrivalled, a quick skywards blast on gravel doesn't seem worth the risk, especially after all the recent rain. I press on towards Chilas.

Within a few hundred metres, the tarmac unexpectedly gives way to mud and loose rocks. I slither through the morass, inch by inch, hoping that tar seal will return round the next bend. Instead, adding insult to injury, it begins to rain. Less than three metres wide, the trail hugs a steep rock face, following its contours away from the river towards a tight u-bend where a stony stream pours across our path. With my heart in my mouth, I crunch over it then turn back towards the Indus. The road rapidly becomes covered in water-filled potholes, so large, I'm forced to balance the bike on the protruding slivers of earth between their edges. It's foul.

Swathes of sand form our next obstacle but fortunately, they're so saturated we can skim over the top without bogging down. We toil on but with only half an hour to go 'til sunset, the steep gorge in tandem with heavy rain brings premature darkness upon the highway and I'm forced to stop to turn on my lights. I can't think of a worse place to be at night:.. the sheer drop to my right plunges a couple of hundred metres straight into the river and the occasional oncoming vehicle completely destroys my night vision as we squeeze past each other. On top of this, I'm at the fringes of Kohistan, which is far from the safest place for a solo western traveller. It's frightening how quickly the easy-going ride has become hazardous and I feel extremely vulnerable.

After another hour, my headlamp and torch being the only lights on the trail, I come to a tiny village. Slowing, I look around for somewhere to spend the night. Men's voices begin shouting and as I peer into the gloom, three leather jacket clad police, all armed to the teeth, step out of a shelter and point torches at me. One of them, with his black beret, shoulder length hair and wispy black beard, closely resembles Che Guevara. He queries what I'm doing. Without answering his question, I ask if there's somewhere I can sleep.

"Sorry, no hotels. Only in Chilas. It is 30 kilometres more."

"Is it safe?"

The soft tone of his voice is more reassuring that his words.

"We have patrols on the road. You will be there soon."

The mud which has hindered progress thins and long stretches of old KKH, with its original 1960s surface badly cracked and patchily repaired, appear with increasing regularity. Still thrown around like a rag doll, I can at least get into 2nd gear! Three times police jeeps pass, their headlights casting eerie reflections on the valley walls and sporadically angling into the night sky like searchlights as they bump over potholes. Seriously concerned for my safety, I repeat, like a mantra,

"I arrive safely in Chilas... I arrive safely in Chillas."

With immense relief, I make it to the town's short central strip. Several hotels line both sides and I ride its full length, searching for one that looks suitable. The town ends suddenly and with only inky darkness ahead, I brake hard. Car lights illuminate me from behind then a navy ute screeches to a halt alongside.

"Where are you going?" asks a concerned policeman. "You cannot go further tonight. You must stay here."

I explain my search for an acceptable hotel, adding that I'd accidentally overshot the town centre.

"Please follow us, we'll show you a place where you can safely park your bike."

Thinking to myself that Pakistan's police must surely be some of the friendliest in the world, I shadow them back to town and into the courtyard of the Shangrila Hotel where they introduce me to an identically attired, machine-gun equipped security guard who promises to protect the Matchless with his life. As I throw the cover over her, I glance at the clock which reads 8.10pm... it's taken nigh on 3 3/4 hours to ride the last 65km!

Reinvigorated by a steaming shower, I exchange money at reception then head to the restaurant. My window seat is close to a large table around which a party of 26 sit. Throughout the time it takes to order and eat my meal, the group continuously debate a subject in urdu, three times voting with unsatisfactory results. After forty minutes, a decision's finally reached and they begin to get up and filter out of the room. Several smile or nod as they pass so I ask one the reason for their heated discussions.

"We are all on a bus heading to Islamabad. Snow on Babusar made us turn around and as a result, our journey will take one more day and night, which we must all pay for. We were voting on how to apportion the costs."

Despite the challenges and dangers of travelling on my own, this reminds me of a plus side. I might not always make the right decisions but at least they're my own. I can also make them instantly and without either consultation or explanation. The man smiles and wishes me goodnight.

Day 47. Chilas to Uchar Nala
police checkpost. 74 miles.

I inspect the Matchless every morning without fail, looking for loose nuts and bolts, examining the rear chain and tyres and checking the oil. Every third day or so I monitor the points and spark plug and assess the state of the air filter. Today, however, I also need to track down a rattle that's become more noticeable over the last couple of days. I guess right first time, the cause is the primary chain which, hidden within its oil-bath chaincase, has stretched. I've never adjusted this kind of setup before and the process involves loosening the gearbox and moving it backwards within the frame until the correct chain tension's achieved. With caution, I loosen all the securing nuts then carefully push the gearbox in the direction of the rear wheel. The chain becomes suitably taut and I quickly lock everything back into place. It couldn't have been simpler!

With my pockets crammed full of leftover paratha from breakfast, I thank the nightwatchman for looking after the Matchless and head to the eastern edge of town. After filling up at Chilas's sole petrol station, PCO Petroleum, I ride about 100m to a barrier manned by police. Parking the bike at the roadside, I'm led downhill through a shady coppice to an concealed office where my photo's taken and my details logged on a computer. This will alert all police patrols who will expect me at each checkpost along the way. Ten minutes later, they show me back to the road and the barrier's raised. Surprised, I ask,

"I don't need an escort?"

"No, not today. No tension... everything is OK."

"It's definitely safe for me on my own?" I doublecheck.

"Yes, no tension in Kohistan at the moment and anyway, we have mobile police units on the highway."

Far from reassured, I set off.

At first, the surface is pretty much as it was in the latter stages of last night's ordeal, a narrow strip of cracked ancient tarmac, but at least I can see where I'm going today. In reality, I'm far more concerned about my security than the condition of the road. Soon I spot an approaching police vehicle, a navy Toyota HiLux whose driver gives me a wave. Then I notice that the odd shape behind his cab is actually a makeshift turret, another policeman's head and arms poking out from inside it. Pressed into his shoulder is the butt of a heavy machine gun, its tripod legs squarely planted on the driver's roof. It hardly smacks of "no tension" to me.

Traffic is light. Occasionally there's an overweight Bedford lorry, a slowly chugging relic from the 1960s that's been flamboyantly decorated in a way unique to Pakistan, an infrequent car or the odd light van. On a bend I come up behind a rattling pickup truck with what appears to be a giant cage hanging over all the edges of its cargo bay. It's impossible to see if it's carrying anything as, redolent of the *Child Catcher's* decorated wagon in *Chitty Chitty Bang Bang*, the outside is completely covered by flapping black cloth cheerfully decorated with colourful appliqué, embroidery and pennants. After slithering through a tiny village, its bazaar a mudbath tantamount to the third day of rain at *Glastonbury Festival*, I pass a lone man cradling a machine gun who's sitting on a rock at the edge of the road. Completely dressed in black, with a black blanket over his shoulders and a black scarf tied turban like around his head, he looks positively intimidating.

Twice we veer sharply inland and have to ford streams before turning back towards the Indus, its murky waters 100 metres down a sheer rocky bank. The third water crossing is more major. Here, the road has been relaid with square concrete slabs so that the river, which thunders down the mountainside as a waterfall, courses over it. I stop the bike to gauge the risks. It's almost a foot deep and travelling exceedingly fast, but if everything else has managed to cross, then so can I. The flow is so swift there's no need to worry about creating a bow wave so I backtrack for 20m then go for it, entering the torrent in 2nd gear. As it makes contact with the side of the bike, water shoots into the air, soaking my calves, knees and lower jacket, but I'm through within seconds and, as the air filter has remained dry, continue on my way.

The aftermath of yesterday's heavy rain becomes more troublesome as the frequency of deep potholes, filled with frothy brown water, increases. I weave around their edges until they become so large, it's impossible to find a path which avoids them and I have no option but to blindly ride through their centres. In the distance, as I wend my way downhill, a goat herd is being led up the highway. Reaching them, I slow down and let them filter around me, waving and saying hello to three shepherds as we pass. From time to time I see people walking along the roadside and to every one of them I wave, doing my utmost for Anglo-Khoistan relations. My fears recede as the smiles, waves and calls of,

"As-salamu alaykum," reassure me and I begin to relax.

The police presence is consistent, with checkposts roughly every 20km and a passing patrol at least once between each of them. Some of the checkpoints require me to stop and show my passport, others just wave me on, at each an officer repeating more of less the same phrase,

"No tension... all OK."

In the early afternoon, 12km before the town of Dasu, I pass an open checkpost, its lone officer squatting beside a wall. Minutes later, the KKH narrows and I peer over the verge. A rickety rope suspension bridge with gaping spaces between the warped planks of wood that serve as footboards, precariously crosses the broad river. Thinking I wouldn't fancy walking across it, I take a tight bend and come upon a yellow Volvo excavator being used to dig up the roadside. Tooting my horn, I wave at its driver who gives an identical response, then continue following the highway which has clearly been blasted out of the rock face. Across the valley ahead there's a clear view of the Indus which, in the far distance, opens out beneath a wide, vertical bank.

Before my eyes, the entire bank seems to be melting into a chocolate mudslide about a hundred metres wide. Like an optical illusion, the entire embankment appears to be collapsing. Braking hard, I stop beneath an overhang. As I reach up to undo the lock on my helmet camera, I realise something's definitely wrong. My attention's torn off the spectacle as 100m ahead, a pile of rocks crashes down onto the road. A deep rumbling sound echoes all around the valley, punctuated with sharper cracks so frequent they resemble machine-gun fire. My brain finally registers that this is an earthquake, its tremors unfelt due to the Matchless's throbbing engine.

With uncertainty, I select gear, ride out from my shelter and pull up next to the knee high barrier along the edge of the road, constantly straining my neck to look up and around for imminent threats. I stop the engine. The sounds are terrifying and I watch in fear-gripped incredulity as rocks cascade down the mountain face on the far side of the river, leaving straggling wisps of dust resembling dry ice in their wake.

Another shower of rocks tumbles onto the road ahead. Without any rational thought, I kick the bike over, turn around and begin riding back in the direction of the excavator. The echoing noise of landslides diminishes but occasionally there's a huge crunch as a big rock lands on the riverbank and sounds similar to rifle shots as smaller ones turn head over heels, hitting outcrops on their way down the slopes. Another landslip has blocked the highway. Leaving the engine running I leap off and frantically clear a trail through, pushing the larger rocks out of the way, then ride precariously over the tops of slippery slate like stones and round the bend.

The digger comes into sight. It appears undamaged, however, embedded in the tarmac just a few metres away is a boulder easily the size of a domestic washing machine. The dazed driver, clutching a visibly painful left hand, walks into the middle of the road. I park the bike between the excavator's caterpillar tracks, the safest place I can think of, then approach the young man.

"My wrist is broken. It hurts so much," he says through gritted teeth.
Leading him to shelter behind the Volvo, I locate my First Aid kit and pull out some bandages. Strapping his wrist up tightly, I make a sling to support his arm and put it round his neck.

Everything has fallen quiet. Both very shaken, we swap experiences.

"That is a bad earthquake," he says in a quivering voice. "I thought that big rock was going to land on us, so I jumped out. Then a smaller one came down and hit my wrist."

"You need a hospital. Hopefully someone will come along soon who can can take you," I tell him.

"There's a small hospital in Dasu. It's not far," he replies, wincing as he tries to make his wrist more comfortable.

After a few minutes we retreat into our individual worlds of shocked contemplation and as I lean against the digger, I reflect on what a near miss I've just had. We emerge from behind the excavator as the noise of an engine rouses us. A small van comes into view and halts next to the fallen boulder. Bustling with energy, a solid man in his thirties jumps out and greets us. The excavator driver says something in Urdu and, taking a second look at me, the van driver realises that I'm a foreigner. I must appear quite frightened as his first words to me are,

"Do not be afraid. You are safe with me. You are my brother… come, we will go forward together... come brother!"

His voice is steady and reassuring and I trust him implicitly.

Hauling the Matchless backwards out of her sanctuary, I climb on and begin following the van, the injured driver now safely ensconced in its passenger seat. We halt moments later in front of the first landslip. The path I'd previously cleared isn't sufficient for the van, so putting the Matchless on her side stand, I help the driver clear a wider route. It doesn't take long and we set off once more, soon passing the spot where I'd stopped during the earthquake. A hundred metres further, our progress is arrested by the slide I'd watched coming down. Covering the full width of the road, it's a good 15m long. I hide the Matchless under a solid-looking precipice and begin moving rocks, all the while turning over and over in my head the thought that had I been travelling even a fraction faster, I could well have been at this point during the earthquake. The consequences of that don't bear thinking about.

While we're working, a car and a pickup arrive and four more men join in. It takes about 10 minutes to create two parallel tracks before we bounce through the obstruction in convoy. A long bend commences 50m further on but as we enter it, we're brought to another standstill. This rockslide is momentous, at least 40m long. Not one single inch of tarmac can be seen through it and although much of the surface is covered in small stones and flat chunks that resemble broken roof tiles, there are many larger rocks, most the size of a football but several as big as a bedside cabinet. We hear loud cracks above us and desperately run for cover, pressing ourselves hard against the cliff wall as stones fly through the air, careering over the road's edge and down the riverbank. When all's silent again, we look at each other and laugh, doubtless the natural release of our nervous tension, then return to our task. Sweating in my jacket, gloves and helmet, I nonetheless keep everything on, thinking it may offer some protection should there be after-shocks and further landslides. Together with two others, we set to shifting a boulder, rolling it over the the edge and watching as it plummets downhill.

The man who had called me brother works like a Trojan and is soon well in front of the rest of us. Standing upright to stretch my back, I notice he's stopped and is staring ahead. I stumble forwards to join him. He's reached a point in the bend where he can see a long stretch of straight road. Forty metres away, an old pickup truck has been crushed, its cab roof flattened by an enormous slab of rock. Four men are pulling a bloody body out of the wreckage and two others have already set off in the direction of Dasu carrying another corpse. I feel sick, tears coming to my eyes in awareness of their families' forthcoming grief. Realising that the camera's still fixed to my helmet, I immediately remove it and put it in a pocket. Quietly returning to our labours, we clear two thin lanes forward but as I work, it's impossible to tear my mind away from the mangled truck. I'm badly shaken. One of our group asks if I'm OK and I explain how close I'd been to this scene.

"Nature is a powerful thing. It is Allah's will that you have survived. In this you had no say."

Preoccupied with my own thoughts, I nod back to him.

'There but for the grace of God... the luck of the draw... in the right place at the right time... it is Allah's will... the stars are aligned.' These and other jumbled notions fly through my head as I nervously walk back to the Matchless, never taking my eyes off the hillsides above for more than a couple of seconds at a time.

"Come brother, follow me. Very slowly," my friend encourages me as he starts his van and edges into the rockfall.

I kick the Matchless over, but she fails to fire. The other two vehicles are now underway as well, wriggling their way across the stony surface. I kick again and again, getting increasingly agitated as my companions disappear from sight. The old girl always starts first or second time and I can only guess that in my haste, I've flooded the engine. Cursing, I turn off the fuel, clear the carb with the throttle fully open, then try again. She starts and I apprehensively move forward onto the slip. It's hard going, with both front and rear tyres sliding all over the place. The exhaust note I usually revel in now sounds petrifyingly loud as I'm aware its reverberations could trigger further landslides. Halfway round the bend, a man runs towards me, a dull black AK47 held wide in his right hand. Wearing a brown leather jacket and a Chitrali-type hat, he signals me to a halt.

"Go back! Go back! Turn around, not safe here."
I try to explain that I'm travelling with the group that have just passed him, but he's resolute.

"It is not safe for you. You must go back and find the police... now... go!"
I don't know who or what he is but I'm in no position to argue and he plainly has my best interests at heart. However, going back isn't so simple as it's impossible to turn the bike around in the middle of the rockslide. Seeing that I'm struggling, he grabs hold of the rear frame and pulls backwards. I ride a foot forward then he tugs me back again. Between us, we complete a 7-point turn during which I only just manage to keep the bike from falling over, my leg muscles burning with the strain. In a state of primal fear, I weave my way back over the rocks and onto the comparative safety of tarmac. Pausing, I look over my shoulder but the man's already disappeared from sight around the bend. I ride on, over the two lesser slides and back past the excavator, all the while trying to keep the engine revving as lightly as possible and repeatedly scanning the surrounding slopes for danger.

Passing over another pile of rocks, I ride round a corner and come upon a parked police truck. Two uniformed officers with rifles stand beside it along with a third man toting a machinegun. He's dressed in black salwar kameez, a dark grey suit jacket and a black baseball cap with Commando written on it worn askew on his head. Out of the three, he's the only one who speaks any English.

"Stay with us," he says. "Please, sit in the car and relax."
I take in his steady eyes, his kind face, the calm tone of his voice and feel reassured. Climbing off the Matchless, I tell him about the man who stopped me on the rockslide.

"He is probably like me, a special security officer. We do not wear uniforms. Come... sit."

He opens the door and I slump onto the passenger seat. The driver, an older man with a crinkly moustache, has a brown woollen shawl around his shoulders and completely wrapped over the top of his head. He looks like a hobbit. As a controller's voice crackles over the radio set, I shut my eyes, totally shattered.

After 10 minutes, we're joined by another police car and a discussion ensues about what to do with me.

"We think it's best you come to our police station. You can stay with us until the road is open again," explains the special security officer, whose name is Yousaf.

Putting my helmet back on, I retrieve the bike and after a short wait, follow the first truck west for half a kilometre. We stop beside the wall where I'd seen a policeman just minutes before the earthquake. Behind it, immediately below road level, is a white concrete blockhouse. I ride down a dirt trail and stop as close to its door as possible. Yousaf helps unload the bike then together we manhandle her inside. Pushing the frame tight against the corridor wall, I throw my cover over her and let out a deep sigh.

One of the officers shows me to my first floor quarters, a damp room with one window and two doors leading to small balconies, neither of which close properly. There's plaster hanging from the walls and ceiling and mould creeping upwards from the floor. Two charpoys, simple rope beds, and a clothesline are the only furniture. It's the basic of basics but I feel protected and am exceedingly grateful to be here. The policemen have to head straight back out to see if they can assist injured or stranded motorists so I'm left in the hands of Yousaf and the station cook. His outside kitchen is a small stone shed which I have to bend almost double to enter. Smoke from the spitting log fire clings to the underside of the corrugated iron roof and I sit on a footstool sipping a glass of sweet milky chai while the cook makes bread. After three more drinks I'm much steadier and head back to my room.

Now dark, I dig out the InReach and type messages home letting people know I'm safe. At first the unit can't find a satellite but once I walk outside and point it skywards, it beeps and 'sent' appears on the screen. Almost immediately, one pings back from Brendan.

"Mr. G. The earthquake was on BBC News. Glad you're safe."
Jane doesn't watch the news but my parents do and would be fraught if they didn't hear from me. Thank goodness I have the InReach.

Later in the evening, I hear a vehicle pull up outside, the only sound to come from the highway during the last couple of hours. An officer comes to my room and requests I follow him downstairs. I'm shown into the mess where I shake hands with three men.

"I am the captain of the police in this territory," the oldest says.

"Thank you, sir, for your hospitality here. I would like to compliment you on your men. They've looked after me brilliantly," I tell him.

"You want to make a complaint about my men and how they have looked after you?" he says in a calm, flat tone. "What complaint do you have?"

"No. not complaint... compliment. They've been excellent."

The two other officers chime in,

"Compliment sir, he wants to compliment us."

"Ah, sorry for the misunderstanding, it has been a long day and my hearing is not very good... it was damaged years ago when I served with UN peacekeeping troops in Kosovo."

I tell him that the earthquake has already been on the BBC news and ask what information he has on its severity in this locale.

"The situation is not entirely clear yet, but most deaths seem to have occurred on the road due to rocks falling. On my stretch of the highway there have been 10 reported deaths so far."

I explain that I'd seen the remains of the truck where two people had died.

"That was very sad. There were actually five killed there. Three who were travelling in the open back of the truck were swept off by the force of the landslide and carried over the edge. Their bodies were found close to the river. You were very lucky not to be there."

After another cup of tea, the police excuse themselves as they have to once more patrol the road. It's heavily blocked 3km to the west and in several places on the far side of Dasu. I return to my room and attempt to read by torchlight but find it hard to concentrate. Out on the KKH there's no movement and trapped between landslides, countless people will be trying to sleep in their cars, vans and buses. I'm acutely aware of how uncomfortable and frightened many of them must feel. Another patrol comes in and one at a time the officers climb the stairs to say hello. Warmly shaking my hand, each calls me "brother". I feel safe and incredibly fortunate to be in their care. Cocooned in my sleeping bag, I search for meaning in my survival today, but unable to find any, drift into a troubled sleep.

My 'brother' at the rockfall 100m ahead of where I'd stopped during the quake.

Day 48. Uchar Nala police checkpost to Keyal police station. 21 miles.

The KKH is ghosty quiet as I rouse myself. Downstairs, the rooms are empty but Yousaf is up on the road and shouts,

"Good morning," as I head towards the outhouse kitchen.

The fire's flaming red and fresh paratha and chai are on offer. Sitting in the doorway out of the smoke, I lick the ghee off my fingers and contemplate the brightening sky. A far away buzzing sound seems to be drifting up the river, so I get up and walk to where I can see the sky, spotting the distant dot of a helicopter flying along the valley. Rapidly growing in size, I watch it turn a circle just beyond our building, hover for a moment, then begin to descend. Intrigued, I pick a path between rocks and head down the riverbank towards it. With rotors spinning fast, it lands on a flat area where a long line of heavy earthmoving equipment is parked. A soldier clad in khaki fatigues hops out and makes a beeline for me. As he approaches, he salutes.

"Good morning sir. We would like to borrow some of your bulldozers to clear the highway. Are your drivers here?"

I laugh, informing him of my humble status as a guest of the police. Bang on cue, Yousaf arrives and introduces himself to the soldier, quickly explaining that the plant belongs to a Chinese work crew who are tasked with upgrading the road. Unfortunately, they've recently returned to China before the passes become blocked with snow and have taken all the keys with them. With no time to waste, the soldier thanks us and climbs back into the helicopter which promptly takes off, its distinctive whirring quickly fading as it heads further up the gorge.

Warming my hands on a second cup of chai, I hear the approach of a truck from the direction of Chilas. It's immediately followed by the sound of many more so I make my way to the bottom of the path and gaze at the long line of vehicles driving past, Yousaf eagerly waving them on. A major obstruction has obviously been cleared and it's easily five minutes before the tail of the convoy has passed. A police pickup comes to a halt and I'm asked to join the occupants at the roadside.

"There are still blockages beyond Dasu, but they will most likely be cleared by the time you get there," the senior officer tells me. "Please get ready to leave. Yousaf will escort you some of the way."

I ask for more news of the earthquake.

"The radio's reporting a 7.5 magnitude earthquake with its epicentre in Afghanistan. It seems the shake originated at very deep levels, so not too many houses are destroyed. We don't know the number of people that have been killed yet but many are injured, especially as a result of landslides."

I thank him again, and, not having slept all night, he goes inside to lie down.

My bags are already packed and it doesn't take long to get the Matchless out of the building and ready to depart. Starting at the third prod of her kickstarter, I ride up the path and wait for Yousaf's transport to arrive.

"Thank you for everything you've done for me," I tell him. "Everybody in Kohistan, and further north too, has been so kind and friendly."

"It's my honour," he replies, hand on heart. "But it would be the same if I were travelling in your country, so everything is equal."

It's awkward to explain that wandering Pakistani visitors to the UK might not necessarily be treated with the same benevolence and ready friendship that I've received in Pakistan, even before yesterday's crisis. Silence would feel like a lie and it seems important that I try to elucidate some of the differences in our cultures. The best I can come up with is,

"In Pakistan, people still have time to give to others. Many of us in the UK are so busy, and so focused on our own lives, we don't have that same time in hand. And as many people from different countries and backgrounds already live there, you wouldn't stand out in the same way as I do here. Of course, there are many good people in the UK too, but I'm embarrassed to say that I doubt you would be welcomed to the same extent. It seems to me that in Pakistan, people have open hearts and they meet strangers with interest and a willingness to do their best for them. These are rare and precious attributes."

"We have open hearts," he muses. "Yes, I like that... it is true, we do."

Within a couple of minutes, a man comes along the road on a small motorbike. Yousaf steps out, flags him down and after a few words, hitches a ride. Climbing onto the back, he slings his AK47 across his chest, turns his baseball cap back-to-front, then signals for me to lead on. Soon we arrive at the crushed pickup, the dark red stain on the rocks next to the passenger's door making me wince. It's tough going riding over the many landslides, which are only marginally clear, and picking our way through the numerous waterlogged and potholed sections before we finally reach the outskirts of town. Having taken more than an hour to cover 12km, we pull up at a busy central checkpost. The three policemen on duty greet me warmly,

"We are very pleased to see you," one says. "Yesterday, when you failed to arrive, we were worried for your safety. When we heard on the radio that you were at Uchar-Nala, we were all relieved. Please, have a Coke with us."

None of the surrounding eateries, despite all sporting Coca-Cola signs, have any in stock, so we settle for a round of chai. Thanking the police for their hospitality, we set off again, Yousaf now riding shotgun in the open back of a truck. We cross the Indus then head uphill through the main section of Dasu's crowded bazaar. When the buildings eventually peter out, the truck pulls over and Yousaf clambers out to say goodbye. I think back to how reassured I was by his presence yesterday and find it hard to communicate the depth of my gratitude to him.

"Come and see us again," he says as we shake hands in farewell.

At this point, there's a transformation in the road. Unblemished jet black tarmac takes over from the shattered surface of the old KKH I've travelled on for the last 200km. Hallelujah! My joy's soon tempered, however, by the frequency of rockfalls I need to skirt and the amount of broken glass that lies in glistening patches, a sad indication of the number of cars damaged by falling rocks. In less than 20 minutes, I corner a tight bend and come to a rapid halt behind a long line of vehicles. Easing past them, I arrive at a police post.

"The road is blocked ahead," a policeman tells me. "Men are working on it but I don't know how long it will be before you can proceed."

I thank him then stand outside, deliberating whether to wait here or ride to the front of the queue. A hand touches my right arm,

"Salamu alaykum. Which country?" a man asks.

I reply, and he smiles, handing me two boiled eggs from a bag he's carrying.

"Please... eat," he says, before leaving me to join his family on a nearby crowded bus.

Sitting down to peel them, a large shadow falls over me and I look up to see four men in smart shirts and jeans, each with a huge grin plastered across his face.

"Hello... don't you remember us?" one asks.

I tentatively shake my head, saying,

"Sorry,"

"In Sost. May the force be with you, Master Skywalker!" says another and they all laugh.

I jump up and shake their hands.

"Good to see you again," the tallest says. "I'm very glad you are safe."

I apologise for not recognising them.

"You must excuse us, we had an advantage over you. In Sost, we were dressed in our Pakistani clothes... salwaar kameez. Now we're travelling back to our homes in Lahore, we're dressed in our city clothes," one of them explains.

We chat for a while and they tell me about their rough night sleeping on the bus, waiting for the road to reopen. Then a shout goes up. A bulldozer has almost finished clearing a way through and with calls of,

"Good luck," the four of them run back to their transport.

I don my helmet and gloves and fire the bike up.

Thanks to the motorcycle's manoeuvrability and the generosity of my fellow travellers, who all wave me forward, I reach the front of the line. The bulldozer, pushing the final rocks over the edge as I approach, reverses out of the way. Following a Landcruiser and a 'Child-Catcher' pickup, which I now see carries hundreds of live chickens behind its gay coverings, we're the third through. The sky's clear and blue, the valley sides verdant with bushes and trees and in the distance, brilliant white peaks crown the skyline. It's a fantastic place to ride a motorcycle! I can see for miles ahead, the empty road snaking along its cutout in the mountainside, hundreds of metres above the river. Soon, however, we come to more rockfalls which I have to edge around, and in a couple of places, nervously ride over, my fears again raised by the thought of the Matchless's exhaust triggering a landslide.

Fifteen minutes later, the KKH is logjammed again with parked vehicles. There's another major obstruction and the tailback stretches far into the distance. Riding to the front, I'm confronted by a boulder the size of a domestic garage. It's obviously detached itself from the rockface and fallen only a matter of feet onto the highway but dynamite will be required to shift it. Hundreds more rocks have tumbled around it, rendering the rest of the road impassable. A couple of locals bravely scramble over, dragging their possessions behind them, but there isn't enough room at the edge for me to squeeze the bike through. Prudently retreating in case the area's prone to further slips, I park up with other travellers a couple of hundred metres downhill.

Two men join me.

"Is that a Matchless?" asks the eldest.

Wow, that certainly makes a change from the usual 'Is it a Harley Davidson?'

"I haven't seen one of these in a long time," he continues.

He goes on to tell me how, in the 1960s, his father owned a Matchless. As a schoolboy, he once travelled on the pillion seat from his home in Lahore to the capital, Islamabad.

"I'm 57 now but it was such an exciting adventure that I've never forgotten it."

He's a very amiable chap and we chat for a long time about all manner of things. I ask him the purpose of his current journey.

"I spent all of my working life as an officer in the Pakistan Air Force," he begins. "I found my niche in skiing and for many years was their chief ski instructor, training the Pakistan team for three consecutive *Winter Olympics*. Every year, we would spend weeks at a remote village north of here which has great slopes and I became very attached to the people there. When I retired two years ago," he continues, "I decided I'd like to give something back to that community. There was no school in the village so I bought a building and had it converted. There's now a permanent teacher there and for the first time, the children are receiving an education. I've just visited them with a view to adding further classes and now I'm on my way home."

It's an inspiring tale and I ask him how he raises the funds.

"From my family and friends," he replies. "We all contribute a small amount but it's enough to make a big difference for them."

His companion, who's just returned from getting something from their car, asks where I'm from and about my journey. When I tell him that I've travelled from the UK, he looks me directly in the eye and says,

"Explain to me, please, why Tony Blair is not being prosecuted as a war criminal."

I'm rather taken aback, and as I gabble, trying to formulate a suitable response, he presses on,

"He clearly told lies, sending British troops into Iraq under false pretences. Hundreds of thousands died unnecessarily and illegally. How is this possible? I've just been reading that the publication of the Chilcot report has been delayed again. Another cover up! What are you people doing about it?"

He's clearly challenging me but not in an aggressive way, as he softly holds my right hand in his whilst he speaks.

"I think many people do care about what happened in Iraq, but there's also a lot of apathy. The stuffing was kicked out of British people during the Thatcher years and protests today seem ineffective," I begin in reply.

"Apathy! You should be out on the streets in outrage. This man, and Bush too, need to be prosecuted. If it was Pakistan, millions of us would be on the streets demanding justice."

By now, a crowd of perhaps 30 or 40 people have gathered around, all trying to listen in. The man puts his arm around my shoulder, saying,

"Come, my friend, lets take our conversation somewhere else," and together with the ex-Air Force man, we walk towards the landslide.

"What do you know about American drone attacks in Pakistan?" he asks me, changing the subject.

The truth is, I know very little, only that these pilotless aircraft are flown by remote control from stations within the USA, and have been used in bombing raids in Afghanistan.

"Not just Afghanistan... Pakistan too." the man tells me. Standing next to the cliff face, he fixes me with intense eyes.

"Since 2004, more than 3,300 people have been killed in Pakistan by American drones. Many are innocent men, women and children. Do you know that in 2006, 69 children were killed in a CIA drone strike on their school. I am not a militant, I'm a moderate, I work as a civil servant, but can you see how these indiscriminate killings will actually encourage more people to take up arms and become terrorists. Or perhaps, instead, they might simply be called fighters, because if bombs were raining down from the sky in your country, murdering innocent people, wouldn't you fight against the perpetrators?"

I'm shocked by the statistics he's just quoted. His friend intervenes,

"Enough... he's our guest, not a CIA agent. Let's talk about something else."

"I take your point," I say, acutely aware of my own complacency, promising to look into the facts when I return home.

"Come, let's go back to your bike," suggests the Civil Servant.

As we approach her, a yellow digger turns a corner and makes its way along the road. A cheer goes up and as its two Chinese drivers pass, everyone applauds. We all watch as a soldier meets them at the landslide and together, they climb up the pile of rocks, formulating a plan of action. Soon they begin chipping away at the smaller boulders, shovelling great scoopfuls over the edge accompanied by hurrahs from the onlookers. My arm is tapped and I look round to see a face beaming at me. It's my van driver 'brother' from yesterday! We embrace, both laughing. It seems I've leapfrogged him in the first queue this morning and he's only just caught up, abandoning his van a long way back and walking to the front to see how bad the landslide is. I thank him again for his courageous camaraderie yesterday and introduce him to my present companions.

More than four hours after my arrival, the road opens and I ride forth, this time the very first through. The enormous slab of rock remains in situ but the bulldozer has cleared a path around it that's wide enough for a car or small van but not for buses or trucks. I estimate an hour remains before sunset and the nearest town is only about 30km away. I'm told it has a hotel and I start anticipating a warm shower and comfy bed. With nothing in front of me, I relish riding the Matchless rapidly, braking hard and late into bends and accelerating crisply on their exits. Ahead, I see a police station set back on the run off of a tight bend, a great panoramic view of the valley sides spread out behind it. Two officers flag me down. I'm going so fast that I overshoot, turning around and backtracking to join them.

"Where are you going?" they ask.

"Pattan... a hotel."

"Sorry my friend, not tonight. There are two landslides between here and Pattan and the road is closed."

The news certainly explains the lack on oncoming traffic.

"You must stay with us. It should be open again tomorrow. Come, bring your bike into our offices."

Two planks are produced and with a heave, we roll the Matchless up a short flight of stairs and through the station's front door. The rest of the staff, six in total, are formally introduced. As I unstrap my belongings, I notice one of them carrying some clothes out of an adjoining room.

"Gordon, this is your room tonight," the Superintendent tells me. "The officer who sleeps there will share my room. Please make yourself at home, then join us in 15 minutes for dinner."

Exceedingly grateful, I remove my boots and putting on a pair of sandals they've lent me, enter the small bedroom. After changing clothes and arranging my sleeping bag, I wander outside to watch the sun recede behind the mountains and wave at a succession of vehicles that drive past, thinking that once more they face another night sleeping rough on the road. I'm soon called inside for dinner which is served in the superintendent's room. A cloth has been laid in the centre of the floor and cushions placed around it. The six officers and I make ourselves comfortable as the station cook brings in a plate piled high with roti and a large, steaming pot of daal. We all tuck in.

Two of the men speak good English and translate for the others. They're all exceedingly friendly and immediately put me at ease. Many questions follow about my journey, my experience of Pakistan and how I fared in the earthquake.

"Are your police like us?" I'm then asked.

I look around the group, all sitting on the floor sharing a meal which we eat with our fingers. A corporal sits next to me, our backs resting against the wall. He's a very likeable man who's spread a blanket over our legs to keep us both warm. It's hard to explain just how different our cultures, not just police forces, are.

Next I'm questioned about my family and how many children I have.

"Just one... a boy called Jacques. And you?" I ask, pointing in a circle that encompasses them all.

One by one they tell me how many children they have.

"I have two, a boy and a girl."

""Four,"

"He has six," the superintendent says, pointing at an older officer with blue eyes and a ginger beard who sits opposite me.

"I'm still young, so only two so far," says the corporal.

"Yes, he only has two kids now, but he'll eventually have the most because he has two wives!"

"Two wives?" I ask incredulously.

The corporal nods and smiles.

214

"What's that like?"

"It's very nice in bed," he replies with a grin. "I sleep in the middle between them both and I'm always warm."

A ripple of mirth spreads around the room.

"But two wives can be difficult. Too much tension!" he adds.

By now everyone's laughing out loud and I realise that the corporal's domestic challenges are obviously a frequent source of amusement.

"We all work for six weeks at a time, then return home for a rest. He's always the happiest to come back here," the superintendent explains.

"There is one man in the nearby village who has 31 children. Can you believe it!" the corporal exclaims.

Everyone shakes their head at the thought.

"He has four wives... now that would be too much tension!"

More hilarity ensues.

The conversation continues for the best part of two hours.

"You travel alone? I'm asked.

'Yes, I'm travelling alone," I reply.

"You don't have a friend in Pakistan?"

"No, no friend in Pakistan... Yes," I say, brightening. "Yes I do. I have six friends in Pakistan," pointing at them all. It sounds corny but I'm being sincere and they look genuinely pleased to hear it.

The superintendent stretches his arms high and says,

"It's time for a patrol. Please excuse us, but we have our duties to perform. I hope you sleep well."

Everyone stands up and after shaking my hand, they each file out of the room. I head for bed, another day behind schedule but glad to once again be safe and in such fine company.

215

Day 49. Keyal police station to Abbottabad. 126 miles.

In the middle of the night, I'm woken by the noise of vehicles driving past. They sound as if they're heading uphill which strikes me as good news because it means the road from Islamabad has been cleared. Rising shortly after 7.00am, I amble outside and take deep lungfulls of clear mountain air. On some land to the right of the station are a wooden table and a bench. Within moments of sitting down, the cook arrives with a glass of ubiquitous sweet milky tea. A couple of officers appear, quietly sitting beside me, and minutes later we're joined by three locals. For some time I've been watching one of them, a rather ancient looking man, slowly making his way up the road. The movement of his bandy legs appears painful and he leans heavily on a gnarly walking stick. As he shakily perches opposite me, I take in his long white beard, weathered brown skin and the woollen Afghani hat akimbo on his head. He seems intrigued by me and asks a flurry of questions that the police translate.

"He was hoping you were American because it's his dream to visit New York. Now he knows you've travelled from the UK, he wonders if you can get him a visa to go to London."

I've already been asked several times on this trip for assistance getting visas, albeit nearly always for work. Not sure whether he's joking or being serious, my answer to this old man is nonetheless the same... it's best he asks relatives or family friends living overseas to invite him. The man seems happy with this information and after a further chat with the police, stiffly sets off back towards his village.

Once the bike's outside, I ask the policeman if I can take their photos beside it. They seem pleased at the prospect, however, it's impossible to get them to smile for the camera no matter how much I grin at them. When we're finished and I'm ready to depart, I receive handshakes and well-wishes from them all. Once more sanctuary has been given with nothing asked in return and I feel greatly indebted.

The KKH follows a spectacularly high path that from a distance only appears suitable for tip-toeing mountain goats. Leaving the police station, it immediately begins twisting and turning so extremely that I end up feeling giddy as I repeatedly lean the bike from side to side. After an hour's riding, I reflect that if I've covered more than 100 metres in a straight line I must have blinked and missed it! Then to my surprise, I come up behind another queue of waiting vehicles. Carefully manoeuvring towards the head of the line, I reach a large crowd watching a bulldozer as it scoops damp earth from under a crumbling bank. It looks like a recent slippage, and as I reach the front, the earthmover reverses backwards and a soldier waves me through. With the onlookers now scampering back to their own vehicles, I ride across the flattened soil, hardly able to believe my lucky timing.

Unexpectedly, I'm given an escort, two policemen on a small bike who struggle to keep up with me. At the next check post, they hand me over to a second motorcycling duo, this pair charging to the front and insisting I stay behind them. 15km later we reach Besham City, the southern boundary of Indus Kohistan. It's been such a breathtakingly beautiful region to ride through and despite my fears about security, the people I've met have been fantastic. I feel a sudden pang of regret that I have to leave. My two escorts say goodbye as I park at a barrier which marks the end of their jurisdiction. The next lot, I'm told by the guard, will arrive in 30 minutes time. Finding some shade, I improvise with the only food I have at hand, tucking into a bowlful of my breakfast muesli mixed with powdered milk and filtered river water.

When my escorts come, I ask them if their services are really necessary.

"I've just ridden through Kohistan, nearly all the way without an escort, and that's supposed to be a dangerous place. Surely from here on everything is OK?"

"No sir, no tension in Kohistan at the moment. Here there are Taliban and we must be careful."

Dutifully, I set off behind their battered pickup, inhaling the acrid black fumes from its exhaust. Still following a wriggling route, we drop down to a height of almost 400m where, underneath a sign which says, 'Islamabad, 246km', I'm passed onto another waiting group, this one in a modern and much more powerful SUV. They zoom off and I fall a long way back as we climb round a series of extended switchbacks. At almost 1500 metres, in the depths of woodland, there's another halt where my details are entered in a ledger and yet another police force become my guardians. One of the men looks strangely familiar... he's the spitting image of New Zealand spin bowler, Danny Vettori, right down to wearing the same style of round glasses.

"Hello," I say as I stop by his side. "Do you like cricket?"
I'd fall off my perch if he said no as it's Pakistan's national sport.

"Yes... of course."

"Do you know the Black Caps... New Zealand?"
His face cracks into an impish grin and I guess he knows what's coming, in fact, he beats me to it.

"Yes, I know, I look like Daniel Vettori. Everybody tells me!"

The highway's surrounded by wildflower meadows, conifers are dotted on the hillsides, with some poking through the snow on the last remaining peaks. Excepting the locals' attire and the incomparable decorations on their buses and trucks, we could easily be travelling through the Swiss alps. The road surface, far from new hereabouts, is quite bumpy and I repeatedly bounce up and down on the saddle. Straightening out of a bend, I sense a slight sag under my right buttock. A couple of minutes later, there's a grinding sensation as I sink further into the seat and each subsequent bump draws me further into its depths. A roadside eatery comes into view so, frantically waving to the policeman sitting in the rear of the accompanying pickup, I swerve across the road and screech to a halt. Turning back, my concerned escorts gather round as I unclip the seat cover and peer underneath. Three more springs have broken, two have become partially detached and another has gone awol. What remains is untenable as a motorcycle seat. Using my Leatherman, I attempt to re-bend one of the hooks on the end of a loose spring... it immediately snaps off, evidently work hardened.

"We can find a motorcycle shop in the next town," suggests one of the police. "There you can buy more springs."

I don't want to appear churlish but I doubt there's any hope of that! Instead, I unearth a selection of cable ties from a pannier bag and use three to replace the smaller springs missing from the front and five for the bigger ones gone from the back. Clipping the cover into place, I press down with the palm of my hand. It holds, but for how long? They're good quality cable ties but they weren't designed to withstand the weight of a grown man constantly bobbing up and down on them. Cautiously, I ride on, the now stiffer seat feeling odd but once it's survived the first 15 minutes, my attention moves onto other matters. The engine, so reliable to date, is becoming increasingly difficult to start and, concurrently, easier to stop by the slightest retardation via the ignition lever. On the overrun, the exhaust unnervingly pops and bangs. I begin to fear that the ignition timing has slipped which for me would be a difficult job to remedy.

On the final approaches to Mansehra we become bogged down in traffic. Stuck behind the police pickup, it's hard to make out what's happening ahead and I try dodging from side to side to get a view. All I can see in both directions are stalled minibuses, trucks and cars with people randomly milling between them. In 20 minutes, we move less than 50m, and with the engine spitting hot, I'm fearful that the clutch is about to burn out. Without the police, I'd simply pull into the middle of the road and squeeze through the congestion. Twice I attempt to do this but both times an officer leaps out of the open pickup and tells me to stop, that it's not safe. Getting frustrated, I pull in the decompressor and kick out the sidestand.

"What's wrong?" the driver asks when he gets out of his cab.

I explain about the risks to engine and clutch and my desire to get moving.

"It's not possible. You must not leave us, it is too dangerous!"

It doesn't feel dangerous but I don't want to be a nuisance and have to trust their judgement.

"How far to the city centre?" I ask.

"Not far... maybe three kilometres."

Three kilometers? At this rate that'll take hours, assuming the Matchless survives!

"Is there a hotel there?"

"Yes, of course."

It'll be dark in under an hour's time so I tell them I'll make the hotel my destination tonight if they let me go.

"No way, sorry. Put your bike in our truck. We will take you there and your engine will be preserved."

I don't like it but it seems the best option. I reluctantly agree. It's all hands on deck and in a flash, my bags are detached from the Matchless. The back of the truck has fold-up steel benches along both sides which are promptly lifted up. Two police heave the front wheel inside followed by three of us hoisting the rear. I climb in and awkwardly lever myself onto the saddle while all my bags are loaded tightly around my feet. With a jerk, we set off and rejoin the stop-start crawl forwards. I desperately hold onto a steel roof rail with my left hand, my right firmly on the front brake to stop the bike rolling backwards and forwards. It rocks from side to side, however, and with no better way of bracing myself, my locked legs take the strain. The 3km journey seems to go on forever. My thighs are bashed against the folded benches, I get cramp in my calves and the square edge of the steel rail cuts into my hand. Fumes from the petrol tank make me dizzy and as it turns dark, all I can think of is escape.

We finally stop. Before I can climb off the bike, the tailgate's lowered and a second police vehicle reverses towards us, its tailgate also down.

"You must transfer to this car now. They will take you on," one of the policemen instructs.

Facing forward inside the cab, desperately struggling to keep the bike upright, I've completely lost track of time and of where we are.

"Where's the hotel? Surely we've come 3km?"

"We've passed that hotel," replies the man. "Our radio controller informed us that the hotel in Mansehra has closed down, so we kept going. However, we've reached the end of our area so these chaps have been sent to get you. Let's get your bike moved over."

By now, traffic is sporadic but I don't fancy reloading the Matchless in the dark, let alone riding her.

"How far is the next town?" I ask.

"Abbottabad is about 18 kilometres."

Feeling that I've lost control, I nevertheless realise that staying with them is the best course of action.

The new truck jumps around on the road, braking sharply and taking bends far too fast. I'm thrown from side to side, the bike's squeaking front suspension rocking up and down to the limits of its travel. One of the steel benches drops, crashing into my shin and scraping down the side of one of the front mudguard stays. I'm desperate for it all to end. After 30 hideous minutes we turn off the main road and I hear the scrunch of gravel as the driver brakes to a halt. Once more the tailgate's dropped and to my horror, I see another police truck reversing towards us.

"No, no more," I call out. "Where are you taking me?"

"Wherever you want to go," a sergeant answers. "Your next lift is here. We can take you all the way to Islamabad in relays if you want."

"No! Thank you... please... I want to get out now."

He looks around at the assembled policemen who all seem baffled that I would refuse the luxury of travelling in the back of one of their trucks!

"Is there a hotel nearby?" I ask.

"Yes, We are next to one."

I clamber out to be greeted by a man wearing a shirt and tie.

"It is my hotel, sir. Please come this way and I'll show you our rooms."

Leaving the police, I follow him to the adjoining building, take one look at its smart outer appearance and readily agree to stay without the necessity of looking inside. For an almost unbearable hour and a half, I've longed for the relief of a shower and a comfortable bed. The hotel has both, as well as its own restaurant, and as the police say goodnight, I count my blessings and head for its comforts.

Day 50. Abbottabad to Rawalpindi. 90 miles.

Concerned about the bike's poor running, I decide to stay put until I've done something about it. On Skype last night, Andy had suggested the cause might be an air leak in the exhaust but as removing it involves the fiddly job of taking off the sump guard and crash bars, I choose to carefully check it over instead. It doesn't appear to be loose and I can't see any evidence of an area where it might be blowing. Scratching my head, I look further afield, checking the ignition timing in the time-honoured fashion with a cigarette paper placed between the contact breakers. Although its never highly accurate, it indicates that the points are opening fractionally late but not horrendously so. The magneto chain, when I remove its cover, proves to be very loose. Tensioning it means rotating the magneto a couple of degrees on its platform, a bit of a concern as I'm unsure if this'll have further repercussions for the ignition timing. It also results in my hands getting covered in sloppy grease, so I take the opportunity to add more into the chaincase and gearbox. Next I clean and gap the spark plug then adjust the carburettor air screw, richening the pilot jet setting. Finally, searching for the cause of another rattle, I check the thin dynamo chain. As it's stretched quite a lot I re-tension that as well.

It feels like a good omen when the old girl starts first kick but as I ride out of the courtyard, she simply won't accelerate, as if the choke were fully on. Furthermore, every time I close the throttle, the poor thing backfires horribly. After floundering close to the kerb for less than a kilometre, with two chaotic lanes of traffic squeezing past, I decide to return to the hotel. Dodging oncoming cars, I make a dicey U-turn. Almost immediately to the left, I spot an open-fronted motorcycle repair shop so ride onto the pavement and park outside it. The mechanic and his assistant greet me and using a passerby to act as their interpreter, tell me I'm very welcome to use their facilities. On closer inspection, it transpires that their tiny shop only contains tools, a couple of beat-up scooters, a shelf of spare parts and a desk on which sit cans of oil and grease. All the work carried out on customers' bikes takes place on the pavement, so that's where I set myself up.

Dripping with sweat under the beating sun, I work in my T-shirt reflecting on how, in the mountains only a couple of days ago, that would have been inconceivable. I'm very conscious that my problem-solving methodology is flawed. I should make one change at a time and check the results before trying anything else. However, in these challenging environs and behind schedule to boot, it simply isn't feasible to do this. I'm also aware that I might be dealing with more than one issue, and with that in mind, check and adjust as many things as I can think of. The biggest job involves following Andy's suggestion to take the exhaust off. Scraping my knuckles, I drop the front end of the sump guard and remove the crash bars. The pipe really doesn't want to come out of the cylinder head and I resort to giving it a couple of solid thumps with a wooden block and hammer. Once it's off, I thoroughly clean both ends and, as I don't have any exhaust sealing compound, generously apply silicone before reassembly. Pushing the down tube home proves almost impossible but the mechanic, a slender man in his thirties, joins in and together we relocate it. The crash bars go on easily enough but the sump guard, secured by one of the main engine studs, won't align. Aided by a new interpreter who's waiting for his own bike to be repaired, both the mechanic and his assistant help, two of us using screwdrivers to lever it into position from opposite sides of the bike while the third taps the stud through. Next I reset the air screw to its original position and loosen off the magneto chain in the hope that if moving the magneto has affected the timing, I can put it back. Once everything's tightened up, I kick her over and to a round of applause from the onlookers, she catches, immediately settling into an unfaltering throb.

I'm given a rag to clean my hands then, getting my wallet out, I ask the helpful interpreter how much I should pay the mechanic. He walks over to the two men, now working on a 70cc two-stroke machine, and has a brief conversation with them.

"He will not accept payment for his help. He is very happy you stopped at his shop and is glad that your problem is now resolved. He wishes you well for the rest of your journey."

I respond that I don't feel comfortable with this.

"Please do not offer again, you will insult him. He is honoured to help you," the man explains.

After saying thank you and shaking their hands, I apprehensively ride off the pavement then make a U-turn and open the throttle, sure as eggs are eggs she'll still run like a dog. However, the valiant Matchless responds amazingly, accelerating more crisply than she has in a long time. Unbelievable! The backfiring has completely vanished too.

"That Andy Berry really knows his stuff," I say to myself as I reach Abbottabad's outer districts and hit top gear.

I ride with a huge grin on my face at the sheer pleasure of the bike running so splendidly. However, as the road opens into a dual carriageway, I really have to sharpen up as the fast moving traffic comes as something of a shock... I've become acclimatised to much quieter roads. We soon arrive at the town of Haripur. It's not very big but the main street is mayhem. Two lanes of vehicles heading in each direction are compressed into a bottleneck caused by fruit sellers and purveyors of street food which take up most of the inside lanes. An incredible number of minibuses add to the melee, kerb-crawling and frequently stopping for passengers to board and alight. On top of that are large trucks which block the way ahead as they collect long-distance travellers, their drivers lengthily negotiating fares through open doors before, deal struck, the passenger climbs in and they set off again. Mix in people pushing hand carts or wobbling along on bicycles and every attempt I make to find an easy path through is instantly baulked.

It's after 3.30pm when I reach the far side of town and can move at speed again. Now the road's down to a single lane and much as I love Pakistan's old Bedford trucks, they're a pain in the bum. I have to breathe in the cloying stuke from their exhausts as I sit terrifyingly tight to their rears waiting for my chance to overtake. If, as I do at first, I leave a reasonable distance between us, another truck or a car bludgeons its way past me and fills the gap, paying no heed to safety and forcing me out of the way. Overtaking them on the inside is an option but it's not a method I relish as Pakistani drivers have a tendency to pull over or turn off without any warning, which could leave me in Dickies meadow. There's no respite for the next 40km and by the time I reach the intersection with the main east-west highway, I feel the need to regroup so I buy some oranges at a fruit stall and sit down for 10 minutes of peace.

My route to Rawalpindi follows an extended dogleg and it's at this point that, for the first time since entering Pakistan, I turn east. In the opposite direction, 120km to the west, lies the city of Peshawar and just beyond, the Kyber Pass. Refreshed, I join National Highway 5, a broad concrete road which for large sections is four lanes wide. The spaciousness is a luxury and I enjoy cruising at 75kmph but as we progress, more vehicles join the highway and soon I'm riding amongst fast, hairy-scary traffic. Trucks, for much of the time, completely take up the outside lane and everything else has to overtake them in the inner three. Many lightweight motorcycles join the fray but one in particular catches my attention... three men are sitting on it, each of them tapping on a smartphone, including the driver!

I overtake a small two-stroke bike, a young man driving it with his wife riding sidesaddle on the back, a baby held tightly in her arms and not a helmet between them. As soon as I pull in front, he zips straight back past me, scooting further ahead by weaving between two trucks. A few minutes later, for once in the outside lane, I realise I'm passing him again. He doesn't seem to like it and as soon as he sees me, he revs the little engine hard and shoots forward as though stung by a bee, this time undertaking a car to get ahead. For the next 15km I keep a steady pace yet the same scenario repeats itself several times, the rider running his engine to the max each time he passes me. It's madness and I'm relieved when, as we approach the city, the traffic thickens and inhibits his antics.

I stop for directions, asking for the Grand Trunk Road into Rawalpindi. The man's unable to help. Fifty metres later I try another, explaining that I want to find a hotel within the city centre.

"Very difficult," he replies. "Much better you take this road to Faizabad, it is not so congested and there are some hotels."

He seems to know what he's talking about so I head left as instructed. The road surface immediately turns to pot and within a hundred metres is clogged with buses and minibuses. Crawling forward, I see a modern office complex set back in gardens. Three men standing at its entrance appear to be discussing my paltry progress so I stop to check with them.

"Yes, the hotels are just down there on the right, next to the bus station," a very friendly man tells me.

Rejoining the morass of vehicles, I pick a route inside and around the jammed lines until I finally spy a gap in the concrete central reservation millimetres wider than the bike which I just manage to squeeze through. Navigating round the edge of the bus station, I search for the promised hotels. Eventually I spot them, The Empress and The Grand. Both look mangy and the area's so filthy and noisy that I don't even bother getting off the bike. Turning around, I head back up the road towards Rawalpindi.

With more help from pedestrians and taxi drivers, I find the right road into the city centre. My engine's so stinking hot I can smell the oil and with night now upon me, I have a very hard time finding somewhere to stay. Signposts pointing to 'City Centre' or 'Rawalpindi' would be a great help but the few signs I do notice seem to be for districts. I settle for one called Sadar and hope it's somewhere near the downtown area. Eventually, wilting in the humid atmosphere, I come upon a thriving shopping district. Two men tell me I should go to Flashman's Hotel... with a name like that, how can I resist! They explain that it's no more than 500m along this very street, however, as it's one-way and I'm heading against the flow, I'll have to work my way round the many sidestreets.

After more confusing turns, I locate the hotel but can't find its entrance. I ride twice round the block, cooking my engine both times at three sets of red traffic lights, with no joy. Stopping it, I dismount and ask someone for help.

"Come with me, I'll show you," a young man says and when I begin pushing the Matchless, he drops behind and puts his weight on my luggage to help.

On reaching them, the gates to Flashman's are protected by security guards with metal detectors. Having spent more than an hour and a half searching for a hotel, it feels like a weight's been lifted off my shoulders when I kick out the side stand in front of reception. The air conditioning is bliss but when I approach the desk, I'm completely ignored by the receptionist. After a couple of minutes, I finally succeed in getting the man's attention.

"Can I have a room for one please."

"No, we're full."

I'm gutted, but try again.

"I don't mind paying extra for a bigger room. I'm desperate to find somewhere to stay."

"We're full," he says again, both his voice and demeanour overtly unfriendly.

"Can you help... is there another hotel nearby?"

"I don't know, you'll have to look for yourself."

I'm confused by his surly attitude and at a loss to know what to do. I flop in a nearby armchair and cool down for five minutes, during which time he busies himself without once looking my way. Perhaps he doesn't like foreigners, or grimy bikers, or both, I muse as I head back outside to the bike.

As I'm putting my helmet on, a taxi pulls up, four men climb out and begin unloading their luggage from its boot. As the strange behaviour of the receptionist rankles and I really don't believe him, I ask one of the men if they have a reservation.

"No, but it shouldn't be a problem," he replies.

I can see why he thinks that, as the hotel's absolutely enormous yet its car park is virtually empty. He's very chatty so I tell him what's just happened.

"Let's see if we get a room... I'll let you know."

I push the Matchless out of sight of the reception door, wait a few minutes then peer round the corner. My new friend gives me a thumbs up through the window. Blood boiling, I march inside and confront the receptionist.

223

"Why did you tell me you have no rooms when you've just given one to these men?" I ask, struggling to keep my voice even.

He ignores me, so I ask again, this time adding.

"I want an explanation, please get your manager."

"These men had a reservation and you don't," he says, not looking up from the guest book he's filling in.

"No they didn't... I asked before they came inside. Now please get me your manager."

He straightens and seeing that the four guests are still standing beside me, grudgingly says.

"This is a cantonment area. Foreigners are not supposed to stay in it without police permission, that's why I turned you away."

"You haven't seen my passport, you didn't ask if I've permission to be here, you lied to me about the room and also about these men's reservation. I want to talk to your manager."

"He is not available at the moment, but I will make an exception and find you a room."

The concession is made in such a way that it sounds like he's doing me a huge favour. Were it not nighttime in a city where hotels are hard come by, and were I not exhausted with a blister forming on my left hand from so much clutch work, I'd just walk away. But the hotel's safe and I simply haven't got the energy to search further, so I accept.

The hotel might be called Flashmans but my room's anything but flash and at almost $50, by far the most expensive place I've stayed in since Azerbaijan. The carpets are threadbare, the curtains are thick with dust, the television doesn't work, the bed's lumpy, its springs squeak noisily and the blanket's pockmarked with cigarette burns. There's no hot water in the shower and I soon discover that the Wi-Fi's broken too. What a dump! It's hard to believe that it's run by the PTDC (Pakistan Tourism Development Corporation)... far from a great advertisement for them.

After a hosepipe shower and third-rate meal, I head back outside. The dark area in front of the hotel turns out to be Rawalpindi's cricket ground and at the opposite side is the far end of the one-way shopping street I'd stopped on earlier. Toy and clothing shops dominate, with a frenzy outside a couple of the latter where winter woollens, crammed into large baskets, are on sale. It's impossible not to smile when I get a closer look at the discounted goods everyone's rummaging through... knitted tank-tops, a relic from the 1970s.

Somewhat surprising is the sight of women. A few wearing a niqab, a long headscarf which covers all of the face except the eyes, but the majority in brightly coloured hijab, a scarf which covers the head but keeps the face completely clear. The exception are a couple of women, still in traditional Pakistani dress, who wear nothing on their heads. It's not their attire that has the biggest impact on me though, it's their presence, which makes me realise that, apart from silhouettes through bus and car windows, these are the first women I've openly seen since entering the country a week ago. I spend an hour walking around the busy streets, absorbing the high energy atmosphere, before returning to my cheerless, overpriced lodgings.

Day 51. Rawalpindi to Lahore. 194 miles.

With the Matchless parked outside my room, I spend the first half an hour checking and rechecking the ignition timing, the upshot being that I'm now a hundred percent certain it's slipped and is running retarded. I need to do something about it but as the bike performed so brilliantly yesterday and my work's already cut out with the length of today's ride, I decide to take a chance on it. When I cross into India, I rationalise, it'll be much easier to find a motorcycle shop where, behind closed doors, I can do the job cleanly and uninterrupted.

There are two routes south-east to Lahore. The first is the Grand Trunk Road, commonly referred to as the GT Road, one of the oldest highways in Asia. Its roots can be traced back to the 3rd Century BC although it was under the British in the 19th Century that it was extensively upgraded and had its name changed from Grand Road to Grand Trunk. Before partition in 1946, it spanned the total breadth of India, over 1500 miles from Chittagong, now in Bangladesh, all the way to Kabul in Afghanistan. English author Rudyard Kipling referred to it as '... a river of life as nowhere else exists in the world' and it's probable that just as much teeming life flows along it to this day. The alternative is a new motorway but motorcycles are banned from it and the curving route it takes is almost a hundred kilometres longer. Despite several warnings about crazy traffic on the GT Road, I'm actually quite looking forward to riding it.

Setting out at 10.15am, I quickly find a petrol station and fill up. After paying, I search in the tank bag for sunblock, a large tube that I keep tightly wrapped inside a polythene bag. As I unfurl it, thick white cream splatters everywhere, the cap has popped off and much of the contents have been squeezed out of the tube. Despite my best efforts, I end up in a pickle, smeared with the stuff. Observing my plight, a man comes out of the petrol station and offers me a fresh carrier bag to drop the offending article into and some tissues with which to wipe myself. A little kindness goes a long way... especially in such messy circumstances.

Failing once again to spot any signposts, I come to an intersection where I think I may need to turn right but can't be certain. Halting, I question a man at the roadside.

"As-Salaam-Alaikum."

"Wa-Alaikum-Salaam."

"Do you speak English?"

"Most certainly."

"Great. Please can you tell me if this is the GT Road?" I ask, pointing to the turn off.

"Ah, you are looking for the GT Road. Where are you from?

"I've travelled from the UK."

"Oh, Great Britain. Her Majesty the Queen... very good. And where are you going?"

I tell him... as I do in answer to the rest of his questions about why I've come to Pakistan, my impressions of his country, the places I've visited since arriving, my family and how they feel about me being away from home. At least five minutes pass before I can steer the conversation back to my original question.

"Please can you tell me... do you know which is the GT Road to Lahore?"

"Of course I can tell you. It is my duty to help you. What is your good name sir?"

I laugh at the difficulty of getting a straight answer out of him! I know the guy's not being deliberately obtuse, he's a genuinely nice man who's eager to hear my story, but the truth is that after almost 10 minutes of questions, I'm desperate to get directions and be on my way.

The highway's much emptier than I'd expected and is mostly a reasonable, if at times patched, dual carriageway. Despite my fears for the ignition timing, the bike runs smoothly and as the terrain's almost completely flat, we make great progress, only slowed when a town encroaches onto the road. There, traffic's thickened by the slow clattering progress of horse and carts, sugarcane juice sellers with large flywheel presses atop rickety hand-drawn carts, buzzing auto rickshaws which switch hither and thither between lanes and animals, mostly goats, in the care of children who chase the errant ones with sticks. Combine all that with the usual long distance buses, trucks and minibuses plying their trade, and my safe passage through it requires every ounce of concentration I have. Frequently, most often in the busiest central area, a belligerent inter-city bus blasts through, air-horns blazing, showing no sign of slowing. Watching the ensuing sight of pedestrians and tradesmen running for cover reminds me of pit crews scampering for the circuit's barrier at the start of a Formula One formation lap.

One of the most unexpected sights is the large number of MKI Ford Transit vans being used as minibuses. Congregating at the fringes of towns, they're almost exclusively the more charming early version with round headlights and tall radiator grills, common in the UK from the late 1960s through to the end of the '70s. All right-hand-drive, I notice one of them has a faded GB roundel stuck on its back door, confirming my suspicion that they're second-hand imports from the UK. Much like the omnipresent Bedford trucks, it's fascinating to see that they've been kept running for so long.

Riding non-stop for 130km, I come upon a truck park, a strip of land perhaps half a kilometre in length at the rear of which shops, restaurants and teahouses have set up to service the many drivers who rest there. For some time I've felt the need to get off and stretch my legs and the sight that beholds me as I ride past is the perfect excuse. I slide to a dusty halt in front of a spectacularly decorated Bedford.

Predominantly vibrant scarlet, it's been gloriously overlaid with a combination of intricate tin work and multicoloured hand painting. Along the sides and the rear are hundreds of wooden panels decorated with ornate script, flowers, squiggles, geometric designs, coloured mirror glass and tiny landscape paintings. Embellished with glittering baubles and gaudy trinkets, the door's window is less than a foot square and surrounded by a long row of colourful christmas tree lights. Above the cab is a dominating 3m tall overhang which angles 30 degrees forward and beneath its ornate curved peak, a magnificent pair of peacocks face inwards towards an all-seeing eye. Stylized flowers and love hearts adorn the windscreen surround and along the trailing edges and front mudguard hang all manner of jingling chains and bells. Rising straight up from the front of the bonnet are two dozen whip aerials, each shiny chrome with a dab of red paint at its tip. I adore the idiosyncratic individuality of all Pakistani trucks but this one stands out as exceptionally fabulous.

Its tall, bearded driver, watching from a distance as I walk around in admiration, comes over and invites me to look inside. The cab's completely covered from top to bottom in colourful appliqué, mirrors and crazy lights... it's so all encompassing, I can't even spot the speedometer. By now a crowd has gathered round and through a man who translates, I'm told that the truck dates from 1970 and has been in this driver's possession for over 20 years, ploughing the same route up and down the GT Road with dry goods on board.

"Please sir," he says. "Would you do us the honour of joining us for a cup of tea."
Everyone, including the driver, nods in agreement when he translates his question. How can I refuse.

Later in the afternoon, approximately 60km north of Lahore, I have to stop to cool down. The thermometer's reading 36° and my body's thermostat, dealing with freezing cold temperatures since leaving Dushanbe, is taking its time to adapt. I pull into a petrol station ostensibly to buy a cold drink but take the opportunity to first fill up. Paying the attendant, I push the bike out of the way then walk to the small shop which amongst other signs, has one for Coca-Cola. The door's locked and I see that it's completely bare inside. The attendant joins me and, not speaking English, uses open arms and hands to ask me what I want.

"Coke... Coca-Cola," I say, simultaneously pretending to drink from a bottle.
He shakes his head and looks sorry that he can't help.

A man's voice calls out and, turning around, I notice three young men in tattered clothes sitting on a charpoi, One of them waves me over so, leaving the bike, I walk towards the group. As I approach, the youngest gets up and disappears from sight, returning moments later with a grubby plastic chair which he gestures for me to sit on. They're in the process of dishing up their shared meal from two small polythene bags of curry, a third which holds rice and another in which there's a compressed stack of roti. As they pour the contents onto a large tin plate, they offer me some. I thank them but say no, perfectly content just to sit with them. I feel a tap on my shoulder. When I spin around, a boy holds a chilled bottle of Coke towards me, condensation trickling down its sides. Turning back to the group of men, they gesture for me to take it and I press it satisfyingly against my forehead and cheeks before taking the first swig.

I spend the next 20 minutes quietly relaxing beside them, sipping the icy Coke and enjoying the light, cooling breeze that wafts across the forecourt, the only disturbance the occasional waving of their hands as they waft away the flies. When I feel steadied and ready to leave, I pull some rupees out of my pocket to pay for the drink. All three vigorously shake their heads... we may not share a common language but their message is clear, it's a gift. Thanking them, I return to the bike feeling humbled. As is so often the case, the people who have little share it unconditionally and I'm enriched by the experience.

I've been given the name of a good hotel and have memorized directions through the city to it. Crossing Lahore's outer ring road, I follow signs towards the Lahore Museum, and despite a couple of confusing moments, manage not to lose my way. Traffic's now solid, 4pm friday afternoon not being the best time to arrive in a large city. Motorcycles, scooters and rickshaws are crammed into the tight lanes and traffic lights are particularly challenging as hundreds of bikes squeeze their way to the front of any larger vehicles blocking their paths. Heavily loaded and wider than all of them, it's impossible to emulate their actions and on a couple of occasions I fail to get through on the first change of lights. Then I reach a junction where the 'Old City' is signposted to the left. I reckon I need to go straight ahead but that avenue's blocked by the central reservation. I ride on for a few hundred metres but my inbuilt guidance system keeps telling me I'm heading the wrong way. Pulling over to the side, I turn off the engine and on an intuition, wait for a solution to present itself.

Within thirty seconds, a young man approaches and asks, in English, if he can help. I explain I'm looking for a hotel on The Mall but have lost my way.

"Please, wait here," he says, jogging back in the direction he came from. He soon returns riding a motorbike he tells me he's just borrowed from a friend.

"Follow me. I know the Mall and I'll ask directions to your hotel once we are on it," he says, pressing the starter button and swinging straight out into the heaving traffic.

I give chase as well as I can. We backtrack for a few hundred metres then through a gap between a dozen other bikes, I spot his grey t-shirt and see he's indicating left. We cross several junctions where, beyond each set of traffic lights, he waits for me to catch up. Then, to my delight, we pass *Zamzama*, the ancient cannon featured at the beginning of Kipling's book, *Kim*. Two kilometres further along the jam-packed road, having twice stopped to ask the way, he pulls up at the doorstep of my hotel. It's taken him nearly half an hour to get here but he says he's delighted to have helped.

"Can I have a photo of us and your bike?" he asks, taking out his phone. We pose for the camera, he shakes my hand, wishes me good luck then zooms off to return the motorcycle. Such is Pakistan and its people and in so many ways, I'll be sad to leave them tomorrow.

The front door of the hotel is manned by a delightfully friendly security guard. Once I've signed in, he tells me that the clothes shop adjoining the hotel is closed and begins moving a row of potted plants that divide the path in front of the two buildings, ushering me to park there. It's approximately one metre from his three-legged stool.

"Have no fear, I love your motorcycle. It will be safe with me and I'll tell my friend, the nightwatchman, to take great care of it too."

In the evening, the streets quieten down, I walk back to *Zamzama*, nipping between now speeding vehicles to its resting place, an island in the middle of the road. Cast in 1762, it was at the time one of a pair of the biggest guns made in India. It's impressiveness hasn't diminished with age, the huge cannon's more than 4m long and sits upon colossal wooden wheels. It was used in several battles until being severely damaged in the 1802 siege of Multan after which it was returned to Lahore and forgotten about until being restored and placed at the entrance to the Lahore Museum in 1870. Kipling's book begins with the boy protagonist, Kim, sitting astride the gun and since then, it's commonly been referred to as 'Kim's Gun'. In 1988, after fleeing Gilgit, I'd spent a week in Lahore waiting to cross into India as the land border was only open two days per month. I read *Kim* during that stay and visited the gun on several occasions. Coming back here tonight has evoked many memories of those times.

Walking back towards the hotel, I stop for a meal and after trying five different banks, finally locate an ATM that will accept my credit card, cash being essential for settling the hotel bill. En route, I gape at the rows of Hondas that line the pavement. Easily stretching three street blocks and mostly parked two or three deep, there must be at least a couple of thousand. I realise, in amazement, that they're nearly all identical. How on earth do people ever retrieve their own bikes when they're not only subsumed in this vast red mass, but all finished with exactly the same decals? Surely it must be a major challenge for their owners, except for the few who've painted the machine's pet name onto the petrol tank... 'Red Devil', 'Evil One', 'Don't Make Me Angry' and the rather boastful, 'No.1 Lover'!

Back in my room, I reflect on today being the end of a chapter and prepare myself for the start of a new one tomorrow... India!

Delightfully friendly security officer guards the Matchless, Lahore.

Day 52. Lahore, Pakistan, to Amritsar, India. 41 miles.

The Mall is one of Lahore's most important thoroughfares yet it's uncannily quiet as I step outside the hotel.

"Many Lahoris left last night," explains the yawning nightwatchman whose command of English, like many Pakistanis, is exemplary. "Fiercely contested local government elections will be held this weekend and lots of people have fled the city to avoid the large rallies."

Standing beside him, I watch a cricket match being played across the empty road, the athletic teenage fielders running for safety as a lone car zooms past. Charging straight back into the fray, the fast-paced bowler bounds towards the chalked wicket and releases his tennis ball. It's smacked along the ground through mid-on where a fielder turns on his heels and gives chase, catching it on the rebound off the kerb. Pirouetting, he fires it towards the cardboard box stumps, the batsman only just making it into his imaginary crease at the end of a cheeky second run. It's captivating but I need to get moving... who knows how long today's border formalities might take.

Last night I replaced the micro SD card in my Garmin with a new one that's loaded with detailed mapping for India. When I clip the unit onto the bike and power it up, it shows nothing except empty space so I zoom out, watching as the colourful details of India's road network begin to emerge on the screen. Although conspicuous by its absence from the satnav, my route to the border is very straightforward as all I need to do is continue along The Mall until I hit Canal Road, where I'll turn left and shadow the course of the canal to the city ring road. If all goes to plan, after a kilometre long dogleg, I should end up following a plumb line straight to Wagah Border. The Matchless isn't willing to cooperate, however, as she's reluctant to start.

"Come on, you can do it," says the nightwatchman, stroking her headlamp while I remove the spark plug and give it a clean.

Next try she coughs then apathetically ticks over. I put on my helmet and gloves, hoping the timing hasn't slipped further.

Half way to the border. I stop at a petrol station, as usual pushing the bike to the side once fuelled to measure the requisite amount of upper cylinder lubrication additive. As a crowd of inquisitive men gathers around, I become distracted and soon realise that I've lost track of how much orange liquid I've poured in the tank. They're such an outwardly decent bunch of guys that I've no qualms leaving the bike with them while I spend my final few rupees on a bottle of chilled water from a nearby shop. Returning, they watch, mesmerised as I pour it into my Camelback. Thankfully, the Matchless starts willingly and we say cheerio.

An army checkpoint blocks the final run to the border. Plainly not very busy, the soldiers fire a salvo of questions about the bike.

"Is it a Yamaha?" the first asks.

"No, it's one of those Indian Bullets, is it not?" one of his colleagues chimes in.

"You're wrong, it's a Harley Davidson. How many cc's... 1000?"

Their evident lack of knowledge is unsurprising as the largest capacity bike I've seen since Sost is a 125cc Honda.

Two hundred metres further on, I'm stopped by another squad of troops, this lot wearing sand coloured camo and dark green berets. They're tasked with checking passports and paperwork, giving mine little more than a cursory inspection. Five minutes later they let me go but incredibly, the next check post is only a hundred metres distant and here I need to leave the bike to go inside a concrete blockhouse where more soldiers enter the same details onto their computer. When it's done, all five of them follow me outside to watch me start the bike. To my chagrin, the kickstart spins round against virtually no compression and my boot flies off it. The blasted inlet valve has gummed up again and is stuck open, patently the result of once more putting too much additive into the fuel. My blood pressure rising as I kick and kick, the sergeant takes in how hot and bothered I've become and suggests I sit with them and have a drink of tea. It won't solve the gummed valve issue but it'll probably prevent my own body blowing a gasket, so I strip off my soggy riding gear and sit in the relative cool of their office for 10 minutes, enjoying my last Pakistani chai.

Back outside, one of the soldiers helps me heave the Matchless onto the rear stand, a task that's too difficult on my own when she's fully loaded. I try the same method I'd employed at the Georgian border, rapidly kicking the engine over and over with the spark plug out. After replacing it, I turn the fuel back on and after a dozen or so rapid revolutions, it catches... thank the lord!

I'm soon at the Pakistan immigration building, a place I clearly remember from the 2008 journey on my Royal Enfield. Exiting today is just as simple as then: my passport's stamped within five minutes and after a further ten, I watch as the carnet's rubbered in a fan cooled office. The customs official, who shows no interest in checking bike or belongings, is primarily concerned that I'm leaving Pakistan with good memories.

"I hope you have enjoyed your stay and will visit us again," he says as he hands back my documents and shows me the way out.
You betcha!

Crossing into India is a wholly different affair. Simple green gates on the Pakistan side, decorated with a single white crescent and star from the Pakistan flag, are already wide open. The much taller, ornate gates that mark the entrance to India have been painted the orange, white and green of the Indian flag and are firmly closed. As I slow in front of them, they're partially opened by two soldiers. The gap's only just wide enough for me to squeeze through and while they swing them shut behind me, a third guard indicates I should go to an open-air desk immediately on the left. Here I'm asked to empty my pockets before being thoroughly checked over with a hand-held metal detector. A lengthy form is duly stamped then I'm told to ride to a building several hundred metres away on the right. It's a new single story immigration complex, huge compared to its predecessor, and upon arrival I'm instructed to park the bike close to its front door and remove my belongings. Stacking them high on a trolley, I head inside and feed everything through an x-ray machine then comes immigration where, after a protracted grilling, my passport's franked. So far so good, I think... just forty minutes gone and only customs to clear... 'though I'm not counting my chickens yet!

"Leave your bags here and come with me," says an officer when I tell him I'm on a motorbike.

We walk outside and he instructs me to push her 100m across an empty car park to an area where half a dozen customs officers sit chatting. Upon our arrival, they show no interest in corroborating engine and frame numbers, being far more intent on searching the bike for illegal substances. They ask me to take the headlamp glass out, empty the toolboxes, which haven't been opened once since leaving the UK, and even look inside the air filter!

"Do you have any contraband?" asks the senior plain clothes officer.

"Absolutely not," I say, steadily looking him in the eye.

"No? ... Really?" he says, stretching the vowels of the second word into a disbelieving question. "You must have something. Come on, tell me what you have."

I laugh at his feigned distrust, guessing he must try the same approach with everyone, and firmly shake my head in denial.

"Okay, that's what you say for now. But let's see. Leave your bike here and return to your bags. They'll need to be searched. Oh, by the way, do you have a satellite phone?"

"No," I reply, immediately conscious that my answer's only half true. My InReach, although communicating over the satellite network, isn't strictly a phone but I hope I'm not taken to task on it.

Back inside, there's a ream of paperwork to fill in. When it's completed, I hand it in at the customs desk and push my trolley forward for my belongings to be checked.

"Later... first the bike," says the young lieutenant in charge, Another chap leads me into an office where, without a single word being spoken, he works his way through the carnet process. Eventually, everything's handed back and I can progress to the next stage. Reclaiming my trolley, I join a long line of people waiting, some with even more luggage than me! When I finally reach the front, the lieutenant joins another officer in the search, meticulously scrutinizing every single item.

"And you definitely don't have a satellite phone?"

"No, no phone... just an SOS device," I add, thinking I'd better err on the side of caution.

His ears prick up and he starts questioning me about its capabilities.

"This is very interesting," he says. "I need to show it to the AC. None of us have seen one that can send texts and it sounds much more dangerous than a Spot SOS device."

"Dangerous?" I ask following him outside. "How can it be dangerous?"

"Satellite phones are being used by terrorists and drug smugglers because they're difficult for us to monitor. That's why we're confiscating them."

The word "confiscating" comes as a bit of a shock and I'm immediately on high alert. Losing it would be a disaster.

"Only last week we caught a drug smuggler with 23kg of heroin. He had a

232

sat phone with him," he continues as we reach an office block and walk inside.

Knocking on a door with *Assistant Commissioner* written on it, we enter on hearing a grunt. The AC, a gold aiguillette hanging from his right epaulette, waves me into a seat across his desk and, after a brief conversation with his subordinate, asks for a demonstration. Switching the InReach on, I run through the basic SOS function then show him how the text system works, using one to my family as an example. A conversation ensues between the two officials and I'm still not sure if they're going to try to seize it.

"Thank you for explaining it to me," the commissioner finally says.
Like being on trial, I await his verdict with bated breath..

"I see no reason why you can't bring it into India. Enjoy your stay."
Relief!

More than four hours after passing through India's gates, I ride to the final check post, hand in my clearance certificate, and am released, swinging straight back onto the GT Road. For just a few moments we're the only vehicle on it and as the Attari border compound vanishes from my mirrors, I notice my Satnav coming to life, its screen abundant with detail for the first time in weeks. I halt, set a course for downtown Amritsar, and before accelerating away, squeeze the Matchless's tank between my knees as I exclaim,

"You've made it to India, girl!"

Visible along the roadside, the people's style of dress is noticeably different from Pakistan, with the women in exquisitely coloured saris and the majority of men wearing turbans. The traffic's changed too, the trucks less OTT and motorbikes clearly bigger and faster. Within a few minutes, I overtake a tiny car known as a *Tata Nano*. When first launched in 2005, it cost less than 1 lakh Indian rupees (sub £1000), a price set artificially low to lure India's burgeoning middle-class away from motorcycles. Manufactured so cheaply, they were notoriously fragile when involved in accidents, a trait which author Miles Davis highlighted in his book, *Motorcycle Yoga*, referring to the Nano as a PCD... Population Control Device!

It doesn't take long to reach the suburbs of Amritsar and I remain on the GT Road right into its heart. The hotel I stayed at in 2008 was close to the railway station and after just one minor hiccup from the satnav, when I have to detour around roadworks, I pull up outside of its familiar doors. The Grand Hotel Is owned by a charming man called Sanjay, who by chance is in reception when I enter. Obviously, he doesn't remember me but I remind him that on my previous visit, he kindly allowed me to keep my Royal Enfield at his house as there's no secure parking at the hotel.

"Of course, and you can do the same again. Let's get you in a room then you can follow me there."

Half an hour later, with the Matchless now bare, I sit tight to the rear of his Toyota, weaving along a convoluted network of backstreets. Before I can park up, Sanjay's housekeeper has to secure his fearsome-looking Alsatian, which prowls up and down, glaring forbiddingly and repeatedly baring its sharp teeth. There's little doubt the bike will be safe in this dog's domain!

Amritsar is the capital of the Punjab state and the most important city for

Sikhs. In its centre is Sri Harmandir Sahib (The abode of God), commonly referred to as the Golden Temple, the holiest place of worship in Sikhism. I've visited it twice before and would love to again, however, with so much still to do today, I come to the conclusion that I'll have to give it a miss. After a late lunch, I send an email to one of my contacts at Royal Enfield's office in Delhi. Subramanian Venkatachalam, known to all as Subbu, is one of the company's international team and I've met him several times while working on projects for the company. Passionate about Royal Enfields, he's a friendly chap who, before I left home, offered to give any assistance I might need upon reaching India. My email explains the problem I'm having with the bike and asks if he can recommend a Royal Enfield dealership where I can take it. I explain I'll be able to fix it myself, I simply require a quiet workshop in which to work.

In my room, I spend a couple of intense hours emptying everything out of my bags and deciding which items are no longer needed. All my thermals go for starters, along with tent, sleeping bag (x2!), air mattress, stove and cooking equipment. Packed into a couple of carrier bags, I make for the nearest DHL office which fortunately proves to be a mere 50m away. The young Sikh running it takes over an hour to sort through it all, itemising every article on a consignment certificate before carefully squashing it all into his largest yellow and red DHL box, It's such a tight fit that I actually have to kneel on top of the lid while he tapes it down. The maximum weight I'm allowed to send per package is 10kg, and mine totals 9.7! It isn't going to make an enormous difference to the bike's overall weight, I think whilst crossing the road back to the Grand, but it'll certainly have a big impact on the height of luggage that's heaped behind me which definitely justifies the expense.

It's 9pm before I order dinner and whilst it's being cooked, I check my emails. There's one from Subbu,

'Hi Gordon, our dealers in Amritsar are called *Jaycee Motors*. They're closed on Sundays but their retail manager says they will open their workshop specially to help you. He'll arrange to meet you in the morning. Good luck and best regards, Subbu.'

What a star!

Bang on cue, the receptionist comes to my table, saying that someone's on the phone asking for me.

"Hello Mr. Gordon, Manish Mishra from Jaycee Motors here. I understand you need to use our workshop and I'd like to extend the services of our chief mechanic to assist you. What time would you like to come tomorrow morning?"

I suggest 10 o'clock, and after a brief chat with the receptionist, Manish suggests I'm met at the hotel so that one of his staff can lead me from Sanjay's directly to their store.

Dinner is waiting when I return. I've ordered one of my favourite meals, paneer tikka, pieces of Indian cottage cheese marinated in spices then dry roasted in a tandoor oven. Accompanied by dal makhani, black lentils cooked with red kidney beans in butter, cream and spices, plus garlic naan and a crisp Kingfisher beer, it can't be beaten, a gastronomic celebration of our arrival in India.

Day 53, Amritsar. 0 miles.

Three American men are sitting at a nearby breakfast table and as they get up to leave, one asks if I'd like today's newspaper, *The Tribune*. He brings it over and we get into a conversation. When I ask about their journey, he explains that they're all recently retired and had originally arranged to visit Nepal to work as volunteers for *Habitat For Humanity*, a Christian non-profit organisation set up by former US president, Jimmy Carter, and his wife Rosalind. The organisation's founding principle is that every person should have a decent, safe and affordable place to live, which it seeks to address by building, renovating and repairing houses using volunteer labour and donations. Shortly before they were due to set off, *Habitat for Humanity* postponed their Nepalese project due to safety concerns resulting from recent constitutional changes in the country but as their flights were already booked, the three men decided to make the most of things and tour northern India instead.

As I eat, I flick through the paper and an article jumps out concerning a spate of suicides amongst Punjabi farmers. This is a disturbing topic which I've come across before, having seen *YouTube* videos featuring Dr. Vandana Shiva, an eminent Indian physicist and environmental activist. Dr. Shiva blames India's devastating farmers' suicide crisis on issues surrounding the patenting of GMO seeds by multinational agrochemical and biotechnology corporation, Monsanto. *BT Cotton* is grown from Monsanto's patented cotton seed which has been genetically modified with a 'terminator' gene so it doesn't produce viable offspring seeds, enslaving farmers to buy new seeds every year. It's now the predominant cotton in India due to the destruction of alternatives and the subsequent creation of a seed monopoly. The constantly inflating price of these seeds, their need to be grown in monoculture and the evolution of superweeds and superbugs resistant to BT technology, has made the plight of many farmers desperate, trapped in vicious cycles of debt and crop failures. Since the late 1990s, more than 300,000 farmers have taken their own lives. I consider it to be madness in plain sight and it makes my blood boil!

Jasbir Singh from *Jaycee Motors* arrives at reception just as I finish reading the paper. Despite being called in at short notice on his day off, he's full of bonhomie and can't wait to see my bike. Crash helmet, gloves and tools at the ready, I follow him outside, expecting to leap onto the back of a Bullet. It's a bit of a shock to see that he's riding a scooter.

"It's the shop's run-about," he sheepishly explains.

We're soon bumping along backstreets and after weeks of riding the rigid Matchless, the spongy feel of the scooter's rear suspension is a revelation. In spite of the comfort, 'though, riding pillion to a stranger amidst India's chaotic traffic turns out to be a pretty nerve-racking experience. At Sanjay's house, we struggle to make ourselves heard above the din of the howling guard dog but eventually, after much hollering over the garden wall, the housekeeper takes the hound indoors and I retrieve my bike. Reluctant to start, she finally coughs into life but sounds so seriously akin to a tractor that I wince as we follow Jasbir through the city's streets, desperately wanting the short journey to be over.

We soon reach the Royal Enfield dealership and I'm directed down a steep ramp into the subterranean workshop where Pargat Singh, the chief technician, waits. Neither he nor Jasbir seem perturbed by the Matchless's poor performance, they're intrigued by the bike and keen to help. Pargat's been working on Royal Enfields for five years and has a wealth of knowledge about the newer fuel injected, unit-construction (UCE) Bullets. Of the older bikes assembled in India since 1956, mostly running points ignition like mine, he knows little. I shouldn't be surprised by this. In 2009, when UCE Bullets debuted in India, the company were running at record production levels of just 40,000 machines a year. By contrast, in 2014 they sold 296,000 bikes and despite recent floods in Chennai temporarily slowing production, their target of 500,000 units this year seems highly likely to be met. Less than 6 years on from the new UCE model's introduction, there are far more of them on India's roads than the totality of the preceding 54 years' output. For Royal Enfield, makers of the world's oldest motorcycle in continuous production, it's a remarkable success story. Little wonder Pargat's expertise is focused on the new models.

First job is to clean as much muck off the engine as possible then remove the timing chain cover. The tool I need next, which I don't carry with me, is a puller, a kind of pincer which prizes the magneto pinion off its taper as you tighten it up. The magneto chain hinders progress and it's difficult to squarely locate the puller but after a few attempts, the pinion comes free. Using my Top Dead Centre tool, I set the engine the correct number of degrees before TDC then turn the contact breakers to the point where they're just opening on the compression stroke. With Pargat's assistance, the mag pinion is replaced, pressed home and tightened up. That should be it but when I check the ignition timing, it's dramatically over-advanced. We go through the whole process again and once more the same happens. Andy had warned me that the pinion is prone to shifting when you tighten it but this is ridiculous! On the third attempt we're especially careful but the results are exactly the same.

"Let's try setting it retarded," I suggest. "That might compensate for the way it advances when you tighten it up."
Pargat nods in agreement and we set to work. The first go gives some improvement. Our second try is the best by far, only a smidgin over-advanced. Reasoning that it might take several more attempts to get it any closer, I use a marker pen to draw a sharp black line on the handlebar advance/retard lever, indicating our new compromise running position for fully advanced. Pargat steps back and I kick the bike over. She sounds beautiful... job done!

"Time for lunch," says Jasbir, joining us as we clean our hands. "Why not leave your bike here tonight and collect it in the morning. It'll save you having to face that mad dog again!"
The offer makes good sense so I cover her up and we head out to eat.

When I was much younger and backpacked through India, the Middle East and South East Asia, I was on a very tight budget and would often eat in basic restaurants or at streetside stalls. Several times I paid the price with my health, suffering from repeated bouts of Delhi-belly. three vile giardia episodes, a dose of gastroenteritis and on one very bad occasion, amoebic dysentery which resulted in a three night stay in hospital. I've managed to avoid any serious hygiene-related illnesses since I've been able to afford to eat in better quality establishments, which is critical on a journey such as this. The restaurant Jasbir introduces as having the best food in Amritsar is typical of the eateries I'd once frequented. Open to the pavement, the food is cooked on an open range and sits out waiting to be served, flies buzzing around the pans of cooling curry. On a hard baked floor is a line of steel topped tables with wooden benches for seating. Following my friends inside, we sit under a whooshing ceiling fan and a waiter brings us water in tin beakers. I pass on that, and as there's no menu, rely on Jasbir to order for me. Minutes later, a piping hot plate of butter masala curry and a small stack of buttered naan is placed in front of me. Despite my worst fears, the food is alive with subtle, spicy flavours, the freshest and most deliciously tasty meal I've had on the whole ride and well worth the risk of an upset tummy.

Thanking the two chaps warmly for their time and help, I head back to the hotel and quickly get changed. I've booked a trip to the famous border closing ceremony that takes place every day at the Attari / Wagah frontier post. I'm the only guest taking the tour so I hop into the front seat of a car driven by one of Sanjay's staff and motor 30km west to the border. Known as Beating the Retreat, the lowering of the flags ceremony has been a daily occurrence since 1959 and in recent years has become a major attraction for visitors from both the two host countries and overseas.

As our car draws near, a swarm of people are heading on foot towards the immigration compound. Arranging to meet the driver in the same place at the end of proceedings, I join the excited masses. Ahead, the crowd splits into two, women on the left and men on the right. Both queues lead to thorough security searches, the result of a bomb explosion on the Pakistan side in 2014 which killed over 60 people. Soon I pass the immigration exit point that I'd left only 20 hours ago, then show my passport to a soldier. Foreigner tourists are allowed in the VIP viewing area and I'm shown around the back of the vast grandstands and deposited near the front, close to the gates between the two countries. I take my position, perched on a concrete step halfway up the stand, and absorb the electric atmosphere. There are literally thousands of people squeezed along both sides of the central thoroughfare. Looking over the gates, I can see into the Pakistan zone where just as many are seated in a steep amphitheater, none of which had registered when I rode through. On the left are men, mostly in white or light colours and to the right is the fabulous sight of the women's area, their clothing every colour of the rainbow.

Through loudspeakers, a compere leads chanting on the Pakistan side.

"Pakistan Zindabad!" ("Long live Pakistan!") shouts the crowd.

A swell of sound rises around me as the Indian contingent reply,

"Jai Hind!... Jai Hind!" ("Long live India!").

As the patriotic cries increase in intensity, a Girl Scout group is brought into the middle of the road. They begin dancing and singing, the crowd clapping along. Then the flag running processions commence with the girls, who fly large

Indian flags on wooden poles, racing up to the gates of Pakistan where they pirouette then run back to hand them over to other members of their troop. Through the gates, I can see an entertainer spinning round and round, his shimmering sword whipping the air. The animated Pakistani audience cheer him on enthusiastically.

With 10 minutes to go to the lowering of the flags, the pageant gets into full swing. Members of the khaki-uniformed *Indian Border Security Force*, each over 6' tall and obviously selected for their height, begin marching backwards and forwards, goose-stepping so high as they turn around at the gates that their boots kick above head height... it's an achievement that outstrips even the notorious goose-stepping Basil Fawlty! Their headdresses are bright red, fanning out across their crowns in a way that resembles the comb of a cockerel. Over in Pakistan, equally lanky soldiers of the *Pakistan Rangers* perform the same routine, their uniforms and identical headwear bottle green. Their combined strutting and toing and froing reminds me of the closely entwined mating dance of exotic birds but just when it seems to have reached its peak, the gates are whipped open and a slightly sinister twist ensues. A camouflage-clad soldier from each side, wearing full battle dress and equipped with automatic weapons, marches to the gates. With their two faces just inches apart, they then lengthily and intimidatingly eyeball each other.

After that, the show recommences and with choreographed perfection, soldiers standing millimetres apart on their respective sides of the dividing line begin lowering their national flags. Simultaneously folded, they're handed to officers who ceremoniously march them away. Both gates are firmly closed, not to be opened again until routine border crossing traffic recommences in the morning. The theatre is over and the audience, now hushed, begins to disperse. Amidst the crush, I head away from the compound and back to my driver who's waiting with his engine gunned. Climbing in, I consider the highly charged and exciting entertainment I've just watched... an unmitigated crowd pleaser. However, I feel slightly uneasy about the displays of jingoism and the military facet that verge on aggression. In view of previous wars between the two countries and continued border skirmishes in the disputed Kashmir area, it's a performance that, whilst absorbing, is rather close to the bone.

Back at the Grand, I eat dinner as I pore over maps, planning my route to the Nepalese border. I estimate it should take just three days.

Day 54. Amritsar to Chandigarh. 156 miles.

Another newspaper report grabs my attention as I eat breakfast. On the front page of *The Times of India*, a prominent article reads, 'India has reiterated there was no blockade imposed by the country for supplies moving to land-locked Nepal while asserting the two main entry points were choked on account of unrest in the Terai region of that country following adoption of a new Constitution... India said petrol supplies were halted as trucks were held up at Rauxul and Birganj entry points through which 70 per cent of supplies reach Nepal... External Affairs Ministry spokesperson Vikas Swarup said that nearly two-thirds of all its goods were crossing over from India.'

It's the first I've heard of these problems and I quickly check online reports for verification. Nearly all contradict the Indian government's statement, highlighting the dearth of goods crossing the border, including petrol, and blaming it on the Indian government's negative reaction to Nepal's constitutional change. If it's true, the blockade would seem exceedingly harsh in view of Nepal's recent catastrophic earthquake. On a personal note, the threat of discontinued petrol supplies could severely impact my plans to ride through Nepal and it's a situation I'll need to keep a close eye on.

I catch a ride in a cycle rickshaw to Jaycee Motors where I'm given a rousing sendoff by all the staff. Back at The Grand, I begin the slow process of loading up at the side of the road. A young cycle rickshaw wallah is hanging around nearby, hoping to pick up a fare from a tourist. He asks where I'm going,

"Chandigarh," I reply.

"Ah... New Model City. Very nice. The best in India," he responds.

"You've been there?" I ask.

"Oh no, but everyone in India knows Chandigarh."

Designed from the ground up by Swiss-French architect and urban planner, Le Corbusier, Chandigarh was one of the earliest planned cities to be built in post-independence India and is internationally recognised as being a highly successful development. It's a Union Territory that's ruled directly by the central Indian government and serves as the capital for both the Punjab and Haryana states. I'm looking forward to seeing it.

As I fasten my jacket and tie my kerchief round my neck in preparation for departure, I look up to see a most unexpected road user. Lumbering towards me is a saggy skinned elephant, its mahout, wearing nothing but a simple dhoti and white singlet, perched high on its neck. As it sways past, I smile at the stylized floral decorations painted on its ears and rump in green, orange and white, the colours of the Indian flag. Helmet on, I kick the Matchless over and set off, giving it a wide berth even 'though I'm aware that in working on India's highways and byways, it must surely have developed immunity to the noise and close proximity of traffic.

At first, the GT Road is a sleepy dual carriageway but once it's reduced to a single lane, the worst of India's driving practices come to the fore and I need to keep my wits about me. Similar to Pakistan, the buses are by far the most dangerous as they go flat out, clearing everything out of their path with trumpeting air-horns only to come to a screeching halt a hundred metres later for a new passenger. The cars, however, are a more frequent and persistent hazard. The attitude of the majority of drivers seems to be, 'get out of my way because I'm bigger and more expensive than you... or I'll hit you.' I lose count of the number of times I'm run off the road by faster vehicles tearing up from behind with no intention of slowing, or by an advancing wall of steel as oncoming cars overtake trucks that are already overtaking slow moving rickshaws. On India's highways, the unwritten rule is 'Might is Right' and if you don't get quickly out of the path of anything bigger than you, you risk being flattened. It's not an enjoyable motorcycling experience and my attention is persistently torn between the road ahead and my mirrors.

As if things aren't dangerous enough, lung searing smoke drifts across the road for most of the morning. Punjab is known as India's breadbasket, growing about 10% of the country's rice and 20% of its wheat. In November, farmers typically harvest rice and sow wheat. Inbetween, they set fire to leftover plant debris to clear their fields for the next plantings, a practice known as stubble or paddy burning, which seems to be at its zenith today. The thick choking smoke drifts off the smouldering stalks, making my eyes sting and, at its most intense, obscuring visibility down the road like a thick winter fog.

Unable to sing out loud without inhaling even more smoke, through my head goes my own version of the Bob Dylan and Rick Danko song, *This Wheel's On Fire*.

"This field's on fire,
Rolling down the road..."
It might be a great song but it doesn't do anything to distract me from the acute discomfort of acrid air in my nostrils and lungs.

There's a choice of routes, either cutting cross country on backroads or continuing along the GT Road to the city of Ludhiana before turning east. As I stayed a night in Ludhiana on my *Overland To India* ride and liked the place, nostalgia biases my decision to head that way. It's a mistake. The congestion is appalling, confirming an earlier perception that there are infinitely more cars on India's roads than in 2008. Near the city centre is an improvised intersection where crossing traffic passes underneath a partially constructed flyover. Progress in a straight line would be difficult enough as cars, trucks and tractors vie for the space to move around parked buses but the addition of stalled cross traffic makes forward movement almost impossible. When I finally reach the middle of the junction by inching the bike through a succession of tiny gaps, I'm caught in a total jam. The rider of a Vespa travelling from my right seems to lose control of his clutch lever and his scooter jumps forward a couple of feet, crashing into the rear of my bike. I can't move anywhere so kick out the side stand and worriedly leap off to examine the result. It's a relief to see that my pannier bags have absorbed the full force of the blow without any damage. Like all around, the turban wearing rider is revving his engine and tooting his horn, completely ignoring me as he wriggles into another gap. For him and everybody else, such incidents are inconsequential, merely a fact of life in the city.

Finally turning off the GT Road and heading east on National Highway 5, I enter a more heavily wooded region where fires and smoke recede and traffic thins. Total concentration is still required but the surroundings and quieter roads nevertheless make travel much more pleasant. I spot a small open restaurant with a beautifully restored 350 Bullet parked outside. Pulling over, I say hello to its rider, a young Sikh who recommends the food he's half way through eating. I take his advice, sitting down with him and his companion.

"The Royal Enfield is my father's," he tells me. "He bought it new in 1992. It was a wreck, completely run down. I asked him if I could borrow it then unbeknown to him, gave it to a mechanic in Chandigarh who has completely restored it in just 3 weeks. I'm now riding it to my home village to give it back to him as a Diwali present."

When I've finished my meal, I get up to inspect it. The chrome gleams, the polished alloy crank cases reflect the sun like mirror glass and the pale green gloss paint, although non-standard, is immaculate, suiting the retro style of the bike perfectly. The man prods the kickstarter and it fires beautifully, settling into a deep rhythmic chug.

Back at my table, the waiter comes over for payment. My meal costs 110 rupees, just over £1, however, I have no change so give him a 1000 rupee note. In return I get a thick wad of crumpled, grubby notes which I begin counting as he walks away. I check then doublecheck... in error he's given me 990 rupees. I call him over and, via the Bullet rider, explain his mistake, handing back two 50 rupee notes. The waiter is absolutely flabbergasted and I'm unable to work out if his reaction is a result of embarrassment at his mistake, no laughing matter at a tiny roadside establishment, or my honesty. He shakes my hand so much that for a moment I wonder if he's ever going to let it go.

I reach Chandigarh around 4pm and am immediately impressed by its grid pattern street layout which does wonders for traffic flow. A city of two million without a single traffic jam is incredible in India. However, as a tired motorcyclist searching for a hotel, its design is extremely frustrating in view of the fact that I can't see anything but road, trees, traffic lights and roundabouts. All the residential, business, shopping and governmental areas located within the city's 56 sectors lie hidden from view. Taking a punt and turning off, I head into a built up district. It turns out to be an industrial area. The next quarter I visit, simply signposted 'Sector 22', has small shops, mechanics workshops and tower block housing but no lodgings. When in need of a hotel, a town or city centre is always the safest bet but Chandigarh doesn't seem to have one. As daylight fades, I plunge into a third sector which proves to contain bus and railway stations, eventually locating a shabby hotel with off street parking. It's far from cosy but will have to do.

All is redeemed later when, on foot, I find a barbers shop, a tiny rundown shack where three stylish young men artfully wield scissors. Facing a cracked mirror are old-fashioned swivelling barber's chairs and behind them, a narrow wooden bench for waiting customers. A stained, chipped sink to the right is totally clogged with hair and bristly lather, the byproduct of numerous wet shaves... lovely. However, needs must. My beard's 55 days old and apart from being incredibly bushy, is displaying more than its fair share of white. Scrutinizing it in the mirror, I reckon I'll make a good Father Christmas in not too many years time.

The chap in charge signals me to his chair then selects Western pop music on his MP3 player to make me feel at home. He cuts my hair with flashy snips then spends a good five minutes massaging lather onto my chin. Slotting a new blade into his cut-throat razor, he sets about skilfully removing the fuzz. After the first shave, I'm re-lathered and a second, closer shave is carried out without a single drop of blood being spilt. Out of the corner of my eye I've been watching the man in the adjoining chair having his face creamed and massaged. Without being asked, astringent yellow lotion is dabbed onto my face and a similar treatment commences. After 10 minutes of rubbing, kneading and slapping, I've had enough. Not so the barber, who's keen to begin massaging my head and seems nonplussed by my gesticulations to pay up and leave. I'm nevertheless very pleased with the result and walk into the street feeling like a shorn sheep, resisting an almost uncontrollable urge to leap in the air.

The restaurant at my hotel is far from sanitary. Dried-out leftover food decorates every table and there's a fair amount scattered on the floor, fodder for the thumb-size cockroaches that scuttle in and out of cover. Going for a walk down a nearby backstreet, I find a new Sikh run hotel which has a pristine dining room. The food and company are great and the milky sweets they offer me at the end of the meal, freshly brought from the temple where the owners have just been worshipping, make the evening feel special.

Day 55. Chandigarh to Meerut. 152 miles.

Straight after breakfast, which for the sake of my health I eat at the nearby Sikh hotel, I catch a rickshaw and head to Nek Chand's famous *Rock Garden*. Chand's story is awe-inspiring. Working as a road inspector, he collected discarded items such as broken pottery, glass and metal objects from demolition sites formed during Chandigarh's reconstruction. In a protected forest gorge, he secretly recycled these pieces into unique sculptures, working for eighteen years before being discovered in 1975 by the municipal authorities. By this time his hidden garden extended to over 18 acres but as it was deemed illegal, was set to be demolished. However, backed by an upswell of community support, Chand was able to secure its future as a public space. Indeed, he was even given a job title, a salary and a labour force to assist him develop the garden further. Sadly, he died this June, aged 90.

The entrance fee is just a few rupees. Through the door, I'm instantly transported by the uniquely elegant creations... it feels as if I've stepped into a surreal wonderland. Moving through a dream-like labyrinth of bridges, gullies and waterfalls, the noise of the city disappears and is replaced by birdsong, the sound of trickling water and rustling trees, as well as my own laughter and perpetual "WOW"s! Soon I enter a series of courtyards where hundreds of Chand's singular statues are lined up, each individually encrusted in a colourful mosaic of recycled materials. Emaciated, leggy men give way to armies of long necked women, each with unusually stretched faces that border on alien. Then there are the animals: glorious gaggles of geese, smiling spotty dogs and splendidly stylised white horses. In total, there are over two thousand statues, some so off beat that it's impossible to distinguish between human, beast and fantasy. In my 51 years, I've never seen anything like it and walk around entranced for two utterly consuming hours.

When I set off some time after 11am, the Matchless is still running sweetly. Soon back on the GT Road, which is mercifully 2 and 3 lanes wide, I head towards Ambala before turning cross country on State Highway 12 for fear of the longer but faster route to the border ensnaring me in the jaws of New Delhi. The fields of rice and wheat that have edged the roadside since Amritsar are soon replaced by the swaying knotty green stalks of sugar cane. Here it's harvest time and the road's choked with tractors hauling trailers piled high with the cropped canes. Mills sporadically appear close to a town or a village, the intoxicating smell of molasses emitting from their chimneys and suffusing the warm air.

Turning left, I enter a village that's in total disarray. All signs of tarmac must have vanished from the road many years ago and the resulting mire of hardened mud potholes looks like the aftermath of prolonged artillery fire. The first dip I enter is at least three metres deep and before I can escape its clutches, a car heading the other way dives in, throwing up so much dust it obscures my vision and I find it hard to breath. We go up and down and in and out of the holes while vying for space with the other road users, who emerge from the dusty gloom only at the last moment. The bike is pounded on ridges of baked earth and dodging buses and trucks is decidedly dicey. It's horrendous... god knows what it must be like to live here.

After a couple of hellish kilometres, roadworks take over, the surface comprising hard packed soil and gravel. As the road gradually rises, the verge on my side falls away steeply into a rocky pit. Climbing in 2nd, I see a heavy truck begin ponderously advancing downhill towards me. He's sitting plump in the middle of the road leaving very little room between us and at this point, the drop to my left is at least 3m. A motorbike pulls out from behind it, looking for an opportunity to overtake. Now almost in line with the front of the truck, I brake hard to give the rider time to pull back in behind... but he doesn't. Instead, he rides straight towards me. I'm virtually stationary with nowhere to go between the slow truck's side and the fall to my left. The bike keeps coming and I watch in disbelief as, without slowing, he rides straight into the Matchless, front wheel to front wheel.

Outraged, I stay on my feet, the Matchless bouncing slightly backwards. Including the rider, there are three grown men on his bike and yet it recoils much further back than mine before, almost in slow motion, tumbling over. All three of them lie on gravel under the bike while the truck continues on its way. I'm absolutely bewildered by the rider's ineptitude and start shouting at him. None of the men say a word and while, incensed, I rant in no uncertain terms, they pick themselves up, right the bike and climb back on. My handlebars are out of line with the front wheel by as much as 20° and as I try to digest the damage, concurrently consider accident reports, insurance, swapping names and addresses, calling the police, how I'll get things fixed, in effect, all the normal post accident procedures of home. Of course, no such things happen here... the rider pushes the starter button and without so much as a by-your-leave, rides off! The whole incident, from start to finish, has taken less than a minute.

With other vehicles passing close by, I figure I should quickly get off the road. The front wheel and forks have been so badly knocked out of alignment, however, that when I try to move forward, I almost fall off. Wobbling, my feet paddling along the ground, I steer across the road and up an embankment, stopping close to a row of tents belonging to road workers. My heart's racing, not due to the crash itself but because of the potential consequences. If the forks are bent or the yokes badly twisted or cracked, it will mean the end of the journey. Getting off, I edge my way to the back and using all my strength, haul the bike onto the rear stand, something I've never managed to do fully loaded until now. I dash round to the front to inspect the damage more closely. Everything's so out of line it's impossible to work out exactly where the problem is so, still mumbling about the idiot rider, I locate my toolkit and begin loosening things off: front mudguard; forks; steering head and headlight. By now a crowd of workmen has begun to assemble around the bike, silently staring at me. Once it's all free, I trap the front wheel between my legs and begin pulling the handlebars to try to straighten everything up. Moving away a little, I can see it's shifted more or less back to normal so give it a couple of further tweaks before methodically tightening all the fastenings.

I've no idea if the forks are bent although the side profile seems to suggest not. The crowd has grown to around 40 strong and still no one has spoken, in fact the situation's become so overwhelmingly claustrophobic that I can't face testing her here. Sweating profusely, I struggle into my riding gear then push the Matchless off the stand, almost dropping her as the front tyre bites into gravel. With trepidation, I set off down the embankment and onto the road. As I ride on the gravel, it's hard to be sure if all's okay, but after a couple of hundred metres, I come to a stretch of new tar seal. Accelerating from 2nd into 3rd, I gently pull on the brakes, letting out a deep sigh of relief when the bike rides true and there are no awful noises as the front forks compress. We've been very lucky to escape more serious damage.

My motto when riding in India is that it's better to be wrong and alive than right and dead, meaning that no matter how indignant I feel about other drivers' inconsiderate, mindless or downright dangerous behaviour, or how much I believe that I should have right of way, the best policy is always to acquiesce. It's simply not worth putting my life on the line when I feel I'm right or to prove a point. Incontrovertibly, I know I would come off worst. However, in this instance, I'd done exactly that, giving the other rider plenty of time to pull out of his doomed overtaking manoeuvre, yet he'd still crashed into me in a manner that defied all logic. Although my life wasn't threatened, the expedition to Vietnam certainly was and I feel quite unnerved.

The further east we travel, the more convinced I become that I've made the wrong decision and that my *Garmin* and *Google Maps* were right to suggest a longer route on major roads... the long stretches of ungraded, dust-ridden surface are both tedious and daunting. A small blessing is that outside of towns, fellow road users are few. It being a rural region, I pass numerous carts drawn by oxen or water buffalo. On one particularly challenging section of sun dried mud, as I pull out from behind a wooden flatbed cart drawn by two strapping water buffs, three young men sitting at the front, who've watched my approach over their shoulders, begin egging the driver on. Using his reigns, the lad gees up the bulky creatures in an attempt to race me. For such strapping animals, I'm amazed at their turn of speed but as I pull alongside, the driver takes hold of a whip and begins frantically whipping them. Eyes bulging white and ears pressed back onto their heads, they're already going hell for leather and his frenzied slashes with the whip seem brutal. I feel an urge to stop and whip him to see how he likes it, but bouncing hard on the uneven ground, my best course of action is unquestionably to get away as quickly as possible, ending his cruel competitiveness.

I'd hoped to get much closer to the Nepalese border but upon reaching the city of Meerut, feel that I've had enough for one day. The extensive suburbs lead to a relatively small but intensely packed town centre and a single main high street on which lie several dozen shops, three hotels and a temple. Located smack bang in the middle sits the biggest and best hotel, the Raj Mahal. A regal looking sikh doorman guards the Matchless from curious onlookers while I secure a room for under £20 then helps push her around the back and up a steep ramp into the safety of a laundry room. I'm shown to my bedroom by a porter who switches on the air con and TV. A movie's just beginning and without giving it much thought, I strip off, flop onto the bed and lose myself in its plot, the perfect remedy to the stresses of the day.

The street typically hums at night with the colourful amalgam of life which makes India such a vibrant country to visit. Parked amongst a row of shoppers' motorcycles like an object time-travelled from the Middle Ages, a Hariana cow, an immensely tall ox with wide horns, is tethered to an ancient wooden cart weighed down with sugarcane. Its juxtaposition with the backdrop of neon lit shops selling high fashion, jewellery and smartphones to the bright young things of the recent Indian economic boom typifies the country's immense cultural, economic and environmental incongruities Things seem to be changing fast here, but not fast enough for the pitiful street side salesman I see as I walk further in search of a meal. Slumped on the pavement's edge, his wares, shiny mini top-hats of the kind worn by clowns at the circus, are piled in a cardboard box at his feet. Available in bold red, blue and glittery shocking pink, they're obviously aimed at small children but none pay him any attention as they walk past with their parents. He abjectly wears a red one slightly askew on top of his head, secured in place by white elastic strung under his chin. The dejected sag of his shoulders and the look of misery on his face is pitiful, the appearance of a broken man, yet the playful child's hat he sports somehow makes him look simultaneously comical. Call me a soft touch but I buy one.

Nek Chand's unique sculptures.

246

Day 56. Meerut to Jhankat. 154 miles.

Breakfast is unexpectedly served in my room along with a newspaper in which the editorial continues to decry Nepal's claims of fuel starvation resulting from Indian government policies. I make a mental note to fill up as close to the border as possible, just in case. After shuttling all my gear to the laundry room, I roll the Matchless down the steep ramp and load up. Everything goes swimmingly well and I'm underway by 8:30am, riding through the centre of a fruit and vegetable market before finding the road east. It proves to be a quiet country backroad that passes through picturesque, sleepy villages, where I observe camels being used to move goods aboard carts constructed from the axles and wheels of defunct cars. Thirty kilometres on, a rattling sound develops which seems to be coming from the front of the bike. Pulling over, I feel my way around and identify the source as a loose nut on the central top mounting for the mudguard. It's one of a pair located between the front forks and its partner is already missing. It takes a while to retighten as there's hardly any room to squeeze fingers and a spanner between the tyre and guard but eventually I manage to secure it, aware that I need to find a replacement for the lost one.

After another 20 minutes, I turn onto National Highway 9, a major route that runs due east all the way to my destination, the border town of Banbasa. At first a relatively empty dual carriageway, I open the throttle and motor at speed, settling at a steady 75kmph. The sun's shining, the bike's running fine and although one can never relax while travelling in India, I'm positively enjoying myself. After an hour I hit roadworks. My side of the highway's blocked off so I drop a gear, cross a gap in the middle of the road and join a contraflow. There's more traffic around now and as I ride, with my left leg close to the central concrete barrier, a bus begins to overtake. It's not moving much faster than us and half occupies the lane for oncoming vehicles. Fast approaching from the opposite direction, a truck angrily blasts his horn but doesn't slow. I brake hard and the bus cuts across in front of us, only missing the bike's front wheel by a couple of feet. It avoids a collision with the oncoming truck by an equal amount and I'm mightily glad when the roadworks end and normal lane conditions resume.

In the distance, there's more resurfacing work. A motorbike travelling ahead, obviously wise to the perils of riding in a contraflow, nips through a gap in the bollards and continues along our side of the highway, easily bypassing the workmen who throw bucket loads of steaming liquid tar onto the road before spreading it with brooms. 'What a great idea', I think, angling through the same gap and following him. Within seconds, the Matchless loses all power then cuts out. Coasting to a halt, I get off and squat down next to the engine, wondering if the throttle cable's broken. To my horror, I see petrol streaming down onto the magneto and crankcases. It takes a few moments to realise that it's coming straight out of the bottom of the carburettor and poses a serious risk of fire. Instantly, I turn the fuel taps off then grab a cloth from inside my spare tyre and desperately wipe all the petrol I can off the hot engine. Hugely relieved it's at least safe, I suck in a deep breath and sit down on the road.

Closer inspection reveals that the carb's drain plug has vibrated out. I'm not carrying a spare and without it, the Matchless is a dead duck. I get up and begin running back down the road towards the workmen. For a hundred metres I follow a thin black line in the old tarmac, the petrol stain left in the wake of my bike, praying the plug's not already covered in layers of fresh tar. Where the trail stops, I frantically spin around in a circle looking for the errant plug. Bright and shiny against the grey road, I spot it, pick it up and examine it closely. It's undamaged! As I walk back to the bike, I look to my right and regard the other side of the central reservation where fast-moving vehicles cross each other in the contraflow, thanking my lucky stars that at the crucial moment, I'd opted to come this side of it... being stranded over there, let alone searching for the lost plug, doesn't bear thinking about.

In the afternoon, the dual carriageway swings sharply to the south just beyond the town of Rampur. I pull over and compare the route on my satnav with my paper map. The Garmin's recommendation seems to run a very long way south east before heading north east again. According to the printed version, I can instead continue in a straight line towards the border, a much shorter option. I decide it's the one for me but rather than backtracking to a turnoff on the far side of town, elect to take a shortcut. Working on dead reckoning, I head into dusty backstreets. People stand on their doorsteps openmouthed in amazement as I navigate along tight, sunbaked alleyways so narrow that most cars could barely fit. Wending a path between pedestrians, bicycles and donkeys, I zigzag along a succession of lanes until finally hitting the road east. It doesn't take long to realise that I've not made the best choice... traffic is much busier than on the dual carriageway and the road's in pretty bad shape. However, as the border's only a hundred kilometres away and retracing my steps would be time consuming and hard work, I persevere.

Miserable hours pass while I bounce along in 2nd gear, trapped in long lines of trucks that clatter and shake as they too negotiate the endless potholes, rubble and congested towns. I stop after a while in a village, buy some bananas and sit at the roadside watching a stream of decrepit trucks rattle by. Time's ticking away but it's impossible to rush so, after steeling myself for another battering, I set off again. Increasingly, I become aware of a squeaking sound. At first I think it's the front fork springs that have been affected by all the dust and dirt that's flying around, but as dusk approaches and I pass the side of a lake, the noise seems much louder and more regular. Concerned, I pull over, get off and rev the engine with my ear close to it. It rhythmically squeaks like an old bedspring. Far from happy, I guess it can only be my inlet valve sticking again and decide I'd better stop putting additive into my petrol. Night's creeping up on us and as I straighten, I spot two young men slowly riding towards me on a silver Bullet, their headlight cutting a sharp line through the gloom. Flagging them down, I ask if there's a hotel nearby. Their answer's unequivocally no, so I remount the gallant Matchless and recommence our trek east.

Bouncing for hours on the ghastly road surface has been exhausting work and it's even more wearing in the dark. My satnav says there are still 23km to go to the border town, where I know I'll find a hotel, but in pitch darkness on these roads, it might as well be a 100km. Within minutes, I ride into Jhankat, thinking 'what I wouldn't give for a hotel right now'. On the right appears a three-story building, by far the largest in sight, its frontage dazzlingly trimmed from top to bottom with strings of purple fairy lights. As I slow beside it, I look up in wonder at a neon sign above the front door which glowingly proclaims, Hotel Kamal Regency... who would have imagined it possible in such a small, remote village! Parking up, I enter the reception with renewed energy. Behind a desk draped with garlands of marigold stands a young man with curly black hair.

"Welcome!" he says. "Welcome to the opening night of our hotel. How can I help you?"

"A room please," I request, not even thinking about the price.

"Very good sir, please come this way. You are our very first guest. Number one! Tonight is our opening party with many friends and prominent business people coming to celebrate with us."

Feeling unbelievably fortunate, I suddenly remember the bike and tell him about her.

"Later, when the party's finished, you can park the bike inside here," he assures me, pointing to the far corner.

It's an excellent solution so I return outside, unload and cover up then, with the help of another member of staff, go to my room.

Everything proves to be very new indeed: the light switch isn't yet screwed onto the wall; the bathroom's half finished and there's only cold water... but in the circumstances, I really don't care! The mattress and pillows are covered in polythene and there's builders' dust on the floor which the man sweeps up. When he finally leaves, I catch sight of my ghost-like figure in the mirror, covered with dust from the afternoon's journey, and feel extremely grateful that in this filthy state, the hotel actually let me in. A photo seems appropriate, a record of just how dirty I am. I get my camera out, position it on an empty shelf and set it to self timer. With a flash it takes a shot but when I check, it's only from the neck down. Using a rolled up piece of paper as a wedge, I angle the camera slightly upwards and press the self timer once more. Running back to my position against the far wall, I turn around and at the very moment the flash fires, the camera topples off the shelf, crashing onto the tile floor. I quickly scoop it up to discover that the photo it's just taken will sadly be its last... the lens has broken. Damn!

Time for a shower, I think, but inside the bathroom I can't find a towel. Key in hand, I open the door, press the lock button on the back of the handle, then close the door behind me as I step into the corridor. Downstairs, the manager's busy handing drinks to his guests but after a few minutes, he finds me a brand spanking new white towel. Guiltily taking it from him, I head back to my room only to find that the key won't unlock the door. Figuring they've given me the wrong one, I saunter back to reception. A porter accompanies me upstairs but gets the same result. Next comes the manager with his master key but after ten fruitless minutes, he gives up with an apology, saying,

"Your lock has jammed and we can't undo it. I'll have to call a locksmith from the next town. Please be patient."

The hotel's restaurant isn't open for dinner yet, so in my sweaty, scungy clothes, I sit at a table with my towel and a chilled cola drink called *Thumbs Up*, waiting for the problem to be resolved.

A while later, I'm let back into my room and make the most of a cold shower. Returning to the restaurant for a restorative meal, I send a text to Andy describing the squeaking sound.

'Hi Gordon, it sounds more like a blown cylinder head gasket than a sticking valve. If you recall it's a paltry copper gasket and you'll probably have to replace it. Remember to keep inlet and exhaust pushrods separate. Good luck, Andy.'

After the day I've had, I know I should leave it unchecked until the morning but I can't take my mind off it, so head outside and remove the cover. Rotating the crank, there's an immediate sharp squeak accompanied by a spurt of compressed air that shoots onto my left hand. He's right again and I can't begin to think how I'm going to fix it here.

Dejectedly, I walk back to my room through the dwindling party and put my phone on charge using the only working socket I can find, strangely situated half a metre above the headboard. I decide to get to bed before anything else can go wrong but can't fall asleep as the room is glowing with fairy light purple despite the closed curtains. After finally drifting off, I'm woken abruptly by a sharp pain on my forehead. Needless to say, the combined charger and travel adapter has dropped out of the socket and landed squarely in the middle of my weary noggin. What a day!

Chaos at an Indian railway crossing.

Day 57. Jhankat. 0 miles.

I rise at the crack of dawn so that I can wheel the bike out of the hotel reception before the day's business starts. Standing beside her outside the main doors, it's clear there's no chance of making any repairs here. The dust kicked up by passing vehicles wouldn't be healthy for the stripped down engine and furthermore, I know I'd attract a huge crowd of onlookers within minutes. An alternative venue is required, so after a quick breakfast I venture forth to explore the village. The roadside's lined with a few simple shops, a couple of semi-industrial units and several basic homes. Near the village's eastern boundary, little more than 300m from the hotel, sits a small motorcycle repair shop. There's not even an electric light within its bare walls and like the garage in Abbottabad, all work takes place in the open air. A young mechanic is busy mending a mud encrusted Suzuki so I loiter for a while, watching his attempts to remove its air filter with a screwdriver and hammer. His lack of progress isn't particularly impressive and I soon walk away, convinced it's not the right place for me to fix the Matchless. I try wandering up a few dusty back lanes to see if there's anywhere more suitable but beyond a few houses and small holdings, there's nothing but fields. Returning to the hotel, I order a coffee over which I cogitate over a new plan.

Since arriving in Jhankat, I've been unable to rationalise why such a sizeable hotel has been built here, it seems something of an anomaly in a small village like this. As I begin my second drink, all is revealed. A large bus comes to a halt and around 50 sleepy passengers climb off, heading for the hotel's restaurant and toilets. The bus has travelled from Kathmandu in Nepal and is heading to Delhi and from what I can see written down its flanks, appears to be a regular service. A weary driver is the last off and as he enters the restaurant, he's patted on the shoulder by the hotel manager and given a meal, evidently his reward for transporting customers to the new enterprise. No closer to resolving my own problem, I go to reception where the manager presents me with my bill. He's more than surprised when I tell him I'll be staying another night and looks concerned when I explain the reason and my need to find somewhere quiet to work on the bike.

I retrace my steps through the village but still can't find a likely bolt hole.

"What exactly do you need?" asks the manager when I return.

"Just a small room with good light where I can close the door and hide from prying eyes," I reply.

"Let me think," he says, walking away.

In an effort to prepare myself for what might lie ahead, I return to the restaurant armed with my workshop manual. Half an hour later, the manager sticks his head through the doorway and asks me to follow him. We cross the road to a short line of shops, each a single room unit approximately the size of a UK domestic garage with roller shutter doors. I'm introduced to the owner of one which seems to sell everything from chocolate to animal feed. Together we take a couple of steps to the neighbouring unit where he unlocks the door and lifts it up. It's his storeroom, the walls lined with piles of sacks and half-filled boxes. He switches the light on and begins to move a few things out of the way.

"He cannot speak English but he says you can use this place to fix your bike. Just give him 200 rupees a day for it," the hotel manager explains.

I'm over the moon and begin shaking both men's hands, thanking them profusely. The shop owner looks somewhat surprised by the force of my reaction, but the solution is better than I'd thought possible and it's hard to contain my happiness.

It's almost midday by the time the Matchless is reversed into the middle of the storeroom and I lower most of the door, leaving just a big enough gap at the bottom for fresh air. The petrol tank, crashbars, sump guard, exhaust and carburettor come off in quick succession. When I remove the rocker cover, I'm alarmed that the exhaust valve and valve springs are thickly caked in carbon. Resembling shiny black anthracite in appearance, it's something which definitely needs removing. Not for the first time, I hear rustling somewhere in the depths of the storeroom. Spinning around, I catch a dash of movement in the beam of my head torch as a large, dark, long-tailed rat dives for cover. I'm not squeamish but neither am I overjoyed at sharing the space with such a whopping rodent! Returning to the task at hand, I loosen all the cylinder head bolts then, using a block of wood as a buffer, gently tap the base of the head until it frees and I can lift it off, remembering Andy's advice to keep the pushrods separate and clearly marked when they drop out. The cylinder head gasket, a thin copper ring with asbestos type material sandwiched in its centre, has a scorched area where it has blown. It's just as well I'm carrying a couple of spares.

After lunch, I set about cleaning all the parts as well as I can with a rag and petrol but it's impossible to scrub the carbon off the valves. As I'm not carrying a valve spring compressing tool to take them out, I conclude I'll need to find a shop that can do the job for me. Returning to the hotel to ask for any suggestions, it transpires that one of the waiters owns a Bullet and regularly uses the services of a mechanic in the nearby town of Khatima.

"Very good, very good man," he tells me as he writes the shop name on a piece of paper.

With the heavy cylinder head wrapped in newspaper and carefully stowed in my daypack, I head up the village and flag down a rickshaw. It's one of the more common black and yellow autos with a vinyl covered hood that I liken to dung beetles when I see them scuttling around India's towns and villages. Even though the steel bench seat is covered in foam, it's still pretty hard and I'm jarred and bounced up and down on potholes throughout the 25 minute journey to the town centre. Gratefully emerging from its uncomfortable confines as it stops outside the bike repair shop, I walk towards three men all deeply engrossed in their work. The owner, Mohammed, breaks off from removing the primary cover from a Bullet to greet me. He inspects the cylinder head with interest then hands it over to his son to work on.

It takes the lad several attempts to remove the valve springs and extract the valves, then, without explanation, he deposits it in a plastic bag, climbs aboard a nearby scooter where he traps it between his legs and rides off. I sit anxiously on a wooden bench and watch Mohammed and his assistant at work. It seems the place deals with the full gamut of Indian motorcycles, everything from Hero Hondas to Bajaj Pulsars, TVS to Piaggio scooters. Mohammed's busy replacing the clutch on the Bullet and his sidekick is energetically changing wheel bearings on a TVS Flame, an all too regular necessity in this region, no doubt! A man slowly rides an angular-looking 1980s grey Vespa onto the pavement, his wife sitting sidesaddle on the back seat. The mechanic abandons the TVS and wanders over to watch the man demonstrate that his front light isn't working. Going to the store room, he returns a minute later with a replacement bulb and a screwdriver, swapping the failed bulb over in no time. A few rupees change hands, the man's wife rearranges her sari and climbs back on the scooter, whereupon they quickly disappear amidst the legion of crawling traffic. In India, as in many places where motorcycles are cheap to buy and used as their owners' sole means of transport, routine maintenance is hardly carried out at all... the machine is ridden until something goes wrong then it's taken to a workshop to be fixed. It's also rare for people to work on their own bikes, especially as repair costs seem to be so cheap.

Mohammed's son returns an hour later and proudly shows me the gleaming ports of the cylinder head and the spotless valves. I'm mightily relieved the head's still in one piece and now looks like new. Together, we set about putting the valves back in, a fiddly job as accessibility is poor and two tightly packed cotters are needed to secure each valve. Finally done, I pay the princely sum of 600 rupees (approx. £6) and thank all three men, promising to return and show them the Matchless tomorrow.

Walking towards the town centre, I struggle to find a rickshaw willing to take me back to Jhankat. Several stop when they see my waving hand but each drives off as soon as they realise I'm a one-way trip to a far off village. Beyond the central clock tower, I notice groups of people climbing into collective rickshaws, battered vehicles not much bigger than the one I'd caught here but certainly more industrial and basic looking. I ask a couple of waiting men if any of them goes to Jhankat.

"This one... this one... go," a man shouts, pushing me on the back while he points to a rusty old jalopy.

"Jhankat?" I asked the driver.

In reply, he simply points into the back where three people are already squashed on a pressed steel bench. Reluctantly, they squeeze up and allow me to press myself in next to them. Just as the driver's setting off, another man shouts and waves, flopping next to him on the front seat. Not content with five passengers, he then waits for a young woman to climb on board, her feet squished next to mine but the rest of her body hovering half in and half out of the cab. We finally set off only to stop a couple of hundred metres later for two men to climb onto the rear bumper where they hang on, laughing and chatting to each other. With eight on board, we can't go very fast yet the driver relentlessly ploughs on regardless of the deepest and most hard-edged potholes. Over the course of the next 20 minutes, I discover a means of travel even more painful than riding the rigid Matchless along these fragmented roads. The eight of us cling on for dear life and I collect a bruise the size of a golfball on my left arm.

The stars are already dancing in the night sky when I get off in Jhankat. As he unlocks the storeroom, the shopkeeper indicates on his watch that he'll be closing in an hour's time. I launch into preparing for reassembly but to my dismay, discover that both the replacement cylinder head gaskets have been mangled despite the care I'd taken to protect them when packing in the UK. Selecting the more serviceable looking one, I straighten it between finger and thumb then silicone it into place before attempting the awkward task of fitting pushrod tubes, their four rubber seals and the cylinder head all in one go. Trying to keep the gasket centred is an absolute beggar of a task but eventually it's done and I begin tightening everything down. An hour and ten very sweaty minutes have passed by the time I raise the shutter doors. The shopkeeper simultaneously pulls his shutters down and I uncomfortably suspect he's been waiting for me to make a move. Thanking him for his kindness, I watch him lock everything up before heading across the street to my quarters.

There's nothing to do in Jhankat so after I finish another spicy dinner, I opt for an early bed where I lie below the purple glowing ceiling, hoping I'll make it to Nepal tomorrow.

Day 58. Jhankat, India, to Bhimdatta, Nepal. 21 miles.

Keeping a lookout through the hotel's cafe window, I watch the shop keeper unlock his premises at 7:40am. He's accompanied by two boys in smart school uniforms and when I cross the road to say hello, he formally introduces them as his sons, aged seven and five. They both solemnly shake my hand.

"Which football team do you support?" asks the oldest.

I tell him none in particular, then ask which team he follows.

"A.F.C. Bournemouth," he replies with obvious pride.

The English *Premier League* is broadcast around the world and has a huge following. It's not unusual for a young Indian to have a favourite team in it, but generally people tend to follow one of the big clubs from Manchester, Liverpool or London... a relative minnow like Bournemouth is highly unusual.

"Why?" I ask.

"They are the smallest team and it's their first time ever in the Premier League. This means they cannot survive, but I want them to succeed so much." It's not the answer I expected... supporting the underdog is obviously a widespread philosophy!

I get to work on the Matchless straightaway, attaching the carburettor and exhaust then adjusting the tappets. At this point I figure I should check if there's compression, so I fit the spark plug and turn the engine over. There's an instant 'phwttt' of compressed air accompanied by the same squeaking sound I'd heard just before Jhankat. It's a kick in the stomach and I sink to my knees, my forehead pressed down on the bike saddle.

"What on earth do I do now?" I groan.

After a few moments' reflection, I conclude the deformed cylinder head gasket must be at fault but as the other spare is in worse condition, don't see any point in changing it over. Digging out the appropriate spanner, I test the two cylinder head nuts on the side of the engine where the gasket's leaking. Surprisingly, there's a small amount of movement, possibly the result of it settling overnight, so as carefully as possible, I try to evenly tighten them. With little hope that I've made any difference, I kick the bike over again. There's no feel of escaping air and certainly no squeak.

"Yes!" I exclaim.

Just for good measure, I give all the nuts the tiniest bit more of a tweak. It's the best I can possibly do without a torque wrench and I can only hope it'll hold.

I'd drained the oil out overnight so replace it with fresh 20/50 and a clean oil filter. The sump guard is slow to refit on my own and by the time I've also secured the crash bar, the clock shows just five minutes to midday. Remembering that I have to check out by noon, I dash across the road, frantically scrub my hands clean then grab all my gear and lug it downstairs, stashing it behind the reception desk. Back to finish the bike after lunch, I get the tank on and connect the fuel pipes. Finally, around 1:30pm, I fully open the storeroom door, wheel her outside and, viewed by a rapidly swelling audience, flood the carb and swing my boot on the crank. Nothing happens.

I check the fuel. That's fine, so I move on to seeing if I've got a spark. There isn't one. Pushing the bike back inside and lowering the door to the dismay of the crowd, I unpack my spares bag and change the HT lead. That makes no difference so I try a new spark plug but without any result. Finally, perspiration rolling down my back and off the tip of my nose, I think about the points. Digging out a replacement set, I swap them and readjust the gap. I'm immediately rewarded with a juicy, fat, blue spark. Putting the plug back in, I kick the old girl over and without hesitation, she bursts straight into life. After a couple of minutes, I loosen the rocker oil pipe and right on cue, blobs of clean oil pulse out of it. We're back in business!

Saying a not particularly fond farewell to our furry companion, I go to thank the shopkeeper, 400 rupees in hand. He simply will not take it, so I ask the hotel manager to join us as interpreter. Eventually, when its offered as a present for his two boys, he graciously accepts the payment. Quickly loading the bike, I thank all the hotel staff and wish their new venture well... in the circumstances, I couldn't have asked for a better or more helpful place to stay. Just after 3pm, I ride back onto the road and recommence the jolting, jarring journey towards Nepal.

In Khatima, I locate the motorcycle repair shop and receive an enthusiastic welcome from the staff who lavish attention on the Matchless, forming a group to pose for photographs beside her. Setting off again, I ride north into glorious countryside, overjoyed to be buzzing along a smooth road, its only blemish the contrasting mosaic shade patterns cast by the tall trees that overhang it. There are no squeaks from the cylinder head, the Matchless runs sweetly underneath me and my confidence soars. We soon reach Banbasa, a sleepy little town where I need to turn right towards the frontier, beginning with a 5km run along a narrow lane. I'm amazed by the volume of people heading towards me, on foot, travelling on bicycles and crowded aboard clip clopping horse and carts. For more than a kilometre, I ride beside the still waters of a canal then turn right over the narrow white bridge that crosses it. At its end, there's an immediate turn to the left which marks the start of the Banbasa barrage, a two hundred metre long dam that crosses the Sarda River.

I have a very keen memory of the view across it. In 1988, when first visiting India, I'd bought a red and chrome 350cc Bullet in Delhi and along with my erstwhile partner, Jude, had travelled to Banbasa, our aim being to tour Nepal on the bike. At this very point, a soldier had stopped us, instructing us to turn around. He'd explained that only Indians and Nepalese were allowed to cross this frontier post and that the two international crossings open to foreigners were located at the towns of Sonauli and Raxaul, the closest of the two being 600km east. We'd reasoned, cajoled, pleaded, even spoken to his commanding officer, but they were resolute in their refusal to let us pass. Several hours later, we'd succumbed, turning around to commence a very challenging, but on reflection highly enjoyable, detour. Not leaving things to chance on this journey, I'd carefully checked online that foreigners could now cross here, so it's with a great sense of satisfaction that I turn the front wheel left, click into 1st gear and roll onto the barrage. Too narrow for trucks or buses, it's busy with passenger carrying horse and carts, their wheels rumbling loudly on the loose wooden beams. Rolling off the far end, we descend a small hill and pull up beside the Indian immigration office.

Outside the front door, a young man is working at a desk. He indicates I should join him, completing formalities within ten minutes before directing me to customs, a similar looking building further down the hill. As I halt outside it and pull in the decompressor, two uniformed officials approach.

"Good day sir," says the first, shaking my hand. "Please tell me the year of your motorbike."

"1941," I respond.

"Oh...." They laugh in unison. "Nearly!"

I ask what they mean.

"My friend here guessed your motorcycle was from 1942... he was much closer than me. I thought it was 1970."

Patting me on the back, they indicate I should go inside. Here another man takes over, immediately getting to work on my carnet. He sets a new record... it's stamped and I'm free to go in just over five minutes!

No man's land, about a kilometre long, is a narrow dirt track pulsating with human life. There are crowds of people cycling, walking and pushing luggage on trolleys in both directions and everyone carrying some form of goods or produce. Bottles of orange liquid, which I assume to be petrol, are prominently being carried in the direction of Nepal. There's no barrier as such between the two countries and the free flow of locals, who pass backwards and forwards across the border without passports, is constant. Ahead I spot a lone soldier and, guessing he's Nepalese, ask him where I'll find immigration. He points me towards a wooden villa on the left so, leaving the bike, I walk across its garden and step onto a shady verandah. Through patio doors walks an elderly man, elegantly dressed in a cream coloured long tailed suit coat and matching tailored trousers. On his head he wears a cream Gandhi cap that's pointed at the front and rear and sports a delicate, gold pattern embroidered in a line along both sides.

"Namaste," he says, slightly bowing while placing the palms of his hands together with the fingertips pointing upwards as if in prayer.

I reciprocate, then he asks for my passport. As I already have a visa the immigration process is very simple and once more I'm on my way in about five minutes.

Customs is located in a small hut in which four brown-shirted officials beaver away. A couple of locals lean on a ledge as they complete paperwork for goods they're bringing in from India. Noticing me through a window, one of the officials requests I walk around the side and enter the office. He pushes a chair in front of a workbench, hands over a large book and asks me to record my motorcycle's details. When I stand to show him what I've done, he simply holds out his hand for my carnet. Bish bash bosh, it's stamped and the relevant section torn off in a flash.

"Welcome to Nepal, have a pleasant stay," he says, showing me the door. Fantastic... carnet and customs complete in 3 1/2 minutes!

There's a small money changing office across the way which I make good use of before setting off towards nearby Bhimdatta. According to my clock it's 5.05pm but that means it's actually 5:20pm as Nepal enjoys the peculiar distinction of being 15 minutes ahead of India, the strangest time zone I've ever encountered. The light's fading as I roll into the town centre and after asking directions a couple of times, I jubilantly enter the grand leafy courtyard of the Opera Hotel.

With the Matchless locked, covered and under the watchful eye of a nighttime security guard, I throw off my clothes in a deluxe room. Smiling to myself that some days everything does go right, I step under a steaming hot shower and cover my body in foamy soap. Suddenly, the lights flick off and the water stops. I stand haplessly in the dark, realising it's a power cut. Frothy and towel-less, I grope around for the door to the bedroom to find a towel. Thankfully, however, within about a minute the electricity comes back on and I can rinse myself off. I shouldn't have tempted fate!

Heading out, I treat myself to a wet shave by a skilful barber then curiously follow crowds across a park to where an enormous marquee has been erected. Inside, on a wide stage, a play is being acted out. The audience consists mainly of women and children and although I find it totally impossible to follow the plot, I do enjoy watching the antics of the gaudily dressed actors. Stomach rumbling, I make my way back to the hotel for dinner then head to bed. Three hours later, I can still hear the musicians and actors being broadcast through tannoys and the frequent eruption of massed applause as the sounds from the marquee drift across the town and through my window.

Day 59. Bhimdatta to Lalmatiya. 201 miles.

In the cool of the morning I set about checking the Matchless over, making sure everything has bedded in after the repairs in Jhankat. Looking along the line of parked bikes that extends around the side of the hotel, I spot a cluster of four Royal Enfields, three of which are Thunderbird cruiser derivatives. Their riders soon appear, push them into the open and begin putting on their riding gear. On the Indian Subcontinent, most people ride their motorbikes in their everyday clothes. These guys take it more seriously... all have textile biker jackets and attach strap-on pads onto their knees similar to those used by rollerbladers. One, called Dipu, comes to say hello, explaining that they're all members of the Adventure Riders Assam Motorcycle Club. They've journeyed from their home in Guwahati, the largest city in the east Indian state of Assam, to Nainital, a former British hill station in western India. Up until this point the've travelled solely through India but, he explains, their planned return leg was across Nepal.

"We crossed the border yesterday. In the evening, we spoke to lots of locals about the petrol crisis. Everyone says it's terrible and have advised us to turn around. Apparently, there is black-market petrol but it's very expensive and not easy to find," he tells me with regret plainly audible in his voice.

"If we had more time, we'd cross backwards and forwards into India to refill, but we only have three days left to get home and to our jobs. We're returning across the border to Banbasa now and will go back the way we came."
With approximately 1600km to ride amidst hectic Indian traffic, they're keen to get off, so I wish them bon voyage.

A little while later, in the middle of loading luggage onto the Matchless, two more motorcyclists emerge from the back of the hotel on a pair of UCE Bullets. I flag them down and shake their hands.

"Black-market petrol is too expensive... if you can find it. We're abandoning our journey through Nepal and returning to India," they explain before roaring out of the courtyard.

Both encounters have served to increase my concerns about the Nepalese fuel crisis, for all the claims in Indian newspapers that it's nonexistent. I sit under the shade of a tree and work through my options. I have a fixed date for entering Burma and due to delays in Pakistan and Jhankat, it's no longer possible to make my planned visit to Kathmandu. My revised plan, formulated over dinner last night, was to directly cross Nepal from its most western to most eastern border with India, approximately 1,000km along one road, the Mahendra Highway, or East-West Highway as it's also known. However, without regular supplies of fuel, this'll be impossible. In Khatima I'd filled my tank to the brim as well as adding 3½ litres of spare petrol into my fuel bottles. Being conservative, this should allow me to travel 400km. I can't nip in and out of India to refuel as my Nepalese visa is single entry, so if I don't find anything on the black-market, I'll have to switch routes and continue east on India's highways instead, the idea of which doesn't thrill me. I conclude that I'll stay in Nepal for as long as possible, searching for petrol as my tank empties but leaving myself a bolt hole into India at the next open frontier post, 220km east at Rupaidiha, should I fail to find any.

Formally called Mahendranagar after a Nepalese king, the town's name was changed to Bhimdatta in 2008 when Nepal became a republic. It's a small place of less than 100,000 people with one main road heading in the direction of the morning sun, which I take. As soon as I begin riding, the catchy *America* song, Ventura Highway, enters my head as 'Mahendra Highway, in the sunshine...' which I sing over and over again. Out on the open, straight road, I'm immediately conscious of just how quiet everything is. One or two motorcycles potter around villages but by far the most ubiquitous form of transport is the bicycle. We pass through a sleepy rural region dotted with tidy villages of simple mud brick dwellings surrounded by well tended fields. The sky's vivid blue, the air fresh and fragrant and with such token traffic, it's extremely therapeutic after the stresses of driving in India.

The first major town I come to is quite an eye-opener. Its petrol station is closed and scattered all around are abandoned tractors, buses, trucks and cars, creating a rather eerie, almost dystopian spectacle. Back out in the countryside, we fly along and I'm thrilled by how well the Matchless is performing, her engine quiet yet pulling strongly. Around lunchtime, chugging through a larger village, my right hand mirror flies up in the air as I inadvertently hit a pothole. Somehow, flinging my hand out in a reflex reaction, I manage to catch it then slow to a halt. While reattaching it, a man comes out of his house and asks if everything's okay. He's very chatty and it's easy to bring subject round to petrol.

"It is very bad, especially in Kathmandu where people are queueing for hours to buy Chinese petrol that's rationed to 3 litres per person. But none of it is making its way here to the south. All our petrol stations are empty and as you can see, our bus network has come to a standstill. These politicians don't understand the impact this is having on people."

I ask him if he knows where I can buy black-market petrol.

"I think you must ask in shops."

"Shops?" I reply, somewhat bemused. "What kind of shops?"

"Any... food, general supplies. If there's a chance of making some money, a shopkeeper will certainly sell smuggled Indian petrol."

I thank him for his time and resolve to put his theory to the test as soon as possible.

A bit further on, I halt outside a long row of shops. The first two can't help so, crossing the road, I try a couple more.

"Petrol... no sorry," says a merchant.

Just as I'm about to leave, his voice changes.

"My neighbour... Yes, I think she has petrol. Wait... no, come, I'll show you."

Leaving his shop unattended, he walks 30m along the pavement to another small store and has a few words with its owner.

"Yes, she has petrol. How much do you want?

I don't really know, so say five litres, providing the price is right. From behind the counter, five recycled one litre water bottles are plonked in front of me, the bright orange liquid inside them almost luminous in the sunlight. I hold one high, checking to see if a layer of water is obvious, the specific gravity of petroleum and H_2O being different and causing them to separate. It looks fine and all things considered, the cost seems reasonable at 200 rupees per litre, approximately what I pay in the UK although I believe that's almost twice the usual pump rate here. After carefully pouring the precious fuel into the tank there's still some room at the top, so I buy one more bottle, reasoning that it'll certainly get me through today and well into tomorrow. Contented, I once more set off.

The full extent of the blockade's impact on Nepal's infrastructure is apparent at the next town. Here there are two petrol stations, both of which are clogged with stranded vehicles that spill out onto the road. In the case of the second one, a line of jettisoned buses and minibuses extends for almost a hundred metres. Although I'm enjoying the freedom and peace of empty roads, I hate to think of the long-term repercussions for the country if this continues.

Late in the afternoon, I enter a hilly region where the road climbs, winding from side to side through a pine forest. As the crystal clear air cools, it suddenly occurs to me that I haven't had anything to eat all day. I stop in a tiny village which comprises just a handful of bare wooden houses and smallholdings. One of the buildings has a little open-fronted shop and a cafe on the ground floor where I buy a soft drink and two packets of biscuits, then, sitting at a table with chickens pecking around my feet, I relax. The owner, a young woman with long jet black hair in a ponytail, sits behind the shop counter breastfeeding her baby. An old man with knobbly knees and a hunched back walks up the road driving three cows ahead of him, a large stick brandished in his hand. I'm tempted to ask the proprietor if she has a room for rent, ruminating that no matter how basic the facilities might be, it'd be wonderful to spend a night in such a restful place. However, I've loved every minute of riding today and as there are still a couple of hours of daylight left, I'd really rather get back on my bike and make the most of things. Two wheels easily wins over pastoral tranquility, so I thank my host and climb onto the Matchless.

Back on the plains, with the sun now lost over the horizon, I have absolutely no inclination to stop. Common sense prevails; the road is increasingly occupied by children, people on bicycles, dogs and the occasional flock of goats and in the rapidly diminishing light, it's too risky to keep going. As I roll through a village, I begin to cast my eyes sideways for somewhere to stay. A sign at the edge of the road says, 'The Moon Palace', and I catch a fleeting glimpse of a few tables spread out like an open-air cafe at the rear of a deep garden. Unsure if it's a guest house or simply an eatery, I about-turn, ride up a gravel path and stop. Walking up a concrete ramp, I come to an open area with what appears to be a reception desk. A young man runs out of a side room and skips behind the counter.

"Are you a hotel... a guest house?" I say.

He looks flustered and a little unsure but replies in the affirmative.

"Can I see a room?" I ask, not wholly convinced by his reaction.

He leads me upstairs and into a small room. There's an unmade double bed, a plastic chair and a low table. When he thinks I'm not looking, he kicks sandals towards the door and gathers some clothes off the chair. I stick my head around the bathroom door and notice that the shower looks as if it's recently been used. Nonetheless, the price is more than reasonable and he tells me he'll clean the room for me. Back downstairs, it's already turned dark so I gun the Matchless then ride her up the concrete ramp, parking in the shelter of the hallway.

After a shower, I go to see if the man can recommend somewhere to eat. There are now three young men behind the reception counter, none of them looking any older than 16. They giggle a lot and seem rather excited by my presence. I ask about dinner, which stumps them for a moment until one of them has the bright idea of offering me a beer from the fridge... now you're talking! As I pour it into a glass, a man in his late 30s arrives, excitedly introducing himself as Govinda, the owner.

"Welcome to our home," he says, sitting beside me and pumping my hand with his. "You are our most honoured guest, the first we have ever had stay. We only opened a week ago."

I can't believe this has happened twice in such a short space of time but it does at least explain the strange behaviour of the young men and the unpreparedness of the room, which they've obviously been using themselves. Govinda goes on to explain that the other three are members of his extended family, they're part-time students and his hope for the lodge is that it'll provide them with somewhere to live and a means of earning some money while they study. As for their age, I'd got that completely wrong, they're all over 20... indeed, the fellow that first showed me to my room is his son-in-law, the father of his first grandchild, and is 24. There must be something about the faces of Nepalese men that gives them such youthfulness!

In the daytime, Govinda hopes to serve food to locals and travellers alike but doesn't yet have a chef working at night. Notwithstanding, he makes a phone call and his daytime cook soon arrives, whipping me up an excellent meal in no time. Deeply contented by today's progress, I spend a very pleasant evening with them all, sitting in the reception, chatting and watching a film on television.

Day 60. Lalmatiya to Chandranigahapur. 232 miles.

In the depths of night I'm jolted out of a deep sleep by the blazing 'd-del-er-d... d-del-er-d... dele-dele le-le-de" of musical air horns from a long-distance nightbus raucously announcing its arrival in the village. When it repeats itself a minute later, the decibel level's so torturous that I think a window must be open, so get up to close it. Pulling back the curtains, I'm astounded to see an ornate wooden window frame without a single pane of glass... there's certainly scope for further development in this all too new hotel!

Heading unwaveringly east, the hours of daylight are noticeably shorter with each day that passes. Despite being befuddled by lack of sleep, I'm up and at it before 7am, keen to waste as little riding time as possible. After a swift breakfast of two boiled eggs and a cup of tea, I prepare for departure.

"You are our most respected guest," says Govinda, refusing to let go of my hand in farewell. "You will always be welcome back at the Moon Palace."
I'm touched by his sincerity. He goes on to tell me that I stand the best chance of finding petrol in the next major town, Butwal, which is 100km away. He thinks it'll take me three hours to get there which I find hard to believe. With a wave and a prolonged beep of my horn, I roll back onto the East-West highway where my musical earworm avidly springs forth with 'Mahendra Highway', now stuck, unremittingly, in a groove.

For most of yesterday, the road ran parallel with the seemingly endless line of dark green hills that marks the beginning of the Himalayas. Within a very short time this morning, the highway takes a turn north and in the distance, I see it disappear into woodland as it climbs steeply into the foothills. A large red sign appears on my left, warning of a '15km Accidental Area'. I soon see why, the incline's so severe and the bends so tight that the occasional truck heading up the gradient can't get out of its lowest gear. Overtaking on the short, narrow straights is a challenge on the way up and a harum scarum flaunt with danger on the way down. The level of difficulty's compounded by the pockmarked road surface which has been irrevocably damaged by the steady drops of water that fall from the dense overhead canopy of trees. The jarring impacts and unrelenting vibrations are so intense that anything above 40kmph is unbearable and before reaching the bottom of the descent, I'm already rummaging in the tank bag for a packet of Ibuprofen.

Back on the plains, I stop shortly before Butwal to enquire if anyone has petrol for sale but draw a blank everywhere. As I'm about to leave, a young man on a scooter asks if he can help.

"I bought mine in India," he says. "How much do you need? I have 16 litres at home, you can have as much as you like."
As all he wants is the going rate of 200 rupees, I agree, hopping onto the Matchless and following him. We promptly turn off the highway and trace a twisting course along interconnecting gravel paths that ramble between allotments and houses, pulling up at the rear of a small dwelling where his parents, wife and two children are seated around a table. The man goes into an

outhouse to retrieve his petrol but immediately comes out empty-handed, a somewhat perplexed expression on his face. He begins a conversation with his wife which quickly becomes heated. Visibly fuming, he walks back to me and says,

"I'm very sorry. My wife has given all of my petrol to a neighbour who she said needed it more than we do! I'm so angry, I don't know what to say to you."
There's nothing that can be said, but he kindly leads me back to the main road and with a wave, I continue on my way.

In Butwal's suburbs, which have, as predicted, taken three hours to reach, I get lucky. The first place I try has fuel aplenty, the shopkeeper surreptitiously passing me litre bottles secreted inside blue plastic bags as he anxiously glances from side to side. It's a considerable relief to have a full tank again and as I ride into the city centre, feel certain I'll be able to stay the distance in Nepal. I come to a crossroads with the Siddhartha Highway, a major north-south route that travels over the border from India at Sonauli and goes all the way to Pokhara, the country's second largest city and gateway to the Annapurna mountain range. Traffic's immediately much heavier, mostly consisting of motorbikes crazily overladen with every shape and size of plastic drum and bottle that can possibly be strapped on. Heading south, the bikes speed along, the empty vessels clattering against each other in the wind. By contrast, heading north, they seem to visibly sag under the tremendous weight of the petrol they're carrying and some of the riders have a hard time steering their mounts in a straight line.

Riding 200km cross country towards Hetauda proves to be a mixed bag of reasonable asphalt interspersed with long sections where stones have been implanted in the ground as make-do repairs. Repeated ripples in the tarmac vibrate through the bike and into me but it seems nothing will stop the Matchless, she's somehow able to absorb enormous punishment and I have nothing but respect for her creators, both past and present. The unpredictable antics of the few trucks and buses that share the road with us are scary and the number of smashed up wrecks which festoon the verges, testament to just how poor the general driving standards are. They have stoved-in bodywork, smashed glass and crushed cabs. Several have collapsed roofs, the result of rolling over, and in some cases there's nothing but the remains of a burnt out carcass. Though not culpable, for the umpteenth time I guiltily acknowledge that the effects of the Nepalese petrol crisis are working to my advantage.

For over an hour, the road follows the northern boundary of Chitwan National Park, where roadsigns warn motorists to watch out for elephant, rhino and Bengal tigers. At one point I need to make a toilet stop, parking the Matchless by the side of the road and stepping into the shelter of bushes. I know that tigers are crepuscular predators, they hunt primarily at twilight, and as it's currently the hottest part of the day, any self-respecting big cat will be sound asleep. Tell that to my autonomic nervous system... a small rustle is all it takes for primal fear to stand every hair on my back on end, and I rush to zip up and get back on my bike.

I stop in a village to buy a lunch of bananas, peanuts and a fruit drink.

Standing beside the parked bike, I study the front-end from all angles and conclude that it's twisted, a partial return to the condition caused by the head-on crash in India. Out come the spanners and this time I'm much quicker at straightening everything up. My supply of Nepalese rupees is getting thin, so in Hetsauda, I find a bank to change some euros, then turn south towards the busy border crossing town of Raxaul. For 25km the road meanders up and down, passing through a cool wooded area where a bare earth village lines the wavy tar edges. My attention's grabbed by the sight of a line of bright orange plastic bottles neatly arranged outside a house. I turn around and head back to buy some but the non-negotiable price of 300 rupees, especially so close to the border, smacks of profiteering and I continue on without making a purchase.

The hamlet of Pathlaiya is situated at the junction where the East-West Highway turns east again and the Tribhuven Highway takes over for the final run to the frontier. There's a water treatment plant, a bus stop and a small collection of open fronted wooden shops but none of them seem to be doing any business. Parking up, I enquire at the first if they have any petrol. They don't but the lady in charge asks her teenage daughter to lead the way to a friend's shop. Here they do but it costs 250 rupees, more than I'd really like to pay, so after a little bargaining, I manage to buy 8 litres at 230 rupees apiece. The shopkeeper seems exceedingly happy with the transaction and the girl, pleased to have had the chance to practice speaking English, skips back in the direction of her own family's store.

The Garmin indicates 40 minutes to sunset and my map shows the next town, Chandranigahapur lies 40km away and all things being equal, I should just about make it before nightfall. As I continue, however, the deep woodland that borders the road increasingly casts heavy shadows, bringing on premature darkness. Making it by the skin of my teeth, I enter the town just as the road turns treacherously black. I'm immediately aware of a heavy, choking atmosphere that's caused by the day's waste, including copious amounts of plastic, being burnt in small piles in front of people's shops and houses. It's an unpleasant but common practice carried out in many Asian rural areas at day's end. Through the fug, I make out the words Alpine Hotel and without pausing for thought, swing onto its forecourt.

Inside the reception, a young woman sits on a sofa tapping her smartphone.
"Do you have a room, please?" I ask.
She looks rather taken aback, replying.
"I'm sorry, I don't work here. You need to ask the manager... here he comes."
Apologising for my mistake, I turn to the approaching man who appears delighted to have a guest, immediately offering secure inside storage for the bike. The rooms are cell-like but clean and mosquito free and I don't hesitate to take one. Outside, unloading the Matchless, the woman I'd erroneously thought was hotel staff joins me, explaining that she's waiting for her driver who's out and about searching for petrol. As we get deeper into conversation, she introduces herself as Dr. Shalu, a conservation worker with the *World Wildlife Fund*. She's been here for two days of meetings with community

representatives and local agencies.

"Three rhinos have been spotted in this area in the last week, which is very encouraging as they don't usually stray far out of Chitwan. It's a good sign because this region is a natural corridor for wildlife to move along," she tells me. "However, as anywhere, when wildlife comes into contact with humans there can be problems and we work very hard with communities to minimize the risks to both people and the animals."

I ask about tigers and am pleased to hear that their numbers are on the rise.

"Nepal, India and China have a joint mission to double their tiger populations by the year 2022. We're making good progress, as we are with the elephants which travel this way from Burma and the Eastern Indian states."

At this point, her Landcruiser arrives and the driver puts her bag into its boot. I ask her how the lack of fuel is affecting her work.

"The petrol crisis has repercussions for everybody in Nepal, but there are implications for the environment too. Illegal loggers cross from India, chopping down hardwood trees and smuggling them back across the border. Usually we have ranger patrols that either deter or catch them but with no fuel for their vehicles, our operations have been severely hampered," she explains before climbing into the back seat and wishing me well for the rest of my journey.

I head inside, jaded from the day's ride but delighted to have come so far. I really like Nepal and its people, from whom I've collected more roadside waves than anywhere else to date. They're relaxed, friendly and courteous and the majority seem to speak excellent English, which makes travel so much simpler and interesting. The only guest in the hotel's restaurant, I sit eating a plate of traditional dal bhat, steamed rice and a lentil soup served with chapati. It's simple fare but tasty and nourishing. Thinking ahead, I relish the prospect of another day in this beautiful and most hospitable country.

Motorcycle petrol queue hundreds of metres long, Nepal.
Image extracted from the helmet camera video.

Day 61. Chandranigahapur, Nepal, to Siliguri, India. 228 miles.

"Why is your motorbike so dirty?" asks an intelligent sounding schoolboy.
At a guess ten years old, he's part of a small audience that's wandered in from the road to watch me load up

"It's from 1941," I explain, "and it's not like modern motorbikes because these wheel bearings aren't sealed. It's got big holes that let the gearbox move and these two electrical things, the magneto and dynamo, aren't waterproof."
He keenly follows my explanation.

"Every place I've seen that cleans cars and bikes uses a jet wash, which will only drive water and maybe grit or sand into all those areas. And that would be a big problem."

"Thank you sir," he says earnestly, then begins translating my answer to the people around him. As he finishes, a call goes up from the roadside where a couple of his schoolmates are waiting, so he formally shakes my hand and excitedly runs off to join them.

Exiting the town, we're straight back into forest where translucent tendrils of mist drift ghost-like across the tarmac and troops of monkeys cavort on the verges, occasionally darting out to challenge us, the intruder in their kingdom. Quite a few infants playfully bound around the adults, the sweetest being the tiny ones with huge round eyes, that cling to their mothers' backs. Almost an hour later, the trees thin and agriculture becomes more prevalent, with villages increasing in proportion to the number of small holdings and farms that now seem to sprout everywhere. So far, I haven't seen a single car, truck or bus on the road but with the advent of habitation, the number of bicycles increases significantly along with herds of golden brown goats, skittish cows, plump pigs and placid-looking water buffaloes.

Reaching the town of Mithila, I'm arrested by a sight that makes me pull over and unashamedly stare. There's a petrol station which obviously has fuel for sale, the first I've seen in almost 800 kilometres! From the line of queueing vehicles, I deduce they're only serving motorcycles... there are hundreds of them in a line that stretches as far as the eye can see. Some of the bikes are two or three deep and their riders sit, engines off, patiently chatting with each other. I click into 1st and slowly get under way, awestruck by the length of the queue which continues on and on. It makes me ponder the age of independent transport that we live in. It's so contingent upon fossil fuels and I wonder how things will pan out once the oil starts to dry up and becomes prohibitively expensive for the masses. Electric powered vehicles including motorcycles, which have come on in leaps and bounds in recent times, seem to be the immediate future, providing their limited range is extended, their purchase price dramatically drops and power to recharge their batteries can be derived from means other than burning hydrocarbons. Interesting times ahead... hopefully.

I stop to buy lunch in a small town but again can't find anything but biscuits in the shops. Near where I park the bike, however, a man sells bananas from a handcart. They're the very small, fat ones not much bigger than a swollen thumb that come in huge clamps, so I buy some and make a banana sandwich with leftover chapati from breakfast. A couple of young men wander over for a chat while I'm eating and I ask one of them what I should do with the pile of skins I've amassed.

"Throw them away... here," he says pointing at the ground. "Anywhere... it does not matter."

It does to me as I have a strong aversion to seeing roadsides plastered with litter. Still, they are biodegradable and I don't have anything to carry them in. Feeling hypocritical, I reluctantly drop them close to the kerb. Within moments, two hip high goats appear out of nowhere, sniff out my cast offs and devour them. We all laugh.

"You knew that would happen?" I ask.

"Of course, food never goes to waste here!" the man replies.

Where the sale of petrol was clandestine in the western and central regions, here there's an open market, with many houses and shops lining up rows of full bottles at the roadside, like skittles waiting to be bowled over. I fill up again, spending virtually the remainder of my Nepalese rupees, confident it'll be enough fuel to get me into India. I know we're getting close to the border when larger motorised vehicles begin to dominate the highway. Riding through the town of Mechinagar, we're jostled by buses and cars tightly pressed together within the narrow streets. Out of the blue, the archway signifying the end of Nepal appears and I stop in my tracks. The legalities of leaving the country don't enter my head, instead I reflect on what a wonderful experience crossing this lovely land has been and how brilliantly the bike has covered 1024 kilometres in just three days. My reverie is broken as I catch sight of the clock. 4.10pm and time to get a move on!

My recent run of good fortune continues, with the polite and efficient Nepalese immigration and customs staff processing me in under a quarter of an hour. Things turn to custard, alas, when I descend from the customs hall and join a column of vehicles inching its way across the 200m long bridge that separates the two countries. Pandemonium reigns. It's a single lane in each direction and with everything squished cheek to jowl, nobody can move. Bicycles and bicycle rickshaws are the biggest problem as they carry people and goods backwards and forwards over the frontier. Every conceivable inch of space has a wheel or foot planted squarely in it, including over the central line. Tempers are frayed and the situation isn't helped by the owner of an expensive 4x4 whose constantly honking horn blasts in my ear while he tries to force a path down the wrong side of the bridge. A cyclist falls over, and in a domino effect, two more follow. The driver pays no heed and hand still on horn, continues trying to bully a way through. Baking in the late afternoon sun, I turn my engine off and whenever there's a chance, use my feet to paddle forward. Excruciatingly slow, it takes more than three quarters of an hour to get to the other side. Drenched and exhausted, I put the Matchless on her sidestand and enter the customs office. Ten minutes sees me back on the road, searching for immigration.

With my passport stamped and the sun dipping in the sky, I ride into India for all of 100m before stopping in disbelief as I join the tail of another jam. This one is caused by a bus turning off a side road and a truck that's unwilling to give any quarter. Front bumpers locked, their respective drivers shout furious abuse at each other through open windows. Thoroughly cheesed off, the rest of us sit unmoving, hemmed in by a solid wall of streetside traders that encroach the road with their wares of gaudy Diwali decorations. A policeman finally sets the protagonists right and the bus, losing out, reverses back. This resolves nothing, however, because the road is now closed by a level crossing a further 100m ahead. We wait, and wait, and wait. Darkness falls like a theatre curtain and all around the Diwali decorations flash gaily as the vendors switch their battery powered lights on. Twenty minutes later, an express train rattles past then the gates lift skywards. All hell is let loose as vehicles from both sides of the track clash head on, each set unwilling to squash back into its own side of the road. Absolute mayhem!

Immediately beyond the crossing is a roundabout. I check directions with a policeman who confirms that my destination, Siliguri, is about 35km away and I need to take the first exit. Driving on Indian roads at night is a game of chance in which I never wished to participate. Tonight I don't have any choice so switch my lights on and despite the sweltering heat, don my hi-vis vest. I tentatively move off, going no faster than 2nd gear and keeping tight within the boundary of a narrow run-off area at the edge of the carriageway that's marked with a white line. Across the road, the tailback of trucks waiting to enter Nepal is at least 5km long. They're all carrying dry goods, with not a single petrol tanker to be seen. Most seem to be locked up and empty, their drivers either absent or sleeping underneath their chassis. My narrow hard shoulder has its own dangers, littered with piles of sand or rocks, patches of broken glass, people pushing hand carts or wobbling along on unlit bicycles. Notwithstanding these perils, it's still the safest place as my proper lane is mostly used by oncoming cars and buses speeding towards the border, their blinding headlights inevitably on full beam. I'm extremely scared, especially when the hard shoulder disappears without warning and I narrowly miss dropping down a large hole. I try a new tactic, letting a motorcycle overtake me then following its rear lights at a safe distance. When it weaves, so do I, when the rider hits his brakes, I hit mine. Every few minutes, one'll go too fast, leaving me behind so I simply wait for another to come along and begin trailing that in the same manner.

Beyond the last of the waiting trucks, I feel more confident in my own lane but still take things slowly. We're now in the middle of the countryside where the moonless sky's ink black. Ahead, a car seems to be stopped in the middle of the road and the motorcycle I'm currently following, slows. Large eerie shadows move across their headlights. Water buffalo, I think, but as I draw alongside them, distinguish the formidable silhouettes of elephants, their magnificent ears and trunks clearly outlined as they pass just a few feet ahead of me. I cut my engine and marvel at the splendour as the herd, one by one, plunges into the undergrowth on the other side. A car coming towards us stops and its owner produces a large torch, shining it into the faces of the last three animals. A small one at the rear becomes spooked, turning sharply around and crashing back into the field it's just left. On the other side of the road, one of the beasts trumpets loudly, sending a tingle through me. The youngster that's become separated replies and I see its dark profile moving through the undergrowth immediately to my left. It's been a most extraordinary experience, the stuff of dreams, but I decide to leave, hoping the others will follow suit and give the lone animal the chance to rejoin its family. I'm so elated, my fears are temporarily forgotten and I ride joyfully into the night. In any case, the risks soon become less immediate as, approaching the city, traffic intensifies and slows and street lighting takes over.

Siliguri's a city of half a million that's located in the Darjeeling district of West Bengal. I stop at the first hotel I spot, a good kilometre short of the centre. It's an older establishment on three levels which has basic rooms. I'm sure I could do much better if I travelled further into the downtown area but I simply haven't got it in me, so push the Matchless to a place of safety behind the kitchens and move in. It's taken 1 hour 40 minutes to ride 33km and as I collapse onto my bed, I stretch my right hand upwards to turn on the bedside light lest I fall asleep in my riding gear. I flick the switch but nothing happens. Moments later, my doorbell buzzes so I get up and open it.

"You rang, sir?" enquires a porter.

"Oh, sorry, it was a mistake," I reply, then watch him walk back along the jade corridor, past the long line of cherry red doors that each have a large potted plant to their right. At the far end is the desk where he'll spend the night at our beck and call. It may be a run down hotel but its old fashioned service can't be faulted.

Revived by a cold shower and a hotel dinner, I hop into a rickshaw and set out to buy a camera to replace the one I'd broken in Jhankat. The sole disappointment of the exhilarating journey through Nepal has been my inability to take a single photograph.

Day 62. Siliguri to Alipurduar. 109 miles.

According to my map, there are two routes east, State Highway 31 and National Highway 31C. The two men at reception confuse matters by disagreeing on which is best. I eventually choose the latter assuming that, as part of Asia Highway 1 (AH1), a proposed single route starting in Japan and ending in Bulgaria, at least some if it will have, by now, been upgraded. Once clear of the city, it seems like I've made a good choice. However, we soon hit a detour where a bridge is closed and have to turn off, entering a deep valley. Climbing steeply, the road narrows and begins winding tightly around the contours of the ever narrowing gorge. The tarmac's pitted from water damage and cracked by tree roots and a column of army trucks slows everything further. The owners of cars and motorcycles perform all their normal stunts, including perilously overtaking on blind bends, and the bus drivers are typically up to their usual tricks of steamrollering their way past everyone else. I'm absolutely fed up with it all... I've spent more than six months of my life in India and have always deeply loved the place. However, the state of the roads, the congestion, pollution and devil-may-care attitude of the majority of drivers has become so vexatious, I realise I'm no longer enjoying travelling here, in fact, I'm actively disliking it.

After about half an hour, we reach the tip of the gorge and double back, heading down its far side. Beyond the closed bridge, the highway straightens and opens up, giving me the opportunity to safely overtake the convoy of military vehicles. Speeding along, I look to my left and see a narrow gauge rail track, the Darjeeling Himalayan Railway, a historic 48 mile line first opened in 1881 which still runs veteran British built steam locomotives to this day. It's always been a dream of mine to take the two day return journey through Ghum, India's highest railway station... one day! I continue on, loudly broadcasting my latest topical song, Morrissey's 'Bengali in Platforms', a marked improvement on yesterday's tune which had been an unequivocal low point, The Wurzels' 'I've Got A Brand New Combine Harvester' spawned by the sight of a threshing machine!

The surrounding vegetation changes to densely packed, knee high, dusky green bushes.

"Tea! Tea!" I call out loud, as if anyone's listening.

Verdant tea estates take over from forest and pasture, gracing gently rolling hills that stretch to the horizon. From late morning to late afternoon, the highway's serenely quiet, swooping gracefully between vast plantations, occasionally dotted with colourfully attired workers picking the leaves. I pass some on their way home, a long line of lithe, weathered women who trek the roadside, cotton tea sacks slung across their backs from straps pressed against their foreheads. The cool fresh air, the sweet scented vegetation and the throbbing sound of the Matchless, which faultlessly powers along the empty straights and sticks like glue in the bends, puts a smile back on my face. In the most timely way, the last couple of hours have served to rekindle my love of riding in India!

A mossy sign on the right says, 'Eco Tourism. Jungle Camp.' It sounds like a great idea, so I spin around and turn down a narrow dirt track that leads into dense forest. Crunching on gravel and weaving from side to side to avoid large rocks, I think back to the start of the ride when my freshly restored Matchless radiated a glossy black sheen and immaculate chrome. I wouldn't have dreamed of heading down this trail for fear of blemishing the finish, damaging the frame or buckling a wheel. Two months on, the path's just another bit of rough stuff for her to conquer. A wooden plank bridge with gaping holes crosses a small river and without stopping, I thread the wheels between the gaps and continue towards our goal. Turning a bend around a belt of trees, we arrive in a large flat clearing with simple village dwellings dotted around its perimeter. On the far side stands the eco lodge. I ride over to its surrounding fence only to discover that the sole gate is padlocked and there are four mean looking dogs standing just beyond it. They bark rowdily as I cut the engine then one nips another on its ear. It retaliates and the other two quickly join in a scrap, wildly chasing one another under the stilts of a house. They come to a stop when they hear my voice.

"Hello... Hello. Anyone there?" then turn around and start barking at me.

As I continue calling, a troop of monkeys descend from a tree and the biggest, a rough looking character with a wicked glint in its eye, starts an altercation with one of the dogs. In an instant all four canines unite and a running battle ensues with the primates, who with greater numbers and the ability to dart up trees, have a definite advantage. For a couple of minutes, the madness of ear piercing screeches and yowls, flying legs and lusty dashes plays out, no doubt a boredom induced skirmish that takes place here most days.

A man comes over from the village.

"Caretaker?" he asks.

"Yes please.", I reply, nodding.

"No caretaker... no. Go army. Finish," he replies, waving his hands negatively towards the buildings.

Thwarted, I thank him and climb back on the bike, noticing a diminutive man busy scrubbing the backs of two baby elephants as I retrace my steps past the village.

Returning to the highway, I ride along the deserted road until the turn off to Alipurduar, halting beside a policeman who stands under a sign which reads 'Tiger Reserve'. I check I'm heading the right way, which he confirms, signalling me on with a wave of his hand. I'm not sure where the reserve begins and ends, for within a minute, a string of villages occupies the roadside, growing in density over the ensuing 9km until they merge into the city itself. Here, every building's festooned with colourful illuminations, all of which are in the process of being switched on. I swing into the courtyard of Hotel Dooars Mountain and as I walk up the steps towards its mirror-glass entrance, a firecracker goes off nearby, assaulting my unwitting ears and making me jump. I look at the clock above reception. It's only 4.40pm yet it's already turning dark outside.

"Tonight marks the start of Diwali," says the receptionist when she hands me a room key. "There will be many more fireworks and celebrations over the next 5 days."

Probably the most important festival in Hinduism, Diwali signifies the victory of good over evil, light over darkness. Festivities include lights shining from roofs, doors and windows and letting off fireworks throughout the hours of darkness. More importantly, and in a way like New Year in many parts of the world, it's a time for people to look inwards, reflect on the year past and how, in the year ahead, they can improve relationships and transform their lives spiritually.

After my ablutions, I head out for a walk where I find that most shops have closed early and the pavements are quiet. Not so the road, along which a procession of open backed pickups parade, their cargo bays crammed full of shouting celebrants, some beating drums, others cheering and waving. A barber's shop is still open. The proprietor doesn't seem to have power, the shelf below his mirror loaded with flickering candles. Of late, I've developed a penchant for being wet shaved so enter, settling myself into the shop's lone seat. With my face fully lathered, the man unwraps a clean blade and inserts it into his razor. In the middle of paring a long strip of creamy stubble from under my chin, an air bomb firework explodes just a couple of metres away from the open door. I don't know who leaps the most, him or me, I'm just grateful to have survived the experience without serious injury.

Walking back to the hotel, whooshes and bangs fill the air in every direction as more and more fireworks shoot into the sky. Entering the courtyard, I'm hit by a distorted cacophony of music that's being played at maximum volume through some nearby loudspeakers. I notice a couple of hotel staff leaning over the wall where I've parked the Matchless, so wander over to see what they're up to. They're watching a party in the gaily lit garden of the adjoining house. On a small stage sit three cross-legged musicians playing tabla (bongo style drums), a sarod (lute) and manjira (small cymbals) into microphones, their tempo gradually building while a woman, entranced, dances alongside them in tight circles. As the music speeds up, she begins spinning, her velocity increasing until she resembles a Whirling Dervish, twirling round and round, completely lost in her pulsating, rhythmic meditation. The crowd, thirty deep and mostly seated on the grass lawn, intently clap in time to the now fevered beat. When some unspoken cue passes between the players, the music abruptly stops and a woman catches the rotating dancer as she sways backwards, leading her off the stage and into the appreciative crowd. The cessation of the music reveals just how loud the fireworks have become, the explosions so continuous they merge into one. I head for the hotel restaurant, seeking refuge from the disconcerting din.

Sitting at a central table in the deserted dining room, I order a meal.

"Oh, and a Kingfisher beer too, please," I ask when the waiter's finished writing in his pad.

Five minutes later he returns bearing a silver tray on which sits a bottle disguised by a cloth that's completely wrapped around it.

"This way please, sir," says the waiter, pointing towards a window table in the far corner of the room.

He walks away and arranges cutlery for one on the table, so somewhat uncertain as to why I need to move, I get up and join him. As I sit, he turns, takes hold of a concertina screen that rolls on castors, and unfolds it around me. When I'm completely hidden, he unwraps the bottle of beer, pops the cap and pours half into a glass.

"Thank you sir, enjoy, please," he says, then ducks out from the confines of my little enclave.

Feeling like the town pariah, I toast my reflection in the window, the sheet of glass visibly trembling from the impact of several large booms, and draw in a cold, satisfying mouthful of the illicit tipple!

Lakshmi, the Goddess of Fortune, is invited into people's homes during Diwali.

Day 63. Alipurduar to Guwahati. 198 miles.

Getting dressed, I put on the TV to catch the morning news. There's just been a general election in Myanmar, the first open elections held there since 1990 when the results were violently quashed by the military junta. The Indian news channel reports that pro democracy leader, Aung San Suu Kyi, and her party, the *National League for Democracy* (NLD), is clearly miles ahead of the opposition but with only 20% of the vote counted and potentially up to a week before the final ballots are in, it's still early days. Aung Sang Suu Kyi has been leading the call for democracy since 1988, with 15 of those years spent under house arrest during which time she received the Nobel Peace Prize. However, the generals who've ruled the country with a rod or iron since 1962 still retain the right of veto with guaranteed seats for their representatives within the Burmese Assembly of the Union, so even if the NLD does win the largest share of votes, it's by no means a done deal. Interestingly, Suu Kyi is constitutionally prohibited from holding the office of president as she married a foreign national, deceased Briton Dr. Michael Aris, and has two British born sons. As I'll be crossing into Myanmar in just 5 days time, I'm simultaneously excited at the prospect of Burma's political freedom and nervous about the soundness of my own travel plans at such a precarious time.

Sticking to yesterday's successful route, I retrace 9km back to National Highway 31C, stopping on the way at a tiny bike repair shop to tighten the steering head. Bitterly regretting not carrying the correct large spanner in order to save weight, I borrow a suitable adjustable and tighten the nut, but when I set off once more and ride over a speed breaker, notice little improvement, a solid thunk reverberating into my hands. For the first half an hour, the tree-lined highway continues to delight before transforming into a dual carriageway that's boldly signposted AH1. It's empty. Stretching ahead is nothing but pale, sand coloured concrete, devoid of traffic in both directions. Smearing an extra layer of sunblock on my face to protect it from UV light reflecting off the surface, I accelerate forward, settling into an uninterrupted cruise of 75kmph for the next hour.

In the distance, I see barriers with what appear to be toll booths interspersed between them. Slowing as I approach, I take in signs which proclaim 'Assam' and a vast compound on the left in which are parked hundreds of heavily loaded trucks. On the far side of the barriers is a colossal line of stationary westbound freight vehicles with no sign of anybody collecting their mandatory road duties and local taxes... little wonder the highway was deserted. A policeman steps out of a booth, smiles, and raises the barrier for me. I ride through without stopping.

Assam is the world's largest tea growing region and the leaves produced here are black in colour, their flavour strong and malty. Unlike Darjeeling and India's other vast tea growing region, Nilgiri in Tamil Nadu, where tea's grown in the highlands, Assam's crop is cultivated closer to sea level. As a result, I don't see any tea estates at all, the roadsides at these altitudes mostly flanked with pasture or habitation. The highway soon turns into a trial with short sections of relatively new concrete that aren't in any way properly joined together. This continues for over 50 bone-rattling kilometres and all I can deduce is that several construction companies have been involved in the resurfacing project and no one has budgeted or arranged for the hundreds of segments to be smoothly linked. There are steps of up to 6" off and back onto this new surface, between which disintegrated old road and absolutely awful dust and rocks reign. The Matchless's steering head knocks and clunks and the rear of the frame takes a pummelling as we repeatedly bump up and down. It takes over two and a half hours to overcome the worst of it, which includes adding a further cable tie to my saddle in place of another broken spring, and from then on, in degrees, things start to improve.

The afternoon heats up, the sun beating down incessantly and the air cloyingly humid. Wandering dogs become widespread, mostly skulking around the outskirts of villages but sometimes roving along the highway itself. On the hard shoulder I notice the sorry sight of one's carcass that's being pecked apart by two large asian crows. A few minutes later I come across another wretched creature which looks as if its days are numbered. Tongue lolling out of the side of his mouth, his russet body wavers down the centre of the outside lane, completely oblivious to his imminent demise as horns blast and vehicles swerve sharply around him. Dazed and exhausted, he trots tragically on.

The death toll starts to mount, with five further canine bodies spotted in various states of decomposure, a gory repast for the carrion scavenging birds which flock around them. Whenever possible, I avert my eyes from the macabre sight. Once again running out of daylight, I press on in the hope I'll make Guwahati's city limits before dusk but fail. The highway becomes even more challenging, with children in particular a risk to life and limb as they herd goats and cows home for the night across the speeding lanes. With woodsmoke from kitchen fires permeating the air and oncoming headlights dazzling me, I gird my loins and determinedly focus on reaching my destination in one piece. With the lights of the city now clearly visible, we climb a steep approach towards a bridge. Too late to do anything about it, I discern the shape of a mutilated dog's corpse smack bang in the middle of my lane. A second later, I smack it square on, both wheels bouncing over the gruesome lump, and somehow manage not to fall off. I'm appalled but can't do anything but keep riding and surviving.

I thought that last night was the main Diwali party night, when everyone used all their fireworks, but Guwahati's populace obviously think otherwise. Following signs towards the city centre, the occurrence of bangs and cracks increases exponentially and within a few minutes it's like being in the middle of a shooting match! Ahead, a cycle rickshaw operator is manfully pedalling two large women along in his carriage. A couple of wiry lads at the roadside light firecrackers and throw them into the road directly in his path. They ignite under the wheels with a rat-ta-ta-ta-tat, the passengers visibly jumping in fright and within seconds, my nostrils are filled with bitter flash-powder fumes. It's soon my turn when a different man lobs a banger across the Matchless's front wheel, the detonation point inches from my left foot. In the distance, I then see two groups of youngsters throwing lit crackers across the road, deliberately aiming for each other. I've always been a bit daunted by fireworks and avoid bonfire night as a matter of course. It feels like pyrotechnic anarchy and I'm unashamedly frightened by it. Forcing panic down, I pull up outside of an official looking building. As there's no pavement here, there are no people cavorting with fireworks, although the general sound of mayhem carries on all around. Hurriedly, I search for a hotel on my Sat Nav. It comes up with seven within a 500m radius. I choose the nearest, the Raj Mahal, and click 'Go'. Determinedly blotting out everything else except traffic, I reach its sanctuary within three minutes, riding up a ramp and into the relative safety of its guarded car park.

A 4 star hotel with a room rate to match, the receptionist makes a phonecall when I ask if he has anything cheaper.

"My manager says I can offer you our preferred customer discount of 30% providing you leave before 10am," he says with the phone pressed against his ear.

There's no way I'm going back out onto those streets, no matter how pricey the room is, and such a substantial reduction is very welcome, so I gladly accept.

After my evening meal, in-house of course, I return to my opulent 7th floor room and look out the window. Below I can see the rooftops of surrounding residences on top of which groups of people celebrate with non-stop firework displays. The sky's aglow with flaming bursts of vivid colour and sparkling showers of incandescence, much prettier seen from a safe distance. After a while, I close the curtains and switch on the TV. The evening news broadcast announces continued wins for the NLD and quotes Aung San Suu Kyi as optimistic. The reporter, speaking from Yangon, infers that the outcome of the elections will very much depend on what the army allows to happen, continued international pressure for fairness and change being the key. I lie in bed listening to the persistent barrage of explosions and the wail of police and fire brigade sirens. It's testament to just how demanding the day's ride has been that I manage to get to sleep at all.

Day 64. Guwahati to Dimapur. 181 miles.

I keep finding lots of little jobs to do this morning and consequently make a slow start. Things are not helped when, in the middle of my regular maintenance checks, I make a gruesome discovery. A chunk of decomposing flesh about the size of my hand has been torn off of the poor dead dog I hit last night and is trapped between the sump guard and crankcase. Yuk! Eventually on my way by 10.30am, I find the route out of town and better still, another workshop where I can attempt to tackle the steering head bearings. The mechanic has two suitable spanners but little interest in the task, which by now I think can only be accomplished successfully if the front end of the bike is lifted into the air. He shows no willingness to understand or attempt this and certainly no finesse with the spanners. Once it's tightened, I head out into traffic and almost fall off... it's now so stiff I can barely steer. Spotting another bike repairer, I borrow a spanner and loosen it off a smidgen, which doesn't help much with the clunks it's emitting but does at least make the bike rideable.

Progress is further hindered when I fail to trust the Sat Nav. The route it plots looks strangely at odds with what's printed on my paper map. However, after circumnavigating the city on a wild goose chase, I resign myself to its original course which proves to be right after all. Climbing through a steep wooded area, I come up behind a solo female touring cyclist, her long blonde hair hanging below a headscarf, who's stoically pedalling up the incline. She's the first foreigner I've seen since Amritsar, so I give her a toot and wave as I pass, spotting her reflection cheerfully waving back in my mirrors. The AH1 proves to be a good choice again, especially as here all the small sections have been joined together by patches of recently laid black tarmac. It's such a joy to be riding on one continuous, smooth surface and I give the Matchless's tank a couple of pats in appreciation.

A new Bullet, with several soft bags haphazardly tied around its tail, overtakes me. Both rider and pillion, hidden behind full face helmets, give a big salute as they power ahead. After a couple of hours I spot a layby where men are selling green coconuts from several ramshackle huts. Braking hard, I manage to pull in just in front of the last two. All smiles, the proprietor of the nearest selects a large coconut and with accurate swipes of his hefty machete, chops chunks off its top until a hole appears. Delicately holding the fruit, he inserts a straw then hands it over. Sweet and refreshing, I take my time savouring the milk before giving it back, upon which he cleaves it in half and returns both pieces with a spoon so I can scoop out the soft white flesh.

Back on the highway, I motor for a steady half an hour before seeing two Royal Enfields stopped on the slim hard shoulder. Pulling over behind them, it's obvious that the first, the one that had previously overtaken me, has a broken chain. Its rider gives me a wave then climbs onto the back of the second Bullet, a Good Samaritan who's stopped to help him. They roar off leaving me with the pillion and the stranded bike.

"What happened?" I ask.

"It was scary, we nearly fell off. The chain just snapped."

I give the offending article a closer look. It's completely bone dry and all the rollers are a grey white colour, evidence that they've been scorching hot.

"Didn't you lubricate it?" I enquire.

"No," he says uncertainly. "It's not ours. We're only hiring it."

It transpires that the pair, from the Punjab, set out to ride the breadth of India, border to border, at its widest point. They'd hired the Bullet but didn't think they'd need to carry out any maintenance on their 5000 kilometre trip. I have a couple of spare links in my toolkit which at first I thought might help them out, but the chain's totally unserviceable and in any case, the rider's already on his way to buy a complete replacement. I wish the man well, suggesting he might want to smear a bit of oil on the new chain from time to time lest the same thing occurs again on the ride back west, with potentially worse consequences.

The road forks outside Nilbagan, a town impossible to see from the highway. Both directions lead to my destination, Dimapur, but the one the Garmin suggests is almost 50km shorter than the other. I look on the map, deliberating which to take as it's already mid-afternoon and ultimately I want the easiest to ride. As it's impossible to guess the surface condition in either direction, I turn off the dual carriageway as recommended and head for the hills, telling myself I can always turn back if the tar's in poor shape. Although the road's narrow and winds through hill country and a succession of sleepy villages, the route is picturesque and the blacktop more than passable. By the time potholes begin to appear, I've travelled over 20km and am too committed to turn back. The holes, which I suspect are the result of water rolling off the precipitous banks that line the road, are all in my lane and have been formed in the shape of elongated horseshoes, each up to 10m long. They're not something I dare get my front wheel stuck in and I spend more and more time riding on the wrong side of the road, extremely grateful that there's little approaching traffic.

I'm well and truly out in the sticks when the sun disappears at 4.18pm. I press on, pushing myself to cover as much distance as possible before the last vestiges of daylight vanish but darkness descends fast in these latitudes and by 4.45pm, I can't even see my hand held in front of my face. There are still over 50km to go. Resorting to the successful ploy I'd used on the night run to Siliguri, I latch onto the coattails of a scooter and stick to it like glue for a good 20 minutes before it disappears, as if by magic, on the far side of a bend. I struggle on for another 20 minutes then enter a much larger village where several policemen appear to be hanging around close to a roundabout. Pausing, I check my bearings then take the first exit with 34km still to run.

Sod's law being what it is, the road deteriorates to its worst in this isolated stretch and I'm constantly reduced to 2nd gear. The occasional oncoming vehicle destroys what little night vision I possess and I have to slow to a crawl until it passes for fear of dropping down one of the many deep, stone filled holes. Following a series of gravelly bends, I momentarily slow when I come upon a large tree that's draped across the road, a gap of only a couple of feet of tar seal visible between its top branches and the soil of the far verge. Using trees to block roads is a common modus operandi for bandits in India and I'd fallen foul to it on my 2008 ride somewhere north of a town called Damoh in the central Indian state of Madhya Pradesh. In broad daylight, a gang of thieves had blocked the narrow road with tree trunks and I'd escaped by the skin of my teeth only by using my wits and having the good fortune of riding a large motorcycle with crashbars. It's very unusual for foreign tourists to encounter banditry and on that occasion, I'm certain it wasn't me they were after... I just happened to head down that particular remote road at the wrong time.

Thoughts racing, I asses tonight's risks while still moving. It looks like the tree has only recently come down as there are no broken branches lying around and all the leaves are still on it. Furthermore, I've seen two or three cars heading towards me in the last 30 minutes and I don't think they could easily have got past the obstacle. It's entirely possible that someone not on the side of the angels has called his villainous mates and told them a lone motorcyclist, his bags chock full of goodies, is heading their way and the tree's been felled especially for me. Throwing caution to the wind, I gun the engine, flatten myself to the tank and without pause, tear through the gap, roaring out the other side. Heart hammering in my chest, I glance in the mirrors before taking the next bend but see no movement anywhere. Telling myself it was most likely just an untimely toppled tree, it nevertheless sets me up to feel nervy and vulnerable as I continue alone down this dauntingly dark forest road.

A weight lifts from my shoulders when I see lights ahead, soon arriving under a curved 'Welcome to Nagaland' sign which spans the now narrow track. A couple of soldiers stand in an adjoining hut and one waves me over.

"Hello. Where are you going?" he asks.

I tell him the name of a hotel in Dimapur that I'd looked up online last night.

"Ah, good hotel, very good security for you and your bike."

"Security?" I respond. "Is security an issue here?"

"Oh no, do not worry, us Nagas never hurt foreigners!"

I laugh out loud, very pleased to hear it.

Dimapur centre's an 8km ride and the hotel proves easy to find as it's located close to the city's most well known landmark, a clock tower. As promised, an underground garage is provided with not one but two guards sitting on stools outside its entrance. Checking my watch as I enter reception, I note it's 6.45pm, meaning I've spent two full hours riding in the dark. Before this venture, I'd always strictly avoided travelling at night in India but the short hours of late have derailed such tenets, forcing me to take risks I'm not at all happy with. In my room, my riding gear stuck to my skin by dried sweat, I slump in an armchair watching some mindless TV for half an hour to reduce the adrenalin that's been coursing through my veins. Eventually peeling off my clothes, I carry them into the shower, killing two birds with one stone, then head downstairs to eat.

Day 65. Dimapur. 0 miles.

I've managed to keep one spare day up my sleeve en route to Myanmar to allow for any emergencies. I'd planned to spend it next to the border but am so enchanted by the Hotel Lake Shilloi and its charming Naga staff that I decide to use the day here instead.

Nagaland is a hilly state that borders Myanmar, and like the surrounding states of Assam, West Bengal, Manipur and Arunachal Pradesh, is separated from the main landmass of India by Bangladesh to the south and Nepal to the north, the only link to the region a narrow strip of land a mere 22 miles wide known as the *Siliguri Corridor*. Over breakfast, I look up the Government of Nagaland's official website, which describes the state as "... a land of folklore passed down the generations through word of mouth." Made up of 17 tribes speaking a variety of different Tibeto-Burman languages, the Nagas were the first ethnic group in north eastern India to declare their territory a self-governing state separate from the new nation of India at the time of independence from Britain in 1947. From then on, it endured ongoing conflict between insurgents seeking autonomy for Nagas and the Indian government, however, the last 15 years have seen piecemeal ceasefires and accords that have done much to diffuse the worst of decades of confrontation.

The government website also says that Nagaland is sometimes referred to as 'The Switzerland of the East,' but when I step out onto Dimapur's sultry, choked streets, I find that hard to picture. What I do see, though, is the change in people's appearance, with a majority of faces less Indian and more south east asian in shape and colour, and also a noticeable shift in attire, especially for many women who rather than dressing in saris, favour sarongs. Turning a corner, I behold the arresting sight of two young female soldiers walking down the street fully kitted out in camouflaged battledress complete with clips of ammunition, strapped on radios and other military paraphernalia. Held across their chests are rather sinister looking dull black assault rifles. I'm quite taken aback as, whilst aware that several armed forces now employ women in combat roles, I really hadn't expected to see them here.

In this morning's newspaper, the *Nagaland Post*, I'd read a letter regarding beggars on the streets of Dimapur, the correspondent referring to it as "our beautiful city". I wander around for an hour searching for that beauty but failing to find it. Nagaland's largest city appears, like many others in India, crowded, congested, grimy and strewn with litter. A lot of buildings seem permanently half finished and the electric and telephone systems are evident as spaghetti-like strands of exposed wiring that criss cross the road and straddle the sides of homes and businesses alike. I do, however, manage to find a motorcycle shop on my travels where I'm able to restock with the Matchless's lifeblood, 20/50 oil.

After lunch, I spend almost three hours in the sweltering hotel garage. Every form of maintenance I can think of, including a 'blood transfusion', is done to thoroughly prepare her for the virtually non-stop, 1000-mile ride across

Myanmar. I end by checking, and where necessary retightening, every single nut and bolt. Returning to my room, I study maps for tomorrow's ride south and check the TV news where I learn that the NLD have an unassailable lead in the Myanmar general elections. Landslide victory imminent, Aung San Suu Kyi continues to call for order and calm while the remaining votes are counted and the new government formed.

An hour before sundown I take the book I'd been given in Gulmit onto the 7th floor roof garden and recline in a comfortable wicker chair. The noise of the city, primarily horns and squealing brakes, drifts upwards and through the haze, in the far distance, I can see the Naga Hills and the peak of Mount Saramati. As the golden orb of the sun dips ever lower, I get up, lean on the parapet and absorb the changes that take place moment by moment. Everything softens, the coarse, rough edges of buildings temper, the unsightly steel framed central clocktower looks unexpectedly interesting, even the thirty or so ungainly mobile phone masts dotted hither and thither take on a gentle, more nebulous appearance. Ragged rows of washing strung along nearby rooftops and rafts of exposed powerlines reflect the sun's amber glow and as fires are lit to cook thousands of evening meals, smoke begins spreading across the skyline, further diffusing the previously harsh outlines. Trees, until now unnoticed, suddenly stand out, their foliage thick and dark and near the horizon, the hills lose contact with the ground as their lower slopes become obscured by smoke, giving them a floating, ethereal quality.

Down below, headlights are switched on and brakelights flash deep red, the once noisy traffic now less abrasive and up above, in vivid shades of orange and crimson, the sky is filled with swooping swallows that gracefully skim the tops of the buildings. The transformation from a dirty, noisy, ugly city to a place of elegance, beauty and enchantment takes place in a matter minutes and as I gaze, the words I'd earlier scoffed at, 'our beautiful city', no longer seem so far off the mark.

Day 66, Dimapur to Imphal. 132 miles.

Last night, I undertook some online research into what lies ahead and came upon a quote from a couple of visiting Delhi politicians who decried the condition of the main highway through the states of Nagaland and Manipur, one even calling it a 'national disgrace'. With this at the front of my mind, I drag myself away from the serenity of the hotel knowing that at least there's no maintenance to do before I set off today. Fortune accompanies me to begin with, the road south continuing straight onwards from my lodgings and although there's a bit of morning congestion, mostly caused by logging trucks, I'm soon out in open countryside. I halt to check the route on the Garmin. It says Imphal is 192km and we should get there at 13.50pm... sounds too good to be true!

We begin to ascend a winding road that's just wide enough to let the sun sneak in between the long leafy branches of trees that encompass it. Mostly in 3rd, the torquey Matchless engine pulls solidly and I'm so fully absorbed in the process of riding the many bends, we're at 1200 metres before I realise how big the climb actually is. It's here that I come upon the first solitary, sharp edged hole in the tar seal, the harbinger of rough times ahead. I spend the next hour and a half scrambling along a road surface that soon reaches the point where the patches outnumber the original tarmac. These repairs have mainly been done by hand and consist of flint-like rocks loosely implanted into packed earth, making them dire to ride over.

Cresting a summit just after midday, Kohima, Nagaland's capital, comes into view. At an elevation of 1200 metres, it stretches across a succession of ridges and largely consists of houses stacked layer upon layer down the sheer hillsides. The kaleidoscopic jumble of mainly rusting tin roof buildings, no two of which appear to be the same, reminds me of remote mountain towns I've seen in the the Andes and Himalayas, but definitely not Switzerland. Kohima was the scene of a crucial confrontation involving Japanese and combined British and Indian forces between April and June 1944. Sometimes referred to as the 'Stalingrad of the East', the Battle of Kohima was the turning point in Japan's quest to conquer the 'jewel in the crown' of the British Empire, India. Once relieved, the allied garrison went on to clear the surrounding area, including the key road I'm about to take.

I stop for food in a small shopping district where minibuses constantly pick up and drop off passengers. The limited choice, which amounts to banana, peanuts and biscuits, has recently become something of a staple and I stand beside the bike nibbling away while stretching my legs and back.

"Good motorcycle. Can I ride?" asks a policeman that I instantly mistrust.

I laugh his request off, smiling and shaking my head.

"I want to try," he persists.

"Sorry, it's very heavy."

"No problem. I am good rider," he says, taking hold of the throttle and repeatedly turning it wide open then letting it flick back to the closed position with a loud click.

"The gears and brakes are different from motorcycles here," I say, still smiling and trying to keep things light.

"I am police. Let me ride," he says with more force in his voice.

He begins to swing his leg in an attempt to climb on but is thwarted by the pile of luggage on the back and the press of nearby bodies now enjoying the free entertainment. I drop a half eaten banana and, lifting my knee high, push my leg through the gap above the saddle, narrowly missing the policeman's hip with the sole of my boot. Settling onto the seat, I pull my helmet off the handlebars and slip my head inside it. Seeing his opportunity rapidly disappearing, the policeman becomes officious, asking me what I'm doing here then where I'm going.

"Vietnam," I holler, simultaneously prodding the kickstarter.

The bike fires and while the man's trying to work out what my answer means, I thank him.

"Very nice to meet you...very good... thank you... Kohima police are the best, thank you," I call, grinning like the Cheshire Cat in feigned bonhomie while slipping the clutch and edging my way through the slowly parting crowd. Feeling cheated of a decent rest, I'm nevertheless glad to have got away from a tricky situation so quickly with nothing more than a bit of bluff and bluster.

Continuing east, things are even more trying with sections of road in which patches of rocks protrude by as much as eight inches. As I'm riding uphill, I'm forced into one of these boulder areas by a descending water tanker, liquid sloshing out of an open hatch, that doesn't give an inch. Pushing tight on my tail is an orange and chrome Tata truck with loud music booming from its cab. With my choice of line severely restricted, I bounce off one rock then another, desperately trying to keep my momentum on an ever steepening incline. My front wheel's sharply turned aside by a another large protrusion and I only just manage to rev over it. Sheer good luck together with the Matchless's heavy flywheels keep us upright and as soon as I've recovered my balance, I pull to the side and let the truck pass, panting from the exertion.

Twenty minutes later, there's a similar close call when I just manage to keep the floundering bike from falling over by powering out of a set of crude road repairs that once again wreak havoc with the front wheel. Standing on the footpegs, my muscles ache from the strain and every time we hit rocks, gullies or ridges, I flinch for my poor motorcycle. I repeatedly check the satnav, desperate for my destination to be nearer. At this point it shows there are still 92km to go. After 10 minutes riding over some particularly punishing terrain, my nerves strung out from the wheels recurrently losing traction in the gravel, I discover that my revised distance to destination is now 91km! It's thoroughly disheartening.

In the north Indian state of Ladakh there are numerous isolated, high altitude himalayan passes. One of my fondest memories of travelling between them is the frequent roadsigns that warn motorists to take care. Black text emblazoned on a yellow background, I've photographed, amongst a multitude of other cautionary jewels, 'Darling I want you but not so fast', 'Be gentle on my curves', 'Hospital ceiling are boring to look at. Avoid accident' and 'If you sleep your family will weep'. I spot one redolent of them this afternoon that says 'Bro. Watch your speed'... talk about chance being a fine thing!

The sun goes down at 4.15pm and in under a quarter of an hour it's dark. With 30km still to ride, I'm grateful that at least the highway's straightened out and is on the level. The lunacy of some of my fellow travellers is typified by the auto rickshaw driving out in the middle of nowhere on a moonless night without any lights and a group of men walking three abreast on the road, the badly adjusted headlights of an oncoming truck blinding me so acutely that I only discern their outline and swerve round them at very last moment. As I ride under the welcome streetlights of Imphal, I feel a mixture of relief at my safety and anger at myself for once again failing to make my destination before nightfall. It's 6.20pm when I reach the refuge of the large but extremely friendly Classic Hotel.

Imphal was under siege in 1944 at the same time as Kohima, its strong resistance blunting the spearhead of the Japanese campaign known as *Operation U-Go*. The city played an extended, critical role in Allied wartime operations. As the eastern Indian railhead, troops and provisions bound for the Burmese frontline usually arrived here, having been shipped first to Bombay then hauled overland on India's rail network. It's quite likely this is the way my Matchless arrived in Burma and I'm keen to get out and explore the city centre. Leaving the hotel, I walk several hundred metres in one direction then turn around and do the same the other way. Most Indian cities are mobbed at this time of night, alive with people going about their business. Not here. Untypically, the shops are closed, there are no night markets and the few people who are on the streets seem to be aimlessly hanging around and in some cases, looking rather desperate. After half an hour, failing to discover anything of interest and feeling rather uneasy, I head back to my room.

I received an email from Brendan a couple of days ago asking if I was actually enjoying the trip. Apparently, my reports of persistently bad roads and long, exhausting days suggested otherwise. I'd assured him that despite the challenges, I was having the time of my life. Encounters with people, ever-changing and often beautiful surroundings and long periods of feeling at one with my motorcycle, have given rise to many fulfilling experiences. Yet lying here on the bed yawning, I'm completely enervated. Inspecting the blisters on my left palm and thumb, the consequence of too much clutch work, I reflect on today's remorseless ride and have to admit there was little about it to enjoy. However, reassessing things in light of Brendan's question, I realise that what I'm attempting isn't a holiday, it's more of an expedition and as such, pleasure and satisfaction often come from completing each difficult task I set myself. While long periods of some days simply cannot be enjoyed, overcoming the obstacles they present can. I fall to sleep feeling deeply contented.

Day 67. Imphal to Moreh. 71 miles.

Neither the TV nor the *Manipur Times* has any further news on the Myanmar election, so I'm hoping no news is good news. One front page newspaper article titled, "KSO Indefinite bandh affects vehicular movement along Imphal-Moreh Road" does catch my eye, however. Underneath a blurry photo of a group of young men surrounding a 4x4, the article reads, 'Vehicular movement along the Imphal-Moreh section of national highway 102 came to a grinding halt due to indefinite bandh imposed by the Kuki Students Organisation (KSO).' The students, it goes on to explain, are protesting against their examination centre being moved out of their district. 'Since 6am bandh supporters were seen blocking through road at Tengnoupal prohibiting vehicular movement along the section of national highway. However, vehicles relating to religious purposes and hospital patients were allowed free passage.' At the end of the article, the students' spokesperson threatened to 'continue and intensify the agitation until the concerned authorities relocate the said examination centre.' I've never heard of the term bandh and can only guess from the description that it's a demonstration. As my crossing into Myanmar is arranged for tomorrow morning, I must reach the border by this evening. Anxiety-laden thoughts of rioting students and police holding up miles of traffic loom large in my mind.

"What is a bandh, please?" I ask the receptionist.
She's unable to explain in a way that I can understand, so I show her the newspaper article and ask her what I should expect.

"My advice is do not go. It might be a big problem for you. You should stay here or go somewhere else in India on your trip."

That doesn't help at all, I have no choice as it's the only road to the frontier town of Moreh. Heading to my room, I search online for a definition of bandh. 'Bandh, originally a Sanskrit word meaning 'closed', is a form of protest used by political activists in South Asian countries such as India and Nepal,' *Wikipedia* explains. 'A bandh is a powerful means of civil disobedience. Most affected are shopkeepers who are expected to keep their shops closed, as well as public transport operators of buses and cabs who are expected to stay off the road and not carry passengers. There have been instances when large metro cities have been brought to a standstill.' Checking further, I discover that Tengnoupal is a village of approximately 2,000 people situated at an altitude of 1,450 metres and is noted as an ideal location for nature lovers. It seems a pretty innocuous place and I have no option but to go there, see what's happening and hopefully find a way through.

Negotiating Imphal's fast moving, wide boulevards, I keep my eyes peeled for another motorcycle repair shop as yesterday's trials and tribulations have created more slack at the Matchless's steering head. I can't believe my eyes when, on the opposite side of the road, I spot an open-fronted workshop with a mechanic actually working indoors. Better still, they have two full length hydraulically operated lifts. I go to investigate and immediately note a series of large, framed certificates on the wall that show the owner has undertaken training courses in Japan. The mechanic, a man in his late 20's, is methodically checking the ignition on a modern scooter using a computerised fault diagnostic tool. When he's finished, he walks around the Matchless in seeming awe then asks what the problem is. Enlisting the help of an assistant, they remove a bike from one of the workbenches and wheel mine onto it. We lift the Matchless's front end and a large block of stabilising wood is wedged under the sumpguard. The workbench is jacked into the air and the front forks, pulled down by the weight of the wheel, fully extend. It only takes a couple of minutes to loosen their pinchbolts before first releasing, then retightening, the steering head nut. With the bike back on terra firma, the mechanic suggests I take her for a test ride. Bombing down the highway, I pull the brakes on hard. The forks compress and the unpleasantly familiar clunk has gone. Next I bounce over some rocks, getting the same positive result.

"No money... no payment please. Just photo with your bike," says the mechanic when I return.

He calls his wife and their toddler out of the adjoining building then they gather round the Matchless whilst a colleague takes photos on 3 different mobile phones. I ride off buoyantly, pleased as punch.

The start of today's adventure is pleasantly surprising, with the road east wide, smooth and straight as it crosses expansive, empty plains. After the hellish passage from Dimapur, it's a breath of fresh air. 48km from Imphal, we enter the rambling township of Pallel Mamang Leikai. At an intersection, I'm flagged down by three soldiers who, according to the regimental sign prominently displayed next to their hut, belong to the *Assam Rifles*.

"Where are you going?" asks the officer, hand placed on my right arm.

I answer, showing my passport at his request. I'm nervous he's going to tell me the road's blocked and I can't continue but he simply smiles and says,

"Have a good journey," indicating with a wave that I should carry straight on. Smoothly accelerating, I pass through the town's outskirts and begin climbing into the foothills, a song for today already raucously issuing forth from my lips, *The Jam's* 'Eton Rifles' now supplanted, needless to say, with the name Assam.

I seem to be out here on my own, the roadsides, densely overgrown with trees and creepers, adding to the feeling of seclusion. From time to time, there's a small gap in the foliage where I get a flashing view of the increasingly distant plains, then it's gone and we're back to winding round a succession of tight, uphill curves. The beat of the engine, the assuredness of its pulling power, the feel of the tyres gripping and the brakes biting all come together and I feel completely in harmony with my motorcycle as we climb onwards and upwards along this stunning strip of twisting tarmac. A fine farewell to India!

I've been enjoying the ride so much, the bandh has completely slipped from my mind. Rolling into a hilltop village, I slow down and head along its deserted main street. Into view comes a line of about 20 red plastic chairs positioned back to back and spanning the entire width of the road. Each is occupied by a young person who, without exception, turns and stares my way when they hear the approaching engine. I slow further, advancing cautiously. A couple at the left hand side leap up and whip their chairs out of the way, their immediate neighbours waving me through the gap they've just created. Pausing at the end of the row, I holler,

"I read about you in the newspaper this morning. Good luck!"

In response, I get a cheer and lots of waves. Riding on, I think back to the fears I had this morning: petrol bombs; tear gas; cars being torched and police blockades. The reality is nothing like I imagined, reminding me that this is India, where the legacy of Mahatma Gandhi and nonviolent resistance is, evidently, still strong.

Two more *Assam Rifles* army camps and checkposts follow then the road begins to descend, with airplane window-like views across miles of hilly jungle away to the north. Constantly on the brakes and twisting round a long succession of tight bends, a tremor felt through the handlebars rapidly increases to a judder. I stop to check the brake plates and wheel drums. All are skin-stripping hot, so I take off my jacket and sit at the roadside, delighting in the sound of cicadas that fill the air. Lost in my thoughts, my reverie is broken when I see a small group of boys, the oldest probably no more than six, running towards me, homemade kites flying high above them. I'd overtaken them at least fifteen minutes ago and feel concerned that their parents will be worried as they've strayed so far. Yelping with delight, they engulf me and the Matchless, their kites falling to the ground as they inquisitively gather around, asking questions and then with ripples of laughter, chasing each other. They jump back a few minutes later when, with the brakes no longer close to melting point, I restart the engine. As I set off, I see them turn back in the direction their homes.

Route 102 continues to surprise, steeply ascending the sides of hills, tracking the narrow tops of ridges then plummeting into the depths of jungle. A few small sections are in the midst of reconstruction, mostly a case of widening bends, where bulldozers have taken giant clefts from the hillside to form 10m high embankments of copper coloured clay that shine in the sun. Narrow and covered in old tar, the road's nevertheless joyfully rideable, with yesterday's omnipresent rock-patched potholes blissfully absent. Heading down a long straight, my eye's caught by a line across the way. Already on the brakes, I apply all the pressure I can and slow just in time, dropping over a 20cm sharp-edged step where the ground has subsided and the full width of the road surface cracked. I can't imagine an auto rickshaw, with its small wheels, having a cat in hell's chance of getting over it! In an hour and a half, I see just three other vehicles.

For years I've dreamed of coming to Moreh although I had no preconceptions of what I'd find here, it merely being the setting off point for Burma. First impressions aren't especially good. With no suburbs as such, the centre begins on the eastern side of a river, its main street no more than 300m long. Slowly riding its full length, I look left then right searching for suitable lodgings. There's a feeling of transience to the place, with numerous hotels and eateries dotted between rows of market-style shops. They all look rundown, in fact, many appear closed. None of the hotels have any obvious secure parking so at the far end I turn around and head back up the main drag. On the completion of my fourth pass, I settle for the tall, red brick River View Hotel. A teenage girl appears at the sound of my engine and efficiently shows me a small second floor room with a plain four poster bed and adjoining asian toilet and shower.

"Do you get many tourists here?" I ask her as we walk downstairs.

"No, not many, most tourists stay in the next hotel."

Back beside the bike, I peer over the wall at an establishment that has a 'Recommended by Lonely Planet' sign across its front door. It doesn't look any better than where I am and as the smiling girl is so delightful, I decide to stay here. She returns a few minutes later carrying a hefty wooden ramp with the aid of her younger sister. We position it up the row of steps that lead to the hotel's entrance then without being asked, both girls put their weight onto the back of the bike and help me heave her up and into the hallway. At this point their mother arrives to take payment and issue me with a key.

Once unpacked, I head out to explore. Moreh has a small market that's set to increase in size as cross border trade grows. The advent of the Asian Highway and a planned international railway connection will certainly make an enormous difference over the next two decades. For now, however, there's a very run down atmosphere about the place. I look inside a couple of restaurants but don't feel particularly inspired to eat in either of them, the food looks more 'to die of' than 'to die for'. The final establishment I check out is even worse and the sight of an unmoving male slumped across a table clinches it... it's a pack of freeze-dried expedition food for dinner! Back at the hotel, the girl, now changed out of her school uniform, brings me a flask of boiling water and in no time I'm sitting on a balcony, the sun just about set, eating veggie Lancashire Hotpot.

In the evening, having prepared everything for a 5.30am start tomorrow, I stretch my legs before turning in. Passing several open doors, I see that each room houses three or four young men squeezed onto plain steel bunk beds, their washing hanging on thin ropes. They're Indian itinerant workers who've moved to the border to find work or seek their fortune. Several wave and say hello as I walk past. Out on the street, I head up town but nothing's afoot except for a couple of elderly women sweeping piles of dusty litter off the street with fan-like hand brushes. In the other direction, just over the bridge, a noisy crowd has assembled around the last two shops. I go to see what's happening. Five street betting games are being run concurrently, all brightly lit by floodlights powered off generators at the side of the shops. I stop at one where a group of gamblers sitting on the ground excitedly throw 20 rupee notes onto one of six squares embroidered on a cloth that's spread out before them. The symbols are a heart, a spade, a diamond, a club, a face and a flag. There are corresponding symbols on each side of the six giant dice which the bookmaker, for want of a better description, holds in a basket. When all the bets are placed, he tips the dice out with a flourish. The symbol that appears face upwards on the most dice wins. Hardly a game of skill or knowledge, it nonetheless draws great whoops of delight or groans of dismay from the participants and their watchers. I ask a man standing next to me what the game's called.

"Jhandi Munda! It is Jhandi Munda," he replies, then steps forward to take a freshly vacated patch of ground and his chance to win.

Returning to the hotel, I climb onto my fourposter and tuck the billowy pink mosquito net in on all sides. Lying on a hard, lumpy mattress, I listen to the cheeky chirrup of the resident gecko as it scurries along a wall. Hours later I'm still awake, too exhilarated for sleep to come. Tomorrow will mark the achievement of a significant goal for the journey... Myanmar!

Panoramic views of thick jungle en route to Moreh.

Day 68. Moreh, India, to Gangaw, Myanmar. 180 miles.

Up at the unearthly hour of 5:30am, I scoff a bowl of muesli in my room then head down to the bike, averting my eyes from the spittoons left haphazardly outside each bedroom door. Aware of my early departure, the owner's waiting with the gangplank, telling me through wide yawns that the border crossing is about 15 minutes away. Without delay, I freewheel down it, load up and leave. She must, however, have meant 15 minutes if walking, because within three minutes I come to a wooden pole across the road with a small guardhouse next to it manned by two redoubtable Indian soldiers. A scooter pulls up while I'm filling in a register, its rider explaining that I'd passed customs and immigration back at the end of Moreh's high street and will need to follow him there. Turning around, we're soon sitting opposite each other at a garden table littered with ledgers and paperwork.

"Before we proceed any further, please can I see proof of your arrangements for crossing Myanmar?" he asks.

I produce a booking confirmation, along with an itinerary, which he carefully checks.

"Thank you," he says, stamping my passport. "Quite a few foreign tourists come here hoping to ride into Burma on their motorcycles. We always check they have an escort arranged for the other side, otherwise they will be sent straight back which wastes everybody's time."

With customs formalities completed, I head to the frontier. A minibus is now waiting on the other side of the barrier in front of which three young men hold up a banner which says *Burma Senses*... they're my guide and escort! One of them, a lean young man with a pleasant face and a welcoming smile, ducks underneath the pole.

"Hello Mr Gordon. My name is Kway," he says, shaking my hand.

His name sounds like Joe, but with a slight 'ch' sound in front of the J. He continues,

"I'm your guide for the next week. When you are ready, please come with us, we have a lot to do this morning."

With a wave of farewell to India, I follow their Toyota along a narrow lane then ride over the Indo-Myanmar Friendship Bridge, a box-like steel framed structure which crosses the Yu river. On a handpainted sign is written, 'Welcome to the Republic of the Union of Myanmar' and a grin splits my face in two... another country reached and the next important phase of the journey about to begin.

We stop a short while later and Kway asks me to walk with him to Immigration. Climbing uphill, we enter a large single roomed wooden structure dominated by a central square of tables. It's empty, so we sit and wait. Pointing to a picture on the wall, Kway breaks the ice, saying,

"Do you know who that is?"

I don't, so shake my head.

"He's our old president and his picture will have to come down soon, now that the NLD have won our elections!"

I can tell by the tone of his voice that he's very excited about it and he goes on to confess that he, like most Burmese, never thought there would be such a resounding victory for the opposition.

"It will take three months, we think, for the handover of government but it's great news for our country."

After ten minutes chatting, Kway leaves to see if he can find someone to help us. I wander around the room, looking at various posters describing the attributes and responsibilities of Myanmar citizens. One narration, which is repeated on several of the posters, catches my eye, the gist of it being that, 'a Myanmar man does not envy those with fair skin or dislike those with black skin, he is fair and open-minded to all races, religions and cultures'. It's an excellent maxim and I only wish it was universally observed.

The official who returns with Kway greets me with,

"Mingalaba."

I respond in kind, the greeting being used extensively in Myanmar as a type of blessing, somewhat akin to 'Namaste,' but wishing the other person auspiciousness. The officer's friendly and efficient and after ten minutes we're back with the bike, the minibus and the two other members of our party, Kyee, the driver and 'Captain', the general helper. With smiles as warm and sincere as Kway's, they help transfer all my luggage, bar the tank bag, into the back of the Toyota. We set off for customs, located in another wooden room that, in contrast to immigration, is little larger than a garden shed. Here, an administrator wearing flip-flops, a singlet and a longyi, a traditional Burmese sarong-type wrap, goes through our paperwork. Kway is carrying reams of official-looking documents that need stamping and counter signing before my carnet can be dealt with. Then I notice three A4 photographs of the Matchless being passed over. They're enlarged copies of pictures I'd taken and emailed to *Burma Senses* before leaving the UK. She looks absolutely mint, a far cry from her current state... bless her!

Myanmar is one hour ahead of India and the bike's adjusted clock reads 9.40am as we arrive in the pleasant border town of Tamu. Our first stop is the local transport office where I'm issued with a driving licence, an unusual process that doesn't require me to prove any riding capabilities or competence in the local rules of the road! Travelling a couple of hundred metres further, we halt at a cafe where I'm asked to wait for half an hour while the team go to complete more paperwork on my behalf. I'm given a coffee and a seat in the sun. Myanmar has such a relaxed, peaceful ambience, and after the full-on experience of India, sitting here, listening to music and receiving the occasional friendly greeting from passers-by, is a welcome respite. By the time the others return, I've had three coffees which Kway, reiterating that he'll be my banker until I can change money in Bagan, pays for. I slap on some sunblock and we hit the road.

The India-Myanmar Friendship Road is an old highway recently repaved at a cost of $30 million by the Indian government in order to boost cross-border trade. It's a joy to ride along, with long straights and gently curving bends all coated with smooth tarmac. I get up to 70kmph and sit there uninterrupted for a long stint, only slowing when I reach a decrepit, ancient bridge. Constructed from wooden planks held in place by rusty steel bands, I crunch onto it, noticing immediately that much of the timber ahead is badly splintered or broken. There are even a couple of beams missing, evident as dark holes I need to avoid at all costs, and creakily crossing the central span becomes a test of nerves I'm exceedingly relieved to complete. Several more bridges follow including some formed from square steel plates which are just as treacherous, almost akin to riding on a precarious seesaw as our weight rocks from one plate to another.

"These bridges date back to the time of the British and the war with the Japanese," Kway tells me after I've crossed a particularly rundown one. "They were supposed to be improved by our government at the time the Indians built the new road, but it never happened."

I hope they do something soon as many appear to be on their last legs.

The neat, orderly villages we pass through mostly comprise of wooden frame houses built high on stilts, their walls formed from square palm-leaf panels and their roofs a covering of corrugated iron or thick thatch. There always seem to be people around them, working by the side of the road, busying themselves with livestock or simply buzzing around on ubiquitous Chinese-made scooters, which Kawy tells me cost as little as US $500 new.

"They don't last very long, though," he assures me. "The better quality ones come from Thailand but they cost $800 upwards."

It still sounds ridiculously cheap.

We come to an area where there are hundreds of white, family size shelters arranged in neat rows. Several fields appear to have been joined together and the tents that extend between them form a makeshift town. At the next bridge, where the minibus is awaiting my arrival, I ask Kway about them.

"Western Myanmar has just been struck by the worst monsoon floods in decades. It started in July and didn't end until September. We're in the Sagaing Division now, one of the worst hit regions. Thousands had to flee their villages and haven't been able to reconstruct their homes yet. These are some of the UN shelters that house the victims."

It's news to me, a natural disaster apparently not covered by the massed media, and although the temporary housing looks well organised, I'm sure the people are desperate to return home and to begin rebuilding their lives.

130km later we come to a halt for lunch. I'm thrilled with our progress. Eating boiled eggs and a plate of noodles at a roadside restaurant close to Kale, I reflect on what a great ride it has been, so easy after the bad roads of India. The men I'm travelling with are fantastic too. All three are genuinely friendly and although only Kway speaks English, the other two are good-humoured and most amicable company. I'd initially been shocked, then rather despondent at the costs involved in transiting Myanmar as a solo traveller, but as the three of them sit opposite, eating their meal and including me in their conversation and jokes, I begin to feel glad that a good part of my payment will go towards their wages and expenses. The alternative, flying the bike from Kathmandu to Bangkok, would have cost just as much but without any of the experiences or benefits that come with this overland option.

Alas, things take a turn for the worse when we set off again. Almost immediately, at what are the first traffic lights I've seen all day, we turn right onto a very narrow strip of uneven tar. It's wide enough for only one car or bus at a time and is congested with bicycles, motorcycles, pedestrians and animals. Moreover, its surface is tantamount to cobblestones. Teeth chattering, I slow, my escort soon disappearing into the distance. I find them 20 minutes later pulled off the road.

"What's wrong? Is there a problem?" Kway asks, plainly worried.

"This road's terrible," I say, "Can't we continue along the Friendship Highway?"

"Sorry," he replies. "No. This is the best way. It's much better than the other route."

I find that hard to believe! So that I'm not constantly left behind, trying to catch them up, I request that they follow me, a solution they readily agree to, telling me they'll overtake when we approach any junction.

Over time, the road gets wider then narrows again, its surface sometimes corrugated, occasionally rocky and always dimpled with a profusion of tiny repair patches. Throughout the long hours, judders and shakes disseminate throughout the bike and my body. Eventually, aching all over, I feel I've had enough so pull off the road and entreat Kway to go another way. Pointing at my map, I highlight the road to Monywa which has been printed with a thicker, coloured line that suggests it's a more major route.

"We tried that road once, but turned around. It was broken up and covered with mud. This really is the best way."

I realise that the misery I'm experiencing has much to do with my expectations. Kway's boss, Min Min, with whom I arranged my crossing of Burma, wrote in an email that I could expect good road conditions all the way, that our route would follow a modern, sealed surface. Had I been mentally prepared for bad roads, they wouldn't seem half as bad. Instead, I'm gutted and as always when faced with trying conditions, fearful that they prove too much for the Matchless. I explain this to Kway.

"I'm very sorry, these are the best roads we have in western Myanmar. We are a poor nation and to us, this road is good. There are many that are worse, believe me. Take your time, we will just follow at your pace," he says earnestly, his head hung slightly low.

His humility and obvious concern embarrass me so I stop complaining, swallow a couple of painkillers and get underway again.

A seat spring twangs off then, at another halt, I notice the bolt on one side of the rear stand has shaken itself free and have to use my only spare to replace it. Next stop is at sunset and there are still almost 60km to go. Walking along the road while stretching my legs and back, I notice a large open sided platform with a straw roof that's sitting high off the ground on stilts. It's positioned perfectly to give a dramatic silhouette against the red and purple streaked sky.

"Hey... come... whisky!" shouts a distant voice.

Kway joins me then begins a conversation in Burmese that's shouted backwards and forwards with a group of men sitting in what I'm told is a meeting house.

"They're local farm workers. They heard you speaking English with me and want you to have a party with them. I thanked them but excused us as we still have over two hours to travel." he explains.

I wave and holler my thanks before settling myself back into the saddle for another session.

Continuing in a southerly direction, I ride late into the evening, the Toyota following 20m behind with its headlights on full beam illuminating the way forwards. The road doesn't improve, instead, it becomes a relentless and formidable succession of blind bends, many covered in scattered pebbles, that taxes my powers of concentration as well as physical stamina. Finally, having failed to get into top gear for the last five hours, we roll into Gangaw, pulling up at the front of a hotel. Reassuring me the Matchless will be safe here, the boys nevertheless use their vehicle to block her in. As soon as I'm changed, we head out to eat at an open air restaurant where a bowl of chow mein's quickly washed down with a bottle of *Myanmar Beer*. I'm so jiggered I can hardly speak, so while the other two stay to enjoy a night out, Kway walks back to the hotel with me, explaining that he likes to spend his evenings quietly, studying the teachings of the Buddha and meditating.

"Tomorrow, the road is the same most of the way to Bagan," he tells me rather apologetically.

"Thanks, Kway," I answer him. "This time I won't have high expectations... I've learnt my lesson!"

Temples on the Bagan plains.

Day 69. Gangaw to Bagan. 174 miles.

Another early start, this time to compensate for the road conditions ahead, sees the four of us up at 6.30am. I begin the day in the same manner as usual, with motorcycle maintenance, including the removal of the front numberplate which yesterday's vibrations have damaged to the degree that it's now oscillating wildly. Next, I secure my saddlebags back onto the bike, hoping their weight will reduce the extent to which the rear end bounces then, for the same reason, lower the tyre pressures. Almost ready to leave, Kway stands beside me, today, like the rest of the team, wearing a longyi. He questions me about the bike's past and I reveal the story of her long life in Burma, at which point he begins patting the petrol tank, saying,

"Welcome back. Welcome back home."

A man after my own heart!

Petrol is first, with Kway leading us to a station that sells 95 octane for the princely sum of 48p per litre. Those were the days! We turn south from Gangaw and as warned, the first 60km are on a par with yesterday afternoon's slog. This morning I do at least manage to get into top gear, if only for a couple of minutes! We enter the southern reaches of the Alaungdaw Kathapa National Park, a forest and wildlife sanctuary first established by the British colonial government in the 19th century. Amidst dense jungle and fast flowing rivers sit two huge escarpments, the Ponnyadaung and the Mahudaung. Both have been formed in a north-south orientation and as we approach, the road changes direction due east, which means we meet them square on. Beginning at 400m, the climb up the first is incredibly steep and mostly straight, the Burmese road builders obviously favouring a direct approach over less precipitous zigzags. Standing up on the pegs while weaving around patches of chalk and rocks, I keep the revs high, bringing all my experience from Tajikistan to bear. The minibus is for once left behind, painfully picking a slow path up the incline. In less than 15 minutes we ascend to 950m, reaching a narrow summit then commencing our drop down the other side. The descent is more gradual, consisting of many bends and by the time I reach the flat valley floor, the brakes are spitting hot. When the boys catch up, Kway reveals there's a restaurant in the next village so we head there for lunch, the halt providing plenty of time for the bike to cool before the next ascent.

Sitting outside an eatery waiting for our meal to be cooked, my interest's piqued as I observe a mechanic working on a scooter in front of his nearby hut. He has the rear wheel off and is welding the bike's swinging arm, which I guess has been fractured by the uneven roads. It's not the first two-wheeler I've seen with its wheels or suspension being worked on since arriving in Myanmar and it underlines just how well the Matchless is coping, especially when you consider that these lightweight bikes are only used on short, local runs and have rear suspension into the bargain!

The second cuesta is even more vertiginous, but the indomitable Matchless powers up it without pause in 2nd gear. With the team once more out of sight behind us, we reach its peak at 980m and keep rolling. The road down is a

nuts, coconuts! Assam, India.

Unnecessary speed warnings, Nagaland, India

ge children with homemade kites. Riding to the Moreh border crossing, Manipur, India.

sky? Sunset on the road to Gangaw.

One of over 2,200 temples on the Bagan plains.

The peanut crop being transported on the droveways of Myanmar. 70km north of Bagan.

Fabulous travelling companions, Myanmar. From the left, Captain, Kway, Kyee and Wunna.

Kyi, Yaway, Mo and May Thi Han, Yangon.

Gold leaf being applied to Golden Rock.

dside halt, Thailand.

Between Vientiane and Vang Vieng, Laos.

rthodox petrol station near Phou Khoun, Laos.

A towering karst, central Laos.

Just 48km to the Laos - Vietnam border at Na Meo!

Roadside accommodation, Na Meo border, Laos.

Home made tractor, Vietnam.

Officially in Vietnam!

...ipe break, first day Vietnam.

Celebrating 70 years of independence, Qui Nhon.

...ls of sunflowers by the side of the Ho Chi Minh Road. South of Thai Hua, Vietnam.

Sunset on the South China Sea. Mui Ne, Vietnam.

There are no limits on Vietnamese bikes.

2-wheelers at one set of traffic lights. In front (above left) and behind (above right), Ho Chi Minh C

ge entrance, Cambodia. Delightful Khmer family on the road to Phnom Penh.

English class at the Hope Agency School, Bakod Village, Cambodia.

After the red earth road, Cambodia.

Rice harvest, Bakod village, Cambodia.

Six on a scooter! Cambodia.

Journey's end. Arrival in Bangkok, Thailand.

The Matchless is crated up, Bangkok.

Safely back home. Southampton docks, U

shambles, so badly damaged that in places, it's like a crossing a series of dry stream beds. Fearing the front wheel will wash out on long steep stretches of loose gravel and stones, I leave its brake lever well alone, instead keeping my foot pressed down almost constantly on the rear brake pedal and my centre of gravity as far back as possible. The bike slithers and slides around tight bends but crucially stays upright. Sweating profusely, I get off at the bottom and sit on some grass in the shade of a tree, immersed in the encircling sound of crickets as I wait once more for the others to arrive. When they do come, I tease them about their pathetically slow speed. They laugh along, confident it'll be the last time that I race ahead of them today.

As we skirt along the tops of a succession of sharp ridges, wild jungle gives way to thickets and small holdings that gradually change into full-scale agriculture. Emerald green paddies are soon dominant, the occasional bamboo shelter the only break in the verdant sea of young shoots that extends all the way to the skyline. We stop in another village where I strip off my riding gear and sit outside a house on a plastic chair, a welcome rest from the torrid heat of the sun. Kway produces a bottle of chilled water from the minibus's on-board fridge then a few minutes later, reappears with a surprise present, a huge bar of Thai chocolate he's bought at a nearby shop. Just what the doctor ordered!. I tear off the wrapper and offer it around but there are no takers, so devour half of it and set off, re-energised by a sugar rush.

The road begins to narrow as we enter a wooded area. Soon, the minibus overtakes then slows to a stop. Ahead lies the boundary of a wide floodplain and winding down his window, Kway warns that a bridge has been washed out and I'll need to take care. Descending a baked mud bank, my front wheel digs into sand before jerking forward as we crunch onto the vast, dried out watercourse. 300 metres further, still riding on hardened silt, I approach what little water is left flowing at this time of year, a shallow river no more than 10 metres wide. The Toyota has already crossed and advanced some way further on so I pause, assessing how best to ford it. Coming up quietly from behind, a local scooter rider edges past me then plunges straight into the river without a second thought. The water's instantly half way up his calves and I carefully watch his steady progress until he emerges onto the far bank. I set off after him, aiming to faithfully follow his tracks. The force of the water isn't strong but the jumble of large round stones and treacly sediment that forms the riverbed, invisible through the churned up waters, first deflect then tug at my wheels, causing us to wobble for a moment before the bike stabilizes. As I open up the throttle, the rear wheel slips, spinning for a second before regaining its hold, driving us hard towards the far side and up a muddy slope to safety. The stony, parched watercourse continues for almost half a kilometre before, at a strip of chewed up grass where cows peacefully graze, the road recommences.

Having passed a string of fields packed with radiant yellow sunflowers, we stop for another break, pulling onto one of the wide, soil droveways that border each side of the road. Whist I'm tightening up the headlight which the constant drumming has loosened, I notice two giant shapes slowly advancing along the earthen track towards us. As they get closer, the forms of two sets of huge white bullocks become clear, each pair hauling an overloaded wooden wagon. They're enormous, as are the loads they're both pulling, dark brown dried out bushes piled 2m high. The drivers are sitting, reins in hand, on top of the heaps. We're actually blocking their way forward so they do a synchronised turn, angling across the metalled road towards the track on the other side. The men don't seem the slightest bit fazed by the detour. The lead drover smokes a large cheroot which he leaves in his mouth as he waves at us and the second takes his broad rimmed hat off and playfully doffs it our way. Kway shouts a question at them then translates their answer for me.

"Peanuts. It's the peanut crop. This region is famous for it."

I continue to watch in awe as the gently swaying humped animals pass by, the wheels of the wagons, obviously reclaimed from a vintage truck, rumbling and squeaking into the distance.

When it's time for off, Kway picks up my back protector and holds it out for me to put my arms in, followed by my jacket which is offered in the same manner. A smiling Captain, displaying his customary air of bonhomie, has taken charge of my helmet and gloves, passing each one in turn as I put them on. This has quickly evolved into our normal starting routine, a process that's carried out without any instigation on my part. Their kindness, good-nature and lack of pretension warm my heart and I thank them over and over again for their help.

The closer we get to Bagan, the busier the roads become although cars and heavy vehicles are still not evident. Bicycles and scooters rule, most of them travelling slower than us. Around teatime, we pass a number of villages where a multitude of scooters whizz along beside us. The average age of their riders is alarming... some can only be 10 to 12 years old and I don't imagine any of them hold a driving license, let alone have insurance! Wearing neither crash helmet nor protective clothing, many ride two by two, chattering away to each other. The most worrying are the kids that want to race me, pressing themselves down into a crouch and revving their engines madly. I'd hate any of them to hurt themselves so whenever possible, drop back, allowing them to easily win after which they quickly give up.

At sunset we come to the mighty Irrawaddy River, which rises in the mountains of northern Burma and travels due south for over 2000km, emptying into the Andaman Sea via an enormous delta. It's been used as a commercial waterway for centuries and sustains a diverse range of water life, although recent hydro-electric damming has caused concern for the future of the threatened Irrawaddy dolphin and river shark species. A new bridge opened here in 2012, before which all traffic crossed the river on overcrowded ferries. It begins at the town of Pakokku, infamous as the place where, in 2007, three peacefully protesting monks were tied to lampposts and brutally beaten by soldiers. This incident, and the response by local monks who held a group of soldiers captive until they received an apology from the army, was the catalyst that sparked massed protests by monks all over the country in what became known as the Saffron Revolution. The bridge, which is used by both trains and cars, spans 3.4km and as I ride across it, I'm treated to the spectacle of a flotilla of small fishing boats returning home to the southern shore. The throbbing amber sun, which gives the illusion of hovering millimetres above the watery horizon, catches on their tall curving bows, casting long rippling shadows in front of them. It proves a considerable challenge to pull my eyes away from the entrancing sight and keep them on the road ahead!

My predisposition to sing as I ride often means hollering songs that'd never enter my head at home. There's one ditty I've been deliberately blocking out since crossing the border yesterday, a song I sang many times to Jacques when he was younger. If either the melody or chorus of 'it that must not be named' enter my head, it'll undoubtably plague me for days on end. I've been wholly successful thus far but as I exit the bridge, an overhead gantry displays signs for Bagan to the right and Mandalay to the left. The latter place name swells in my mind, resistance proves futile and out of my mouth blurts,

"... They met one night in the silver light
On the road to Mandalay
Ohhh...... Nellie the elephant packed her trunk
And said goodbye to the circus
Off she went with a trumpety-trump
Trump! Trump! Trump!"
No!!!

The run into Bagan is completed in darkness, the highway full of smelly old trucks, speeding tour buses and ever present scooters. With the Toyota sitting protectively tight to my tail, we enter the township of Nyaung U. I can hardly believe my eyes, there are hundreds of hotel complexes, rows of restaurants, a plethora of cafes and more gift shops than you could shake a stick at. Everywhere I look, animated tourists mill around. With the minibus now leading, we reach our hotel and as I park up, Kway tells me there are upwards of 5000 visitors staying here on any given night. I'm amazed. I came to Bagan almost 20 years ago, staying at a rundown lodge in Old Bagan. There were just five backpackers in the village during the three days I was there. The nearby township of New Bagan was just starting to develop, with a couple of purpose-built Japanese tourist hotels recently opened. Facilities for visitors were non existent at Nyaung U... how times have changed.

After a quick shower, the four of us go in search of a restaurant. The choices are overwhelming and it takes quite some time to decide which establishment we'll eat at. Finally sitting down, I remark that this part of Bagan now looks like a Thai beach resort, but without the sea.

"That's just what it's like," Kway replies. "The only differences being that this is still a religious site, so there are no nightclubs, no all-night parties and I think that Bagan probably attracts older, more serious people."

Despite the immensely swollen number of tourists, Bagan holds a special place in my heart and I'm very excited about looking around it tomorrow.

Day 70. Bagan to Naypyidaw. 178 miles.

Breakfast is served on the hotel's roof terrace where I tuck into fruit, fried eggs and toast. There are about 40 other diners, the sea of their voices made up from a wide range of regional British accents. The colourful, skin-hugging lycra outfits most of them wear are a big clue that they're participants in a cycling tour. I strike up a conversation with a couple from the West Country who confirm they're on a two week organised trip run by a UK company, *Exodus Travels*. Each day, a coach takes them to the start of their ride where bicycles, included in the deal, are waiting. They pedal a pre-planned route, each travelling at their own pace for anything up to 40 miles, at the end of which they hand their bikes back and climb onto the coach which returns them to wherever they're staying. The men I speak with, neither young and athletic nor committed cyclists, explain it's a great way to see a country at grassroots level and make new friends as well. It certainly sounds like it.

Bagan was the capital of the Kingdom of Pagan between the 9th and 13th centuries, the first kingdom to unify the lands that now make up Myanmar. During its zenith in the 11th and 12th centuries, more than 4,000 Buddhist temples, pagodas, stupas and monasteries were constructed on the Bagan plains. Over 3000 had survived into modern times but a major earthquake decimated many of the less stable structures in 1975. What seismic activity failed to topple, erosion, neglect, looting and crass restorations further damaged, resulting in a count of approximately 2,200 edifices remaining today. Now known as *The Bagan Archaeological Zone*, the plains are a breathtaking spectacle, especially at sunrise and sunset when in every direction, the umbrella tops of bell-shaped pagodas punctuate the smouldering skies. It's now Myanmar's main tourist drawcard.

Unlike my visit of almost 20 years ago, when I pedalled everywhere on an archaic open-framed iron bike, there are no shortage of transport options for visitors today. Most common are e-bikes, electric powered mopeds that silently glide between the shrines. Out on the roads, horse and carriages are popular, as are giant guided AC tour buses. For those with deeper pockets, hot air balloons offer a sensational way to view the plains. Accompanied by my companions, I ride to three separate temple complexes, none of which have been restored. I'm not a ruins aficionado, much happier to sit quietly amongst them, absorbing the atmosphere, than studying their history. Looking around from the Matchless's saddle, some of the relics are no taller than me while others tower 30m high. Each structure is unique, be it crumbling brick or weathered stucco, overgrown with moss or daubed in gold leaf, half collapsed or unsympathetically repaired. The sheer scale of the site is awe-inspiring.

Half hidden amongst scrubby bush, the final and largest monastery we visit has a nearby line of ad-hoc, open-sided homes, each timber framed with plastic sheeting for roofs. Spying me resting in front of the temple, two boys run over. Cheeky little chaps with bright eyes and wide grins, both produce a collection of greeting cards that they've hand coloured with felt tip pens. Small for their age at 9 years old, they're chatty but not pushy and I find myself unable to resist buying a set from each of them. Excitedly running off, I can hear them shouting to their parents, no doubt regaling their triumph in extracting a relative fortune from a passing tourist!

I'd intended to visit Old Bagan, the original small settlement where in 1997 I'd fallen in love with an enchanting young Japanese woman called Keiko. However, apart from the ancient monuments themselves, so much has changed here over the last two decades that I decide to leave that memory unsullied, content to have had another magical sighting across the temple studded plains. We head, instead, to a motel in New Bagan where another man joins our party. Wunna works for the *Myanmar Ministry of Hotels and Tourism*, the governmental body responsible for all visitors to the country. Older than the other three, he's more reserved but nonetheless just as friendly, explaining that his role is to smooth out any problems or bureaucracy encountered by independent tourists travelling with their own vehicles. Usually he accompanies them from one border to the other but had to miss the first two days of my journey as he was sitting an exam. Throwing his bag into the minibus's boot, he settles himself alongside Captain in the back... and then there were four!

Patched old road greets me as we turn south. 'Here we go again', I think, resigning myself to more grim vibrations. Thankfully it's short-lived, the surface evening out as it clears the built up area and I'm able to comfortably ride at 70kmph. After half an hour, I notice a couple of tourist complexes at the roadside where traditional Burmese crafts can be seen, such as cotton weaving, hand rolling cigars and the production of the traditional cosmetic, thanakha, a light brown balm made from tree bark that the majority of Burmese women and girls apply to their faces. At the third of these tourist establishments, a demonstration showing how oxen are used to thresh crops is in progress and assembled around is the group of British cyclists I met earlier. As they stand in a circle observing the cattle at work, their identical yellow mountain bikes are being unloaded from a giant trailer.

Travelling along miles of straight road, I gradually creep up on a Burmese Army convoy that's moving just a tad slower than us. Sandwiched between outriding jeeps are three giant tank transporters, their cargo sheeted in khaki tarpaulins, and a dozen troop-carrying trucks. As I pull out and begin a long overtake, I give the Matchless her head and she surges forward. With no oncoming traffic, I manage to stay out in the oncoming lane for half a kilometre, eventually swinging in ahead of the column. Slapping the bike's saddle, it suddenly occurs to me that Matchless G3Ls were often used for convoy escort duty and that mine could possibly have made such a manoeuvre many times before in this country.

"You're probably an old hand at this, eh girl?" I shout above the hum of her engine.

Lunch is taken at a roadside restaurant where I drink a fresh mixed fruit cocktail comprising watermelon, pineapple, mango and crushed ice which is sublime. The Matchless, as always, gets lots of attention from passers-by and from a distance, I observe people stop, lean over and closely inspect her. Over a period of time, I notice that they're all acting in the same manner, studiously analysing one central feature. Intrigued, I wander over towards a group of three men to see what it is they're pointing at, wondering if it's the speedometer, the clock and thermometer, possible even the choke or advance/retard levers. As I draw alongside them I realise that the bike herself is irrelevant to their attentions... it's the folded map of Myanmar squeezed into the clear pouch on the tank bag that's been piquing everyone's interest!

Heading back out into the heat of the day, the road narrows and begins to gently climb. It's an exquisite ride and I become completely lost in the experience. A minibus rounds a corner then motors uphill towards me, the name of a tour company emblazoned in blue letters on its side. It's followed moments later by a pair of BMW R1250 GS Adventures, each one dripping with *Touratech* luggage and accessories. Almost too late, I wave at their equally well kitted-out riders, one of whom notices and lifts his hand in acknowledgement. God only knows what he makes of my old bike! A minute later, a KTM and another BMW zoom past, both their riders failing to spot my raised hand, then soon after, a last one passes at speed, evidently chasing after his companions. It's great to have seen a group of fellow overland motorcyclists, even if their bikes, in comparison, make the Matchless appear decidedly Lilliputian.

Half way through the journey, our road meets the Yangon - Mandalay Expressway, Myanmar's main north-south motorway from which motorcycles and trucks are banned, albeit for different reasons. Opened in 2010, it fails to meet international design, construction and safety standards and has experienced a string of fatal accidents, resulting in it being dubbed 'Death Highway'.

"Don't worry," says Kway as we halt ahead of the first toll booth. "That ban applies to locals on scooters. You are on a bigger bike and will be granted a special dispensation... Wunna is with us in case the police have a problem."

He continues by warning me about the frequent ripple bars that have been sunk into the tarmac. They're here, apparently, to prevent drivers from falling asleep and it soon becomes clear why. Two lanes wide in both directions, the highway is monotonously straight and constructed from almost white concrete. Under clear skies, the glare off it is intensely soporific and within ten minutes I start feeling dozy. Matters aren't helped by the lack of traffic. With only a speeding coach or fast car every five minutes or so, there's nothing to keep my mind occupied. I have to force myself to look from right to left, gazing at the passing fields, or focus down at the black tank bag, anything to soothe my eyes and keep my brain busy. The road markers are in miles and after 40 have passed, I pull off and ride onto the wide grass hard shoulder, desperate for some ocular relief.

Kway has another surprise up his sleeve. After handing me a chilled bottle of water, he produces a large bag of Bagan peanuts which he's bought for me as I was so fascinated by the oxen-drawn crop yesterday. They're quite different from the peanuts I'm used to, only half the size and covered with dark brown husks, but they're really tasty and perfect for restoring energy in the sapping heat, which today has topped 35 degrees. When it's time to get underway again, Wunna unselfconsciously joins in the 'get Gordon dressed' routine, his self appointed role being the bearer of my Camelbak, which he eases over my jacketed shoulders before Captain steps forth with the helmet. It's not at all what I expected when Kway told me a government official would be accompanying us!

To counteract the dazzling road, I try putting my polarised sunglasses on then pulling my tinted goggles down over them. It's a tight fit but the result is well worth it, a dark view of the world that instantly diminishes my stupor. A while later, I spot a 2-wheeler moving slowly at the very edge of the inside lane. It's the first I've seen on the Expressway and catching up fast, I'm tickled by the sight of a shaven-headed monk, billowing along in his plum coloured robes. Seemingly immune to highway regulations, he gives me an exaggerated wave as I toot my horn and bomb past him.

The boys overtake just north of Naypyidaw, leading me off the Expressway and pulling up beside a roadside office. Lots of paperwork is handed over then a policeman climbs onto his bike, signalling I should stay behind him. We head along a completely deserted 12 lane mega-highway lined with immaculately tended flowerbeds, It's one of many that crisscross the vast area of the nation's capital, which is estimated to be around 4,800 square kilometres. Modern office buildings, sprawling convention centres, giant shopping malls and luxurious international standard hotels appear, each super-sized and set well back in its own extensive grounds. Everything's ultra-modern and except for our three vehicles, devoid of all sign of human life. It's like riding across a futuristic, otherworldly planet and it rankles to think all this has been created in one of Asia's poorest countries... no wonder the Myanmar people have fought so long and hard for freedom!

Reaching our hotel 8km later, I park on a huge curving driveway that's covered by a colossal canopy. Appearing from nowhere, three staff run over, taking charge of my bags and carrying them inside while I lock the Matchless up. The hotel looks as though it could sleep a thousand but I'm the only person, bar the staff, in its cathedral-like foyer. In keeping with everything else, my room is rather grand and its air conditioning extremely welcome.

Heading out later for an evening meal, my first pizza since Turkmenistan, Kway fills me in on Naypyidaw.

"It first became the capital of Myanmar in 2006, after the government decided to move from Yangon without giving much of an explanation why. It's a city planned on a greenfield site, and a lot of it is still under construction. Naypyidaw means 'the abode of the king' in Burmese, although we don't actually have a king, but our governmental parliament, the Assembly of the Union, is here."

Driving back to my hotel, we take a straight boulevard that's easily wide and long enough to land a Jumbo Jet and was obviously built for speeding motorcades. Naypyidaw by night seems just as eerily underpopulated as it did in the middle of the day... where is everyone? The boys drop me off, I say goodnight to them then they turn around and drive away. My only discomfort about staying in such a magnificent establishment is that my companions have to sleep elsewhere in cheaper lodgings. It jars on my sense of fairness and egalitarianism that they are relegated to staying somewhere inferior.

Day 71. Naypyidaw to Hlegu Police Station, 213 miles.
To Yangon, approximately 25 miles by minibus.

I wake in the small hours with my throat swollen and inflamed. It slowly registers that I forgot to turn the air-conditioning off last night so cursing myself, get up and do it, My alarm wakes me at 7.00am and with a headache and a raging sore throat, I turn on the TV to search for more information on the General Election. There's nothing relevant on local channels so I try online instead. The results are clear, the NLD has won 86 percent of the seats, which is way more than the 67 percent required when the guaranteed military seats are taken into account. Leader of the last quasi-civilian government, 8th President and former General, Thein Sein, has conceded defeat. Current opinion is that as Aung San Suu Kyi is barred from being president, someone else from her party will be appointed to that role as a proxy, whereas she will most likely become Foreign Minister and act as de facto Prime Minister. It feels a great privilege to be in the country at such a momentous time, although everything's so calm and peaceful that if people didn't on occasion excitedly say to me, "Did you know about our victory in the General Election?" the political metamorphosis would not be evident. To have won by such a majority is incredible, especially as approximately three quarters of Myanmar's population are rural dwellers, largely living off the land. In many villages, domestic electricity is often only produced by generators a couple of hours a day and access to television, let alone the internet, is certainly not a given. The election campaign, carried out at grassroots level by NLD's regional activists, saw Suu Kyi, aged 70, tirelessly travelling the length and breadth of the country to speak at rallies. As a strategy, it obviously worked well.

Several cups of black coffee fail to clear my heavy head and the morning doesn't improve. On checking the bike over, I discover a missing bolt off the rear subframe and a replacement takes forever to find. Then, with all my gear on and ready to depart, the Matchless simply won't start. It's especially embarrassing as three police motorcyclists have shown up to escort us to The Assembly of the Union buildings, Myanmar's legislature, which I'm keen to see if only from the outside. I make all the usual checks, finally pinpointing pitted contact breakers as the problem. I have two more sets of new-old-stock spares in my bags but for the life of me can't locate them. Eventually, the police leave and in frustration, I remove the existing points, polish them with wet and dry paper then put them back. The old girl fires up straightaway and I'm relieved to note that the ignition timing hasn't slipped in the meantime. It's nearly 11am before we get underway.

Taking the ghost-like superhighway west, we soon reach the junction with the Expressway. Stopping just before the toll booths, Kway tells me we have exactly 200 miles to travel before the motorway ends just north of Yangon. The first service station, where he suggests we stop for lunch, is 85 miles south. I think I'll roughly divide the journey into five 40 mile stages, however, with my eyes once more doubly protected and the Matchless running unerringly smoothly, I fly past my first marker and set myself a new goal of making the rest stop in one go. There's not a whisper of wind and the air's so hot, a permanent heat shimmer distorts the highway where it narrows to a point in the far distance. As the miles tick unhurriedly by, I become increasingly concerned about overheating the engine. Just as I'm about to pull off and stop, the minibus overtakes and within a couple of minutes, indicates right. We've made it and as quickly as I can, I find some shade to park up so the engine can begin the slow process of cooling down.

Lunch comprises oodles of noodles washed down with two glasses of sweet, freshly squeezed orange juice. Man-flu is taking hold and as well as the sore throat, I'm now aching from head to foot. Knocking back a couple of paracetamol, I check the Matchless over then get underway again. Myanmar's landscape consists of mountains and a high plateau in the north and forested, hilly, jungle covered areas in the western and eastern regions. Inle lake, a calm body of water surrounded by fishing villages raised on stilts, is northwest of our current position. The Expressway tracks straight down the middle of the central lowland area where there are few distinguishing geographical features. To the right there's agriculture and to the left, grasslands. An occasional village, seen far away, soon vanishes and once more, I've nothing to focus on except the perpetual belt of concrete that unwaveringly rolls underneath our wheels. Often whilst I'm riding, my thinking clears, my worries disappear and problems simply resolve themselves, or appear to anyway. New ideas, theories, dreams and schemes have a tendency to spring forth, a phenomenon I hardly ever encounter driving a car. I think many motorcyclists regularly experience this 2-wheel enhanced state of mind, although today, with my thoughts clouded and my body decidedly crook, it would probably be wise to take any revelations with a pinch of salt!

The space between each mile post is sub-divided by 8 lesser markers. 45 miles later, pulling up for my next break under wilting roadside trees, I question what they are.

"Furlongs," Kway explains. "There are eight furlongs in a mile, and that's what the posts indicate."

I've only ever equated furlongs with school and horse racing, and ask what other strange legacies the British colonists left here.

"Several," Kway says, handing me a bar of Cadbury's chocolate from the fridge. "For example, until 1970 we drove on the left, like you do in Britain. Then the government changed it to the right but most people couldn't afford to alter or upgrade their cars. It's a problem that's been made worse by cheap imports of second-hand cars from Japan, Thailand and Singapore, all of which are right hand drive."

It suddenly dawns on me that their minibus is right hand drive too.

"Whoever sits in the front passenger seat acts as a co-driver, especially when passing parked cars or when overtaking. You'll notice in Yangon that nearly every car is right hand drive and has a spare driver."

The thermometer's fluctuating around 40°C when I decide it's time to take to the road again. The team, as usual, gather my belongings. Captain, who's 6' tall and very strong looking, walks behind me and to my surprise, begins massaging my neck and shoulders. It's excruciating at first but as the tension slowly evaporates, my head begins to clear and once I've got my gear on and the Matchless is running, I'm feeling much better. A petrol stop comes within 30 miles then after a final run of 40 miles, we arrive at our turnoff. It's just after 6pm, the sun's lost for today and the sky's going through its final transformation from wisps of rich reds and purples into deepest indigo. Once clear of the toll collectors, I follow the team along a busy road, make a scary u-turn through a large gap in the central reservation, then head back a couple of hundred metres to enter a police station compound. I have to leave my bike here as 2-wheelers are banned from central Yangon, a law that was instated in 2003 without any reason being given, although rumours for its cause include a motorcyclist making a threatening gesture to a general. In this instance, there's no special treatment for foreign visitors so the bike's locked and covered up beneath a vestibule that's in plain sight of every policeman at the station. She couldn't be safer.

Traffic's far heavier than I expected as we make our way into the city but it's great to sink into the comfort of the minibus's reclining seat, the glass sunroof fully open above us. An hour later, crawling forward, I notice a bus halted by the roadside. It too is a right hand drive secondhand import, but worse, it's passenger doors are also on the wrong side, meaning everyone has to get off and on exposed to the dangers of passing traffic. Even during my second visit here in 2003, rickety old wooden-framed buses dating back to the 1950s plied the streets, their passenger door permanently open at the back. They may have been rattly and smoky but they were definitely safer than this daft arrangement.

Kway turns around from the front seat, gets my attention then points to the left. Dominating the skyline is Myanmar's most famous and most sacred stupa, Shwedagon Pagoda. It's 99 metres tall and, illuminated all round by floodlights, glows gloriously golden. And so it should, it's covered in several tons of gold bricks and gold leaf. It soon disappears from sight behind a row of new high-rise developments and within twenty minutes, we pull up outside my hotel, locate a trolley and wheel all my gear inside. It's going to be very late by the time Wunna is taken to his hotel and the rest of the team reach their respective homes. As I sit in reception waiting for my room key, I try to impress upon Kway that I can easily look after myself tomorrow and they should all have the day off. He takes a lot of persuading, feeling responsible for my welfare and in the end I'm only able to get a partial concession... he'll meet me in the morning to escort me to my friends' home, the others can have some down time. When they leave, I head to the hotel's restaurant for a hot curry, which I hope will help me sweat out my cold, then upstairs to an early bed.

Day 72, Yangon. 0 miles.

As agreed, Kway is in reception at 10.30am. When we walk outside, thinking we're about to flag down a taxi, I'm shocked to see the minibus waiting for us complete with Kyee and Captain.

"They feel it's their duty to accompany you," explains Kway, "and I couldn't persuade them to take a day off."

I don't argue and greet them with warm handshakes before climbing into the back.

Yangon is a sprawling city with a population of around 5 million. Called Rangoon while under British rule, it was also known as 'The Garden City of the East' due to its many fine parks, gardens and lakes. Its fall to the Japanese army in 1942 and recapture in 1945 caused extensive damage, and under the 28 year isolationist rule of military dictator, Ne Win, much of the city's infrastructure deteriorated. Many superb examples of colonial architecture survive nonetheless, including the City Hall, High Court, Port Authority building, the General Hospital, Holy Trinity cathedral and a number of hotels, schools and Anglican and Baptist churches. Rapid economic development in the last decade, however, has changed the face of the city irrevocably, with foreign investment resulting in towering new hotels, offices and shopping malls sprouting up everywhere.

I'm hoping to see quite a few of the sights as I travel to my friends' home this morning and almost immediately, spot the sad sight of the Secretariat, the administrative seat of British Burma. Covering a whole city block, the once magnificent red brick building, some 120 years old, is abandoned, fenced off and overgrown with creepers and trees. Kway tells me that plans are afoot to convert it into a museum and hotel complex which, judging by its present state, will be a colossal undertaking. We carry on for another two blocks then turn left into a bustling city street lined, at ground level, with small shops on top of which sit several floors of concrete flats, all fronted with small steel-railed balconies. The minibus stops and Kway says,

"We're here."

I'm gobsmacked. The Han family's apartment turns out to be only three and a half blocks away from my hotel... I could have walked it in minutes! The quiet residential street I remember has changed beyond recognition and is now thronging with businesses, pedestrians and traffic. It's also horribly noisy, although some of that is due to the music blaring from a loudspeaker placed in the back of a nearby truck. Here collections are being made for monks, who receive new robes and alms as part of the imminent Tazaungdaing Festival, the Festival of Lights, which will be held at full moon in just a couple of days.

I'm greeted by Yaway, one of Kay Thi's two brothers. The other, a sailor, is based in Singapore. As soon as we enter the living room and sit down, he tells me that today is the 16th anniversary of Kay Thi's death, a poignant coincidence. Hair now tinged with grey, he's a quiet, gentle man a couple of years older than me, who's second youngest at number ten in the sibling line up of eleven. He tells me that sister number five, Thanda, a woman who looks so much like her departed sister that on past visits I've had to stop myself calling her Kay Thi, is currently in Mandalay. She's there caring for one of her nieces who's contracted Dengue fever, a mosquito borne virus that's on the rise in Asia. However, her daughter, Suu Kyi, is here and soon joins us. Suu Kyi was six the first time I visited and twelve on the second occasion, taking a day trip with me and her mother which included a boat ride across Yangon harbour. Now 24, she remembers both my previous visits and I'm really touched when a few minutes into our conversation, she disappears into the back room, returning with a perfectly preserved photograph of Jacques as a toddler, which I'd given her all those years ago.

Appearing from the kitchen, laden with trays of food, comes Mo, sister number seven and May Thi, sister number nine. May Thi doesn't speak English but Mo does, chattily updating me on all the family news. Lunch is a luscious array of delicacies they've prepared in my honour, most of the recipes indigenous to the Shan state from where the family originates. There are at least a dozen different dishes and I'm not allowed to skip trying any of them, the fruits coated in desiccated coconut being my favourite. It's all finished off with exquisitely piquant pickled tea and ginger. Conversation switches between the General Election, which everyone talks about with verve, the fast-paced changes in Yangon, and how each family member is faring. Inevitably, our dialogue always returns to Kay Thi and our many fond memories of her.

When the time comes to leave, the four of them line up on their balcony to wave me off. I've been with them for almost four hours and after waving back from the pavement, I turn around to see that my escorts are dutifully waiting 50 metres down the road, the Toyota's air conditioning working at full blast to keep them cool. Not sure whether to feel guilty or moved by their sense of duty, I end up experiencing a mixture of both. Back at the hotel, I dose myself with medicine before setting off in the early evening to collect Yaway en route to Shwedagon Pagoda, best visited after sunset when its marble tile flooring won't burn bare feet. The entrance is up a flight of steps, a pair of giant chinthes, impressive lion-like creatures, guarding the entrance. Inside, we walk around the broad golden terraces at the base of the pagoda in a clockwise direction, a sign of respect in Buddhist tradition by keeping the right of the body towards the object of veneration. As we go, Kway fills me in on its history.

Believed to have been built approximately 2,600 years ago, it's most likely the oldest Buddhist stupa in existence. According to tradition, two merchant brothers met the Gautama Buddha while travelling in northern India and he gave them eight of his hairs as relics. Under the Buddha's direction, the pair journeyed to Burma and, with the help of the local ruler, King Okkalapa, located Singuttara Hill. They found there, as promised, the relics of three previous incarnations of the Buddha which together with the hair, they enshrined in a stupa.

"It fell into disrepair but was renovated and built much taller in the 14th and 15th Centuries," Kway explains. "An earthquake severely damaged it in 1768, knocking the top off it, but it was repaired by the king of the time, who raised it to its current height. Now sitting at the very top, in what's called the diamond-bud, is a 76 carat diamond," he continues.

There's more than one diamond here, though, the pagoda's encrusted in jewels and precious stones. Standing on the flagstones beneath it, I gaze upwards at its many levels, which Kway names for me as terraces; bell; turban band; inverted alms bowl; lotus petals; banana bud; umbrella crown; vane and diamond bud. Its vastness makes it impossible to fully appreciate the scale and splendour from this proximity. Both Yaway and Kway offer prayers as they complete three cumambulations then Yaway explains the significance of the eight corners of the octagonal base of the pagoda. As Wednesday is split into two halves, am and pm, each corner signifies a day of the week. Worshippers pray at the shrine on the corner that corresponds with the day they were born. All around the compound are smaller shrines, each magnificently decorated, as well as giant reclining Buddhas, seated Buddha's with glowing neon halos and swathes of candles, prayer flags and flowers. It's a place that I imagine you'd never tire of visiting.

I admire the magnificent glowing structure for one last time from a distance, gazing across a darkened park as I stand up inside the minibus, my head sticking out of the sunroof. Driving on, I say farewell to Yaway, hoping that it's not another 12 years before I see him and his family again, then after visiting a moneychanger, return to the hotel. Once packed in preparation for tomorrow's ride, I eat another sweat-inducing curry and climb between the sheets.

Yaway and Kway, Shwedagon Pagoda.

Day 73. Yangon to Hlegu Police Station, approximately 25 miles by minibus. To Kin Pun Sakhan, 98 miles.

Travelling through Yangon in the comfort of the Toyota, I look out of the window and realise that here, unlike the rest of the country, a high percentage of the population now wear western clothes, especially younger people. There are, however, many sights that make me feel as though I'm stepping back in time, including the wonderful old trishaws. These pedal-powered taxis are essentially sturdy bicycles with neat sidecars attached in which two passengers can sit back to back. It looks a quaintly old world way to get around, if a little strenuous for the rider in the humid, tropical heat.

Arriving at Hlegu police station, I find the Matchless undisturbed, a splattering of guano from overhead roosting birds decorating her cover. On the latter part of the ride from Naypyidaw, the gearbox had felt a tad clunky so I take a few minutes to ladle more grease into it. Intently concentrating whilst squatting down on my hunkers, I get quite a shock when I tighten the filler cap and stand up. A crowd of at least a dozen police officers is pressed into a tight semicircle behind me. Their daunting appearance transforms as their faces, in unison, dissolve into broad smiles. After cleaning my hands, I climb into my riding gear, thank them all for safely housing the bike then depart behind the minibus.

The road tracks in a north-easterly direction, its sides largely built up as we continue to move through the outer reaches of Yangon's greater metropolitan area. I soon realise that bikes and scooters are once more present on the road, although their riders' practice of running tight against the central reservation is rather disconcerting. I decide to stay with the cars and trucks, picking a path through wavy tar whilst undertaking hundreds of slower moving 2-wheelers. Lovely as it was to visit Yangon, it's brilliant to be back on my bike and in spite of a snotty nose and thick head, I revel in the sensation of warm air flowing past me and a joyous feeling of freedom.

From the town of Bago, which boasts another splendid ancient pagoda, we turn sharply to the south and enter quieter countryside. Shady palms are dotted amongst rice paddies and low-lying orchards, the road cutting a straight path between the fields. After nearly 80km of non-stop riding, I need a rest, halting under a tree and climbing into the minibus for a welcome blast of cold air. While the others stretch their legs, I talk with Kway, asking him how long he's been a guide.

"For two years. Before that, I studied engineering at University but when I graduated, I discovered I was the worst engineer in the world! I started my first job and left after just a couple of months... it wasn't a good career choice. But I love being a guide," he tells me. "I've led groups, mostly of motorcycles but sometimes 4x4s, from one border to another probably a dozen times now. You're the first person travelling on his own 'though. My biggest problem is getting bikers to slow down and stick together, a lot of them ride like they're in a race." he continues.

Needless to say, the same can't be said of the Matchless! Kway takes his job very seriously, studying in time off between trips to further advance his knowledge of Myanmar and its history. I compliment him on his command of English, which pleases him.

"I can understand American English easily, Australian too, but I found many British accents very hard at first. I bought all seven *Harry Potter* films on DVD and watched them over and over, which helped me a lot. Now I can grasp most of what English, Irish and Welsh people say. But Scottish accents... I'm sorry, that sounds like another language!"

We get under way again and around an hour later stop for lunch. Up until this point, the fresh fruit juices and shakes I've had in Myanmar have been sublime but today's is a bit of a let down. It's heavily laced with condensed milk and sugar cane syrup, so teeth-tarnishingly sweet it's totally undrinkable. While we're eating, the police show up, somehow alerted to my presence. They want to check our paperwork, which Kway produces with a flourish. Wunna, earning his crust, has a quiet word with them and we're soon left in peace.

Heading due east through thick jungle, our narrow road arrives at a small checkpost. It appears we're expected, and after filling in a brief form, two uniformed motorcycle police are detailed to shepherd us into town. With caterwauling sirens and revolving blue and red lights, one bike leads and another follows at the rear. The 5km journey to our hotel is undertaken at a snail's pace and it's almost impossible to get out of first gear as we chug along at under 20kmph. In the town centre, visiting tourists turn and stare as we pass them at the pace of a cortege... it's acutely embarrassing. I discover a problem the minute I dismount in the hotel compound. Although today's journey has been on reasonable roads, the bike's still been shaken by numerous small repair patches resulting in another crack in the rear number plate carrier. This time it's terminal, the plate hanging on only by a solitary cable tie and its taillight wiring. The thin metal's broken in so many places, I'm certain it can't be welded so I take it off and carry it to my room where, counting my lucky stars, I remove the remainder of the cash taped to the back of it. Unbeknown to me, Mr. Fixit, Kway, organises the town's sole motorcycle mechanic to call by and I'm taken by surprise when he suddenly shows up. We quickly agree that the number plate and light fitting can be bolted directly on to the mudguard and make arrangements to visit his workshop later in the evening.

Kin Pun Sakhan is little more than a village that's become a major tourist destination because of its proximity to Kyaiktiyo Pagoda, more commonly referred to as *Golden Rock*. As soon as I'm changed, I meet up with Kway, Captain and Kyee and set off for the bus depot. Here, I watch in amazement as an open-backed truck departs for the pagoda, 49 passengers squeezed onto seven benches that run from side to side in its open cargo bay. The instant it leaves, another pulls up next to a platform and we, together with more visitors and pilgrims, climb up steps and take our pews. It's so packed in the back that my inner thighs are pressed tightly together, the bones of my hips hard up against the men each side of me. There is, however, a sense of adventure and fun, a 'we're all in this together' spirit as the truck lurches forward and bumps onto the street. Over my shoulder, I notice the next truck pull forward, a new crowd waiting to climb aboard.

Starting from close to sea level, the 14 kilometre drive to the top of Kyaiktiyo Hill at 1,100m is incredibly steep, the ultra low geared truck revving hard as it swings round a series of switchbacks. Embracing the often sheer sides of the creeper covered rock wall, the road suddenly drops, nosediving downhill then, after banking round a bend, commences a fresh climb. My stomach struggles to catch up with the rapid changes in direction and as the driver keeps his foot flat to the floor, I join in with the rest of the passengers, sucking in deep breaths and exhaling with laughter... it's like an extreme theme park ride! Three quarters of an hour later, we reach the upper terminus and everyone clambers breathlessly down. Here awaits a welcome serenity. After being issued with visitors passes and removing our shoes, we walk uphill, the pleasant feeling of warm tiles under our bare feet. Ambling past guesthouses and kiosks that flank each side of the ridge-top path, we emerge into a large open space. Ahead, set against the staggering backdrop of distant plains and steamy jungle, sits the *Golden Rock.*

It's an enormous boulder, approximately 7.6m high and with a circumference of roughly 15m that, over centuries, visiting worshippers have completely covered in layers of gold leaf. On its top sits a shimmering pagoda, itself 7.5m tall, which, according to legend, also houses one of the Buddha's hairs. The most amazing feature of the boulder is its precarious location, perched on the edge of a giant granite outcrop which juts out from the cliff face. It looks as though the boulder might topple off at any time, indeed, so much of its mass overhangs the edge of its resting place that I fear the force of people currently rubbing gold onto its landward side could be enough to tip the balance and set it catapulting downhill. Of course it doesn't, the rock's been here for millennia and survived goodness know how many earthquakes.

"The contact point between the boulder and the platform is about one square foot," Kway tells me in awe.

It's an astonishing spectacle.

Today being a Saturday, the top of the ridge is packed with visitors who've come to see the gravity-defying wonder at sunset. The few foreign tourists are greatly outnumbered by thousands of Burmese pilgrims and monks who are here to pray. Many will spend the night camping at the summit and as we walk towards the rock itself, we pass rows of makeshift shelters, little more than thin raffia mats separated by scarves hung from cliffside railings, where families, some spanning three generations, are encamped. Across the way, the quirkily named *First Yoe Yoe Lay Company* can supply bedding to those without any. The place is infused with an almost mystical aura as incense drifts thickly across the ridge and on a narrow deck constructed immediately below the boulder, crowds of devotees kneel in prayer. The atmosphere's so potent that I wish I too was staying the night, but when the last rays of sunlight turn the hazy skies pink and the rock's golden vibrance transmutes to smouldering bronze, it's time to leave. The final trucks are scheduled to depart at 6pm and as the alternative walk will take over 4 hours, we hurry back to secure our places.

After our slalom ride downhill, we reach the hotel and I prepare the Matchless for a short journey to the mechanic's workshop. Following the police and the minibus beyond the high street, we quickly turn onto a lane that leads along the side of an open field. Apart from one of two dim lightbulbs in nearby shacks, everything is intensely dark. One hundred metres further on, we come to rest outside a shed-like building clad in palm fronds that's lit by a solitary glowworm light bulb. Power is provided by a single plug socket that runs off a rattling generator and on the ground lies a smattering of beat-up tools. Swinging straight into action, the mechanic gauges the curvature of the mudguard then commences grinding a couple of pieces of steel to form spacers. The light's so poor that Kway steps forward and uses his mobile phone as a torch to help the man see what he's doing. With the spacers fabricated, an electric drill replaces the grinder in the power socket and holes are swiftly drilled into the rear number plate and mudguard. I'm feeling under the weather so seat myself on a chair outside, viewing progress in a removed way, as though it was someone else's motorcycle, not mine. Two bolts secure the number plate through the spacers and onto the mudguard and in a jiff, the excess thread is sawn off them.

Out of the blue, I'm hit on the side of the face by a bright green flying creature that's been drawn in by the light. At least 2 inches long, it settles on my leg and I curiously inspect it until, moments later, a second crashes into Kways hand then propels itself across the small room.

"Are these what you eat? I ask him, referring to a conversation we had a couple of days ago about insects being a delicacy in Myanmar.

"No, these are grasshoppers. It's crickets we eat," he replies.
The thought of crunching crispy fried critters doesn't quite do it for me, although I believe they're an excellent and cheap source of protein. Most importantly, the Matchless is now fit to fight another day and after paying the mechanic and posing with him for a couple of photos beside her, we head back to the hotel.

Dinner is an unremarkable affair with cold rice and warm beer, the latter problem solved by the waiter nipping out to get a replacement bottle from a neighbour's fridge. The evening's prematurely curtailed by a powercut so I head for bed. Tomorrow will be my final day in Myanmar and, more significantly, the last with my wonderful companions. I lie awake pondering how I can thank them enough when the time comes to part.

One of the Golden Rock trucks
loading up with passengers.

321

Day 74. Kin Pun Sakhan, Myanmar, to Mae Sot, Thailand, 182 miles.

Seen in broad daylight, last night's repairs are utilitarian but sturdy. I rewire the taillight and whilst I'm doing the stock maintenance, discover the points gap has opened up significantly. It's a fiddly job to reset correctly and the team wait patiently close by, jumping into action as soon as I'm finished to help me get ready for the off. As Wunno threads the straps of the *Camelbak* over my outstretched arms, I say,

"I'm going to find it really strange without you guys tomorrow."

They all smile and Captain pats me on the back. Before we leave, Kway points to a section of today's journey on the map which, he warns me, will be testing for the bike. It's a 50 mile stretch of very poor road that there's no way around... something to look forward to!

The two police motorcyclists from yesterday tear themselves away from the comfort of the hotel restaurant where they've been drinking tea. They say hello, then Kway translates their next words.

"He says they are your VIP escort."

I think they're joking but Kway assures me they're being serious. Lights a flashing, we ride out of the courtyard and straight into a traffic jam of tour buses and Golden Rock trucks ensnared in a colossal tangle. The first outrider, who's had his new machine for less than a week, struggles. Unused to its size and weight, he lacks the confidence to ride between the almost stationary vehicles and twice stalls. Ten minutes pass before, fearing my engine will overheat, I squeezed past him and ride on, weaving around the immobilised vehicles until I'm clear of the town. I wait for 15 minutes in the shade of a bus shelter before the others catch up and we can continue, back in our original dawdling convoy formation with both escort bikes' sirens wailing.

Upon reaching their checkpost, we say cheerio to the officers and recommence our southbound journey. The roads and scenery are unchanged from yesterday, the only noticeable difference being the prevalence of huge empty trucks heading back to Thailand. Painfully retarded through urban areas, they drive foot-to-the-floor along straight stretches of open road, making overtaking them a heart-in-mouth manoeuvre. In the towns, progress is further hampered by the number of motorcycle rickshaws that unpredictably stop to pick up and drop off customers. Their design is unknown to me, the sidecars huge, each with two wooden benches that can easily seat six people. Above them, propped up by four corner posts, are large canopies. From afar, they look like garishly decorated fourposter beds on wheels.

Turning east around midday, the road soon goes to pot, the first 25km taking us almost an hour. By the time we stop in a village for lunch, the Matchless's front forks are twisted so whilst my food's being cooked, I carefully straighten them out. The restaurant's a quiet, open-air establishment that mostly caters for travellers heading to and from Thailand and we have it to ourselves. My meal arrives looking worryingly like dog food but, to my surprise, turns out to be very tasty.

"Well, that was a lot better than it looked," I say to Kway without caution then immediately realise that the cook come waiter, a pleasantly smiling middle-age lady, is standing right next to me. Looking up, I guess from the hurt expression on her face that she understands English. As I'm cringing, Kway jumps in with words of thanks in an attempt to smooth things over and I leave with my tail firmly between my legs.

The next 45km of road make the Matchless feel like a washing machine on the full-spin cycle and my fingers, wrists and arms all go numb. Close to two hours after leaving the restaurant, I pull in at what I think is a cafe only to be told it's a petrol station. At this minute the bike's fine, it's me that needs replenishment. Fortunately they sell chilled drinks, so we grab one apiece and perch ourselves side by side on a bench seat waiting for the feeling to come back in my extremities. After a while, I ask the boys to stand next to the bike so I can take a photograph of them. They dutifully form a line but when I click the shutter button, Captain, ever the joker, shoots his arms up into the air. Standing beside him is his polar opposite, Kyee, the driver, who calmly waits while I attempt another. He's only 20 but has been driving for 5 years. Kyee possesses two of the most essential traits for a tour bus driver, those of being very cautious and totally unflappable. On the far side is Wunna, a steady man of few words who's always willing to lend a helping hand. The stand out act, however, is Kway, who's dedicated to his job, doing everything in his power to make my crossing of Myanmar a success. Down to the smallest detail, he's highly attentive without being in the slightest bit obsequious, genuinely interested in my trip and always cheerful and positive. A more gentle, upbeat, accommodating and friendly group of men I could not have hoped to meet! Photos complete, they immediately gather around, helping me into my riding clothes with well practiced proficiency.

The ensuing 18km eat up an hour but as we emerge onto the far side of one deplorably rough section, I spot an alluring line of deep grey tar seal in the distance, the start of the new Thai-made road that leads to the border. Eagerly, I accelerate hard but a sixth sense alerts me that the engine, which has run with virtually no airflow over it for the last four hours, might be just about to nip up. It could well be my imagination but I follow my gut instinct and release the throttle, immediately looking for somewhere to stop. The road's built on a steep embankment so I slow to the point where I can roll off its hard shoulder then, at an angle, track down a grassy bank. Halting at the first place I can park the bike on her sidestand, I see the minibus, hazards flashing, has drawn up at the top of the bank and everyone's piling out, soon joining me as I lie back on the grassy verge. Sometime later, when we're all at risk of dozing off, we rouse ourselves and put our backs into pushing the Matchless upwards to the roadside. Retrieving the last of my luggage from the back of the Toyota, I strap it on and prepare to leave. Next stop, the border!

The final run is 40km and although it involves climbing over a 600m high hill, the superb road makes it a breeze. In what seems barely more than the blink of an eye, we arrive at Myawaddy, riding through busy streets as people go home from work. We pull up in front of a large building that straddles the road, its roofs elaborately edged with gold painted ornaments. Customs is in an office to the right and immigration is housed on the left, with the yellow, green and red horizontally striped flag of Myanmar flying above the central, road-spanning building. Kway and Wunna accompany me inside where my carnet's speedily processed and passport stamped. I return back outside to say goodbye, warmly shaking everybody's hand and at the same time giving each person a preprepared roll of Kyat as a thank you. In truth, money can't express how much their comradeship has meant to me.

After being helped into my gear for the last time, I prod the crank and the Matchless starts straightaway. Captain gives me his customary thumbs up and I straddle the saddle. Following a final wave, I gently let out the clutch, roll underneath the government offices and onto the Thai Myanmar Friendship Bridge. It climbs high over the Moel river, the orange ball of the setting sun shining brightly down its centreline. Upon reaching the middle of its curving span, a broadening strip of chevrons appear on my side of the road which divert me over the left and I note, as I slowly descend, matching markers doing the opposite for westbound traffic. I'll have to remember to ride on the left from now on! Approaching the Thai immigration offices, I'm conscious that I should be feeling jubilant... reaching Thailand is such an important landmark in the journey, indeed, Vietnam is now only one more country away. I don't, tears are welling up in my eyes and I'm bereft at leaving my four friends behind, acutely aware it's unlikely I'll ever see any of them again.

Smartly dressed, ultra efficient Thai officialdom takes charge, handing me two forms to complete. Once my photo's taken, I get a stamp in my passport and can progress to customs. Here, I complicate matters unnecessarily. The official hands me temporary import papers for my motorcycle, which I duly complete, guessing at what half of the questions really mean as they're written in pidgin English. There's a nominal fee due for processing it, which I pay using a single US Dollar bill, then I'm told I'm free to go. I fail to realise that this actually does mean go, as these documents replace my carnet, so unwittingly move onto the next customs window, present my carnet and after several confused conversations, persuade someone to fill it in and stamp it. It's only at this point that another brown suited officer arrives, explaining my folly.

"When you leave Thailand," he tells me, "Nobody will want to stamp your carnet and you will need to insist that it gets done."
In all, the arrivals process has taken about an hour and by the time I leave, night has settled upon the frontier post, not that that makes things any cooler, it's still sweltering.

The road immediately enters a thriving night market that, flashing with coloured lights, resembles a fairground. There doesn't appear to be any accommodation in the area so I ride through it, pausing half a kilometre ahead at a set of traffic lights. A man on a scooter pulls up alongside so I ask him where I can find a hotel. At first he doesn't understand but grasps my meaning when I perform the customary snoring act. He attempts to point out some directions then, as the lights turn to green, indicates I should follow him. Travelling under bright overhead lighting, something I haven't seen in open countryside since Europe, he slows 4km later and points to a fork I should take on the right. Shouting my thanks, I swing across the road and soon enter the township of Mae Sot. Almost immediately, I spot a small boutique hotel on the left which, the manager informs me, has one last chalet room available. I take it, grateful that he accepts Visa as I don't yet have any Thai Bhat. Directly across the way, he tells me, is a restaurant that also accepts plastic which means I can eat without the tedium of traipsing around town in search of an ATM.

With the Matchless secured close to my room door, I head out for dinner. Thailand seems so modern and uncluttered compared with Myanmar, the streets and pavements spotlessly clean, well lit and meticulously maintained. I'm exceedingly proud of my motorcycle for making it here and tell myself, as I head for bed, that it's time to look forward again... if our luck holds out, we'll be at the Vietnamese border in about a week's time!

About to set off behind the police escort, Kin Pun Sakhan, Myanmar.

Day 75 Mae Sot to
Thung Salaeng Luang National Park. 206 miles.

Underway immediately after breakfast, I ride to an ATM to stock up on Baht then join the eastern highway. Fuel is a priority and as soon as possible I pull into a *Shell* garage where two things immediately jump out. The first is the impressive array of petrol grades on sale, which includes E20, a mix of 20% ethanol and 80% low octane fuel that would have my engine glowing red hot within ten miles. The second is the plenitude of staff wielding the pumps, five young women in smart uniforms and matching baseball hats. Thailand's unemployment rate is phenomenally low at 0.6%, a figure partly achieved by companies offering low paid work to young people like these and also attributable to the lack of any meaningful unemployment benefit, which results in many Thais working part-time or becoming self-employed and entrepreneurial.

In the late 1980s, I spent a month backpacking around Thailand. During the following decade, I returned at least twenty times on business trips centred around buying textiles in Bangkok and exporting them to New Zealand. Undisputedly exotic, it boasts misty, jungle-clad mountains in the north and pristine beaches and enchanting tropical islands in the south. Now a modern, easy country to travel in, the people are hospitable, the food is great and the infrastructure efficiently geared to support the 29 million tourists who come each year to, amongst a plethora of other activities, snorkel, visit sacred temples and ride elephants.

In spite of my many visits, I never fully connected with Thai people, especially the younger generation who always seemed predisposed to giggling because I was a foreigner, colloquially known as a 'farang'. They thought me weird and didn't understand me. On occasions, I'd found this kind of reaction annoying and so today, resolve to try really hard to make a better go of it. When I say,

"Fill her up, please," and the pump attendants fall about laughing, I join in. When they shyly look away instead of answering a question, I calmly try again, determined not to be a grumpy old man. With the transaction satisfactorily complete and a little progress made on the interaction front, I head out into bright sunshine and am soon climbing through a heavily wooded area.

Route 105's wide, well sealed, and sweeps round long, fast bends as it dramatically rises and falls. Within 10km I spot the sign I've been looking for. It says 'Magic Hill'. Over breakfast, the hotelier had told me about this place and I'm intrigued to see its party piece for myself. Pulling up where a yellow line's been painted across the highway, I take in our position at the bottom of a dip... from this point the road clearly climbs in both directions. With the bike in neutral and no traffic in sight, I let go of the brake lever and begin to roll forward. Raising my feet onto the foot pegs, we slowly build up momentum. I begin chortling... it's true... vehicles do roll uphill on Magic Hill! Stopping, I get off and look around, squatting down to check the plane of the road. The obvious answer has to be that it's an optical illusion but I can't see how, it does appear to be a genuine upwards slope. Observing my study of the road surface, a passing motorists stops sharply, and with his hazard lights flashing, reverses back towards me.

"Magic Hill!" a man shouts through his open window.

I respond with a thumbs up.

"Look!" he adds, a huge grin across his face.

He makes a U-turn then drives back to the yellow line. Swinging over to my side of the road, he begins waving through his window, indicating that I should cross over the road and watch him from the opposite verge. I do, laughing out loud as his car begins rolling uphill, boot first! When he stops next to my bike, I run over and shake his hand, thanking him for the demonstration. Grinning, he about-turns and continues merrily on his way. According to last night's host, magnetism has been ruled as the cause of the phenomenon. I leave, none the wiser but greatly entertained.

Thailand's roads are distinctly quiet compared with Pakistan, India and Myanmar, primarily because drivers don't incessantly blare their horns as a matter of course. Patience, lane discipline and consideration for other motorists are also evident... it's quite a culture shock. Descending to the plains, the air's so hot that I don't much feel like lunch so opt for two rounds of chocolate *Cornetto*, eating them under a large umbrella at the side of a petrol station while the Matchless is cooled by the gentlest of zephyrs. Back underway, the road widens into a dual carriageway that, in towns, expands to a broad six-laner. Traffic lights become increasingly prevalent and as I spot each set in the distance, do my level best to reach them at green, whether that means speeding up or slowing to a crawl. Adjacent to each set of lights is a large digital timer which painfully ticks down the seconds until the lights change again. Being caught when they just turn red is a torment because the next change will be three full minutes away, with traffic from the left crossing on its own before traffic from the right gets its turn. Sometimes I stop the Matchless, taking a chance on her readily restarting whilst so hot, but when conditions are right, I cheekily turn left into the free filter, make a smart one-eighty and, with lights hopefully still in my favour, turn left again, and continue in my original direction.

In the middle of the afternoon, I spot a small restaurant set back beside a row of tall poplars. Parking the Matchless in shade, I head indoors, pile my jacket and helmet onto a chair then inspect the range of foods laid out beneath a glass counter. Displayed in stainless steel bowls is a wide variety of ingredients but I've no idea what most are or how to order a meal made from them. A young woman, her jet black hair beautiful tied in a long plait, tries to help. When I fail to comprehend her words, she changes tack, and after a good five minutes studiously studying her smartphone, comes up with the word, 'Noodle'.

We both laugh, probably for different reasons, but it's not exactly enlightening. The only other customers, a Thai couple, join in, the woman making suggestions about what I should order in stilted English. I'm extremely grateful and the result, which centres around chilli sauce on stringy threads of rice vermicelli, is fresh tasting with a lip-tingling afterburn. Back beside the Matchless preparing to depart, I'm once again poignantly conscious of the absence of my Burmese friends and their helping hands.

Now designated Highway 12, the road climbs, skirting along the northern boundary of a national park. The temperature falls from sizzling to just plain hot and the fragrant smells from the nearby forests fill the air. According to the satnav, sundown will be upon us in less than an hour so I keep my eyes peeled for somewhere to stay. At the summit of a long ascent, there's a strip of strung out houses and eateries, amongst them a baby pink VW T2 campervan that's on display next to some garishly painted chalets and a restaurant. Looking like a cross between a psychedelic holiday camp and the children's TV show, *Balamory*, the accommodation has nevertheless come at just the right time. My allotted cabin is shocking magenta on the outside but totally conventional inside. Crucially, the bike can be parked right next to its door, out of sight of the road... and just as importantly, the office, as I desperately need to do an oil change!

Within half an hour, I'm showered and the last of the hot oil is slowly dripping from the oil tank into a plastic bottle secured in place with gaffer tape. I head to the restaurant where the waiter, an earnest young man who carefully considers every word before speaking, offers me a menu. Thankfully, there's an English translation for each dish but as some of the choices are unusual sounding, I ask him for a series of explanations. Finally, I quiz him about the 'fish of the day', which is 'Dolly fish with red Thai sauce'.

"Do Dolly fish come from a river or from the sea?" I enquire.

His brow furrows as he tries to understand the question then suddenly, a look of comprehension spreads across his face,

"Dolly fish come from supermarket," he replies.

Fair enough!

Rest stop, Thailand.

Day 76. Thung Salaeng Luang National Park, Thailand, to Vientiane, Laos. 220 miles.

Fresh oil and a clean filter are first on the agenda, swiftly followed by tappet adjustment and a few extra pounds of air in the tyres courtesy of my foot pump. I'd expected the knobbly rubber on the rear wheel to have worn out by now but it's still going strong, coping with the high temperatures and coarse tar-seal remarkably well. Less prone to wear, the chunky enduro front tyre has probably 7mm of tread left and I'm hoping both will see me through to the journey's end. Failing that, I'm still carrying the tyre I'd used to cross Europe as a backup. It's almost 10am by the time it and the rest of the bags are securely strapped on board and I'm ready to leave.

The highway soon drops down to the plains where it becomes Asia Highway 2 (AH2), a proposed development that links Denpasar, the capital of Indonesia, to Europe, merging with AH1 to cross Myanmar and India. Similar to yesterday's roads, it's a fast dual carriageway on which cars are few and far between in the countryside and we're only slowed by exasperatingly prolonged waits at traffic lights when passing through towns. The temperature builds, soon touching 40°, and, feeling the effects of dehydration after only a couple of hours, I stop to replenish my *Camelbak* with another 3 litres of chilled water. Checking the *Garmin*, I'm chuffed to see that we've already covered 130km, one of the longest non-stop distances thus far. Pressing on, the highway abruptly changes to single lane before I'm halted at a barrier that's manned by soldiers. It's the entrance to another National Park, this one the domain of elephants, the officially recognised symbol of Thailand. As poaching has caused such a marked fall in the animals' numbers and illegal logging shrunk their habitat, its encouraging to see the area being so heavily protected.

The 50km long strip of tar seal that wends through the park rises and falls spectacularly, beginning not much above sea level and rising to 940m before plunging 200m in one mad dash, a hurtling descent that the freewheeling Matchless makes in under a minute. The same happens again and again and no matter how much momentum we build on the downslopes, we're soon reduced to crawling on the way back up, the invisible force of gravity all too keen to pull us back down again. I'm concerned about labouring the bike but over time it strikes me that the fresh oil must be working a treat as the engine's exceedingly quiet, even when chugging up severe inclines. Nearing the park's eastern boundary, the road continues to fall for long, flying stretches, not levelling out until we reach another set of guarded gates at an altitude of 120m. Here, one of the soldiers speaks to me but I can't make out what he says. I cough and my ears pop loudly... the cold I caught in Burma together with the sudden changes in altitude have been playing tricks with my hearing and normal noise levels instantly resume, including the familiar sound of the G3L's engine resolutely ticking over.

At a sprawling service station, I eat an improvised lunch of a cheese toastie followed by an obligatory Thai *Cornetto*. As I'm finishing, a preposterously overladen Toyota Hi-Lux ute pulls in. Chrome railings have been welded all around its cargo bay and cab roof and the resultant space filled to overflowing with hessian wrapped produce. On top of that, precariously contained by a tarpaulin and strong netting, are more burgeoning layers of king-size cabbages that, wedge-shaped, culminate in a skyscraper of a pile at its tail. I've seen many grossly overburdened vehicles during the last couple of months but this caps them all... the tops of the rear wheels have completely disappeared within the wheel arches!

The satnav throws up the option of a shortcut which chops a substantial corner off the route I'd originally planned to follow, reducing it by 67km. Experience to date on less well developed road networks has taught me to avoid such alternatives like the plague, their surfaces inevitably poor with severe repercussions for both bike and body. In Thailand, however, I figure it's worth the risk and turn left where indicated. Although narrower, it proves to be a good decision and as the Matchless relentlessly motors north east through farmland, I become completely lost in my own world of untroubled thoughts. Our next break comes after approximately 100km and this time I park squarely in front of a giant white sitting Buddha that, including its plinth, is a good 10m tall. There's nothing else in sight bar fields and trees, an impressive setting in which to lean back on a saddlebag, listen to the cicadas and eat a banana.

We ride through Phu Wiang National Park, one of the world's largest dinosaur graveyards, then join the main northbound highway. A brisk 50km run sees us closing in on the city of Nong Khai and the border with Laos, which is formed by the mighty Mekong River. I visited Nong Khai in 1988, staying several nights in a ramshackle wooden hotel that enjoyed uninterrupted views over its opaque green waters. At that time, Laos was a closed communist country with no access for foreign tourists and I remember quizzically buying bizarre postcards in Nong Khai's market showing the Moscow Underground and a USSR military radio operator that had been smuggled over the border. Every evening, as I sat on my balcony, a Laos armoured motorboat, its large outboards churning up water, would patrol up and down the river. I'd longed to see the mysteries of the land that was just a stone's throw away. Since then, things have changed for the better and entry is now straightforward. Avoiding Nong Khai itself, I veer to the left and follow signs for the Thai-Lao Friendship Bridge.

Thai immigration is swamped with pedestrians, buses, cars and trucks all vying for the attention of a handful of hassled officials. As the queue at the passport booths are at least 20 deep, I head for customs first, locating the office and asking for someone to deal with my carnet. Two men curiously inspect it then tell me the only person authorised to stamp it is having his dinner. I'm instructed to leave it on his desk and return once my passport's stamped. At the immigration booth I'm asked for the temporary import licence I was issued at Mae Sot and I wonder, apart from my motorcycling gear, how the official knows that I have one. Nonetheless, I hand it over and receive the appropriate triangular purple exit stamp in my passport. I head back to customs, anticipating a long wait but am pleasantly surprised to find that my carnet's been duly completed and I'm able to move on straightaway.

The delight which evaded me when crossing into Thailand engulfs me now.

"Almost there!" I yell at the Matchless, over enthusiastically slapping her tank as we power round a bend towards the start of the bridge.

A tailback of stationary cars comes into view and I have to haul on the brakes to avoid piling into the back of them. Edging my way to the head of the line, I halt in front of a barrier that's been lowered across the road. As I kill the engine, a single headlight materialises like a cyclops high above the centre of the bridge and floats down the middle of the road. In amazement, I realise it's a train. As unexpectedly as it appeared, it obliquely veers off and disappears from sight, the sound of its clanging bogies quickly drowned by revving car engines. I boot the kickstarter and the Matchless joins in the din. As the barrier flies up, the race is on. Three lanes of speeding cars streak ahead, all jockeying for the position of top dog as they reach the bridge proper and are forced into single file. I'm way behind the front runners but care not as I'm treated to a captivating spectacle of the sun's final amber rays reflecting off the water in a glorious splurge of twinkling colours.

Laotian bureaucracy is a mixed bag. First I need to buy a visa, a burgundy sticker that covers a full page of my passport and costs $35. With the corresponding entry stamp on the following page, I'm instructed to go and find customs, which transpires to be exactly where I've parked the bike. My carnet causes a lot of head scratching and in the end, a bright young woman leaves her booth and asks me to follow her. We go from one office to another, traipsing backwards and forwards across the broad compound until we finally find someone with the authorisation to fill it in. He may have the requisite number of gold pips on his epaulettes but he doesn't have a clue what to do, so while the young woman interprets, I point to the empty boxes on the form and suggest what he should write. All that remains is an official stamp to seal the document. This causes further consternation. He opens a drawer crammed full of all shapes and sizes of rubber stamps and begins inspecting each one. Clearly he has no idea which is appropriate and eventually the woman, using her initiative, points to one that's already been discarded and recommends he uses that. A bright red floral design blooms on the paper and to be honest, I don't really care what its true purpose is as I deduce the authorities at the exit post will more than likely be just as clueless. Returning back to the bike, I thank the soldier who's guarded her and the young woman who'd so patiently helped me, then ride out of the immigration area and onto the dark road.

Within minutes I'm encountering the renowned friendliness of the Lao people. Turning towards Vientiane, I pass a scooter piloted by a woman accompanied by two smiling boys, both in school uniform, one in front and one behind her. With their engine at full stretch, they briefly overtake so that all three of them can wave! The road into the city is at least 20km and the streetlights that illuminate it sporadic and weak. Nonetheless, the boulevards are wide, a legacy of the city's time as a place of importance in French Indochina. As my satnav doesn't have mapping for Laos, I slot into the busiest flow of traffic, finally arriving at the city's ceremonial heart, Ave Lane Xang, an arrow-straight, six lane boulevard. Glowing golden at one end is the ornate temple, Wat Si Saket, and at the other, beautifully lit by vivid blue spotlights, sits Patuxai Monument. I become frustrated by the dearth of hotels and at a set of traffic lights, ask a couple on a scooter if they know of one. They do, a large, Soviet-type complex just around the corner. It looks bleak and uninviting and without even entering the building, I swing out of its driveway and resume my search. Two convoluted loops of the inner city ensue, neither of which produce any results... I must be losing my touch!

It's after 8pm and the humidity levels are stupefyingly high. I resign myself to the inevitable, backtrack to the rejected lodgings, the Chaleunxay Hotel, and ask to see a room. It's bare but clean and will suffice. However, when I return downstairs, the suggested parking for my motorcycle proves to be on open land.

"I'm sorry," I say to the receptionist, "I won't sleep a wink if I leave it there."

"No problem," he replies. "You can bring it inside," and to my amazement, he holds the front door wide open, indicating I should park her in the middle of the lobby. Tentatively wheeling her in, I'm a little edgy in case a more senior member of staff comes along and quashes the arrangement. Rocking her onto the rear stand, I throw the cover over as quickly as possible, partly in a deluded attempt to somehow disguise her but mainly to diminish the smell of hot oil and petrol fumes that threaten to pervade the foyer.

"Leave it, it's okay" the receptionist says.

What an understanding man!

The hotel can't change money so I set out to find a bank and somewhere to eat. Within a hundred metres is an enormous, modern building with a bright blue neon sign fortuitously reading 'ANZ Bank' across its front. On the corner of one of its walls sits an ATM. It's ideal as my bank account in New Zealand is actually with ANZ, so I dig the relevant card out of my moneybelt. When I select 400,000 kip (approximately US$50), however, I'm shocked to find there's a 10% withdrawal fee. Affronted, I cancel the transaction and leave, searching for a money changer. My sense of direction and good fortune seem to have deserted me and with increasingly weary legs, I walk for almost an hour without finding a single one open. Eventually, I stumble upon an ATM that only charges 5% commission and although it's still an outrageous fee, go for it.

Giving up hope of finding somewhere to eat, I return to my hotel where, on overhearing me talking to the receptionist, a helpful Vietnamese guest gives me directions to a backstreet restaurant that's less than a two minute walk away. Turning a corner, I stop in my tracks at what lies before me. Set in the middle of a small roundabout is That Dam, the Black Stupa, a stone monument that looks as though it's been formed in a giant jelly mould. To its right is a fabulous looking brasserie, Chateau Du Laos, with plenty of open-air seating and waiters at hand. Tired and hungry as I am, I can't resist circumnavigating the stupa which, lit from below with powerful floodlights, looks curiously hairy. Closer inspection shows that it's completely overgrown with stalky weeds, which I imagine by daylight don't look so alluring but tonight give the stupa a peculiar hirsute appearance that I really like. Finally taking a seat, I order a meal of Pad Thai and my first bottle of *Beer Laos*. While listening to a group of musicians play on acoustic guitars, I sink into my seat, gazing at the stupendous view and feeling contented to the core.

Day 77. Vientaine. 0 miles.

A Vietnamese tourist visa is valid for three months from its date of issue meaning I'd have had to apply for one too close to my departure date to reliably get my passport back in time. A 15 day 'Visa On Arrival' was introduced in June for UK citizens but it was unclear if this was only for air passengers or if it would be granted at land borders too... even the London Vietnamese embassy was in the dark. Straight after breakfast, I catch a tuk-tuk, a three-wheeler taxi, to the nearby Vietnam embassy. Contrary to what I'd read online, it transpires that they need 48 hours to issue a tourist visa, time I don't have as I need to meet the Hanoi based agent who's arranged entry paperwork for the Matchless at the Vietnam border in just four days. I offer to pay for an expedited service but that's changed too and the facility is no longer available. However, the ever-so-polite consular official does assure me I'll be given a visa at any land border, including the remote northern one I intend to use. Here's hoping!

Sun hat on, I wander around baking hot streets for a couple of hours and eventually locate the old city. It's chockablock with tourist and backpacker haunts but that does at least mean I get a good espresso. Lunch, however, I take at the same restaurant as last night, its fresh mango shakes and prime position opposite That Dam making it too good to miss. In the afternoon, I explore a couple of wats, Buddhist temples dripping with elaborate gild, then head to Patuxai Monument, also known as Victory Gate, the war memorial in honour of those who fought for independence from France in the 1940s and early '50s.

Set in its own gardens, with Lane Xang boulevard separating into two carriageways that wrap around it, it's immediately apparent that the building's design mirrors that of the Arc de Triumph in Paris, albeit with a Laotian architectural twist. Above the giant arches are towers topped with classically south east Asian tile roofs crowned with golden vanes, traditional masonry ramparts and a panoply of statues depicting mythological creatures that are part human, part bird. The story behind its construction is amusing. The memorial was built using diverted American concrete and funding, both of which had been given to the Kingdom of Laos' government to build a new airport in Vientiane. This misappropriation earned the building its nickname, 'the vertical runway'. As I turn a corner, music erupts behind the memorial and I watch in delight as a musical fountain spurts choreographed jets of water into the air.

Vientiane's an eminently walkable city that's languid, picturesque and awash with a charismatic blend of Sino, Franco and Soviet influences. Late in the afternoon, I relax for half an hour below the spinning ceiling fan in my room then take another tuk tuk, this time to *The Cope Visitor Centre*. The goal of the Cooperative Orthotic and Prosthetic Enterprise (COPE) is to ensure that people with physical disabilities have free access to a quality prosthetic limb service at local level. Walking around the centre, I read case studies of people born with disabilities or who need help due to recent injuries, such as motorcycle crashes. Many of these success stories are inspiring but the overwhelming impact derives from reports on those who've suffered injuries caused by UXOs, unexploded ordinance.

Between 1964 and 1973, while the war in Vietnam was in the news every day, US planes dropped over 2 million tonnes of bombs on Laos in what became known as The Secret War. This is more than was dropped in the entirety of the Second World War and made Laos the most heavily bombed country, per capita, in history. Much of the ordinance that rained down from the skies was in the form of cluster bombs, repulsive weapons that until today I knew nothing about. The average cluster bomb consists of a hollow shell packed with hundreds of small submunitions or bomblets, in many cases fitted with a parachute or streamer to slow its descent and aid dispersement over a wide area. In Laos, most of these bomblets, or 'bombies' as they are called here, were anti-personnel devices, although large numbers of incendiary submunitions were also dropped on villages to start fires. Killing and maiming tens of thousands of innocent people, each one of these bombings broke international laws, a fact which raises many fundamental questions.

Spread over vast rural regions, as many as 30% of these miniature bombs, that's an estimated 80 million devices, failed to explode in Laos! I'm bewildered by what I'm reading and double-check the numbers... 270 million bomblets dropped, 80 million unexploded. From 1973 to 2008 it's estimated there have been as many as 20,000 cluster bomb related deaths and injuries in the country and despite efforts to educate people of the dangers and clear large areas of land, many still die or are maimed by them today. What brings sanity to the despicable insanity is the work COPE is doing. One example on display is a homemade, coarse wooden stump that a farmer fabricated after he stood on a 'bombie' and lost his lower leg. He lived with it for almost 30 years before being introduced to COPE. He now has a made-to-measure, and therefore far more comfortable, prosthetic.

On the walls are many photos of survivors along with their heartrending stories, including one about a Lao fisherman called Mr. Ta. It reads,
'In 2004, Ta was out fishing with his two sons, aged 6 and 10. He found a bombie lying on the ground. He knew it was dangerous but he had heard that the explosive made it easy to catch fish. He sent his children behind a tree and crawled up to the bombie. As soon as he touched it, it exploded. His sons dragged him into his boat and rowed him back to the village. In total, it took nine hours for them to reach medical help. Ta lost not only both his arms and an eye but all of his family's livestock to pay for his treatment. For four years, Ta described how he had to "eat like a dog." Since being brought to COPE by the team at PCL (a UXO clearance organisation) he has received arms and is now able to help his family and try to rebuild his life. He has become an advocate for the ban on cluster munitions and travelled to Oslo to watch the signing of the treaty.'

The treaty referred to is the *Convention on Cluster Munitions* (CCM) which was adopted in Dublin in May 2008 and ratified in Oslo later the same year. Countries that sign up to the convention are obliged to 'never under any circumstances use cluster munitions; develop, produce, otherwise acquire, stockpile, retain or transfer to anyone, directly or indirectly, cluster munitions.' 107 states have so far signed it, with The Lao People's Democratic Republic being one of the first. Along with several other major players in the armaments industry, such as China and Russia, the United States of America has refused to be a signatory and continues to manufacture and stockpile these abhorrent weapons. They've been used many times since The Secret War, including in Lebanon, Yugoslavia, Iraq and Afghanistan.

On the way out, I walk past a pile of decommissioned bombies, several of which are painted bright colours... it's little wonder so many children have been tempted to their death by assuming they are toys. The psychopaths who think it's acceptable to commission and use these weapons, the faceless, cold-hearted corporates who make money from them and the self serving politicians who don't stand up to be counted when it comes to doing the right thing, should be dragged to Laos and made see the results of their actions. It's not only sickening, it's totally unforgivable. In truth, it is beyond belief to the vast majority of decent human beings.

To my surprise, the tuk tuk driver that brought me here has waited an hour and a half for my return. I told him not to bother when he dropped me off but obviously tourist money is good money and he's been happy to wait, giving me a huge gummy smile as I climb inside and perch on a bench seat. After another meal sitting opposite the shaggy stupa, I wander back to my room, my thoughts still very much at the COPE Visitor Centre, then make myself focus, researching tomorrow's route before turning in.

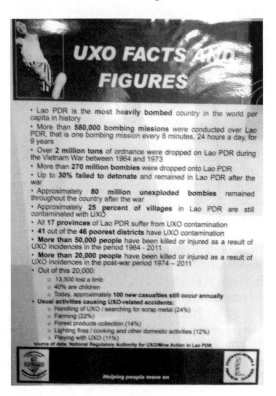

Harrowing statistics from the COPE Visitor Centre.

335

Day 78. Vientiane to a village 5 miles south of Phou Khoun. 167 miles.

Finding my way out of the city proves more difficult than I'd imagined and I'm soon lost. A businessman on a scooter acknowledges me as we sit side-by-side at red lights, so I ask him the way to north-bound Highway 13.

"Follow me," he responds.

When the lights change to green, he alters his direction, sharply cutting across a lane and forking left. The course he takes turns right, left and right again, eventually merging with a more major road. Slowing until I draw alongside him, he indicates that I should continue straight on then, with a smile, deftly makes a life-threatening U-turn and heads back towards the city centre.

The sprawling outer reaches of Vientiane seem to go on forever and I soon discover why so many oncoming cars are splattered red. Every hundred or so metres, the road's broken up by a line of potholes, all brimming with muddy red water, the result of a nighttime downpour. At first it's easy enough to weave around them but as their frequency multiplies, this becomes more difficult and soon my boots and trousers are caked in cayenne coloured mud which, in direct sunshine, hardens like quick drying cement. The uneven rocky terrain and gouged tarmac is hard work and I soon fall into a familiar pattern of persistently shifting gears and overtaxing the brakes.

80km into the journey, I need a breather so fittingly park under the drooping leaves of a banana tree to eat a couple of bananas I'd bought earlier. When I set off again, the roadsides press tightly in and we begin a shallow climb. It doesn't take long to reach the summit of a hill where I'm greeted by an absolutely exceptional vista. Ahead are a trio of tower karsts, giant limestone outcrops that rise vertically, like supernatural islands, from the surrounding flat landscape. Caused by erosion and weathering, they're hundreds of metres tall and although some shadowy patches of white sedimentary rock still show on their ragged, cave-peppered sides, they're mainly covered in a tangle of creepers impenetrable to the eye.

Descending to the plains, I arrive at the tourist hotspot of Vang Vieng, a well known stopping point on the so-called South East Asia backpacker 'banana-pancake trail'. Dwarfed by a spine of towering rock faces, the town sits snugly on the banks of the Nam Song river amidst a tapestry of emerald paddies. Just a few years ago, Vang Vieng became one of the world's more unusual party destinations for young travellers. Things got out of control and during the summer of 2011, there was a spate of fatalities where stoned tourists were let loose on swings, slides and zip-wires over the river. Apparently, unregulated riverside bars were serving revellers with alcoholic drinks laced with opium and hallucinogenic mushrooms known as 'Magic Shakes'. Despite the welcome boost to their coffers, many locals were unhappy, complaining that the cocktail of all-night music, drunkenness, nudity and toxic drug scene conflicted with their cultural values. The Laos government eventually intervened, closing down many of the suspect businesses, and Vang Vieng cleaned up much of its act. Since then, the focus has shifted towards eco tourism, with karst climbing, kayaking and caving all now popular attractions.

Riding up the main drag, I spot a cafe flanked by a line of colourful chalkboards promoting the speciality of woodfired pizza. Parking the Matchless outside, I plonk down at an empty table. Two menus are immediately produced, one offering a wide choice of food including a range of pizzas and the other listing pretty much the same fare but with cannabis a constituent ingredient in every dish. I look around at the other diners, five relaxed, short and singlet-wearing backpackers spread around two tables. None of them look wasted, they're either engrossed in reading paperbacks or tapping away on tablet computers. I opt for a non-psychoactive Margherita pizza with added pesto and a mixed fruit shake. As I wait for their arrival, three minivans drive past, each crammed with a dozen or so backpackers. Strapped onto their roofs are rows of inflated tractor tyre inner tubes and they're obviously off to do Vang Vieng's popular river activity, tubing, which involves dreamily floating downstream for a couple of hours inside the inner tubes. Great fun in this heat!

The state of the narrow highway progressively improves and throughout the afternoon we steadily climb. Passing through a succession of isolated villages, I note that the houses are mainly single room dwellings, constructed from dark timber and raised on knee high stills. I slow as I progress through each settlement because children often play at the roadside and in some cases run alongside me, hooting and cheering. At the edge of one village, all the able-bodied adults appear to be collectively working in an adjoining paddy. At least 30 people with partially submerged limbs are stooped, scything the crop, their colourful clothes a sight to behold in the golden light. In the next village, a gurgling waterfall splashes down a rock face and three young women, all wrapped in multicoloured sarongs, shower underneath it. Further along, I receive a bright wave from a woman and a tentative one from the infant on her hip. Amongst a nearby crowd of kids, a young boy enthusiastically demonstrates his wooden spinning top for me and as it whizzes down the middle of the road, his buddies exuberantly chase after it. Each village offers a feast for the eyes and soul, and for a while I think it's a shame there isn't a place to stay in any of them... then I have a rethink, remembering what Vang Vieng endured.

Reaching an altitude of 1300m, I pause to look around. The sun's now hidden by the surrounding mountains which, as they're immersed in dense, steamy jungle, have a dark, almost menacing air. From here, we descend dramatically, falling without pause to 500m before starting a fresh ascent. Our only other companions on the wildly undulating and wriggling roads are trucks, all well past their use-by dates and struggling to make the gradient. One by one I overtake them until, with a clear view of the fading sky ahead, the satnav shows 1400m. Once again, I'm running out of daylight and as I pull into a settlement of about a dozen small properties, pigs and chickens roaming freely along the verges, wonder how much further I can continue before it becomes pitch black.

The last building in the village is a rambling single-story eatery that spans the crest of the hill and has a commanding view down a valley, now possessed by ghostly shadows. I have to pinch myself as I make out the words 'Guest House' on its yellow *Beer Laos* sponsored restaurant sign. What a godsend! I swing into the courtyard, stop the engine and dismount. Upon hearing the noise, a shy young girl runs out followed by her heavily pregnant mum. I'm shown a room, which passes muster, and a coal shed where I can secrete the bike. Unloading as quickly as possible, I dart back to the unlit shed and in the gloom, drag a couple of sacks of coal out of the way, move a scooter to one side and a bicycle to the other, which creates just enough space to shoehorn the Matchless down the middle.

The last remaining light in the sky is a sliver of translucent primrose and turquamarine that fizzes close to the horizon. All around, the dark outlines of the karsts and hills have been subsumed by velvet night. My sky-gazing is interrupted by a short squeal of brakes accompanied by the scrunch of tyres on gravel as a lone cyclist comes to a rapid halt in front of the building. I go over to say hello and he introduces himself as Bruno from Calais. I must've overtaken him during the last climb, possibly while he himself was being overtaken by a truck... with his bright yellow hi-viz top, I don't see how else I could have missed him. Both of us sweaty and grimy, we agree to meet up for dinner once we've showered.

Egg fried rice and a couple of *Beer Laos* is the order of the day. Sitting opposite each other in the cavernous restaurant, Bruno tells me about his trip, a three month sojourn commencing in Kuala Lumpur, Malaysia, and taking in that country, Thailand, and as much of Laos as possible before he catches a flight home from Bangkok. We trade stories, laugh at our misfortunes and pass on useful information gleaned on the road. Again, I'm aware just how much more I have in common with touring cyclists than with backpackers these days, and despite the differing physical challenges we face, I feel a definite sense of fraternity with them.

A long-distance bus travelling from Vientiane to Luang Prabang, Laos's former royal capital, pulls up outside. Twenty or so Lao passengers disembark, noisily flooding the restaurant in a quest for food. Bruno and I are the only two overnight guests and we both decide it's time to get some rest, agreeing to meet up for breakfast at 7am.

With sleep slowly overtaking me, I ruminate affectionately about the 74-year old, lionhearted Matchless, which is still running faultlessly. Our goal, Vietnam, is just a couple of days away, and although I shouldn't count my chickens...

Day 79. A village 5 miles south of Phou Khoun to Namnern. 164 miles.

The restaurant's stores are devoid of coffee... Bruno to the rescue. He nips back to his room and, as only a Frenchman would, produces some freshly ground beans from his panniers. After a monster size omelette and two fortifying cups of coffee apiece, he loads up and, whilst I'm still going through my checks and routine adjustments, mounts his bike. We agree to keep a look out for each other and he quietly pedals off, soon disappearing from sight behind thick, woolly clouds.

As it rained heavily during the night, the road's damp and slippery so I ride with care, headlight on and my speed tempered on the long downhill stretch that lies just beyond the guest house. Phou Khoun is a small place built around a key junction, the main road splitting at the only roundabout I've seen since Vientiane. 120km to the north is Luang Prabang and 280km beyond that, China. I take the second exit, turning to the east on Highway 7. Within a hundred metres the village ends and as I haven't seen petrol for sale since Vang Vieng, I ask a pedestrian, a lean woman with a baby strapped to her back, where I can buy some. She simply points to the road ahead. I thank her then check my fuel tank, noting with alarm that what's left in the bottom wouldn't fill a teapot.

Setting off, I'm on high alert, scanning the dim sides intently for a sign or telltale forecourt but after 10km of misty hilltop riding, nothing's emerged. Entering a village that's positioned along the top of a ridge, the fog's now so thick it's hard to see more than 5m ahead. I stop to ask directions from a villager who's leading a water buffalo by a rope. He indicates I'll find petrol on the left, somewhere close ahead. 'Thank goodness,' I think, having been on tenterhooks expecting the engine to cough, splutter and expire at any moment. I ride forth in anticipation but see no station, no petrol pumps and watch in dismay as the houses peter out. Continuing further proves fruitless so with all the strength my legs can muster, I make a 3-point turn then coast back down the hill to preserve what bit of fuel I've got.

Reentering the silent village, I suddenly discern the faint silhouette of a scooter, its seat hinged up and a hose poking into its bowels. The petrol station's nothing more than a small breezeblock shop, its sides built up from bamboo and its roof covered in rusty corrugated iron... no wonder I missed it! The righthand side is open fronted, selling everything from cigarettes to tarpaulins, seeds and biscuits. The left half, approximately 2m wide, is solid to hip level above which, through a giant glassless window, I spy two dented 48 gallon drums. Above both are cylindrical glass vessels, one empty, the other half full of ruby red liquid. The scooter rides off and one of the two women that runs the shop asks me how much benzine I want. My request for 10 litres is turned down, apparently the glass cylinders can only measure 6 litres at a time, so I go for that. The other woman, dressed in a strawberry love heart jumper, vigorously works a hand pump, drawing liquid up into the cylinder until it reaches a mark just below the top. As I move the tank bag aside and lift off my petrol cap, the first lady wields a thick rubber tube, removing her thumb from the end just as she pushes it into the tank. The siphoning effect begins and I watch in fascination as the red liquid slowly drains into my bike.

Another woman has stopped to watch, chatting and laughing with the others then trying to communicate with me in a chirpy, melodious language. Bent almost double, she looks ancient but is effortlessly carrying a huge bundle of heavy firewood in a woven sling on her back. She gives me a grin, revealing more gums than teeth, then makes a sassy remark to her two friends which sets them off giggling. I join in the laughter... what else can I do? On paying, the price proves to be only a few Kip higher per litre than I paid in Vientiane and more than worth it for the uniqueness of the experience.

After an hour or so the cloud evaporates and I ride across a plateau which for the first time today allows me to use top gear. I begin to wonder if Bruno was an apparition that, phantom-like, vanishes when on his bike and is only seen late in the evening or first thing in the morning. Approaching the two hour mark, I feel certain that, like last night, I've somehow passed him, maybe when he was having a pee in the bushes. One thing's for sure, he's definitely not been hidden by overtaking trucks this morning because there hasn't been another vehicle on the road thus far. Then, just as I've resigned myself to having missed him, I spot his bright lycra top in the distance. Freewheeling downhill, he's hotly pursued by a local lad pedalling manically to keep up on his rickety old bike. Overtaking, I toot my horn and he comes to a stop, as does the boy who leans on his handlebars looking somewhat perplexed.

"He's my shadow!" exclaims Bruno. "He started following me half an hour ago and has cycled very hard to stay with me since."

He gives the youngster a thumbs up and gets one in return. We chat for a few minutes more, wish each other bon voyage, then hit the road again. Looking in my mirrors as I roar ahead, I can't help smiling at the sight of the phlegmatic Bruno being trailed by his avid acolyte.

I have lunch in a small restaurant in Phonsavan, the capital of the Xiangkhoang Province. The town's name rather poetically translates to 'hills of paradise' and it's well known as the closest habitation to the Plain of Jars, a vast area over which ancient giant vessels, some as tall as 3m, are scattered in clusters. Mostly chiselled out of sandstone, archaeological evidence suggests they date from between 200BC and 500AD. Local legend has it that the jars were made to distill an alcoholic brew whereas modern archaeologists argue it's more likely they were funeral urns. The fact is, nobody can say with any certainty why they exist. Many of the smaller jars have been carried off by souvenir hunters and just as many large ones were destroyed by American carpet bombing during the Secret War but around 2,500 examples still remain, spread over approximately 90 sites. Sadly, only a few of these locations are accessible, and even then, from within clearly marked safe areas. The vast majority are still riddled with unexploded cluster bombs. As intriguing as they are, my priority today is to get within striking distance of the Vietnamese border so with energy levels replenished by a hearty meal, I kick the Matchless over and continue heading east.

The 55km leg to Maung Kham takes roughly an hour and is on the best roads I've experienced in Laos. Vibrations greatly diminished, I revel in the sensation of covering ground smoothly, flowing round bends and powering up gentle hills, all the while untroubled by any concerns about the bike, which is running like clockwork. There's no doubt either that I'm excited by the thought of successfully making it to Vietnam, which produces butterflies in my stomach every time I think how close we are. In Maung Kham's unsophisticated centre, I stop at a store to buy a cold drink and ask directions as, according to my map, we need to turn off Route 7 somewhere around here. Three people simultaneously point towards a lane which cuts off at right angles. I look at it apprehensively... it's plumb straight for as far as the eye can see, climbing steeply and reducing in size to little more than a farm track. Taking a deep breath, I remount and turn onto it.

Beyond the first kilometre, the road corkscrews, tightly winding round the heavily wooded mountainside. I keep the Garmin set to altimeter mode, watching it keenly as we ascend from 540m to 1000m then keep going. At 1250m we re-enter cloud. The road's only just wide enough for a single car, not that I see many, and as we climb ever higher, the thicker the cloud becomes and the chillier it gets. At 1550m it's hard to see more than a few metres ahead and everything, including my clothes, feels decidedly damp. After two hours of travelling no faster than 30kmph and anticipating that vehicles might fly hazardously round blind bends at any moment, my concentration's stretched to the limit and I feel the cold taking its toll. Shivering, I stop and dig my only woollen top out of the bottom of a dry bag, something I never dreamed I'd be doing in the tropics, As expediently as possible I get underway again, the poor visibility now compounded by the inevitable onset of dusk.

For the last hour I pin my hopes on Namnern having lodgings, counting down the distances from 36 to 24 to 18 kilometres on milestones intermittently seen at the roadside. Thoroughly soaked, there are still 12km to go when I break through the cloud base. Within minutes, it turns properly dark but at least the air warms as I descend, which is exactly what my stiff muscles and aching hands need. Finally, I cross a small bridge and reach my destination, a place of fewer than a hundred dwellings that has a small market square with two places to eat. In one, I spot a group of European-looking travellers so ride over and call out to them, asking where they're staying.

"Ya, here" replies one, pointing right. "One hundred metres that way. I hope there is a room for you as we are all sleeping there. Come back and have a beer with us soon!"

Their guesthouse, it transpires, is the only accommodation in Namnern and to my considerable relief has one room left... saved again! I gratefully take it and after a revitalising shower, head out for dinner.

Walking along a short avenue, I glance into a shop. At the rear is the owner's communal living space, a single, sparsely furnished room where the family obviously eat, sleep and work. In the next store, behind small piles of sweets, biscuits and blankets, two children studiously apply themselves to their homework at a wooden table that's lit by a weak overhead bulb. All around are their family's few possessions, a rail of clothes, a couple of chairs, a bed shrouded by a mosquito net and a scooter. The shutters of the adjoining dwelling are also rolled up, revealing a woman who sits in the middle of the room, methodically pulling and pushing the arms of a stout wooden weaving loom, a similar array of basic belongings tidily arranged in the small living area. Her two children are playing in the street, throwing a ball backwards and forwards to each other which I automatically catch and throw back to them, much to their amusement.

Continuing on, I arrive at the restaurant only to find that the other visitors have vanished. The owners, a young couple with a two-year-old boy, grin from ear to ear as they show me to a table, making me feel most welcome. There are probably a dozen tables in the restaurant, all empty apart from mine, and in one corner is the family's own space, a couple of chairs, a desk and a small TV set. I ask for a menu but there isn't one in English so between us we work out a dish of vegetable fried rice with egg, which I watch being flash cooked in a sizzling wok. It's scrumptious. As I'm finishing, the party of tourists returns and I learn they're a group of retirees from Bavaria on a two-week guided bicycle tour of northern Laos. They order a round of drinks, which the restauranteur purchases from a nearby shop, then on my recommendation, request seven replications of the meal I've just eaten, pleasing the owners no end. I enjoy their company for a while, but when the third round of beer is ordered, make my excuses as I'm pooped and need a clear head for the ride to the border tomorrow. Sauntering back to the guest house, I hear distant shouts of "Prost" as the cyclists ebulliently quaff more bottles of *Beer Laos*.

Day 80 Namnern to Na Meo Border. 118 miles.

As I'm loading, the Germans make ready to leave, filing out of the guesthouse and into a minibus which will transport them to the start of the day's ride, their bikes jammed into a second minivan. Not one of them's escaped a sore head from following copious amounts of beer with local rice wine but nonetheless, they all manage a feeble "auf wiedersehen" as they pass.

Namnern's prize possession, as far as I'm concerned, is its lone petrol pump where I top up with strangely viscous blood-coloured petrol. Now seen in daylight, the village is at the bottom of a deep gorge. Starting at 550m on a road that's barely wide enough for a single vehicle, we don't stop climbing until 1400m, the poor Matchless pulling hard in second gear the whole way. Next we skip along the tops of ridges followed by a series of short ascents and descents, the road constantly twisting and often doubling back on itself. My chest is tight, my head thick and my reactions slow, a combination of the cold from Myanmar and the effects of being in the clouds for so long yesterday. I feel barely more than a passenger and riding with so little focus and finesse is precarious, the verges are riven with cracked, flaky tar and many of the bends are littered with gravel. In lieu of a caffeine fix, I decide to boost my biochemistry with an appreciative outlook... the sun's out, there's not a patch of fog to be seen and the mighty Matchless is running impeccably.

Quaint villages come and go, strung out along the attenuated lanes that skim the ridges and skirt tapering valley floors. Their tiny dwellings are made from thick chunks of timber, readily available from the all encompassing rainforest. Penned livestock are abundant and free-ranging chickens roam around, several dashing in front of the bike for no apparent reason. When a kamikaze cockerel does the same, making a last second charge from one side of the road to the other, he manages to hang onto his life by little more than a hair's breadth. So 'why did the chicken cross the road?'... to put the wind up the overland motorcyclist!

In one village I decide to take a break, pulling up at its sole convenience store. A couple of local women perch on crudely made stools on my side of the counter and they watch me curiously as I walk the length of the display, searching for something to eat. The selection of snacks, as ever, comprises sweets and biscuits. I buy a couple of each, enjoying the chocolate wafers but almost gagging on the banana flavoured ones, which breaks the ice, making the women laugh. Sitting on a spare stool, I contemplate my toes for a while, content to be stationary, and while it proves impossible to communicate further with the villagers, their demeanour is open and amicable. As I rise to leave, they both wave, one of the women holding the plump hand of her tiny baby and waving that too.

Underway again, I spot Na Meo written on a milestone for the first time... just 105km to go! In Sam Nuea, I search without luck for a place to eat or get a drink, circling the town's main streets three times in vain. Eventually conceding defeat, I top up with benzine and depart once more due east. Vieng Xia, just 55km from the border, is surrounded by more monumental limestone cliffs. I pause at the junction to its historic town centre where a large restaurant has been built beside a pond. It's closed so, flagging, I turn off towards the town, looking for an alternative... and hit gold. There's a small backstreet cafe with a laid-back ambiance where the family who own it are themselves eating a late lunch. One of them, a young man in his early twenties who speaks English, jumps up and sets to serving me. As well as egg fried rice and bananas, they have fresh coffee, or *Coffee Laos* as he calls it. It's made the Turkish way, with the thick grounds settled at the bottom of a glass. Three rounds later, my grogginess is exorcised and I'm ready for the last part of the ride to Vietnam.

The narrow lane degrades as the kilometres pass, frequently covered in dried mud, dung and gravel. But my spirits are so high I hardly notice and furthermore, I'm uplifted by the number of people who wave from their roadside houses as I roar through a succession of tiny villages, some no more than half a dozen single room thatched dwellings. Today must be washing day, judging by the number of clotheslines I see festooned with vibrantly coloured clothes. On the level for the first time since Vientiane, we weave through paddies that are punctuated by towering karsts blanketed in creepers, dodge around sleek cattle as they wander along the verges, and wave at children playing ball across the road. The tots who want to run beside my bike put the fear of God into me. Just one of them tripping and falling sideways could be calamitous and I vacillate between choosing to speed up or to crawl along as the best strategy.

Counting the mileposts, I'm increasingly excited as the numbers drop from double to single figures. Having passed no sign of habitation for the last few kilometres, I'm rather surprised to round a bend and come upon a shop and an open fronted restaurant. There's nothing else in sight apart from a cluster of concrete buildings about 200 metres further on the left which, it slowly dawns on me, must be the Laos customs and immigration offices. We've made it! As I ride towards them, I feel a surge of joy and a fervent urge to plant a kiss on the Matchless's tank... she's been utterly incredible! Managing to restrain myself, I park up at immigration to check their opening time tomorrow, which proves to be 7am.

"Where is Na Meo town and a guesthouse, please?" I ask the official, a pleasant young man in a peaked cap.

"Na Meo is in Vietnam, they have accommodation there," he replies. "You can cross now, there's still time."

As entry conditions for motorcycles are stringent and the arrangement with my escort is not to meet until tomorrow morning, it's not an option.

"I am sorry," continues the officer when I explain, "but there is nothing I can do. Maybe the restaurant can help you."

Concerned, I ride a couple of hundred metres back to the two buildings. A woman in the eatery tells me they have no accommodation and suggests I ride back to Vieng Xia. That'll take two hours, mainly in the dark.

"Could I sleep on your floor?" I ask.

Her reply is firmly in the negative. Feeling deflated, I approach the neighbouring shopkeeper. At first he also says no, but seeing the look of desperation on my face, relents. At the roadside immediately to the left of his shop is a small open bamboo platform with a sloping woven roof propped up by four thick canes. I watch, hardly daring to believe my good luck as he lays a bedroll across half of it then rigs up a mosquito net. Perfect! One of the immigration officers arrives and, using him as a translator, I offer payment for my open-air lodgings. All the man will accept is 50,000 Kip, approximately £2.50, even though I try to pay more. Exceedingly grateful for his kindness, I park the Matchless beside my makeshift refuge and unload some essentials into it, an upswell of elation engulfing me again as I test my bedroll for comfort.

Changing, a challenging task that involves publicly wriggling out of my bike pants, I wander over to the restaurant which is rapidly filling with immigration and customs staff. Many have just finished an interdepartmental football game and those that didn't play have shut up shop early and joined them at two long tables which completely fill the space. I sit at a small table outside, looking in and counting the diners. The last two stragglers arrive making a total of 44. I sit unattended, the two members of staff run off their feet laying heaped platters along the middle of each table while a couple of senior officers make long speeches. Judging from the pained expressions on most of the faces, they're exceedingly boring.

After a cheer and a relieved round of applause, a toast is made then everyone begins to tuck in. I'm still unable to catch the attention of a waiter but am unconcerned, content to watch the goings on in front of me. A young uniformed man gets out of his seat and invites me to join the party, a couple of his colleagues encouragingly waving me over at the same time. A spare chair is found and placed at the head of the table and as I'm sitting down, a plate and chopsticks appear in front of me.

"Eat, please eat," says one of the men and before I know it, an empty glass has been produced and beer sloshed into it.

There's tofu, a green spinach-like vegetable and my favourite, bamboo shoots packed with sticky rice. Each time my plate nears empty, more food's spooned onto it and I end up having to keep tabs on my beer intake because every time I put my glass down, it's topped to the brim. They're a splendid bunch of people, chatty and full of jokes, especially at the expense of immigration who lost 6-2! An hour and a half later, as the karaoke and serious drinking competitions commence, I give my sincere thanks and head for an early bed, collecting so many handshakes my right hand begins to ache.

Outside, I discover that the other half of my platform is now occupied by seven Vietnamese construction workers, all young men who've purchased two crates of beer and are sitting in a circle smoking, talking and drinking. I say hello, shake all their hands, climb under my mosquito net and, although it's not yet 9pm, fall straight to sleep. I'm jolted awake by two of the construction workers in a drunken brawl. The platform shakes as punches are thrown in every direction and one man falls backwards, landing on my netting which sags precariously. The shopkeeper's wife rushes over and screams, which stops them in their tracks. One of the protagonists walks into the road cradling his head and the other struts around, the unabated flow of adrenaline evident in his twitchy movements. A couple of the lads apologise to me and, in the face of a further tongue lashing from the woman, they all leave for wherever it is they sleep.

I manage to doze off again only to be woken by the untuneful wailing of the karaoke. Getting up, I cross the road to have a pee in the bushes, bombies very much on my mind as I step one pace out of sight. It's now 10.30pm and six people are left in the restaurant, stridently giving their all into the microphones. I laugh, shaking my head as I walk back towards my encampment. I'd imagined a very quiet night here, the gentle background sound of crickets for company, but as I settle down again, the disturbances fade into insignificance... all that matters is I've made it safely to the Vietnam border with both myself and my beloved motorcycle still intact.

Dramatic scenery in central Laos.

Day 81. Na Meo border, Laos, to Mai Chau, Vietnam. 77 miles.

At 3am I'm wrested out of my slumbers by the sharp sound of someone chopping wood. Switching on my torch, I see the shopkeeper axe a few more sticks then poke them into an open fire on which he's barbecuing thin slivers of meat. I roll over and, lullabied by the gentle quacking of nearby penned ducks, fall back to sleep. At 4am the shop lights go on followed by a flashing TV screen set loudly to a music channel. Laotian pop music booms unwelcomed through open shutters so I turn over and put a finger in my ear. At 5.20am, a rooster starts strutting his stuff, jubilantly proclaiming the dawn within inches of my head and by his third cock-a-doodle-doo, the other cockerels are wholeheartedly joining him. I decide to throw in the towel and drag myself out of bed. Once I've dressed and loaded the bike, I grab a basic breakfast at the restaurant and, with plenty of time to spare, coast down towards immigration.

Exiting Laos proves a streamlined process as two of the officers I met last night take me through the process. The customs staff, as I envisaged, have never seen a carnet so I again demonstrate how to fill one in. As before, I'm sure the rubber stamp they use is for a completely different purpose but who cares! My departure from Laos is rather an anticlimax as the rules don't allow me to ride the bike. Instead, signs instruct me to push her between two barriers and out of the compound. Once clear, I fire her up and motor the short distance into Vietnamese jurisdiction, heralded by a parade ground type square. Halting in front of an office block, all my concerns about getting a visa on arrival come flooding back and I nervously climb the steps to the immigration hall. I needn't have worried, the cheerful official rubbers my passport without even requiring me to fill in any paperwork. The stamp shows today's date, 29th November, and underneath it he handwrites the length of my permitted stay, 15 days.

My escort is nowhere to be seen and the immigration chap recommends I stay well clear of customs until he arrives, suggesting I get myself a drink at a small cafe on the opposite side of the square. I don't have any Vietnamese dong yet but the proprietor, who seats me at a wobbly outdoor table, says he's happy to accept payment in kip. A few minutes later I'm presented with a traditional Vietnamese coffee. This consists of a glass beaker on top of which sits a pressed aluminium funnel-shaped, gravity-fed distiller with coffee grinds packed in the bottom. Hot water is poured in at the top and I enjoy the distinct pleasure of watching the liquid slowly filtering through, dripping a lovely fresh brew into the glass. Life can be good!

As I finish the drink, a soldier accompanies a young man across the square. They stop at my table and he introduces me to Hung, a well groomed 20-year-old MotoTours Asia representative who carries a thick file of documents under his arm. In quick time, customs approve our entry and after I've ceremoniously signed some legally binding documents which, I'm gravely informed, forbid the sale of my motorcycle, I'm free to go. I've often anticipated what this moment would feel like... it's such an achievement for my old motorbike and the fulfilment of a personal ambition for me. Surprisingly, I don't experience the high I'd imagined. Perhaps that's because I'd felt such exultation when reaching the border yesterday or maybe it's simply down to the practicalities of a new day and a whopping 320km ride ahead. I am, however, filled with a deep sense of gratitude towards all the people in the UK who'd believed in me and made the journey possible.

Beneath the unmistakeable Vietnamese flag, a gold star on a bold red background, I pose for a couple of photos next to the Matchless then get ready to leave. It's a happy coincidence that MotoTours is the only company in Vietnam that uses Royal Enfields and I'm delighted that Hung will riding one to Hanoi.

"There are roadworks for the first fifty kilometres," he tells me whilst climbing aboard his bike.

Oh joy!

The first 10km are horrendous. I get stuck behind a column of construction trucks which kick up engulfing clouds of powdered chalk that float in suspension like thick smog. Within minutes, I'm completely white and coughing chestily. Once I finally succeed in overtaking them all, I begin to count down the kilometres to the good road. We slither over long sections of coarse gravel and slog through tracts of claggy clay, only occasionally getting up speed on short, newly completed strips. Fifty six kilometres pass yet we're still in the construction zone, with Hung well ahead and out of sight. Labouring through turgid mud, I take a detour around a section that bulldozers are grading and unexpectedly wedge the bike in a narrow, high-sided rut. There's no way forward so I try to push backwards, thinking I'll start again and build up more momentum. Looking down to check if the sumpguard has grounded, I'm dismayed to see my left trouser leg and boot are soaked in oil, jet black against the rest of my now mottled white clothing. Considerably more perturbing is the sight of the engine, which is also swathed in oil.

I kill it and within a minute, a roadworker appears, helping me haul the Matchless backwards out of the gloop. Together, we ease her slowly downhill to the bottom of the slope where I put her on the sidestand and frantically search for a cause, which doesn't take long. The copper oil pipe that feeds the rockers has a 10cm flexible rubber section to help it cope with engine vibrations. One of the two jubilee clips that secure it has chewed through the rubber and oil must have been pumping out of the open end for quite some time. Just a few more miles without oil circulating would have spelt disaster... getting stuck in that mud turned out to be extremely fortuitous!

Thankfully I have a spare pipe buried in my panniers and set to work replacing it. Although my pants and boot are quick to wipe, it takes a while to clean the residue of oil off the cylinder and crankcase, all the time my now returned escort hopping from one foot to the other in agitation.

"As I'm slower than you, why don't you follow me," I suggest.

"No, I am the guide, you must follow me... and go faster," comes his curt reply.

'This is not going well,' I think, in no small part because I'm used to travelling on my own at a pace that's mechanically sympathetic to my motorcycle, but also due to Hung's inflexibility and lack of empathy.

The good road that follows doesn't last long. Despite my protests, Hung, who's a bit of a boy racer, takes a cross country route that, after 25 km of narrow, rippled lanes, leads to another stretch of road construction. This lot lasts for over 40km and is seriously tough, with mile after mile of slimy red mud, water and slippery stone tracks that edge around half built bridges. Twice I show him my map, explaining that a longer route on good roads will be far faster for my rigid machine but he just doesn't get it, insisting that the shortest route is the most interesting, he's the guide and I must follow where he says. Vietnam is renowned for its excellent highways and my frustration builds as hour after hour we struggle along a track that's as bad as anything I've experienced to date. My plea that this cannot be the only workable option between a city of seven million and its nearest international border falls on deaf ears and I'm sorely tempted to let him ride off and go my own way.

Bumping cautiously along a stretch made up of pebbles sunk into sunbaked dirt, I watch Hung once more accelerate away in his well established pattern of racing in front then every so often waiting impatiently for me to catch up. In the distance I see him suddenly fall off, the Bullet spinning around on the ground underneath him. I quickly catch up and help him heave the bike upright. As well as broken indicators, the gear change pedal is flopping uselessly against the engine case, the Enfield's jammed in first gear and there's nothing we can do about it here. Thankfully, Hung's unhurt but we're forced to travel very slowly for the next 40 minutes, which in the circumstances is no bad thing. Eventually, we enter a drawn out village where there's a small roadside mechanic's shop. The Bullet's engine cases are removed and the problem immediately becomes apparent… the gear lever is connected to a selector fork by a rod which has detached with the impact of his fall. It's reconnected in a jiffy. I donate some silicone sealant as the mechanic has run out, then we sit and wait for half an hour while it cures.

As I get up to stretch my legs, two young tourists ride leisurely past on a pair of Honda Wave step-through scooters, their backpacks strapped onto the rear seats and covered in thick polythene sheeting. The man's wearing shorts, a long-sleeved T-shirt and a beanie crash helmet, the woman a pair of thin cotton leggings with similar upper attire.

"Look at them!" I exclaim.

"What?" Hung responds. "Oh them. You'll see lots of backpackers like that in Vietnam. Don't you know? It's a very popular way to tour here. There are always thousands of foreigners riding local motorbikes."

It's the first I've heard of this so I ask Hung for more information.

"They buy a cheap second-hand bike and usually ride it from Ho Chi Minh City to Hanoi, or vice versa, before putting an advert on the wall of a backpackers' hostel and selling it to another traveller. Many of the bikes have gone backwards and forwards between the two cities for years and regularly break down."

I comment on the pair's inappropriate riding gear, remarking that Hung himself wears protective clothing and a proper crash helmet.

"So many tourists have never ridden a motorbike before and there are a lot of accidents. You'll see them wearing nothing but shorts and sandals. It's a big problem."

There's no doubt in my mind that Hung's recent fall was caused by slick road tyres being used on slippery, off-road terrain, with a few too many revs thrown in. The two scooters I've just seen will undoubtedly have even less tread on their tyres and I can only hope the scantily dressed riders will be able to stay upright.

"They can take those bikes into Laos and Cambodia, but not into Thailand," Hung finishes.

A light goes on in my head. Only a handful of foreigners have crossed into Vietnam on their own motorcycles in recent years and I'd been surprised that nobody in Laos had found it unusual that I was riding there. Now I know why... they're used to seeing tourists crossing back and forth on their Vietnamese machines.

"Those two were on 110's" Hung adds while oil is being poured into the Bullet. "You will see many on 50cc bikes, which they ride as fast as they can, and even you will be able to overtake them!"

It's a revelation that adds a whole new element of interest to my journey here and I hope I'll have the chance to meet up with some of these newly initiated motorcycle travellers in the days to come.

Our mishaps have cost us over two hours and the appallingly slow road conditions have hampered progress by just as much. Thirty minutes before sunset, we emerge from backroads, joining a lovely wide strip of sumptuous asphalt. Hanoi is still more than 150km away and although that should be on better roads, the journey could easily take three more hours, possibly longer considering the city's notoriously congested streets. Tuyen, the man in charge at the MotoTours office in Hanoi, phones Hung and suggests that for our safety, we sleep at a homestay in a nearby village. At first I'm not keen but when I consider my escort's zestful riding style and the uncertain territory that lies before us, decide it's probably a wise proposition.

Following a chequered course along dykes that straddle a patchwork of paddies, we arrive at a quiet collection of houses, an authentic Vietnamese farming village except for one recent addition, the incongruous, ultra modern, neon-lit bar aimed at overnighting tourists. We park in the courtyard of a traditional stilt house where Hung is evidently known to the owner, a slender young woman with a tell-tale baby bump. She's incredibly welcoming, showing me where Hung and I will sleep in a large lounge on the first floor that's completely finished in polished timber. Two futons have been spread on the carpet with, suspended from the ceiling, voluminous mozzie nets that drape elegantly around them. Underneath the stilts is the guest bathroom and across the way, the kitchen. She tells me her mother will cook a meal of our choosing when she calls round later. It's idyllic. Just as I begin to unload the bike, Hung realises he's left his backpack at the mechanic's shop, a good half an hour ride away. Cursing, he climbs back on his Bullet and goes to retrieve it. I push the Matchless under cover and head for a shower.

Spick and span and savouring a mango juice, I get out my phone and make the most keenly anticipated calls of the expedition, letting Derek, Andy, and Andrew Engineering know that the Matchless has made it.

Before I set off for India in 2008, Alan said to me, "It's a long way to go for a curry Gordon." Ahead of this ride, he'd changed his message to, "It's a long way to go for vegetable spring rolls." Maybe, but the ones I'm served tonight are decidedly worth the wait. Hung hoes into his meal too, part way through taking a phonecall from his uncle who owns the tour company. He's reprimanded in no uncertain terms for making a poor choice of route, the vociferous, disembodied voice telling him there were three other roads we could have taken to Hanoi, all of them in much better shape. The lad looks somewhat battered when he eventually hangs up and I feel rather sorry for him. We share a couple of cold bottles of a local brew, *Bia Hà Nội,* Hanoi Beer, putting the challenges of the day behind us and looking forward to a better ride tomorrow.

Fellow travellers on the quiet Ho Chi Minh Road, Vietnam.

Day 82. Mai Chau to Hanoi. 93 miles.

The windows have been open all night allowing cooling flurries of air to penetrate the mosquito nets. Feeling well rested, I go downstairs to breakfast on banana pancakes and fresh coffee made by the grandmother of the household, a willowy lady with the most lovely smile and crinkly, kind eyes. After some Matchless maintenance I begin to load. The grandmother says goodbye as she leaves for work at the family's smallholding, a daily routine she shares with her husband and son. As she departs on her scooter, I take in her unorthodox crash helmet, a quintessentially Vietnamese cone shaped straw hat known hereabouts as a nón lá.

Negotiating our way across the rice paddies, I stop to take a photo, enjoying the peaceful sound of burbling water channeling along the irrigation ditches and the sight of small birds catching insects on the wing. Immediately ahead, the main road turns and begins to track up the side a towering mountain. Giving the Matchless a fistful of revs, I chase after Hung and begin to climb. As the acclivitous highway heads skywards, we enter the clouds, and still it keeps going. Near the summit, I overtake the spectre-like shape of a tourist on a moped, an enormous backpack strapped to his back. Wearing a pork-pie hat, a tan leather coat and smoking a cigarette while moving at not much more than walking pace, he looks a cool kind of dude who gives the appearance of not having a care in the world. We stop at a viewing point where no views are actually visible through the murk and I watch him freewheel past, his engine switched off. Close to his tail comes a group of five loaded scooters, each with a Vietnamese flags fluttering on the back. The riders haphazardly weave around, lightheartedly chatting to each other and seemingly oblivious to the threats posed by overtaking traffic.

"They are not foreigners, they're young Vietnamese tourists," Hung tells me before we set off again.

Back on the plains, the sun lies hidden but the humidity rises. We pass through a succession of towns where Hung slows right down, my sat nav showing he's doing 30 to 32kmph. When I try to overtake, he gets angry, waving me back. I call a halt and once more we have words.

"What's the speed limit in these towns please Hung?"

"Some are forty, some fifty," he replies.

"Then why are we travelling at thirty?"

"Because my speedometer is broken," he answers.

"It's a really bad speed for my engine, my gearing's different from yours and I'm either over-revving in second or labouring in third. Let me go ahead, then you can follow me at forty or whatever the signs say."

"No I cannot let you to go in front, it's not allowed in Vietnam."

It's the umpteenth time he's said no to me riding ahead. I'm going to be travelling on my own for the next ten days or so and I explain it'll be irrelevant who or what I'm in front of or behind then.

"No, I'm in front," he repeats, bringing an end to the matter.

As the kilometres pass, I reflect upon the many Hollywood films made about the Vietnam War: *Platoon; Apocalypse Now; Full Metal Jacket; Casualties of War* and *Good Morning Vietnam* springing to mind. An enduring feature of them all is their nostalgic soundtrack, each packed with iconic songs from the late 1960s and early 1970s. The works of *Creedence Clearwater Revival, The Doors, Martha & the Vandellas, Smokey Robinson and the Miracles, The Beach Boys, James Brown, Jefferson Airplane* and *Aretha Franklin* are all given a hearty airing... although in my enthusiasm I probably rake up a few songs that aren't actually from the movies.

Along the way, I see two-wheelers being used in the craziest of ways. One young boy sits between his mother's legs holding a bowl of food from which she's somehow managing to feed him as she pilots the bike. Families of three on one machine are ubiquitous and four far from rare, and in one case I see two children sound asleep, the boy's head flat against the tiny instrument panel and the girl sandwiched between her parents with her lolling head supported by her mother's hand. There are bikes massively overladen with crates of dogs, pigs or ducks and one that wobbles through the centre of a town carrying nine earthenware Alibaba type pots, each half a meter tall, that are tied onto a bizarre looking wooden frame. Another, a scooter loaded with hulking slabs of polystyrene, looks as if it might float into the air at any moment and in complete contrast, a battered old Minsk that leaves plumes of blue smoke in its wake is so burdened with crates of bottled water that it's little short of a miracle it doesn't implode. Talking or tapping on smartphones is endemic and I soon stop noticing.

With 60km left to go, I catch Hung up. He's waiting at a turn off but before I reach him, he guns his engine and sets off down a narrow lane that's in pretty poor nick. I bounce along after him, tooting my horn and waving which I continue doing for about a kilometre until he's nowhere to be seen. I'm certain he's spotted me in his mirrors so I pull over and wait. He finally comes back, a sour look on his face.

"What's the problem?" he asks.

"Why are we going on this smaller road?" I respond.

"Because this road is a shortcut and there is less traffic."

I remind him that over breakfast we agreed to follow the main road all the way.

"Yes, but I always go this way," he replies, sulkily.

"Are there any roadworks?"

He looks uncomfortable and mumbles,

"Yes."

"I'm sorry Hung. Go this way if you want but I'm heading back to the main road. I have the address of your office and I'll meet you there."

Peeved and silent, he restarts his engine and rides back to where we turned off, then, without pausing, turns straight onto the Hanoi highway. I must be his nightmare customer!

I've read a couple of online reports that describe Hanoi's traffic as bedlam so as we approach I steel myself for the worst. The final 25km run to its centre becomes progressively congested and once we're in the city proper, we're mired in two wheelers, hundreds at a time in any direction. It doesn't take long to grasp the unwritten rule. I am responsible for everything in front of me and no matter how stupid, inconsiderate or downright dangerous others might be... if they're in front of me and I hit them, it's my fault. What happens behind me is someone else's problem! The challenge of negotiating the madness turns out to be a thoroughly enjoyable one and I find myself roaring with laughter at the absurdity of some of the riders' antics. The Matchless does brilliantly, sitting with her engine ticking over for minutes on end as the sheer volume of bikes sometimes means we're stuck at traffic lights for two changes in a row.

Unsurprisingly, Hung's almost impossible to follow, though his bright green backpack gives me an intermittent pointer amidst the multitude of riders. I keep going straight, eventually finding him at the roadside where he's looking back, trying to pick me out. Each time he spots me, he zips off again, weaving around slower bikes, dodging inbetween buses, undercutting cars then sprinting through lights just as they change. He doesn't have 'Racing Boy' stickers on his crash helmet for nothing! I put his strange insistence to always be in the lead out of my mind and concentrate wholly on safety.

The MotoTours offices are in a quiet narrow street, the buildings crowding in from both sides. Tuyen, in his mid-20s with shoulder length black hair, bounds down the stairs and warmly shakes my hand. He opens broad doors and together we wheel the Matchless through, parking her alongside an ensemble of seven Royal Enfields. As soon as I've taken my riding gear off, we head across the road to a small cafe. Tuan, the company's founder and Hung's uncle, joins us for coffee, telling me about the origins of their business which go right back to the formative years of tourism in Vietnam and the tours they do today, many of which are along jungle trails on Honda dirt bikes. They chose Royal Enfields as an alternative touring machine because of the bike's unique heritage and it has worked out well for them, with many groups of foreign visitors booking a tour simply for the experience of riding a Bullet here.

Tuyen suggests I leave the Matchless with them overnight as my hotel has no off road parking, which is an excellent idea. So far I've only paid a deposit for their services so Hung is tasked with showing me to my hotel before taking me to a money changer. We nip along a series of back streets on his scooter then, after checking in and dropping off my bag, ride to a shop that does foreign exchange. I'm not happy with the rate they offer as it's far worse than what I've seen online so, much to Hung's chagrin, begin walking towards a nearby busy tourist district to find an alternative. In the third shop I get an excellent rate, walking out with twenty two million dong stashed in various pockets, a multi-millionaire... but not for long! Back at my hotel, sitting in a corner of reception, I count most of it into Hung's hands then we say goodbye. We've crossed swords so many times over the last couple of days and I'm happy and relieved to be free again.

When I first visited Hanoi in 1995, the streets were jammed full of bicycles that flowed, almost as one, redolent of a large crowd pouring out of a football ground except on two wheels. My next visit wasn't until 2004, by which time motorcycles outnumbered them, but not by much. In the evening, I meet Tuyen and his quiet girlfriend Nga for a couple of *Tiger Beers* at a pavement bar. I remark on these changes to Tuyen, asking him how he defines himself as a biker in a country of 90 million people and 37 million motorbikes.

"To the Vietnamese, riding your motorbike or scooter is like eating or like drinking water. You don't consider it anything special... most adults do it every day without thinking. It's not the bike I choose to ride or the clothes I wear that define me, the only thing that sets me apart as a biker is that I do long distance touring, because just about everyone else only uses theirs for short runs or work," he explains.

The area we're in is crammed full of tourists, hundreds of them sitting in rows on tiny footstools that line the roadsides, drinking, using their phones and people-watching. The noise of their chatter reminds me of a buzzing beehive.

"But look more closely," says Tuyen. "You will see a large number of Vietnamese amongst them. This area has become a fashionable place to hang out for young Hanoi people as they like the association with foreign visitors... they call it International Corner."

He's right, the more I look, the more Vietnamese faces I can see.

"The same thing's starting to happen with motorcycle touring. Because so many foreign backpackers ride the length of Vietnam, it's become cool for groups of Vietnamese friends to do similar tours in their holidays, but of course they don't have to sell their scooters afterwards."

I tell him about the group I saw yesterday.

"Exactly. They nearly always have our flag flying on the back of their bikes!"

I ask why he thinks riding between Saigon and Hanoi has grown into such a phenomenon, despite the concomitant risks.

"Top Gear!" he exclaims. "Quite a few intrepid backpackers did it before 2008 but once Clarkson, Hammond and May had travelled from Saigon to Hạ Long Bay on crappy old bikes, the concept went global and now it's on many people's bucket list."

Before we say goodnight, we arrange to meet in the morning for a farewell coffee, at which time Tuyen promises to draw me a map of the easiest route out of the city. I head back to the hotel but can't settle in bed, my mind too stimulated by the prospect of the long ride south, so I get up and put on my clothes. Wandering the quietening streets, I absorb the atmosphere and attempt, unsuccessfully, to recognise buildings or features from my previous visits. I eventually return to my room, the kaleidoscopic thoughts settled and my mind much calmer.

Day 83. Hanoi to Thai Hua. 171 miles.

Beginning the day without the Matchless close by feels decidedly odd. Following a quick breakfast, I carry my riding gear and clothes bag downstairs then ask the receptionist to call me a taxi. After all the miles travelling here, it's quite strange to climb into its back seat and passively watch the roads and traffic. Tuyen is awaiting my arrival and watches with interest as I go through the preparations for today's ride which include tensioning the loose dynamo chain and topping up the oil. When my bags are loaded, we wander across the street for a final coffee.

As promised, Tuyen draws a sketch map of my route out of the city. I work through it with him, memorising the turns: first left, first right, right again after three sets of traffic lights, fork onto highway, 30km later go left onto the Ho Chi Minh Road, which he writes onto a separate piece of paper as 'Đường Hồ Chí Minh'. Whilst we're talking, the cafe owner, a slight, grey-haired man, passes our table, a smartphone in his hand. Hanging along the front of the cafe is a chain of ornate birdcages containing delicate, chirping songbirds. Keeping these little feathered creatures is a longstanding pastime in Hanoi, many people actually taking their caged pets to parks where they can meet up with others. These excursions are especially important for young birds as it gives them the chance to learn songs from older birds, however, the cafe owner has brought a 21st Century invention to bear on this process. Holding his phone high, he uses an app to play a recording first to one species of bird, then, selecting a different recording, to another. It's the loveliest use of technology I've witnessed, though slightly marred by the birds' unnatural and imposed captivity.

I wheel the Matchless out of the entranceway and start her up. It's only been 20 hours since I last rode my beloved motorcycle but the sound of her engine and exhaust sends a shiver down my spine and I'm overjoyed to be reunited. With a shake of his hand I say farewell to Tuyen and start putting into practice the memorised sequence of turns. The first two take place on quiet backstreets but the next leads onto a heaving main road. Soon we're flowing along a major route that heads west then forks towards the main southbound highway, although not fully onto it. On the other side of a barrier, sporadic cars, buses and trucks speed along pristine concrete. The two-wheelers remain confined within two separate, and infinitely busier, lanes that run parallel to them. As Hanoi's suburbs thin, giant dusty concrete factories start to appear, their smoking chimneys casting a sickly pallor over the surrounding land. After 30km I come to a rather confusing intersection so stop in front of a roadside trader to ask directions. Predictably, my pronunciation of 'Doung Ho Chi Minh' flops woefully and I'm glad to have Tuyen's piece of paper at hand. I present it and get an instant response, including lots of pointing to the left. The problem is, there's no left turn so I head right instead, make a convoluted about-turn at a set of traffic lights, then finally join the Ho Chi Minh Road.

Ahead of me lie three choices of route. The Ho Chi Minh Road takes an inland course between Hanoi and Ho Chi Minh City, which was formerly known as Saigon. It passes through many rural areas and National Parks and much of it has recently been re-tarred. It's also an interesting route as certain sections of it were built upon stretches of the fabled Ho Chi Minh Trail, which was a network of footpaths, lanes, jungle trails and mountain tracks initially used by the Viet Minh during the First Indochina War. Much of the original trail is in Laos and some even cuts through Cambodia, travelling from north to south in vast, thinly populated regions of thick jungle and rainforest as well as over the Annamite mountains. The National Front for the Liberation of Vietnam, commonly referred to as the Vietcong, and the People's Army of Vietnam (PAVN) employed it extensively throughout the Vietnam War to secretly move troops and supplies. Inevitably, it was heavily bombed by American planes.

My second option is to attempt to follow as much as possible of this wartime trail. Maps are available that show which paths and tracks to take although many have, over the years, become impassable, assimilated back into wild jungle. To do this route justice, however, I would need at least twice as much time and Vietnamese entry restrictions would make it impossible to cross backwards and forwards into Laos on my imported bike. Consequently, it'd mean buying or renting a local one, preferably a dirt bike as the southern rainy season has only just ended and many trails will be muddy. The third alternative is to follow National Route 1A, the main trans Vietnam highway that hugs the coast, calling in at many of the country's major cities. Beginning at the Chinese border in the north and continuing all the way to Năm Căn at the southern tip of the country, some 350km south of Ho Chi Minh City, it's mostly a dual carriageway and is extremely busy with trucks and cars.

In light of a long conversation with Tuyen, my final decision is to follow the Ho Chi Minh Road south for roughly 600km then head to the coast, taking National Route 1A the remainder of the way to Saigon.

After a petrol stop, I settle into some steady riding. At first there's a mixed bag of traffic but within an hour, having passed through a couple of small towns, it thins and the roadsides become lined with sugarcane and rice. Some of the paddies are deeply flooded and as we cruise along, my attention's caught by the sight of a herd of giant water buffalo covered in slimy mud heaving themselves out of the water and up onto one of the dividing banks. Soon after, I spot a shady rest stop at the far side of a village and decide to let the Matchless cool and grab some lunch. The only food available is freshly baked baguettes. I buy one but leave it sitting on my table whilst working my way through a much needed iced drink. A small bus pulls in, its dozen or so passengers clambering off and buying up the remaining bread. As one of the cafe workers sets to washing the bus, its driver enjoys a cigarette, walking up and down the road to stretch his legs. A short time later, he comes over, has a brief conversation about my bike then disappears back onto the bus. Once all its passengers have boarded, the driver reemerges carrying a couple of bananas which he puts on the table in front of me, pointing towards my bread. It's a unexpected gift and after thanking him profusely, I make myself a huge banana sandwich.

From here on, my travelling companions are scooters, mostly ridden by women or teenagers, and a seemingly endless stream of cyclists. Oxen drawn carts are common too, some steered by men dressed characterfully in olive green uniforms with matching coloured pith helmets, a throwback to the helmets worn by the Viet Minh and the PAVN, which in turn were copied from those worn by French colonists. The cyclists and pedestrians are the most friendly, many giving me waves and sometimes shouting greetings as I ride past. The Matchless, for once, is the fastest machine on the road and I have to reign in her power as I approach other two-wheelers from behind due to the lackadaisical riding habits of their owners, which mostly involve weaving across the road while using their phones or chitchatting to friends on nearby bikes. From time to time, small karsts appear in the surrounding countryside, all of them showing much more exposed limestone than those previously seen in Laos. I stop for another drink opposite a particularly splendid one and, in need of a sugar boost, survey the cafe's counter display, settling for a slab of compressed sesame toffee that does its level best to remove all my fillings in one hit.

An hour before nightfall, I approach a township that my map indicates as being quite substantial. Although the Ho Chi Minh Road is supposed to run straight through it, when I get there I find only a closed-down business premises, a couple of houses and a bus stop. Two school girls sit nearby on a parked scooter so I ask them where I can find Thai Hua. They point down a dirt track that turns off to the right, telling me it's a few kilometres along it. Setting off, I bounce over hardpacked ruts for 10 minutes, riding on top of a steep embankment with paddies on either side. Eventually, I arrive at an intersection encircled by a cluster of buildings and needing a hotel, stop to pick the brains of a group of people queuing beside a vegetable stall. In unison, they point down the track I've just travelled along and indicate I should then turn south. After kangarooing my way back, I regain the Ho Chi Minh Road, turn right and in less than half a kilometre, pull up outside of a large roadside hotel... needless to say, it was blatantly visible when I asked the two girls directions to Thai Hua!

A muscular young man wearing a singlet and jeans comes to the reception desk. His arms and shoulders are covered in dramatic, almost intimidating, dragon tattoos but his demeanour and voice are genteel and soft. Under his guidance, I chain my bike to his scooter then head to my room, a strange set up as there's no glass in the window that opens into the corridor. Instead, it's protected by stout wooden staircase balusters and reminds me of a prison cell! His sister, who has a ponytail the length of her back, comes to check everything's okay then tells me there's a restaurant by the roadside just 15 minutes walk away if I'm hungry. When am I not?

There's no moon tonight and I set off down the highway on foot, the only visible light emanating from my torch and the coruscating stars, the broad, arcing smudge of the Milky Way running at right angles across my path. After ten minutes, I hear the deep, throaty sound of an approaching vehicle's engine. It sounds like a bulldozer but all I can see heading towards me is a tiny bobbing torch-like beam approximately 2m off the ground. Stepping onto the grass verge, I discern the outline of a home-made tractor as it passes, its diesel generator positioned above go-kart like front wheels. The vehicle's sole lighting is the weak headtorch strapped around its driver's forehead... so much for health and safety!

Three side-by-side restaurants come into view, all of them family homes where food is offered in an extended, open dining area at the front. The first two don't have any guests but the third hosts two truckers who watch TV while they eat. Adhering to the rule of thumb that the most popular restaurants are generally the best, I plump for it. The elderly couple whose home it is are completely baffled by my demonstrative attempts to communicate with them. Eventually, they make a phone call to their daughter who can speak a little English and she relays my order of egg fried rice to her parents. Sitting down, I begin to wait. Half an hour passes before my meal is brought, a bowl of plain rice, a greasy fried egg and a plate of steamed spinach! The man looks apologetic but it's all he can offer so, dousing everything in soy sauce and chillies, I force it down.

Across the road is a small wooden shack lit by a single light bulb where a woman and her two children live. On a table slightly to one side are piled green skinned oranges. They're obviously not anticipating any passing trade at this time of day and become very excited when I appear out of the dark and buy a kilo of fruit. Back in my room, I supplement the meagre meal with the surprisingly sweet oranges followed by some more of the chewy sesame block I bought in the afternoon and turn in, hoping there's better cuisine to come!

Day 84. Thai Hua to Son Trach. 199 miles.

This morning I decide it's time to replace the rear chain with my spare. It's endured almost 10,000 miles of some pretty horrendous conditions and is now showing signs of wear. I've used a *Tutoro* automatic oiler throughout the ride which has undoubtedly contributed to the chain's long life. In yesterday's dusty conditions, I had it set at a fast drip rate and as a result the chain is thoroughly soaked in oil, making removing it without gloves a messy job. With the new one on, I spend five minutes cleaning my hands before loading up and getting underway. The arresting sight of fields vibrantly rippling with two metre high sunflowers soon draws me to a halt. It seems to be something of a local attraction as many cars and scooters have pulled over to admire the swaying, yellow heads. I join them, snapping photos of the Matchless against the cheery backdrop until a policeman blows his whistle and tells me in no uncertain terms to move on. I beat a hasty retreat.

We soon enter a remote region, the road rising and falling, kilometre after kilometre. Here even the bicycles and scooters allay and for the first time in days, I enjoy a feeling of isolation. The occasional village we motor through has several dwellings with cafe signs prominently displayed outside, but none are open or even appear to have tables and facilities. After seeing a dozen such places, I begin to wonder if there's some kind of government subsidy for having a cafe, even if it never opens. This sets me thinking about communism in Vietnam. It is, after all, supposed to be a single party, marxist-style communist state yet private enterprise and entrepreneurialism undoubtedly thrive everywhere. I don't have the perspicacity into how it pans out so resolve to try to get some clarification from any locals I meet.

I come upon a large open fronted shop which at first glance appears to sell a range of farming supplies. Several tables and seats occupy its entrance so I slow, turn around and go to see if I can get a coffee. Two men silently regard my approach and when I greet them and make gestures for food and drink, one gets up, saunters to a fridge and brings me a bottle of beer, evidently all they have. Thanking them, I pass on their kind offer and return to the Matchless where I'm not quite fast enough to prevent a dog from cocking his leg and peeing down the front wheel! The two men, spotting the event, fall about laughing... the ignominy!

140km after setting off, I finally come to a reasonably sized town. By now I'm hungry and much in need of a break, so I turn off the Ho Chi Minh Road and head towards its centre. A lengthy reconnoitre draws a blank so, thwarted and hungry, I return back to the highway. No further habitation's evident during the next hour and I continue to ride through gently rolling, lush countryside. Casually checking my satnav, I see I've ridden almost 200km without letting the Matchless properly cool and experience the first twangs of concern... it's not just me that needs a break. Ten minutes later, as we begin to ascend a small hill, I sense a momentary loss of power. It's little more than a blip and could easily be caused by something in the petrol or even a slight blockage in the air filter but I can't take the risk so cut the engine and coast to a halt.

360

Parking at the optimal angle to take advantage of the lightest of breezes, I sit on a barrier, my head shaded by the leaves of an overhanging tree and my legs stretched out in the blazing sun. After a couple of minutes a scooter pulls up and its rider dismounts, quickly unstrapping a petrol powered strimmer off the side of the bike then filling it with fuel from a can. He walks over to where I'm sitting, nods, pulls a drawcord and, engine buzzing noisily, begins cutting back the roadside grass little more than a metre away from me. I get up and go for a stroll, incredulous that even here, out in the wilds with not a sign of civilization for miles, Sod's law still prevails.

I give it half an hour and set off again, nervously anticipating a reemergence of the glitch. Gradually, when all's plainly hunky dory, I relax back into the groove of riding, enjoying travelling through the tranquil, leafy countryside. 40km later I halt for another break, and flumping down on the edge of a concrete drainage ditch, gobble the last of my oranges and Bagan peanuts. Nothing moves for fifteen minutes save for a couple of girls who cycle past, both wearing light blue, surgical face masks. It's an unusual sight to the European eye but common practice in Asia when people think they are ill or have a cold, a wise courtesy to prevent spreading their infection to others.

Underway again, the scenery begins to change as agriculture succumbs to the wilds of forest and spectacular karsts. Around 4pm, I decide I need to give the Matchless another cooling halt. Passing through an area overgrown with jungle, I randomly select a place to pull over, put the bike on her side stand and plant my bottom on a large stone. As I'm relaxing, I notice movement a little further along the road so wander down to see what's happening.

I arrive at a village made up of small wooden shacks partly hidden by trees and creepers. Two women and a boy are standing in front of a small store with a fold down front flap that's a couple of metres square. Inside, a girl in her school uniform sits at a round plastic table concentrating on her maths homework. Her mother, the proprietress, is talking with the two women while they wait for a bus, which duly arrives. The shop's supplies are spartan, a few packets of biscuits, some confectionery, pens, exercise books and a couple of toys. I ask for a drink of Coke. The lady opens the lid of her fridge, a chilly bin which sits on the floor, to give me the choice from her modest selection of three small bottles of water and two cartons of a brightly coloured purple liquid. I opt for H2O and a packet of biscuits. The woman appears very pleased to have picked up some unexpected business and her daughter, looking up from her books, says,

"Hi... sorry, bye," when I say thanks to them before returning to the bike.

As we continue, pasture appears with increasing frequency and, with an hour to go until sunset, the road starts to fill with people herding their animals. One young woman wearing a nón lá drives a golden brown calf down the centre of the road with a stick while carrying two heavy baskets on a wooden yolk that rhythmically bounces on her shoulders. Set against a backdrop of emerald paddies and limestone cliffs, it'd be hard to find a more poetic or stereotypical image of rural Vietnam. With 45km to go to our destination, we enter Phong Nha-ke Bang National Park, a UNESCO World Heritage site that's the second largest karst region on earth and famous for its vast cave and grotto systems. The serpentine road immediately begins to climb, winding round ever tightening curves whilst affording the most fantastic views of towering chalk outcrops. Dramatically silhouetted against the now iridescent sky, I'm compelled to stop and appreciate them, despite the time pressure to get to a town before dark.

After bombing down the other side of the hill, I reach the valley floor and stop to swap to nighttime goggles and switch on my lights. Twenty minutes later, a huge marquee comes into view. Generators provide power for lighting and loud music, which booms from within its vinyl walls. A party's in full swing and dozens of celebrants have spilled out onto the roadside in their Sunday best, drinking, talking and in some cases, dancing. I pause to ask where I'll find a hotel and am immediately swamped by jolly partygoers, many of them slightly drunk. Finally, a sober male voice takes charge, shouting above the din that I need to go 10km further. By now, there's not a glimmer of daylight left but my luck's in... a large lorry trundles past, lighting the way ahead and I quickly set off behind it, matching its pace and using it for protection from wandering animals and unlit tractors. We eventually come to a junction where, to the right and over a bridge, the first bright lights of a township come into view. Suspended near the summit of a rocky, vertical karst is an illuminated string of tall white letters which proclaim Phong Nha-ke Bang, my refuge for the night.

I ride slowly along the town's main drag, overwhelmed by the number of backpackers' hostels, hotels, cafes, restaurants, moneychangers and tour operator outfits that hem both sides of the street. At the far end there's the large *Heritage By Night* hotel, smartly set back within its own car park. A cut above most of the other establishments, I decide a bit of a splurge is on the cards and pull in. Walking up the steps to reception, I'm surprised to be greeted by a young Dutchman who's employed as assistant manager. He shows me to a huge modern room with two double beds and a separate shower that by itself is larger than the bedroom I slept in yesterday. It's the equivalent of £12 per night, a no-brainer.

Parked, unloaded and clean, I set off to get something to eat. Some of the bars and restaurants are full to overflowing but there's a new pizzeria in town which boasts a wood-fired clay oven, a sure winner for me. The only downside to eating at this stylish venue is that just one pizza can be cooked at a time. I order mine and move into the back room which is set up with reclining chairs, coffee tables and a lounge bar. From an eclectic drinks menu, I order a mango, lime and dragonfruit juice from the owner, a young American lady who encourages me to sit back, listen to music and relax while I wait for my food.

As I watch the woman at work, I consider all the people who've visited South East Asia, especially Thailand, as holidaymakers and have returned to live there, in many cases setting up tourist orientated businesses. They must face many unforeseen challenges, especially overcoming the legalities of starting a new venture in a land with different laws, regulations and language, but I can fully understand their motivation... work must be so much more enjoyable when you're living in paradise.

Day 85. Son Trach to Huế. 138 miles.

The highway splits in two at Phong Nha-Ke Bang National Park, branching into the the Đường Hồ Chí Minh Đông (East) and Đường Hồ Chí Minh Tây (West). The latter takes a remote, mountainous route with barely any habitation and not a whiff of petrol to be found on the 220km transit to the town of Khe Sanh and its Vietnam War US combat base, which is now a museum. It's supposed to be a stunningly beautiful journey, though slow and rough going. The former is in superior condition, curving east towards the coast then paralleling National Route 1A. I choose the eastern road, immensely keen to travel beside the South China Sea. Today's target is the former Vietnamese capital city of Huế, a notorious battleground during the Vietnam War. It was once the seat of power of Nguyen Dynasty emperors and parts of their Imperial Palace still survive.

To my surprise, the road's largely devoid of cars and two-wheelers as it passes through serene farmland and sleepy villages. The most exciting moment occurs when, stopping for petrol, I see the station sells 20/50 oil... a telling revelation of my priorities! However, a much more adrenaline pumping incident happens half an hour later when a couple of buffalo crash through the undergrowth and lurch onto the road, stumbling to their feet just a few metres ahead of me. Swerving on reflex, I watch in my mirrors as they disappear into the bushes on the other side of the highway, my heart still pounding. Carefully checking coordinates on my satnav and keeping a close eye on the printed map, I stop when we reach 17° North, the 17th parallel. It was here that the *Vietnamese Demilitarized Zone* (DMZ) was established at the end of the First Indochina War. Taking the form of a strip of land a couple of kilometres wide that stretched across the full width of the country, it was an area of demarcation between The Democratic Republic of Vietnam (North Vietnam) and the Republic of Vietnam (South Vietnam) and was heavily bombed during the Vietnam War. Visitors are not encouraged to go wandering willy-nilly in this region as enormous quantities of unexploded ordinance remain uncleared.

The Matchless steadfastly puts kilometre after kilometre behind us and just south of the city of Dong Ha, with only 65km left to travel to our destination, we swing onto the trans-Vietnam highway. My survival instincts switch to red alert in anticipation but to my amazement, rather than mayhem I find relative decorum. The trucks sedately travel exclusively in a long, strung-out chain in the outside lane and along with sporadic cars, I vigilantly undertake them. Two-wheelers occupy the hard shoulder but the risks of collision with parked vehicles, bicycles coming the other way and scooter riders travelling with their brains in neutral are just too high for me to take.

Passing through a small town, I slow to the speed limit of 40kmph. Just ahead I see a policeman step out from behind his car and flag down a young man on a bike whom I assume is going too fast. At the last moment, the rider accelerates and weaves around the policeman who spins around and throws his baton. It lands squarely in the middle of the lad's back and bounces off but he continues without even turning round to look. I slow even further, not wanting in any way to antagonise this particular policeman but, to my delight, as I pass he gives me a beaming smile then salutes!

Huế has a population of around 350,000 and flanks both sides of the wonderfully named Perfume River. The highway leads to the modern Da Vien bridge which I cross. Working from my memory of a map I'd viewed online last night, I track north east for a kilometre to an area where all the hotels and restaurants are located. The choice of accommodation is mind boggling and I ride several times around large city blocks trying to decide which might be the most suitable. On my third pass of a tall hotel that's tightly packed in amongst several others, I stop to talk with a tourist who's sitting outside smoking a cigarette.

"There's no parking," he says, "but I've been here for two months now. The boys that run the place are great and I'm sure they'll find somewhere to put your bike."

After settling the Matchless onto her stand, I join the man at his table. He tells me he's from Finland and is enjoying an extended stay here because his girlfriend, also Finnish, is taking a three month study course in the city. At this point, a couple of young Vietnamese men come out of the hotel and we set to discussing quarters for my bike.

"Leave it outside now," one says, "then in the evening we can pull it into the lobby. It will be perfectly safe."

Later, chatting to the Finn and drinking a coffee, I get some maintenance out of the way so that I'm free to explore the citadel in the morning. There are quite a few jobs that need doing, including re-polishing the contact breakers and changing the air filter. I also notice that the oil level is dropping with increasing regularity which confirms the suspicion I've had that the engine's burning oil. It also looks and smells contaminated and I feel certain a rebore will be on the cards when I get the bike back to the UK. For now, an oil change seems prudent. When all's done, I secure her with the chain and cover her up.

An hour before sunset, I walk along the riverbank, treating myself to a mango ice cream on the way. There are several luxury international hotels nearby, all with a line of waiting trishaws, locally known as cyclos, parked in their driveways. Outside one, about 20 Korean tourists all sit on upholstered bench seats ahead of their individual cyclo drivers. Several of the passengers are grossly overweight and as they set off down the road, I can see their wiry, featherweight riders struggling to get the pedals moving, let alone steer the contraptions which appear as manoeuverable as Victorian perambulators. A couple of the older cyclo drivers look as though they're about to expire but somehow they keep going, soon swallowed up in swelling crowds of scooters.

As daylight fades, I approach the Truong Tien Bridge, a 115 year old iron bridge with a superstructure of six large curving bowstrings. Stopping at its southern end, I gaze in awe at the traffic that's crossing... there are no cars at all, simply thousands upon thousands of motorbikes and scooters. Climbing on top of a buttress, I sit with my feet dangling over the edge and take in the sight of the wall-to-wall two-wheelers moving as one in an unending, fluid motion that oozes slowly over the bridge.

When it's fully dark, I jump down and begin to walk back through a riverside park. A young woman steps forward and asks if I speak English. Looking around, I see several others of a similar age engaged in exactly the same activity. Slightly cautious about her motives, I nod.

"I am a medical student," she says by way of explanation. "And I need to practice English. Can I talk with you please?"

She looks and sounds genuine so I agree, chatting for ten minutes about life in the UK and her studies and aspirations.

"When I qualify as a doctor, I want to work in America," she tells me.

I've been itching to ask someone about Vietnam and communism but when I grab the opportunity, she looks perplexed and twice evades the question.

"How often do you come here to do this?" I ask.

"Most nights. I enjoy talking to tourists, they are always relaxed and friendly."

Naturally... they're all on holiday!

"Are there no male medical students?" I eventually ask, noticing that everyone who's collared a passing tourist is female.

"Yes, but they're either too lazy to come or prefer to go out drinking with their friends instead of learning English."

It sounds a perfectly plausible answer. A fellow student comes to join her and after a couple more minutes, tummy rumbling, I make my excuses. They both thank me for my time whilst politely shaking my hand and say good night.

Heading back to the nexus of the tourist quarter, I'm overwhelmed by the number of restaurants to choose from. Some employ attractive young women to stand on the pavement, handing out menus and trying to engage people in conversation. I pass these by, settling instead for a restaurant that advertises a free dessert of fresh passionfruit with each main course ordered. Watching the flocks of visitors walk past, I wonder how much of an impact tourism has had on the country in recent years. Back in my room, I do a bit of online research. Nearly eight million tourists came here last year and the largest number, I'm surprised to see, were from China. More critically, the influx of visitors, and the infrastructure that has developed around them, has shifted Vietnam's economy from one that's agrarian to one based more on service industries. It's such an exquisitely beautiful and culturally vibrant place that I only hope, as visitor numbers continue to rise, the essence of Vietnam, everything which makes it so special and attracts travellers in the first place, doesn't become totally consumed and irrevocably distorted.

Day 86. Huế to Hoi An. 86 miles.

When I get up, it turns out there's a powercut and, somewhat befuddled, I dress by torchlight. Breakfast is served in the hotel lobby and I stumble downstairs just in time to roll the bike outside so that the tables can be put out and laid. As soon as I've eaten, I flag down a cab and set off for The Citadel, the colossal fortification which encompasses the former imperial city. Surrounded by a moat and immense ramparts, the restored remnants include long, tile-roofed open-sided buildings containing photographs and sketches from its royal past. There are temples, beautifully embellished gateways and gardens, walkways bordered by large ornamental urns as well as Thai Hoa Palace and the gloriously named Hall of Supreme Harmony. Entrance to the area known as The Forbidden Purple City, so named as the emperor was the only man who could enter it, is marked by a tall, cast iron gate with delicately painted panels running along its top. During the Nguyễn dynasty, any man who dared to go beyond this threshold was sentenced to death... the only people allowed to visit were empresses, servants, concubines and eunuchs of the court. During the Tet Offensive of January 1968, the Viet Cong and PAVN launched a nationwide attack on South Vietnamese and American forces. In Huế, the battle raged for a month and severe damage was caused to both the palace and the wider city.

Once I've viewed the main buildings and strolled through a couple of gardens, I decide to walk back to the hotel, absorbing as much of the city's ambience as possible in the half hour stroll. With the electricity still off, packing involves checking then double checking I've got everything by the rapidly dwindling light of my torch. Outside, just when I'm ready to leave, the Finnish guy I met yesterday arrives, plonking himself at the table directly behind my exhaust.

"I wouldn't sit there," I warn, "it might get a bit smoky."
He just smiles, waves his pack of cigarettes and replies,
"I don't think it can be any worse than these... anyway, I love the smell of napalm, I mean exhaust fumes, in the morning!"
We say goodbye and I set off, partly following directions given by the hotel staff and partly relying on my satnav. As it's not mapped for Vietnam, I set it to compass mode, something I often do when finding my way in and out of cities, and hey ho, before I know it, I've given voice to today's ditty, REM's 'Stand'.

"If you are confused, check with the sun
Carry a compass to help you along...
Stand in the place where you live
Now face North
Think about direction, wonder why you haven't before."
It stays with me for a long time, even when I join up with the National Highway.

After a while we come to a large hill where the road shrinks to single lane and is clogged with slow moving trucks and buses. Overtaking is touch-and-go due to the ever present threat of vehicles careering downhill but staying amongst the stop-starting traffic is mind numbing not to mention bad for the lungs. I take my chances, nipping in and out of the line when I dare, but it's far from enjoyable. Back on the plains, I pass a foreign couple riding a scooter. All they're wearing are t-shirts and shorts... they don't even have crash helmets, which is against the law. The highway's so empty I begin to wonder where all the heavy vehicles have gone. I soon find out... they're queued up on the next hill. A sinuous tailback of trucks nudges skywards, the narrow road they're on carved out of a bleak rock face. At the base of the hill are roadworks and as I approach, I watch a scooter nip through a gap between concrete blocks then continue along a totally empty and obviously new stretch of asphalt. On a hunch that he's taking a shortcut, I follow him. The deserted, dusty road curves round a bend, leading to a splendid new tunnel. Unlit, I can just make out the scooter's taillight so switch my lights on and follow him inside. A couple of minutes later, I emerge into bright sunshine, nip through another barrier, and gleefully rejoin the main highway having completely bypassed the jammed hill. Happy Days!

A small open-air restaurant sits just before a major fork in the road. Spotting two tourists at a table, and a nearby bike heavily weighed down with a pair of giant backpacks, I park up and go to say hello. Unfortunately, they're just about to leave. After establishing they're American and that the food is good, I take a seat and place an order while they pay their bill.

"Are you riding from Hanoi to Ho Chi Minh City?" I ask as they say goodbye.

"No, just from Huế to Hoi An today," one replies.

"Aren't you concerned about getting injured if you fall off?" I ask, pointing to their minimalist attire of t-shirts, shorts and open sandals.

"We're not committed like you," the taller one replies.

It's a strange adjective to use when it comes to safety and I'm quite baffled.

"Have you seen what road rash and skin grafts look like?" I say, immediately conscious that I probably sound self-righteous. "Even a short slide down the road at forty could see you in a Vietnamese hospital for a long time."

They both shrug and smile so I shake their hands and wish them well. I watch in amazement as they turn and mount their respective motorbikes, neither of which has any luggage. From another table, a Vietnamese man gets up and climbs aboard the scooter carrying their backpacks, nods at them and together all three set off. Guessing he's their guide, it's interesting to note that he, at least, has the good sense to wear a crash helmet.

The fork in the road quickly disappears into the Hải Vân Tunnel, a 6km long route that cuts beneath a spur of the Annamite mountains. Two-wheelers aren't allowed through it so I veer right, heading for the 21km Hải Vân Pass, which charmingly translates as 'ocean cloud pass'. As I begin to climb, the slopes teem with rich vegetation and wildflowers and from a motorcyclist's point of view, the winding strip of tar is rapturous to ride, turning back on itself several times as it scales the heights. Looking north from the summit, which stands at 486m, the panorama is sensational. A crystal lagoon is followed by a horseshoe bay beyond which an uninterrupted straight line of perfect white sand and calm turquoise ocean fade into the distant blurred horizon. At the start of the descent I come upon a group of a dozen or so well-tanned backpackers, each with their own local motorbike. They're parked up taking rounds of group photos. All adhere to the standard dress code of shorts and t-shirt with a marked absence of crash helmets. I wave but don't stop, rather concerned that I'm becoming a protective clothing elitist!

The descent is steep and twisting and I revel in the sensation of fresh sea air filling my lungs as I swoop round one bend after another. On the level again, I'm soon sucked into the heat of the city of Da Nang and near its widely dispersed centre, fail to find any signposts. I figure that as long as I keep the ocean to my left, I can't go wrong, but a roundabout with five exits and no clear sight of the sea completely throws me. After circuiting it twice, I pull up outside a shop and ask directions from a policeman who simply shrugs his shoulders and walks away. A student pulls up on a motorbike and asks if he can help. He speaks excellent English and soon directs me across the Han River and due south, paralleling the beach resorts around Non Nuoc, infamously known as *China Beach* during the Vietnam War.

The approach to Hoi An is on tight country lanes. The historic port's centre is suddenly upon us and at waterfront crossroads, I look left to restaurants and houses. To the right there's a street market where cone-hatted Vietnamese women sell fruit and vegetables and beyond that, gift shops piled high with T-shirts and souvenirs. Straight ahead is a narrow concrete bridge that passes over the shimmering waters of the Thu Bon River. I ride slowly over it, noting a rather posh looking resort hotel in well-tended grounds nestled on the far shore but beyond that, little else. The residential area soon thins out so I turn around, go back over the bridge and swing right but apart from more housing, there's little to be seen. Looping back, I try the opposite direction and beyond the market and souvenir sellers, find a long line of restaurants and bars but no hotels. The afternoon's stifling, the Matchless's temperature rising accordingly, and the huge number of tourists walking the streets belie the dearth of accommodation, begging the question... where are they all staying? Keen to make as much of what daylight remains, I head back over to the bridge and ride into the grounds of the resort hotel. The nightly rate of $40 is more than I was hoping to pay but the combination of safe parking, beautiful gardens, ritzy rooms and proximity to the river seduces me and I cough up.

Hoi An owes its backwater, old-world charm to the Thu Bon River silting up in the latter part of 19th Century. This prevented larger ships from reaching its docks, effectively stunting the town's growth and preserving its old centre as effectively as if it were submerged wholesale in aspic. Tightly packed with characterful Japanese merchants' dwellings, it remained unchanged until tourists began to arrive in the 1990s. Crossing the bridge on foot, I soon reach the quayside where long, flat-bottomed boats are being loaded with local workers heading home. Almost every one of them has a scooter or bicycle and the first boat is crammed full of them. This doesn't prevent more people from trying to squeeze theirs on board and as its engine note deepens and it prepares to depart, a motorcyclist frantically pushes his bike up a ramp as two youngsters heave their bicycles over the side and scramble on. I watch it chug away from the shoreline to be replaced within moments by another, the whole chaotic process starting all over again. The sun has now disappeared and as I look down the estuary from a small footbridge, the sky's turning feathery blue, edged by translucent yellow. On the far bank, an enterprising woman is selling small leaf boats with candles in them to two female tourists. With a sense of occasion, they ease them into the water and watch the tide carry them gently downstream towards the ocean.

I sit for a while watching the darkness creep in then, remembering I'm on a small island, set off on a circuitous walk accompanied by a knee-high dog that, pert tail trembling, keeps looking hopefully upwards for a treat. As I approach the footbridge from the opposite direction, I pass two stores that sell rice paper Chinese lanterns. They're all lit up, the shopfronts cascading with exquisite colours. Back over the bridge, I find a restaurant with a pavement table and as I eat, watch the throng of visitors walking past... in their thousands! Replete, I explore an inland area, arriving at the town's renowned covered bridge which was originally built in the 16th Century by the Japanese community to link up with the Chinese enclave. It's a solid, chunky, arched structure that's guarded by a pair of weathered monkey statues on one side and a similarly aged pair of dogs on the other. Only a few metres wide, it's dark and atmospheric inside but once I emerge from its western entrance, my eyes are assaulted by lines of brightly illuminated gift shops. I quickly turn around, heading back to a quieter quarter for a nightcap in one of the many bars that line the waterways then retreat to make the most of my sumptuous lodgings.

Trying to squeeze more bikes onto a packed ferry, Hoi An.

Day 87. Hoi An to Quy Nhon. 191 miles.

This morning's one of the few occasions I find it hard to motivate myself to get on the bike. The hotel's darned comfy and the surrounding port area so quaint and characterful that I dally, taking a leisurely stroll after an unhurried breakfast. Fortunately, the Matchless seems to be coping much better with eastern Vietnamese tarmac and there's little maintenance to do before we can hit the road. Crossing back over the river, we hang a left, soon exiting the town and following the banks of one of the many creeks that flow into Hoi An's estuary. Gradually narrowing, the road's little more than a lane by the time it reaches National Route 1A and isn't deemed significant enough to be worthy of a junction. Instead, it passes through a dark, concrete underpass then continues on to the west. Taking a nearby turn to the north, we ride a few kilometres, work round a succession of minor roads and finally join the highway.

It's appallingly busy and most motorcycle riders seem to have had the sense to avoid it. Coping with the trucks is manageable as they're all going slower than the Matchless and as before, most prefer the outside lane. The inter-city and tourist coaches and the cars, however, charge past at terrifying speeds. Just as I've tuned in to their pace and the general conditions, the driver of a black Nissan L200 that's heading up the northbound carriageway throws his pickup through a gap in the central reservation in a tyre-squealing U-turn. His window's down and our eyes meet but that doesn't stop him swinging round in front of me. All I can do is haul the brakes on and brace myself, screeching to a standstill as he unwaveringly completes his turn then slowly motors south. Fuming, I catch him up, giving him a piece of my mind through his open window. He gazes back, nonplussed, totally unmoved by the life-threatening situation he just put me through. A couple of minutes later he turns off and heads down a dusty farm track and I enter one of the many small towns scattered along the highway. Thankfully, traffic slows to a more sedentary pace and equilibrium is restored.

After another hour or so of full-on concentration, I spy a large restaurant and pull over for lunch. Ordering quickly, I sip an iced drink whilst waiting for a stir-fry to arrive. A young man enters, takes one look at me and heads straight to my table.

"Can I join you?" he asks.

"Absolutely... please..." I say, pointing to the seat opposite. Taking off his jacket, he plonks his crash helmet and daypack onto a spare chair.

"Where are you from?" I ask, assuming his answer will be one of Vietnam's major cities.

"Seoul," he replies. "Korea."

I'm flabbergasted and also secretly ashamed that I'd assumed he was Vietnamese purely because of his skin colour and facial features. Jon, it transpires, is a student who's just completed a three month placement in a Japanese IT company's offices in Ho Chi Minh City.

"For my vacation I'm riding from Hanoi to Ho Chi Minh on a motorbike but I was meant to do it more slowly on a bicycle. About a month ago, I was on the back of my friend's scooter and we were knocked off. I hurt my right leg and its not yet strong enough to pedal."

I ask him about his bike so he leads me outside and points to a decrepit old blue Yamaha two-stroke that wears the story of a hard life on its scratched, dented and rusty bodywork.

"I picked it up for $250 and so far, so good. It can only do 60kmph but to be honest, I'm too scared to go any faster, especially when I'm trying to navigate at the same time, which means holding my iPhone in my left hand!"

A warm, smiley chap, Jon's on a tight deadline to reach Ho Chi Minh City and his flight home.

"I'll need a couple of days to sell the bike and collect some of my things then I'm off... and my bike will probably be off as well, travelling back to Hanoi with another backpacker."

Whilst we eat, we talk about the challenges of Vietnam's roads, as well our destinations today which in my case I haven't yet decided upon. Like Jon, I'm heading to Nha Trang but as that's almost 550km from Hoi An, will need to stop somewhere midway. Jon has already settled on the city of Quy Nhon and, studying my map, it looks like a reasonable target for me too. We head outside again and wish each other good luck followed by shouts of,

"See you on the road."

I leave while Jon returns inside to send some texts home.

Well into the afternoon's long, straight, stretch, something suddenly feel wrong. The problem becomes clear when I pull over and inspect the bike. Two empty straps hang limply where the bag that contains the Matchless's cover should be. Hopping back on, I turn a tight circle and, grateful the traffic is lighter in this region, slowly backtrack, my wheels tight to the kerb as I search for the missing luggage. Nervously keeping one eye on oncoming vehicles, I feel a complete hypocrite having cursed so many other motorcyclists for doing this very same thing. However, from the other side of the carriageway it'd be completely impossible to spot the black bag amongst the long weedy grass, copious litter, abandoned tyres and string of workshops that border the road. After 3km, my nerves can't stand any more cars and buses bearing down on me so reluctantly call a halt and in a gap in the traffic, spin around once more. Scanning from left to right I retrace our route but the cover, I finally concede, is gone. When underneath it, my precious motorcycle became invisible and I rue its loss.

In the next hour, I stop at two small shops that re-cover scooter seats but neither has full bike covers and when I think about it more rationally, I realise that two-wheelers are so common in Vietnam nobody bothers to cover them for security or weather protection. I need to find an alternative but for now, refocus my mind on riding safely. The highway's been as smooth as a billiard table for hundreds of kilometres but out of the blue, we hit an unseen ripple in the concrete. An almighty graunching sound accompanied by an odd sensation from my seat warns me there's a problem and thinking I've broken yet another saddle mattress spring, I pull over to take a look. When I try to lift one side of the seat cover up, the saddle itself rises into the air accompanied by a repeat of the same unwelcome sound. One of the two large coil springs that connect the rear of the saddle to the bike's frame has completely broken in half. It's a serious problem but most fortunately, the manner in which it's snapped means the top half of the spring nestles neatly into the spiral of the bottom half when I push the saddle down and as long as I don't hit too many more bad bumps, it should suffice.

It's well known that listening to loud rock music while you're driving will probably make you drive faster. Out in flat, nondescript countryside, I'm overtaken by a flash young man astride a customised black scooter and, without thinking, am quickly roused into Montrose's 70's epic, 'Bad Motor Scooter'. When the song changes tempo, I furiously hum the guitar's speeding power chords, enthusiastically nodding my head to the rhythm... and inadvertently twisting the throttle. Before I know it, I'm zooming up behind the black scooter and, glancing at the Gamin, am shocked to see 87. The heavy metal reprise suddenly silent, I snap the throttle shut and berate myself for getting so irresponsibly carried away.

As light begins to fade, I observe workers in rice paddies, the straw of their conical hats highlighted against the rich green shoots by the dipping sun. It's so much the iconic Vietnamese pastoral scene that, cliched though it may be, I pull over to take a photograph. I'm unable to get a good angle when I try to include the Matchless in the shot so noticing the solid concrete central reservation is raised about a metre high, run over and scramble up it. Standing tall, I prepare to take the photograph but the gusting wind catches me and blows me right off. Thankfully I land safely and begin to clamber back up again but realise my folly as another strong gust of wind plucks at my jacket and an artic whizzes past, so give up. An epitaph of '...cut short in his prime by a puff of wind' just isn't the ending I envisage for myself.

The approaches to Quy Nhon go on and on and from the outskirts to the city centre is almost 20km. In the dark, I sweep along wide boulevards lined with trim gardens and finally arrive at the seafront where, I've been assured by two sets of helpers, there are plenty of hotels. At the far end of a large curving bay, I discover three narrow, four-storey guest houses packed tightly together. The young man at reception in the first is hopeless, unable to tear his eyes off his smartphone long enough to let me into the ground floor car park. I simply walk out and try the next. Here the mother and son owners couldn't be more helpful but they don't have a car park and four scooters are already shoehorned into their lobby. The three of us push the Matchless up a ramp but no matter how hard we try, cannot squeeze her in. They're very apologetic and I'm disappointed not to be able to stay with them. The final hotel has underground parking and this one is run by and energetic girl who bounces down the stairs, keenly showing me where I can store the bike. After allocating the room, she follows me back to the garage to help carry my bags into the lift. Bitterly regretting not searching harder for the errant cover, I relate the tale of its loss and she listens sympathetically. A few minutes later, whilst in my room slowly stripping off sticky clothes, I hear a tap on the door. The young woman has found an old sheet in the laundry room which, she tells me, I can use as a replacement. I'm delighted and dash downstairs to put it to immediate use.

At the receptionist's recommendation, I walk to a nearby cafe for something to eat. The only other customers are three young Vietnamese, two men and a woman, deep in conversation. One of the men and the woman soon leave and when I ask the waiter for help with the menu, the remaining man offers his assistance. He's called Nam and is a student from Ho Chi Minh City who's home visiting his family. Inquisitive about my journey, he speaks English most eloquently, which he explains he's learned largely online. After a couple of minutes I tell him I'm struggling to get answers from the Vietnamese I've met about how communism works in their country... can he tell me? He nods, talking with knowledge and passion.

"After the war ended, the embargoes placed on my parent's generation by America crippled our country for twenty years and it was only by moving away from a marxist model, allowing in foreign investors and opening up to globalisation, that we could escape destitution."

He elucidates that Vietnam was victorious in war but defeated in peace by the might of Washington's sway over its allies, the UN, the World Bank and the IMF. Its hard won right to live by its own ideals succumbed to a financial stranglehold, first changing into a market economy with a socialist orientation then finally to neoliberalism hidden beneath a wafer thin red veneer. To add insult to injury, the government was forced to drop its claims for recompense for war crimes and the monstrous results of 75 million litres of herbicides dropped by US planes, most notably agent orange, which resulted in widespread defoliation, the death and maiming of upwards of 400,000 people and countless subsequent birth defects.

Nam concludes, "Corruption, profiteering and nepotism are now endemic, especially amongst officials involved in selling off our resources and state industries. Communism has not existed here for the last two decades. What we have instead is rigid state control over many aspects of our lives combined with an uncontrolled free market economy, the worst of both worlds. Government spending on education and health care has almost collapsed and many farmers are losing their land. From the outside, our economy is booming but for millions of Vietnamese, life is as hard as it ever has been. It was never meant to be like this but the story is now the same as everywhere else in the capitalist world... the rich get richer and the poor get poorer."

His phone rings and after a brief conversation, he tells me he has to go home as his mother needs his help. I warmly shake his hand and watch him depart on his scooter, the richer but also the sadder for having met him.

Back at the hotel, I check the sheet which, elasticated at its corners, is doing a sterling job of covering the front two thirds of the bike. I give her a pat, grateful as always that she's got us safely through another day, then retire for the night. It's hard to settle, however, with Nam's descriptions of the shocking repercussions of Vietnam War atrocities ringing in my ears. As with the devastating use of cluster bombs in Laos, my blood boils at the governments and corporates who think it's neither here nor there to inflict such devastation on others.

Day 88. Quy Nhơn to Nha Trang. 144 miles.

I grab breakfast in *Barbara's Kiwi Cafe and Backpackers*. Whilst hoeing into a stack of pancakes, I'm tapped on the shoulder and turn around to see Jon's face grinning down at me! It turns out he'd spent the night here in a four dollar dorm, having reached the city about an hour and a half after me.

"The highway was too dangerous in the dark," he says, "so I took the slower but quieter coast road."

At this point we're joined by an Italian called Tom who's also travelling on a locally bought motorbike and was Jon's roommate last night. Tom's a pretty zany character, animately bemoaning the fact that he needs to reach Hoi An today but his bike is poorly.

"It goes 45kmph flat out," he reveals. "There's a problem with the carburettor and I'm too scared to try to repair it."

I offer to have a look, not that I'm any great shakes at mechanics, but the problem is beyond my skill levels as one of the carb studs has sheared off and has been bodged back on by a roadside repair shop. I offer silicone to help seal it but that's already been done. The bike's a $150 shambles, a 50cc Chinese-made 2-stroke that's been hand painted black with slapdash large red stars unequally sprayed on each side of the petrol tank. It's a miracle it runs at all... there again, anyone unable to see beneath the layers of oily muck and torn fork gators on the Matchless might think exactly the same.

As we drink coffee, Tom divulges that he tried to ride his BMW F650GS from Italy to Vietnam last year. Unable to get a visa for Turkmenistan, he'd sailed across the Caspian Sea to Kazakhstan but had been turned back at the China border. He had a Chinese visa but was unaware that travellers with their own vehicles needed prearranged paperwork and an escort.

"I was gutted but had no option other than return home. I flew into Asia this time but spent too long in Thailand which is why I'm desperately rushing this part of my trip. But one day I'll ride back here on my own bike!"

I wish them both well, joking with Jon that we'll no doubt bump into each other again in Nha Trang, then go to get the Matchless prepped for the day ahead.

Once clear of the city, the highway runs straight, wide and flat with no distractions except for the occasional trundle through a speed-restricted town. We make excellent progress in the first part of the morning, only slowing our pace when the highway turns back towards the sea and begins to twist along the tops of several rocky escarpment's where light rain begins to fall. Twice I halt to put on my waterproofs then change my mind as a sea breeze blows the rainclouds away and things quickly dry up again. When the rain persistently returns, I wriggle into my wet weather gear to the racket of a nearby karaoke joint. The road becomes treacherous, with mud dragged off adjoining farm tracks making it slippery and fine mizzle drifting in off the ocean drastically reducing visibility. Vietnamese riders are few and far between, except in the towns where they don flimsy see-though polythene capes that, when they're sitting on their scooters, protect their chests, laps and legs but leave half of their backs exposed.

Ravenous, I spot a roadside eatery just as the sun peaks through the clouds and the rain abates. A car I'd recently overtaken swings into a neighbouring parking space. The passengers, a woman and two children, head for the restaurant whilst the male driver comes over to look at the Matchless. Struggling out of my waterproofs, I say hello from the opposite side of the bike.

"You've got a leak here," the man says.

The bike is completely caked with oil that over the weeks has seeped out of the primary chain case and spread all over the engine, attracting a thick layer of road grime along the way. The almost catastrophic rubber hose failure just beyond the Vietnamese border has done little to help the situation. Unconcerned, I reply,

"It's okay... it's no problem."

"Not a problem? It looks bad to me... it might catch fire," he responds with alarm in his voice.

"It's only oil," I counter, sitting on the tarmac to wriggle out of the last bit of rainsuit.

"No... it's not oil, it looks like petrol and its dripping onto your exhaust. You'd better come and look."

Finally taking notice, I get up and join him. He's right... petrol's dripping from the timing side petrol tap, steadily splashing down onto the hot exhaust pipe! Grabbing a cloth from inside my pocket, I hurriedly wipe it up, simultaneously attempting to turn the tap off. To my horror, I realise it's already in the off position and the more I open and close it, the worse the leak becomes. Recognising my plight, the man runs over to the restaurant and after a quick word with the staff, returns with an empty water bottle. Hands soaked in petrol, I whip the hose off the carburettor and drop it into the neck of the bottle. Unfortunately, I filled up earlier in the morning so there's a lot of fuel in the tank and despite tightening the fuel tap with my spanner, I'm unable to stem the flow. Wedging the bottle into position, I dash over to the restaurant to scrounge some more and while the helpful man joins his family inside, slowly drain the tank dry.

Wheeling the machine to the far corner of the car park, I sit on a step and, with a lineup of six assorted fuel-filled bottles next to me, remove the petrol tap. Close inspection reveals that the top O-ring has perished and I don't have a spare. Fortunately, the thoughtful designers of the G3L blessed the bike with twin fuel taps and the obvious solution is to seal up the failed one and only use the one on the other side. Drying it with tissues, I completely bung it with silicone then head inside to order lunch whilst I wait for it to cure. The man and his family prepare to leave so I get up to thank him... without his keen eye and intervention who knows what would have happened. Allowing a good hour for the silicone to set, I reinsert the tap and refill from the bottles of petrol. It works, not a single drip escapes and I drum into myself that it's critical I remember to only use the left hand tap henceforth.

I've already passed many billboards displaying images of Ho Chi Minh. Mid-afternoon, I stop for a rest below a couple of different ones and get the chance to study them more closely. The first is in a stylized Soviet genre with illustrations of a miner holding a posy of flowers high in the air, a young female agricultural worker, a navy sailor and a child who looks as if he's some sort of boy scout. All stand below a red flag with the star of Vietnam and a hammer and sickle emblem. In the background, Ho Chi Minh, an adopted name meaning 'he who has been enlightened', is depicted signing a document. The second has a picture of Ho making the radio broadcast that declared Vietnam's Independence. It's dated the 2nd of September 1945 and celebrates the 70th anniversary of the creation of the Democratic Republic of Vietnam. In view of last night's conversation with Nam, it's difficult to place them in context, or accept them as anything but propaganda,

Next stop is Nha Trang. In 1998 I stayed there for three nights and remember it as a sleepy seaside town beside a wide curving bay with a halo of golden sands. It had a laid back atmosphere, beautiful unspoiled surroundings and a handful of budget hotels and restaurants. I have a clear memory of lazing outside a peaceful cafe every evening, drinking my favourite fresh fruit shake which was made from jackfruit. Although jackfruits aren't in season, I'm nonetheless really looking forward to seeing the place again. According to the map, there are two turnoffs I can take so I opt for the first as it looks like the more scenic approach. It proves slow going, the narrow road weaving tightly for a few kilometres before finally reaching the seafront. With dusk softly falling and a brilliant full moon magnified as it appears to hover just above the road, I ride along a curling bay enjoying an idyllic silhouetted view of dainty fishing boats bobbing in the gently lapping waves. Arriving at a collection of seaside buildings, I pull up outside a busy cafe and approach a group of Vietnamese men, asking them where I'll find a hotel. Even though my memory is of a quiet place, this actually looks too small for Nha Trang.

"Ten kilometres more. Just keep going, you can't miss it," I'm told by a man who points towards the end of the shore.

The bike casts lengthy shadows in the moonlight and as I round a headland, before me is a scene that leaves me dumbstruck. Soaring into the heavens is an agglomerative hodgepodge of vast glittering skyscrapers. Nha Trang is no longer a backwater town, it's a glitzy resort city. Like a popped balloon, all hope of recognising anything familiar whooshes out of me. The place has undergone a transformation so profound that only the sweep of the bay, the outline of its islands and the shadowy ring of surrounding hills have endured. A miscellany of affluent visitors, package holidaymakers and backpackers fills the streets, indisputably outnumbering locals. Passing several blocks of international hotel chains, plush resort complexes and stacked serviced apartments, I turn at right angles to the waterfront then backtrack down second and third tier streets. These are more tightly packed, bristling with smaller hotels, restaurants, cafes, bars and tourist orientated shops. It's almost overwhelming.

On the right I spot a tall hotel with a fully lit subterranean car park. Usually I'd halt the Matchless near the front door and check the room rates first but here, places with parking such as this are a rarity so I swing straight down the ramp and into the garage, almost certain I'll be staying the night. As the lift door opens into the foyer, the first thing I notice is a giant, gaily lit Christmas tree which, to my eyes, looks oddly out of place. Lavishly furnished, the hotel appears more plush and expensive than I expected and as I walk to the reception desk, I begin to have doubts. Three uniformed members of staff man the desk and at the front is a sign that displays the room rates:

Standard Room: 600,000 dong.

Superior Room: 900,000 dong.

Suite: 1,200,000 dong.

"Please can I have a standard room," I say to the smiling young woman who greets me.

"I'm sorry sir, all our standard and superior rooms are full. We only have suites left."

Inwardly groaning, I try to do a quick calculation of what 1.2 million dong equates to… even said quickly it sounds like an awful lot.

"You have motorcycle?" the lady says, taking in my attire.

"Yes, it's downstairs in your car park. Is there another hotel near here you can recommend that's a little cheaper but also has parking?" I ask.

"Okay. Here's what I can do," she replies after a moment's pause. "If you want to stay with us, I will give you a suite for the price of a standard room."

My wallet's out of my pocket before you can say Jack Robinson.

I don't even bother to go and inspect it, instead, accompanied by a helper, I return to the garage to collect my belongings. In his forties, the porter's a diminutive man, no more than 5 foot tall and thin as a beanpole. Once everything's piled into the lift, he pushes the button for the seventh floor then, as we begin to ascend, turns towards me and with an inquisitive look, claps his hands twice in quick succession. It's the kind of sound one would equate with a period drama where the maitre d' might call for the attention of one of his waiters. Alone with him in a lift, I have no idea what it means so just ignore it. As the doors open, with a certain panache, he does it again and as I look towards him, he questioningly raises an eyebrow. Clueless, I smile, nod and begin to gather my helmet and tank bag. The keyless entry provides access to the most opulent and spacious lodgings of the ride, including two king size beds and a circular bath large enough for four. It's the kind of place where porters expect tips, so while the man ferries in the last of my dry bags, I rummage through my pockets for a couple of notes. Once more, the man gives his strange double clap, the look on his face clearly demanding an answer.

"I'm sorry, I don't understand. What are you clapping for?" I ask.

Standing with his back against the wall, he claps again and says,

"Lady… you know…?" then maintaining a serious expression on his face, launches into a series of rhythmic pelvic thrusts. "You want lady?"

The sight of his homunculus form, smartly dressed in white shirt and black tie, performing such overtly suggestive movements catches my funny bone and in spite of myself, I burst out laughing.

"No, no thank you," I manage to say, shoulders shaking, and hand him his gratuity.

Nha Trang is a noisy party town, the streets crushed with visitors and people trying to sell things to them. I need a new battery for my video camera's microphone and after dinner, search several shops in vain. Someone suggests I try a pharmacy. I find one, standing at a counter next to a tall German backpacker who's buying dressings, antiseptic cream and antibiotics. What ails him is plain to see, there are bandages around both his knees, his left wrist and right elbow and I can't resist asking what happened.

"I fell off my scooter," he replies, "and I think the wound in one of my knees is infected."

I sympathise, having the sensitivity to keep my opinions on tourist motorcycle safety to myself. Once stocked up, he hobbles stiffly out of the door. I leave empty handed and turn in the opposite direction, eventually reaching the seafront. Taking off my shoes, I walk on the cool, soft sand and relish the sound of breaking waves and the familiar smell of the ocean. At least some things haven't changed.

Day 89. Nha Trang to Mui Ne. 143 miles.

A different porter helps transfer my luggage to the basement, where, before loading up, I have to remove and polish the contact breakers again. The tappets need adjusting, the spark plug gets a spruce up and I fit a freshly washed air filter too. After topping the tank with oil I decide my next priority is to buy some more and do an oil change tonight. The porter returns as I'm strapping everything down and, pointing to my sheet, asks its purpose. I explain about the lost cover then question whether the hotel could sell me another, which would ensure the bike's fully concealed in future. Leading me to a small laundry room where three women are busily working, he has a word with one of them. Smiling shyly, she disappears into a storeroom and promptly returns with a double sheet in her hands. I get my wallet out but they refuse payment and lightheartedly shoo me away... it's a gift.

Light rain has been falling intermittently since I woke and I've been equivocating whether to put my waterproofs on ever since. In the end, I decide not to and set off in a well-timed dry patch. As the crow flies, highway 1A is about 10km west of the city but rather than heading straight to it, I decide to take a coastal diversion that links up with it 40km further south. Filling the tank with petrol, I buy three litres of oil and find my way out of the city easily enough but from there become confused by a series of junctions and roundabouts, none of which have signposts. Worse still, having initially tracked inland, the road winds back to the ocean and into the wild, wet weather that's now blowing forcefully off it. Soaked within seconds, I pull up at a shack shop and, sheltering under a tin canopy that the rain's noisily bouncing off, climb into my waterproofs. Setting off again, it appears I'm the only rider mad enough to brave the elements until I come upon a local on a moped. Dressed in flip-flops, shorts and a sodden T-shirt that clings to his torso like a second skin, he's slowly tracking the edge of the gutter, squinting fixedly through the tropical downpour and looking thoroughly miserable.

A complex concatenation of byways eventually deposits us at the small town of Cam Rahn, its high street immersed in murky brown water. The Matchless just makes it through, her engine submerged half way up its casings, and I breath a deep sigh of relief that she doesn't stall in the middle of the deepest, filthiest part of the floodwater. At a set of lights, we turn onto the national highway which here, I'm delighted to see, is a dual carriageway virtually devoid of traffic. Neckerchief pulled up to protect my face and clear goggles on, I accelerate through the intense rain, my vision instantly obliterated by a semi-translucent, grey veil of precipitation. An hour later, nothing's changed and I'm absolutely amazed that the engine and electrics are coping so brilliantly, never missing a beat. The knobbly tyres are also gripping impressively, not once giving me pause for concern. Only one car overtakes us and one by one we pass three trucks, all of which throw huge rooster tails of spray off their wheels. The song which pertinently pushes its way through my grey matter is *ELO's* 'Showdown', especially its chorus,

"It's raining, all over the world..." which expresses exactly how it feels at this moment.

No major towns exist along this tract of highway and although many sections are in the middle of being upgraded, I almost always have the contraflows, some of which are kilometres long, to myself. In the early afternoon the deluge gradually thins, the clouds begin to lift and patches of weak blue sky peak through. Somewhere near the coast but not in clear sight of it, I spot a roadside rest stop and gratefully pull over for a much needed break.

The restaurant comprises half a dozen outside tables and a kitchen that's no more than a quadrant of waist high brick walls under a corrugated tin roof which is raised on stout posts. The teenage lad who comes to serve me doesn't have a menu and can't speak English so I act out a suggestion that I go to the kitchen to point at ingredients. He readily agrees and there I meet two women I assume to be the cooks. Remembering how fresh the fish has been over the last couple of days, I fancy a seafood stir-fry but I'm not sure how to communicate it to them until suddenly, I have a brainwave. Gesticulating for a pen and paper, which are quickly produced, I begin drawing... fish and squid are easy but my prawns degenerate into amorphous blobs. Pointing to their rice steamer and nodding, it's apparent they've grasped the gist of my request and, priding myself on my artwork, I return to my table.

With steam rising off my drying gloves, I sit warming my bones in the sun, sipping a glass of Coke and after hours of uninterrupted concentration, slowly unwind. One of the ladies appears carrying a plate of rice, another of cooked vegetables and a bowl of salad. Returning to the kitchen, she reappears moments later with a large plate piled high with squid rings drizzled with a light dressing. It's more than I usually have for dinner, let alone lunch, but it looks and smells great so I get stuck in. A couple of minutes later, I look up to see the young man carrying another large dish which, when placed in front of me, holds ten enormous tiger prawns cooked in a spicy sauce. My eyes on stalks, I crunch into one to discover it's utterly divine. Wondering if I'm going to be able to finish such a feast, I diligently set to work. Out of the blue, the first woman reappears bearing an earthenware pot which is ceremoniously deposited centre table. She lifts the lid to reveal soup complete with a whole fish measuring about 20cm. I shake my head in disbelief... they've taken my pictures literally! With the language barrier that exists between us, I don't attempt to explain the misunderstanding for fear of causing confusion or offence. Smiling to myself, I guess they must think overland biking makes you hungry! Soon the three of them join me carrying their own meals, all of which are infinitely more modest than mine. With lots of smiles, we eat companionably. I offer some of my prawns and squid around the table but they politely shake their heads and continue chomping at their own food.

Making a valiant effort, I polish everything off apart from half the rice and some of the greens. Full to almost bursting, I ask for the bill with more than a little trepidation. When it's presented, I look in amazement at a figure which converts to just under £4. For this modest price, the rudimentary kitchen has produced the most unexpected, most delicious and best value meal of the journey. I'm only glad I don't have to zip my waterproofs over my bulging stomach!

In direct sunlight, the asphalt dries astonishingly fast and keeping to the *ELO* theme, my song switches seamlessly to 'Mr Blue Sky'. 50km north of my destination, the beach retreat of Mui Ne, the highway takes a major direction change, heading cross country and I begin searching for the turnoff to the coast. In a rare town centre, I pass one intersection but it looks decidedly minor so continue a little further, stopping outside a bar to ask for guidance. Here a dozen or so older men, all shirtless and sporting an aged variety of smudged tattoos, sit at a long outside table playing cards and drinking beer. It doesn't take long to work out that they're as drunk as skunks yet I persist longer than good sense tells me I should. One of the rowdier fellas gets up, demanding I pay him $100 to lead me to Mui Ne. His breath reeks and he repeatedly sways into me while pushing my chest with a nicotine stained hand. Two others rise, staggering in my direction just as a passer-by comes to the rescue, pointing back down the road and indicating I should take the turnoff I've already passed. Hopping back on the bike, which starts on cue, I roar away from the den of iniquity post-haste.

A couple of back roads lead to a bridge which crosses a small estuary, both banks lined with blue and white wooden fishing boats. At anchor in the mouth of the harbour are at least 50 more, all with pronounced, steeply curving bows which give them an ancient appearance. Immediately upon exiting the bridge, the road transforms into the DT716B, a stellar new stretch of dual carriageway that's concrete perfection. For 23km it's all mine, save for the occasional road-gang working on some unfinished section, although even here there's no diminution in my pleasure as the other side of the central reservation is always complete and fully operational. I believe Mui Ne and its beaches are still relatively undeveloped but this level of investment in infrastructure smacks of Nha Trang style expansion in the near future. Giant sand dunes appear with increasing frequency on both sides of the highway, many of them twice the size of a house, and as the sun once more sinks towards the horizon, I begin searching for the seaside. Eventually, assisted by some workers who point me down a narrow country road, I follow a circuitous course into a small town and find the shoreline. Riding south, the road changes into a leafy lane where all the beachfront accommodation's situated, a kilometre long strip of low-rise resorts set back in well tended gardens. Turning around after a while, I head back to one which looked smaller and slightly less salubrious than the rest. Pulling up inside its sandy courtyard, I'm greeted by a staunch Russian man who introduces himself as the under manager.

"Our hotel is for Russian package holiday makers, which is why I work here. None of the Vietnamese staff can speak Russian," he says in response to my question about his nationality.

He takes an instant shine to the Matchless and when asked if he can recommend a suitable nearby hotel, says,

"Stay here, it's no problem. We can work something out for you and your motorcycle will be safe with our security guard."

Removing my helmet, I follow him indoors and receive a welcome blast from the cool air conditioning.

I'm handed over to a Vietnamese receptionist and I ask the room rate.

"Fifteen dollars," he replies.

The place looks amazing for that price so I readily agree. He takes me to the room, which is smart and comfortable, then leads me back to reception to complete registration. Once done, I go outside to unload the bike then park her in a covered shelter close to the night guard. Walking back through the foyer, the receptionist waves me over and asks if I can pay the bill in advance.

"Fifty dollars please," he says as I extract my credit card.

I ask him to write it down as his accent is strong and I think I've misheard. On paper I can plainly see $50 and it's clear that I got it wrong first time around. Too exhausted to reload the bike and search elsewhere, I endeavour to explain my error and ask if a cheaper option is available. The Russian steps in, makes a phone call to his boss, then offers a discounted rate of $35, which is very decent considering the fault was mine. The receptionist, however, is displeased with the arrangement. Obviously, I'm not the usual type of guest they get here and thinking the worst, he follows me back to the room, clipboard in hand, and makes a detailed inventory of every single item in it, which he then asks me to sign... not exactly a vote of confidence!

Postponing the oil change until tomorrow, I clean up then go for a walk but can't find a way through to the beach as the seafront's completely obstructed by tourist complexes. Restaurants and cafes occupy the landward side so I wander into one for something to eat. After today's lunch, all I can face is mango juice and a banana pancake. Checking the Matchless is OK, and thanking the nightwatchman for guarding her, I return to my room and am out like the proverbial light the instant my body's horizontal.

Day 90. Mui Ne to Ho Chi Minh City. 130 miles.

Seen in daylight, the manicured hotel grounds contain a lavishly appointed outdoor swimming pool surrounded by luxurious sun loungers. Bypassing it, I enter a grand dining room packed with noisy Russian holidaymakers. Like a fish out of water, I sit at a corner table people-watching and eating breakfast fit for a king. Alexander, the Russian under manager, is there, busy smoothing things out for his guests. In a quiet moment, however, he reveals he's fed up with the job, working twelve hours a day, seven days a week endlessly sorting out petty problems. Pastures new beckon him. Replete, I locate the guarded entrance to the beach and walk barefoot along the shoreline, giving myself a good dose of negative ions before heading to the rear of the complex and setting about the overdue oil change.

With so few miles to go and a far from suitable environment to do the job, I cheat, simply draining the oil tank then refilling it with fresh lubricant. The oil filter remains unchanged and I don't even attempt syringing the oil out of the bottom of its retaining cylinder. Vacating my room, I head to reception to collect my passport. The woman can't find it and after ten minutes of searching, enlists the help of another member of staff. Together they twice empty every drawer behind the counter as well as thoroughly searching the back office to no avail. Alexander is called to unlock the safe but it can't to be found there either. Starting to get worried, I ask them to contact the mistrustful receptionist who took it from me last night. Alexander does this immediately, rousing him from his slumbers. Eventually, it drops out from within a file that contains my signed property list. Although I'm hugely relieved, forty minutes have been wasted and half the morning's gone before I hit the road.

Turning onto the leafy avenue, I go no more than a kilometre before something forcibly strikes me on the top of my crash helmet, giving me the fright of my life. Skidding to a halt, I jump off and look around. There's nothing in the road but above I see a large overhanging tree that's dripping with mangosteen, one of which must have chosen exactly the wrong moment to drop. It's hardly the most auspicious start to the day's ride.

Following the seafront, the Matchless's engine purrs and I smile... a smile that soon slips when we merge onto Highway 1A, which is heaving with trucks. There are so many, they occupy both lanes and make for highly demanding riding as I thread the bike in and out between them. Stopping to refuel, I'm astounded by the sight of two motorcycles that are already filling up. They're both being used as delivery vehicles carrying heavy, folded clothing in bulky rectangular sacks each of which roughly equates to the size of a large suitcase. I estimate there are the equivalent of six of these on the back of each machine, piled high above the heads of the riders. As if that weren't already too much, both have half-size bags hanging over the front wheels, on top of the handlebars and in the floorwells. Once finished, the pump attendant has to pile the final packages onto each rider's knees! The weight they're carrying is hard to rationalise and how they ever manage to manoeuvre the bikes is beyond me... they make the Matchless look positively anorexic.

In the middle of the afternoon, I halt in a narrow, dusty recess at the side of the highway where pedestrians take their lives into their hands as they cross both road and railway lines to reach their village. Sitting under a tree, I still my mind as the engine cools. Unexpectedly, a step-through motorcycle turns into the same area, a huge empty steel cage fixed to a wooden platform on the back. Its rider, a man in his 30s, makes a phone call and a couple of minutes later, another bike arrives, This one's piloted by a woman who looks like a farm worker and squashed inside the near identical cage on her bike are a dozen or so oinking piglets. One by one, the man plucks them out by their ears, inspects them and despite their squealing protests, weighs each one on mobile scales. They're finally transferred into his cage except for a couple of runts, which he disdainfully throws back into the woman's cage. Negotiations commence in earnest, the woman becoming quite agitated until a deal's finally brokered. Cash changes hands and the piglets ride off.

The closer we get to Ho Chi Minh City, the greater the traffic woes become. The road has widened, separating into more clearly defined lanes for cars, trucks and buses, with a narrow lane for bikes that's segregated by a low concrete dividing wall. Intimidating as the larger vehicles are, I feel far safer with them than amongst the mass of two wheelers, so stay out of their designated channel. The road forks and without any signposts to follow, I'm torn between the two directions. Stopping to buy fruit, I ask the man who serves me which way I should head for Saigon. He laughs, indicating to one road then the other,
"This one Saigon... this one Saigon too!"
As the left option seems marginally quieter, I plump for it.
Riding into the sun virtually non-stop for two hours, I'm feeling decidedly baked. With an indicated 20km still to go, I spot a drinks shack at the roadside and pull off. My Camelbak's empty for the second time today but the proprietor doesn't have any water for sale, the grubby old fridge, which from its appearance could possibly pre-date the Vietnam War, contains only fizzy drinks. I settle for a chilled Coke and flop onto a seat, its once stylish cover oily and torn. The tumbledown place is built from a motley collection of discarded timber, tin roofing and worn out furniture, a temporary structure on dusty waste ground strewn with litter. The mother and son who run it are, however, lovely, making me feel very welcome and even bringing me a miniature packet of tissues to wipe the sweat from my brow and oil off my hands. The contrast between this set up and the luxurious hotels I've recently stayed in couldn't be much more extreme, but its uncomplicated, hospitable and obviously poor owners are without doubt as genuine and friendly as anyone I've met on the entire journey.
Underway again, I sense that the edge has dropped off the bike's performance, a situation which isn't helped by the overwhelming volume of two-wheel traffic gradually grinding to a near standstill as we enter the city's outer suburbs. I can't make my way through to the car lanes which are flowing relatively freely, because I'm totally jammed in, especially at traffic lights. At one particular two-minute red light halt, I stand tall and look ahead. There must be

500 bikes in front of me and turning around, I'm amazed to see at least as many queued up behind, with more joining the distant tail by the second. It's incredible. Two or three junctions later, waiting for another change to green, I can smell the hot oil of my engine and feel its heat radiating onto my shins and feet which begin to cook. When the lights change, the old girl simply won't start and whilst I frantically kick, a mass of two-wheelers squeezes around us. She finally catches but by the time I make it to the front, the light's have changed again.

Ho Chi Minh City is divided into 19 districts and according to my rather small scale map, the area I'm looking for is in District 1. Twice I stop to ask where I am but the city's so vast and densely populated that all the people can tell me is to keep going straight on, which I do, crossing the wide Dong Nai River then the smaller Saigon River. Light is fading and with not a clue which district I'm in, I turn off at a random junction to seek advice. Beside the entrance to a large shopping mall stand four uniformed security guards. Pulling up, I ask if this is District I. None of them speak English so I get out my map but it proves no help either. The youngest of the men takes it upon himself to assist me, typing a message on his phone which it then translates to:
'Cannot stop here. Come with me please.'
I follow him to the far side of an underground car park entrance where he hands me the phone. I type that I'm looking for District 1 and, with my destination now clear, he returns to his mates where a lot of head scratching ensues. A few minutes later he comes back with a complex route on Google Maps that should at least help me find a way through the next couple of major intersections. When I come to leave, however, the Matchless won't start and a quick inspection reveals there's no spark. Cursing for not being able to find my replacement contact breaker sets, I once again remove the old ones, and with sweat streaming off me, work by torchlight. The young security guard becomes increasingly concerned but when everything's reassembled and the bike finally bursts into life, he enthusiastically slaps me on the back.
He types one last message onto his phone.
'You wait 7.30pm, my friend come take me home. You follow to hotel.'
It's an exceedingly kind offer but as that's an hour and a half away, I decide to press on alone. My helper has an unpronounceable name but along with one of his colleagues, teaches me how to enunciate the syllables of the street I'm heading to, Pham Ngu Lao, which has extra emphasis on the final word. Once I have it down to pat, they both shake my hand and, with the gallant Matchless starting upon the first prod of my foot, I rejoin the fray.

Within a kilometre we arrive at a massive intersection where a crossflow of traffic heads underneath a wide flyover. It's chockablock with motorcycles and scooters trying to move in opposing directions and a lone traffic cop standing on a portable pedestal with the impossible job of controlling them. Tightly packed at a standstill, I get the attention of a girl on a pink scooter immediately to my right.
"Pham Ngu Lao?" I ask, stretching the last word and sounding like a wailing

cat as I simultaneously point to the left.

"Yes, that's the way to Pham Ngu Lao, but it's not direct, just follow the one-way system for maybe three kilometres then ask again," she replies sweetly in the most articulate English!

Without the policeman's say so, someone zooms forward and all hell breaks loose as hundreds of two-wheelers follow, vying for clear space, weaving between vehicles crossing at right angles and completely swamping the poor officer. He gives up on containment but bravely stands his ground whilst the hordes swarm around him. It's so utterly bonkers I begin belly-laughing whilst, like everyone else, I dodge this way and that before making it to the relative safety of a one way street.

I stop three further times to check my bearings and on every occasion, the people speak enough English to be able to either confirm or clarify my route. Eventually we swing onto Pham Ngu Lao street, which, along with a number of alleyways that branch off it, forms the main tourist area. Drenched in perspiration, I ride up and down the busy sidestreets looking for suitable lodgings and eventually, on a narrow alleyway packed with restaurants that spill onto the pavements, spot what I'm looking for, a hotel with an underground garage. I nip in to check it's affordable then ask the concierge to open the garage gates. When I return outside, a tourist is squatting down, carefully inspecting the Matchless's engine. He turns out to be a Scottish motorcyclist and former Matchless owner to boot. Bubbling with bonhomie, he enthuses about the bike but alas, with my energy levels at rock bottom and my belongings strewn up the hotel steps, I need to get everything safely put away and myself checked in, so we say a cheerful goodbye.

Whilst I'm showering, the heavens open and when I later step outside, the roads are awash with puddles. I wander the lively streets for a while, keenly absorbing the buzz of Vietnam's commercial and cultural heart. As Saigon, it was the capital of the Republic of Vietnam until, on the 30th April 1975, it fell to communist PAVN forces. Shortly afterwards, its name was changed to honour Ho Chi Minh, who'd died almost six years earlier. With a population of over ten million, it's a densely crowded place, although this being the tail end of the wet season there aren't as many tourists packing the bars and cafes as at other times of the year. I inspect several stalls selling street food but decide to eat at a table outside an eatery just across the road from my hotel. Sipping a glass of Bia Saigon, I reflect on my first visit here twenty years ago and how it's unwise to look back and compare those quiet, charming times with the fizzing firecracker of the current era. Like plums and prunes, they both have their merits.

Enjoying the ambience later than I really should, I finally buy some food for breakfast in a 24-hour convenience store then go to bed, memorising an easterly route out of the city from my tablet screen. Our arrival here marks the end of one chapter in the journey and tomorrow will be the start of a new one, heading for Cambodia and ultimately Bangkok from where I'll ship the bike home. For the last week she has been increasingly showing signs of wear and I only hope she's going to make it.

Day 91. Ho Chi Minh City, Vietnam, to Karod Village, Cambodia. 215 miles.

Up with the eastern lark, I work like a trooper to get ready, gleefully wheeling the bike out of the garage just after 6am. My aim is to exit the city before traffic builds... fat chance! As soon as I merge onto a wider avenue, I'm engulfed by droves of bikes and scooters which, like me, seem to be following a left, right, left series of turns. Unlike last night, however, everything flows more freely and after half an hour, my chosen route links up with good ol' Asia Highway 1. Here the two-wheelers are again corralled into a narrow side strip that's lined with small businesses and minor turnoffs. Abused by all and sundry, it's painfully slow and smacks of high risk. As on previous days, I stay out in the multi-lane section reserved for cars. It's all but empty and I bomb along at 70, only hindered momentarily by infrequent sets of traffic lights.

Close to the city's outer limits, a policeman steps into the road and flags me down, leading me towards his car and a couple of other waiting officers. In broken English he reprehends me for flouting the law, gesticulating furiously that I should be travelling with the other bikes. I see no point in arguing as he's plainly right but I try explaining that for me, the inner lane is just too dangerous. It falls on deaf ears and he waves a colleague over who's armed with an official-looking book. Opening it at the relevant page, he shows me a list of regulations and fines and I gulp at the one he points to. It says one million dong! I've less than fifty thousand left in change and my exit appointment at the border is in under two hours time... try explaining that when you don't speak Vietnamese. I give it my best shot and he seems to understand the problem but insists I was breaking the law and must face the consequences. Then, like a light going on, it dawns on him that I'm riding a foreign registered bike. His eyes shine and I can almost see him adding up the additional penalties he can impose.

"Motorcycle papers," he says staunchly.
Fortunately I have them all to hand. I pass everything over and watch with bated breath as he begins flipping through the wad of special import licences and government documents. He seems placated, even impressed by the array of official letterheads, stamps and signatures and after checking my passport, hands them all back. Pointing down the road, he says in a much less stern manner,
"OK... go. Have good two more hour Vietnam."
Firmly indicating I should stay in the nearside scooter lane, he smiles then heads back out into the road to collar the next miscreant.

The border lies little more than 60km east but I somehow miss the turnoff, only realising half an hour later when the road tracks north. Making a U-turn, I ask directions from a variety of people but each seems to have a different perspective on where the crossing is and how I should get there. Maybe it's just that my pronunciation of Muc Bai isn't good enough but the result's the same, time slips away. Finally I find someone who can speak a little English and, as luck would have it, is also heading my way on his bike. He leads me down a bumpy red earth trail which I've been down once but had turned back up because it looked like a dead end lane that would only lead to an isolated village. Stopping after 5km, he tells me to turn left at the end of the road then departs, bouncing across an irrigation channel before circuiting a large field. I stop half a dozen more times to enquire if I'm on track and each informant tells me where to go... but only as far as the next junction where I need to stop and ask somebody else. Progress is excruciatingly slow and when I finally make it to the frontier and its huge immigration building, I'm almost an hour late for my appointment with the agent from *MotoTours*, Mr. Thai.

The moment I come to a standstill, a rather harassed looking man bounds over.

"You are Mr. Gordon? I am very worried for you. Are you okay?"
I explain my convoluted route and apologise, at which point he completely calms down.

"It is okay. I have something for you," he says, handing me a package that's been sent by Andrew Engineering.
I was supposed to collect it in Hanoi but the post had been slow, taking over three weeks to come from the UK. It's an additional gasket set, including a well protected cylinder head gasket, all reassuring to have but with hindsight I wish I'd asked them to include a new set of contact breakers too.

First we walk to customs which is strangely located behind a sprawling bar that serves both beer and spirits. Here Mr. Thai efficiently takes over then, after 10 minutes, leads me to passport control. I join the back of a long queue, watching in fascination as a couple of well-groomed people walk straight to the front of the line and approach the first immigration window that becomes free. They're turned away, the money poking out of the tops of their passports evidently rejected by the official. It doesn't deter them, however, they simply jump straight to the next window that becomes available and this time the note disappears and they're promptly processed!

When I'm through, I apologise again for keeping the agent waiting then quietly push the Matchless the last few metres out of Vietnam. I feel rather deflated as I wheel her across no man's land, poignantly aware that this marks the end of my primary objective, riding overland to Vietnam. That's it... for this trip at least.

Coming to a halt at the Cambodian check post, my spirits are soon lifted by the thrill of entering a new country and all the possibilities it entails. There's a bit of a crush at the office which sells visas, a flock of tourists having just emptied off a bus. Buying a visa, another sticker that takes up a whole passport page, is straightforward and costs $30. I saunter across the road to the immigration building and join a queue to get it stamped. Unlike anywhere else on the journey, this involves electronic fingerprints being taken which seems rather incongruous given the size and status of Cambodia and the remote nature of this border crossing. Once done, I retrieve the Matchless and push her over to customs, handing my carnet to the first man I meet.

"Please, sit here and wait," he tells me pointing towards a table and chairs, adding,"Would you like a drink?"

Dipping into a cool box, he pulls out a chilled bottle of water and courteously removes the plastic seal before handing it over. He soon returns accompanied by a colleague. Sitting across the table, they discuss certain aspects of my paperwork before duly completing it and five minutes later, without even glancing towards the bike, give it back and tell me I'm free to go. Excellent!

Cambodia is noticeably poorer than Vietnam. The roadside dwellings and businesses are much more down at heel and the highway's narrow and well worn. It's infinitely quieter too, all that motors past us in the first half an hour is a bus, two 4x4's and a handful of scooters. Having changed some euros into riel with a money changer fanning herself inside a baking hot hut just beyond the frontier, I begin looking for somewhere to get lunch. The only sizeable town I pass through doesn't have anywhere obvious to eat so I press on, turning around when I pass a small open-fronted tin shack with bananas, coconuts and watermelons hanging outside. Rolling to a halt, I park on the chalky verge beside it.

Out in the middle of nowhere, the shop's run by a enchanting, dark-skinned Khmer woman who has a round, kind face. She's sitting cross-legged on a long wooden bench that stretches most of the way across the shopfront and behind her I can see a bicycle, a scooter, a stove and a bed. Her stock consists of water, a couple of cartons of Angkor beer, a plucked chicken hanging from a hook and a large tin teapot together with some glasses on a tray. She's assisted by her nine-year-old daughter who, while her mum's busy, takes care of an exceptionally cute one-year-old boy. Flopping into a plastic chair, I watch the lady expertly machete the top off a coconut then, after passing it and a straw to me, continue with her work. Blending rice and grated coconut in a bowl, she rolls the mixture inside long green banana leaves then ties them closed with twine. Meanwhile, the girl dances around with the toddler in her arms, the perfect surrogate mum. It might be stark and basic but it's an enormously relaxing place to be.

After eating a couple of bananas, I ask what I need to pay. The mother shows me three fingers, meaning the cost is 3000 riels (about $1) but unused to the currency and still thinking in the large denominations of Vietnamese dong, I mistakenly hold out 30,000 riels made up from two 10,000 and a couple of 5,000 notes. It's a relative fortune, ten times the amount asked, but the girl shakes her head and simply extracts one 5,000 note from my hand and passes it to her watching mum, who already has two 1000 notes waiting in change. It strikes me they can't have much in the way of ready cash and it would have been so easy for them to take advantage of my mistake. Looking into both their eyes, I see not a trace of guile, just innate integrity and openness. Before leaving, the family pose for photographs, their faces reflecting genuine friendliness. It's such a brief encounter but as I set off once more, I realise it's one I'll treasure.

Just over a hundred kilometres from the border, the road transforms into a wonderful stretch of new concrete, curling into the distance then sweeping up and over the recently opened, 2km long Neak Loeung suspension bridge, a gift from the Japanese government to the people of Cambodia. Building up as much momentum as the Matchless can muster, we begin to climb, overtaking a horse and cart near the towering crest. Casting my eyes over the edge, a magnificent view of the Mekong River opens up before me, its dark green waters lazily making their way towards the Vietnamese border.

Rising on the Tibetan plateau, the river travels over 4000km and provides vital irrigation, fishing and bulk transport opportunities for the many barges that navigate its deep channel. However, recent and forthcoming hydroelectric dams in China, Laos and Cambodia, while generating much needed power, threaten the natural flow of the river with as yet unknown consequences for the people who live downstream. Changes to its seasonal flow pattern are most likely to have the greatest impact on those living close to Tonlé Sap lake, located in the centre of the country. Such is the volume of water travelling down the Mekong during the annual monsoon, it causes a prodigious back flow up the 100km long river which exits the lake, increasing its surface area from a minimum of 2,700km² up to as much as 16,000km² and leaving mineral rich deposits on farmland as it gradually recedes. I only hope the governments, investors and engineers in the respective countries involved have studied the results of similar schemes on the Aral Sea and planned their new developments with care and consideration.

Traffic starts to build as we near the capital, Phnom Penh, and the torrid humidity and relentless sun get to me. Pulling in for petrol, I park the bike, grab a plastic chair and after stripping my gear off, sit back in the shade. The station's run by three lively teenagers, one of whom brings me a bottle of cold water. Noting how hot I look, he soon returns with another, which, after asking my permission, he sprinkles from his hand down the back of my neck and over my head. The other two laugh, 'though obviously with me, not at me, and after 20 minutes, I feel much cooled and ready for the off again.

To my surprise, I come upon my intended turn off within 30 seconds of resuming the ride, forking onto National Route 2. My paper map's only detailed enough to get a general overview of where to head so last night I memorised an online route to my destination, a volunteer-run project approximately 75km due south of Phnom Penh. Weaving between smoky old trucks while dog-legging 20km west is hard yakka and, intensely focused on picking my way through one particularly lumbering string of vehicles, I overshoot the turn off south onto Route 3. After checking my position a couple of kilometres further on, I turn back and locate it. This southern highway's quieter and, accompanied only by a long shadow of man and machine to my left, I clock up 40 smooth, unhindered kilometres. Passing through a small town, lines of open backed pickups are filling up with people going home from a sprawling central market and several wave as they watch me ease my way past.

The address I'm aiming for is Street 22, National Road No. 3, Bakod Village, Leay Bour Commune, Tramkak District, Takeo Province, which at first appears detailed enough to be an easy find but is, in reality, decidedly illusive. Bakod village consists of only a handful of small houses surrounded by fields and isn't known by anyone more than a few kilometres away, so I start big, aiming for

Tramkak district. The first three people I ask have never heard of it and, energy levels depleted, I pull into a roadside rest stop to buy a coconut. Here I get lucky. A man sitting at the back talking with the owner's children turns out to be a schoolteacher who speaks English very well. He's never heard of the school I'm heading to but writes its address in Khmer for me. Re-energised by the syrupy drink, I thank him and set off once more, riding for another twenty minutes before coming to a settlement built around a crossroads. The junction seems to be in just about the right position on my mental map so I show a local the paper with the Khmer address on it. Recognising Leay Bour commune, he confirms that I should turn left.

I'm still too far away for anyone to know of Bakod but a couple more impromptu checks get me nearer to Leay Bour. Stopping by chance at a small shop, a man recognises the name and points down a stony, dirt track a short distance ahead. I take it, riding in a perfectly straight line with the setting sun reflecting off the flooded paddies and creating striking silhouettes from a line of leaning palm trees. Reaching the compound of a Buddhist temple, I ask two boys on a bike if they can direct me to Bakod.

"You want Hope Agency?" one of them asks. "I go there... we will show you." They set off, bouncing along the trail for a half a kilometre before turning left. Stopping, the boy says,

"My house here, the school there," he calls, pointing to the left and with, "See you," about-turns and pedals off.

Within a minute, I arrive at the entrance, riding through its gates just as two volunteers, a man and woman on a dilapidated motorcycle with a pronounced misfire, are leaving. Stopping to say hello, they tell me to head inside where I'll find four more volunteers. I do, half-heartedly chased by a couple of stray dogs who've made the school their home. Parking in the volunteers' recreation area, I turn to see a man and a woman recumbent in hammocks and another man seated beside a table. They leap up and come over to greet me.

The project was set up in 2010 by Jason Han, a local lad who left home at the age of 14 when his parents were unable to afford for him to go to school. After a brief episode living on the streets of the capital, he worked as a house-boy then in a factory. One of Jason's brothers, who'd been put in an orphanage as his parents were unable to feed all of the family, had the good fortune of being adopted by an American couple. Jason was sponsored by his brother's new family and travelled to the US to study at a university. A decade or so later, having managed a Cambodian orphanage for a short time, he returned to his home community with a mission to assist local children, providing them with free education. Reasoning that learning English would help broaden their horizons and provide greater opportunities when they become adults, he set up the Hope Agency school. It's funded and staffed by visiting foreign volunteers who stay from as little as a week to up to several months at a time. Many return for second and third spells. I'd first encountered the project 15 months ago when my lovely step-daughter, Surya, taking a gap year before commencing a degree in international development, spent six weeks volunteering here.

Spanning an area the size of one and a half football pitches, the school comprises a grassy playing area, three small wooden classrooms and a large accommodation block for volunteers. In front of this sits their recreation area and kitchen, a key facility as the school regularly feeds some of the children as well as the teachers. At the front of the recreation area are two open-roofed toilet and shower rooms and to the back of the grounds a smattering of fruit trees, a goat pen and Jason's tiny cottage. As today's classes have finished and the children already left, I sit for a while with the volunteers, hearing about their varied motivations for coming to the school, the classes they teach and the children that have captured their hearts.

Jason, an upbeat man with laughing eyes and a near permanent smile, arrives on his scooter. Straightaway, he sets to cooking the evening meal which tonight is a celebratory one as three of the volunteers are due to return home in two days time. While he's in the kitchen, I sit chatting with the six teachers, Josh from Australia and the other five, Brad, Mikey, Terry, Lorna and Jess, from the UK. The next few weeks are going to be hectic for the three that remain but more volunteers are due to arrive in January. Even though the school's obviously run on a shoestring, Jason reveals he's going to cook a meal for the hundred or so children who will visit tomorrow afternoon to commemorate Cambodia's Human Rights Day, The kitty's empty so we all pledge $10 to make the best of the party.

Without my knowledge, Jason enlists Lorna's help to make a bed up for me, a kind gesture for a weary biker, then heads to bed himself. After a quick walk to the village store to procure some cans of beer, we sit around the softly lit dining table and play a fun game of pontoon with matchsticks for money. The stakes are ten cents a go and at the end of the night the banker converts the matchsticks to riel, donating all his takings to the school fund. It's a highly enjoyable way to spend a couple of hours and I go to bed happy with not only the day's ride but the warm reception I've received here.

The volunteers plus a smiling Jason Han, second from the left.

Day 92. Hope Agency School, Bakod village. 0 miles.

Waking in the night to go to the loo, I shuffle past the Matchless which, cloaked in her two white sheets, has taken on a ghost-like appearance in the brilliant moonlight. When I rise again, the sun's only just up and the air's deliciously cool. After breakfast, Jason appears, discussing today's agenda. As the morning's free and we won't need to prepare for the children's' party until mid-afternoon, we're all invited to his parent's home to participate in the first day of their rice harvest. It's an exciting opportunity to contribute to an important annual event, however, it does present a dilemma for a couple of the volunteers who haven't had vaccinations against Japanese encephalitis. The mosquitoes that carry the virus usually breed in rural areas, particularly where there are flooded rice fields or marshes, and although they tend to bite between sunset and sunrise, there's still a risk. I had a course of the expensive vaccine, two injections a month apart, before leaving the UK. The two volunteers who haven't been inoculated weigh up the odds during a group discussion and decide to take the risk.

In high spirits, we troop across the fields, sticking to the narrow raised walkways between each paddy and reach Jason's small family home after about twenty minutes. Here we watch a group of colourfully dressed workers, mostly children and young adults, chatting and laughing as they harvest the rice. They've already laid bare a quarter of the field. Whipping off our shoes, we wade into the knee-high, warm water and spread ourselves out between the different work groups. At first, our tasks involve gathering the hand-tied sheaves of rice and carrying them to the side of the paddy where they begin to dry in the sun.

After a while, I ask one of the young men I'm helping if I can have a go at cutting the rice. He gives me a quick demonstration, which involves the deft use of toes to hold the rice whilst bending over and scything it underwater. It's satisfying work and I've soon got the hang of it but before I get too carried away, remind myself to temper my enthusiasm... it would be more than unfortunate were I to injure my foot with the 20cm curved blade of the scythe. Straightening up after tying my third sheaf, I stretch my already stiff spine and guess that a few hours of this must play hell with the back. I notice at this point that Jason and a couple of the others are cutting the odd stalks that have been missed by the advancing line of workers.

"Is it important not to leave them in the ground before you sow next year's seeds?" I ask him in ignorance.

"No, not at all. Cambodia is a very poor country and each stalk has a small spoonful of rice on it. So much effort goes into growing it and we cannot afford to let any go to waste. The missed crop could feed a family for weeks and it would seem like a crime to squander it," he earnestly replies, bending over once again to gather up an overlooked clump of several stalks.

After an hour, we're all called over to the house where a simple meal of noodles and vegetables is being served by Jason's delightful mother. While we eat, she expertly demonstrates how to thresh the rice the traditional way, using her very muscular feet. It's a skill I doubt could be mastered overnight. Then it's back into the paddy for another hour before carrying all the drying sheaves to a garden area where they're not at risk of falling back into the water. Hot and drenched in sweat, the six of us recline in chairs in front of the house, relaxing while Jason's dad, a diminutive man with a smile almost as broad as his face, prepares fresh coconut milk for us to drink. Although only two thirds of a single paddy have been harvested this morning, each of us confirms how fulfilled we feel by our labours, although doing it for weeks on end would be an entirely different matter. We eventually meander back to the school, the golden panorama of ripe rice only interrupted by the occasional islands of houses or palms.

After a quick lunch, I wander down to the village shop with three of the teachers where we sit on bench drinking Coke and chatting. The shop owner's husband, a spindly, elderly man, is repairing his scooter, a Honda step-through that's had a hard life. The drive sprocket's lying on the earthen floor, one of its securing bolts having sheered off. He sets about reattaching it with a nail, which he bends into shape using the back of an axe for a hammer. Once done, he slips the chain back on without removing its split pin. Squatting next to him, I test the strength of the job. The sprocket wobbles all over the place but he just smiles, happy to have something that works at all. Looking closer, I see that the swinging arm has snapped off at some point in the machine's chequered history and been welded back in place and the rear chain's not only worn out but rigid with rust. Earlier this morning, I'd topped up the Matchless's gearbox with the last of my grease and had put the tub in a rubbish bin. Running over to the school, I'm glad to find it's still there and pick it out. Back at the shop, I use a finger to scoop up as much of the residue as possible then smear it along the old chain. The man goes for a smoky test ride, giving me the thumbs up when he shakily comes to a halt a few minutes later.

Whilst finishing off my drink, a rickshaw bounces past carrying a curly-haired woman with a pleasant expression who's wearing a flamboyant, floral dress.

"Who's that... Mary Poppins?" shouts Brad.

All three of us jump up and hurriedly make our way over to the school, keen to see if a new volunteer has just arrived. When we get there we meet Julia, an Englishwoman who volunteered at the school for three months earlier in the year. Her return is a flying visit, staying just a few days to say hello to some of her favourite children and bringing them photos from her first stay.

Throughout the afternoon, the school's cook and her sister toil over the enormous task of cooking for a hundred plus children on a tiny range. Rice noodles constitute the bulk of the meal, with a watery vegetable stew to accompany it. The keenest children begin to arrive around 3 o'clock, running around and playing games with the volunteers. I join in, chasing a couple, participating in an improvised game of volleyball then talking with some of the boys who are considerably more knowledgeable about British football than I am. When the majority of the children have arrived, we set up a serving table and begin dishing up the food, my allotted task being to pull equal size clumps of sticky noodles out of a giant steel cauldron and slap them down into disposable bowls. Once gravy's ladled on top, they're handed to the grinning kids, who eagerly wait in a straggling line. Before even half of the meals have been served, some of the hungry ones return to the side of the queue, asking if they can have seconds. There's no skimping on portions and tummies are soon filled to the brim.

Music plays on loudspeakers and the children run around having fun, talking with some of the parents or sitting with the volunteers. The cheery, party atmosphere continues until sunset, then in small groups, the children drift off home, most walking or bicycling down the lane or across the paddies. By 7.00pm, all is silent. The cook, bless her cotton socks, hasn't forgotten us and a separate pot of noodles and sauce awaits our return to the kitchen.

For the rest of the evening I relax with the volunteers, talking for a long time with Julia about her fascinating life, a good deal of which has been spent running a guest house in the Philippines. She starts a new appointment as an English teacher at a school in another Cambodian district in about a week's time, a job she envisages will last a year. After that, she's open to whatever comes her way. Her happy-go-lucky, positive approach to life is infectious, although, she confesses, her own grown-up children and grandchildren don't think so, wishing she'd settle down in a place that, to their thinking, is safer, i.e. the UK! Before bed, I decide to stretch my legs and go for a walk. I'm warned that nearby village dogs will be very territorial in the dark but armed with my torch, a couple of hefty stones in my pocket and a large staff donated by one of the local translators, I set off down the lane. Within 200 metres I'm confronted by three fierce hounds so, reflecting on Shakespeare's words 'discretion is the better part of valour,' I slowly turn and amble back.

I'd originally planned to leave early tomorrow, bypassing Phnom Penh and putting some good miles under my belt before nightfall. However, the school's atmosphere is seductive and I dearly want to see the children being taught. On the spur of the moment, I decide to postpone my departure until after the first classes, which start at 1pm for the youngest pupils, then ride the short distance to the capital. I could happily stay longer, despite the basic facilities, but I need to leave time up my sleeve before my flight back to the UK, which I've now booked, leaving Bangkok in just eight days.

Day 93. Bakod Village to Phnom Penh. 56 miles.

My body clock's used to early starts so I am the first up. As I'm washing my breakfast plate, Julia emerges from the girl's dorm. Impressively travelling with her own yoga mat, she commences a series of slow stretches whilst I head for the play area and begin the onerous task of cleaning up the aftermath of the party. There are dozens of sets of cups, chopsticks and bowls to collect, many of the latter containing sloppy remnants of food together with an assortment of drowned insects. Once she's limbered up, Julia joins me then, one at a time, the rest of the yawning volunteers make an appearance and the work incrementally speeds up. When the heavy wooden tables have been returned to the classrooms and the final scraps of litter binned, we head back to the recreation area for a well deserved coffee.

I spend a contented time checking the bike over and loading her up then sit with Jason for a while, discussing the Hope Agency project. The underlying problem they face is lack of funding. The school operates on a pittance, a situation that's not helped by the primary source of its volunteers, a UK based agency that connects prospective participants with a variety of schemes around the world. They subtract a substantial operating and marketing charge from the fees that volunteers pay then often take weeks, and sometimes months, to pass the residue on to the school. What Jason really needs is a steady supply of volunteers who find the school directly, not via a third party, and some additional donations so he can invest in better facilities for both the international visitors and the children. The place isn't slickly run or ultra professional but that's part of its charm. The critical factor is that the children are benefiting from their additional education.

I'm intrigued by how Jason copes with the constantly changing faces that surround him.

"I enjoy it very much. A lot of volunteers stay for just a short time but the ones who remain longer and make a real impact on the school usually keep in touch on Facebook. Many come back to see us again, like Julia. This is a particularly quiet time. At Christmas, most people head home, but at the busiest times we can have as many as thirty volunteers, which is great for the children as there are enough people to teach arts and crafts, play games, take them on trips and also work on improving the amenities here."

He ends our conversation by explaining that his immediate priority is to acquire some computers so he can begin teaching the children computer skills. At the moment, however, he doesn't have enough funds to do this.

When Jason leaves to visit his parents, kindly offering to collect the pair of socks I'd absentmindedly left drying on a tree beside their house, I consider the words of Henry David Thoreau, 'There is no more fatal blunderer than he who consumes the greater part of his life getting his living.' Although money is part of the picture, Jason appears to have achieved a balance, seemingly untroubled by the challenges he faces and in no way consumed by the need to work longer hours, earn bigger wages, amass possessions or accrue wealth. I walk to see the baby goats at the back of the compound accompanied by one of the dogs, aptronymically called Scabby Dog, and reflect on the busy 7 day weeks I so often work at home.

The first classes commence at one o'clock, all of them for pupils aged between 4 and 6. Ross, Lorna and Jess go to greet their students then set them to work, which mostly involves responding to oral prompts and questions. None of the three have had any formal teacher training, they simply picked things up from their fellow volunteers and Jason when they got here. As a back up. there are two local translators plus Jason who help, especially the older children, understand grammar and tenses. The children interact enthusiastically with the volunteers and each other, 'though of course there's always the odd cheeky monkey who sits at the back of the class making it their job to test the teacher's sense of humour! A couple of the kids are exceptionally bright, their hands eagerly shooting into the air in answer to every question, but I'm impressed by how each of the teachers manages to include everyone in the lessons and how enjoyable they seem to be.

At the end of the 45-minute classes, I climb into my riding gear, fondly wish everyone well, then ride through the gates. Once again I'm chased by the friendly gang of school dogs including my favourite, the characterful alpha-male of the pack known as Dusty, a brown short haired dog with blonde wisps around his ears, muzzle and permanently wagging tail. With front suspension squeaking loudly, I negotiate the earthen lanes, crossing paths with a bullock cart driven by a young boy as we skirt around the walls of the village temple. Eventually regaining the sealed main road, I backtrack my route from a couple of days ago and am soon speeding north on Highway 3.

After a short coconut stop, I cross Highway 2 and head north west. Phnom Penh irrevocably draws us into its heart, congested approach roads soon giving way to wider, free-flowing boulevards. The vehicles which assemble at the frequent sets of traffic lights are an odd mix of secondhand imports, worn out oldies and a smattering of luxurious modern cars. Unlike Vietnam, the two-wheelers have free reign within the lanes. Their riders squeeze around queued cars and rickshaws to get to the front at each intersection then, demonstrating almost prescient anticipation, race forth milliseconds before the lights actually change. I find I've become something of a rickshaw connoisseur, captivated by the many variations on a theme evident throughout Asia. Here the manpowered variety are identical to Vietnam's, with the passenger(s) sitting on a comfy seat in front of a bicycle. The tuk tuks, however, are unique. The passenger cabins are large, unwieldily contraptions lined with benches that are hitched to the backs of motorcycles or scooters via a ball socket mounted on their rear seats and towed like caravans.

Today I'm navigating by a small scale map in a guide book, the relevant page progressively harder to read each time I smear it with additional layers of oil and grime off my gloves. Eventually, I arrive at the area I'm aiming for, a grid pattern of streets lined with hotels, bars and restaurants immediately north of the Royal Palace. For a change, there's still some daylight left and I unhurriedly try two smart looking hotels. Neither can offer parking but at the third attempt, a receptionist tells me I can put the bike on the pavement in a segregated area reserved for hotel guests and worker's machines. It's within a couple of metres of the outdoor security desk and seems the best option, so I accept, quickly parking up and deploying my sheets. The attendant is friendly and promises he'll pass word to the night guard to keep an extra look out for the Matchless, which will give me peace-of-mind well deserving of a good tip.

During colonial times, Phnom Penh was hailed the 'Pearl of Asia', the most beautiful French-built city in Indochina. Formed around the confluence of the Tonlé Sap and Mekong rivers and the distributary of the Bassac river, the city's currently home to around one and a half million people, a significant percentage of the country's total population of approximately 15 million. During the Vietnam War, refugees flocked here to escape the fighting that spilled over the border and by 1975, its population had virtually doubled. The Khmer Rouge, the army of the Communist Party of Kampuchea, held the city under siege for more than a year and when it finally succumbed, forcibly evacuated everybody. Brutally, they condemned all its inhabitants, irrespective of political persuasion, wealth, education, profession or health, to make a massed death march. As the Pol Pot regime sought to return the country to an agrarian economy, a high percentage of these city dwellers were placed in forced labour camps or communal farms. The Vietnamese Army drove the Khmer Rouge from Phnom Penh in 1979 and over the following two decades the population gradually returned. In recent times, foreign investment has resulted in many new developments and tourism is increasingly having an economic impact.

Two memorials to the millions who died during the four years of Pol Pot's Kampuchea can be found within Phnom Penh's city limits. Nearby is Tuol Sleng Genocide Museum, a former school which, under Khmer Rouge hegemony, became the notorious S-21 prison camp. It was a place of torture for anyone connected with the former government or foreign agencies plus the likes of intellectuals, academics, professionals and monks. The other site is 10km south of the city centre at Choeung Ek, one of Cambodia's infamous 'killing fields' where thousands were slain and buried en masse in shallow graves. Surya visited the site when she volunteered at Hope Agency and I clearly remember her phone call home that evening and how upset and disturbed she was for a long time afterwards. I've no desire to visit either place, I'm already aware of the atrocities and would rather invest my energy in hoping for a brighter future for the people of Cambodia.

Heading out for dinner, I chat with the nightwatchman then stroll to a nearby restaurant he recommends. The tables are tightly packed and mine's next to one occupied by three backpackers, two young American women and a European man who are in the middle of an emotional discussion about their love triangle. It's impossible not to overhear every word and I vacillate between acute embarrassment, sympathy... and burning curiosity! Once they leave, I while away the best part of an hour people-watching then take a leisurely stroll back to the hotel, passing a closed fruit and vegetable market where the sweetly aromatic scent of durian still hangs heavily in the sultry air.

Day 94. Phnom Penh to Siem Reap. 201 miles.

The day begins with a surreptitious oil change. Hidden under the sheets, the blackened oil drips into a bottle whilst I eat breakfast and clear my room. By chance, the area the hotel's situated in lies close to the northbound highway, National Route 6, and navigating out of Phnom Penh proves a doddle, especially as it's Saturday morning and traffic's light. After circling an impressive Wat, I join a wide boulevard, cross the Tonlé Sap river, then for a while parallel the banks of the Mekong. After 40km of leisurely riding on a broad dual carriageway, the course of the river turns north east and we continue due north. the sun shining brightly as the Matchless glides over silken asphalt.

The near straight highway cuts a silver line through miles of rice paddies and I ride contentedly for a while before breaking for a drink and to fuel. The petrol station owner and his family are drinking tea in an air conditioned room adjoining their office. Once I've paid for my petrol and a bottle of Coke, he invites me inside to join them at a table made from the lacquered cross section of a giant hardwood tree trunk. I receive welcoming sampeahs from three seated adults and two children, all placing their palms together in a prayer-like fashion and gracefully bowing their heads. Their faces show welcoming smiles but, when it becomes apparent that none of them speak English and I know no more than two words in Khmer (chomreabsuor, hello and au koun, thank you}, a stilted silence descends. In unison, they suddenly begin talking again and resume their prior conversation as if I'm not here. I sit placidly, enjoying my drink and the cool temperature. Despite our inability to communicate, I feel peaceful and completely at ease in their company.

At Kampong Thma, a town located 20km further north, the road forks with Route 6 turning firmly north east. Within a few hundred metres the tarmac ends and powdery, red dust takes over. At first I assume it won't last long and feel sorry for the adjoining householders who have to endure asphyxiating clouds of airborne earth until such time as the road's repaired. After a quarter of an hour, however, corrugations erupt in earnest and, bounced and battered, I realise that this is a long term state of affairs. By now, the highway's stretched to the width of a British six-lane motorway yet it's completely unpaved. I build up a mighty sweat, manoeuvring the bike from side to side, testing out smoother lines which all prove illusory whilst stuck in second gear. Cars and intercity buses are a constant torment. Bombing along in order to skim the tops of the washboard, they create huge palls of dust that stick to my moist face like glue and forms rock-like obstructions up my nose. The surrounding fields and houses are tainted dark red and I wonder how the locals ever manage to keep themselves clean. 45km of non-stop dirt takes almost an hour and a half to negotiate and by the time some tarmac makes an appearance, I'm exhausted.

Turning east at another fork in the road, I accelerate on beautiful black asphalt and ponder stopping for a rest, reasoning that the Matchless's hot engine could probably do with some respite as well. Bang on cue, it cuts out. Slipping into neutral, I allow the bike to coast, spying in the near distance a

399

shack-shop with a couple of chairs outside it. I roll to a halt and put the beleaguered machine onto her stand, drop my helmet and gloves onto a chair then take a slow, long look at my mount. Both it and the luggage are caked in red loam and when I look down at my jacket and pants, so am I. Glancing in one of the mirrors, I see my face and guffaw... except for two panda-like, white skin goggle rings that circle my eyes and overlap the bridge of my nose, it too is smeared red. I don't even touch the bike, but instead, remove my jacket and walk wearily to the shop front in search of a drink.

In a state of unexpected equanimity, I sit for a while then get up and test the kickstarter. There's absolutely no resistance and instantaneously, I figure out the cause of the problem. Last night, whilst sorting through my bags, I came upon the bottle of fuel additive last used in India and I'd put some in the tank at my recent petrol stop, thinking it a bit of extra insurance for the engine. As before, it's gummed the inlet valve open. I sit down again and continue to sip my drink, watching the shopkeeper work her pedal sewing machine which occupies at least half the storefront. She's sewing a man's shirt and to the right of her is a small pile of similar garments she's obviously completed today. Although there's not another building in sight along the roadside, through the trees behind the shop I can just make out the shape of several small wooden dwellings belonging to a tiny village. One of the residents, a teenage girl, is walking along a footpath quietly singing to herself but as she arrives at the front of the shop, she screams at the sight of me, dropping the container she's carrying. Hurriedly picking it up, she smiles shyly, says hello, then begins filling the vessel with water from a ground level tap. When she's done, she gives a little wave then runs back down the path, giggling.

With the engine cooled, I employ the tactic used at Wagah border, taking the plug out and spinning the crank. When I replace the plug, there's still no compression but after a couple of kicks, she nevertheless fires up. Satisfied, I thank the shopkeeper for letting me stay, don my riding kit then take my leave. Moving smoothly through the gears, I click into top and open the throttle wider, climbing from 45 to 55kmph. As suddenly as before, the engine cuts out and again I haul in the clutch lever... we've only gone half a kilometre!

If the stars were with me coasting to the shop an hour ago, they're well and truly in my favour this time as less than 200m ahead is a petrol station and the bike has just enough momentum to reach the pumps before coming to a lifeless stop. I buy 4 litres then park the Matchless in some shade and plant myself on a step next to her, patiently waiting for the engine to cool. Twenty minutes later, I get her going again and this time she all but purrs as we climb up to cruising speed and sit there, not once changing gear during the next 60km.

I take a break at a roadside rest stop where a long line of businesses cater for the needs of bus travellers and devour my second coconut of the day. Then, with little more than an hour of daylight left, I set off on what I hope will be the final run into Siem Reap. Alas, I don't make it, the darkness stealing visibility as I slow for a third long stretch of roadworks. Arriving in a village, I aim for the only source of light, steering the Matchless off the road and down a bank before coming to a halt outside a thriving, if wall-less, shop. It seems to be the heart of the community, frequented by pedestrians who appear like ghouls out of the dark and scooter riders who buy a litre of petrol at a time in recycled water bottles. I sit next to the shopkeeper's husband, a wrinkled, barebacked man who seems pleased to have my company, slapping my thigh several times while smiling broadly. After I've munched my way through a whole packet of chocolate biscuits, he points towards the invisible road and asks,

"Siem Reap?"

I nod, at which he gets up, finds pen and paper, then writes, '45km'.

I'm so comfortable amongst the shop's lively comings and goings that I don't want to move, but with time ticking away, I finally rouse myself, taping my torch onto the front dry bag and slipping a battery operated flashing red light into a rear pocket of the saddlebags for added safety.

The bike's jolted so badly by further stretches of roadworks, the torch soon angles uselessly up into the night sky. The moon's not yet made an appearance and my headlight isn't good enough to pick out the many ridges and potholes that blight our path, so I stop to re-tape the torch back into position. Within moments, I'm assaulted by a swarm of insects, some of them two inches long, which crash into my face and helmet as I bend down towards the light. Gladly underway again, I muster all the concentration I can as hardly any of the other two-wheeled road users appear to value lighting. Two scooters in succession have no taillight and another, which carries a man, a woman and her baby, is lit solely by the flashlight in the woman's hand. Further on, in pitch darkness, I pass two bicycles, two teenagers astride each one, chatting away as they carelessly weave all over the road, not a light between them. It's a tremendous weight off my mind when, 10km from the Siem Reap's centre, street lighting commences.

Siem Reap is Cambodia's premier tourist destination, the stepping off point for visitors to nearby Angkor Wat which, at just over 400 acres, is the largest religious monument in the world. Originally built in the 12th Century as a Hindu temple dedicated to Vishnu, it was quickly transformed into a Buddhist temple but over the ensuing centuries, its prominence waned in line with the declining fortunes of the Khmer Empire. Although never totally abandoned, many of its structures fell into disrepair as jungle slowly overtook it. For the two million plus international visitors that come here each year, the jungle's imposition holds a certain charm and in one temple in particular, Ta Prohm, giant tentacle-like tree roots still climb down walls in spectacular fashion. One obvious result of all the recent international attention is the development of Siem Reap itself, which is unrecognisable from my previous visit in 2004. I'm spoilt for choice by the profusion of hotels that border the main drag, riding around in a couple of circles before making a decision. The receptionists in the first two large establishments I try say they're full, although neither appear to be especially busy. At the third, the Freedom Hotel, the staff manage to see beyond my dishevelled state and find me a room, and just as importantly, a safe place for the bike squeezed in a garage next to the owner's car.

It's almost 10pm by the time I've peeled my sticky clothes off and stained a white towel with streaks of red. The hotel restaurant has closed for the night so, with the help of the receptionist, I catch a tuk tuk. It takes me a couple of kilometres to a cluster of bars and restaurants that are still open and I choose a trattoria. Pooped, I flop into a seat and order spaghetti. Only one other table's occupied and like last night, it's impossible not to overhear the conversation of the two men sitting at it. Talking loudly with a northern British accent, one of them, who comes from Brendan's home town of Chesterfield, is complaining about the price of his meal.

"That's almost two dollars fifty!" he says in disgust. "Too much for Cambodia. I'm right fed up, it's totally blown my budget for today. Let's get out of 'ere tomorrow!"

I'll also be moving on tomorrow, but for a different reason... just 150 kilometres away is the border with Thailand, which I plan to cross on what should be the penultimate day's ride of the journey.

The start of the 45km long red earth highway, Cambodia.

Day 95. Siem Reap, Cambodia, to Aranyaprathet, Thailand. 110 miles.

Over breakfast, a moment (or two) of mental arithmetic divides the current estimation of 2,000,000 annual visitors to Angkor Wat by 365 and comes up with a daily average of almost 5,500 tourists at the site. I walked around the magnificent ruins last time I was here and unique as the place is, I'm not tempted to go back for a second helping. The truth is, although it renders me a philistine, I'd much rather be on my motorcycle than milling around crumbling temples surrounded by crowds of people.

Happy to be on my way again, I load up and turn west. Reaching the outskirts of Siem Reap, I pass the most preposterous use of a motorcycle I've seen on the whole journey. A simple 125cc machine is towing two wooden flatbed trailers, one behind the other, both of which are stacked high with kingsize mattresses... there must be at least twenty! I slow for a closer look, the rider smiling and waving as the bike's droning engine toils, dragging the monstrous load at a laborious 15kmph.

Although the road is narrow, it has recently been resealed, tracking in a near straight line for over 100km towards the Thai border. Along the verges are a succession of beautifully ornate arches, some of which mark the entrance to religious sites and others which straddle dusty trails leading to distant villages. I saw a simple one astride the turn off for Bakod village and spotted a couple yesterday whilst I was negotiating the red earth road. However, the structures in this region are far more artistically decorated and I soon stop to take photographs of one.

The archway is superb, intricately covered in gold painted bas-relief, its hemispherical pediment bedecked with ornamentation that resembles stylized sun flames. Behind it is, by comparison, a rather plain temple. Presently, two inquisitive boys approach me, politely watching whilst I put my helmet back on. I ask one of them if he'll take a photo of me alongside the Matchless, which is positioned at right angles to the arch. His bewildered expression and awkwardness as he holds the camera tells me he doesn't know what it is, let alone how to operate it. Much to his relief, I take it back, then snap a photo of him. He's tickled pink when I show him the result, the only downside being I've no way of giving him a copy as my question of "email?" receives more blank stares.

The next archway I halt beneath is entirely different, bridging an earthen trail that cuts between fields to a settlement somewhere beyond the horizon. Painted pale gold, the top is formed from two nāgas, mythical serpents, with a second smaller pair crowning lesser arches on each side. The only other prominent features across the entirely flat terrain are lofty sugar palms that shoot skywards out of the quivering heat haze. Further along, I pull up beside another, this one dark brown which, if anything, is even more striking against the sand coloured track it spans. It has two small nāgas at the periphery of the arch and a golden relief of the Buddha in its central tympanum. All are highly individual and I spend large chunks of the morning admiring and photographing each one I see.

Today's lunch stop is at a quiet place and as on many previous occasions I'm the sole patron. Enjoying some relief from the sun under a bamboo sunshade, I get my camera out of its pouch to look more closely at one of the photos I'd recently taken. It's of the Matchless, no less, positioned under a light blue temple archway that's guarded by a pair of stone chinthes. By chance, a scooter had ridden past just as I clicked the shutter button and I'd inadvertently snapped an image of the woman rider with what I assumed to be her family squeezed around her. Although I only caught a fleeting glance of them riding away, there appeared to be four on the seat, some achievement considering it's only a narrow strip of foam approximately 60cm long. When I zoom in on the photo, I begin head counting. There's a little boy at the front sitting between his mum's legs, a girl in a yellow top, a girl in a pink dress and a teenager in black hanging on at the back. That makes five! Double-checking, I increase the zoom to maximum and notice a previously unseen leg topped with red shorts that's poking out from directly behind the mother. Making a careful recount, I can hardly believe what I'm seeing... there are six bodies sandwiched on the seat. Goodness knows how the one on the back is managing to stay on!

After another hour of hot riding, I spot a snack shack at the roadside and decide to pull over for a cold drink. Precariously balancing the Matchless on a steep, sandy slope, I strip off my jacket and step under the shop's canopy. For sale are an assortment of dried delicacies as well as packets of sweets and biscuits, none of which appeal, but the proprietor smartly produces a Coke from a fridge when I ask for a cold drink. Sitting down on a nearby stool, I suck through a straw whilst condensation trickles down the side of the bottle, onto my hand and up my arm. Taking in the surroundings, there's little around except baked, scrubby fields. Sitting just a few metres away at the extremity of the shade are three local women who I'm conscious have been watching and talking about me.

"Where you from?" asks the nearest, a lady probably in her thirties with a broad, smiling face under tied-up black hair.

When I tell her, she translates my response and for some reason all three of them burst into laughter. Several more questions follow, relating to my home, where I'm going and if I'm on my own. After further chatter and giggles, the woman enquires,

"You... married?"

I've never been married so answer "no", which adds to the hilarity. I'm about to mention Jane when the translator's friends nudge her in the ribs and I'm propositioned,

"You marry me... I good wife!"

By now all three are doubled up, holding their stomachs, and their mirth is so infectious I find myself laughing with them. Although it's quite common for European men to have an Asian wife, especially from Thailand, I assume this is just a bit of tourist baiting and I'm sorely tempted to say yes, just to see her reaction. Instead I tell her I'm not available and in any case, I'm way too old for her. Ready to leave, I sampeah and all three respond in kind then, waving to them from the bike, I head to the final frontier.

Poipet is a bustling town where Cambodian traders, pushing handcarts backwards and forwards across the border on day passes, bring cheap and often secondhand Thai goods into Cambodia. Because of its proximity to Angkor Wat, the place is also busy with tourist coaches travelling between Bangkok and Siem Reap. Cambodian immigration sits at a large roundabout but when I try to turn towards it, an official steps out and directs me back down the road to the hidden customs building. There's no faffing around here. In a small office, a uniformed man bows, takes my carnet and with a quickfire stamp... stamp... stamp... hands it back. It's another new record, this time under a minute! Back at immigration, I park the bike and join a long queue, half of which is made up of excited backpackers. Once my passport's endorsed with an exit stamp, I push the bike towards the Thai compound where things get rather more complicated.

The first set of customs officials sit me at an outside table, instructing me to fill in two sets of badly photocopied import licenses identical to the those I'd completed when arriving from Myanmar. It takes a further 15 minutes to have them approved. Positioned in direct sunlight and by now baking hot, I'm regretting that I didn't strip off when I arrived but fortunately, just as the heat's becoming overwhelming, I'm given the documents and told I can leave. Joyfully, I remount the bike only to be halted round the next corner by another official. Here they need to input the paperwork onto a computer and unfortunately, there's a problem. Putting the bike on her sidestand, I sit on a kerbstone and wait. By the time I realise I've overheated, it's almost too late and I feel decidedly faint. Quickly shedding my clothes, I vigorously waft myself with a map. Observing my flushed cheeks, a kindly official appears with an iced bottle of water, most of which I pour over my head and down my back. When I'm feeling better, I get up and check the thermometer... it reads 39 degrees in the shade!

Almost an hour later, an eloquent woman comes over to explain the hold up. Their computer shows that the Matchless is already in Thailand and after checking the stamps in my passport, she had to phone the Nong Khai border post where I exited to Laos. It has taken the staff there half an hour to find the relevant paperwork and belatedly update their system. I'm only glad that this time I refrained from producing my carnet... that really would have added to the confusion!

Until reaching Thai customs, the day's ride had been completely undemanding. Once free of the border, the challenges continue to mount, although in a rather unexpected way. The main road west is lined with hotels that are mostly set back in leafy clearings. The first two I try offer accommodation in perfectly adequate cabins. One has a room rate of 250 bhat and the other, 300, which equates to £5 and £6 respectively. Being so cheap, neither has credit card facilities. I only have 200 bhat in my wallet and had failed to spot a moneychanger at the border so am reluctantly forced to move on and try more lodgings. Riding up and down the road, I check out three further establishments, all of which accept plastic but are fully booked. Eventually heading into Aranyaprathet centre, I pull up at an expansive, modern hotel close to the railway station. It has rooms and payment facilities but nowhere to put the bike! More than an hour and a half after leaving the customs compound, spirits sagging and my body wilting, I set the satnav to take us to the Indochina Hotel which, according to several billboards, is the town's one and only 4 star accommodation.

Pulling off the road onto a curving entranceway, my first thought is, 'Oh dear, this is going to be expensive!' The place is far grander than anywhere else in the locale and even has uniformed parking attendants and porters. To my delight, I'm directed to park the bike opposite the front doors, in full view of the doormen and reception. Even better, a luxury double room costs just £19 and comes complete with towels rolled into the shapes of two swans that nestle on the bed, beaks touching.

Later, I sit in the restaurant staring vacantly ahead like a space cadet. I'm so bushed I can hardly read the menu and squinting in vain, eventually give up and ask the waiter to help. Tomorrow will be the last day of the journey, a fact which I can hardly contemplate. As soon as I've eaten, I head for bed, out for the count within minutes, the TV still on.

Day 96. Aranyaprathet to Bangkok. 180 miles.

It may be the last day of the ride but that doesn't mean I can skimp on maintenance, in fact, Murphy's Law being what it is, it's probably more important than ever today! A freshly washed air filter, re-tensioned chain, topped up oil, re-gapped spark plug and a spot of air in the tyres don't take long and I'm soon loading up, preparing to leave. With all my gear on except crash helmet and gloves, I go through the well established starting routine then swing the kickstart over compression. The engine catches first kick... considering everything I've put her through over the last 95 days, it's little short of a miracle. Paying no heed to what passers-by might think, I wrap my arms around her tank, choked. What a brilliant motorcycle!

After 40km of easy-going dual carriageway, I pull into my favourite brand of Thai petrol station, ostensibly to fill up but, more truthfully, to have my first chocolate Cornetto since Laos. Not hanging around, I promptly set off again, putting in another 60km stint on easy-going roads that are light on traffic. Puttering along, I spot a temple adorned by a sublimely sculptured golden Buddha head standing at least 3m tall. Within a couple of minutes a roundabout shows up so I make an about turn and head back towards the temple. Pulling up in its leafy grounds, I pop the bike on her stand, stretch my back then wander around, admiring the stupas and golden effigies. A mangy, short haired dog appears round a corner and instantly seems out of sorts with my presence, timidly approaching then hurriedly backing away again. When he gets too close I gently shoo him back, which he doesn't like. He starts barking, calling up reinforcements, and within seconds three further dogs appear. Now much bolder, he closes in, as do his cohorts, all of them showing their teeth and barking. I retreat to the Matchless and fortunately, the sound of her firing up makes them recoil so I roar out of the compound before they have time to give chase.

As I turn onto the main southbound highway to Bangkok there's a noticeable shift in the volume of traffic, with cars and long-distance buses being the worst as they plough along at breakneck speeds. The closer we get to the city, the more frequently major intersections and traffic lights delay us and at each of them, I join long queues of vehicles waiting for countdown timers to tick through the seconds and the lights to change colour. The traffic eventually becomes so heavy I take to the narrow hard shoulder and along with the other bikes, undertake the stalled lines that wait behind each set of signals. After almost an hour of taxing concentration, I pull over, deciding to let the engine cool thoroughly before making a final thrust to the capital.

Parking on a grassy bank, I look up to a huge freestanding billboard which sports a picture of King Bhumibol Adulyadej. Crowned in 1946, he's currently the world's longest reigning head of state and in 1987 was conferred with the noble title *King Bhumibol the Great*. Highly revered by the majority of Thais, many of whom look upon him as being akin to a deity, there are glorified images of Bhumibol and his wife, Queen Sirikit, everywhere you look. They span the roads on colourful overhead gantries, line the streets in ornate frames atop of lampposts and like here, grab the attention of passing motorists. Some show the king regally attired in royal robes, others depict him at work, dressed in a smart business suit whilst signing official paperwork. The one I'm parked underneath is a less formal picture, however, portraying him as a man-about-town dressed in flannels and a sports coat, a broadsheet newspaper tucked under his arm and a large Nikon camera in his left hand. The picture presents him like an affluent Westerner, not a Thai, and I wonder how his subjects are supposed to relate to him via this portrait. Maybe that's not the purpose... old Kingy and Queenie are the world's richest Royals, with an estimated wealth of over $30 billion and no tax to pay on their annual income. Furthermore, they're protected by Thai lèse-majesté laws which make it a crime to violate the so called dignity of a reigning sovereign resulting in many of their critics being thrown into gaol. While the heat in Matchless's engine gradually dissipates, I can't help thinking what a crazy world we live in.

Now four lanes wide, the southbound carriageway splits with two roads forking off to the left, another to the right and a fourth swooping onto and up a steep ramp. Volatile traffic's darting every which-way, and pressed tight to my left, is a scooter with an ungainly street food sidecar attached that's furnished with a gas wok. It has a flat rear tyre and is wobbling jerkily as it crawls forwards. My satnav indicates the route I should take with a thick pink line but the junction's so complicated I can't work out which one it means in the few seconds I have to scrutinize it. Forced to make a decision, I plump for the ramp which takes me skywards, depositing me onto an overhead expressway.

It opens up beautifully, three wide lanes in both directions and much less traffic than down below. Gleefully I accelerate up to 75kmph, thinking that in today's steamy 37°C heat, the Matchless's baking engine is going to love the improved airflow. After a couple of minutes, I become aware that I'm the only motorbike on the road and it slowly sinks in that there's probably a good reason for that... like they're not allowed! As the kilometres pass, I grow increasingly uneasy, aware that I should get off it as soon as possible.

The first exit sign I come to has the unmistakable symbol for an airport. Looking ahead and over the barrier, I see the familiar outline of Don Muang, Bangkok's old International airport that I've used many times in the past. Now I know where I am... I'm on the 22km long Don Muang Tollway, an expressway that leads directly to the centre of the city. I've travelled along it on many occasions in taxis and know that down below us, the same journey could take hours longer. By the time these thoughts have been fully processed, the junction has passed and along with it my chance to avoid almost certain trouble. The next exit, it transpires, is beyond a tollbooth and as I approach the line of kiosks, I watch a motorcycle cop in a tight fitting chocolate brown uniform step out and begin waving at me. I ride over to him and stop. He looks stern and my heart sinks ... a hefty fine seems inevitable this time, and so close to the end of the journey too!

As he doesn't speak English I adopt full ham acting mode, giving the performance of a lifetime as I portray how I became confused at the junction then, whilst I was riding, discovered there were no other motorcycles. Incredibly, he laughs along with me, patting me on the back, his kind face showing empathy with my predicament. Talking into his radio, he summons help, signalling for me to wait at the railed side of the road. Within minutes, a highway maintenance pickup arrives, roof mounted amber lights flashing boldly. I'm told to follow him so thank the policeman with a warm handshake and depart behind my escort. It immediately zooms off, virtually disappearing from sight until the driver realises how slowly I'm travelling, at which point he brakes dramatically for me to catch up. 7km later, at the next off ramp, he releases me and I'm free to go.

Free, in this case, is a relative term because now I'm in the midst of Bangkok's notorious evening rush-hour traffic. Bangkok has been classified as the second most congested city in the world behind Mexico City and it's estimated that there are now upwards of nine million vehicles registered within the metropolis and its surrounding provinces. However, the city's streets are thought only able to cope with approximately one and a half million vehicles at any given time and the resulting traffic jams waste fuel worth millions of baht every day. The Garmin says I still have 18km to go, which should be fun...

Everything moves incredibly slowly except for the motorbikes which slip in and out of the crawling lanes. As much as possible I do the same but it's far from easy on my laden machine, a relative porker compared to the nippy lightweights locals ride. Using my feet for balance as I edge between parked cars and stationary buses, I weave the Matchless inside and out, pressed hard against either the central reservation or the kerb. Crawling over sharp humpbacked bridges that span narrow canals, I ride under an overpass then over an underpass, squeezing the bike into the tiniest gaps just to keep some forward momentum. An hour passes, the sky becomes dark, the street lights go on and still there are 5km to go to reach the district of Banglamphu and a hotel I booked online last night, one of the few budget accommodations with off-street parking.

All of a sudden I see the closed off entrance to Bangkok's famous backpacker mecca, Khaosan Road, and realise we've arrived. Pausing, I look down its heaving length, mobbed with hordes of shambling pedestrians, purveyors of street food and stalls selling everything from fake student ID cards and pirate CDs to hippy clothes and silver jewellery. Moving on then turning left, I spot the sign for *Banglumpoo Place* and slowly ride under its covered entrance, halting beside the hotel reception window.

A hotel seems an innocuous place to finish the expedition, neither exotic nor epic, but the end it is. I sit in silence, not wanting to get off the bike. A lady comes out of reception and, handing her my camera, I ask if she'd mind capturing the moment. Still I'm glued to the saddle, embodying a dichotomy of elation at having completed the ride and absolute sorrow that it's over. I'm shaken out of my daze by the receptionist who, handing back my camera, enquires,

"Checking in?"

I climb off and as I push the Matchless to a corner, remember the words Simon Warner said to me before I set off,

"Even when they were totally worn out, they still kept going."

He wasn't wrong!

With the bike secured for the night and the luggage piled up in my room, I flop into a chair and call home to let everyone know I'm safe. That done, I phone the trusty trio of Andy, Derek and Andrew Engineering to pass on the news that the bike has made it. Sweat congealing and my clothes turning stiff, I stay rooted in the seat, unable to stir as thoughts about the journey overwhelm me.

What remains? What is impressed upon me? The landscapes; the mountains, deserts and seas; the fabulous architecture and awesome roads; dramatic changes in flora; variations in smells and cuisine; the challenges of tough terrain and the strains of negotiating crazy traffic. There's been delight in riding my motorcycle day after day and a certain pride in keeping her going. However, I realise that, on this journey, something has impacted me more profoundly than ever before. The people. For despite adversity; extremes of climate; earthquakes; cluster bombs; landmines; dictatorships; appalling living conditions; severely limited opportunities and, in many cases, harsh poverty, I have witnessed the strength, resilience, kindness and sheer decency of these fellow humans and seen, firsthand, their indomitable spirits.

Before I set off for Vietnam, I knew this book would be dedicated to my dear friend Kay Thi... but as I come to the end of telling my journey's tale, I realise there is another dedication which needs expressing, one which Kay Thi would have wholly embraced. This book is also dedicated to the good hearted, perennially enterprising, innately valiant and truly remarkable human spirit because, no matter what is thrown at it, it will somehow, as the people I've met on my three month ride have so richly shown me, manage to, "pick itself up, dust itself off, and start all over again".

Epilogue

I have three days in Bangkok before my flight back to the UK. The primary task is shipping the bike, something I've organised on the wing whilst travelling. My contact, an efficient Thai lady called Nisarat, provides directions to a contractor who will crate her up for the long sea journey. I set off the next day, a 30km crawl through the centre of Bangkok that takes almost two hours, then watch, captivated, as a team of four lean young men set to work with planks and powertools. Strapping the Matchless firmly onto a platform, they enfold her in enough clingfilm to wrap a thousand sandwiches then build an open sided crate around her, telling me it's made this way so Thai customs can see inside. It looks more like a pen for transporting sheep than a motorcycle and concerned about its strength, I encourage them to write 'Top Load Only' around its flanks.

When they're done, I complete all the necessary paperwork and pay the shipping fee, which equates to roughly £400. Helpfully, they call me a taxi, but leaving my beloved motorcycle behind tugs hard at my heartstrings and while no one's looking, I stick my hand into the crate and, over the layers of polythene, pat her petrol tank farewell.

Once I've bought a couple of presents, I'm at a loss to know what to do with myself. I take a boat down the river and wander through parks and Chinatown but still feel in a state of limbo. In the end, I settle for escape via a good book and spend hours sitting outside a cafe, time slowly ticking by.

Finally on the aeroplane, I avidly follow the route we're taking. The map on the screen in front of me accurately shows our path across many of the countries I'd ridden through such a short time ago. Looking out of the window at the appropriate times, I spot the bright line of the Expressway somewhere between Naypyidaw and Yangon, the lush plains of northern India, the icy peaks of Pakistan, the golden desert of Turkmenistan and finally, when we cross the Caspian Sea at sunset, the shimmering lights of Baku. 'All those miles,' I think as I look down from on high.

Arriving at Manchester airport on a bitter cold December evening, I'm met by Jane and Jacques. Jacques exuberantly shouts through the open car window,

"Gordon May, where do you think you're going?"
As I look around trying to locate him, he jokingly continues,

"Over here, you old geezer!"
I'm overjoyed to see them. Climbing into the car, Jacques's dog, Rosie, jumps onto my lap and begins licking my hands and face. Jacques, like most youngsters in the UK at this time of year, can talk of little else but Christmas and all the presents he hopes to get. His life's so utterly different from those of the children I've recently met and I just nod my head and make non-committal sounds as the list grows. Their relief at having me safely back is written on their faces and I'm only glad I was able to honour my promise to Jacques to make it home before Christmas Day.

Unlocking my front door, I'm greeted by bright lights and a noisy TV, all courtesy of timer plugs that, rather strangely, make the place feel as if I've never been away. Before going to bed, I switch on my computer and whilst 7,224 emails download, send one to Nisarat, asking for an update on my bike which should have been picked up by the shippers today. There's no way I'm going to be able to fully relax until I have my most magnificent, stoic, trustworthy and marvellous Matchless safely back in my hands.

Suppliers: Motorcycle

Matchless Parts and Consumables
Almost all parts used in the restoration of the bike, including new crankshaft axles, oil pump, clutch, sprockets, bushes, bearings, fork stanchions and springs, wheel spindles and brake shoes, as well as a plethora of small components and fixings, were provided by AMC parts specialists **Andrew Engineering**. They even specially fabricated a stronger rear wheel bearing and axle arrangement for my rigid Matchless.
Formed in 1980, the company manufactures a wide range of high quality replacement parts for both AJS and Matchless and offers a friendly, knowledgeable and fast service. I cannot recommend them highly enough. However, the owners, Malcolm and Joan Lee, are due to retire in the next couple of years so it's a case of making the most of their parts and excellent service whilst still available.
Contact: www.andrew-engineering.co.uk Tel: (+44) 01942 888848

Chain
I used Iwis *Megalife* chain from **Sprockets Unlimited.** This chain has a coating that ensures it doesn't rust and special sintered bushes, which means it can be run dry or with minimal lubrication when necessary, useful in sandy conditions. I was very pleased with the life of the first chain, which endured 10,000 tough miles with little adjustment. Iwis chains are made in Germany from high quality, quenched, tempered and case-hardened steels. They are pre-stretched with shouldered pins and have a high fatigue strength and superior wear resistance. As well as the drive chain, **Sprockets Unlimited** also provided the Matchless with new magneto, dynamo and primary chains, all of the highest standard. Because of the lateral movement caused by the engine shock absorber, they recommended a speedway primary chain made by Regina which was flexible enough to allow this degree of movement. It only twice needed adjusting on the whole ride.
Contact: www.sprocketsunlimited.com Tel: (+44) 01386 831341

Powder Coating
Riding a military-looking motorcycle in the sensitive borders regions of Central Asia could have been problematic so I decided to civilianise my Matchless. **Redditch Shotblasting** did a brilliant job, powder coating everything high gloss black. The finish is excellent, but that's what you would expect from the company's owners, classic motorcycle enthusiasts Dave and Porl Joynes, as they've been in business for 40 years. They also had a couple of dents knocked out of my tank. Superb service.
Contact: www.redditchshotblasting.co.uk Tel: (+44) 01527 529659

Tyres
Finding dual sport tyres for classic 19" wheels is a challenge! On the front I fit a **Mitas E07** enduro tyre which has an excellent reputation for both on and off road use. It ran the whole journey and still has plenty of tread left. The **Mitas H02** is a classic motorcycle tyre which I used on the rear through Europe and the Caucasus. When the going got tough, I changed it for a **Heidenau K67** Trials tyre, which had brilliant grip off road and to my surprise, on road too, in both scorching heat and extremely wet conditions. It stayed on all the way to Vietnam. All were supplied by **Tyre-Finder.** Their simple website has a downloadable PDF listing the tyres they supply and the friendly service and advice given by the owner, Mick, is excellent. Mick's also a regular attendee at many classic motorcycle shows and autojumbles in the UK.
Contact: www.tyre-finder.co.uk Tel: (+44) 07796 188283 or 0845 2301966

Wheels
Hidden under thick green paint, my bike's rims and spokes were badly rust damaged. I sent the hubs to wheel experts **Central Wheel Components** who rebuilt them using new British steel rims and spokes powder coated gloss black, a brilliant finish. The resulting wheels took an enormous pounding and never let me down. The company provided spare spokes for the journey, which weren't needed
Contact: www.central-wheel.co.uk Tel: (+44) 01621 841100

Oil
Using fully synthetic oils in classic engines is a much debated topic. Naysayers contest that you should only use the grade of oil originally specified by the maker. I decided, after much research, to use a synthetic and I'm glad I did. I chose **Silkolene Comp 4 Synthetic** ester based engine oil. It's especially good for performance engines running in hot climates. It's also suitable for many vintage and classic engines where monograde oils were originally specified and has been successfully used in roller bearing engines like mine. Oil experts, **Opie Oils,** supplied it, along with excellent advice.
Contact: www.opieoils.co.uk Tel: (+44) 01209 202944

Ultrasonic cleaning
The Matchless's alloy engine cases were in poor condition, oil stained and corroded. I sent them to **CC's Carburettor Cleaners** who specialise in ultrasonic and vapour cleaning. Using high pressure water and fine blasting media, they returned the crankcases, rocker box and timing chaincase to a lustrous satin finish... better than new! CC's are experts at cleaning old carburettors, as well as larger components such as cylinder heads and wheels, using safe and gentle processes. A highly recommended family business with a fast turnaround and very friendly service.
Contact: www.carbcleaning.com Tel: (+44) 05602 051339

Magneto & Dynamo
Both the Matchless's Lucas N1 magneto and 6 volt dynamo were restored by expert, **Tony Cooper** of Halesowen, West Midlands. Tony, known as 'The Mag Man', was a long time exhibitor at classic motorcycle shows and autojumbles but now only works from home. His skill and experience gave me enormous peace of mind and both units were 100% reliable, running for many hours a day in extremes of climate.
Contact: (+44) 0121 5592405

Cables
On the rides to India and Egypt I needed special cables making to accommodate non-standard fittings on the bikes. However, the Matchless was much simpler to equip and I was able to get off the shelf items from **JJ Cables**, a long established company making cables for all types of British motorcycles. They all fit perfectly and none broke. JJs are a regular attendee at Stafford, Kempton Park and Founders Day motorcycle events.
Contact: Tel: (+44) 01926 651470

Automatic Chain Oiler
I've used a manually operated **Tutoro chain oiler** in the past and found it excellent at extending chain life. Tutoro have now developed a very clever automatic chain oiler which is simple to install and operate. The oiler has an adjustable flow rate to account for different riding conditions and is leakproof when the bike's stationary. It's one of the simplest and best bits of kit I used on the Matchless.
Contact: www.tutorochainoiler.com Tel: (+44) 01594 841097

Air Filter

My previous rides to India and Egypt taught me to value a good air filter. Sandy and dusty road conditions en route to Egypt were superbly dealt with by **Ramair pod filters,** so I used the same on the Matchless. They have a unique multilayered Aeriform material that ensures maximum filtration and come pre-oiled & ready to fit. Importantly, they can be washed and reused many times over. I carried three on the ride to Vietnam and they gave great service.

Contact Tel: www.ramair-filters.co.uk (+44) 01980 623401

Exhaust

I struggled to find an exhaust solution for the bike as it needs an early-type downpipe that sits above the footpegs. Then I tried **Armours**, a long established and renowned British motorcycle parts manufacturer. They produce exhaust systems in the UK from heavy, high grade steel with a top quality chrome finish. Their stock includes a wide range of Matchless exhausts (among many other makes of British motorcycles) including one produced to the original WWII pattern. It's well made, solid and fit perfectly onto the bike!

Contact: www.armoursltd.co.uk Tel: (+44) 01202 519409.

Mirrors

I've used stainless steel fittings on the bike where possible. **Halcyon Design & Manufacturing**, famous for their aviator and motorcycle goggles, produce beautiful stainless handlebar and bar-end mirrors. I fitted a pair of their *Stadium 850* handlebar mirrors which are authentically classic and were surprisingly untroubled by vibration.

Contact: www.classicpartsltd.com Tel: (+44) 01920 486032

Number Plates

In the UK, pre-1973 cars and motorcycles can use old style numberplates with silver or white letters on a black background. Mine were made by specialists, **Tippers Vintage Plates**. The numerals are die pressed, highly polished aluminium on a stove-enamelled black background.

They look stunning, far superior to the stick-on white letters you often see applied to the rear numberplates of many classic bikes. Unfortunately, I lost one of the two curved front number plates en route, but that was down to me not securing it properly.

Contact: www.tippersvintageplates.co.uk Tel: (+44) 01726 879799

Battery

Lead acid batteries tend to be big and heavy, a large 18 A/H battery can weigh over 3.5kg. I used a compact **Shorai Lithium Ion** 18 A/H battery which weighs just 0.5kg. It holds its charge for a year without maintenance and can be recharged in approximately 10 minutes via a special charger. With twice the service life of a lead acid battery, using one was a no-brainer! Mine was supplied by UK importers and classic motorcycle and performance parts specialists, **Carrot Cycles,** who are, through years of working with lithium Ion technology, experts in the field .

Contact: www.carrotcycles.co.uk Tel: (+44) 01522 595975

Fuel Taps & Ethanol Resistant Hose

Carrot Cycles is a UK web-based business specialising in quality classic motorcycle consumables. They supplied two new 1/8 Gas traditional push/pull fuel taps, a fuel filter and **ethanol resistant fuel hose** to suit.

Contact: www.carrotcycles.co.uk Tel: (+44) 01522 595975

Indicators

I'm usually happy to use hand signals whilst riding my classics locally. However, on long international journeys it has always seemed prudent to fit indicators. **Paul Goff**, a specialist supplier of classic motorcycle electrical parts, provided two pairs of classic-looking indicators, a matching relay and an unobtrusive handlebar switch.
Contact: **www.norbsa02.freeuk.com Tel: (+44) 01494 868218**

Headlight and brake switch

The headlight that was attached to the Matchless when I bought her was not original and its blackout mask made it unsuitable for this ride. Andy and Sean of Midland's based **Kidderminster Motorcycles** supplied a replica Lucas MU42 6½" headlight as well as a period looking brake light switch.
Contact: **www.kidderminstermotorcycles.co.uk Tel: (+44) 01562 66679**

Pinstriping

The first post war Matchless G3Ls had beautiful pinstriping along the full length of their petrol tanks. As I've civilianised mine, I opted for the same look. Rob Evans of **Shropshire Classic Sprayers** did a wonderful job recreating the lines from a period advertisement. He also lacquered the finished job to prevent damage from fuel spills, which was just as well!
Contact: **www.restorebike.co.uk Tel: (+44) 07800 863969**

Crankshaft

My existing cast iron flywheels were badly bruised and the replacements I bought online had a hairline fracture. Dudley based experts, **Alpha Bearings,** have been making crankshafts for 70 years. They fabricated new flywheels from Sheffield billet steel, incorporating a needle roller big end on an oversize crankpin, jig ground and significantly stronger than the original. The Matchless's bottom end was bombproof!
Contact **www.alpha-bearings.com Tel: (+44) 01384 255151**

Fuel Catalyst

My motorcycle was originally built to run on leaded petrol. To cope with poor quality, low octane unleaded petrol, I used a **Spitfire Fuel Catalyst.** This helped the engine run cooler, protected the exhaust valve and assisted power output when the fuel was low grade. It didn't gum up the Matchless's inlet valve either, unlike the liquid additive I used on part of the journey. You just drop it in your petrol tank and forget about it.
Contact: **www.spitfirefuelcatalyst.co.uk Tel: (+44) 01403 754173**

Light Bulbs

As I wanted to run the bike all day with my lights on, I used an LED tail light and LED pilot bulb as daylight running lights. For the main beam, I installed a 6 volt LED H4 dipping bulb, which puts out a pure white light with a consumption rating of only 3.2 amps. These were supplied by **Classic Dynamo & Regulator Conversions.**
Contact: **www.dynamoregulatorconversions.com**

Engine Rebuild

The Matchless's engine was carefully restored by classic motorcycle engineer, **Andy Berry** of Preston, UK. Andy also restored my 2008 'Overland To India' Royal Enfield engine which proved so reliable. His attention to detail and workmanship are top class and his knowledge of classic motorcycle engineering invaluable to this project.
Contact email: **ajb1962@hotmail.co.uk Tel: +44 (0)1772 788077**

Carburettor

I fit the Matchless with a new **MK1 Concentric Premier carburettor** from **The Amal Carburettor Company.** Made to exceedingly high standards, it's slightly larger than the WWII Amal carbs so not 100% original for my bike. However, having a wholly reliable, no fuss, easy to set up carburettor was, and is, priceless. It came with Amal's proprietary **'Stay Up Float'**, and excellent idea. I carried an **Amal Repair Kit** just in case anything needed working on and a selection of jets to cope with the extremes of altitude, all from the same supplier. Worth every penny!
Contact: www.amalcarb.co.uk Tel: (+44) 01722 412500

Accessories

Brendan Layton of **Motorbikebits** provided a **handlebar brace**, great for attaching my satnav and clocks. He also supplied **bar-end weights**, not that the Matchless vibrates... much!. My choice of alarms was limited due to using a 6 volt battery. Brendan supplied a compact but loud **alarm** that runs off a 9 volt disposable battery. I surreptitiously mounted it at the rear of the bike. Just the job.
Contact: www.motorbikebits.co.uk Tel: (+44) 07914 783197

Speedometer

My **Smiths 80mph Chronometric Speedometer** is a mechanical work of art that was fully serviced by **Philip Woods.** Along with his father, David Woods, Philip also offers completely restored Smiths speedometers on an exchange basis for your old one. As well as working by post, he can be seen at London's Kempton Park autojumble and Netley Marsh Eurojumble.
Contact: www.chronometricspeedos.co.uk Tel: (+44) 01903 724509

Electronic Regulator

I used a 12 volt **JG electronic regulator** on my ride to India as it allowed my 6 volt dynamo to charge a 12 volt system. They're Bullet-proof. The Matchless has an earlier, lower output dynamo and I was advised to keep it running on 6 volts. An appropriate 6 volt JG unit was supplied by **Dave Lindsley**, who is very knowledgeable about classic motorcycle charging. It worked perfectly.
Contact: www.davelindsley.co.uk Tel: (+44) 01568 617750

Electronic Ignition Magneto Repair / Upgrade Kit

My Matchless's ignition runs on a magneto and its failure would have meant the end of the journey. However, a spare unit would have been exceedingly cumbersome and heavy to carry. Instead, I packed a **Thorspark** electronic ignition unit as a back up. It's compact, lightweight and easily fits into the end cap of the magneto. Even if the Matchless's dynamo had failed, the Thorspark would have run the bike all day on one charge of its 6 volt battery. As it transpired, I didn't need to use it but it gave me peace of mind and saved carrying a spare magneto.
Contact: www.sussexmotorcycles.com/thorspark Tel: (+44) 01273 491362

New Old Stock Parts

I needed a replacement cylinder, piston, small end and push rods to complete the Matchless's restoration. London based **Russell Motors** have been in business for over 50 years and still have genuine WWII Matchless parts squirrelled away in dark corners of their premises. Les Myers knows the machines inside out and was able to find the parts I needed, still caked in thick layers of army protective grease!
Contact: www.russellmotors.co.uk Tel: +44 (0)207 2281714

Welding

Derek took all the parts that needed welding, including crash bars, luggage rack and bracketry, to **Lavis Engineering of Widnes.** The work was efficiently carried out to a high standard by the team of Gary, Danny, Liam and Aaron.

Contact: Tel: (+44) 0151 423 4443

Suppliers: Bike Equipment

Gel Pad

I was so stiff and sore on the ride to India that I estimate I must have ridden at least 10% of the journey standing up. On my return to the UK I set about solving the problem. The result is the **Supreme Comfort Seat Gel Pad.** Made from medical grade gel (a hi-tech viscoelastic polymer that prevents friction between the seat and skin, distributes weight evenly, gives a floatation effect and reduces vibration), the pad simply clips on top of any existing seat.

The horrendous terrain on parts of the ride to Vietnam resulted in more than half the saddle's mattress springs and one of its two main coil springs breaking. Despite this, I never had a numb bum, even when riding as many as 10 hours a day.

Contact: Supreme Comfort Seats, www.motorcyclegelpad.co.uk

Tools

After years of fiddling around with secondhand tools of average quality, I now have a set of the best, thanks to British manufacturer **Britool**.

My bike uses Whitworth fixings exclusively and the Britool combination spanner set and 6 piece socket set covers every nut and bolt on it. Obviously, Britool produce all metric sizes too, several of which I carried for taking off the sump guard and crash bars that Derek made. I have never used such superbly made tools and they feel as though they will last a lifetime. When some serious spannering was required in Jhankat, it was reassuring to have such fine tools to do it with.

Contact: www.britool.com Tel: (+44) 01142 917266

Bike Cover

A good cover not only protects your bike from the elements, it can act as an extra deterrent to prying eyes and hands. Being able to securely cover up when you want to explore a new place gives peace of mind and makes for a more enjoyable trip too. I used a bike cover from **Specialised Covers** on my rides to India and Egypt. Both were fantastic The company produce excellent made to measure bike covers but the Matchless easily fits inside one of their standard sizes. The covers are waterproof, ultra light and clip under the bike front and rear for added security.

Contact: www.specialisedcovers.com Tel: +44 (0)1943 864646

Tank Bag

Essential for keeping maps, camera, adjustable spanner, sunblock, guide book, mobile phone and various other bits and bobs at hand. After much deliberation I plumped for a **Wolfman Explorer Lite Tank Bag** from motorcycle touring and adventure products suppliers, **Winding Roads.** It stayed securely in place, no matter how tough the road conditions, and after cleaning looks as good as it did at the start of the ride.

Contact: www.windingroads.co.uk Tel: +44 (0)1332 865006

Satellite Navigation:
I used a **Garmin Montana 600 Moto**. My previous Garmin Zumo took 6 years of abuse and was still going strong. However, I chose a new Montana because it also works as a handheld satnav, can run on AA batteries as well as being powered by the bike, can leave breadcrumbs for you to trace your route back and has a large 4" screen. It was superb. Garmin's mapping for Europe was faultless and although its maps for India and South East Asia are not yet comprehensive, their level of detail is growing all the time.
Contact: www.garmin.com/en-GB

Sat Nav Lockable Mounting Bracket
I've always felt sat navs are vulnerable when mounted on a bike. The **Touratech** mounting bracket for the Garmin Montana has vibration damping (essential on my old Matchless!) and is also lockable. It's a very well made piece of kit that gave me peace of mind both when riding and when leaving the Montana in situ, such as when going into a petrol station to pay.
Contact: www.touratech.co.uk Tel: (+44) 01639 841765

Clock and Thermometer
I like to know the time when riding without having to stop, take off my glove and roll up a jacket sleeve. Checking the temperature, especially the extremes of freezing or blistering hot, is very useful too. My waterproof clock and thermometer were beautifully made in England from billet aluminium by my friend, Phil, of **Time4Bikes.** Both miraculously survived the pounding dished out by the roads of Ukraine and Central Asia.
Contact: www.time4bikes.com Tel: (+44) 01327 340513

Luggage Straps
Made in Australia, **Andy Strapz** have so many benefits over bungees: there are no metal hooks so there's virtually no risk of eye injury; they don't roll off or cut into luggage; gear can be packed and unpacked in seconds; they hold firmer yet under less tension due to their width and they are kinder to paint and bodywork. They also fold away into a very small package. I used a pair of 1250mm long *Strapz* to hold my rack bag onto the rear luggage rack.
Contact: www.andystrapz.com

Rok Straps
I've tried many ways to hold awkwardly shaped odds and ends on bikes in the past, with only limited success. **Rok Straps** do the job superbly as they're specially designed for motorcycles. The larger pair of *Motorcycle Stretch Straps* I took can hold up to 40KG. They're fully adjustable and can be fitted any number of ways. I also used several pairs of smaller *Adjustable Pack Straps* which were a flexible way to secure dry bags, spare tyre and even the rear stand when it worked loose. The products are excellent and I can't recommend them highly enough.
Contact: www.rokstraps.com

Cylinder Head Temperature (CHT) Gauge
Being stuck in congested cities, held up at traffic lights or slogging along muddy trails can be problematic for an old air cooled engine with a cast iron head. I fitted an **Aircraft Spruce Micro1000 CHT pyrometer** to warn me of impending doom. It's superbly accurate and even self compensates for changes in ambient air temperature. Mine was imported into the UK by Aircraft Spruce agents **Airworlduk.**
Contact: www.shop.airworlduk.com Tel: (+44) 01296 714900

Rack Pack

I needed a versatile holdall bag to carry my clothes, computer and general travel accessories. **Lyon Equipment**, of Sedbergh in the Lake District, provided me with the perfect solution; an **Ortlieb 49 Litre *Rack Pack***. Ortlieb make superb outdoors equipment, tried and tested by travellers for over 25 years. Although initially designed for touring bicyclists, the *Rack Pack* has been awarded 'highly recommended' and 'top-product' status in several European motorcycling magazine tests. It was excellent on the ride to Vietnam, never once letting rain, dust or sand into my equipment. I also used a number of **PS490 heavy duty Dry Bags** for carrying tools, oil and grease. These also performed magnificently.

Contact: www.lyon.co.uk (list of UK dealers available on the website)

Lock

Securing your motorcycle, especially at night, is crucial, but it wasn't possible to carry a huge, heavily armoured chain on this journey. A good compromise was a hardened steel cable lock. Mine came from online motorcycle accessory shop, **Motorbikebits.**

Contact: www.motorbikebits.co.uk Tel: (+44) 07914 783197

Pannier Bags

The toughest saddlebags I could find were ***Expedition Pannierz*** from Australian company, **Andy Strapz.** They're constructed from heavy weight, truck side, polyester reinforced canvas and have a variable capacity from about 15 to 25 litres per bag via a roll top system. They are easy to secure and light, weighing in at just 2KG. When I crashed in Kyrgyzstan, I was able to kick one of the bags out of the way with my free boot and release my trapped left leg, something I'd previously been unable to do with hard luggage.

Contact: www.andystrapz.com

Pump and Tyre Sealant

I needed a compact but efficient foot pump. **Bike It** produce a **Mini Foot Pump** which, weighing in at just 300 gms, fit the bill perfectly. Before setting off, we also injected **Slime tyre sealant** into both inner tubes. Guaranteed to instantly seal punctures of up to 1/4 inch, it gave peace of mind from roadside puncture repairs. Both were supplied by Brendan Layton of **Motorbikebits**. Brendan has a large stall selling a plethora of motorcycle accessories at most of the UK's major bike shows and is very helpful.

Contact: www.motorbikebits.co.uk Tel: (+44) 07914 783197

Neoprene Handlebar Comfort Grips

Old British thumpers are renowned for vibrating and my hands certainly can ache after a full day's ride. I used a set of **Grip Buddies** on the way to Vietnam which made a marked difference. As well as reducing vibration, they fill your hand far more than standard skinny rubber grips, resulting in surprisingly increased levels of comfort. Well worth the money.

Contact: www.originalbeemerbuddies.com

Suppliers: Rider Equipment

Jacket

I was really proud to wear my **Barbour *International* jacket.** Made from 100% waxed cotton, the jacket has been in production since the 1930s when it was used by a succession of British teams in the Olympics of motorcycling, the International Six Days Trial. I used one on the rides to India and Egypt and found it breathed superbly well in hot climates. On the journey to Vietnam, I used an International with sewn in pockets for body armour. It was extremely comfortable and looked great, even when covered in layers of white chalk and red dust. It's voluminous pockets also came in very handy.
Contact: www.barbour.com Tel: (+44) 0191 455 4444

Boots

I used **Alt-Berg** Original Hogg Lites. They were absolutely superb, as they were on the rides to India and Egypt. They're designed as a dual purpose bike and walking boot, making them ideal for touring. The beauty of these boots is that they are made to measure, so the fit is perfect. For a fitting you can visit Alt-Berg, as I did, at their premises in Richmond, Yorkshire. It's a bonus that their shop is surrounded with great motorcycling countryside. Alternatively, you can see their stand at one of the UK's major bike shows. I was very impressed to meet a fellow biker in their shop who had brought his 6-year and 120,000-mile-old Alt-bergs in for a resole. Now that's longevity!
Contact: www.altberg.co.uk Tel: (+44) 01748 850615

Trousers

I wanted riding pants that breathed well in hot climates, had knee, thigh and hip protection and would dry quickly if riding through rain in climates too hot to wear waterproofs. I settled on made-to-measure **Police Air Mesh Kevlar pant**s from US Kevlar riding clothes specialist, **Motoport.** The Air Mesh kevlar at the front is wonderfully breathable and 10 times stronger than leather. The stretch kevlar at the back is supremely comfortable. I also bought an **Aero-Tex waterproof, windproof and breathable liner,** which was very useful when the temperatures fell below freezing. They came with a 7 year guarantee and I'm thrilled with them.
Contact: www.motoport.com Tel: (+1) 760 7521048

Rain Suit

I packed a **Jofama** *Wet Stop Rain Suit* just in case the weather turned against me. The suit is exceedingly well designed, with zippers that come up to the knee for ease of getting on and a main zip that runs diagonally across the chest, almost down to the knee. The waist is elasticised for comfort and there is a fold-away hood hidden in the collar. A very nice touch are the large Hi-Vis stripes that run across the sleeves, back and chest area. It was invaluable in Britain whilst running the bike in and priceless when called on when riding in the rain at Colditz. Jofama are made in Sweden to the highest standards and much of their gear looks in keeping with classic motorcycling.
Contact: www.jofama.se (list of UK & international dealers available on the website)

Body Armour

I've tried hard-shell armour in the past and always found it too stiff and uncomfortable. I simply couldn't believe just how light and easy-to-wear **Forcefield** gear was when I first tried it on; I could hardly tell it was there! And unlike any other armour I've encountered, it's even reusable after an impact. I used a Forcefield *Sport-Lite L1* back protector. It's soft, light and breathable and was perfect for long distance riding. I also used Forcefield *performance upgrade inserts* which I slipped into pockets sewn into my jacket's shoulders and elbows. I was fortunate to land quite softly when I crashed in Kyrgyzstan, but felt reassured at all times to be wearing such high quality protectors.

Contact: www.forcefieldbodyarmour.co.uk Tel: (+44) 01933 410818

Waterproof Overgloves

Dry hands, and in winter warm hands, make all the difference on a long journey. **Rain-Off** produce guaranteed 100% waterproof overgloves with welded seams that have the dual benefit of increasing finger warmth by as much as 50%. Made in New Zealand, they are a great product that I really missed after losing them in the Ukraine.

Contact: www.rain-off.com Tel: (+64) 9 817 3356

Gloves

Lewis leathers have a proud heritage of making leather clothing for aviators and motorcyclists and their quality is just as legendary as their styling.

I've always owned thick, chunky biking gloves, which would have been far too hot for this journey. The Lewis gloves are unlined and made from the softest hide imaginable. Now I know what it means when people say 'it fits like a kid glove'. Surprise bonuses were the increased sense of feel and control of the handlebars and how easily I could get them off, even on the hottest days. The company have a specialist shop in London, which sounds like a great place to meet other motorcyclists as well as checking out their classic riding gear.

Contact: www.lewisleathers.com Tel: (+44) 0207 4020863

Riding Clothes

I wear **Icebreaker** pure **New Zealand Merino wool** clothes just about every day, summer and winter. They're just so practical and very comfortable. The beauty of Merino wool is that it's super warm when layered, yet remarkably cool in hot climates. It naturally breathes and resists body odours; you can wear it day after day in tough outdoor conditions without getting whiffy!

Icebreakers are especially good for motorcycling. I wore a ***Men's Tech Lite 150*** t-shirt under my biking gear, with a ***Apex*** **long sleeve top** for extra warmth when necessary. These are great biking tops as you can zip the neck up and pull the sleeves down using thumb loops on colder days. I also used I**cebreaker Merino trunks, socks, leggings and long sleeve base layer** when it got cold in the mountains. I went for days on end in 30° to 40°C heat wearing the same t-shirt. Not once did I detect a hint of body odour!

Contact: www.icebreaker.com

Travel Clothes

I only had enough room in my luggage for two changes of clothes. **Rohan** travel clothes were inimitably suitable. They are extremely rugged yet very packable and easy to care for. They also look smart however tough the conditions.

I took a pair of ***Bags***, Rohan's iconic multi-function travel trousers. They weight just 335 grams and have a lightning fast drying time of 3 hours. To keep me looking presentable, I also packed a classy short-sleeve shirt made from a mixture of cool bamboo and cotton. Rohan specialise in very well-designed travel accessories too. I wore an ***All Terrain Money Belt*** that from the outside looks just like an regular belt for holding your trousers up.

Contact: www.rohan.co.uk

Goggles

I've been riding with **Halcyon** goggles for over 20 years; they are comfortable and allow great peripheral vision. In my opinion, the style of their split lens goggle compliments a classic bike perfectly. For the trip I used a pair of soft leather *MK49 Deluxe* goggles with tinted lenses to cope with the bright sunshine and a similar pair with clear lenses for night use. I removed the visor from my helmet and wore my goggles all the time as they provide great protection from dust. After 11,500 very tough miles, there's still not a scratch on the lenses.
Contact: www.classicpartsltd.com Tel: (+44) 01920 486032

Hydration System

Some days I drank up to 6 litres of water. Finding room to carry that volume of liquid, as well as stopping frequently enough to drink it, could have been problematic. A lightweight backpack-type hydration system was the perfect answer. **Camelbak** are market leaders in these products, whether they be for motorcyclists, bicyclists, walkers or general sports use. I used a *3 litre Lobo*, which is simple in design and style and didn't look too out of place on the back of a classic motorcyclist. With my open face helmet, it was very easy to drink on the go as well.
Contact: www.zyrofisher.co.uk (UK Distributor) Tel: (+44) 01845 521700

Helmet

I entrusted my head protection to a **Cromwell** *Spitfire*. Now made in Italy, these beautifully designed helmets are light, comfortable and exceed the latest EU standards. - it even has a stainless steel outer shell. It looks in keeping with my bike and I've been thrilled with it! Mine was supplied by **Barry Vincent**. Barry has many years experience working in the crash helmet industry and is a regular sight at major UK motorcycle shows, where he sells Cromwell helmets alongside his other well-known line, **Vac-Bag**, which I also highly recommend. Barry is a friendly and helpful chap who offers great service as well as excellent prices.
Contact: www.vac-bags.co.uk Tel: (+44) 08443 303013

Satellite Communications

Keeping in touch when out of cell phone coverage can save your life and certainly give peace of mind to loved ones at home. I used a **Delorme In Reach** satellite communications device. It allows 2 way text messages over the satellite network and also has an SOS button should you get in serious trouble. Being able to use it in remote mountain regions or when crossing seas was a real boon. Delorme offer several packages, including monthly opt-in, opt-out ones. Once you've bought the device, you only pay for their services when you know you'll be using it.
Contact: www.inreachdelorme.com

Camping

Multi-tool

I've found **Leatherman** multi-purpose tools invaluable in the past. The **Leatherman Blast** has a saw, scissors and bottle / can opener tools and is ideal when camping. The file and needlenose pliers came in handy on my bike too. An essential piece of kit.
Contact: www.leatherman.co.uk

Tent

After considerable research I settled on the **Force Ten Argon 200** semi-geodesic tent. It ticks all the boxes: can be pitched inner only on hot nights; is free-standing and is very strong thanks to its unique pole structure. At just 1.75kg it's also very light. Roomy enough for all my bike gear and me, it's by far the best tent I've ever owned and of such high quality I know it'll last for years.
Contact: www.force-ten.co.uk

Stove

The **Primus Omnifuel stove** can run off virtually any fuel - LP Gas, naptha, gasoline/petrol, diesel, kerosene, aviation fuel and even a BSA Bantam petrol & 2-stroke oil mixture! Designed to work well in the most demanding conditions including extreme altitudes and high or low temperatures, it's a real gem. The extra litre of petrol carried in its fuel bottle ensured the Matchless made it to a petrol station on several occasions.
Contact: www.primus.eu

Camp Food

I took a tasty selection of **Be Well Expedition Food** high energy, freeze dried meals on the ride. Made in the UK, each meal weighs just 125g before adding boiling water and provides 600Kcal. Although I joked, "Camp food agin!" I actually enjoyed each meal and found them both nutritious and filling.
Contact: www.bewellexpeditionfoods.com

Mattress

A self-inflating mattress is essential for insulation and a restful night's sleep. UK based manufacturer **Multimat** make the best! I used a **Summit 25/38** mat that's a comfy 38mm thick at my torso, weighs just 895g and packs into a very compact fleece lined sack that doubles up as a pillowcase. It can safely insulate down to -60°C, a great piece of kit!
Contact: Multimat, www.multimat.uk.com
(list of UK dealers available on the website)

Sleeping Bag

I needed an affordable down sleeping bag that was lightweight and would pack really small. The **Vango Venom 300** fit the bill perfectly (880 gms and 25x16 cm before compression). With a comfort range of 0 to +25 °C, it certainly kept me snug and cosy throughout the journey.
Contact: www.vango.co.uk

Dry Bag

I used two **Ortlieb Dry Bags** on the ride. Heavy duty and fully waterproof, a tube-shaped **PS490 Dry Bag** carried all my camping equipment, which weighed in at under 4.5kg. Undeniably, they are essential luggage for motorcycle and camping trips.
Contact: www.lyon.co.uk

Cookware

I used a lightweight but durable **Vango stainless steel cook kit** on the journey. These are manufactured tough to provide years of use with little or no maintenance - perfect for me! The one person set includes a frying pan, 2 pots and a cup that all nestle into each other to save space.
Contact: www.vango.co.uk

Water Filter

Waterborne illnesses can range from the mildly irritating to the seriously dangerous. I use a **Sawyer Mini water filter** as a straw or attached to a proprietary **Sawyer Squeeze** pouch. The heart of the Mini is a 0.1 micron hollow fibre membrane filter that is guaranteed to last for 100,000 gallons. Furthermore, in hot climates it saves wasting endless plastic water bottles.

Sawyer also provided me with an **Extractor Pump Kit,** which safely removes poisons from snake bites, bee and wasp stings, mosquito bites & more. Fortunately, I didn't need to use it, but Sod's law being what it is, I know that if I hadn't packed it...

Contact: **www.sawyereurope.com** Tel: **(+44) 07786 067533**

Essentials

The AJS & Matchless Owner's Club

The AJS & Matchless Owners Club caters for individuals and families who have an interest in either AJS or Matchless motorcycles. The club produces its own monthly magazine, the Jampot, that is distributed to over 3,600 members worldwide as well as having its own spares scheme to assist owners in keeping their machines in top working order. A number of social activities are organised at international, national and local levels. Each year members of the club organise an International Rally in May, a UK National rally in August and a second national 'back-to-basics' rally in October. As well as these rallies, there are a number of local sections throughout the UK that organise their own evening and week-end social activities.

Contact: **www.jampot.com**

Matchless W.D. Spare Parts List Database

A search engine that allows owners to examine and compare the information contained in 16 of the Matchless G3-WO and G3L spare parts lists issued between 1939 and 1944. Compiled and run by enthusiast, Simon Warner.

Contact: **www.matchlesswd.co.uk**

Horizons Unlimited

A website that is so much more! **Horizons Unlimited** is dedicated to the overland motorcycle traveller and is packed full of useful information. Its forum, **The Hubb**, offers great support to travellers, including information on overland bikes, travel equipment, safety, border crossings, paperwork etc. The website organisers and members also arrange several meetings around the world where you can get together with like-minded motorcyclists. There's even a regular inspiring ezine. It's a highly useful and comprehensive resource for any traveller.

Contact: **www.horizonsunlimited.com**

Accommodation

One of the best travel bargains is access to the **Hostelling International** network. Join your own country's **Youth Hostel Association** and you automatically can stay at more than 4000 hostels in 80 countries. Members can be any age and prices are very reasonable, especially in cities. Youth hostels are clean, safe and a great place to meet fellow travellers.

Contact: **UK YHA, www.yha.org.uk   Hostelling International, www.hihostels.com**

Carnet De Passage

It's not only the rider that needs a passport... for some countries the bike needs one too! To temporarily import my motorcycle into Pakistan, India, Nepal, Myanmar, Laos and Cambodia I required a Carnet De Passage. The ever-helpful Carnet team at the **RAC** arranged this document for me. In summary, I paid a fee, a deposit and an insurance premium to guarantee I would not sell the bike. 100% of the deposit and 50% of the insurance was refunded on return of correctly completed Carnet.

However, the RAC stopped offering this service shortly after my return home and UK residents are now advised to use the German motoring organisation, **ADAC,** instead.
Contact: www.adac.de
Search for "Carnet De Passages English Information"
A PDF application form is available to download

Life Insurance

It's just about impossible to get a new life insurance policy from any of the big, mainstream insurance providers when you tell them you'll be riding a motorcycle to off-the-beaten-track places. It's especially difficult if you'll be away for a long time or work in a dangerous industry. Alan Knowles of **Cura Financial Services** was absolutely brilliant, taking the time and trouble to assess my needs on an individual basis and creating the right policy for me.
Contact: www.specialrisksbureau.co.uk Tel: (+44) 0800 5677450

Travel Insurance

Most insurers don't provide travel insurance for overlanding on a motorcycle. **Carole Nash** insurance offer a comprehensive motorcycle travel package that's just the ticket and only costs about the same as regular worldwide travel insurance without motorcycling. They even fly your panniers, leathers and helmet home with you in the case of a serious accident.
Contact: www.carolenash.com/other-insurance/travel Tel: (+44) 0800 8047952

Motorcycle Insurance

'How do they do it?' is the question I ask myself every year when I renew my bike insurance with **Carole Nash**. Fully comprehensive classic bike cover, including a take-you-home breakdown recovery service from anywhere in the EU, costs an astonishingly low price.
Contact: www.carolenash.com Tel: (+44) 0800 8047952

Trailer

Moving the Matchless around to have work done to it was made easy using a **Motolug** collapsible trailer. Superbly designed and constructed to a high standard in the UK, the **Motolug S7** folds away into the boot of my car or garage when not in use. I'll be displaying the Matchless at several classic bike shows over the next couple of years, courtesy of Motolug.
Contact: www.motolug.com Tel: (+44) 0800 043 7106

Workshop Manuals

I got an original Matchless WWII workshop manual and parts book from **Steve Brown** of **Classic Motorcycle Manuals**. Steve also supplied a high quality reproduction Matchless G3L rider's handbook. His website shows many of the books and manuals he sells, although he's contactable by phone if you can't find what you're looking for.
Contact: www.classicmotorcyclemanuals.com Tel: (+44) 07908 616818

Useful Information

Black Sea Ferry
UKR Ferry have regular sailings across the Black Sea linking Ukraine with Bulgaria, Turkey and Georgia
Contact: www.ukrferry.com/eng/schedules

Caspian Sea Crossings
When I made my journey, there were no ferries across the Caspian Sea. I arranged a berth on a freighter with the very helpful **Vika** (Victoria), who works at the Baku port ticket office.
Contact Tel: +994 50 420 0905 or +994 55 266 5354

However, since then a new Turkmenistan ferry called Berkarar has commenced sailings. An online reservation service run by the **Azerbaijan Caspian Shipping Company** started in October 2016 but there are no reports available on its effectiveness yet.
Contact: https://public.acsc.az/online/payment/index/en/

Crossing China
Although things are slowly changing, most travellers wishing to cross China with their own vehicle need to use a guide / escort service. I used Kashgar based **Newland Travel** who were considerably less expensive than some of the others I contacted. I was very pleased with their flexibility, communication and service.
Contact: www.kashgarsilkroad.com

Crossing Myanmar
It's simply not possible visit or cross Myanmar with your own car or motorcycle without using an agency to complete all the paperwork and escort you, border to border. I used Yangon based **Burma Senses**. They were superb every step of the way through the planning stages and their staff on the ground were outstanding.
Contact: www.burmasenses.com

Taking Your Own Motorcycle Into Vietnam
Entering Vietnam with a foreign registered motorcycle isn't possible without an agency making all the arrangements for you. I could only find two companies that offered the service and only **MotoTours Asia** would allow me to ride independently once I'd crossed the border. Although there was a clash of personalities between myself and the representative who met and escorted me from the Laos border, the company was totally professional, all the bureaucratic paperwork was perfectly prepared and executed and their head office staff were very flexible and friendly. MotoTours Asia organise guided tours of Vietnam on Royal Enfield Bullets. The bikes looked new and well maintained.
Contact: www.mototoursasia.com

Motorcycle Shipping From Bangkok
I sent countless emails to Thai shipping agents and only one bothered to reply. **Nisarat Khongphetsak Schmidt of KPS International Trade (Thailand)** arranged everything, including the bike being custom crated for the impending sea journey. KPS's price was 1/8th of the air freight quote I received from a UK based specialist and Nisarat's service was top drawer.
Contact: www.kpsthailand.com Tel: (+66) 2 8327025
email: nisarat@kpsthailand.com

Hope Agency School

75km south of Phnom Penh, **Hope Agency** is a school funded and run by volunteers with the aim of teaching English to underprivileged children from the surrounding villages. Their mission is: "to combat the cycle of poverty by empowering women, children and the community through access to education and subsequent sustainable employment opportunities. Hope Agency strives to create a bright and better future for these disadvantaged people".

For more information about the school, sponsoring a child, making a donation or volunteering as a teacher, go to their website where you'll see many photographs of the children and school.

Contact: www.hopeagency.org

For further information, photographs and links to all of the suppliers and agencies on these pages, visit www.overlandtovietnam.com

Guest Speaker

If you are a member of a motorcycle club, motoring organisation or any group that would like Gordon to give a talk and slideshow about this journey, or the *Overland To Egypt* or *Overland To India* rides, please get in touch by email.

Contact: speaker@overlandtovietnam.co.uk

Gordon giving an 'Overland To India' talk at Royal Enfield's Rider Mania event in Goa, November 2013.

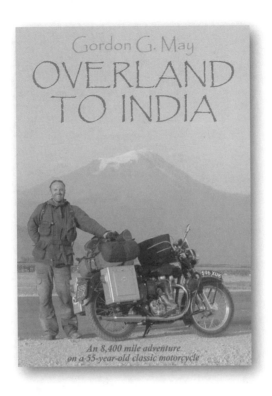

A total of 8,400 miles from Manchester, UK to Chennai, India, in just under seven weeks. A challenge on most vehicles, but on an antiquated 1953 Royal Enfield Bullet...

"Your bike belongs in a museum, not on the road," was how one doubter tried to discourage Gordon from undertaking this journey. Despite intense heat in excess of 40°C, a crash in the Baluchistan desert and some of the worst roads and driving standards on the planet, Gordon's old Bullet did indeed make it triumphantly to the current Royal Enfield factory in Chennai.

In his first travel book, Gordon describes in detail the restoration of his motorcycle and the build up to departure, the larger-than-life characters he met and the many challenges he faced. He also recounts the more personal highs and lows of life on the road. Above all, *Overland To India* is a heartwarming book that illustrates human kindness and hospitality and encourages other riders to take their own motorcycles on a long-distance journey.

New Second Edition includes additional chapters: most frequently asked questions; 'How To Guide' for those wishing to ride to or from India today; route planning guide; spare parts list plus an additional 40 b&w photographs.

256 pages including 8 pages of colour photographs, £9.95 from
www.overlandtoindia.co.uk

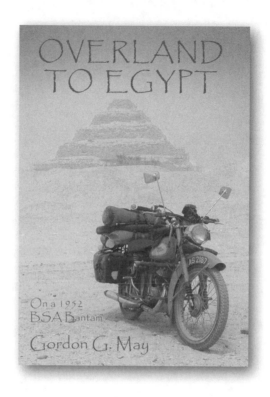

"To Egypt... on a Bantam! Are you joking?" This was the response to author Gordon May's idea to ride one of BSA's diminutive 2-stroke motorcycles, a modified 1952 D1 called Peggy, to the land of the Pharaohs.

Gordon's first attempt at the ride, which took him across the Swiss Alps, ended prematurely in north eastern Italy due to an engine failure. However, he recovered his spirits, set about rebuilding the engine and six months later, having learned from his mistakes, set off once more. This time, crossing through Tunisia and Libya, the ride was a success and after many challenges, Gordon and Peggy jubilantly made it to The Pyramids in Cairo. The return trip, via Jordan and Syria, was also not without its tests, but with determination and a never-say-die attitude, he was able to safely return the Bantam to the UK.

In *Overland to Egypt*, Gordon describes the preparations for both journeys, the trials and tribulations of keeping the fragile BSA running, and takes the reader, as if they were riding pillion, on a journey through the landscapes, architecture, food, and even aromas of the countries he passes through. But most of all, it is a heartening account of the ordinary and extraordinary events that take place on a long distance motorcycle journey, where humanity, trust and the goodwill of strangers have a profound impact on the visitor.

Paperback, 278 pages including 8 pages of colour photographs. £9.95 from: **www.overlandtoegypt.co.uk**

PEGGY IRIS THOMAS

A Ride in the Sun

OR

GASOLINE GYPSY

A DOG IS A GIRL'S BEST FRIEND

Highly Recommended - Gasoline Gypsy by Peggy Iris Thomas

"So many people have dreams like mine," the author writes. "Dreams of satisfying that inner voice that says 'Go on, quit that job, take the plunge and see if it really is greener on the other side of the hill.'" Here is the refreshing story of someone who did take the plunge; who landed in Halifax in the spring of 1951, with her BSA motorcycle, Oppy, and her Airedale, Matelot, on the pillion, and set off to explore Canada, the United States and Mexico. Loaded on Oppy was camping equipment, food, a variety of clothing and a typewriter – everything she needed to secure complete independence. Before they turned homeward once more Peggy and Matelot were to pitch their tent in such strange places as a vacant lot in downtown Los Angeles, a Mexican village bar room, a mosquito-infected Louisiana swamp, and on the heights of New Jersey's Palisades.

She was travelling on a strict budget, so from time to time she worked – typing night telegrams, making plywood (backbreaking work this), serving milk-shakes, acting as a 'car-hop' at a road-house. And everywhere Senorita Motorsicilista went she met curiosity and great kindness. She tells of her experience in a cheerful and likeable book, full of infectious enthusiasm, which will appeal to everyone who warms to a tale of real-life adventure.

226 pages including 4 pages of photographs, £9.95 from
www.gasolinegypsy.co.uk

1945 advertisement for the civilian Matchless G3L